Tomart's Price Guide to
20th Century
BOOKS

by John Wade

Photography by Tom E. Tumbusch

TOMART PUBLICATIONS
Division of Tomart Corporation
Dayton, Ohio

Dedicated to Bibliophiles Everywhere

Acknowledgements

Special thanks to Tom Tumbusch for encouraging me to write this book and for photography.

Hats off to Bob Welbaum for editing and typography, Elisabeth L. Cline, T.N.Tumbusch and Nathan Zwilling for photo scanning and enhancement, and T.N.Tumbusch for layout, design, and final project coordination.

Thanks to the following fine collectors and dealers for providing information and/or books for photography: Russ Bernard, Don Leet, George Budd, Dick Miller, Roger Stephens, Tom Tumbusch, T.N.Tumbusch, Gary Overmann, Bob Raymond, Jay Small, Dan Nagel, Wes Cowan, and Richard Dickson. Thanks also to these libraries for use of resources: Hamilton County Public Library, Middletown Public Library, and the Cincinnati Natural History Museum.

Prices listed are based on the author's experience and are presented as a guide for information purposes only. No one is obligated in any way to buy, sell or trade according to these prices. Condition, rarity, demand and the reader's desire to own determine the actual price paid. No offer to buy or sell at the prices listed is intended or made. Buying and selling is conducted at the consumer's risk. Neither the author nor the publisher assumes any liability for any losses suffered from use of, or any typographical errors contained in, this book, The numeric code system used in the book is not consistent with previous collectible guides published by Tomart Publications. All value estimates are presented in U.S. dollars. The dollar sign is omitted to avoid needless repetition.

First printing, 1994

© Copyright 1994, John Wade. Photography © Copyright 1994 Thomas E. Tumbusch.

All rights reserved

Published by Tomart Publications, Dayton, Ohio 45439-1944

No part of this book may be reproduced, transmitted, or stored in any form or by any means, electronic or mechanical, without prior written permission from the publisher, Tomart Publications, 3300 Encrete Lane, Dayton, OH 45439-1944

Library of Congress Catalog Card Number: 93-60872

ISBN: 0-914293-25-7　　　　　　　　　　　　　　　　　　Manufactured in the United States of America

1 2 3 4 5 6 7 8 9 0　8 7 6 5 4 3 2 1 9 0

TABLE OF CONTENTS

INTRODUCTION

This book is a compilation of some of the most collectible books published in the 100-year period from 1893-1992. After all the promotion has died down, these are the titles, authors, photographers, and artists which have captured enough of a following to be collected. In some cases these are signed limited editions, but for the most part they are normal titles some publisher deemed worthy of print.

Here too, in more than a thousand photographs, is a hundred years of publishing techniques, graphic styles, and subject matter. Certainly, there are many other types of valuable books. Old manuscripts and rare books published before 1900 are probably the most prized possessions, but are out of reach of most book collectors. Local city and county registries are valued for genealogical purposes. Occult, erotic, and religious titles also have avid collectors. The purpose of *Tomart's Price Guide to 20th Century Books*, however, was to concentrate on mainline publishing which received mass distribution as it was done in any given time period. Limited editions listed are mainly by authors and artists who gained fame through sales of more traditional books. All books pictured are from private collections. Given the resources, a beginning collector can still build an outstanding book collection of the titles listed herein.

History

Book collecting is as old as book publishing itself. In medieval times, collectors bought fine examples of ancient Roman and Greek texts, Egyptian papyri, and illuminated manuscripts. During the 1700s, English collectors got excited over incunabula ("books for the cradle": books printed before 1500). Later, great collections of early English books (before 1600), and the first books printed in America (1640s-1660s) were amassed by wealthy tycoons like J. Pierpont Morgan.

Most collectors started accumulating 20th century books in the 1950s. Before that, collectors of Americana wanted only books from the 18th and 19th centuries. Collectible modern first editions were by Melville, Hawthorne, Twain and possibly the earliest "firsts" by Hemingway, Faulkner and Steinbeck. Collectible poets were William Butler Yeats, Percy Bysshe Shelley and Walt Whitman. Thus, at the midpoint of the 20th century nearly any volume by L. Frank Baum, the Walt Disney Studio or Edgar Rice Burroughs could be purchased for several dollars in a used-book store. Interest in science fiction, fantasy and detective fiction was slight during this period.

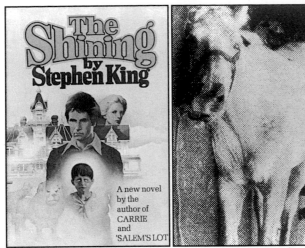

Books need not be old to be collectible. First editions of Stephen King's novels, written as recently as the 1980s, can be worth hundreds of dollars depending on condition. Limited editions of his works are valued as high as $3000-$5000. Above: *The Shining* and *My Pretty Pony* (slipcover of trade edition).

Recent Trends

Several changes in the art and technology of printing in the transition from the 19th to the 20th centuries have stimulated interest in collecting 20th century books. Also, establishment of limited-edition fine presses has created an artificially low supply. By combining high quality books with low printing numbers, many publishers have been able to ignite maximum collector interest. The Limited Editions Club, founded in 1929, is the most famous of these presses, but many others begun in the late 1800s as an alternative to mass-produced industrial-age books are important. Among these are The Grolier Club (1884), The Doves Press (1900), The Riverside Press (1896), The Kelmscott Press (1891), The Ashendene Press (1894), and The Roycrofters (1896). Then trade publishers got into the collecting market by offering many of their authors' latest works as limited editions before the regular trade (mass market) editions appeared. For example, *The Hamlet* by William Faulkner was offered as a 250-copy signed edition in box before the first trade edition appeared.

Dust jackets first appeared in the mid-1800s on a few books as plain wrappings of manila or tissue with brief printing. Pictorial dust jackets started appearing in the late 1800s. Publishers and book sellers believed these jackets would help promote the books as well as add protection. They were right; books stood out on store shelves and collectible appeal was enhanced. In many cases, both the dust jacket and front cover for books from the early 1900s are pictorial. By the mid-twentieth century, however, pictorial cloth covers were dropped for plain covers. In today's world of book collecting a dust jacket in good condition is paramount to realizing maximum value in 20th Century titles. The first American edition of Stephen King's first novel *Carrie* is worth $200-300; without a dust jacket it may be worth $50. The first American edition of *Salem's Lot* in dust jacket is worth $500-700; without, its value is only $100-150.

Further advances in printing technology like the engine-driven rotary printing press, photolithography, mechanical binding, and the linotype machine have made it possible for more people to own and treasure inexpensive yet colorful books.

New realms of writing, almost non-existent during the nineteenth century, were created. These include science fiction, detective/mystery, protest poetry, series novels and stories, Black poetry and novels, American Indian writing, spy/cold war novels, and western romance novels. Mystery and science fiction make up about one-third of current novels, followed by horror, romance, western/frontier, and spy/cold war novels.

The mystery genre began in the 19th century. Edgar Allen Poe wrote *Murders in the Rue Morgue* (Bos 1841) and *Tales* (Bos 1845); both books featured a detective named Chevalier C. Auguste Dupin. Sir Arthur Conan Doyle is famous for his Sherlock Holmes stories set in Victorian England. Among the most collectible modern mystery writers are Earl Derr Biggers, Agatha Christie, Raymond Chandler, Dashiell Hammett, Ellery Queen and lately Tony Hillerman and Sue Grafton.

Science fiction also started in the 19th century. Early common themes were rocket trips to the moon and the earth's core. Jules Verne wrote *From the Earth to the Moon* and *Journey to the Center of the Earth*, and Edgar Rice Burroughs authored *At the Earth's Core*. Among the most collectible science fiction writers are Isaac Asimov, Robert Heinlein, Frederic Pohl, and Andre Norton.

Highly sought-after children's books include the *Oz* stories and other titles by L. Frank Baum and *Little Black Sambo* by Helen Bannerman.

A relatively new collectible art form is children's literature. *Alice in Wonderland* by Lewis Carroll first appeared in 1865. Since then, children's books have been profusely published. Classics like Aesop's Fables and Mother Goose Stories have gone through innumerable editions. L. Frank Baum's Oz series, Walt Disney's works and Helen Bannerman's *Little Black Sambo* are among the most sought-after children's books. Some children's stories are embellished by the great illustrators of the 20th century: Arthur Rackham, Maxfield Parrish, Edmund Dulac and others. The first printings of the Newbery and Caldecott Award winners are desired by collectors. Dr. Suess books have lately become in demand.

Some books have additional value as cross-collectibles. The book shown at left is valuable both for the author, Nathaniel Hawthorne, and the illustrator, Maxfield Parrish. Disney books are sought after both by book collectors and Disneyana enthusiasts. Multiple demands for these books increase their collectibility.

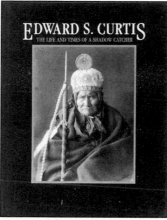

Sports, photography, and other topical books have become a relatively recent trend in collector interest.

The sudden popularity of sports books is a surprising recent trend. In the 1960s, most baseball card collectors wanted early cards issued by the tobacco and candy companies, but didn't show much interest in other memorabilia. A Babe Ruth uniform could be bought for $500 (it is now worth over $50,000) and most baseball books (including early annuals and histories) sold for less than a ticket to a game. Now it's a different story.

Other trends which generate interest in book collecting include novels used as a basis for films (*Jurassic Park*) and author-created paraphernalia like posters, photographs, cards, and book signings to complement and promote their books.

The most collectible living author is Stephen King. A high school teacher whose first story was published in the 1960s, his firsts are worth as much as those of most 18th and 19th century authors. Even books from the 1980s are valuable. Sue Grafton's first "alphabet" mystery *A is for Alibi* (NY 1982) is worth a minimum of $1,000.

This explosion in value over the last 40 years also extends to almost all topical books: golf, photography, natural history, etc. What were once considered ordinary "used books" are now very collectible as rare early books disappear from the market. Another factor is the tremendous growth in the number of people who collect some type of book.

Book and Publishing Terms

A book is a collection of printed sheets pasted, stapled, or sewn together. These sheets are usually enclosed in some kind of cover made of paper, cloth/boards, leather/boards, and occasionally wood or metal. A book has a spine, which is the part bound together, and a fore edge, top edge, and bottom edge. The endpapers and flyleaves are the paper sheets which enclose the printed pages. The backstrip is the spine's cover and normally is imprinted with the author and title. The head-band is a cloth strip laid between the backstrip and spine. A book's edges may be decorated with color by staining. For example, a first edition might have a red-stained top edge.

Book covers are protected by dust jackets: a paper, glassine, or plastic sheet laid over the front and back covers. Dust jackets can be printed, pictorial, or plain. A slipcase is an open-ended box with the book's backstrip showing. A detachable cover is called a portfolio. Books come in several common sizes: folio (10" X 12" and up), one half folio (9" X 11" to 14" X 16"), quarto (about 8" X 10"), and octavo (about 6" X 8"). Smaller sizes, such as duodecimo (4" X 6"), also occur, but are less common.

Inside the book, the copyright page is always the reverse side (verso) of the title page and usually indicates whether the book is a first or later printing.

Book publishers also have their share of unique terms. A first edition is the first time an original manuscript appears in print-ed book form. This term applies to all copies in the first print-ing. As an example, a publisher decides to initially print 5,000 copies. If he later prints more, these copies are not firsts even though they may be identical to the original print run. In later printings there is usually some indication as to which edition, printing, or impression (these terms are synonymous) the book is from. Issues or states are simply variations in printing or bind-ing within an edition. A first edition second issue may vary from the first issue in minute ways...spelling corrections or a change in cover color. The number of copies of a limited edition is always fixed, normally to 1200 copies or less.

A limited edition may or may not be a first edition. Some books are initially published as a limited edition; this edition is automatically a first. Other books appear as a limited edition after the first edition. "Limited" means the book will never be reprinted again in this format. A limited edition always has this denoted somewhere in the book...sometimes in the front before the title page or in the back after the last page of text. Usually this denotation includes the number of copies printed. Individual copies can also be numbered. For example, "77 of 500" means 500 copies were printed and this copy is number 77 of 500. Limited editions are frequently signed by the author, illustrator, etc, beneath the limited-number statement.

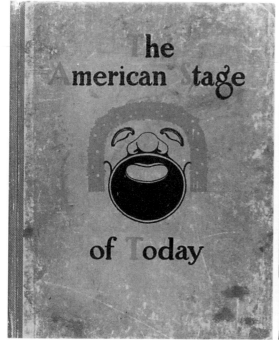

Standard Novel Size

Whitman Big Little Book

Common book sizes, shown to scale. Left to right: folio, quarto (4to), octavo (8vo), and duodecimo (12mo).

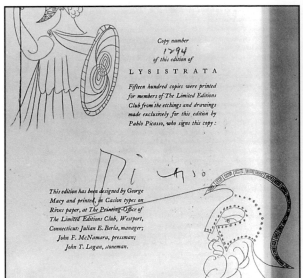

Signature page from a limited edition of Pablo Picasso's *Lysistrata*.

More than just an autograph, a unique drawing by the illustrators greatly increases this book's value.

A pre-publication review copy of Arthur C. Clarke's *2010*.

Features adding value over the price for a first edition are signed & inscribed copies and review & advance copies. Signed trade editions are worth much more than unsigned editions if the author is of any renown. But any editions of a book, including later reprints, are more valuable signed. How valuable depends on the autograph's value combined with the book's scarcity and desirability. *The Old Man and the Sea* by Ernest Hemingway (NY 1952) is worth about $300 in fine condition in dust jacket. But Mr. Hemingway's autograph is valuable. If he signed the book and added an interesting anecdote on the flyleaf, the book might be worth more like $2000. An unsigned copy reprinted by the Book of the Month Club (BOMC) might be worth about $10. Books having long inscriptions or anecdotes may be worth more than those with just a signature. Books inscribed by an author to a famous person are valuable by association. For example, a book inscribed by William Carlos Williams to Allen Ginsburg is worth much more than if it is inscribed to a fan. Signed posters, prints and such ephemera as postcards or advertising displays are collectible and sometimes very valuable. A postcard signed by Ernest Hemingway from his Key West home is an example.

Review and advance copies are special books given to book reviewers, editors, and distributors before the actual first edition is sent to bookstores. The science fiction novel *Alas Babylon* by Pat Frank (NY 1959) is worth $200-250 as a first edition; a more scarce advance copy in plain paper wrappers without a dust jacket is $600-800 (see Modern First Editions).

Determining First Editions

One problem in collecting first editions is the reprint. Reprints are books printed after the first edition. These can be a later printing by the original publisher or a book reprinted by a publisher specializing in reprinting books. Publishers don't state clearly when their books are not first editions, and some reprint publishers even strive to imitate the design of the original first edition. Among these are the BOMC, Book Club Editions, and Science Fiction Book Club. Very often these reprints are almost identical to the first editions, including the statement on the verso of the title page proclaiming it a first. The binding and printing may be virtually identical. Frequently the dust jacket design is identical and the title page may even state the original publisher and identify it as a first edition. Without a dust jacket, sometimes the only way to tell is to look for variant or cheaper cloth covers, slightly thinner paper or a

smaller volume. For instance, the original edition of *Carrie* by Stephen King is in a burgundy cloth, but many of the reprints are in boards. To further complicate matters for recently printed books (1970 or later), the reprint houses often bought the remainders from the original publishers, and replaced the original jackets with their own. Thus the book itself may be the actual first printing.

Here are some guidelines for identifying most first editions:

a. The dust jacket should state the original publisher's price.

b. The flaps of the dust jacket should not be blank but should have a brief biography of the author and synopsis of the book.

c. In most cases the imitators identify themselves on the dust jacket flap, but many recent publications after 1960 do not have this.

d. For BOMC's editions the top edge is normally unstained with no headband. There is usually a small indented dot or mark on the lower corner of the back cover, but many times this dot has disappeared. The dust jacket flap should state BOMC.

e. There should be no statements of further printings on the copyright page and the copyright date should be the same or earlier than the date on the title page. Some publishers print the statement "First Edition" on the copyright page. Other publishers print a code letter or monogram on the copyright page to denote firsts. For example, Charles Scribners & Sons used the letter "A" between 1929 and 1973.

f. After 1960, publishers started using a number code on the copyright page. If the book is a first edition, the numerals 10-9-8-7-6-5-4-3-2-1 appear. If the book is a second printing or second edition, the numeral 1 is deleted. If the numerals 10-9-8-7-6-5-4 appear, this means the book is a fourth printing. Many publishers started using this code, with some variations: Random House deletes the number "1", so its first edition is 0 9 8 7 6 5 4 3 2.

It also helps to become familiar with publishers. Among the many publishers of the most collectible post-1950 first editions are: Abrams, Ace, Arkham House, Avalon, Avon, Bantam, Crown, Dell, Doubleday, Dutton, Fantasy Press, Garden City, Gnome Press, Harper and Row, New Era, Prentice Hall, Putnam, Random House, Scribners, and Simon & Schuster. Doubleday was the major hardback publisher of first editions during the 1950s and 1960s. Ace was the major paperback first-edition publisher. Publishers such as Grosset & Dunlap, A.L. Burt, Triangle Books, Modern Library and others reprint books in an entirely different format. The design of the binding, dust jacket, and illustrations are usually so totally different that anyone can easily identify it as a reprint.

Many reprints are valuable and collectible. Most collectors prefer the first edition but will settle for and even pay a fair amount for later printings depending on the book. Grosset & Dunlap reprints of the Edgar Rice Burroughs' Tarzan series and the Zane Grey western fiction series from the 1920s and 1930s can be worth $10 to $150 in dust jacket. The Modern Library reprints of John Steinbeck, William Faulkner and others are collectible in dust jacket and may be worth $20-40 apiece.

There are many other important details for identifying first editions, and issues and states within the first edition. The following references are invaluable sources of information on U.S. and British publishers and authors. Also see Books About Books.

Johnson, Merle, *American First Editions*, NY 1936 (reprinted)
Cutler, B.D., *Modern British Authors*, NY 1930
Tannen, Jack, *How to Identify and Collect American First Editions*, NY 1976 (reprinted and revised)
Zempel, Edward N., *First Editions: A Guide to Identification*, Peoria 1984.

 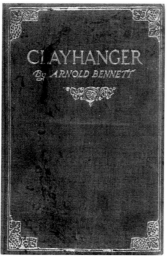

Chipped dust jackets and soiled covers are among the forms of damage which can decrease a book's collectible value.

Condition

Condition is critically important. A book in fine condition in its dust jacket may be worth ten times one in good condition without the jacket.

Books are usually graded as mint, fine, very good, good, fair, or poor. A book in mint condition is totally unused, never opened, right off the store shelf or from the box. Fine refers to a book that appears very close to mint but has been opened and may have slight shelf wear such as slightly bumped corners or a crinkled backstrip. Very good is somewhere between fine and good. Good is a book that has obviously been opened and handled with light soiling, creasing of some pages, a faded spine, and very minor defects. A book in fair condition is faded and frayed with soiling, possible stains and small tears. The spine may be loose or shaken with some pages ready to pull out. A book in poor condition is so bad it's not only uncollectible but hardly readable.

Buying and Selling

There are many ways to buy and sell collectible books: auctions, house sales, library sales, rummage sales, used-book stores and rare-book dealers. There is no best way to buy. All methods have advantages and disadvantages.

At the high end of the scale are auctions. Many auction houses have regular sales of rare and collectible books. Several are Swann Galleries, 104 East 25th St., New York, NY 10010;

Sotheby's, 1334 York Ave., New York, NY 10021; Christie's, 502 Park Ave., New York, NY 10022; Butterfield & Butterfield, 220 San Bruno Ave., San Francisco, CA 94103; and Skinner, 357 Main St., Bolton, MA 01740. These houses deal mainly in the rarest and most valuable books. Most books sold at auction are normally worth over $100 each. Many are worth over $1,000. Auction houses publish catalogs and will accept mail bids in addition to bids from the floor. Books can also be consigned to an auction house for a commission on books sold (usually 10-15 percent) and sometimes a buyer's premium of about 10 percent. There are other expenses such as shipping, insurance, catalog photography, and so forth. There is also no guarantee the books will sell.

Next are outlets devoted exclusively to books. Library sales are held by public and college libraries to sell deacquisitioned or donated books in order to raise money. Rare- and used-book dealers frequently have shows in arenas and civic centers. Most used-book stores keep hours and are listed in the phone book. Rare-book dealers have stores or offices and keep regular hours or are open by appointment. Many rare-book dealers sell through the mail and send out catalogs. They also advertise in book trade publications, listing either books they are searching for or books for sale. The main weekly book collectors' magazine in the U.S. is *AB Bookman's Weekly*, P.O. Box AB Clifton, New Jersey 07015.

Book dealers buy good books and pay according to their need for merchandise. If they have a ready client and can "turn" the books in several weeks, they'll pay more than if they think the books are going to be hard to sell. Sometimes book sellers send out "quotes" to dealers and collectors. They list all pertinent information about the book(s) on a post card or letter and wait for a response. Usually the book is returnable if incorrectly described. Many dealers are collectors and will pay a substantial amount for a prized book. With rare- and used-book dealers (and auctions), prices are higher and professional expertise is available.

Here is a list of reputable collectors and dealers based on the author's personal experiences:

Russ Bernard 7229 Longwood Ct., Cincinnati, OH 45239, (513) 521-0517 (6 PM-8 PM): L. Frank Baum, his pseudonyms & related Oziana, J.R.R. Tolkien, older fantasy (juvenile or adult), R.F. Schulkers-Seckatary Hawkins books, books illus by J.W. Smith, W. Pogany, W.H. Robinson, Tenggren, R. Lawson, Pyle, Nielsen, Moon, Lathrop, Peat, Timlin, J. King, Parrish, H. Clarke, etc.

The Book Shoppe 2818 Wayne Ave, Dayton, OH 45420, (513) 252-2276: 6 rooms of out-of print & Antiquarian books in all fields. Always wanted: Ohio history, Civil War, Oz books, pre-1800 subjects, pre-1950 movie material.

Ellen & George Budd 6910 Tenderfoot Lane, Cincinnati, OH 45249-1041: Collectors & dealers, old postcards, bird books, Arm & Hammer soda cards.

Collector Book & Print Gallery 1801 Chase Ave, Cincinnati, OH 45223, (513) 542-6600, Wed-Sat 3-6, Sun 1-5: Modern art & literature, ephemera, sports, children's, local history, Americana, autographs, Jack London & Black writers.

Cowans American Views 103 Marian Lane, Terrace Park, OH 45174: Stereo views, Daguerrotypes, fine 19th century photographica.

Mostly Baseball - Dick Miller 8010 Nob Hill Drive, Ft. Thomas, KY 41075: Baseball books, ephemera, memorabilia, publications. Send 75¢ SASE for sale lists. Buying pre-1960 baseball items.

Dealer list continues on next page...

Gary Overmann Books of the Ages Mail Order, 4764 Silverwood Drive, Batavia, OH 45103: Deals in & collects children's books illustrated by Arthur Rackham, N.C. Wyeth, Tasha Tudor, Jessie Willcox Smith, Michael Hague, Edmund Dulac, Robert Lawson, Maxfield Parrish, & other finely illustrated books.

Jay Small 1169 N. Bolton, Indianapolis, IN 46219, (317) 359-1209: Indiana history & Americana, real photo postcards.

T & S Books 1545 Scott Blvd., P.O. Box 14077, Covington, KY 41014, (606) 261-6435: Used, rare, & collectible books.

John Wade P.O. Box 11560, Cincinnati, OH 45211: Books, photographs, letters & documents, magazines, advertising about early sports, transportation, exploration, and entertainment.

Finally, there are many less-expensive hit-and-miss sources. House sales are private-owner sales of part or entire contents of estates. They usually advertise in the local newspapers. Rummage sales are often held by schools and churches and sell donated household goods. Another type of rummage sale is the "flea market": a private owner's sale of household goods at a central location such as a park or drive-in theater. Sometimes antique dealers will have books in their stores or antique malls. Books can turn up at any of these places, although good books are much harder to find and the consumer is buying "as is."

HOW TO USE THIS PRICE GUIDE

The prices in this guide are based on auction prices realized, dealer prices and the advice of experts. In that sense the guide is accurate, but the rare-book trade is volatile and a few prices may stand still or go down slightly while others will increase dramatically. Therefore, what values are going to be 15 years from now cannot be predicted. The trend is for all collectible books to go up in value just like any other collectible, with high-demand books realizing loftier prices.

Although there are some entries for limited editions, later printings, and revised and special editions, most prices are for first trade editions. A first trade edition is the first printing of a book made available to the public with the intention that reprints will follow. This edition is rare because few copies were printed, few copies of the first printing were bought or the books are so old and fragile few remain. Demand also increases if the book is a now-great author's first effort or the initial appearance of an unusual topic.

If a book has a later date on the title or copyright pages than is listed in this guide, it means this is a later printing and is usually worth less.

If the abbreviation DJ appears after the date, the price range is for a copy in dust jacket. If DJ does not appear, the book either does not have one or its original existence is unknown.

To some extent, determining value and condition is subjective. That is, not all collectors will agree on the value, and may differ on what is "fine" condition. Some collectors say a bumped corner, the slightest fading, or paper aging brings the condition down, while others are not as critical. Differences in value may also be the result of regional interests. Certain books may bring higher prices in specific parts of the U.S. or overseas. For example, interest in Jack London is higher in California than Ohio, and Gene Stratton-Porter's popularity is stronger in Indiana than England. Interest in Texas history is naturally stronger in Texas than elsewhere. Some collectors or dealers will pay more for books in their speciality. A collector of L. Frank Baum children's books will usually pay a higher price for this type than a collector of all children's books.

This guide is organized by category. Most categories are self-explanatory. But some require a few words of introduction:

Disneyana includes books published since the 1930s under Walt Disney's name, as well as books on Disney characters.

Baumiana & Oziana covers books written by L. Frank Baum with emphasis on his Wizard of Oz series.

Children's books are not a separate category. They are listed under Modern First Editions, Artists and Illustrators, Disneyana, and Baumiana & Oziana.

All categories are alphabetized according to author, editor, illustrator, or artist, then by the first word of the title after "The" or "A." In a few cases an entry is by title or a book series, such as "American Guide Series" in Americana. Authors are cross-referenced when listed in more than one category.

All entries are assumed to be first or limited editions unless otherwise stated. In some cases, limited editions are listed before the first trade edition because the limited edition is the first printing from the manuscript. For example, James Joyce's *Ulysses* in Modern First Editions is first listed as a limited edition. This is followed by many later printings, including the first trade editions and those from foreign countries. Some long titles have been shortened and subtitles deleted to save space. (Also, some books do not have their complete titles on the cover.) Dates that are estimated or do not appear on the title or copyright pages are in parentheses. Unless otherwise noted, the price range is for books in very good to fine condition.

ABBREVIATIONS & DEFINITIONS

Place of Publication

Albu	Albuquerque
Balt	Baltimore
Bos	Boston
Can	Canada
Chi	Chicago
Cinti	Cincinnati
Clev	Cleveland
Col	Columbus, OH
Eng	England
Fr	France
Ger	Germany
Ind	Indianapolis
LA	Los Angeles
Lex	Lexington
Lon	London
Minn	Minneapolis
NY	New York
NZ	New Zealand
Okla Cty	Oklahoma City
Phil	Philadelphia
Prov	Providence, RI
SF	San Francisco
Tor	Toronto
Wash	Washington

Book Sizes

12mo	duodecimo	(about 4" X 6")
8vo	octavo	(about 6" X 8")
4to	quarto	(about 8" X 10")
1/2fol	one half folio	(9" X 11" to 14" X 16")
fol	folio	(10" X 12" and up)

Miscellaneous

b&w	black and white
bds	boards
BOMC	Book Of the Month Club
cl	cloth
cr	copyright
cy/cys	copy/copies
DJ(s)	dust jacket(s)

ed	edition		pseud	pseudonym
eg	example		pub	publish/publisher
end pprs	end papers		sp	spine
frontis	frontis piece		tp	title page
gr	green		VG	very good (condition)
G & D	Grossett & Dunlap		vol	volume(s)
illus	illustration(s)		w/	with
imp	impression		w/o	without
intro	introduction			
litho(s)	lithographs(s)			
lea	leather			
lbl	label			
ll	linen-like			
lp	large paper			
lt	light			
meas	measures (size)			
nd	no date listed			
np	no place			
orig	original			
p/pp	page/pages			
photog	photographer			
pict	pictorial			
p-o	paste-on			
por	portrait			
ppr	paper			
promo	promotion			

Definitions

Paste-on: Paper pictorial label mounted on the front cover, usually a portrait or scene.

Point(s): The characteristics that identify the edition, issue or state, e.g., changes in text, incorrect spelling, etc.

Second printing before publication: A statement sometimes found on copyright pages. The publisher decided to print more copies before the book was released.

Serified type: Type with small points or "serifs."

Signature: Folded sheet divided into leaves to form pages, e.g., a sheet folded once becomes a four-page signature. Almost all books consist of signatures sewn or pasted together.

Stamped: Imprint of letters or pictures made in the cover. "Gold stamped" is gold print; "blind stamped" is an imprint without any color added.

Tipped in: Color plate or photograph mounted to a blank leaf.

Vellum: Animal skin used for some covers or a parchment.

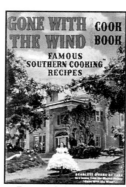

Cloth Cover styles, left to right: pictorial cloth, decorative cloth, and cloth with paste-on.

Pictorial Cover styles, left to right: pictorial wrappers, pictorial boards, pictorial dust jacket.

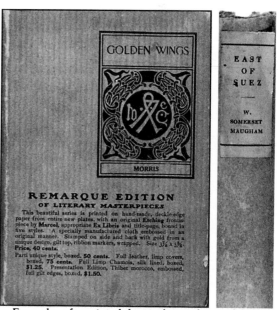

Book with slipcase (at left) and folder (background).

Examples of a printed dust jacket and spine label.

AMERICANA

Americana is any book relating to the exploration, settlement and military history of America. Americana is also called "USiana," a term coined by Wright Howes, a premier dealer and collector of Americana. Howes published a major guidebook for collectors entitled *USiana 1750-1950* NY 1954.

During the 16th through the 19th centuries, Americana dealt primarily with the adventures and exploits of the English, French and Spanish in the New World. The first English book about America appeared in Antwerp in 1520. American Indians and Afro-Americans were among the first settlers of America, but there were few extensive, detailed descriptions of their lives and cultures until the 19th century. Examples are George Catlin's *Letters and Notes on the Manners, Customs, and Conditions of the North American Indians* (NY 1841) and the many books about slavery and the underground railroad that surfaced before and after the Civil War.

In the mid-1800s, the U.S. Government commenced publishing such scientific works on exploration and Indian culture as Randolph Marcy's *Exploration of the Red River of Louisiana* (Washington 1854), John Charles Fremont's *Report of the Exploring Expedition to the Rocky Mountains in the Year 1842* (Washington 1845), and the annual BAE (Bureau of American Ethnology) Reports beginning in 1879.

Coinciding with this government enterprise, many commercial publishers expanded into books about the American West. Favorite topics included Texas, California, western states in general, the Plains Indians, the life of the cowboy, new national parks like Yosemite and Yellowstone, western lawmen and outlaws, and the Mexican War. In the early 1900s, Frederic Remington and Charles M. Russell were major illustrators of cowboys, Indians and western life. Books about hunting and gold prospecting in Alaska gained popularity in the 1890s.

The 20th Century witnessed the establishment of many publishers who dealt primarily in Americana. These included Arthur H. Clarke & Co. (Cleveland & Glendale), The Caxton Press (Caldwell, ID), The Grabhorn Press (San Francisco) and The University of Oklahoma (Norman). Many of the books were historical reprints of 18th and 19th century imprints and first-time printings of 18th and 19th century manuscript journals and diaries.

Some highly collectible topics of 20th century writers are steamboating, the Pony Express, wild west shows, outlaws, mountain men, "Buffalo Bill" Cody, George Armstrong Custer and the Civil War.

Civil War books are among the most published Americana. More of them have been sold in the past ten years than in the ten years following the war itself. The most valuable are regimental histories published during the Civil War until the early 1900s. These were usually penned by veterans who served in those regiments. Depending on scarcity and demand (Confederate and western regimentals are more desirable than those of New England), values can range from $50 to several hundred dollars. Books illustrated with photographs taken during the Civil War by Matthew Brady and others are also in demand.

Other categories of Americana, many of which are beyond the scope of this price guide, are:

1. City, Town and Village Histories
Almost every community in the U.S. has a published history. Some were written 150 years ago and others may be only several years old. Sizes range from large multi-volume sets to pamphlets of less than ten pages. Their values depend on scarcity, demand, the amount of information contained (including illustrations like street scenes and portraits) and the print quality. A typical village history of a few pages done in the 1940s-80s may be worth $5 to $20, while a large multi-volume set published in the early 1900s might bring $75 to $300.

2. County Histories
Most were published between the 1860s and the 1920s. Many have recently been reprinted and sell for $40 to $100. Original county histories are usually valued from $50 to $200, depending on scarcity, amount of information, and illustrations.

3. County Atlases
These are large folio-sized books with township, village and town maps. Also named "plat" books, many have views of homesteads, buildings and street scenes. The most valuable were done between the 1850s and about 1910 by speciality publishers like The Lewis Historical Publishing Co. of Chicago. The maps are often hand-colored with original lithographs of scenes and portraits. These atlases may range from $75 to $300 for some rare western and southern counties. Later atlases usually have color-printed maps and halftone photos of scenes and portraits; these may range from $50 to $150.

4. American Guide Series (see listings under this heading)
These are state and city guides which were originally published between 1937 and 1942 as part of the Federal Writers Project of The Works Progress Administration. The state guides were reprinted many times during the 1940s-1980s.

5. Bureau of American Ethnology (BAE) Reports and Bulletins
The U.S. Government published scientific reports about the American Indian annually from 1879 to the 1920s. Many of these volumes are prized for their fine maps and chromolithographs of artifacts, Indian portraits and scenes. Along with these are hundreds of BAE bulletins which were usually monographs. Most are small volumes dealing with the artifacts and traditions of a certain tribe, but a few are as large as the BAE Annual Reports. A good example is *The Handbook of American Indians North of Mexico* (Washington 1910) by Frederick Hodge.

The condition of Americana books is important, but not as crucial as with Modern First Editions. Books with dust jackets are more valuable, but in most cases the value of a jacketless book is at least 50% of the book in jacket and most likely 70% to 80%. Slightly later printings are nearly as valuable unless the book was written by a famous author. Then it becomes like a Modern First: collectible because of the author and not the content.

The following listings are alphabetical by author or edition. For BAE Reports see Powell, J. W. and for WPA Guides see American Guide Series.

Abbott, Charles Conrad
AA1010 **Ten Years Digging in Lenape Land** Trenton 1912 100 - 150
Abdy, Harry B.
AA1060 **On the Ohio** NY 1919   40 - 60
Adams, Andy
AA1110 **Anthony Reed Cowman** Bos 1907, DJ   100 - 150
AA1121 **The Log of a Cowboy** Bos 1903, DJ, 1st state
             w/o entry for map on List of Illus   250 - 350
AA1122 Bos 1903, DJ, later state   100 - 150
AA1124 Bos 1927, DJ   30 - 50
AA1126 Bos 1931, DJ   30 - 50
AA1128 NY 1981   20 - 30
AA1140 **The Ranch on the Beaver** Bos 1927, DJ   100 - 150
AA1150 **Texas Matchmaker** Bos 1904, DJ   100 - 150
AA1160 **Wells Brothers The Young Cattle Kings**
             NY 1911, DJ   100 - 150
AA1162 NY, early 1900s, G & D reprint, DJ   30 - 50
AA1170 **Why the Chisholm Trail Forks** Austin 1956, DJ   50 - 75
Adams, Ramon F.
AA1310 **Come and Get It** Norman 1952, DJ   50 - 75
AA1320 **Cowboy Lingo** Bos 1936, DJ   75 - 125
AA1330 **A Fitting Death for Billy the Kid** Norman 1960, DJ 30 - 50
AA1340 **The Old Time Cowhand** NY 1961, DJ   30 - 50

AA1350	**The Rampaging Herd** Norman 1959, DJ	200 - 300
AA1360	**Six Guns and Saddle Leather** Norman 1954, DJ	100 - 150
AA1370	**Western Words** Norman 1944, DJ	50 - 75

Aiken, James

AA1510	**The Journal of...** Norman 1919, wrappers	100 - 150

Aken, David

AA1610	**Pioneers of the Black Hills** Milwaukee 1920s, wrappers	100 - 150

Aldrige, Reginald

AA1710	**Life on a Ranch** NY 1884, wrappers	300 - 500
AA1712	NY 1966	30 - 50
AA1720	**Ranch Notes in Kansas** Lon 1884	300 - 500

Alexander, E. P.

AA1810	**Military Memoirs of a Confederate** NY 1907	100 - 150

Alexander, Hartley

AA1910	**Sioux Indian Painting** Nice 1938, 2 vol, portfolios, 400 cys	800 - 1200

Alexander, John Brevard

AA2010	**The History of Mecklenburg County From 1740 to 1900** Charlotte 1902	100 - 150
AA2020	**Reminiscenses of the Past Sixty Years** Charlotte 1908	100 - 150

Allen, Dr. William A.

AA2210	**Adventures with Indians and Game or Twenty Years in the Rocky Mountains** Chi 1903	200 - 300

Alter, J. Cecil

AA2310	**James Bridger** Salt Lake City 1925, 1000 cys	100 - 150
AA2312	Col 1951, DJ	30 - 50

Alvord, Clarence Walworth

AA2410	**The First Explorations of the Trans-Allegheny Region by the Virginians** Clev 1912	150 - 250
AA2420	**The Mississippi Valley in British Politics** Clev 1917, 2 vol	150 - 250

American Guide Series

These books were written and published as a part of the Federal Writers Project of the W.P.A. (Works Progress Administration) during the 1930s and early 1940s. They are mostly state and city guides. Most original editions have been reprinted many times between the 1940s and 1980s. Reprints still have collectible value but are not worth as much as the first editions. Later printings are usually worth $25 to $40 in dust jacket and bring slightly less without the dust jacket.

State Guides - various unstated writers - 1st editions.

AA2500	**Alabama** NY 1941, DJ	40 - 60
AA2510	**Alaska** NY 1940, DJ	40 - 60
AA2520	**Arizona** NY 1940, DJ	50 - 75
AA2530	**Arkansas** NY 1941, DJ	40 - 60
AA2540	**California** NY 1939, DJ	50 - 75
AA2550	**Colorado** NY 1941, DJ	40 - 60
AA2560	**Connecticut** NY 1938, DJ	30 - 50
AA2570	**Delaware** NY 1938, DJ	30 - 50
AA2580	**Florida** NY 1939, DJ	40 - 60
AA2590	**Georgia** NY 1940, DJ	30 - 50
AA2600	**Idaho** NY 1937, DJ	50 - 75
AA2610	**Illinois** Chi 1939, DJ	30 - 50

AA2620	**Indiana** NY 1941, DJ	30 - 50
AA2630	**Iowa** NY 1938, DJ	50 - 75
AA2640	**Kansas** NY 1939, DJ	30 - 50
AA2650	**Kentucky** NY 1939, DJ	30 - 50
AA2660	**Louisiana** NY 1941, DJ	30 - 50
AA2670	**Maine** NY 1937, DJ	30 - 50
AA2680	**Maryland** NY 1940, DJ	30 - 50
AA2690	**Massachusetts** NY 1937, DJ	30 - 50
AA2700	**Michigan** NY 1941, DJ	50 - 75
AA2710	**Minnesota** NY 1938, DJ	40 - 60
AA2720	**Mississippi** NY 1938, DJ	40 - 60
AA2730	**Missouri** NY 1941, DJ	30 - 50
AA2740	**Montana** NY 1939, DJ	50 - 75
AA2750	**Nebraska** NY 1939, DJ	50 - 75
AA2760	**Nevada** Portland 1940, DJ	50 - 75
AA2770	**New Hampshire** Bos 1938, DJ	50 - 75
AA2780	**New Jersey** NY 1939, DJ	30 - 50
AA2790	**New Mexico** NY 1940, DJ	50 - 75
AA2800	**New York** NY 1940, DJ	30 - 50
AA2810	**North Carolina** Chapel Hill 1939, DJ	30 - 50
AA2820	**North Dakota** NY 1938, DJ	50 - 75
AA2830	**Ohio** NY 1940, DJ	30 - 50
AA2840	**Oklahoma** Norman 1941, DJ	40 - 60
AA2850	**Oregon** Portland 1940, DJ	50 - 75
AA2860	**Pennsylvania** NY 1940, DJ	50 - 75
AA2870	**Rhode Island** Bos 1937, DJ	30 - 50
AA2880	**South Dakota** NY 1938, DJ	50 - 75
AA2890	**Tennessee** NY 1939, DJ	30 - 50
AA2900	**Texas** NY 1940, DJ	50 - 75
AA2910	**Utah** NY 1941, DJ	50 - 75
AA2920	**Vermont** NY 1938, DJ	50 - 75
AA2930	**Virginia** NY 1940, DJ	30 - 50
AA2940	**Washington** Portland 1941, DJ	50 - 75
AA2950	**West Virginia** NY 1941, DJ	30 - 50
AA2960	**Wisconsin** NY 1941, DJ	30 - 50
AA2970	**Wyoming** NY 1941, DJ	50 - 75

City Guides

AA3100	**New York City** NY 1939, DJ	40 - 60
AA3150	**Washington D.C.** Wash 1937, DJ	40 - 60

Amsden, Charles

AA3260	**Navaho Weaving** Santa Ana 1934	200 - 300
AA3262	Albu 1948	100 - 150
AA3264	Chi 1964	50 - 75

Anderson, Capt. John

AA3360	**History of the 57th Mass. Vols.** Bos 1896	150 - 250

Andrews, Matthew Page

AA3410	**The Founding of Maryland** Balt 1933, DJ	50 - 75
AA3420	**History of Maryland** NY 1929, DJ	100 - 150
AA3430	**Virginia The Old Dominion** Garden City 1937, DJ	40 - 60

Andrist, Ralph K.

AA3510	**Long Death The Last Days of the Plains Indian** NY 1964, DJ	30 - 50

Anthony, Irvin

AA3610	**Down to the Sea in Ships** Phil 1924, DJ	50 - 75
AA3620	**Paddle Wheels and Pistols** Phil 1929, DJ	30 - 50

AA1060

AA2520

AA2620

AA2920

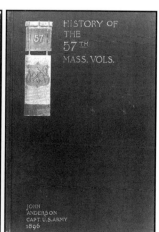

AA3360

AB0210   AB1160

Applegate, Frank
AA3710   Indian Stories From the Pueblos Phil 1929, DJ   75 - 125
AA3720   Native Tales of New Mexico Phil 1932, DJ   75 - 125

Applegate, Jesse
AA3810   A Day with the Cow Column in 1843 Chi 1934   100 - 150

Armstrong, Moses Kimball
AA3910   Early Empire Builders of the Great West
St. Paul 1901   75 - 125

Armstrong, Nevil
AA4010   Yukon Yesterdays Lon 1936, DJ   75 - 125

Arnold, R. Ross
AA4110   Indian Wars of Idaho Caldwell 1932, DJ   50 - 75

Arthur, John Preston
AA4210   Western North Carolina Raleigh 1914   100 - 150

Arthurs, Stanley
AA4310   The American Historical Scene NY 1936   30 - 50

Asbury, Herbert
AA4410   The Barbary Coast Garden City 1933, DJ   15 - 25
AA4420   The French Quarter NY 1936   40 - 60
AA4430   The Gangs of New York NY 1928, DJ   50 - 75
AA4440   The Great Illusion Garden City 1950, DJ   15 - 25

Ashe, Samuel (editor)
AA4510   Biographical History of North Carolina
Greensboro 1905-17, 8 vol, 750 sets   800 - 1200

Ashley, Clifford W.
AA4610   The Yankee Whaler Bos 1926, DJ   75 - 125

Athearn, Robert G.
AA4710   Forts of the Upper Missouri Englewood Cliffs
1967, DJ   30 - 50
AA4720   Rebel of the Rockies New Haven 1962, DJ   30 - 50
AA4730   William Tecumseh Sherman and the Settlement
of the West Norman 1956, DJ   30 - 50

Atherton, Gertrude
AA4810   California NY 1914   30 - 50

Avey, Elijah
AA4910   The Capture and Execution of John Brown
Elgin, IL 1906   50 - 75

Ayers, James J.
AA5010   Gold and Sunshine: Reminiscences of Early
California Bos 1922, DJ   50 - 75

Babbitt, Charles Henry
AB0110   Early Days at Council Bluffs Wash 1917   75 - 125

Bacon, Edwin Munroe
AB0210   The Connecticut River NY 1906   75 - 125

Bailey, Kenneth P.
AB0310   The Ohio Company of Virginia and the
Westward Movement Glendale 1939   100 - 150

Bailey, Washington
AB0410   A Trip to California in 1853 Leroy 1915,
wrappers   300 - 500

Baity, Elizabeth
AB0510   Americans Before Columbus NY 1951, DJ   30 - 50

Bakeless, John
AB0610   Daniel Boone NY 1939, DJ   20 - 30
AB0620   The Eyes of Discovery Phil 1950, DJ   20 - 30
AB0630   Lewis & Clark, Partners in Discovery NY 1948, DJ   20 - 30
AB0640   Spies of the Confederacy Phil 1970, DJ   20 - 30

Baker, C. Alice
AB0710   True Stories of New England Captives,
Carried to Canada During the Old French
and Indian Wars Cambridge 1897   75 - 125

Baker, Hozial
AB0810   Overland Journey to Carson Valley, Utah
SF 1973, DJ   100 - 150

Bancroft, Hubert Howe
AB0910   The Works of Hubert Howe Bancroft
SF 1886-1890, 39 vol   3000 - 5000
Individual volumes from this set are worth $75-125 each with some
2 volume titles worth about $150 - 200. For example: **History of the
Northwest Coast** SF 1886, 2 vol, $150-200 (vol 27 & 28).

Bandelier, Adolf F.
AB1010   Contributions to the History of the Southwestern
Portion of the U.S. Cambridge 1880   200 - 300
AB1020   The Delight Makers NY 1890   150 - 250
AB1022   NY 1918, DJ   40 - 60
AB1030   The Gilded Man NY 1893   250 - 350
AB1040   Indians of the Rio Grande Valley Albu 1937, DJ   75 - 125

Bandini, Joseph
AB1110   A Description of California in 1828 Berkeley
1951, 400 cys   150 - 250

Banta, R. E.
AB1160   The Ohio NY 1949, DJ   20 - 30
AB1161   NY 1949, DJ, limited ed, signed   40 - 60

Banta, S. E.
AB1210   Buckelew: The Indian Captive Mason
1911, 50 cys   2000 - 3000
AB1212   Kerryville 1964, wrappers   100 - 150

Banta, William
AB1310   Twenty Seven Years on the Frontier or Fifty
Years in Texas Austin 1893, wrappers   2000 - 3000

Barnard, Evan G.
AB1410   A Rider of the Cherokee Strip Bos 1936, DJ   50 - 75

Barnes, Will C.
AB1510   Apaches and Longhorns LA 1941, DJ   100 - 150
AB1520   Tales From the X-Bar Horse Camp Chi 1920   100 - 150

Barney, James
AB1610   Tales of Apache Warfare Phoenix 1933,
wrappers   200 - 300

Barrett, Ellen C.
AB1710   Baja California 1535-1956 LA 1957,
50 cys, box   300 - 500
AB1711   LA 1957, 500 cys   100 - 150
AB1720   Baja California II 1535-1964 LA 1967   100 - 150

Barry, Ada Loomis
AB1810   Yunini's Story of the Trail of Tears Lon 1932, DJ   200 - 300

Bass, W. W. (editor)
AB1910   Adventures in the Canyons of Colorado
Grand Canyon 1920, wrappers   200 - 300

Bates, Finis L.
AB2010   Escape and Suicide of John Wilkes Booth
Memphis 1907   100 - 150

Beard, Dan
AB2110   Hardly A Man Is Now Alive NY 1939, DJ   50 - 75

Bechdolt, Frederick
AB2210   Giants of the Old West NY 1930, DJ   50 - 75
AB2220   Tales of the Old Timers NY 1924, DJ   50 - 75
AB2230   When the West Was Young NY 1922, DJ   50 - 75

Beck, Henry Charlton
AB2310   Forgotten Towns of Southern New Jersey
NY 1936, DJ   50 - 75

Beebe, Lucius
AB2410   The American West NY 1955, DJ   30 - 50

AB2420 **Hear the Train Blow** NY 1952, DJ 50 - 75
AB2430 **Mansions on Rails** Berkeley 1959, DJ 75 - 125
AB2440 **U.S. West: The Saga of Wells Fargo** NY 1949, DJ 30 - 50

Bell, Horace
AB2510 **On the Old West Coast** NY 1930, 20 cys, box 200 - 300
AB2511 NY 1930, DJ (1st trade ed) 50 - 75
AB2520 **Reminiscenses of a Ranger** Santa Barbara 1927, DJ 50 - 75

Benedict, Carl P.
AB2610 **A Tenderfoot Kid on Gyp Water** Austin 1943 200 - 300

Bennett, Estelline
AB2710 **Old Deadwood Days** NY 1928, DJ 30 - 50

Bennett, George
AB2810 **Early Architecture of Delaware** Wilmington 1932 200 - 300

Benton, Frank
AB2910 **Cowboy Life on the Side Track** Denver 1903 150 - 250

Berry, Rev. Chester D.
AB3010 **Loss of the Sultana and Reminiscences of the Survivors** Lansing 1892 100 - 150

Berry, Don
AB3110 **A Majority of Scoundrels: An Informal History of the Rocky Mountain Fur Company** NY 1961, DJ 75 - 125

Besson, Maurice
AB3210 **Les "Freres De La Coste", Filibustiers & Corsaires** Paris 1928 200 - 300
AB3220 **The Scourge of the Indies, Buccaneers, Corsairs & Filibusters** Lon 1929, 960 cys, DJ 250 - 350

Biggers, Don H.
AB3310 **Biggers Chronicle** Lubbock 1961, 500 cys 75 - 125
AB3320 **From Cattle Range to Cotton Patch** Abilene, early 1900s, wrappers 500 - 700
AB3322 Bandera 1944, wrappers 75 - 125
AB3330 **German Pioneers in Texas** Fredericksburg 1925, DJ 100 - 125
AB3332 Fredericksburg 1983, DJ 20 - 30
AB3340 **Shackleford County Sketches** Albany 1974, 100 cys, box 300 - 500

Bixby-Smith, Sarah
AB3410 **Adobe Days** Cedar Rapids 1925 30 - 50

Black, Glenn
AB3510 **Angel Site** Ind 1967, 2 vol, slipcase 75 - 125

Blackbird, Andrew
AB3610 **History of the Ottawa and Chippewa Indians of Michigan** Ypsilanti 1887 250 - 350

Blackford, W. W.
AB3710 **War Years With Jeb Stuart** NY 1945, DJ 50 - 75

Blackmar, Frank
AB3810 **Spanish Colonization in the Southwest** Balt 1890 100 - 150

Blair, Emma
AB3910 **Indian Tribes of Upper Mississippi Valley** Clev 1911, 2 vol 200 - 300

Bledsoe, A. J.
AB4010 **Indian Wars of the Northwest** SF 1885 300 - 500

Boas, Franz
AB4110 **Handbook of American Indian Languages** Wash 1911 75 - 125

Boatright, Mody
AB4210 **Backwoods to Border** Dallas 1943 30 - 50
AB4220 **From Hell to Breakfast** Dallas 1944 30 - 50
AB4230 **Gib Morgan, Minstrel of the Oil Fields** El Paso 1945, 1000 cys 75 - 125
AB4240 **Tall Tales From Texas Cow Camps** Dallas 1934 250 - 350

Bolton, Charles
AB4310 **On the Wooing of Martha Pitkin** Bos 1894, 35 cys 200 - 300
AB4311 350 cys 100 - 150

Bolton, Herbert Eugene
AB4410 **Anza's California Expeditions** Berkeley 1930, 5 vol, DJs 300 - 500
AB4420 **Athanase de Mezieres and the Louisiana-Texas Frontier** Clev 1914, 2 vol 400 - 600
AB4422 NY 1970 50 - 75
AB4430 **Bolton and the Spanish Borderlands** Norman 1964, DJ 50 - 75

AB4440 **Coronado and the Turquoise Trail** Albu 1949 150 - 250
AB4450 **Coronado: Knight of the Pueblos and Plains** NY 1946, DJ 50 - 75
AB4460 **Defensive Spanish Expansion** 1930, wrappers 50 - 75
AB4470 **Font's Complete Diary: A Chronicle of the Founding of San Francisco** Berkeley 1933 200 - 300
AB4480 **Guide to Materials for the History of the United States in the Principal Archives of Mexico** Wash 1913 200 - 300
AB4490 **Mission as a Frontier Institution in the Spanish-American Colonies** El Paso 1962, wrappers 20 - 30
AB4500 **Rim of Christendom** NY 1936, DJ 100 - 150
AB4510 **Spanish Activities on the Lower Trinity River 1746-1771** Austin 1914, wrappers 25 - 50
AB4520 **Texas in the Middle Eighteenth Century** Berkeley 1950, DJ 200 - 300
AB4522 NY 1962, 400 cys 50 - 75
AB4524 Austin 1970, DJ 30 - 50

Bolton, Reginald Pelham
AB4610 **Indian Life of Long Ago in the City of New York** NY 1934 75 - 125
AB4620 **Relics of the Revolution** NY 1916 200 - 300

Bordeaux, William
AB4710 **Custers Conqueror** pub Smith & Co., 1930s 100 - 150
AB4720 **Sitting Bull** 1920s, wrappers, 7 pp 50 - 75

Botkin, B. A. (editor)
AB4810 **Sidewalks of America** Ind 1954, DJ 20 - 30
AB4820 **A Treasury of Western Folklore** NY 1951, DJ 20 - 30

Bourke, John G.
AB4910 **Apache Campaign in the Sierra Madre** NY 1886, wrappers 400 - 600
AB4912 NY 1955, DJ 25 - 50
AB4920 **On the Border With Crook** NY 1891 300 - 500
AB4922 NY 1892 75 - 125
AB4924 Col 1950, DJ 50 - 75
AB4926 NY 1980 30 - 50
AB4930 **MacKenzie's Last Fight With the Cheyennes** Governor's Island, NY 1890 150 - 250
AB4940 **Medicine Men of the Apache** Pasadena 1971, DJ 30 - 50
AB4950 **Snake Dance of the Moquis of Arizona** NY 1884 300 - 500

Bowman, Elizabeth Skaggs
AB5010 **Land of High Horizons** Kingsport 1938, DJ 30 - 50

Bowman, Isiah
AB5110 **The Pioneer Fringe** Wash 1931 30 - 50

Boyd, Julian
AB5210 **Indian Treaties Printed by Benjamin Franklin 1736-1762** Phil 1938, slipcase 250 - 350

Braddy, Haldeen
AB5310 **Cock of the Walk** Albu 1955, DJ 75 - 125
AB5320 **Pancho Villa at Columbus: The Raid of 1916** El Paso 1965, DJ 25 - 50

Bradford, John
AB5410 **Historical Notes on Kentucky** SF 1932, 500 cys 250 - 350

Bradley, Glen Danford
AB5510 **The Story of the Pony Express** Chi 1913 50 - 75

Bradshaw, Herbert
AB5610 **History of Prince Edward County, Virginia** Richmond 1955, DJ 50 - 75

Bratt, John
AB5710 **Trails of Yesterday** Lincoln, NE, 1921 200 - 300

Brayton, Matthew
AB5810 **The Indian Captive** Clev 1860, wrappers 800 - 1200
AB5812 Fostoria 1896 150 - 250

Brewer, J. Mason
AB5910 **Snuff Dipping Tales of the Texas Negro** Austin 1956, 400 cys 200 - 300

Brewer, William H.
AB6010 **Up & Down California in 1860-64** New Haven 1931, DJ 50 - 75

Briggs, L. Vernon
AB6110 **Arizona and New Mexico 1882, California 1886, and Mexico 1891** Bos 1932 150 - 250
AB6112 Ann Arbor 1966 30 - 50
AB6114 NY 1966 30 - 50

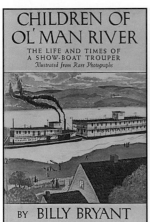

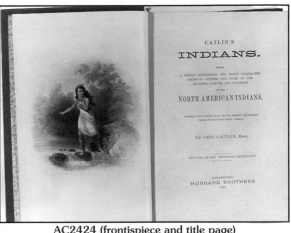

AB8460	AB9260	AB9270

AC2424 (frontispiece and title page)

AB6120 **California and the West** Bos 1931 — 150 - 250

AB6130 **History of Shipbuilding on the North River, Plymouth County, Massachusetts** Bos 1889 — 200 - 300

Brigham, William T.
AB6210 **Ancient Hawaiian Stone Implements** Honolulu 1902 (possibly several vol), each vol — 150 - 250

Brill, Charles J.
AB6310 **Conquest of the Southern Plains** Oklahoma City 1938, DJ — 75 - 125

Brininstool, E. A. (Earl A.)
AB6410 **Crazy Horse** LA 1939, DJ — 75 - 125
AB6420 **Fighting Indian Warriors** Harrisburg 1953, DJ — 30 - 50
AB6430 **Fighting Red Cloud's Warriors** Col 1926, DJ — 50 - 75
AB6440 **Troopers with Custer** Harrisburg 1952, DJ — 50 - 75

Brinton, Daniel G.
AB6510 **Essays of an Americanist** Phil 1890 (American Indian Culture) — 75 - 125

Brisbin, James
AB6610 **The Beef Bonanza** Phil 1881 — 250 - 350
AB6612 Norman 1959, DJ — 20 - 30
AB6620 **Beldin, The White Chief** Athens 1974, DJ — 15 - 25

Britt, Albert
AB6710 **Great Indian Chiefs** NY 1938, DJ — 40 - 60

Broder, Patricia
AB6810 **The American West** Bos 1984, DJ — 75 - 125

Bronson, Edgar B.
AB6910 **Love of Loot and Women** NY 1917, 100 cys, slipcase — 200 - 300
AB6920 **Red Blooded Heroes of the Frontier** NY 1910 — 50 - 75
AB6930 **Reminiscences of a Ranchman** NY 1908 — 150 - 250

Brooks, Elbridge S.
AB7010 **The Story of the American Indian** Bos 1887 — 50 - 75
AB7020 **The True Story of George Washington** Bos 1895 — 50 - 75

Brose, David
AB7110 **American Woodland Indians** NY 1985, DJ — 30 - 50

Brothers, Mary
AB7210 **Billy the Kid** Farmington 1949, wrappers — 30 - 50
AB7220 **Pecos Pioneer** Albu 1943 — 75 - 125

Brower, Jacob V.
AB7310 **Memoirs of Explorations in the Basin of the Mississippi** St. Paul 1898-1904, 300 cys — 500 - 700

Brown, Dee
AB7410 **Bury My Heart at Wounded Knee** NY 1970, DJ — 30 - 50
AB7420 **Gentle Tamers: Women of the Old Wild West** NY 1958, DJ — 20 - 30
AB7430 **The Settlers West** NY 1955, DJ — 30 - 50
AB7440 **Westerners** NY 1974, DJ — 20 - 30

Brown, James S.
AB7510 **California Gold: An Authentic History of the First Find** Oakland 1894 — 300 - 500
AB7520 **Life of a Pioneer** Salt Lake City 1900 — 150 - 250

Brown, Jesse and A. M. Willard
AB7610 **The Black Hills Trails** Rapid City, SD 1924 — 200 - 300

Brown, John
AB7710 **Twenty Five Years a Parson in the Wild West** Fall River 1896 — 200 - 300

Brown, John H.
AB7810 **Encyclopedia of the New West** Marshall 1881 — 1000 - 1500
AB7820 **History of Texas From 1685 to 1892** St. Louis 1892, 2 vol — 800 - 1200
AB7830 **Indian Wars and Pioneers of Texas** Austin 1896 — 700 - 1000
AB7840 **Life and Times of Henry Smith: The First American Governor of Texas** Dallas 1887 — 150 - 250
AB7850 **Political History of Oregon** Portland 1892, 1 vol — 500 - 700

Brown, John P.
AB7910 **Old Frontiers: The Story of the Cherokee Indians** Kingsport 1938 — 100 - 150

Brown, Mark
AB8010 **Before Barbed Wire** NY 1956, DJ — 50 - 75
AB8020 **Flight of the Nez Perce** NY 1967, DJ — 50 - 75
AB8030 **The Frontier Years: L.A. Huffman, Photographer of the Plains** NY 1955, DJ — 50 - 75
AB8040 **Plainsmen of the Yellowstone** NY 1961, DJ — 50 - 75

Brown, Robert L.
AB8110 **Empire of Silver: A History of the San Juan Silver Rush** Caldwell 1968, DJ — 30 - 50

Brown, Samuel J.
AB8210 **In Captivity: & Etc.** Mankato 1896 — 1000 - 1500

Brown, William C.
AB8310 **The Sheepeater Campaign in Idaho** Boise 1926, 50 cys — 300 - 500

Bruffey, George A.
AB8410 **Eighty-One Years in the West** Butte 1925, wrappers — 100 - 150

Bryant, Billy
AB8460 **Children of Ol' Man River** NY 1936, DJ — 40 - 60

Buck, Franklin A.
AB8510 **Yankee Trader in the Gold Rush** Bos 1930, DJ — 30 - 50

Buley, R. Carlyle
AB8610 **The Old Northwest: Pioneer Period 1815-1840** Ind 1950, 2 vol, slipcase — 50 - 75

Bulloch, James D.
AB8710 **The Secret Service of the Confederate States in Europe** NY 1959, 2 vol, slipcase — 100 - 150

Bunton, Mary T.
AB8810 **A Bride on the Chisholm Trail in 1886** Austin 1939, DJ, 200 cys — 100 - 150

Burch, T. P.
AB8910 **Charles W. Quantrell** Vega 1923 — 50 - 75

Burdette, Mary
AB9010 **Young Women Among Blanket Indians** Chi 1898 — 150 - 250

Burdick, Usher
AB9110 **Some of the Old-Time Cowmen of the Great West** Balt 1957, DJ — 50 - 75

Burke, John M.
AB9210 **Buffalo Bill From Prairie to Palace** Chi 1893 — 150 - 250

Burman, Ben Lucien
AB9260 Blow for a Landing Bos 1938, DJ   30 - 50
AB9270 Steamboat Round the Bend Bos 1935, DJ   30 - 50
Burnett, W. R.
AB9310 Adobe Walls NY 1953, DJ   50 - 75
AB9320 Bitter Ground NY 1958, DJ   50 - 75
Burns, John H.
AB9410 Memoirs of a Cow Pony Bos 1906   300 - 500
Burns, Walter
AB9510 The Robin Hood of El Dorado NY 1932, DJ   30 - 50
AB9520 Saga of Billy the Kid Garden City 1926, DJ 30 - 50
AB9530 Tombstone Garden City 1927, DJ   30 - 50
Burroughs, Stephen
AB9610 Memoirs of the Notorious Stephen Burroughs
        NY 1924   30 - 50
Burt, Struthers
AB9710 Diary of a Dude Wrangler NY 1924, DJ   50 - 75
Butterfield, Consul Wilshire
AB9810 History of Brule's Discoveries and Explorations
        1610-1626 Clev 1898   150 - 250
AB9820 History of George Rogers Clark's Conquest
        of the Illinois and the Wabash Towns 1778
        and 1779 Col 1904   100 - 150
Buttree, Julia M.
AB9910 The Rhythm of the Redman in Song, Dance
        and Decoration NY 1937, DJ   50 - 75
Campbell, J. L.
AC0510 Idaho and Montana Gold Regions Chi 1965, DJ 30 - 50
Campbell, John C.
AC0610 The Southern Highlander and His Homeland
        NY 1921, DJ   30 - 50
Campbell, Patrick
AC0710 Travels in the Interior Inhabited Regions of
        North America Tor 1937   100 - 150
Canfield, Chauncey L. (editor)
AC0810 The Diary of a Forty Niner NY 1906   150 - 250
Canfield, Captain S. S.
AC0860 History of the 21st Regiment Toledo 1893 200 - 300
Cannon, J. P.
AC0910 Inside of Rebeldom: The Daily Life of a Private
        in the Confederate Army Wash 1900   75 - 125
Carey, A. Merwyn
AC1010 American Firearms Makers NY 1953, DJ   30 - 50
Carey, C. H.
AC1110 History of Oregon Chi 1922   100 - 150
Carr, John
AC1210 Pioneer Days in California Eureka 1891 150 - 250
Carrington, Frances C.
AC1310 My Army Life and the Fort Phil Kearney
        Massacre Phil 1910   75 - 125
Carroll, H. Bailey (translator)
AC1410 The Texan Santa Fe Trail Canyon, TX 1951, box 100 - 150
AC1420 Three New Mexico Chronicles Albu 1942,
        557 cys   100 - 150
Carson, Christopher
AC1510 Kit Carson's Own Story of His Life Taos 1926 50 - 75
AC1512 Chi 1935 (republished as Kit Carson's autobiography) 20 - 30
Carson, James H.
AC1610 Life in California Tarrytown NY 1931, DJ 100 - 150
Carstarphen, J. E.
AC1710 My Trip to California Louisiana, MO 1914 100 - 150
Carter, Captain Robert G.
AC1810 Four Brothers in Blue Wash 1913   700 - 1000
AC1812 Austin 1978, DJ   30 - 50
AC1820 Massacre of Salt Creek Prairie and the
        Cowboy's Verdict Wash 1919, wrappers   300 - 500
AC1830 The Old Sergeant's Story Winning the West
        From the Indians and the Bad Men in
        1870-1876 NY 1926   300 - 500
AC1840 On the Border with MacKenzie Wash 1935 2000 - 3500
AC1842 NY 1961, 750 cys, slipcase   150 - 250

AC1850 On the Trail of the Deserters Wash 1920,
        250 cys, wrappers   200 - 300
AC1860 Pursuit of Kicking Bird Wash 1920, wrappers,
        100 cys   700 - 1000
Cartland, Fernando
AC2010 Southern Heroes Poughkeepsie 1897   50 - 75
Casler, John
AC2110 Four Years in the Stonewall Brigade Guthrie,
        OK 1893   200 - 300
Castaneda, Carlos
AC2210 The Teachings of Don Juan/A Yaqui Way of
        Knowledge (1st book) Berkeley 1968, DJ 75 - 125
Castaneda, Carlos E.
AC2310 Mexican Side of the Texas Revolution Dallas
        1956, DJ   50 - 75
AC2312 Austin 1970   50 - 75
AC2314 Wash 1971, 500 cys   50 - 75
AC2320 Our Catholic Heritage in Texas 1519-1936
        Austin 1936-1958, 7 vol   2000 - 3000
AC2330 Report of the Spanish Archives in San
        Antonio, Texas San Antonio 1937   200 - 300
Catlin, George
AC2410 George Catlin, Episodes From Life Among the
        Indians and Last Rambles Norman 1959, DJ 30 - 50
AC2420 The Manners, Customs and Condition of the
        North American Indians Lon 1841, 2 vol 800 - 1200
AC2422 Lon 1857, 2 vol   200 - 300
AC2424 Lon 1892   100 - 150
AC2425 Phil 1892   100 - 150
AC2426 Edinburgh 1926, 2 vol, DJs   400 - 600
AC2428 Minneapolis 1965, 2 vol, slipcase   50 - 75
Catton, Bruce
  BMOC reprints are worth about half a first printing.
AC2510 The American Heritage Picture History of the
        Civil War NY 1960, DJ   40 - 60
AC2512 NY 1982, DJ   15 - 25
AC2520 Army of the Potomac Garden City 1951, 3 vol, DJs 50 - 75
AC2530 The Coming Fury NY 1961, DJ   30 - 50
AC2540 Grant Moves South Bos 1960, DJ   20 - 30
Caughey, John Walton
AC2580 Gold is the Cornerstone Berkeley 1948, DJ 30 - 50
Celiz, Fray Francisco
AC2610 Diary of the Alarcon Expedition into Texas
        1718-1719 LA 1935, 100 cys   300 - 500
Chabot, Frederick C.
AC2710 Early Texas Album Austin, 1929, 50 mounted
        photos, 50 cys   2000 - 3000
AC2720 Pictorial Sketch of Mission San Jose De San
        Miguel De Aguayo San Antonio 1935, 12 cys 2000 - 3000
Chambers, Harvey
AC2810 The Last Stand of the Nez Perce NY 1962, DJ 50 - 75
Chapman, Arthur
AC2910 The Pony Express NY 1932, DJ   50 - 75

AC2512

AC2580

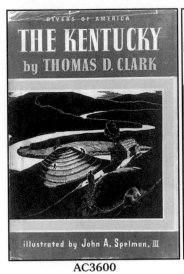
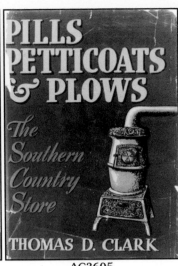
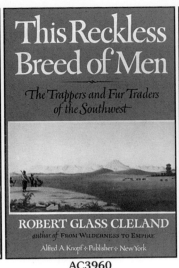

AC3600	AC3605	AC3960	AC4630

Charlevoix, Pierre F. X.
AC3010 Journal of a Voyage to North America
     Chi 1923, 2 vol   250 - 350

Charnay, Desire
AC3110 The Ancient Cities of the New World NY 1887 100 - 150

Chittenden, Hiram Martin
AC3210 The American Fur Trade of the Far West
     NY 1902, 3 vol   400 - 600
AC3212 NY 1935, 2 vol   150 - 250
AC3220 History of Early Steamboat Navigation on
     the Missouri River NY 1903, 2 vol, 950 cys 200 - 300
AC3230 Yellowstone National Park Cinti 1899   30 - 50

Claiborne, John Herbert
AC3310 Seventy Five Years in Old Virginia NY 1905 100 - 150

Clappe, Louise
AC3410 California in 1951; 1852 SF 1933, 2 vol, 500 cys 250 - 350

Clark, Stanley
AC3510 The Life and Adventures of the American
     Cowboy Providence 1897, wrappers   200 - 300

Clark, Thomas D.
AC3600 The Kentucky NY 1942, DJ   30 - 50
AC3605 Pills Petticoats & Plows NY 1944, DJ   20 - 30
AC3610 South Carolina The Grand Tour Columbia
     1973, 499 cys, slipcase   150 - 250

Clark, W. P.
AC3710 The Indian Sign Language Phil 1885   100 - 150

Clark, Walter (editor)
AC3810 Histories of the Several Regiments and
     Battalions From North Carolina in the
     Great War 1861-65 Raleigh 1901, 5 vol 250 - 350

Clay, John
AC3910 My Life on the Range Chi 1924, DJ   200 - 300

Cleland, Robert Glass
AC3960 This Reckless Breed of Men NY 1963, DJ   20 - 30

Clev, Richard
AC4010 Voyages of a Merchant Navigator NY 1886 75 - 125

Clum, Woodworth
AC4110 Apache Agent Bos 1936, DJ   75 - 125

Coates, Harold, Wilson
AC4210 Stories of Kentucky Feuds Knoxville 1942   40 - 60

Coates, Robert M.
AC4310 The Outlaw Years NY 1930, DJ   20 - 30

Cody, Louisa Frederic
AC4410 Memories of Buffalo Bill NY 1920, DJ   75 - 125

Cody, William F. ("Buffalo Bill")
AC4510 Buffalo Bill's Life Story NY 1920, DJ   50 - 75
AC4520 Life and Adventures of Buffalo Bill Chi 1917, DJ 75 - 125
AC4530 The Life of the Honorable William F. Cody
     Hartford 1879   75 - 125
AC4540 The Story of the Wild West and Campfire
     Chats Chi 1888   75 - 125

AC4550 True Tales of the Plains NY 1908   50 - 75

Coffin, Charles Carleton
AC4610 The Boys of '61 Bos 1892   50 - 75
AC4620 The Boys of '76 NY 1876   50 - 75
AC4630 My Days and Nights on the Battlefield Bos 1887 75 - 125

Cohn, David
AC4710 New Orleans and its Living Past Bos 1941 75 - 125

Cole, Fay Cooper
AC4810 Rediscovering Illinois Chi 1937, DJ   50 - 75

Coleman, John Winston
AC4910 The Casto Metcalfe Duel Lex 1950, wrappers 20 - 30
AC4920 Historic Kentucky Lex 1967, DJ   30 - 50
AC4930 Kentucky a Pictorial History Lex 1971, DJ   20 - 30

Collier, John
AC5010 Patterns and Ceremonials of the Indians of the
     Southwest NY 1949, DJ, 1475 cys, signed 100 - 150

Collins, Dennis
AC5110 The Indians Last Fight; or the Dull Knife Raid
     Girard, KS, early 1900s   300 - 500

Collins, John S.
AC5210 Across the Plains in '64 Omaha 1904 200 - 300

Collins, Mrs. Nat
AC5310 The Cattle Queen of Montana St. James,
     MN, 1894   1200 - 1800
AC5312 Spokane, early 1900s   200 - 300

Collins, Lt. R. M.
AC5410 Chapters From the Unwritten History of the
     War Between the States St. Louis 1893 250 - 350

Collison, W. H.
AC5510 In the Wake of the War Canoe NY, early 1900s, DJ 50 - 75

Connelley, William E.
AC5610 Quantrill and the Border Wars Cedar
     Rapids 1910   100 - 150
AC5620 The War With Mexico 1846-47 Topeka 1907 100 - 150
AC5630 Wild Bill and His Era NY 1933, DJ   100 - 150

Connolly, A. P.
AC5710 A Thrilling Narrative of the Minnesota Massacre
     and the Sioux War of 1862-1863 Chi 1896 300 - 500

Conover, Charlotte
AC5810 Memoirs of the Miami Valley Chi 1919, 3 vol 75 - 125

Conover, George W.
AC5910 Sixty Years in Southwest Oklahoma
     Andarko 1927   100 - 150

Constanso, Miguel
AC6010 The Spanish Occupation of California SF 1934 200 - 300

Cook, Frederick
AC6110 General John Sullivan's Indian Expedition
     Auburn 1887   100 - 150

Cook, James H.
AC6210 Fifty Years on the Old Frontier New Haven
     1923, DJ   100 - 150

AC6220 Longhorn Cowboy NY 1942, DJ 75 - 125

Cook, John R.
AC6310 The Border and the Buffalo Topeka 1907 100 150

Coolidge, Dane and Mary
AC6410 Arizona Cowboys NY 1938, DJ 30 - 50
AC6420 The Navajo Indians Bos 1930, DJ 75 - 125
AC6430 Old California Cowboys NY 1939, DJ 50 - 75
AC6440 The Rain Makers Bos 1929, DJ 30 - 50
AC6450 Texas Cowboys NY 1937, DJ 50 - 75

Cooper, Courtney Riley
AC6510 Annie Oakley NY 1927, DJ 50 - 75

Corlett, William Thomas
AC6610 The Medicine Man of the American Indian
Balt 1935, DJ 40 - 60

Cornplanter, Jesse J.
AC6710 Legends of the Longhouse Phil 1938, DJ 50 - 75

Cossley-Batt, Jill L.
AC6810 The Last of the California Rangers NY 1928,
200 cys 200 - 300
AC6811 NY 1928, DJ (1st trade ed) 50 - 75

Costanso, Miguel
AC6910 The Spanish Occupation of California
SF 1934, 550 cys, slipcase 200 - 350

Coulter, E. Merton
AC7010 Travels in the Confederate States: A
Bibliography Norman 1948, DJ 75 - 125

Coursey, O. W.
AC7110 Wild Bill (James Butler Hickok) Mitchell,
SD 1920s 100 - 150

Couts, Cave J.
AC7210 From San Diego to the Colorado in 1849
LA 1932 200 - 300

Coves, Elliott (editor)
AC7310 History of the Expedition Under Command
of Lewis & Clark NY 1893, 4 vol, 200 cys 800 - 1200
AC7320 Journal of Jacob Fowler NY 1898, 950 cys 200 - 300
AC7330 New Light on the Early History of the Greater
Northwest NY 1897, 3 vol, 1000 cys 500 - 700
AC7332 Minneapolis 1965, 2 vol 75 - 125

Cowan, Robert E.
AC7410 A Bibliography of the History of California
and the Pacific West, 1510-1906 SF 1914,
250 cys, box 600 - 800
AC7412 SF 1933, 3 vol 500 - 700
AC7420 The Forgotten Characters of Old San
Francisco SF 1938, 500 cys 100 - 150
AC7422 LA 1964, DJ 50 - 75

Cox, Jacob Dolson
AC7510 Military Reminiscences of the Civil War
NY 1900, 2 vol 150 - 250

Cox, James
AC7610 Historical and Biographical Record of the
Cattle Industry St. Louis 1895 5000 - 7000
AC7612 NY 1960, 2 vol, 500 cys, box 300 - 500

Coy, Owen C.
AC7710 Pictorial History of California Berkeley 1925 200 - 300

Creswell, R. J.
AC7810 Among the Sioux Minn 1906 100 - 150

Crocket, George L.
AC7910 Two Centuries in East Texas Dallas 1932 200 - 300

Crook, George
AC8010 General George Crook Norman 1946, DJ 50 - 75
AC8020 Resume of Operations Against Apache Indians
1882 to 1886 Omaha 1886 200 - 300

Crotty, D. G.
AC8110 Four Years Campaigning in the Army of the
Potomac Grand Rapids 1894 100 - 150

Croy, Homer
AC8210 Jesse James Was My Neighbor NY 1949, DJ 50 - 75
AC8220 Trigger Marshall: The Story of Chris Madsen
NY 1958, DJ 30 - 50
AC8230 Wheels West NY 1955 DJ 30 - 50

Cruse, Thomas
AC8310 Apache Days and After Caldwell 1941, DJ 50 - 75

Cunningham, D.
AC8410 Antietam Springfield 1904 75 - 125

Cunningham, Eugene
AC8510 Buckaroo Bos 1933, DJ 50 - 75
AC8520 Famous in the West El Paso 1926, wrappers 200 - 300
AC8522 Dallas 1958, 500 cys 50 - 75
AC8530 Triggernometry: A Gallery of Gun Fights
NY 1934, DJ 100 - 150
AC8532 Caldwell 1941, DJ 30 - 50

Curtis, Edward S. (also see Photography)
AC8610 In a Sacred Manner We Live NY 1972, DJ 30 - 50

Curtis, Natalie
AC8710 The Indian's Book NY 1907, DJ 200 - 300
AC8712 NY 1935, DJ 100 - 150

Cushing, Frank H.
AC8810 My Adventures in Zuni Santa Fe 1941,
400 cys, DJ 300 - 500
AC8812 Palo Alto 1970, DJ 30 - 50
AC8820 Zuni Folk Tales NY 1901, NY 1931, DJ 100 - 150

Cushman, H. B.
AC8910 A History of the Choctaw, Chickasaw and
Natchez Indians Greenville, TX 1899 300 - 500

Custer, Elizabeth B.
AC9010 Boots and Saddles NY 1885 75 - 125
AC9020 Tenting on the Plains NY 1887 50 - 75

Custer, George Armstrong
AC9110 My Life on the Plains NY 1874 200 - 300
AC9112 NY 1876 150 - 250
AC9114 St. Louis 1886 100 - 150
AC9116 Norman 1962, DJ 30 - 50
AC9130 Wild Life on the Plains and Horrors of Indian
Warfare St. Louis 1883 200 - 300
AC9132 St. Louis 1891 100 - 150

Cutter, Donald
AC9210 Malaspina in California SF 1960, 1000 cys 150 - 250

Dabney, Wendell P.
AD1010 Cincinnati's Colored Citizens Cinti 1926 100 - 150

Dacus, J. A.
AD1110 Life and Adventures of Frank and Jesse
James St. Louis 1880 300 - 500

Dale, E. E. (Edward Everett)
AD1210 Cow Country Norman 1942, DJ 50 - 75
AD1220 Frontier Trails: The Autobiog. of Frank M.
Canton Bos 1930, DJ 75 - 125
AD1230 Frontier Ways: Sketches of Life in the Old
West Texas 1959, DJ 30 - 50
AD1240 Indians of the Southwest Norman 1949, DJ 30 - 50
AD1250 Range and Cattle Industry Norman 1930, 500 cys 300 - 500
AD1252 Norman 1960, DJ 30 - 50

Dale, Harrison C.
AD1410 The Ashley-Smith Explorations and the
Discovery of a Central Route to the
Pacific 1822-1829 Clev 1918 250 - 350
AD1412 Glendale 1941 150 - 250

Dalton, Emmett
AD1510 When the Daltons Rode Garden City 1931, DJ 100 - 150

Damon, Samuel C.
AD1610 A Journey to Lower Oregon and Upper
California 1848-49 SF 1927, 250 cys 200 - 300

Dane, G. Ezra
AD1710 Ghost Town NY 1941, DJ 30 - 50

Darlington, Mary Carson (editor)
AD1810 Fort Pitt and Letters From the Frontier
Pittsburgh 1892 200 - 300

David, Ellis
AD1910 A Commercial Encyclopedia of the Pacific
Southwest Oakland 1915 150 - 250

Davidson, Gordon
AD2010 The North West Company Berkeley 1918 200 - 300

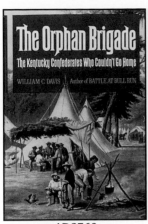

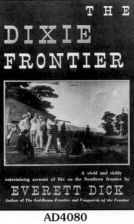

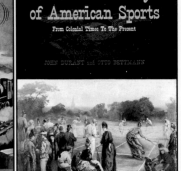

AD2760	AD3060	AD4080	AD7112	AD7360

Davidson, Levette J.
AD2110 Rocky Mountain Tales Norman 1947, DJ   30 - 50

Davis, Britton
AD2210 The Truth About Geronimo New Haven 1929, DJ 75 - 125

Davis, Burke
AD2310 Grey Fox - Robert E. Lee and the Civil War
          NY 1956, DJ   30 - 50
AD2320 Jeb Stuart, The Last Cavalier NY 1957, DJ   30 - 50
AD2330 They Called Him Stonewall NY 1954, DJ   20 - 30

Davis, Mary Lee
AD2410 Uncle Sam's Attic Alaska Bos 1930, DJ   20 - 30

Davis, S. L.
AD2510 Authentic History of the Klu Klux Klan
          1865-1877 NY 1924, DJ   50 - 75

Davis, Sam P.
AD2610 The History of Nevada Reno 1913, 2 vol   800 - 1200

Davis, W. W. H.
AD2710 The Fries Rebellion 1798-99 Doylestown 1899 100 - 150

Davis, William C.
AD2760 The Orphan Brigade NY 1980, DJ   20 - 30

Davis, William Heath
AD2810 Seventy Years in California SF 1889   300 - 500
AD2812 SF 1929   200 - 300
AD2814 SF 1967, DJ   200 - 300

Davis, William J. (editor)
AD2910 The Partisan Rangers of the Confederate
          States Army Louisville 1904   150 - 250

Dawson, Nicholas
AD3010 California in '41 Texas in '51 Memoirs
          Austin 1910   700 - 1000

Dayton, Fred Erving
AD3060 Steamboat Days NY 1939, DJ   50 - 75

De Shields, James T.
AD3110 Border Wars of Texas Tioga, TX 1912   300 - 500

De Soto, Hernando
AD3210 The Discovery of Florida SF 1946, 280 cys   200 - 300

De Tonty, Henri
AD3310 Relation of Henri De Tonty Concerning the
          Explorations of La Salle Chi 1898   250 - 350

De Wolff, J. H.
AD3410 Pawnee Bill 1902   150 - 250

Delane, Alonzo
AD3510 Across the Plains and Among the Diggings
          NY 1936, DJ   50 - 75

Dellenbaugh, Frederick S.
AD3610 The North Americans of Yesterday NY 1906   75 - 125

Dengler, Hermann
AD3710 American Indians Tribes of the Prairies and
          the East NY 1923, DJ   50 - 75

Denny, Arthur A.
AD3810 Pioneer Days on Puget Sound Seattle 1888   200 - 300
AD3812 Seattle 1908, 850 cys   150 - 250

Densmore, Frances
AD3910 Chippewa Music Wash 1918   30 - 50

AD3920 Pawnee Music Wash 1929   30 - 50
AD3930 Seminole Music Wash 1956   30 - 50

DeVoto, Bernard
AD4010 Across the Wide Missouri Bos 1947, box   100 - 150
AD4011 Bos 1947, DJ (1st trade ed)   20 - 30
AD4020 House of the Sun-Goes-Down NY 1928, DJ   30 - 50
AD4030 Journals of Lewis and Clark Bos 1953, DJ   30 - 50
AD4040 Year of Decision 1846 Bos 1943, DJ   20 - 30

Dick, Everett
AD4080 The Dixie Frontier NY 1948, DJ   20 - 30

Dickins, James
AD4110 1861 to 1865, by an Old Johnnie Cinti 1897 150 - 250

Dienst, Alex
AD4210 The Navy of the Republic of Texas
          1835-1845 Temple, TX 1909   300 - 500

Dietz, August
AD4310 The Postal Service of the Confederate States
          of America Richmond 1929   500 - 700

Dimsdale, Thomas J.
AD4410 The Vigilantes of Montana Helena, MT 1915   75 - 125
AD4412 Norman 1953, DJ   30 - 50

Dobie, J. Frank (also see Books About Books)
AD4510 Apache Gold and Yaqui Silver Bos 1939,
          265 cys, box   1500 - 2500
AD4511 Bos 1939, DJ (1st trade ed)   75 - 125
AD4513 Bos 1949, DJ   30 - 50
AD4520 As the Moving Finger Writ Dallas 1955, 300 cys 75 - 125
AD4530 Ben Lilly Legend Bos 1950, DJ   100 - 150
AD4532 Lon 1952, DJ   50 - 75
AD4540 Between the Comanche and the Rattlesnake
          Dallas 1955, wrappers   40 - 60
AD4550 Bob More Austin, 1965, 500 cys, slipcase   200 - 300
AD4561 Coronado's Children Dallas 1930, DJ, 1st state
          w/o "clean" in dedication   75 - 125
AD4562 Dallas, 1930, DJ, later printings   25 - 50
AD4564 NY 1931, DJ   20 - 30
AD4566 Dallas 1980, 300 cys, slipcase   800 - 1200
AD4580 Cow People Bos 1964, DJ   50 - 75
AD4590 Coyote Wisdom Austin 1938, DJ   250 - 350
AD4592 Dallas 1965, DJ   20 - 30
AD4600 Flavor of Texas Dallas 1936, DJ   200 - 300
AD4610 Folklore of the Southwest Okla Cty 1924,
          wrappers   200 - 300
AD4620 Frontier Tales of the White Mustang Dallas
          1979, 395 cys   100 - 150
AD4640 I'll Tell You a Tale Bos 1960, DJ   30 - 50
AD4650 Legends of Texas Austin 1924, DJ   200 - 300
AD4660 Longhorns Bos 1941, DJ, limited ed, signed 1000 - 1500
AD4661 Bos 1941 (1st trade ed), DJ   75 - 125
AD4663 Bos 1951, DJ   25 - 50
AD4670 Lost Mines of the Old West: Coronado's
          Children Lon 1960, DJ   40 - 60
AD4680 Man, Bird and Beast Austin 1930, DJ   75 - 125
AD4682 Dallas, 1965, DJ   15 - 25
AD4690 Mustangs Bos 1952, 100 cys w/original
          drawing, box   3000 - 5000
AD4691 Bos 1952, DJ (1st trade ed)   150 - 250

AD4700	**On the Open Range** Dallas 1931, 750 cys	800 - 1200
AD4701	Dallas 1931, DJ (1st trade ed)	75 - 125
AD4710	**Rattlesnakes** Bos 1965, DJ	40 - 60
AD4720	**Tales of Old Time Texas** Bos 1955, DJ	75 - 125
AD4730	**Tales of the Mustang** Dallas, 1936, 300 cys, box	2000 - 3000
AD4740	**Texan in England** Bos 1945, DJ	75 - 125
AD4750	**Texas and Southwestern Lore** Austin 1934, DJ	100 - 150
AD4760	**Tongues of the Monte** Garden City 1935, DJ	200 - 300
AD4762	Bos 1947, DJ	75 - 125
AD4770	**Vaquero of the Brush Country** Dallas 1929, DJ	300 - 500
AD4780	**Voice of the Coyote** 1949, DJ	100 - 150
AD4782	Bos 1950, DJ	25 - 50
AD4790	**Wild and Wily: Range Animals** Flagstaff 1980, 100 cys, slipcase	300 - 500
AD4791	Flagstaff 1980, DJ (1st trade ed)	25 - 50

Dockstader, Frederick
AD4910	**Indian Art of the Americas** NY 1973, DJ	50 - 75

Doddridge, Joseph
AD5010	**Notes, on the Settlement and Indian Wars, of the Western Parts of Virginia and Pennsylvania Etc.** Wellsburgh, VA 1924	100 - 150

Dodge, Grenville M.
AD5110	**Biographical Sketch of James Bridger, Mountaineer, Trapper and Guide** Kansas City 1905	200 - 300
AD5111	NY 1905, wrappers	200 - 300
AD5121	**How We Built the Union Pacific Railway** Council Bluffs, IA, early 1900s, 1st issue w/o printer's name on forepage	200 - 300
AD5130	**Wonderful Story of the Building of the Pacific Roads** Omaha 1889, wrappers	150 - 250

Dodson, W. C.
AD5210	**Campaigns of Wheeler and His Cavalry 1862-1865** Atlanta 1899	200 - 300

Donan, P.
AD5310	**Gold Fields of Baker County, Eastern Oregon** Portland 1898, wrappers	300 - 500

Donoho, M. H.
AD5410	**Circle-Dot, A True Story of Cowboy Life 40 Years Ago** Topeka 1907	150 - 250

Doten, Dana
AD5510	**The Art of Bundling** NY 1938	30 - 50

Douglas, C. L.
AD5610	**Cattle Kings of Texas** Dallas 1939	300 - 500
AD5611	Dallas 1939, rawhide cover	500 - 700
AD5613	Dallas 1968, DJ	50 - 75
AD5620	**Famous Texas Feuds** Dallas 1936, DJ	150 - 250
AD5630	**Gentlemen in the White Hats** Dallas 1934, DJ	150 - 250
AD5640	**James Bowie** Dallas 1944, DJ	100 - 150

Douglas, David
AD5710	**Journal Kept by David Douglas During His Travels in America 1823-27** Lon 1914, 500 cys	250 - 350

Douglas, Frederic H.
AD5810	**Indian Art of the United States** NY 1941, DJ	50 - 75

Dow, George Francis
AD5910	**The Arts and Crafts in New England** Topsfield 1927, DJ	200 - 300
AD5920	**The Pirates of the New England Coast** Salem 1923, DJ	150 - 250
AD5940	**Slave Ships and Slaving** Salem 1923	200 - 300
AD5941	Salem 1923, 97 cys	300 - 500
AD5943	Salem 1927, DJ	100 - 150
AD5950	**Whale Ships and Whaling** Salem 1925, 950 cys	200 - 300
AD5960	Salem 1925, 97 cys	300 - 500

Downie, William
AD6110	**Hunting For Gold** SF 1893	300 - 500

Drago, Harry S.
AD6210	**Great American Cattle Trails** NY 1965, DJ	30 - 50
AD6220	**Great Range Wars** NY 1970, DJ	30 - 50
AD6230	**Legend Makers** NY 1975, DJ	30 - 50
AD6240	**Outlaws on Horseback** NY 1964, 150 cys, box	150 - 250
AD6250	**Red River Valley** NY 1962, DJ	30 - 50
AD6260	**Road Agents and Train Robbers** NY 1973, DJ	30 - 50
AD6270	**Wild, Wooly and Wicked** NY 1960, 250 cys	150 - 250
AD6272	NY 1960s, DJ	50 - 75

Drannan, Capt. William F.
AD6410	**Thirty-One Years on the Plains and in the Mountains** Chi 1899	250 - 350

Driggs, Howard R.
AD6510	**The Pony Express Goes Through** NY 1935, DJ	30 - 50

Drips, Joseph H.
AD6610	**Three Years Among the Indians in Dakota** Kimball, SD, 1894, wrappers	1000 - 1500

Driver, Harold
AD6710	**Indians of North America** Chi, 1961, DJ	20 - 30

Du Bois, W. E. B.
AD6810	**The Gift of Black Folk in the Making of America** Bos 1924, DJ	200 - 300
AD6820	**The Souls of Black Folk** Chi 1903, DJ	300 - 500
AD6830	**Suppression of the American Slave Trade** (1st Book) NY 1896	800 - 1200

DuFlot De Mofras, Eugene
AD6910	**Travels on the Pacific Coast** Santa Ana 1937, 2 vol	200 - 300

Duke, Basil W.
AD7010	**History of Morgan's Cavalry** Cinti, 1867	200 - 300
AD7012	NY 1906	75 - 125
AD7020	**Reminiscences** Garden City 1911	100 - 150

Dunbar, Seymour
AD7110	**A History of Travel in America** Ind 1915, DJ	50 - 75
AD7112	NY 1937, DJ	50 - 75

Dunlap, William
AD7210	**History of the Rise and Progress of the Arts of Design in the United States** Bos 1918, 3 vol	200 - 300

Dunn, J. P.
AD7310	**Massacres of the Mountains A History of the Indian Wars of the Far West** NY 1886	300 - 500

Durant, John & Otto Bettmann
AD7360	**Pictorial History of American Sports** NY 1952, DJ	20 - 30

Dustin, Fred
AD7410	**The Custer Tragedy** Ann Arbor 1939	300 - 500

Duval, John C.
AD7510	**Adventures of Big Foot Wallace** Phil 1885	500 - 700
AD7512	Austin 1947, DJ	50 - 75
AD7514	NY 1983	20 - 30
AD7520	**Early Times in Texas** Austin 1892, wrappers	300 - 500
AD7522	Dallas 1935, DJ	30 - 50

Dyer, Mrs. D. B.
AD7610	**Fort Reno** NY 1896	200 - 300

Dyer, Frederick H.
AD7710	**A Compendium of the War of the Rebellion** Des Moines 1908	150 - 250

Earle, Alice Morse
AE1010	**Colonial Dames and Good Wives** Bos 1895	50 - 75
AE1020	**Costume of Colonial Times** NY 1924	40 - 60
AE1030	**Curious Punishments of Bygone Days** Chi 1896	50 - 75
AE1040	**Old Time Gardens** NY 1911	40 - 60
AE1050	**The Sabbath in Puritan New England** NY 1891	50 - 75
AE1060	**Stage Coach and Tavern Days** NY 1900	50 - 75

Eaton, Rachel Caroline
AE1210	**John Ross and the Cherokee Indians** Menasha, WI 1914	200 - 300

Eckenrode, Hamilton J.
AE1310	**The Revolution in Virginia** Bos 1916	100 - 150

Edwards, Billy
AE1410	**Gladiators of the Prize Ring, or Pugilists of America** Chi 1895	150 - 250

Edwards, Philip Leget
AE1510	**The Diary of Philip Leget Edwards** SF 1932, 500 cys, DJ	150 - 250

Eisenchiml, Otto
AE1610	**The Civil War** NY 1956, 2 vol, box	50 - 75

Elfer, Maurice
AE1710	**Madam Candelaria Unsung Heroine of the Alamo** Houston 1933, wrappers	50 - 75

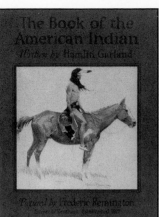
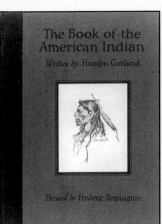
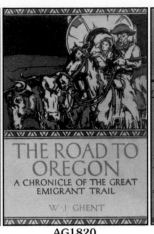
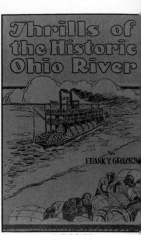

AF1660   AG1210 Dust jacket (left) and cover (right)   AG1820   AG4060

Elliott, David S.
AE1810   Last Raid of the Daltons Coffeyville, KS
       1892, wrappers   600 - 800
AE1812   Coffeyville 1954 (facsimile reprint)   50 - 75

Elliott, W. W.
AE1910   History of Arizona Territory SF 1884   1000 - 1500

Ellsworth, Lincoln
AE2010   The Last Wild Buffalo Hunt NY 1916   75 - 125

Elman, Robert
AE2110   The Great American Shooting Prints NY 1972, DJ 75 - 125

Englehardt, Zephyrin
AE2210   The Franciscans in California Harbor Springs
       1897, wrappers   200 - 300

Esmeralda, Aurora
AE2310   Life and Letters of a Forty-Niner's Daughter
       SF 1929, 1600 cys   50 - 75

Espejo, Antonio de
AE2410   New Mexico Lancaster 1928, 200 cys   300 - 500

Esquemeling, John
AE2510   The Buccaneers of America Lon 1911, DJ   50 - 75

Essholm, Frank
AE2610   Pioneers and Prominent Men of Utah
       Salt Lake City 1913   100 - 150

Evans, Bessie
AE2710   American Indian Dance Steps NY 1921   75 - 125

Falconer, Thomas
AF1010   Letters and Notes on the Texan Santa Fe
       Expeditions 1841-42 NY 1930   250 - 350

Feder, Norman
AF1110   American Indian Art NY 1960s, DJ   200 - 300

Fehrenbach, T. R.
AF1210   Comanches NY 1974, DJ   50 - 75

Ferguson, Russell J.
AF1310   Early Western Pennsylvania Politics Pittsburgh
       1938, DJ   50 - 75

Fess, Simeon D.
AF1410   Ohio the History of a Great State Chi 1937, 5 vol 100 - 150

Fewkes, Jesse Walter
AF1460   Hopi Katcinas Drawn by Native Artists
       Chi 1962, DJ (reprint of 1899-1900 Bureau
       of Ethnology Report: see Powell, J.W.)   30 - 50

Fife, Austin
AF1510   Saints of Sage and Saddle Bloomington 1956, DJ 30 - 50

Finerty, John F.
AF1610   War Path and Bivouac Chi 1890   100 - 150

Finger, Charles J.
AF1660   The Distant Prize NY 1935, DJ   20 - 30

Fish, Daniel
AF1710   Lincoln Bibliography NY 1906, 75 cys, box   200 - 300

Fisher, Owen
AF1810   The North American Indians NY 1967, DJ   30 - 50

Fisher, Vardis
AF1910   Idaho Caldwell 1937   200 - 300

Fister, R.
AF2010   Golden Book of the Osages Clev 1950, box,
       45 RPM record, 15 medals   200 - 300

Fite, Emerson D.
AF2110   A Book of Old Maps Delineating American
       History Cambridge 1926, DJ   300 - 500

Fletcher, W. A.
AF2310   A Rebel Private, Front and Rear Beaumont,
       TX 1908   800 - 1200

Forbes, Alexander
AF2510   California: A History SF 1919, 250 cys   500 - 700
AF2512   SF 1937, 650 cys, DJ   200 - 300
AF2514   SF 1939   75 - 125

Forbes, Edwin
AF2610   Thirty Years After: An Artists Story of the
       Great War NY 1890, 4 vol   200 - 300

Foreman, Grant
AF2710   Advancing the Frontier Norman 1933, DJ   150 - 250
AF2720   Indians and Pioneers Norman 1930, DJ   200 - 300
AF2730   Pioneer Days in the Early Southwest Clev 1926 200 - 300

Forrest, Earle R.
AF2810   Arizona's Dark and Bloody Ground Caldwell
       1936, DJ   75 - 125
AF2820   Missions and Pueblos of the Old Southwest
       Clev 1929, DJ   150 - 250

Fowke, Gerard
AF2910   Archaeological History of Ohio Col 1902   50 - 75

Frederick, J. V.
AF3010   Ben Holladay, The Stagecoach King
       Glendale 1940   100 - 150

Freeman, Douglas Southall
AF3110   Lee's Lieutenants NY 1942, 3 vol, DJs   150 - 225
       ea vol w/DJ   50 - 75
       ea vol w/o DJ   30 - 50

French, Capt. W. J.
AF3210   Wild Jim, The Texas Cowboy and Saddle
       King Antioch 1890, wrappers   800 - 1200

French, William
AF3310   Some Recollections of a Western Ranchman
       Lon 1927, DJ   300 - 500
AF3312   NY 1928, DJ   300 - 500
AF3314   NY 1965, 750 cys, 2 vol, slipcase   100 - 150

Fridge, Ike
AF3410   History of the Chisum War...Cowboy Life
       on the Frontier Electra, TX 1927, wrappers   500 - 700

Frink, Margaret A.
AF3510   Journal of the Adventures of a Party of
       California Gold Seekers Oakland 1897   600 - 800

Fulkerson, H. S.
AF3610   Random Recollections of Early Days in
       Mississippi Vicksburg 1885, wrappers   600 - 800

Fuller, C. L.
AF3710   Pocket Map and Descriptive Outline History
       of the Black Hills of Dakota and Wyoming
       Rapid City 1887, wrappers   800 - 1200

Fuller, Emeline
AF3810 **Left by the Indians** Mt. Vernon, IA 1892,
    wrappers   300 - 500
AF3812 NY 1936, 200 cys   100 - 150
Fulmore, Z. T.
AF3910 **History and Geography of Texas** Austin 1915 150 - 250
AF3912 Austin 1935   50 - 75
Fundaburk, Emma (editor)
AF4010 **Sun Circles and Human Hands** Luverne 1957, DJ 50 - 75
Funkhouser, W. D.
AF4110 **Wild Life in Kentucky** Frankfort 1925   100 - 150
Fynn, A. F.
AF4210 **American Indian as a Product of Environment**
    Bos 1907   50 - 75
Garavaglia, Louis A.
AG0910 **Firearms of the American West 1803-1865**
    Albu 1984   75 - 125
AG0920 **Firearms of the American West 1866-1894**
    Albu 1985   75 - 125
Garces, Francisco
AG1010 **On the Trail of the Spanish Pioneer** NY 1900,
    2 vol, 950 cys   250 - 350
Gard, Wayne
AG1110 **Along the Early Trails of the Southwest** Austin
    1969, 250 cys   200 - 300
AG1120 **The Chisholm Trail** Norman 1954, DJ   75 - 125
AG1130 **Frontier Justice** Norman 1949, DJ   75 - 125
AG1140 **Sam Bass** Bos 1936, DJ   100 - 150
Garland, Hamlin
AG1210 **The Book of the American Indian** NY 1923, DJ 200 - 300
Garner, James W.
AG1310 **Reconstruction in Mississippi** NY 1901   150 - 250
Garrard, Lewis H.
AG1410 **Wah-To-Yah, and the Taos Trail** Cinti 1850 2000 - 3000
AG1412 SF 1936, 550 cys, box   200 - 300
AG1414 Glendale 1938, DJ   50 - 75
AG1416 Norman 1955, DJ   20 - 30
AG1418 Palo Alto 1968, DJ   50 - 75
Garrett, Pat F.
AG1510 **The Authentic Life of Billy, the Kid** Santa Fe
    1882, blue wrappers w/misnumbered pages &
    ad in back   3000 - 5000
AG1512 NY 1927, DJ   75 - 125
AG1514 NY 1946, wrappers   30 - 50
AG1516 Norman 1954, DJ   30 - 50
Gerhard, Peter
AG1610 **Pirates in Baja California** Mexico 1963, 500 cys,
    wrappers   30 - 50
AG1620 **Pirates on the West Coast of New Spain**
    1575-1742 Glendale 1960   75 - 125
Gerstaecker, Friedrich
AG1710 **California Gold Mines** Oakland 1946, 500 cys 150 - 250
AG1720 **Scenes of Life in California** SF 1942, 500 cys 150 - 250
Ghent, W. J.
AG1810 **The Early Far West** NY 1936, DJ   30 - 50
AG1820 **The Road to Oregon** NY 1929, DJ   30 - 50
AG1822 NY 1934, DJ   30 - 50
Gifford, Edward W.
AG1910 **California Indian Nights Entertainment**
    Glendale 1930   75 - 125
Gilbert, Paul T.
AG2010 **Chicago and its Makers** Chi 1929   200 - 300
Gillett, James B.
AG2110 **Six Years with the Texas Rangers** Austin 1921 150 - 250
AG2112 New Haven 1925   75 - 125
AG2114 Chi 1943   20 - 30
Gillmor, Frances
AG2210 **Traders to the Navajos** Bos 1936, DJ   50 - 75
AG2212 Albu 1952, DJ   30 - 50
Gilmore, James R.
AG2310 **Personal Recollections of Abraham Lincoln**
    and the Civil War Bos 1898   75 - 125

Glasscock, C. B.
AG2410 **Bandits and the Southern Pacific** NY 1929, DJ 50 - 75
AG2420 **The Big Bonanza** NY, DJ   20 - 30
AG2430 **Gold in Them Hills** NY 1930s, DJ   20 - 30
AG2440 **Lucky Baldwin** NY 1930s, DJ   20 - 30
Glazier, Captain Willard
AG2510 **Down the Great River** Phil 1888   20 - 30
Goddard, P. E.
AG2610 **Indians of the South West** NY 1921, DJ 50 - 75
Goldsmith, Oliver
AG2710 **Over Land in Forty-Nine** Detroit 1896   1000 - 1500
Gookin, Frederick W.
AG2810 **Daniel Gookin 1612-1687** Chi 1912, 202 cys 150 - 250
Gordon, M. L.
AG2910 **Experiences in the Civil War** Bos 1922   75 - 125
Gordon, Maurice
AG3010 **Aesculapius Comes to the Colonies** Ventnor, NJ
    1949, DJ   50 - 75
Gorrell, J. R.
AG3110 **A Trip to Alaska** Newton, IA 1905, gr wrappers 200 - 300
Goss, Charles Frederic
AG3210 **Cincinnati the Queen City 1788-1912**
    Chi 1912, 4 vol   250 - 350
AG3220 **Cincinnati the Queen City** Chi 1912, 2 vol
    (supplement)   125 - 200
Gould, E. W.
AG3310 **Fifty Years on the Mississippi** St. Louis 1889 200 - 300
Gove, Captain Jesse A.
AG3410 **The Utah Expedition 1857-58** Concord, NH
    1928, 50 cys   300 - 500
Grabhorn, Jane Bissell (editor)
AG3510 **A California Gold Rush Miscellany** SF 1934,
    550 cys   200 - 300
Graham, William A.
AG3610 **The Custer Myth: A Source Book of Custeriana**
    Harrisburg 1953, DJ   100 - 150
AG3620 **The Official Record...of Major Marcus A. Reno**
    Pacific Palisades, CA 1951, 2 vol 500 - 700
AG3630 **The Story of Little Big Horn** Harrisburg 1941, DJ 100 - 150
Grant, Blanche
AG3710 **Kit Carson's Own Story** Taos 1926, wrappers 150 - 250
AG3720 **When Old Trails Were New - The Story of**
    Taos NY 1934, DJ   50 - 75
Grant, U. S.
AG3810 **Personal Memoirs** NY 1885-86, 2 vol,
    large paper cy   200 - 300
AG3811 NY 1885-86 (trade ed)   50 - 75
Graves, Richard S.
AG3910 **Oklahoma Outlaws** Okla Cty 1915, wrappers 75 - 125
Graves, W. W.
AG4010 **Annals of Osage Mission** St. Paul, KS 1935 150 - 250
Grayson, Frank
AG4060 **Thrills of the Historic Ohio River** Cinti (early
    1900s), wrappers   50 - 75
Green, Ben K.
AG4110 **Back to Back** Austin 1970, 850 cys, slipcase 150 - 250
AG4120 **Ben Green Tales** Flagstaff 1973, 1250 cys, 4 vol 150 - 250
AG4130 **Color of Horses** Flagstaff 1974, 150 cys, box 300 - 500
AG4131 Flagstaff 1974 (1st trade ed) DJ   75 - 125
AG4140 **Horse Tradin** NY 1967, DJ   75 - 125
AG4150 **Some More Horse Tradin** NY 1972, 350 cys, box 150 - 250
AG4160 **Thousand Miles of Mustangin** Flagstaff 1972,
    150 cys, Box   300 - 500
AG4161 Flagstaff 1972, DJ (1st trade ed)   75 - 125
AG4170 **Village Horse Doctor West of the Pecos**
    NY 1971, DJ   100 - 150
AG4180 **Wild Cow Tales** NY 1969, 300 cys, slipcase 300 - 500
AG4181 NY 1969, DJ (1st trade ed)   75 - 125
Green, Jonathan S.
AG4310 **Journal of a Tour on the Northwest Coast of**
    America in the Year 1829 NY 1915, 150 cys 500 - 700

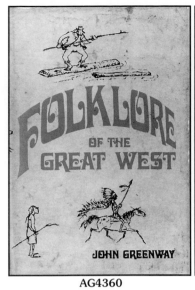

| AG4360 | AH3011 (frontispiece) |

Greenway, John
AG4360 Folklore of the Great West Palo Alto 1969, DJ   20 - 30

Greer, James K.
AG4410 Bois D'Arc to Barb'd Wire Dallas 1936, DJ   200 - 300
AG4420 Colonel Jack Hays NY 1952, DJ   150 - 250
AG4430 Grand Prairie Dallas 1935, DJ   200 - 300
AG4440 A Texas Ranger and Frontiersman Dallas
          1932, DJ   200 - 300

Gregg, Alexander
AG4510 History of the Old Cheraws Columbia, SC 1905 200 - 300

Gridley, Marion
AG4610 Indians of Yesterday NY 1940, DJ   30 - 50

Griffin, James B.
AG4710 Archeology of the Eastern United States
          Chi 1952, DJ   75 - 125
AG4720 The Fort Ancient Aspect Ann Arbor 1943, DJ   75 - 125

Grinnell, George Bird
AG4810 Blackfoot Lodge Tales: The Story of a Prairie
          People NY 1892   150 - 250
AG4820 The Cheyenne Indians New Haven 1923, 2 vol   150 - 250
AG4830 The Fighting Cheyennes NY 1915, DJ   200 - 300
AG4840 The Indians of Today Chi 1900   300 - 500
AG4850 Passing of the Great West NY 1972, DJ   50 - 75
AG4860 Pawnee Hero Stories and Folk Tales NY 1893   75 - 125
AG4870 Two Great Scouts and Their Pawnee Battalion
          Clev 1928   100 - 150

Grinnell, Joseph
AG5010 Gold Hunting in Alaska Elgin 1901, wrappers   100 - 150

Guernsey, Alfred & Alden, Henry
AG5210 Harper's Pictorial History of the Civil War
          Chi 1894, 2 vol   150 - 250

Haberly, Loyd
AH1010 Pursuit of the Horizon: A Life of George Catlin,
          Painter and Recorder of the American Indian
          NY 1948, DJ   30 - 50

Hafen, Le Roy R.
AH1110 Broken Hand, The Life Story of Thomas Fitzpatrick,
          Chief of the Mountain Men Denver 1931   200 - 300
AH1112 Denver 1973, DJ   50 - 75
AH1120 The Far West and the Rockies 1820-75
          Glendale 1954-61, 15 vol   1000 - 1500
AH1130 Handcardts to Zion Glendale 1960   75 - 125
AH1140 Mountain Men and the Fur Trade of the
          Far West Glendale 1965-72 10 vol/DJs   800 - 1200
AH1150 The Old Spanish Trail Glendale 1954   100 - 150
AH1160 The Overland Mail, 1849-1869 Clev 1926   150 - 250
AH1170 Overland Routes to the Goldfields Glendale 1942 100 - 150
AH1180 Powder River Campaigns and Sawyers
          Expedition 1865 Glendale 1961   75 - 125
AH1190 Relations with Indians on the Plains Glendale 1959 75 - 125
AH1200 Western America NY 1941, DJ   50 - 75

Hakluyt, Richard
AH1310 The Principal Navigations, Voyages, Traffiques
          and Discoveries of the English Nation Glasgow
          1903-05, 12 vol, 100 sets   800 - 1200
AH1312 Lon 1927-28, 10 vol   300 - 500
AH1314 Lon 1932 8 vol (Everyman's Library)   150 - 250
AH1316 Cambridge 1965, 2 vol, DJs   150 - 250

Halbert, Henry S.
AH1410 The Creek War of 1813 and 1814 Chi 1895   300 - 500

Hale, John
AH1510 California As It Is SF 1954, 150 cys   250 - 350

Hale, John P.
AH1610 Trans-Allegheny Pioneers Cinti 1886   100 - 150

Hale, Will
AH1710 Twenty-Four Years a Cowboy and Ranchman
          in Southern Texas and Old Mexico Hedrick,
          OK Territory 1905, wrappers   4000 - 6000

Haley, J. Evetts
AH1810 Fort Concho on the Texas Frontier
          San Angelo 1952   100 - 150
AH1820 The Heraldry of the Range Canyon, TX 1952   100 - 150
AH1830 Life on the Texas Range Austin 1952   100 - 150

Hall, Bert L.
AH1910 Round Up Years Pierre, SD 1954   100 - 150

Hallenbeck, Cleve
AH2010 Alvar Nunez Cabeza de Vaca Glendale 1940   200 - 300
AH2020 Journey of Fray Marcos de Niza Dallas 1949, DJ 250 - 350
AH2030 Land of the Conquistadores Caldwell 1950, DJ   50 - 75
AH2040 Legends of the Spanish Southwest Glendale 1938 100 - 150
AH2050 Spanish Missions of the Old Southwest
          Garden City 1926, DJ   50 - 75

Hambleton, Chalkley J.
AH2110 A Gold Hunters Experience Chi 1898   250 - 350

Hamilton, W. T.
AH2210 My Sixty Years on the Plains NY 1905   150 - 250

Hammond, George Parker (editor)
AH2310 Narratives of the Coronado Expedition
          Albu 1940   100 - 150
AH2320 Noticias De California SF 1958, 400 cys   100 - 150
AH2330 Oregon's History of 16th C. Exploration
          LA 1928   100 - 150

Hanly, J. Frank
AH2410 A Day in the Siskiyous Ind 1916   30 - 50

Hanson, Joseph Mills
AH2510 Conquest of the Missouri Chi 1910, DJ   75 - 125

Hardin, John Wesley
AH2610 The Life of John Wesley Hardin Seguin, TX 1896 150 - 250
AH2612 Norman 1961, DJ   30 - 50

Harlan, Jacob Wright
AH2710 California '46 to '88 SF 1888   150 - 250

Harlow, Alvin F.
AH2810 Old Post Bags NY 1928, DJ   150 - 250
AH2820 Old Towpaths NY 1926, DJ   150 - 250
AH2830 Old Waybills NY 1934, DJ   150 - 250

Harlow, Neal
AH2910 The Maps of San Francisco Bay SF 1950,
          375 cys   800 - 1200

Harman, S. W.
AH3010 Hell on the Border Ft. Smith, AR 1898,
          green wrappers   400 - 600
AH3011 Ft. Smith, AK 1898, cloth   500 - 700

Harpending, Asbury
AH3110 The Great Diamond Hoax SF 1913   75 - 125

Harris, Sarah Hollister
AH3210 An Unwritten Chapter of Salt Lake 1851-1901
          NY 1901   300 - 500

Harrison, Fairfax
AH3310 Virginia Land Grants Richmond 1925   50 - 75

Hart, John A.
AH3410 History of Pioneer Days in Texas and Oklahoma
          Guthrie 1906   300 - 500
AH3510 Pioneer Days in the Southwest Guthrie 1909   200 - 300

Hastings, Frank S.
AH3610 A Ranchman's Recollections Chi 1921, DJ   150 - 250
Haven, Charles T.
AH3710 A History of the Colt Revolver NY 1940, box   200 - 300
AH3711 NY 1960, DJ (1st trade ed)   50 - 75
Havighurst, Walter
AH3810 Annie Oakley of the Wild West NY 1954, DJ   30 - 50
AH3820 Upper Mississippi NY 1937, DJ   30 - 50
Hawley, W. A.
AH3910 The Early Days of Santa Barbara NY 1910   150 - 250
Headley, John W.
AH4010 Confederate Operations in Canada and New
         York NY 1906   100 - 150
Hebard, Grace R.
AH4110 The Bozeman Trail Clev 1922, 2 vol   250 - 350
AH4120 Sacajawea Glendale 1933, 750 cys   150 - 250
AH4130 Washakie Clev 1930   100 - 150
Hebison, W. C.
AH4210 Early Days in Texas and Rains County Emory,
         TX 1917, wrappers   300 - 500
Heckewelder, John
AH4310 A Narrative of the Mission of the United
         Brethren Among the Delaware and Mohegan
         Indians Clev 1907, 160 cys   250 - 350
Hendricks, George
AH4360 The Badman of the West San Antonio 1959,
         DJ (revised ed)   20 - 30
Hennepin, Father Louis
AH4410 A New Discovery of a Vast Country in America
         Chi 1903   100 - 150
Henry, Alexander
AH4510 New Light on the Early History of the Greater
         North West NY 1897, 3 vol   500 - 700
AH4520 Travels and Adventures in Canada and the
         Indian Territories Bos 1901, 700 cys   200 - 300
Herndon, William H.
AH4610 Herndon's Lincoln Chi 1889, 3 vol   300 - 500
Hewett, Edgar L.
AH4710 Ancient Life in the American Southwest
         Ind 1930, DJ   50 - 75
AH4712 NY 1943, DJ   30 - 50
AH4720 The Chaco Canyon and Its Monuments
         Albu 1936, DJ   50 - 75
AH4730 The Pueblo Indian World Albu 1945, DJ   50 - 75
Hewitt, Randall H.
AH4810 Across the Plains and Over the Divide NY 1906 150 - 250
Heyerdahl, Thor
AH4910 American Indians in the Pacific NY 1953, DJ   100 - 150
Hill, Alice Polk
AH5010 Tales of the Colorado Pioneers Denver 1884   200 - 300
Hilton, A.
AH5110 Oklahoma and Indian Territory Along the
         Frisco St. Louis 1905, wrappers   200 - 300
Hinkle, James F.
AH5210 Early Days of a Cowboy on the Pecos
         Roswell 1937, wrappers   500 - 700
Hinman, Wilbur F.
AH5310 The Story of the Sherman Brigade Alliance 1897 50 - 75
Hittell, Theodore
AH5410 History of California SF 1897, 4 vol   300 - 500
Hodge, F. W.
AH5510 Handbook of American Indians North of
         Mexico Wash 1907, 2 vol   200 - 300
Hodge, Gene Meany
AH5610 The Kachinas Are Coming LA 1936   200 - 300
AH5612 Flagstaff 1967, DJ   75 - 125
Holbrook, Stewart H.
AH5710 Holy Old MacKinaw NY 1938, DJ   30 - 50
Holden, W. C.
AH5810 Alkali Trails Dallas 1930, DJ   100 - 150
Hollister, Uriah S.
AH5910 The Navajo and His Blanket Denver 1903   150 - 250

Holmes, Roberta E.
AH6010 The Southern Mines of California SF 1930,
         250 cys   300 - 500
Holmes, W. H.
AH6110 Handbook of Aboriginal American Antiquities
         Wash 1919   30 - 50
Holsey, Albon L.
AH6210 Booker T. Washington's Own Story of His Life
         and Work 1915   30 - 50
Honig, Louis O.
AH6310 The Pathfinder of the West: James Bridger
         Kansas City 1951   100 - 150
AH6320 Westport, Gateway to the Early West North
         Kansas City 1950, 525 cys   100 - 150
Horan, James D.
AH6410 The McKenney-Hall Portrait Gallery of
         American Indians NY 1972, DJ   50 - 75
Horgan, Paul
AH6510 Great River: The Rio Grande in American
         History NY 1954, 2 vol, 1000 cys   100 - 150
AH6511 NY 1954, 2 vol, box (1st trade ed)   50 - 75
Hosmer, James K.
AH6610 Cass's Journal of the Lewis and Clark
         Expedition Chi 1904   150 - 250
Hough, Dr. Walter
AH6710 The Hopi Indians Cedar Rapids 1915, DJ   50 - 75
Howard, Helen
AH6810 War Chief Joseph Caldwell 1941, DJ   30 - 50
Howard, McHenry
AH6910 Recollections of a Maryland Confederate
         Soldier Balt 1914   300 - 500
Howard, Oliver O.
AH7010 Famous Indian Chiefs I Have Known NY 1908   150 - 250
AH7020 My Life and Experiences Among Our Hostile
         Indians Hartford 1907   150 - 250
Howbert, Irving
AH7110 The Indians of the Pikes Peak Region NY 1914 75 - 125
Howe, Henry
AH7210 Historical Collections of Ohio Cinti 1902, 2 vol 50 75
Hubbard, Harlan
AH7310 Shanty Boat NY 1954, DJ   30 - 50
Hubbard, Rev. William
AH7410 Narratives of the Indian Wars 1675-1699 NY 1913 30 - 50
Huckel, J. F. (editor)
AH7510 American Indians First Families of the Southwest
         Kansas City 1920, wrappers   50 - 75
Hughes, Langston (also see Modern First Editions)
AH7610 A Pictorial History of the Negro in America
         NY 1963, DJ   30 - 50
Hughes, Richard B.
AH7710 Pioneer Years in the Black Hills Glendale 1957 100 - 150

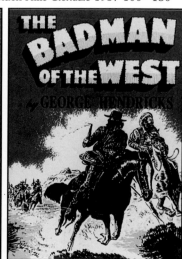

AH3820   AH4360

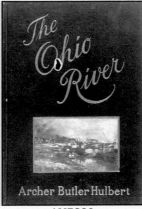

| AH7310 | AH7510 | AH7830 | AH8010 (spine, cover, and interior illustration) |

Hulbert, Archer B.
AH7810 **Forty Niners** Bos 1931, DJ 50 - 75
AH7820 **The Niagara River** NY 1908 50 - 75
AH7830 **The Ohio River** NY 1906 75 - 125

Hulbert, Winifred
AH7910 **Indian Americans** NY 1952, wrappers 30 - 50

Humfreville, James L.
AH8010 **Twenty Years Among Our Savage Indians**
Hartford 1897 (orig ed w/color plates) 300 - 500
AH8012 Hartford 1899 50 - 75
AH8014 NY 1903 50 - 75

Hungerford, Edward
AH8110 **Daniel Willard Rides the Rails** NY 1938, DJ 30 - 50
AH8120 **Locomotives on Parade** NY 1940, DJ 30 - 50
AH8130 **The Story of the Baltimore and Ohio Railroad**
NY 1928, 2 vol, DJs 75 - 125
AH8140 **Wells Fargo** NY 1949, DJ 30 - 50

Hunt, George M.
AH8210 **Early Days Upon the Plains of Texas**
Lubbock 1919 150 - 250

Hunt, Rockwell
AH8310 **California and Californians** Chi 1930, 4 vol 75 - 125
AH8320 **Oxcart to Airplane** LA 1929, DJ 30 - 50
AH8330 **Personal Sketches of California Pioneers**
Stockton 1962, 500 cys 100 - 150
AH8340 **A Short History of California** NY 1929, DJ 30 - 50

Hunter, J. Marvin
AH8410 **The Album of Gun-Fighters** Bandera, TX
1951, DJ 100 - 150
AH8412 1959, DJ 50 - 75
AH8420 **Peregrinations of a Pioneer Printer** Grand
Prairie 1954, DJ 100 - 150
AH8430 **The Trail Drivers of Texas** San Antonio
1920-23, 100 cys, 2 vol 1000 - 1500
AH8431 San Antonio 1920-23, 2 vol (1st trade ed) 300 - 500
AH8433 Nashville 1925, 100 cys, 2 vol, DJs, box 500 - 700
AH8435 NY 1963, 750 cys, 2 vol, box 150 - 250

Hurston, Zora Neale
AH8510 **Dust Tracks on the Road** Phil 1942, DJ 200 - 300

Hyde, George E.
AH8610 **The Early Blackfeet and Their Neighbors**
Denver 1933 75 cys, wrappers 150 - 250
AH8620 **Indians of the High Plains** Norman 1959, DJ 50 - 75
AH8630 **The Pawnee Indians** Denver 1934, 100 cys,
2 vol, wrappers 200 - 300
AH8632 Denver 1951, DJ 50 - 75
AH8640 **Rangers and Regulars** Denver 1933, 50 cys,
wrappers 150 - 250
AH8650 **Red Cloud's Folk** Norman 1937, DJ 100 - 150
AH8652 Norman 1957, DJ 30 - 50
AH8660 **Spotted Tail's Folk** Norman 1961, DJ 50 - 75

Ide, Simeon
AI2010 **The Conquest of California A Biography of
William B. Ide** Oakland 1944, 500 cys, DJ 100 - 150

Inman, Henry & William F. Cody
AI2220 **Buffalo Jones' 40 Years of Adventure**
Topeka 1899 300 - 500

AI2231 **The Great Salt Lake Trail** Topeka 1898,
blue 1st state binding 250 - 350
AI2232 later state binding 150 - 250
AI2240 **The Old Santa Fe Trail** Topeka 1897 200 - 300
AI2242 Topeka 1913 50 - 75
AI2250 **Stories of the Old Santa Fe Trail** Kansas City
1991 (1st book) 150 - 250

Inverarity, Robert Bruce
AI2410 **Art of Northwest Coast Indians** Berkeley 1950, DJ 50 - 75

Ivins, Virginia W.
AI2610 **Pen Pictures of Early Western Days**
Keokuk, IA 1905 150 - 250

Jackson, Clarence S.
AJ1010 **Picture Maker of the Old West** NY 1947, DJ 75 - 125

Jackson, George
AJ1110 **Sixty Years in Texas** nd (1908), 322 pp 300 - 500
Dallas 1908 200 - 300

Jackson, Joseph Henry
AJ1210 **Anybody's Gold: The Story of California's
Mining Towns** NY 1941, DJ 50 - 75
AJ1220 **Bad Company** NY 1949, DJ 50 - 75
AJ1230 **Tintypes in Gold: Four Studies in Robbery**
NY 1939, DJ 50 - 75

James, Frank
AJ1310 **The Life and Trial of Frank James** NY 1883 200 - 300
AJ1320 **The Only True History of the Life of Frank
James. Written by Himself** Pine Bluff, AR 1926 100 - 150

James, Fred
AJ1410 **The Klondike Gold Fields and How to Get
There** Lon 1897, wrappers 500 - 700

James, George Wharton
AJ1500 **California** Bos 1919, DJ 50 - 75
AJ1510 **The Grand Canyon of Arizona** Bos 1910, DJ 50 - 75
AJ1520 **In and Around the Grand Canyon** Bos 1900,
500 cys 250 - 350
AJ1530 **Indian Blankets and Their Makers** Chi 1914, DJ 200 - 300

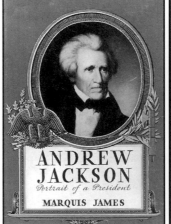

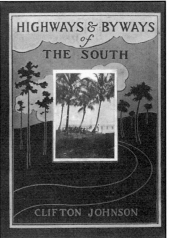

| AJ1700 | AJ2610 |

24

AJ1532	NY 1937, DJ	100 - 150
AJ1540	Indians of the Painted Desert Region Bos 1903	75 - 125
AJ1550	Practical Basket Making Pasadena 1910	75 - 125
AJ1560	What the White Race May Learn From the Indian Chi 1908	100 - 150
AJ1570	The Wonders of the Colorado Desert Bos 1906, 2 vol	150 - 250

James, Jr., Jesse

AJ1620	Jesse James My Father Clev 1906	100 - 150

James, Marquis

AJ1700	Andrew Jackson Ind 1937, DJ	30 - 50
AJ1710	Cherokee Strip NY 1945, DJ	30 - 50
AJ1720	Life of Andrew Jackson Ind 1933, DJ	30 - 50
AJ1731	Sam Houston: The Raven Ind 1929, DJ, 1st ed w/o "Pulitzer Prize Winner" on DJ	75 - 125
AJ1732	Ind 1929, DJ (later printing)	30 - 50

James, Thomas

AJ1810	Three Years Among the Indians and Mexicans St. Louis 1916, 365 cys	200 - 300

James, Will S.

AJ1910	27 Years A Mavrick or Life on a Texas Range Chi 1893	800 - 1200
AJ1920	Cowboy Life in Texas Chi 1893	200 - 300
AJ1922	Chi 1898	75 - 125

Jane, Calamity

AJ2010	Life and Adventures of Calamity Jane Livingston, MT 1896	500 - 700

Jenkins, Howard M.

AJ2110	Pennsylvania Colonial and Federal Phil 1903, 3 vol	200 - 300

Jenkins, John H. (also see Books About Books)

AJ2210	Along the Early Trails of the Southwest Austin 1969, DJ	30 - 50
AJ2220	I'm Frank Hamer Austin 1968, 300 cys	150 - 250
AJ2222	Austin 1980, DJ	30 - 50
AJ2230	Recollections of Early Texas Austin 1958, DJ	75 - 125

Jennings, N. A.

AJ2310	A Texas Ranger NY 1899	500 - 700
AJ2312	Dallas 1930	100 - 150
AJ2314	Austin 1958, DJ	40 - 60

Jocknick, Sidney

AJ2410	Early Days on the Western Slope of Colorado Denver 1913	200 - 350

Johnson, Captain Charles

AJ2510	A General History of the Robberies and Murders of the Most Notorious Pirates NY 1926, DJ	75 - 125

Johnson, Clifton

AJ2610	Highways & Byways of The South NY 1904	30 - 50

Johnson, Guion

AJ2710	Ante-Bellum North Carolina Chapel Hill 1937, DJ	75 - 125

Johnson, Harrison

AJ2810	Johnson's History of Nebraska Omaha 1880	150 - 250

Johnson, L. F.

AJ2910	Famous Kentucky Tragedies and Trials Louisville 1916	75 - 125

Johnson, Sidney

AJ3010	Some Biographies of Old Settlers Tyler, TX 1900	200 - 300
AJ3020	Texans Who Wore the Grey Tyler, TX, nd	500 - 700

Jones, Charles C.

AJ3110	The Dead Towns of Georgia Savannah 1878	150 - 250
AJ3120	The History of Georgia Bos 1883, 2 vol	250 - 350
AJ3130	The History of Savannah, Georgia Syracuse 1890	250 - 350

Jones, Daniel W.

AJ3210	Forty Years Among the Indians Salt Lake City 1890	100 - 150

Jones, Herschel

AJ3310	Adventures in Americana NY 1928, 2 vol	300 - 500

Jones, Jonathan H.

AJ3410	Indianology: A Condensed History of the Apache and Comanche Indian Tribes San Antonio 1899	500 - 700

Jones, Terry L.

AJ3510	Lee's Tigers Baton Rouge 1987, DJ	20 - 30

Jordan, Philip D.

AJ3610	The National Road NY 1948, DJ	40 - 60

Josephy, Alvin (editor)

AJ3710	The American Heritage Book of Indians NY 1961, DJ	20 - 30
AJ3720	The Indian Heritage of America NY 1966, DJ	20 - 30

Judd, A. N.

AJ3910	Campaigning Aganist the Sioux Watsonville, CA 1906, wrappers	800 - 1200

Kane, Harnett T.

AK1010	Bayous of Louisiana NY 1944, DJ	20 - 30
AK1020	Gallant Mrs. Stonewall NY 1957, DJ	20 - 30
AK1030	Natchez on the Mississippi NY 1947, DJ	20 - 30
AK1040	Plantation Parade: The Grand Manner in Louisiana NY 1945, DJ	20 - 30
AK1050	Queen New Orleans NY 1949, DJ	20 - 30
AK1060	Spies for the Blue & Gray NY 1954, DJ	20 - 30

Katz, D. Mark

AK1210	Custer in Photographs NY 1985, DJ	150 - 200

Kaufmann, Helen L.

AK1260	From Jehovah to Jazz NY 1937, DJ	20 - 30

Keleher, William A.

AK1310	The Fabulous Frontier Santa Fe 1945	100 - 150
AK1320	The Maxwell Land Grant Santa Fe 1942	200 - 300

Keller, Allan

AK1360	Morgan's Raid Ind 1961, DJ	40 - 60
AK1370	Thunder at Harper's Ferry Englewood Cliffs 1958, DJ	40 - 60

Kelley, Joseph

AK1410	Thirteen Years in the Oregon Penitentiary Portland 1908, wrappers	100 - 150

Kelly, Charles

AK1510	Old Greenwood: the Story of Caleb Greenwood Salt Lake City 1936, 350 cys, DJ	250 - 350
AK1520	The Outlaw Trail: A History of Butch Cassidy and His Wild Bunch Salt Lake City 1938, 1000 cys, DJ	200 - 300
AK1522	NY 1959, DJ	50 - 75
AK1530	Salt Desert Trails Salt Lake City 1930	100 - 150

AJ3510

AK1260

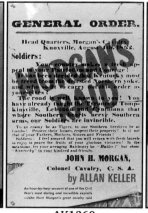
AK1360

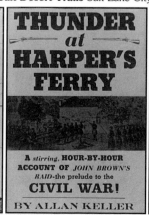
AK1370

AK1814

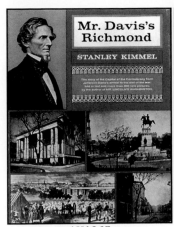
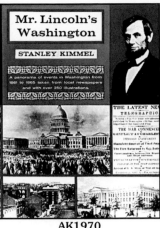

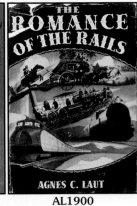
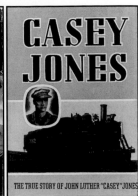

AK1965   AK1970   AK1960   AL1900   AL2610

Kendall, George W.
AK1610 Narrative of the Texan Santa Fe Expedition
        Austin 1936, 2 vol   100 - 150

Kennedy, William
AK1710 Texas Ft. Worth 1925   100 - 150

Kephart, Horace
AK1810 Our Southern Highlanders NY 1913   50 - 75
AK1812 NY 1926   30 - 50
AK1814 NY 1949, DJ (revised ed)   20 - 30

Kidd, J. H.
AK1910 Personal Recollections of a Cavalryman
        Ionia, MI 1908   250 - 350

Kimmel, Stanley
AK1960 The Mad Booths of Maryland NY 1940, DJ   50 - 75
AK1965 Mr. Davis's Richmond NY 1958, DJ   25 - 35
AK1970 Mr. Lincoln's Washington NY 1957, DJ   25 - 35

King, Blanche Busey
AK2010 Under Your Feet NY 1939, DJ   50 - 75

King, Frank M.
AK2110 Longhorn Trail Drivers LA 1940, 400 cys 200 - 300
AK2120 Wranglin' the Past LA 1935, 300 cys   200 - 300

King, Jeff
AK2210 Where the Two Came to Their Father: A Navajo
        War Ceremonial NY 1943, 2 vol, wrappers 800 - 1200

Kino, Fr. Eusebio
AK2310 Las Misiones de Sonora Y Arizona Mexico
        1913-22, wrappers   200 - 300

Kirby, W. S.
AK2410 The Drummer Boy of the Ozarks West Plains,
        MO 1893, wrappers   50 - 75

Kneale, Albert W.
AK2510 Indian Agent Caldwell 1950, DJ   50 - 75

Kneedler, H. S.
AK2610 The Coast Country of Texas Cinti 1896, wrappers 200 - 300

Knoblock, Byron W.
AK2660 Banner Stones of the North American Indians
        La Grange 1939   200 - 300

Knox, Dudley W.
AK2710 Naval Sketches of the War in California
        NY 1939, 1000 cys   300 - 500

Knox, Thomas
AK2810 Boy's Life of General Grant Akron 1907   20 - 30

Kroeber, Alfred L.
AK2910 Handbook of the Indians of California
        Wash 1925   250 - 350
AK2912 Berkeley 1953   100 - 150

Kurz, Rudolph Friederich
AK3010 Journal of...An Account of His Experiences Among
        Fur Traders and Indians Wash 1937, wrappers 200 - 300

Kuykendall, Ivan L.
AK3110 Ghost Riders of the Mogollow San Antonio
        1954, DJ   400 - 600

La Bree, Ben (editor)
AL1010 The Confederate Soldier in the Civil War
        1861-1865 Louisville 1895   300 - 500

La Farge, Oliver
AL1110 The Changing Indian Norman 1942, DJ   75 - 125
AL1120 Laughing Boy Bos 1929, DJ   50 - 75
AL1130 A Pictorial History of the American Indian
        NY 1957, DJ   30 - 50

La Frantz, F. W.
AL1210 Cowboy Stuff NY 1927, 500 cys, slipcase 300 - 500

La Salle, Nicolas de
AL1310 Relation of the Discovery of the Mississippi
        River Chi 1898, 269 cys   300 - 500

La Salle, René Robert Cavelier
AL1410 Relation of the Discoveries and Voyages of
        Cavelier de La Salle Chi 1901, 227 cys 300 - 500

Lancaster, Robert A.
AL1460 Historic Virginia Homes and Churches
        Phil 1915, DJ   200 - 300

Langsdorff, George H.
AL1510 Narrative of the Rezanov Voyage to Nueva
        California 1806 SF 1927, 260 cys   250 - 350

Larkin, Thomas O.
AL1610 California in **1846** SF 1935, 550 cys   200 - 300

Laroque, Francois A.
AL1710 A Journal of Francois A. Laroque from the
        Assiniboine to the Yellowstone **1805** Ottawa
        1910, wrappers   300 - 500

Larpenteur, Charles
AL1810 Forty Years a Fur Trader on the Upper Missouri
        NY 1898, 2 vol   200 - 300

Laut, Agnes C.
AL1900 The Romance of the Rails NY 1936, DJ   30 - 50
AL1910 Vikings of the Pacific NY 1905 DJ   40 - 60

Layne, J. Gregg
AL2010 Western Wayfaring LA 1954   30 - 50

Le Sueur, Meridel
AL2110 North Star Country NY 1945, DJ   20 - 30

Lea, Tom
AL2210 Hands of Cantu Bos 1964, 100 cys/Levant 2000 - 3000
AL2211 Bos 1964, DJ (1st trade ed)   75 - 125
AL2220 The King Ranch Bos 1957, slipcase   200 - 300
AL2221 Kingsville 1957, 2 vol, rag paper/slipcase 2000 - 3000
AL2222 Kingsville 1957, "Saddle Blanket Edition," 12 cys 6000 - 8000
AL2230 Land of the Mustang Austin 1965   50 - 75

Leahy, Ethel C.
AL2310 Who's Who on the Ohio River and its Tributaries
        An Ohio River Anthology Cinti 1931 200 - 300

Leckenby, Charles H. (editor)
AL2410 The Tread of Pioneers Steamboat Springs,
        CO 1944   125 - 200

Leckie, William H.
AL2510 The Buffalo Soldiers Norman 1967, DJ   50 - 75

Lee, Fred J.
AL2610 Casey Jones Kingsport 1939, DJ   30 - 50

Leeth, John
AL2710 A Short Biography of John Leeth, with an
        Account of His Life Among the Indians
        Clev 1904, 267 cys   100 - 150

Lehman, Herman
AL2810 Nine Years with the Indians Bandera 1927   150 - 250
AL2811 Austin 1927   100 - 150
Leigh, William R.
AL2910 The Western Pony NY 1933   400 - 600
Leonard, Lewis Alexander (editor)
AL3010 Greater Cincinnati and its People Chi 1927, 4 vol 150 - 250
Lewis, Lloyd
AL3110 Sherman, Fighting Prophet NY 1932, DJ   50 - 75
Lewis, Meriwether & William Clark
AL3210 History of the Expedition Under the Command
        of Captains Lewis and Clark etc NY 1893, 4 vol 500 - 700
AL3212 Chi 1902, 2 vol   100 - 150
AL3220 Original Journals of the Lewis and Clark
        Expedition 1804-1806 NY 1904-05,
        8 vol, atlas   2000 - 3000
Lewis, Oscar
AL3310 Sea Routes to the Gold Fields NY 1949, DJ   30 - 50
AL3320 Silver Kings NY 1947, DJ   50 - 75
Lilly, Eli
AL3360 Prehistoric Antiquities of Indiana Ind 1937, DJ 125 - 200
Lincoln, Abraham
AL3410 Collected Works of... New Brunswick 1953-55,
        9 vol   250 - 350
AL3420 The Life and Public Services of Gen. Zachary
        Taylor Bos 1922, 435 cys   300 - 500
Linderman, Frank B.
AL3510 Blackfeet Indians: Pictures by Winold Reiss
        St. Paul 1935   125 - 200
Lindsey, C. H. Forbes
AL3560 Daniel Boone Backwoodsman Phil 1909   20 - 30
Linn, John J.
AL3610 Reminiscensces of Fifty Years in Texas NY 1883 200 - 300
AL3612 Austin 1936   50 - 75
Little, James A.
AL3710 What I Saw on the Old Santa Fe Trail
        Plainfield 1904, wrappers   150 - 250
Lobb, Allan
AL3760 Indian Baskets of the Northwest Coast
        Portland 1978, DJ   30 - 50
Lockwood, Frank
AL3810 The Apache Indians NY 1938, DJ   100 - 150
AL3820 Arizona Characters LA 1928, DJ   100 - 150
AL3830 Pioneer Days in Arizona NY 1932, DJ   100 - 150
Long, A. L.
AL3910 Memoirs of Robert E. Lee His Military and
        Personal History NY 1887   100 - 150
Long, John
AL4010 Voyages and Travels of an Indian Interpreter
        and Trader Clev 1904   200 - 300
AL4012 Chi 1922   20 - 30
Lorant, Stefan (editor)
AL4110 The New World: The First Pictures of America
        NY 1946, DJ, box   150 - 250

Lothrop, S. K.
AL4160 Treasures of Ancient America Geneva 1964, DJ 75 - 125
Lowie, Robert H.
AL4210 The Crow Indians NY 1935   75 - 125
AL4220 Myths and Traditions of the Crow Indians NY 1918 50 - 75
Luce, Edward S.
AL4310 Keogh, Comanche and Custer St. Louis 1939, DJ   75 -
125
Lummis, Charles F.
AL4410 King of the Broncos NY 1897   100 - 150
AL4420 Land of Poco Tiempo NY 1893   50 - 75
AL4430 Mesa, Cañon and Pueblo NY 1925, DJ   50 - 75
AL4440 Pueblo Indian Folk Tales NY 1910, DJ   100 - 150
Lumpkin, Wilson
AL4510 The Removal of the Cherokee Indians From
        Georgia Wormsloe, GA 1907, 2 vol, 500 cys 100 - 150
Luttig, John C.
AL4610 Journal of a Fur Trading Expedition on the
        Upper Missouri St. Louis 1920, 365 cys   200 - 300
AL4612 NY 1964, 750 cys, DJ   50 - 75
Lyman, George D.
AL4710 John Marsh, Pioneer NY 1930, 150 cys   150 - 250
AL4711 NY 1930, DJ (1st trade ed)   30 - 50
AL4720 Ralston's Ring NY 1937, DJ   50 - 75
AL4730 The Saga of the Comstock Lode NY
Macartney, Edward Clarence
AM0110 Grant and his Generals NY 1953, DJ   20 - 30
MacCurdy, George
AM0210 A Study of Chiriquian Antiquities New Haven 1911 200 - 300
MacGregor, Frances Cooke
AM0310 Twentieth Century Indians NY 1941, DJ   30 - 50
Mack, Effie
AM0410 Nevada: A History of the State Glendale 1936,
        250 cys   150 - 250
MacKay, Malcolm S.
AM0510 Cow-Range and Hunting Trail NY 1925, DJ   300 - 500
MacKaye, Percy
AM0560 Tall Tales of the Kentucky Mountains Lon 1930, DJ 40 - 60
MacKenzie, Alexander
AM0610 Voyages From Montreal, on the River St.
        Lawrence, Through the Continent of North
        America NY 1902, 2 vol, 210 cys   300 - 500
MacKenzie, George Norbury
AM0710 Colonial Families of the United States of
        America Balt 1907, 6 vol   250 - 350
AM0712 Balt 1966, 6 vol   150 - 250
MacLay, Edgar S.
AM0810 A History of American Privateers NY 1899   30 - 50
Macon, T. J.
AM0910 Reminiscensces of the 1st Company of Richmond
        Howitzers Richmond 1909   150 - 250
Magoffin, Susan Shelby
AM1010 Down the Santa Fe Trail and Into Mexico
        New Haven 1926, DJ   150 - 250

AL3560

AL4430 (w/o DJ)

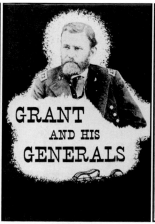
AM0110

AM0560

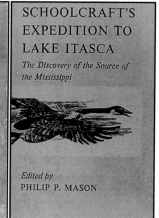
AM2460

AM3960   AM5960

Magovn, F. Alexander
AM1110 **The Frigate Constitution and Other Historic
        Ships** Salem 1928, 97 cys   300 - 500
AM1111 Salem 1928, DJ (1st trade ed)   75 - 125
Mahan, A. T.
AM1210 **The Navy in the Civil War** NY 1883   150 - 250
Mails, Thomas E.
AM1310 **Mystic Warriors of the Plains** NY 1972,
        250 cys, DJ, box   200 - 300
AM1311 NY 1972, DJ (1st trade ed)   75 - 125
AM1313 NY 1991, DJ   50 - 75
AM1320 **The People Called Apache** Englewood Cliffs
        1974, DJ   150 - 250
AM1330 **Pueblo Children of the Earth Mother**
        Garden City 1983, 2 vol, DJ   100 - 150
AM1340 **Sundancing at Rose Bud & Pine Ridge**
        Lake Mills 1978, DJ   75 - 125
Majors, Alexander
AM1410 **Seventy Years on the Frontier** Chi 1893,
        wrappers   300 - 500
Malone, James
AM1510 **The Chickasaw Nation** Kansas City 1919   100 - 150
Mangam, William D.
AM1610 **The Clarks of Montana** NY 1939, wrappers   300 - 500
Manly, William Lewis
AM1710 **Death Valley in '49** San Jose 1894   300 - 500
Marquis, Arnold
AM1810 **A Guide to America's Indians** Norman 1974, DJ 20 - 30
Marriott, Alice
AM1910 **Hell on Horses and Women** Norman 1953, DJ   30 - 50
AM1920 **Maria: The Potter of San Ildefonso** Norman
        1948, DJ   50 - 75
AM1922 Norman 1963, DJ   30 - 50
AM1924 Norman 1976, DJ   20 - 30
AM1930 **The Ten Grandmothers** Norman 1945, DJ   50 - 75
Marshall, James
AM2010 **Santa Fe: The Railroad That Built an Empire**
        NY 1945, DJ   30 - 50
Marshall, William I.
AM2110 **Acquisition of Oregon and the Long
        Suppressed Evidence About Marcus
        Whitman** Seattle 1905, 2 vol   200 - 300
AM2112 Portland 1911, 2 vol   150 - 250
Martin, Paul S. (author, editor)
AM2210 **Indians Before Columbus** Chi 1947, DJ   20 - 30
Marvin, Frederic R.
AM2310 **Yukon Overland: The Gold Digger's Handbook**
        Cinti 1898, wrappers   200 - 350
Mason, Otis T.
AM2410 **Indian Basketry** NY 1904, 2 vol   500 - 700
Mason, Philip P. (editor)
AM2460 **Schoolcraft's Expedition to Lake Itasca** Lansing
        1958, DJ   30 - 50

Mason, Richard Lee
AM2510 **Narrative of Richard Lee Mason in the Pioneer
        West** NY 1915, 160 cys   200 - 300
AM2512 NY 1915, 10 cys   300 - 500
Masters, Edgar Lee
AM2610 **Along the Illinois** Prairie City, IL 1942   50 - 75
Mathews, A. E.
AM2710 **Pencil Sketches of Colorado** Denver 1961   75 - 125
Mathews, John Joseph
AM2810 **Osages Children of the Middle Waters**
        Norman 1961, DJ   30 - 50
AM2820 **Wah-Kon-Tah** Norman 1932, DJ   30 - 50
Matthews, Sallie Reynolds
AM2910 **Interwoven, A Pioneer Chronicle** Houston 1936 700 - 1000
AM2912 El Paso 1958, 1500 cys, DJ   200 - 300
AM2914 Austin 1977, DJ   30 - 50
AM2916 College Station 1982, DJ   20 - 30
Matthews, Washington
AM3010 **Navajo Legends** Bos 1897   150 - 250
AM3020 **Navajo Myths, Prayers and Songs** Berkeley 1907 100 - 150
Maxwell, James A. (editor)
AM3110 **America's Fascinating Indian Heritage**
        Pleasantville 1978, DJ   20 - 30
Maxwell, William Audley
AM3210 **Crossing the Plains: Days of '57** SF 1915,
        wrappers   200 - 300
Mazzanovich, Anton
AM3310 **Trailing Geronimo** LA 1926, DJ   75 - 125
McAdams, Wm. (William)
AM3410 **Records of Ancient Races of the Mississippi
        Valley** St. Louis 1887   50 - 75
McAfee, Robert B.
AM3510 **History of the Late War in the Western Country**
        Bowling Green 1919, 300 cys   150 - 250
McCauley, J. E.
AM3610 **A Stove-Up Cowboy's Story** Dallas 1943,
        700 cys, DJ   400 - 600
McClellan, George B.
AM3710 **McClellan's Own Story** NY 1887   50 - 75
McClintock, John S.
AM3810 **Pioneer Days in the Black Hills** Deadwood 1939 100 - 150
McClintock, Walter
AM3910 **Old Indian Trails** Bos 1923   100 - 150
AM3920 **The Old North Trail** Lon 1910   100 - 150
McClure, Alexander
AM3960 **The Authentic Life of President McKinley** NY 1901 20 - 30
McConnell, H. H.
AM4010 **Five Years a Cavalryman** Jacksboro 1880   500 - 700
AM4012 NY 1970   30 - 50
McConnell, Joseph Carroll
AM4110 **The West Texas Frontier** Jacksboro 1933   200 - 300
McConnell, W. J.
AM4210 **Early History of Idaho** Caldwell 1913, DJ   100 - 150
McCorkle, John
AM4310 **Three Years With Quantrell** Armstrong 1914,
        wrappers   300 - 500
McCracken, Harold
AM4410 **Alaskan Bear Trails** NY 1931, DJ   200 - 300
AM4420 **The American Cowboy** Garden City 1973,
        300 cys, box   300 - 500
AM4421 Garden City 1973, DJ (1st trade ed)   50 - 75
AM4430 **The Charles M. Russell Book** Garden City
        1957, 250 cys, box   700 - 1000
AM4431 Garden City 1957, DJ (1st trade ed)   50 - 75
AM4440 **The Frank Tenney Johnson Book** Garden City
        1974, 350 cys, box   300 - 500
AM4450 **Frederic Remington's Own West** NY 1960,
        167 cys, box   400 - 600
AM4460 **George Catlin and the Old Frontier** NY 1959,
        250 cys, box   300 - 500
AM4461 NY 1959, DJ (1st trade ed)   75 - 125
AM4470 **Portrait of the Old West** NY 1952, DJ   50 - 75
McGee, Joseph H.
AM4610 **Story of the Grand River Country 1821-1905**
        Gallatin, MO 1909, wrappers   200 - 300

McIntire, Jim
AM4710 Early Days in Texas: A Trip to Hell and Heaven
    Kansas City 1902   300 - 500

McKay, M. N.
AM4810 When the Tide Turned in the Civil War
    Ind 1929, DJ   75 - 125

McKay, Richard C.
AM4910 South Street: A Maritime History of New York
    NY 1934, 200 cys, box   200 - 300
AM4911 NY 1934, DJ (1st trade ed)   50 - 75

McKenney, Thomas L. and James Hall
AM5010 History of the Indian Tribes of North America
    Edinburgh 1933-34, 3 vol, DJs, box   500 - 700

McKim, Randolph H.
AM5110 A Soldier's Recollections: Leaves From the
    Diary of a Young Confederate NY 1911   100 - 150

McKnight, George S.
AM5210 California 49er: Travels From Perrysburg to
    California Perrysburg, OH 1903, wrappers   200 - 350

McLaughlin, James
AM5310 My Friend the Indian Chi 1896   75 - 125

McLeod, Alexander
AM5410 Pigtails and Gold Dust Caldwell 1947, DJ   30 - 50

McMurtrie, Douglas C. (see Books About Books)

McNicol, Donald M.
AM5510 The Amerindians NY 1937, DJ   20 - 30

McReynolds, Edwin C.
AM5610 The Seminoles Norman 1957, DJ   30 - 50

McWhorter, Lucullus Virgil
AM5710 The Border Settlers of Northwestern Virginia
    From 1768 to 1795 Hamilton 1915   100 - 150
AM5720 Crime Against the Yakimas Yakima 1913,
    wrappers   200 - 300
AM5730 Hear Me My Chiefs Caldwell 1952, DJ   200 - 300
AM5740 Yellow Wolf: His Own Story Caldwell 1940, DJ   200 - 300

Mercer, A. S. (Asa Shinn)
AM5810 Banditti of the Plains Cheyenne, WY 1894   3000 - 5000
AM5812 SF 1935, 1000 cys, slipcase   150 - 250
AM5814 Norman 1954, DJ   30 - 50
AM5816 pulp reprints late 1800s-early 1900s   25 - 75
AM5830 Banditti of the Plains; or, The Cattlemen's Invasion
    of Wyoming in 1892 Sheridan 1930, wrappers   75 - 125

Merrick, George B.
AM5910 Old Times on the Upper Mississippi Clev 1909   100 - 150

Merritt, Raleigh H.
AM5960 From Captivity to Fame Bos 1929, DJ   50 - 75

Meyers, William H.
AM6010 Journal of a Cruise to California and the
    Sandwich Islands SF 1955, 400 cys, DJ   300 - 500
AM6020 Naval Sketches of the War in California
    1846-47 SF 1939, 1000cys   250 - 350
AM6030 Sketches of California and Hawaii SF 1970,
    450 cys   200 - 300

Miles, Charles
AM6110 Indian and Eskimo Artifacts of North America
    Chi 1963, DJ   30 - 50

Miles, Gen. Nelson A.
AM6210 Personal Recollections and Observations
    Chi 1896   250 - 350
AM6212 Chi 1897   150 - 250

Miles, William
AM6310 Journal of the Sufferings and Hardships of
    Capt. Parker H. French's Overland
    Expedition to California Chambersburg 1851   3000 - 5000
AM6312 NY 1916, 250 cys   100 - 150
AM6314 Wash 1970, 490 cys   50 - 75
AM6316 Austin 1979   20 - 30

Miller, Benjamin S.
AM6410 Ranch Life in Southern Kansas and the Indian
    Territory NY 1896   500 - 700

Miller, Francis T. (Trevelyn)
AM6510 The Photographic History of the Civil War
    NY 1912, 10 vol   250 - 350

Miller, Joaquin
AM6610 An Illustrated History of Montana Chi 1894,
    2 vol   300 - 500
AM6620 Overland in a Covered Wagon NY 1930, DJ   50 - 75

Miller, Joseph
AM6710 Arizona Indians NY 1941, DJ   50 - 75

Miller, Lewis B.
AM6810 Crooked Trail Pittsburgh 1908   300 - 500
AM6820 Saddles and Lariats Bos 1912   150 - 250

Mills, W. W. (William W.)
AM6910 Forty Years at El Paso 1858-1898 Chi 1901   300 - 500
AM6911 El Paso 1962, DJ (1st trade ed)   100 - 150

Mills, William C.
AM7010 Archeological Atlas of Ohio Col 1914   200 - 300
AM7020 Certain Mounds and Village Sites in Ohio
    Col 1907, 4 vol   300 - 500
AM7030 Ohio Archaeological Exhibit at the Jamestown
    Exposition 1907 Col 1907   50 - 75

Mitchell, John D.
AM7110 Lost Mines of the Great Southwest Phoenix 1933   100 - 150

Monaghan, Jay (editor)
AM7210 The Book of the American West NY 1963, DJ   40 - 60
AM7220 The Great Rascal - Ned Buntline Bos 1952, DJ   30 - 50

Monks, William
AM7310 History of Southern Missouri and Northern
    Arkansas West Plains, MO 1907   150 - 250

Monteiro, A.
AM7410 War Reminiscences by the Surgeon of Mosby's
    Command Richmond 1890   150 - 250

Moore, Clarence B.
AM7510 Certain Aboriginal Remains of the Black
    Warrior River Phil 1905   150 - 250

Moore, Clement B.
AM7610 Aboriginal Sites of Tennessee River Phil 1915   200 - 300
AM7620 Certain Aboriginal Mounds of the Georgia
    Coast Phil 1897   200 300

Moore, Edward A.
AM7710 The Story of a Cannoneer Under Stonewall
    Jackson NY 1907   150 - 250

Moore, Dr. James
AM7810 A Complete History of the Great Rebellion
    NY, nd (about 1900)   20 - 30

Moorehead, Warren K.
AM7910 Archaeology of Maine Andover 1922   50 - 75
AM7920 Prehistoric Implements Cinti 1900, 2050 cys   100 - 150
AM7930 The Stone Age in North America Bos 1910, 2 vol   200 - 300
AM7940 Stone Ornaments Used by Indians in the
    United States and Canada Andover 1917   100 - 150

Morfl, Juan A.
AM8010 History of Texas Albu 1935, 2 vol   700 - 1000

Morgan, Dale
AM8110 Jedidiah Smith NY 1953, DJ   75 - 125
AM8120 Jedediah Smith and His Maps of the
    American West SF 1954   700 - 1000

Morgan, James Morris
AM8210 Recollections of a Rebel Reefer Bos 1917   100 - 150

Morgan, Lewis H.
AM8310 The Indian Journals of Lewis Henry Morgan
    Ann Arbor 1959, DJ   75 - 125
AM8320 The League of Ho-Dé-No-Sav-Nee or Iroquois
    NY 1922   100 - 150

Mourelle, Francisco Antonio
AM8410 Voyage of the Sonora in the Second Bucareli
    Expedition to Explore the Northwest Coast
    SF 1920, 230 cys   150 - 250

Muir, John
AM8510 A Thousand Mile Walk to the Gulf Bos 1916,
    DJ, box   400 - 600
AM8520 Travels in Alaska Bos 1915, DJ   100 - 150

Muller, Dan
AM8610 My Life With Buffalo Bill Chi 1948, DJ   30 - 50

Mumey, Nolie (also see Books About Books)
AM8710 Bloody Trails Along the Rio Grande Denver
   1938, DJ   100 - 150
AM8720 History of the Early Settlements of Denver
   Glendale 1942, 500 cys   100 - 150
AM8730 March of the First Dragoons to the Rocky
   Mountains in 1835 Denver 1957, 350 cys 100 - 150
AM8740 Old Forts and Trading Posts of the West
   Denver 1957, 500 cys   100 - 150
AM8750 Pioneer Denver Denver 1948   100 - 150
AM8760 Poker Alice Denver 1951, 500 cys, wrappers 100 - 150
AM8770 The Teton Mountains Denver 1947 75 - 125

Murray, Keith A.
AM8910 The Modocs and Their War Norman 1959, DJ 75 - 125

Myers, John M.
AM9010 Death of the Bravos Bos 1962, DJ 50 - 75
AM9020 Doc Holliday Bos 1955, DJ   50 - 75
AM9030 The Last Chance, Tombstone's Early Years
   NY 1950, DJ   50 - 75

Myrick, Herbert
AM9110 Cache La Pudre NY 1904   150 - 250
AM9120 NY 1905, 500 cys   400 - 600

Napton, William B.
AN1010 Over the Santa Fe Trail, 1857 Kansas City
   1905, wrappers   250 - 350

Neese, George M.
AN1110 Three Years in the Confederate Horse Artillery
   NY 1911   150 - 250

Neihardt, John G. (see Modern First Editions)

Nelson, John Louw
AN1210 Rhythm For Rain Bos 1937, DJ 50 - 75

Newmark, Harris
AN1310 Sixty Years in Southern California 1853-1913
   NY 1916   75 - 125

Ningler, L. (translator)
AN1410 Voyages en Virginie et en Floride Paris 1927,
   100 cys   200 - 300

Nordenskiöld, G.
AN1510 The Cliff Dwellers of Mesa Verde
   Stockholm 1893   400 - 600

Noyes, Alva J.
AN1610 In the Land of Chinook: or, The Story of Blaine
   County Helena 1917   150 - 250
AN1620 The Story of Ajax: Life in the Big Horn Basin
   Helena 1914   300 - 500
AN1622 NY 1966   30 - 50

Obregon, Baltasar de
AO1010 Obregon's History of 16th Century Explorations
   in Western America LA 1938   100 - 150

O'Connor, Richard
AO1110 Bat Masterson Garden City 1957, DJ 30 - 50
AO1120 High Jinks of the Klondike Ind 1954, DJ 30 - 50
AO1130 Hood, Cavalier General NY 1949, DJ 50 - 75
AO1140 Pat Garrett Garden City 1960, DJ 30 - 50

Ogle, Ralph H.
AO1210 Federal Control of the Western Apaches
   1848-1886 Albu 1940   50 - 75

O'Kane, Walter, C.
AO1310 The Hopis Norman 1954, DJ   30 - 50

Older, Mr. & Mrs. Fremont
AO1410 The Life of George Hearst, California Pioneer
   SF 1933   500 - 700

Oldroyd, Osborn H.
AO1460 A Soldier's Story of the Siege of Vicksburg
   Springfield 1885   150 - 250

Omwake, John
AO1510 The Conestoga Six-Horse Bell Teams of Eastern
   Pennsylvania Cinti 1930   75 - 125

Ormsby, Waterman L.
AO1610 The Butterfield Overland Mail San Marino 1942, DJ 50 - 75

Ortega, Luis
AO1710 California Hackamore Sacramento 1948, DJ 50 - 75

Osborn, Samuel
AO1810 The Dark and Bloody Ground: A History of
   Kentucky Bristol 1907, wrappers 100 - 150

Osgood, Ernest Staples
AO1910 The Day of the Cattleman Minn 1929, DJ 150 - 250
AO1912 Minn 1954, DJ   30 - 50

Otero, Miguel
AO2010 My Life on the Frontier 1864-1882 NY 1935,
   400 cys   150 - 250
AO2020 The Real Billy the Kid NY 1936, DJ 100 - 150

Packard, Wellman & G. Larison
AP1010 Early Emigration to California Bloomington
   1928, wrappers   400 - 600

Paine, Albert Bigelow
AP1110 Queen of the Comstock NY 1929, DJ 50 - 75

Palmer, H. E.
AP1210 The Powder River Indian Expedition 1865
   Omaha 1887   300 - 500

Palou, Fray Francisco
AP1310 The Expedition into California of the Venerable
   Fray Junipero Serra SF 1934, 400 cys 150 - 250
AP1311 1000 cys, DJ   75 - 125
AP1320 Historical Memoirs of New California Berkeley
   1926, 4 vol   250 - 350

Parker, Aaron
AP1410 Forgotten Tragedies of Indian Warfare in Idaho
   Grangeville, ID 1925, wrappers 200 - 300

Parker, Arthur C.
AP1510 The Indian How Book NY 1927, DJ 50 - 75
AP1520 The Life of General Ely S. Parker Last Grand
   Sachem of the Iroquois and General Grant's
   Secretary Buffalo 1919   200 - 300

Parker, Henry W.
AP1610 How Oregon Was Saved to the U.S. NY 1901,
   wrappers   75 - 125

Parkman, Francis
AP1710 The Works of ... Bos 1910, 13 vol 300 - 500

Parsons, Elsie (editor)
AP1810 American Indian Life NY 1927, DJ 75 - 125

Parsons, John E.
AP1910 Firearms in the Custer Battle Harrisburg 1953, DJ 100 - 150
AP1920 The First Winchester NY 1969, DJ 75 - 125
AP1930 Henry Deringer's Pocket Pistol NY 1952, DJ 50 - 75
AP1940 Peacemaker and its Rivals NY 1950, DJ 75 - 125

Pattie, James O.
AP2010 Personal Narrative...During an Expedition
   From St. Louis...Cinti 1831 20000 - 30000
AP2012 Clev 1905, 250 cys   150 - 250
AP2014 Chi 1930   20 - 30

Paul, Elliot
AP2060 A Ghost Town on the Yellowstone NY 1948, DJ 20 - 30

Paxson, Frederic Logan
AP2110 History of the American Frontier Bos 1924, DJ 50 - 75
AP2120 The Last American Frontier NY 1930, DJ 50 -75

Payne, Doris
AP2210 Captain Jack, Modoc Renegade Portland 1938, DJ 75 - 125

Payne, John Howard
AP2310 Indian Justice: A Cherokee Murder Trial at
   Tahlequah in 1840 Okla Cty 1934 200 - 300

Peake, Ora B.
AP2410 Colorado Range Cattle Industry Glendale 1937 100 - 150

Pearson, Edmund (editor)
AP2510 The Autobiography of a Criminal (Henry Tufts,
   Revolutionary War) NY 1930 50 - 75

Peet, Frederick
AP2610 Personal Experiences in the Civil War NY 1905,
   50 cys   200 - 300

Peithmann, Irvin
AP2710 Broken Peace Pipes Springfield 1964, DJ 20 - 30

Pelzer, Louis
AP2810 Cattlemen's Frontier Glendale 1936, DJ 100 - 150

Penn, William
AP2910 Fruits of Solitude Chi 1906   30 - 50
Perez de Villagra, Gaspar
AP3010 History of New Mexico LA 1933, 665 cys   100 - 150
Peterson, Harold
AP3060 American Indian Tomahawks NY 1965, DJ   40 - 60
Peterson, Wm. J.
AP3110 Steamboating on the Upper Mississippi
        Iowa City 1937, DJ   200 - 300
Petter, Rodolphe
AP3210 English-Cheyenne Dictionary Kettle Falls, WA
        1913-15, 100 cys   300 - 500
Phillips, Ulrich B. (editor)
AP3310 American Negro Slavery NY 1918, DJ   100 - 150
AP3320 Plantation and Frontier Documents 1649-1863
        Clev 1909, 2 vol, 150 cys   250 - 350
Pinkerton, Allan
AP3410 The Spy and the Rebellion NY 1883   75 - 125
AP3420 Thirty Years a Detective Hartford 1884   100 - 150
Pinkerton, William A.
AP3510 Train Robberies, Train Robbers, and "Hold Up"
        Men Chi 1907, wrappers   100 - 150
AP3512 Ft. Davis 1968   20 - 30
Pleasants, W. J.
AP3610 Twice Across the Plains 1849-1856 SF 1906 700 - 1000
Point, Nicolas
AP3710 Wilderness Kingdom NY 1967, DJ   30 - 50
Polley, J. B.
AP3810 Hood's Texas Brigade NY 1910   300 - 500
AP3820 A Soldiers Letters to Charming Nellie NY 1908 200 - 300
Pollock, J. M.
AP3910 The Unvarnished West Lon 1911   300 - 500
Pond, Frederic Eugene
AP4010 Life and Adventures of Ned Buntline NY 1919 100 - 150
Porter, Lavinia
AP4110 By Ox Team to California Oakland 1910   600 - 800
Powell, H. M. T.
AP4210 The Santa Fe Trail to California 1849-1852
        SF 1931, 300 cys   1500 - 2500
Powell, J. W.
AP4310 Canyons of the Colorado Meadville, PA 1895 1200 - 1800
Powell, J. W. (editor, director)
        Annual Reports of the Bureau of Ethnology Published for
the Smithsonian Institute, Washington, D. C., these large folio volumes
are bound in olive green cloth, gold stamped, and have an Indian por-
trait on the cover. Published annually from 1879 to the 1920s, they
are usually illustrated with maps and lithographic and half-tone plates.
The early volumes contain fine-color lithography and are highly col-
lectible. Later reports were not under the directorship of J. W. Powell.
AP4401 1 (1879-80)   200 - 300
AP4402 2 (1880-81), 2 vol   250 - 350
AP4403 3 (1881-82), 2 vol   250 - 350
AP4404 4 (1882-83)   150 - 200
AP4405 5 (1883-84)   150 - 200
AP4406 6 (1884-85)   150 - 200
AP4407 7 (1885-86)   100 - 150
AP4408 8 (1886-87), 2 vol   150 - 250
AP4409 9 (1887-88)   100 - 150
AP4410 10 (1888-89)   150 - 200
AP4411 11 (1889-90)   150 - 200
AP4412 12 (1890-91), 2 vol   175 - 250
AP4413 13 (1891-92), 2 vol   150 - 225
AP4414 14 (1892-93), 2 vol   175 - 250
AP4415 15 (1893-94), 2 vol   175 - 250
AP4416 16 (1894-95), 2 vol   150 - 225
AP4417 17 (1895-96), 2 vol   175 - 250
AP4418 18 (1896-97), 2 vol   200 - 300
AP4419 19 (1897-98), 2 vol   175 - 250
AP4420 20 (1898-99)   150 - 200
AP4421 21 (1899-1900)   100 - 150
AP4422 22 (1900-01), 2 vol   125 - 200
AP4423 23 (1901-02)   250 - 350
AP4424 24 (1902-03), 2 vol   175 - 250
AP4425 25 (1903-04), 2 vol   200 - 275

AP4426 26 (1904-05)   100 - 150
AP4427 27 (1905-06)   125 - 200
AP4428 28 (1906-07)   50 - 75
AP4429 29 (1907-08)   50 - 75
AP4430 30 (1908-09)   50 - 75
AP4431 31 (1909-10)   50 - 75
AP4432 32 (1910-11)   50 - 75
AP4433 33 (1911-12)   50 - 75
AP4434 34 (1912-13)   50 - 75
    Later volumes are worth about $50 - 100 depending upon the num-
ber of plates and thickness of text. The Government published many
other collectible reports, some of which are listed in this guide under
Author, Editor or Director.
Price, George Frederick
AP4510 Across the Plains with the Fifth Cavalry
        NY 1883   300 - 500
AP4512 NY 1959, 750 cys   100 - 150
Price, Samuel
AP4610 The Old Masters of the Bluegrass Louisville 1902 100 - 150
Prosch, Charles
AP4710 Reminiscences of Washington Territory
        Seattle 1904   200 - 300
Pyle, Howard (also see Artists & Illustrators)
AP4810 Book of the American Spirit NY 1923, DJ, box 200 - 300
AP4820 Howard Pyle's Book of Pirates NY 1921, DJ   150 - 250
Quaife, M. M. (Milo Milton)
AQ3010 Absalom Grimes, Confederate Mail Runner
        New Haven 1926   50 - 75
AQ3020 Chicago and the Old Northwest 1673-1835
        Chi 1913   150 - 250
AQ3030 Chicago's Highways Old and New Chi 1923   50 - 75
AQ3040 The Development of Chicago 1674-1914
        Chi 1916, 175 cys   150 - 250
AQ3050 Pictures of the Gold Rush in California Chi 1949 20 - 30
AQ3060 Yellowstone Kelly New Haven 1926, DJ   100 - 150
Quarles, Benjamin
AQ3210 Frederick Douglass Bos 1948, DJ   30 - 50
AQ3220 The Negro in the American Revolution
        Bos 1961, DJ   30 - 50
AQ3230 The Negro in the Civil War Bos 1953, DJ   30 - 50
Quick, Herbert
AQ3410 American Inland Waterways NY 1909, DJ   50 - 75
AQ3420 Mississippi Steamboatin' NY 1926, DJ   30 - 50
Radin, Paul
AR1010 The Story of the American Indian Garden City
        1937, DJ   20 - 30
Rafinesque, C. L.
AR1110 Walam Olum or Red Score the Migration Legend of
        the Lenni Lenape or Delaware Indians Ind 1954 75 - 125
Raine, William McLeod
AR1210 45 Calibre Law Evanston 1941, DJ   30 - 50
AR1220 Cattle Garden City 1930, DJ   50 - 75
AR1230 Famous Sheriffs and Western Outlaws
        NY 1929, DJ   50 - 75
AR1232 NY 1944, DJ   30 - 50
AR1240 Guns of the Frontier Bos 1940, DJ   30 - 50

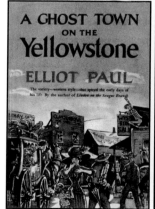

AP2060   AP4403 (spine and cover, Vol. 1 of 2)

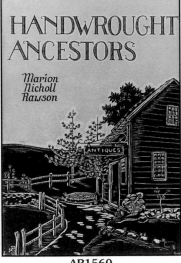

AR1010	AR1560	AR2334	AR3410

Randall, E. O.
AR1310 The Serpent Mound, Adams County, Ohio
Col 1905   50 - 75

Rankin, M. Wilson
AR1410 Reminiscences of Frontier Days Denver 1938   150 - 250

Rascoe, Burton
AR1510 Belle Starr, "The Bandit Queen" NY 1941, DJ   50 - 75

Rawson, Marion Nicholl
AR1560 Handwrought Ancestors NY 1936, DJ   30 - 50

Raymond, Dora
AR1610 Captain Lee Hall of Texas Norman 1940, DJ   30 - 50

Reagan, John H.
AR1710 Memoirs, with Special Reference to Secession
and the Civil War NY 1906   200 - 300

Reed, Nathaniel
AR1810 The Life of Texas Jack Tulsa 1936, wrappers   700 - 1000

Reed, S. G.
AR1910 History of Texas Railroads Houston 1941   300 - 500

Reed, Wallace P.
AR2010 History of Atlanta, Georgia Syracuse 1889   100 - 150

Reichard, Gladys
AR2110 Spider Woman NY 1934, DJ   50 - 75

Reid, James D.
AR2210 The Telegraph in America NY 1879   150 - 250

Remington, Frederic (also see Artists & Illustrators)
AR2310 Collected Writings of Garden City 1979, DJ   50 - 75
AR2320 Crooked Trails NY 1898, DJ   300 - 500
AR2322 NY 1923, DJ   100 - 150
AR2330 Done in the Open NY 1892, w/"Frederick"
instead of "Frederic" on front cover   700 - 1000
AR2331 NY 1892, 250 cys   1200 - 1800
AR2333 NY 1902   300 - 500
AR2334 NY 1903   75 - 125
AR2340 Drawings NY 1897, box   400 - 600
AR2341 NY 1897, 250 cys   700 - 1000
AR2343 NY 1898   300 - 500
AR2350 Frederic Remington's Own West NY 1960,
167 cys, box   400 - 600
AR2351 NY 1960, DJ (1st trade ed)   50 - 75
AR2360 Frontier Sketches Chi 1898   500 - 700
AR2361 Akron 1898   300 - 500
AR2370 Men with the Bark On NY 1900   150 - 250
AR2380 Pony Tracks NY 1895   300 - 500
AR2382 Col 1951, DJ   50 - 75
AR2384 Norman 1961, DJ   30 - 50
AR2386 Norman 1977, wrappers   15 - 25
AR2410 The Way of an Indian NY 1906, 1st state
w/p 9 correctly numbered & yellow-lettered cl   200 - 300

Rich, Virtulon
AR2510 Western Life in the Stirrups Chi 1965   30 - 50

Richardson, R. N. (Rupert N.)
AR2610 The Comanche Barrier to the South Plains
Glendale 1933, DJ   200 - 300
AR2620 Frontier of Northwest Texas 1846-1876
Glendale 1963, DJ   100 - 150
AR2630 The Greater Southwest Glendale 1934, DJ   75 - 125
AR2640 Texas: The Lone Star State NY 1943, DJ   100 - 150
AR2642 Englewood 1958, DJ   30 - 50

Richman, Irving B.
AR2710 Ioway to Iowa Iowa City 1931   20 - 30

Riddle, Jeff
AR2810 The Indian History of the Modoc War and the
Causes That Led To It 1914   200 - 300

Ridge, John R.
AR2910 Joaquin Murieta, the Brigand Chief of
California SF 1932, 400 cys   100 - 150

Ridings, Sam P.
AR3010 The Chisholm Trail Guthrie, OK 1936, DJ   200 - 300

Riegel, Robert E.
AR3110 The Story of the Western Railroads NY 1926, DJ 50 - 75

Rister, Carl C. (Coke)
AR3210 Baptist Missions Among the American Indians
Atlanta 1944, wrappers   30 - 50
AR3220 Border Captives: The Traffic in Prisoners by
Southern Plains Indiana 1835-1875 Norman
1940, DJ   200 - 300
AR3230 Border Command; General Phil Sheridan in
the West Norman 1944, DJ   50 - 75
AR3240 Comanche Bondage Glendale 1955, DJ   150 - 250
AR3250 No Man's Land Norman 1948, DJ   30 - 50
AR3260 Oil! Titan of the Southwest Norman 1949, DJ   50 - 75
AR3270 Southern Plainsmen Norman 1938, DJ   100 - 150
AR3280 The Southwestern Frontier 1865-1881
Clev 1928   250 - 350

Rittenhouse, Jack D.
AR3330 American Horse-Drawn Vehicles LA 1948, DJ 150 - 250
AR3340 Cabezon: A New Mexico Ghost Town Santa Fe
1965, DJ   50 - 75
AR3350 The Man Who Owned Too Much Houston
1958, 450 cys, box   100 - 150

Robertson, Frank G. & Beth Kay Harris
AR3410 Soapy Smith NY 1961, DJ   20 - 30

Robertson, John W.
AR3460 Francis Drake and Other Early Explorers
Along the Pacific Coast SF 1927, 1000 cys   300 - 500

Robinson, Charles Edson
AR3510 A Concise History of the United Society of Believers
Called Shakers East Canterbury, NH 1893   200 - 300

Robinson, Doane
AR3610 History of South Dakota Mitchell 1907   50 - 75

AR3620 A History of the Dakota or Souix Indians
        Aberdeen 1904   75 - 125
Robinson, John and George F. Dow
AR3710 The Sailing Ships of New England 1607-1907
        Salem 1922-28, 3 vol   500 - 700
Rock, Marion Tuttle
AR3810 Illustrated History of Oklahoma Topeka 1890   500 - 700
Rollinson, John K.
AR3910 Hoofprints of a Cowboy and a U.S. Ranger
        Caldwell 1941, DJ   75 - 125
AR3920 Pony Trails in Wyoming Caldwell 1941, DJ   100 - 150
AR3930 Wyoming Cattle Trails Caldwell 1948, 1000 cys 125 - 200
Roosevelt, Theodore
   (Wrote numerous books on hunting, the American West, politics and
history - about 70 titles)
AR4010 Big Game Hunting in the Rockies and on the
        Great Plains NY 1899, 1000 cys, in tan buckram 500 - 700
AR4011 in leather   700 - 1000
AR4020 Hunting Trips of a Ranchman NY 1885, 500 cys   300 - 500
AR4021 NY 1886 (1st trade ed)   200 - 300
AR4023 Lon 1886 (1st English ed)   200 - 300
AR4025 NY 1897   100 - 150
AR4027 NY 1910   50 - 75
AR4040 The Naval Operations of the War Between
        Great Britain and the United States
        1812-1815 Bos 1901   150 - 250
AR4041 Lon 1901   150 - 250
AR4050 Naval War of 1812 (1st book) NY 1882   200 - 300
AR4061 Ranch Life and Hunting Trail NY 1888, DJ, 1st
        state in tan buckram w/green & gold stamping   400 - 600
AR4062 later states stamped in brown & gold   200 - 300
AR4064 NY 1915, DJ   100 - 150
AR4080 The Rough Riders NY 1899   250 - 350
        signed by Frederic Remington   800 - 1200
AR4090 Who Should Go West? NY 1927, 75 cys   200 - 300
AR4101 The Wilderness Hunter NY 1893, 1st state
        w/chapter headings in brown   200 - 300
AR4102 NY 1893, 200 cys   300 - 500
AR4110 The Winning of the West NY 1889-96, 4 vol,
        1st issue w/last word of p 160, vol 1 "diame-"
        & 1st word p 161 "ter"   600 - 800
AR4112 NY 1900, 4 vol   75 - 125
Root, Frank A. & W. A. Connelley
AR4210 The Overland Stage to California Topeka 1901   200 - 300
Rosen, Peter
AR4310 Pa-Ha-Sa-Pah or the Black Hills of South
        Dakota St. Louis 1895   200 - 300
Ross, Alexander
AR4410 Adventures of the First Settlers on the Oregon
        Clev 1904   200 - 300
AR4420 Red River Settlement Minn 1957, DJ   50 - 75
Ross, Harvey L.
AR4510 The Early Pioneers and Pioneer Events of the
        State of Illinois Chi 1898   150 - 200
Rothert, Otto A.
AR4610 History of Mulenberg County, Kentucky
        Louisville 1913   200 - 300
AR4620 The Outlaws of Cave-in-Rock Clev 1924   150 - 250
AR4622 Clev 1927   125 - 200
Russell, Carl P.
AR4710 Firearms, Traps & Tools of the Mountain Men
        NY 1967, DJ   50 - 75
AR4720 Guns on the Early Frontiers Berkeley 1957, DJ 50 - 75
Russell, Charles M.
AR4810 Back Trailing on the Old Frontiers
        Great Falls 1922   300 - 500
AR4820 Cow Range and Hunting Trail NY 1925, DJ   200 - 300
AR4830 Cowboy Artist Pasadena 1948, 600 cys, 2 vol   250 - 350
AR4832 NY 1957, DJ   75 - 125
AR4840 Good Medicine Garden City 1929, DJ, 134 cys   1200 - 1800
AR4841 Garden City 1930, DJ (1st trade ed)   75 - 125
AR4850 Master Portfolio of Western Art Helena 1965,
        500 cys   150 - 250
AR4860 More Rawhides Great Falls 1924, wrappers   300 - 500
AR4862 Pasadena 1946, DJ   75 - 125

AR4864 Pasadena 1954, DJ   50 - 75
AR4870 Pen and Ink Drawings Pasadena 1946, 2 vol   300 - 500
AR4880 Pen Sketches Great Falls 1898   1500 - 2500
AR4890 Rawhide Rawlins Stories Great Falls 1921,
        wrappers   400 - 600
AR4892 Pasadena 1946 Lea   150 - 250
AR4900 Seven Drawings by... El Paso 1950, 675 cys   400 - 600
AR4910 Studies of Western Life (1st book) Cascade,
        MT 1890   2000 - 3000
AR4912 Spokane 1919   300 - 500
AR5000 Trails Plowed Under Garden City 1927, DJ   150 - 250
AR5002 Garden City 1928, DJ   100 - 150
AR5004 Garden City 1936, DJ   75 - 125
AR5006 NY 1944, DJ   50 - 75
AR5020 Western Types Great Falls, 16 prints,
        envelope, box   300 - 500
Russell, Don
AR5110 The Lives and Legends of Buffalo Bill Norman
        1960, DJ   50 - 75
Russell, Morris
AR5210 Western Sketches Lake City, MN 1904,
        wrappers   300 - 500
Russell, Osborne
AR5310 Journal of a Trapper Boise 1914, 100 cys   500 - 700
AR5312 Portland 1955, 750 cys   100 - 150
Russell, Virgil Y.
AR5410 Indian Artifacts Casper 1951   50 - 75
AR5420 Casper 1970   20 - 30
Ruxton, George
AR5510 Life in the Far West Norman 1951, DJ   30 - 50
AR5520 Wild Life in the Rocky Mountains NY 1932, DJ   30 - 50
Rynning, Thomas
AR5610 Gun Notches NY 1931, DJ   75 - 125
AR5620 Chi, nd, DJ (A.L. Burt reprint)   30 - 50
Sabin, Edwin L. (also see Golf: Fiction, Humor & Poetry)
AS1010 Building the Pacific Railway Phil 1919, DJ   100 - 150
AS1020 Gold Phil 1929, DJ   50 - 75
AS1030 Kit Carson Days 1809-1868 Chi 1914, DJ   200 - 300
AS1032 Chi 1919, DJ   100 - 150
AS1034 NY 1935, 2 vol, glassine DJs, 1000 cys   150 - 250
AS1036 later printings w/DJs   20 - 30
AS1050 On the Plains With Custer Phil 1913, DJ   75 - 125
AS1052 later printings w/DJs   20 - 30
AS1060 Wild Men of the Wild West NY 1929, DJ   100 - 150
AS1062 later printings w/DJs   20 - 30
AS1070 With Carson & Fremont Phil 1912, DJ   75 - 125
AS1072 later printings w/DJs   20 - 30
AS1080 With George Washington into the Wilderness
        Phil 1924, DJ   50 - 75
AS1090 With Sam Houston in Texas Phil 1916, DJ   50 - 75
Sale, Edith Tunis
AS1210 Manors of Virginia in Colonial Times Phil 1909 100 - 150
Sales, Father Luis
AS1310 Observations on California 1772-1790
        LA 1956, 300 cys   50 - 75
Samuel, Ray, Leonard V. Huber & Warren C. Ogden
AS1360 Tales of the Mississippi NY 1955, DJ   20 - 30

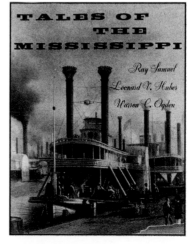

AS1360

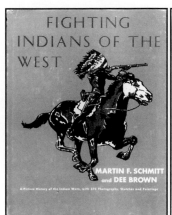

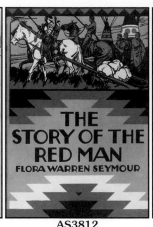

| AS2812 | AS3240 | AS3310 | AS3812 | AS5810 |

Samwell, David
AS1410 Captain Cook and Hawaii SF 1957, 750 cys   75 - 125
Sanchez, Nellie Van de Grift
AS1510 Spanish and Indian Place Names of California
        SF 1922, DJ   50 - 75
Sandburg, Carl (also see Modern First Editions)
AS1610 Abraham Lincoln - The War Years NY 1926,
        2 vol, box   500 - 700
AS1612 NY 1939, 4 vol, box   400 - 600
Sandoz, Mari
AS1710 The Battle of Little Bighorn Phil 1966, 249 cys 150 - 250
AS1711 Phil 1966, DJ (1st trade ed)   20 - 30
AS1720 The Beaver Men NY 1964, 185 cys   150 - 250
AS1721 NY 1964, DJ (1st trade ed)   20 - 30
AS1730 The Buffalo Hunters NY 1954, DJ   75 - 125
AS1740 The Cattlemen NY 1958, 199 cys, box   200 - 300
AS1741 NY 1958, DJ (1st trade ed)   50 - 75
AS1750 Cheyenne Autumn NY 1953, DJ   75 - 125
AS1760 Crazy Horse NY 1942, DJ   75 - 125
AS1770 Hostiles and Friendlies Lincoln 1959, DJ   30 - 50
AS1780 Old Jules (1st book) Bos 1935, DJ   75 - 125
AS1790 Old Jules Country NY 1965, 250 cys   150 - 250
AS1791 NY 1965, DJ (1st trade ed)   20 - 30
AS1800 Slocum House Bos 1937, DJ   50 - 75
AS1810 The Tom Walker NY 1947, DJ   50 - 75
Santee, Ross (also see Golf: Fiction, Humor & Poetry)
AS1910 Apache Land NY 1947, DJ   50 - 75
AS1920 Cowboy NY 1928, DJ   75 - 125
AS1930 Hard Rock and Silver Sage NY 1951, DJ   50 - 75
AS1940 Lost Pony Tracks NY 1953, DJ   50 - 75
AS1950 Men and Horses NY 1926, DJ   150 - 250
Santleben, August
AS2010 A Texas Pioneer NY 1910   300 - 500
Sass, Herbert R.
AS2110 Hear Me, My Chiefs! NY 1940, DJ   30 - 50
Saunders, James E.
AS2210 Early Settlers of Alabama New Orleans 1899   200 - 300
Saxon, Lyle
AS2310 Lafitte the Pirate NY 1930, DJ   75 - 125
Schaffer, John G.
AS2410 The Early History of the Wells Fargo Express
        Berkeley 1922   50 - 75
Scharf, John Thomas
AS2510 The History of Delaware Phil 1888, 2 vol   200 - 300
AS2520 The History of Maryland Balt 1879, 3 vol   200 - 300
AS2530 History of the Confederate States Navy NY 1887 150 - 250
AS2532 Albany, 1894   100 - 150
AS2540 The History of Western Maryland Phil 1882,
        2 vol   200 - 300
Scharmann, H. B.
AS2610 Overland Journey to California NY 1918   200 - 300
Schmidtz, Joseph
AS2710 Texan Statecraft 1836-1845 San Antonio
        1941, 200 cys   300 - 500

Schmitt, Martin F. & Dee Brown
AS2810 Fighting Indians of the West NY 1948, DJ   50 - 75
AS2812 NY 1950s reprint, DJ   30 - 50
Schoolcraft, Henry R.
AS2910 The Indian Tribes of the United States
        Phil 1884, 2 vol   200 - 300
Schreyvogel, Charles
AS3010 My Bunkie and Other Pictures of Western
        Life NY 1909, box   1500 - 2500
Schultz, James Willard
AS3110 My Life as an Indian (1st book) NY 1907   150 - 250
AS3120 The Sun God's Children Bos 1930, DJ   75 - 125
AS3130 With the Indians in the Rockies Bos 1912   75 - 125
Schwatka, Frederick
AS3210 Along Alaska's Great River NY 1885   75 - 125
AS3212 Chi 1898   50 - 75
AS3220 Children of the Cold Bos 1899   50 - 75
AS3230 In the Land of the Cave and Cliff Dwellers
        NY 1893   50 - 75
AS3240 Summer in Alaska Phil 1891   75 - 125
Sell, Henry & Victor Weybright
AS3310 Buffalo Bill and the Wild West NY 1955, DJ   30 - 50
Serven, James
AS3410 Conquering the Frontiers Tucson 1972, DJ   30 - 50
Seton, Ernest Thompson
AS3510 The Birch Bark Roll of the Woodcraft Indians
        NY 1906, wrappers   150 - 250
AS3520 The Gospel of the Redman Garden City
        1937, DJ   150 - 250
AS3530 Lives of the Hunted NY 1900   50 - 75
AS3540 Wild Animals I Have Known NY 1898, 260 cys   200 - 300
AS3541 NY 1898 (1st trade ed)   75 - 125
Seton, Julia M.
AS3610 Indian Creation Stories Santa Fe 1952   50 - 75
Severance, Frank H.
AS3710 An Old Frontier of France NY 1917, 2 vol, DJs 100 - 150
Seymour, Flora Warren
AS3810 The Story of the Red Man NY 1929, DJ   30 - 50
AS3812 NY 1934, DJ   20 - 30
Shaw, R. C.
AS3910 Across the Plains in Forty-Nine Farmland,
        IN 1896   200 - 300
Shea, John Gilmary
AS4010 Early Voyages Up and Down the Mississippi
        Albany 1902   75 - 125
Shields, G. O.
AS4110 The Battle of the Big Hole NY 1889   200 - 300
AS4120 The Big Game of North America Chi 1890   100 - 150
AS4130 The Blanket Indian of the Northwest NY 1921,
        500 cys   200 - 300
AS4140 Cruising in the Cascades Chi 1889   75 - 125
AS4150 Hunting in the Great West Chi 1884   75 - 125
Shinn, Charles Howard
AS4210 Graphic Description of Pacific Coast Outlaws

	SF, nd (late 1800s), wrappers	300 - 500
AS4212	LA 1958, DJ	30 - 50
AS4220	**Mining Camps** NY 1885	150 - 250
AS4222	NY 1948, DJ	30 - 50
AS4230	**Story of the Mine** NY 1896	100 - 150

Shipman, Mrs. O. L.
| AS4310 | **Taming the Big Bend** Marfa, TX 1926 | 200 - 300 |

Short, John T.
| AS4410 | **The North Americans of Antiquity** NY 1880 | 75 - 125 |

Siebert, Wilbur Henry
AS4510	**Loyalists in East Florida** Deland, Fl 1929, 355 cys, 2 vol	150 - 250
AS4520	**The Mysteries of Ohio's Underground Railroads** Col 1951	30 - 50
AS4530	**Underground Railroad From Slavery to Freedom** NY 1898	150 - 250

Silverberg, Robert
| AS4610 | **Mound Builders of Ancient America** Greenwich 1968, DJ | 50 - 75 |

Simmons, Leo
| AS4710 | **Sun Chief** New Haven 1942, DJ | 30 - 50 |

Simpson, C. H.
| AS4810 | **Wild Life in the Far West** Chi 1907 | 20 - 30 |

Simpson, Elizabeth M.
| AS4910 | **Bluegrass Houses and Their Traditions** Lexington 1932, DJ | 100 - 150 |

Sipe, C. Hale
| AS5010 | **The Indian Chiefs of Pennsylvania** Butler, PA 1929 | 150 - 250 |
| AS5020 | **The Indian Wars of Pennsylvania** Harrisburg 1929 | 150 -250 |

Siringo, Charles A.
AS5110	**A Cowboy Detective** Chi 1912, signed	400 - 600
	unsigned	250 - 350
AS5112	Chi 1912, 2 vol, wrappers	150 - 250
AS5120	**A History of Billy the Kid** Santa Fe 1920, wrappers	1000 - 1500
AS5130	**Lone Star Cowboy** Santa Fe 1919, DJ	250 - 350
AS5141	**Riata and Spurs** Bos 1927, DJ, 1st issue w/"1927" on tp	300 - 500
AS5142	later issues	250 - 350
AS5144	Bos 1931, DJ	75 - 125
AS5150	**A Texas Cowboy** Chi 1885, wrappers	7000 - 10000
AS5151	Chi 1885, cloth	3000 - 5000
AS5153	Chi 1886	1000 - 1500
AS5155	NY 1890	300 - 500
AS5157	NY, pub by Ogilvie (late 1800s)	150 - 250
AS5159	NY 1950, DJ	100 - 150

Smedley, William
| AS5310 | **Across the Plains in '62** Denver 1916 | 150 - 250 |

Smith, Buckingham
| AS5410 | **The Discovery of Florida** SF 1946, 280 cys | 300 - 500 |

Smith, Captain James
| AS5510 | **The Generall Historie of Virginia, New England & The Summer Isles** Glasgow 1907, 100 cys | 300 - 500 |

Smith, Charles H.
| AS5610 | **The History of Fuller's Ohio Brigade, 1861-1865** Clev 1909 | 150 - 250 |

Smith, Charles W.
| AS5710 | **Journal of a Trip to California** NY 1920 | 100 - 150 |

Smith, DeCost
| AS5810 | **Martyrs of The Oblong and Little Nine** Caldwell 1948, DJ | 40 - 60 |

Smith, James E.
| AS5910 | **A Famous Battery and Its Campaigns, 1861-64** Wash 1892 | 100 - 150 |

Smith, Wallace
| AS6010 | **Garden of the Sun: A History of the San Joaquin Valley 1772-1939** LA 1939 | 100 - 150 |
| AS6020 | **Oregon Sketches** NY 1925, DJ | 30 - 50 |

Smith, Mrs. White Mountain
| AS6110 | **Indian Tribes of the Southwest** Stanford 1933, DJ | 75 - 125 |

Smith, William
| AS6210 | **Historical Account of Bouquet's Expedition Against the Ohio Indians in 1764** Cinti 1907 | 100 - 150 |

Smith, William
| AS6310 | **History of Southwestern Ohio** NY 1964, 3 vol | 75 - 125 |

Smith, Z. F.
| AS6410 | **History of Kentucky** Louisville 1886 | 100 - 150 |

Snow, Edward Rowe
AS6510	**Great Storms and Famous Shipwrecks of the New England Coast** Bos 1943, DJ	50 - 75
AS6520	**Pirates and Buccaneers of the Atlantic Coast** Bos 1944, DJ	50 - 75
AS6530	**Romance of Boston Bay** Bos 1944, DJ	50 - 75

Sonnichsen, C. L.
AS6610	**Alias Billy the Kid** Albu 1955, DJ	50 - 75
AS6620	**Outlaw, Bill Mitchell Alias Baldy Russell** Denver 1965, DJ	50 - 75
AS6630	**Roy Bean; Law West of the Pecos** NY 1943, DJ	50 - 75

Sorrel, Gen. G. Moxley
| AS6710 | **Recollections of a Confederate Staff Officer** 1905 | 200 - 300 |

Sowell, A. J.
AS6810	**Capt. John F. Tom** np, nd (Seguin, TX, 1906), wrappers	700 - 1000
AS6820	**Early Settlers and Indian Fighters of Southwest Texas** Austin 1900	1500 - 2500
AS6830	**History of Fort Bend County** Houston 1904, 100 cys	300 - 500
AS6840	**Life of Big Foot Wallace** Austin 1899	250 - 350
AS6842	Austin 1957	50 - 75
AS6844	Austin 1977	30 - 50
AS6850	**Rangers and Pioneers of Texas** San Antonio 1884	800 - 1200
AS6852	NY 1964, 750 cys	75 - 125

Speakman, Harold
| AS6910 | **Mostly Mississippi** NY 1927, DJ | 30 - 50 |

Spears, John R.
AS7010	**American Slave Trade** NY 1900	75 - 125
AS7020	**Capt. Nathaniel Brown Palmer** NY 1922, DJ	50 - 75
AS7030	**History of Our Navy** NY 1897	75 - 125
AS7040	**History of the Mississippi Valley** NY 1903	75 - 125
AS7050	**Illustrated Sketches of Death Valley** Chi 1892	200 - 300
AS7060	**Story of the New England Whalers 1640 to 1901** NY 1910	100 - 150

Spotts, David L.
| AS7210 | **Campaigning with Custer** LA 1928, 800 cys | 200 - 300 |

Sprague, Marshall
| AS7260 | **Money Mountain** Bos 1953, DJ | 20 - 30 |

Spring, Agnes Wright
AS7310	**A Bloomer Girl on Pike's Peak** Denver 1949	50 - 75
AS7320	**Caspar Collins** NY 1927, DJ	75 - 125
AS7330	**The Cheyenne and Black Hills Stage and Express Routes** Glendale 1949	150 - 250
AS7340	**William Chapin Deming of Wyoming** Glendale 1944	75 - 125

Spurr, Josiah Edward
| AS7390 | **Through the Yukon Gold Diggings** Bos 1900 | 150 - 250 |

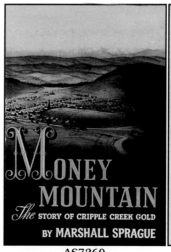 

AS7260   AS7390 (frontispiece)

Squires, W. H. T.
AS7440 The Days of Yester-Year in Colony and
Commonwealth A Sketch Book of Virginia
Portsmouth 1928   50 - 75
AS7450 Through Centuries Three, A Short History of
the People of Virginia Portsmouth 1929   50 - 75

Standard, Mary Newton
AS7510 Colonial Virginia Phil 1917   100 - 150

Standing Bear, Chief
AS7610 My People the Sioux Bos 1928, DJ   50 - 75

Starbuck, Alexander
AS7710 History of the American Whale Fishery Etc.
Waltham 1878   500 - 700
AS7712 NY 1964, 2 vol, 50 cys, box   300 - 500
AS7713 NY 1964, 2 vol, box (trade ed)   75 - 125

Steedman, Charles J.
AS7810 Bucking the Sagebrush NY 1904   300 - 500

Steele, James W.
AS7910 The Klondike Chi 1897, wrappers   200 - 300

Steele, John
AS8010 Across the Plains in 1850 Chi 1930   100 - 150
AS8020 In Camp and Cabin: Mining Life and Adventure,
in California Etc. Lodi, WI, wrappers   300 - 500

Steele, Matthew Forney
AS8110 American Campaigns Wash 1909, 2 vol, wrappers 150 - 250

Stephens, Lorenzo Dow
AS8210 Life Sketches of a Jayhawker of '49 San Jose
1916, wrappers   200 - 300

Stern, Philip Van Doren
AS8310 The Man Who Killed Lincoln NY 1939, DJ   30 - 50

Stevens, Walter B.
AS8410 Centennial History of Missouri St. Louis 1921,
2 vol   100 - 150

Stewart, Hilary
AS8510 Totem Poles Seattle 1990, DJ   30 - 50

Stirling, Matthew (editor, director)
AS8610 Indians of the Americas Wash 1955, DJ   20 - 30

Stone, Henry Lane
AS8710 Morgans Men Louisville 1919, wrappers   100 - 150

Stone, William H. (Hale)
AS8810 Twenty Four Years A Cowboy and Ranchman
in Southern Texas Hedrick 1905   200 - 300
AS8812 Norman 1959, DJ   50 - 75

Strahorn, Mrs. Carrie A.
AS8910 15,000 Miles by Stage NY 1911   300 - 500
AS8912 NY 1915   200 - 300

Stratton, R. B.
AS9010 Life Among the Indians SF 1935, 550 cys   150 - 250

Streeter, Floyd Benjamin
AS9110 Ben Thompson NY 1957, DJ   30 - 50
AS9120 Kaw NY 1941, DJ   50 - 75
AS9130 Prairie Trails and Cow Towns Bos 1936, DJ   300 - 500
AS9132 NY 1963, DJ   30 - 50

Stuart, Granville
AS9210 Forty Years on the Frontier Clev 1925, 2 vol,
slipcase   300 - 500
AS9212 Glendale 1957, DJ   100 - 150

Stuart, Robert
AS9310 The Discovery of the Oregon Trail NY 1935, DJ 50 - 75

Sullivan, Maurice S.
AS9410 The Travels of Jedediah Smith Santa Ana,
CA 1934   250 - 350
AS9412 NY 1936   150 - 250

Sullivan, W. John L.
AS9510 Twelve Years in the Saddle Austin 1909   300 - 500

Sutton, J. J.
AS9610 History of the Second Regiment, West Virginia
Volunteer Cavalry 1861-65 Portsmouth 1892 200 - 300

Swasey, William F.
AS9710 The Early Days and Men of California
Oakland 1891   250 - 350

Sweetser, M. F.
AS9810 King's Handbook of the United States Buffalo 1891 30 - 50

Tallent, Annie D.
AT1510 The Black Hills St. Louis 1899   200 - 300

Tarbell, Ida M.
AT1610 Early Life of Abraham Lincoln NY 1896   30 - 50
AT1620 The History of the Standard Oil Company
NY 1904, 2 vol   300 - 500
AT1630 The Life of Abraham Lincoln NY 1902, 2 vol   50 - 75

Tarrant, Sargeant E.
AT1710 The Wild Riders of the 1st Kentucky
Louisville 1894   250 - 350

Tate, Allen
AT1810 Jefferson Davis, His Rise and Fall NY 1929, DJ 100 - 150

Taylor, Joseph Henry
AT1910 Sketches of Frontier and Indian Life Pottstown,
PA 1889   400 - 900

Taylor, Robert Lewis
AT1960 Vessel of Wrath NY 1966, DJ   20 - 30

Taylor, Thomas U.
AT2010 Jesse Chisholm Bandera, TX 1939   150 - 250

Taylor, Zachary
AT2110 Letters of Zachary Taylor From the Battle-Fields
of the Mexican War Rochester 1908, 300 cys   150 - 250

Thissel, G. W.
AT2210 Crossing the Plains in '49 Oakland 1903   200 - 300

Thomas, Henry W.
AT2310 History of the Doles-Cook-Brigade, Army of
Northern Virginia Atlanta 1903   200 - 300

Thomas, Lewis F.
AT2410 The Valley of the Mississippi Illustrated in a
Series of Views St. Louis 1948, 300 cys   200 - 300

Thompson, David
AT2510 David Thompson's Narrative of His
Explorations in Western America
1784-1812 Tor 1916, 550 cys   800 - 1200

Thompson, Peter
AT2610 Narrative of the Little Big Horn Glendale 1974 75 - 125

Thompson, R. A.
AT2710 Conquest of California Santa Rosa 1896   150 - 250

Thruston, Gates P.
AT2810 Antiquities of Tennessee Cinti 1890   75 - 125

Thwaites, Reuben Gold (author & editor)
AT2910 Afloat on the Ohio Chi 1897   75 - 125
AT2920 Frontier Defense on the Upper Ohio, 1777
to 1778 Madison 1912   100 - 150
AT2930 Historic Waterways: Six Hundred Miles
of Canoeing Down the Rock, Fox, and
Wisconsin Rivers (1st book) Chi 1888   250 - 350
AT2940 Original Journals of the Lewis and Clark Expedition
1804-1806 NY 1904-05, 8 vol, 790 cys   2000 - 3000
AT2942 NY 1959-60, 8 vol   300 - 500
AT2944 NY 1962, 2 vol   150 - 250
AT2950 The Revolution on the Upper Ohio, 1775
to 1777 Madison 1908   75 - 125

Tilghman, Zoe A.
AT3110 Marshall of the Last Frontier Glendale 1964   50 - 75
AT3120 Outlaw Days Okla Cty 1926, wrappers   50 - 75
AT3130 Quanah Okla Cty 1938, DJ   75 - 125
AT3140 Spotlight: Bat Masterson and Wyatt Earp as U.S.
Deputy Marshalls San Antonio 1960, wrappers   20 - 30

Tourgee, Albion W.
AT3310 The Story of a Thousand Buffalo 1896   200 - 300

Townsend, William H.
AT3360 Lincoln and his Wife's Home Town Ind 1929, DJ 50 - 75

Townshend, R. B.
AT3410 The Tenderfoot in New Mexico Lon 1923, DJ   100 - 150
AT3411 NY 1924 (1st U.S. ed)   75 - 125

Triplett, Frank
AT3510 The Life, Times and Treacherous Death of
Jesse James Chi 1882   300 - 500

Truett, Velma Stevens
AT3611 On the Hoof in Nevada LA 1950, 1st state w/o
    "Nevada Publications" on sp   150 - 250
AT3612 2nd state   75 - 125

Turner, Mary
AT3710 These High Plains Amarillo 1941, 150 cys   300 - 500

Twitchell, Ralph Emerson
AT3810 History of the Military Occupation of the Territory
    of New Mexico From 1846 to 1851 Denver 1909 100 - 150
AT3820 The Leading Facts of New Mexican History
    Cedar Rapids 1911-12, 2 vol, 1500 cys   300 - 500
AT3822 Albu 1963, 2 vol   200 - 300
AT3830 Old Santa Fe Santa Fe 1925   150 - 250
AT3840 The Spanish Archives of New Mexico
    Cedar Rapids 1914, 2 vol   700 - 1000

Udell, John
AU2010 Journal of John Udell, Kept During a Trip
    Across the Plains LA 1946, 35 cys, signed   150 - 250
AU2011 750 cys   100 - 150
AU2013 New Haven 1952, 200 cys, wrappers   75 - 125

Underhill, Ruth
AU2210 The Navajos Norman 1956, DJ   30 - 50

Upton, Richard
AU2410 Fort Custer on the Little Big Horn 1877-1898
    Glendale 1973   50 - 75

Vail, Isaac Newton
AV0040 Alaska: Land of the Nugget Why? Pasadena 1897 200 - 300

Van de Water, Frederic F.
AV0080 Glory-Hunter, A Life of General Custer
    Ind 1933, DJ   100 - 150

Vaughn, Robert
AV0120 Then and Now, or 36 Years in the Rockies
    Minn 1900   200 - 300

Vespucci, Amerigo
AV0160 Letter of Amerigo Vespucci Describing
    His Four Voyages to the New World
    SF 1926, 250 cys, box   300 - 500

Vestal, Stanley
AV0200 Big Foot Wallace Bos 1942, DJ   50 - 75
AV0205 Dobe Walls Bos 1929, DJ   50 - 75
AV0210 Happy Hunting Grounds Chi 1928, DJ   30 - 50
AV0215 James Bridger, Mountain Man NY 1946, DJ 30 - 50
AV0220 Queen of Cow Towns: Dodge City NY 1952, DJ 50 - 75
AV0225 Short Grass Country NY 1941, DJ   30 - 50
AV0230 Sitting Bull Bos 1932, DJ
AV0235 Wagons Southwest NY 1946, DJ   30 - 50
AV0240 Warpath Bos 1934, DJ   50 - 75

Visscher, William Lightfoot
AV0280 The Thrilling and Truthful History of the
    Pony Express Chi 1908   75 - 125

Vogel, Virgil
AV0320 American Indian Medicine Norman 1970, DJ 20 - 30
AV0325 Indian Place Names in Illinois Springfield 1963 20 - 30

Vorhees, Luke
AV0360 Personal Recollections of Pioneer Life on the
    Mountains and Plains of the Great West
    Cheyenne 1920   150 - 250

Wachtel, Hubert
AW1010 Who's Who in Indian Relics Dayton 1960 150 - 200

Wagner, Lieut. Col. A. L.
AW1110 The United States Army and Navy: Their
    Histories Akron, OH 1899   200 - 300

Wagner, Henry R. (also see Books About Books)
AW1210 The Cartography of the Northwest Coast of America
    to the Year 1800 Berkeley 1937, 2 vol, box 600 - 800
AW1220 The First American Vessel in California
    LA 1954, 325 cys   100 - 150
AW1230 The Plains and the Rockies SF 1920 w/pamphlet 300 - 500
AW1231 SF 1921 (1st trade ed)   100 - 150
AW1233 SF 1937, 600 cys   200 - 300
AW1235 Col 1953, 75 cys, box   100 - 150
AW1250 The Spanish Southwest 1542-1794 Berkeley
    1924, 100 cys   400 - 600
AW1252 Albu 1937, 2 vol, 401 cys   300 - 500

AW1260 The Spanish Voyages to the Northwest Coast
    of America SF 1929, 25 cys   600 - 800
AW1261 SF 1929 (1st trade ed)   150 - 250

Walgamott, Charles S.
AW1410 Reminiscences of Early Days Twin Falls, ID
    1926-27   150 - 250

Walker, Tacetta
AW1510 Stories of Early Days in Wyoming: Big Horn
    Basin Casper, WY 1936   75 - 125

Wall, Bernhardt
AW1610 Following Fra Junipero Serra and Others
    Sierra Madre, CA 1943, 200 cys   300 - 500

Wall, Oscar
AW1710 Recollections of the Sioux Massacre Lake City,
    MN 1909   150 - 250

Wallace, Ernest
AW1810 The Comanches: Lords of the South Plains
    Norman 1952, DJ   50 - 75

Wallace, Susan E.
AW1910 The Land of the Pueblos NY 1888   100 - 150
AW1912 NY (Hurst reprint-early 1900s)   20 - 30

Walsh, Richard
AW2010 The Making of Buffalo Bill Ind 1928, DJ 30 - 50
AW2012 NY (1930s reprint) DJ   20 - 30

Walters, Frank
AW2110 Book of the Hopi NY 1963, DJ   75 - 125
AW2120 The Earp Brothers of Tombstone NY 1960, DJ 50 - 75
AW2130 Masked Gods: Navaho and Pueblo
    Ceremonialism Albu 1950, 300 cys   200 - 300
AW2131 Albu 1950, DJ (1st trade ed)   75 - 125
AW2140 The Story of Mrs. Virgil Earp NY 1960, DJ 50 - 75

Walters, Lorenzo D.
AW2210 Tombstone's Yesterday Tucson 1928, DJ 150 - 250

Walton, William
AW2310 The Captivity and Sufferings of Benjamin
    Gilbert and His Family 1780-83 Clev 1904 100 - 150

Ware, Eugene
AW2410 The Indian War of 1864 Topeka 1911 200 - 300
AW2412 The Lyon Campaign in Missouri Topeka 1907 150 - 250

Washington, Booker T.
AW2510 The Future of the American Negro Bos 1899 200 - 300
AW2520 Story of My Life and Work Naperville 1900 100 - 150
AW2530 Up From Slavery NY 1901   100 - 150

Watson, Douglas S. (editor)
AW2610 California in the Fifties SF 1936, 850 cys, DJ 800 - 1200
AW2620 The Spanish Occupations of California
    SF 1934, 550 cys   200 - 300

Watts, J. L.
AW2710 Cherokee Citizenship Muldrow, OK Territory
    1895, wrappers   200 - 300

Wauchope, Robert
AW2810 Handbook of Middle American Indians
    Austin 1964, 4 vol   150 - 250

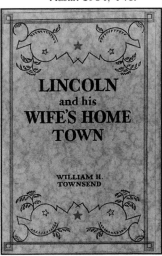

AT3360

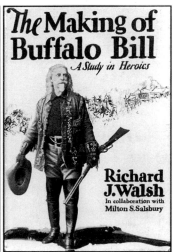

AW2012

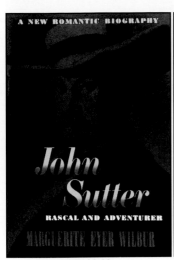
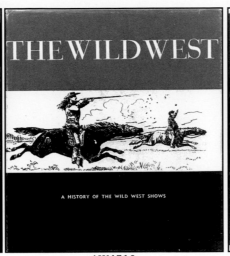
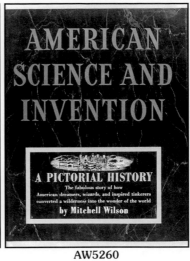
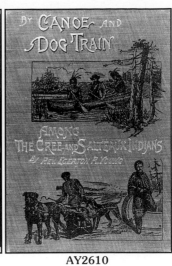

AW4360	AW4510	AW5260

AY2610

Way, Frederick
AW2910 **She Takes the Horns** Cinti 1953   50 - 75

Wayland, John W.
AW3010 **Historic Homes of Northern Virginia and the Eastern Panhandle of Western Virginia** Staunton, VA 1937   100 - 150

Webb, Walter Prescott
AW3110 **The Great Frontier** Bos 1952   100 - 150
AW3120 **The Great Plains** Bos 1931, DJ   100 - 150
AW3130 **Story of the Texas Rangers** NY 1957, DJ   30 - 50
AW3132 Austin 1971, DJ   20 - 30
AW3140 **Texas Rangers** NY 1935, 250 cys, slipcase   800 - 1200
AW3141 NY 1935, DJ (1st trade ed)   100 - 150
AW3150 **Texas Rangers in the Mexican War** Austin 1975   50 - 75

Wellman, Paul I.
AW3310 **Dynasty of Western Outlaws** NY 1961, DJ   75 - 125
AW3320 **The Indian Wars of the West** Garden City 1954, DJ   30 - 50
AW3330 **The Trampling Herd** NY 1939, DJ   75 - 125

Wendt, Lloyd
AW3410 **Lords of the Levee** NY 1943, DJ   30 - 50

West, George A.
AW3510 **Tobacco, Pipes and Smoking Customs of the American Indians** Milwaukee 1934, 2 vol   300 - 500

West, John C.
AW3610 **A Texan in Search of a Fight Being the Diary and Letters of a Private Soldier in Hood's Texas Brigade** Waco, TX 1901   400 - 600

Wetmore, Helen Cody
AW3710 **Last of the Great Scouts: The Life Story of Col. William F. Cody, "Buffalo Bill"** Duluth 1899, 1st issue w/267 pp   300 - 500
AW3711 later issue w/296 pp   150 - 250
AW3712 Duluth 1899, 500 cys, signed "Buffalo Bill"   1500 - 2500
AW3713 NY 1899   100 - 150

Wheat, Carl I.
AW3810 **Books of the Gold Rush** SF 1949   250 - 350
AW3820 **The Maps of the California Gold Region 1848** SF 1942   1000 - 1500
AW3830 **The Pioneer Press of California** Oakland 1848   200 - 300

Wheeler, Col. Homer
AW3910 **Buffalo Days** Ind 1925, DJ   50 - 75

White Horse Eagle, Big Chief
AW4010 **We Indians** NY 1931, DJ   50 - 75

Whittaker, Milo Lee
AW4110 **Pathbreakers and Pioneers of the Pueblo Region** 1917   100 - 150

Wierzbicki, F. P.
AW4210 **California As It Is and As It May Be** SF 1933, DJ, 500 cys   200 - 300

Wilbarger, J. W.
AW4310 **Indian Depredations in Texas** Austin 1890   800 - 1200

AW4312 Austin 1935   100 - 150

Wilbur, Marguerite Eyer
AW4360 **John Sutter** NY 1949, DJ   20 - 30

Wilcox, Frank
AW4410 **Ohio Indian Trails** Clev 1933   125 - 200
AW4412 Kent 1970   50 - 75

Wilder, Mitchell
AW4510 **The Wild West: A History of the Wild West Shows** Ft. Worth 1970, DJ   30 - 50

Willcox, R. N.
AW4610 **Reminiscences of California Life** Avery OH 1897   200 - 300

Willert, James
AW4710 **Little Big Horn Diary** La Mirada, CA 1982, 500 cys   150 - 250

Williams, Joseph
AW4810 **Narrative of a Tour From the State of Indiana to the Oregon Territory** NY 1921, 250 cys   100 - 150

Williams, Llew
AW4910 **Dalton Brothers in Their Oklahoma Cave** Chi 1893   150 - 250

Williams, Samuel Cole
AW5010 **Adair's History of the American Indians** Johnson City 1930, DJ   50 - 75

Williamson, James J.
AW5110 **Mosby's Rangers** NY 1895   250 - 350
AW5112 NY 1909   150 - 250

Wilson, Elijah N.
AW5211 **Among the Shoshones** Salt Lake City, nd (early 1900s), 1st issue w/222 pp   300 - 500
AW5212 2nd issue w/247 pp   200 - 300

Wilson, Mitchell
AW5260 **American Science and Invention** NY 1954, DJ   20 - 30

Wilson, Neill C.
AW5310 **Silver Stampede** NY 1937, DJ   75 - 125
AW5311 **Treasure Express** NY 1936, DJ   50 - 75

Wilson, Obed G.
AW5410 **My Adventures in the Sierras** Franklin, OH 1902   150 - 250

Wilson, Woodrow
AW5510 **George Washington** NY 1897   100 - 150
AW5521 **A History of the American People** NY 1902, 1st ed w/"Oct 1902" on cr page, 5 vol   125 - 200

Wilstach, Frank J.
AW5610 **Wild Bill Hickok** NY 1926, DJ   50 - 75

Wilstach, Paul
AW5710 **Hudson River Landings** Ind 1933, DJ   30 - 50
AW5720 **Potomac Landings** Ind 1932, DJ   30 - 50

Wiltsee, Ernest
AW5810 **Gold Rush Steamers** SF 1938, 500 cys   150 - 250
AW5820 **The Pioneer Miner and the Pack Mule Express** SF 1931, DJ   100 - 150

AW5830 **The Truth About Fremont** SF 1936, DJ 100 - 150

Winchell, N. H.
AW5910 **The Aborigines of Minnesota** St. Paul 1911 300 - 500

Windsor, Justin
AW6010 **A Narrative and Critical History of America**
Cambridge 1889, 8 vol 200 - 300

Winkler, A. V.
AW6110 **The Confederate Capital and Hood's Texas**
Brigade Austin 1894 300 - 500

Winther, Oscar
AW6210 **Express and Stagecoach Days in California**
Palo Alto 1935 150 - 250
AW6220 **The Great Northwest** NY 1947, DJ 50 - 75
AW6230 **The Old Oregon Country** Stanford 1950, DJ 150 - 250
AW6240 **The Trans-Mississippi West** Bloomington 1942 50 - 75
AW6250 **Via Western Express & Stagecoach** Stanford
1945, DJ 75 - 125

Winthrop, T.
AW6410 **Canoe and the Saddle** Tacoma 1913 150 - 250

Wise, George
AW6510 **Campaigns and Battles of the Army of**
Northern Virginia NY 1916 200 - 300

Wislizenus, Frederick
AW6610 **A Journey to the Rocky Mountains in the**
Year 1839 St. Louis 1912, 500 cys 200 - 300

Wissler, Clark
AW6710 **Indian Cavalcade** NY 1938, DJ 30 - 50
AW6720 **Indians of the Americas** Garden City 1953, DJ 20 - 30

Wood, Frederic
AW6810 **The Turnpikes of New England** Bos 1919, DJ 75 - 125

Wood, James H.
AW6910 **The War, Stonewall Jackson, His Campaigns**
and Battles, The Regiment, As I Saw Them
Cumberland, MD, nd (early 1900s) 150 - 250

Wood, Norman
AW7010 **Lives of Famous Indian Chiefs** Aurora 1906 75 - 125

Woodruff, W. E.
AW7110 **With the Light Guns in '61-'65** Little Rock 1903 200 - 300

Woodward, C. Vann
AW7210 **The Burden of Southern History** Baton Rouge
1960, DJ 50 - 75
AW7220 **Mary Chesnut's Civil War** New Haven 1981, DJ 75 - 125

Woodward, W. E.
AW7310 **Meet General Grant** NY 1928, DJ 20 - 30

Woolen, William Watson
AW7410 **Inside Passage to Alaska 1792-1920**
Clev 1924, 2 vol 200 - 300

Wooten, Dudley G. (editor)
AW7510 **Complete History of Texas** Dallas 1899 150 - 250
AW7520 **A Comprehensive History of Texas 1865**
to 1897 Dallas 1898, 2 vol 2000 - 3000

Wright, E. W. (editor)
AW7610 **Lewis and Dryden's Marine History of the**
Pacific Northwest Portland 1895 500 - 700

Wright, Robert M.
AW7710 **Dodge City, The Cowboy Capital** Wichita
1913, 344 pp 200 - 300
AW7712 Wichita 1913, 342 pp 100 - 150

Wright, Capt. T. J.
AW7810 **History of the 8th Regiment, Kentucky**
Volunteer Infantry St. Joseph 1880 200 - 300

Wyeth, John A.
AW7910 **Life of Gen. Nathan Bedford Forrest** NY 1899 200 - 300

Wyeth, John B.
AW8010 **Oregon; or A Short History of a Long Journey**
Clev 1906 200 - 300

Wyllys, Rufus K.
AW8110 **Arizona** Phoenix 1950, DJ 50 - 75

Yeary, Mamie
AY2010 **Reminiscences of the Boys in Gray,**
1861-1865 Dallas 1912 200 - 300

Yoakum, Henderson K.
AY2210 **History of Texas** Austin 1935, 2 vol 100 - 150

Young, Colonel Bennett H.
AY2410 **The Prehistoric Men of Kentucky** Louisville
1910, wrappers 200 - 300

Young, Rev. Egerton R.
AY2610 **By Canoe and Dog Train** Cinti (1900) 50 - 75

Young, Harry
AY2810 **Hard Knocks: A Life Story of the Vanishing**
West Portland 1915 150 - 250

Young, Jesse Bowman
AY3010 **What a Boy Saw in the Army** NY 1894 50 - 75

Young, L. D.
AY3210 **Reminiscences of a Soldier of the Orphan**
Brigade np, nd (Louisville 1916) 200 - 300

Zaccarelli, John
AZ1010 **Zaccarelli's Pictorial Souvenir Book of the**
Golden Northland Dawson 1908, wrappers 100 - 150

ARTISTS & ILLUSTRATORS

Many 20th century artists dabbled in magazine and book illustrating. A good example is Pablo Picasso, who illustrated for *Verve* magazine and did *Lysistrata* by Aristophanes for the Limited Editions Club. He designed posters and postcards as well. Numerous illustrators were also fine painters and sculptors: Maxfield Parrish, Rockwell Kent, N.C. Wyeth, Frederic Remington, Norman Rockwell, and Aubrey Beardsley to name a few. Original works by these illustrators may be worth $10,000 to $500,000.

Several major artists who illustrated their own books are Salvador Dali, Marc Chagall, and Henri Matisse. One of the most expensive books of the 20th century is *Jazz* (Paris 1947) by Henri Matisse. It's worth over $40,000, and sells for over $100,000 with the accompanying portfolio of prints. Marc Chagall illustrated for *Verve* magazine; several issues showcased his biblical stained-glass designs. This was followed by *The Jerusalem Windows* (NY 1962), a very popular book among art collectors; it brings over $1000. Salvador Dali wrote and illustrated many of his own books beginning in the 1940s. *Hidden Faces* (NY 1944) and *The Secret Life of Salvador Dali* (NY 1942) are two examples. His books are collected as marvelous illustrations of surrealistic art.

Much of the impetus for beautiful books illustrated by contemporary artists began in France around the turn of the century. "Livre D'Artiste" is a French word for hand-made books done in close collaboration among the artist, writer, publisher, typographer, printer, and binder. Ambroise Vollard was a famous French publisher who created books with color lithographs by Picasso, Matisse, and Braque. The "Limited Editions Club," an American publisher, produced fine limited-edition books from 1929 to the 1960s. They were illustrated by such great artists as Picasso, Matisse, and others.

A very popular magazine for artists was *Verve* (1937-1960). Large and colorful, it was published by Teriade, a French book publisher. *Verve* was sold by subscription on an irregular basis in France and the USA, and featured Pablo Picasso, Marc Chagall, Pierre Bonnard, Georges Braque, Henri Matisse, and others. Needless to say, issues have become very collectible with some bringing over $300. The last double issue (*Verve* 37 & 38) by Chagall is worth $4000 to $6000.

The most widely collected illustrators...and the ones which tend to be most expensive...are Arthur Rackham, N.C. Wyeth, Rockwell Kent, Kay Nielsen, Maxfield Parrish, Willy Pogany, Frederic Remington, Harrison Fisher, Edmund Dulac, and Maud Humphrey. Some of their books appeared as sumptuously bound and printed limited editions. For instance, most of Rackham's books first appeared as gold-stamped/vellum-bound signed limited editions, thus adding to their rarity and appeal.

Some classic writings which have gone through profuse editions (each by a different artist or illustrator) are Aesop's Fables, Arabian Nights Entertainments, Hans Christian Andersen's Fairy Tales, Grimm's Fairy Tales, Alice in Wonderland, and The Rubaiyat of Omar Khayyam.

RA2510 (cover w/ signed print)

RA3050 (w/o DJ)

RA3080 (w/o DJ)   RA7520 (w/o DJ)

Children's book illustrators are also coming to the forefront of book collecting. Any books illustrated by Jessie Willcox Smith, Beatrix Potter, Johnny Gruelle, John R. Neill, or W.W. Denslow may bring $50 to over $1000 for very rare examples.

Many collectors buy illustrated books by category. Some focus on the *Scribners Illustrated Classics*, a series of famous stories published by Charles Scribners & Sons from the early 1900s to the 1940s. They were illustrated by such talents as N.C. Wyeth, Maxfield Parrish, and Jessie Willcox Smith and were uniformly bound in pictorial dust jackets. Other collectors want books published by the Limited Editions Club or Heritage Press; still others focus on certain artists and illustrators. Some of the interest is regional. English collectors prefer fantasy artists Arthur Rackham, W.H. Robinson, and Walter Crane, while western U.S. collectors like Frederic Remington and Harrison Fisher. Some collect the Caldecott Award Winners. The Caldecott Award is for the best children's book published in the U.S. and has been given annually since 1938.

Condition is paramount for art and illustrated books: missing plates, stained covers, or torn pictorial paste-ons decrease value. The presence of the dust jacket can make some books a lot more valuable, especially from the early 1900s.

The following listings are by artist, author, or title. Editors' or authors' names may appear in parentheses after the title. Also see seperate listing for *Verve* magazine.

Adams, Charles
RA1010	Home Bodies NY 1954, DJ	20 - 30

Aldin, Cecil
RA2010	Black Beauty Lon 1912	50 - 75
RA2020	Dog Day Lon 1902	50 - 75
RA2030	A Dog Day NY 1906	50 - 75
RA2040	My Dog Lon 1913	100 - 150
RA2050	Old Inns NY 1921	50 - 75
RA2060	Old Manor Houses Lon 1923	50 - 75
RA2070	Our Friend the Dog NY 1913	50 - 75
RA2080	Two Little Runaways Lon 1898	100 - 150
RA2090	The White Puppy Book Lon 1917	50 - 75

Alvar
RA2510	Alvar (Jacques Lassaigne) Barcelona 1970, DJ, signed, print inserted	250 - 350

Anderson, Anne
RA3010	Aladdin and the Wonderful Lamp Lon 1920, DJ	50 - 75
RA3020	Ali Baba and the Forty Thieves Lon 1920, DJ	50 - 75
RA3030	Ann Anderson's Fairy Book Lon 1928, DJ	75 - 125
RA3040	The Golden Story Book Lon 1933, DJ	50 - 75
RA3050	Heidi Phil 1923, DJ	125 - 175
	w/o DJ	40 - 60
RA3060	Lie-Down Stories Lon 1919, DJ	75 - 125
RA3070	Sleeping Beauty Lon 1928, DJ	40 - 60
RA3080	The Water Babies Lon 1930, DJ	100 - 150
RA3082	NY, nd, DJ	125 - 175

Anderson, C. W. (Clarence William)
RA3510	Billy and Blaze NY 1936, DJ	50 - 75
RA3520	Black, Bay and Chestnut NY 1939, DJ	40 - 60
RA3530	Throughbreds NY 1942, DJ	40 - 60

Artzybasheff, Boris
RA5010	Aesop's Fables NY 1933, DJ	50 - 75
RA5020	The Apple Tree NY 1926, DJ	50 - 75
RA5030	The Circus of Dr. Lao NY 1935, DJ	50 - 75
RA5060	The Fairy Shoemaker NY 1928, DJ	75 - 125
RA5070	Feats on the Fiord NY 1924, DJ	75 - 125
RA5080	The Forge in the Forest NY 1925, DJ	75 - 125
RA5090	Gay Neck NY 1927, 1000 cys	100 - 150
RA5100	Ghond, the Hunter NY 1928	50 - 75
RA5110	Herodotus NY 1929, DJ	50 - 75
RA5120	Poor Shydullah NY 1931, DJ	50 - 75
RA5130	Seven Simeons NY 1937, DJ	50 - 75
RA5140	Verotchkas' Tales NY 1922, DJ	50 - 75

Audubon, John James (also see Birds)
RA6510	Journal of John James Audubon (Howard Corning) Bos 1929, 2 vol, 225 cys	200 - 300
RA6520	The Original Watercolor Paintings by John James Audubon for the Birds of America (M. Davidson) NY 1966, 2 vol, slipcase	300 - 500

Austen, John
RA7510	Adventures of a Harlequin Lon 1923	50 - 75
RA7520	As You Like It Lon 1930, DJ	75 - 125
RA7530	Daphnis & Chloe Lon 1925	100 - 150
RA7540	Hamlet Lon (1920s), 60 cys	400 - 600
RA7542	Lon 1922, (1st trade ed)	75 - 125
RA7544	NY 1922	100 - 150
RA7560	The Personal History of David Copperfield NY 1935, slipcase	30 - 50
RA7570	Tales of Past Times Lon 1922	50 - 75

Avery, Milton
RA8510	Milton Avery (Hilton Kramer) NY 1962	150 - 250

Bailey, Mildred L.
RB1010	Queen Tiny's Little People (Claude Wetmore) NY 1914	50 - 75

Bannerman, Helen (also see Modern First Editions)
RB1210	Little Black Sambo Chi 1905 (w/intro by L. Frank Baum	75 - 125

Beardsley, Aubrey
RB1510	Aubrey Beardsley (Brian Reade) NY 1967, DJ	30 - 50

RB1520	Aubrey Beardsley: Selected Drawings NY 1967	30 - 50
RB1530	The Early Work and the Later Work Lon 1901, 2 vol	500 - 700
RB1532	Lon 1920, 2 vol	300 - 500
RB1540	Fifty Drawings NY 1920, 500 cys	300 - 500
RB1550	Nineteen Early Drawings Lon 1919, 150 cys	500 - 700

Beckmann, Max

RB1710	Catalog Raisonné of His Prints Bern 1990, 2 vol, DJs, slipcases	300 - 500

Beerbohm, Max

RB1910	A Book of Caricatures Lon 1907	200 - 300
RB1920	Observations Lon 1925	200 - 300
RB1922	Lon 1926, 280 cys	400 - 600
RB1930	A Survey Lon 1921, 275 cys	300 - 500

Bellows, George W.

RB2110	His Lithographs NY 1927	200 - 300
RB2120	The Paintings of George Bellows NY 1929, 2000 cys, DJ	500 - 700

Betts, Ethel Franklin

RB2310	Babes in Toyland NY 1924, DJ	150 - 250
	w/o DJ	100 - 150
RB2320	The Complete Mother Goose NY 1909	100 - 150
RB2330	Fairy Tales From the Brothers Grimm NY 1909	150 - 250
RB2340	The True Story of Humpty Dumpty NY 1905	100 - 150

Birch, Reginald B. (also F. H. Burnett, Modern First Editions)

RB3110	Giovanni and the Other (F.H. Burnett) NY 1892	50 - 75
RB3120	Little Lord Fauntleroy NY 1886, 1st issue w/De Vinne imprint	300 - 500
RB3122	NY 1911 (F. H. Burnett)	50 - 75
RB3130	Little Men (L.M. Alcott) Bos 1901	50 - 75
RB3140	The Would Be Goods (E. Nesbit) NY 1901	100 - 150

Blake, William

RB3510	All Religions Are One Lon 1970, 36 cys	400 - 600
RB3512	LON 1970, 600 cys	150 - 250
RB3520	America: A Prophecy Lon 1963, 20 cys	1500 - 2500
RB3522	Lon 1963 (trade ed)	400 - 600
RB3530	Blake's Innocence and Experience (Joseph Wicksteed) Lon 1928, DJ	50 - 75
RB3540	Pencil Drawings (Joseph Wicksteed) Lon 1927, 1550 cys, slipcase	100 - 150

Bonnard, Pierre

RB4010	Correspondences of Pierre Bonnard Paris 1944, 1000 cys	400 - 600
RB4020	Couleur de Bonnard Paris 1947 (Verve 17/18)	300 - 500
RB4030	Lithographie (Claude Roger-Marx) Monte Carlo 1952, wrappers	300 - 500

Boston, Peter

RB4310	Treasure of Green Knowe NY 1958, DJ	40 - 60

Botticelli, Sandro

RB4610	Sandro Botticelli (Yukio Yashiro) Lon 1925, 3 vol	250 - 350

Boylan, Grace & Ike Morgan

RB4910	Kids of Many Colors Chi 1901	100 - 150

Bradley, Will

RB5210	The American Stage of Today NY 1910	125 - 175
RB5220	The Ashes of Empire NY 1898	75 - 125
RB5230	Earth Breath Lon 1897	200 - 300
RB5240	The Legend of Sleepy Hollow NY 1897	100 - 150

RB5250	Peter Poodle NY 1906	400 - 600
RB5260	Rip Van Winkle NY 1897	100 - 150
RB5270	The Rubaiyat of Omar Khayham NY 1897	100 - 150
RB5280	War is Kind NY 1899	500 - 700
RB5290	Young Lives Lon 1899	100 - 150

Brangwyn, Frank

RB5510	The Book of Bridges Lon 1925	50 - 75
RB5520	The Rubaiyat of Omar Khayham Lon 1919	75 - 125
RB5522	Lon (nd), limp lea/box	50 - 75

Bransom, Paul

RB5810	The Argosy of Fables NY 1921, DJ	100 - 150
RB5820	The Wind in the Willows NY 1913, DJ	150 - 250
	w/o DJ	75 - 125

Braque, Georges

RB6210	Braque (Raymond Cogwiat) NY 1980, DJ	100 - 150
RB6220	Braque Lithographie Monte Carlo 1963, wrappers, slipcase	1000 - 1500
RB6230	Cahier de Georges Braque 1917-1947 Paris 1948, 95 cys	2000 - 3000
RB6231	Paris 1948, 750 cys	800 - 1200
RB6233	Paris 1955, 95 cys	1000 - 1500
RB6234	Paris 1955, 750 cys	500 - 700
RB6250	Carnets Intimes Paris 1955 (Verve 31/32)	300 - 500
RB6260	Georges Braque, His Graphic Works (Raymond Cogwiat) NY 1961, DJ	150 - 250
RB6270	Hommage de Georges Braque (Raymond Cogwiat) Paris 1964, 350 cys	500 - 700
RB6280	The Intimate Sketchbooks of Georges Braque (Raymond Cogwiat) NY 1955 (Verve 31/32)	300 - 500

Bratby, John

RB6410	Breakdown NY 1960, DJ	50 - 75

Brock, H. M. (Henry Matthew)

RB6610	The Book of Fairy Tales Lon (early 1900s)	100 - 150
RB6620	The Book of Nursery Tales Lon 1934	100 - 150
RB6630	The Deerslayer NY 1900	50 - 75
RB6640	Treasure Island NY 1928	40 - 60

Brown, Ethel P.

RB7010	Catching Up with the Circus NY 1926	75 - 125

Brundage, Francis

RB7510	The Baby's Biography NY 1893	75 - 125

RB2310

RB3110

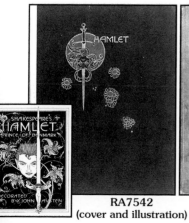

RA7542
(cover and illustration)

RB1010

RB1510

RB4910

RB5260

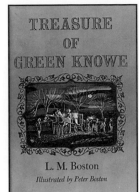

RB4310   RB6610   RB7540   RB7550   RB9010

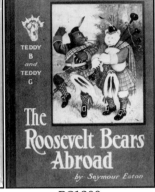

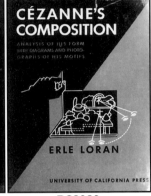

RB9020   RC1300   RC1310   RC2020   RC2585 (back)

RB7520	**The Baby's Book** Lon 1904	75 - 125
RB7530	**Belles & Beaux** NY 1896	75 - 125
RB7540	**Royal Children of English History** NY (early 1900s)	25 - 35
RB7550	**What Happened to - Tommy.** NY (1920s)	30 - 50

Buffet, Bernard
RB8010	**Bernard Buffet** (Maurice Rheims) Nice 1983, DJ	125 - 200
RB8020	**Buffet** (Gerhard Reinz) NY 1968, DJ	100 - 150
RB8030	**Lithographies de Bernard Buffet 1952-1966** Paris 1967	500 - 700
RB8040	**Oeuvre Grave** Paris 1967	250 - 350

Bull, Charles Livingston
Illustrated for Jack London: *Call of the Wild, White Fang, Before Adam*, etc. See Jack London in Modern First Editions.
RB8510	**Country Cousins** NY 1927	40 - 60
RB8520	**Horsemen of the Plains** NY 1910	50 - 75
RB8530	**Kindred of the Wild** Bos 1902	50 - 75
RB8540	**Kootenai Why Stories** NY 1926	40 - 60
RB8550	**More Wild Folk** NY 1924	40 - 60
RB8560	**Red Fox** Bos 1905	50 - 75

Burd, Clara
RB9010	**A Child's Garden of Verses** (Robert Lewis Stevenson) Akron, 1929, wrappers	30 - 50
RB9020	**Little Men** Phil 1928, DJ	30 - 50

Caldecott, R. (Randolph)
RC1010	**The House That Jack Built** Lon 1879	50 - 75
RC1020	Some of Aesop's Fables w/Modern Instances NY 1883	75 - 125

Calder, Alexander
RC1110	**Animal Sketching** NY 1927	40 - 60
RC1120	**Selected Fables** (Jean De La Fontaine) NY 1957, DJ	100 - 150
RC1130	**Three Young Rats and Other Rhymes** (James Sweeney) NY 1944, limited ed	75 - 125

Campbell, Floyd V.
RC1300	**The Roosevelt Bears Abroad** Phil (early 1900s)	200 - 300
RC1310	**The Roosevelt Bears Their Travels and Adventures** (Seymour Eaton) Phil 1906	200 - 300
RC1320	**Teddy-B & Teddy-G The Bear Detectives** (Seymour Eaton) Phil 1909	200 - 300

Cassatt, Mary
RC1510	**Mary Cassatt** (Adelyn D. Breeskin) Wash 1970	1000 - 1500

Catlin, George
RC1710	**The George Catlin Indian Gallery & Etc.** (Thomas Donaldson) Wash 1887	200 - 300

Cézanne, Paul
RC2000	**Cézanne** (Bernard Dorival) Bos 1948, DJ	75 - 125
RC2010	**Cézanne** (Joachim Gasquet) Berlin 1930	100 150
RC2012	Paris 1926	100 - 150
RC2020	**Cézanne's Composition** (Erle Loran) LA 1959, DJ	50 - 75
RC2030	**Die Zeichnungen Von Paul Cézanne** (Adrian Chappius) Olten 1962, 2 vol	100 - 150
RC2040	**The Drawings of Paul Cézanne** (Adrian Chappius) Greenwich 1973, 2 vol, slipcase	200 - 300
RC2050	**Le Maitre Paul Cézanne** (Georges Riviere) Paris 1923	100 - 150
RC2060	**Paul Cézanne** (Ambroise Vollard) Paris 1914, 150 cys, Japan paper	3000 - 5000
RC2061	Paris 1914, 200 cys, vellum	3000 - 5000
RC2062	Paris 1914, 1000 cys	1500 - 2500
RC2070	**Paul Cézanne** (Eugenio D'Ors) Paris 1930, wrappers	100 - 150

Chagall, Marc
RC2510	**The Bible** (illus) NY & Paris 1956 (Verve 33/34)	4000 - 6000
RC2520	**The Biblical Message** NY 1973, DJ, slipcase	200 - 300
RC2530	**The Ceiling of the Paris Opera** (Jacques Lassaigne) NY 1966, DJ, w/separate print in pocket	300 - 500
RC2540	**Ceramics & Sculptures of Chagall** Monte Carlo 1972	400 - 600
RC2550	**Chagall** (Ives Bonnefoy) Paris 1962	150 - 250
RC2560	**Chagall Lithographie** (Fernand Mourlet) Monte Carlo 1960-74, 4 vol	10000 - 12000
RC2570	**Chagall: Vitraux Pour Jerusalem** Paris 1961 (catalog) wrappers	50 - 75
RC2571	Paris 1961, 300 cys, signed, wrappers	200 - 300
RC2580	**Chagall's Posters** (Charles Sorlier) NY 1975, DJ	300 - 500
RC2585	**Daphnis & Chloe** NY 1977, DJ	75 - 125
RC2590	**Diary of a Horse** (Claire Goll; drawings by Chagall) NY 1956, DJ	250 - 350
RC2600	**Drawings and Watercolors for the Ballet** (Jacques Lassaigne) NY 1969, DJ	125 - 200
RC2610	**Drawings for the Bible** NY & Paris 1960 (Verve 37/38)	4000 - 6000
RC2620	**É Légie des alizés** (L.S. Senghor) Paris 1969, 450 cys, wrappers	150 - 250
RC2630	**Homage to Marc Chagall** (G. San Lazzaro) NY 1969, DJ	150 - 250
RC2640	**The Jerusalem Windows** NY 1962, DJ	1000 - 1500
	w/o DJ	800 - 1200

RC2650	**Le Cirque d'Izis** (Jacques Prevert) Monte Carlo 1965, DJ	150 - 250
RC2660	**Le Message Biblique** Paris 1972, DJ, slipcase	200 - 300
RC2670	**Marc Chagall** (Franz Meyer) NY 1963, DJ	150 - 250
RC2680	**Monotypes** (Jean Leymarie) Geneva 1966, 100 cys, orig etching	1000 - 1500
RC2690	**My Life** NY 1960, DJ	50 - 75
	signed	150 - 250
RC2700	**The World of Marc Chagall** (Roy McMullen) Garden City 1968, DJ	75 - 125

Christo

RC3150	**Christo** (David Bourdon) NY 1970, DJ	300 - 500
RC3160	**Valley Curtain, Rifle Colorado 1970-1972** (David Bourdon) Stuttgart 1973	200 - 300

Christy, Howard Chandler

RC3410	**The American Girl** Bos 1906	75 - 125
RC3420	**The Christy Girl** Ind 1906	125 - 175
RC3422	NY (early 1900s) Grosset & Dunlap reprint , DJ	100 - 150
RC3430	**The Courtship of Miles Standish** Ind 1903	40 - 60
RC3440	**Dolly Dialogues** NY 1901	50 - 75
RC3450	**Evangeline** Ind 1905	50 - 75
RC3451	Ind (about 1914)	40 - 60
RC3460	**Lady of the Lake** Ind 1910	100 - 150
RC3470	**The Lion and the Unicorn** NY 1899	40 - 60
RC3480	**Old Gentlemen of Black Stock** NY 1900	40 - 60
RC3490	**An Old Sweetheart of Mine** Ind 1902	30 - 50
RC3500	**Our Girls** Bos 1907	50 - 75
RC3510	**The Princess** Ind 1911	50 - 75
RC3520	**Riley Roses** Ind 1909	50 - 75
RC3530	**Wanted, A Chaperone** NY 1902	30 - 50

Clarke, Harry

RC4010	**Fairy Tales by Hans C. Andersen** Lon 1916	200 - 300
RC4011	NY 1916	200 - 300
RC4014	NY 1930	125 - 200
RC4030	**Tales of Mystery and Imagination** NY 1920	100 - 150
RC4032	NY 1933	75 - 125
RC4040	**The Year's at the Spring** Lon 1920, 250 cys	800 - 1200
RC4041	NY 1920	150 - 250
RC4042	Lon 1920, DJ (1st trade ed)	100 - 150

Coffin, Robert P. Tristram

RC4410	**On the Green Carpet** Ind 1951, DJ	20 - 30

Constable, John

RC4510	**Constable and His Influence on Landscape Painting** (C.J. Holmes) NY 1902, 350 cys	300 - 500

Corbett, Bertha

RC4810	**The Sunbonnet Babies' Book** Chi 1902	75 - 125

Corot, J. B. C.

RC5110	**Corot** (Julius Meier-Graefe) Berlin 1930	100 - 150

Cory, Fanny Y.

RC5410	**Jackieboy in Rainbowland** (William Hill) Chi 1911	40 - 60
RC5420	**Just Rhymes** NY 1899	50 - 75
RC5430	**Pete and Polly Stories** Chi 1902	50 - 75

Cox, Palmer

RC5710	**The Brownie Year Book** NY 1895	75 - 125
RC5720	**The Brownies at Home** NY 1897	100 - 150
RC5730	**The Brownies: Their Book** NY 1897	75 - 125
RC5740	**Jolly Chinee** NY 1900	50 - 75
RC5750	**Palmer Cox's Queer People** NY 1888	75 - 125
RC5755	later printings	40 - 75

Crane, Walter

RC6510	**The Art of Walter Crane** Lon 1902	200 - 300
RC6520	**Baby's Bouquet** Lon 1878	125 - 200
RC6522	Lon 1910	75 - 125
RC6530	**Baby's Own Aesop** Lon 1887	100 - 150
RC6540	**The Bases of Design** Lon 1898	100 - 150
RC6550	**The Christmas Child** Lon 1888	100 - 150
RC6552	Lon 1902	50 - 75
RC6560	**Cinderella's Picture Book** Lon 1897	100 - 150
RC6565	**Don Quixote** NY 1932	30 - 50
RC6570	**Flora's Feast** Lon 1899	125 - 200
RC6580	**The Flower Wedding** Lon 1905	150 - 250
RC6590	**The Flowers in Shakespeare's Garden** Lon 1906	100 - 150
RC6600	**The Four Winds Farm** Lon 1887	75 - 125
RC6610	**Grimm's Fairy Tales** Lon 1888	100 - 150
RC6620	**The History of Reynard the Fox** Lon 1897	50 - 75
RC6630	**Ideals in Art** Lon 1905	50 - 75
RC6640	**King Arthur's Knights** Lon 1911	150 - 250
RC6650	**Masque of Days** Lon 1901	100 - 150
RC6660	**The Old Garden** NY 1894	75 - 125
RC6670	**Renascence: A Book of Verse** Lon 1891, 44 cys, vellum	500 - 700
RC6671	Lon 1891 100 cys	250 - 350
RC6672	Lon 1891 (1st trade ed)	100 - 150
RC6680	**Rumbo Rhymes** NY 1911	100 - 150
RC6690	**Slate and Pencil-vania** Lon 1885	150 - 250
RC6700	**Triplets** Lon 1899, 750 cys, vellum	300 - 500
RC6710	**A Wonder–Book for Girls and Boys** Lon 1893	100 - 150
RC6711	Cambridge 1893, 250 cys, vellum	300 - 500

RC2590

RC2700

RC3420

RC3450

RC3451

RC4041 (cover and frontispiece)

RC4410

RC4810

RC5410

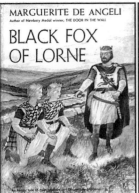

| RC6565 | RC6570 (cover and title page) | | RD2010 | RD2020 |

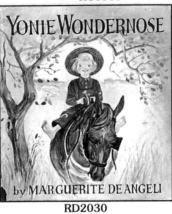

| RD2030 | RD4040 (w/o DJ) | TD4140 | RD4530 | RD9010 |

RC6712 Cambridge 1893 (American trade ed) 100 - 150

Dali, Salvador
RD1000 **Dali's Mustache** NY 1954, DJ 100 - 150
RD1010 **Fifty Secrets of Magic Craftsmanship**
  NY 1948, DJ 300 - 500
RD1020 **Hidden Faces** NY 1944, DJ 100 - 150
RD1022 Lon 1973, 100 cys, pamphlet, box 300 - 500
RD1030 **La Conqueste de Irrational** Paris 1935 3000 - 5000
RD1040 **Les Metamorphoses Erotiques** Paris 1969,
  1200 cys, slipcase 200 - 300
RD1050 **The Secret Life of Salvador Dali** NY 1942,
  DJ, 119 cys, drawing, box 1500 - 2500
RD1051 NY 1942, DJ (1st trade ed) 200 - 300

De Angeli, Marguerite
RD2010 **Black Fox of Lorne** Garden City 1956, DJ 30 - 50
RD2020 **The Door in the Wall** Garden City 1949, 1st issue
  DJ w/no seal 100 - 150
  1st issue DJ w/seal 50 - 75
RD2030 **Yonie Wondernose** NY 1944, DJ 40 - 60

De Kooning, Willem
RD2500 **De Kooning** (Harold Rosenberg) NY 1974, DJ 800 - 1200
RD2510 **Drawings** NY 1967, 100 cys, signed 400 - 600
RD2520 **Willem De Kooning Drawings** (Thomas B. Hess)
  Greenwich 1972, DJ 300 - 500

Degas, Edgar
RD3000 **Degas** (Denis Rouart) Paris 1948, wrappers,
  slipcase 150 - 250
RD3010 **Degas** (Daniel Rich) NY (1970s) DJ 50 - 75
RD3020 **Degas** (Ian Dunlap) NY 1979, DJ 30 - 50
RD3030 **Degas Dancers** (Lillian Browse) Lon 1950, DJ 100 - 150
RD3040 **Degas et Son Oeuvre** (P.A. Lemoisne) Paris
  1946-49, 4 vol, 980 cys, slipcases 3000 - 5000
RD3050 **Degas Monotypes** (Eugenie Janis) Greenwich
  1968, DJ 75 - 125
RD3060 **Degas Sculpture** (John Rewald) NY 1956, DJ 250 - 350
RD3070 **Degas: Works in Sculpture** (John Rewald) Lon
  1944, DJ 200 - 300
RD3080 **Edgar Degas** (Pierre Cabanne) Paris 50 - 75

Delacroix, Eugene
RD3510 **Delacroix** (Raymond Escholier) Paris 1926-29,
  3 vol, wrappers 300 - 500

Denslow, W. W. (also see Baumiana & Oziana)
RD4010 **The Arkansas Planter** NY 1896 50 - 75

RD4020 **Billy Bounce** G.W. Dillingham, NY (1906), 16
  plates, yellow cl 200 - 400
RD4023 later printings, (1906) 125 - 175
RD4030 **Denslow's Animal Fair** NY 1904 100 - 150
RD4040 **Denslow's Mother Goose** NY 1901, 1st ed, 1st
  issue: pict bds, *Humpty Dumpty* text begins
  on verso of dedication leaf 300 - 500
  w/DJ 800 - 1500
RD4043 later issues, NY 1901 250 - 350
RD4050 **The House That Jack Built** NY 1903 150 - 250
RD4060 **Humpty Dumpty** NY 1903 250 - 350
RD4070 **Jack and the Beanstalk** NY 1903 100 - 150
RD4080 **The Jeweled Toad** Bobbs-Merrill, Ind (1907),
  12 color plates, pict bds 400 - 750
RD4090 **The Night Before Christmas** NY 1902 200 - 300
RD4092 NY 1915 100 - 150
RD4100 **Old Mother Hubbard** NY 1903 100 - 150
RD4110 **The One Ring Circus** NY 1903 100 - 150
RD4120 **The Pearl and the Pumpkin** G.W. Dillingham,
  NY (1904), 1st ed, 1st state: 16 color plates,
  lt green cl, end pprs printed in blue 200 - 300
RD4130 **Simple Simon** NY 1904 100 - 150
RD4140 **The Teddy Bear's Christmas** np 1908,
  wrappers (advertising premium) 200 - 350
RD4150 **When I Grow Up** NY 1909 125 - 175

Detmold, E.
RD4510 **The Arabian Nights** Lon 1924, DJ 300 - 500
RD4512 NY 1925, DJ 200 - 300
RD4520 **The Fables of Aesop** Lon 1909 150 - 250
RD4530 **Fabre's Book of Insects** NY 1936, DJ 50 - 75
RD4540 **The Jungle Book** Lon 1908 125 - 175
RD4541 NY 1908 125 - 175
RD4543 NY 1913 100 - 150
RD4550 **Life of the Bee** Lon 1911 150 - 250
RD4552 NY 1912 125 - 175
RD4560 **The News of Spring** NY 1913 100 - 150
RD4570 **Pictures From Birdland** Lon 1899 150 - 250
RD4580 **Rainbow Houses for Boys and Girls** Lon 1923 100 - 150

Dine, Jim
RD5500 **Jim Dine Complete Graphics** Lon 1970,
  3 signed color prints 1000 - 1500

Duchamp, Marcel
RD7050 **La Mariee Mise a Nu Par Celibataires Meme**
  Paris 1934, 20 cys 20000 - 30000

RD7051	Paris 1934, 320 cys	4000 - 6000
RD7060	**Not Seen and or Less Seen Of** NY 1965, 100 cys, wrappers	400 - 600
RD7070	**Notes and Projects for the Large Glass** NY 1969, glassine DJ	250 - 350

Duerer, Albrecht

RD7550	**The Little Passion** Vienna 1971, 140 cys	500 - 700
RD7560	**Zeichmungen** Berlin 1883-1929, 7 vol, 300 sets	3000 - 5000

Dufy, Raoul

RD7910	**Aquarelles et Dessins** Paris 1947	500 - 700
RD7920	**Dessins et Croquis** Paris 1944, 199 cys	500 - 700
RD7930	**Ten Color Collotypes After Watercolours** Lon 1961, 200 cys	200 - 300

Dulac, Edmund

RD8410	**The Bells and Other Poems** Lon 1912, 750 cys, vellum	600 - 800
RD8411	Lon 1912 (1st trade ed)	150 - 250
RD8420	**The Daughters of the Stars** Lon 1939, 500 cys, DJ	500 - 700
RD8421	Lon 1939 (1st trade ed)	150 - 250
RD8430	**Dreamer of Dreams** Lon 1915	200 - 300
RD8440	**Edmund Dulac's Fairy Book** NY 1916, 350 cys	400 - 600
RD8441	NY 1916 (1st trade ed)	75 - 125
RD8442	Lon 1916	75 - 125
RD8450	**Edmund Dulac's Picture Book** Lon 1915	125 - 175
RD8460	**Fairies I Have Met** Lon 1910	125 - 175
RD8470	**A Fairy Garland** NY 1929	100 - 150
RD8480	**The Green Lacquer Pavillion** NY 1926	50 - 75
RD8490	**The Kingdom of the Pearl** NY 1920, 675 cys	300 - 500
RD8500	**The Magic Horse** Lon 1911	150 - 250
RD8510	**My Days with the Fairies** Lon 1913	150 - 250
RD8520	**The Novels of Charlotte, Emily and Anne Bronte** (1st book illustrated) Lon 1905, 10 vol	300 - 500
RD8530	**Picture Book of the French Red Cross** Lon 1915	200 - 300
RD8540	**Princess Badoura** Lon 1913	150 - 250
RD8550	**The Rubaiyat of Omar Khayam** Lon 1909, 750 cys, vellum, box	1000 - 1500
RD8552	Lon 1910 (1st trade ed)	200 - 300
RD8554	NY 1932, slipcase	25 - 35
RD8570	**Sinbad the Sailor and Other Stories from the Arabian Nights** Lon 1911, 500 cys	700 - 1000
RD8572	Lon 1914 (1st trade ed)	200 - 300
RD8580	**The Sleeping Beauty and Other Fairy Tales** Lon 1910 (1st trade ed)	200 - 300
RD8590	**The Stealers of Light** Lon 1916	100 - 150
RD8600	**Stories from the Arabian Nights** Lon 1907, 350 cys, vellum	400 - 600
RD8602	Lon 1908	125 - 175
RD8603	NY 1908	125 - 175
RD8610	**Tanglewood Tales** Lon 1918, 500 cys, vellum	700 - 1000
RD8611	Lon 1918 (1st trade ed)	200 - 300
RD8614	Lon 1938	100 - 150
RD8630	**Tannhauser** Lon 1909	150 - 250
RD8640	**The Tempest** Lon 1908, 500 cys, vellum	800 - 1200
RD8641	Lon 1908 (1st trade ed)	250 - 350
RD8650	**Treasure Island** Lon 1927, 50 cys, vellum	1200 - 1800
RD8651	NY 1927, slipcase (1st U.S. trade ed)	200 - 300

Dwiggins, Clare Victor

RD9010	**Only a Grain of Sand** Phil 1905	30 - 50

Edwards, George Wharton

RE2010	**Hans Brinker** NY 1933, DJ	40 - 60
RE2020	**The Princess Pocahontas** (Virginia Watson) Phil 1922	100 - 150

Ernst, Max

RE6000	**Histoire Naturelle** 1926, 306 cys	
RE6002	Cologne 1965, 700 cys	300 - 500
RE6004	NY 1972, 1200 cys	200 - 300

Fabergé, Karl

RF1050	**The Art of Karl Fabergé** (Marvin C. Ross) Norman 1965, DJ	200 - 300

Feiffer, Jules

RF2510	**The Phantom Tollbooth** (Norton Juster) NY 1961, DJ	100 - 150

Feininger, Lyonel

RF3010	**Lyonel Feininger** (Hans Hess) NY 1961, DJ	250 - 350

Fisher, Harrison

Illustrated hundreds of books, magazines, and postcards.

RF5010	**American Beauties** NY 1909	200 - 300
RF5020	**The American Girl** NY 1909	300 - 500
RF5030	**American Girls in Miniature** NY 1912, box	100 - 150
	w/o box	50 - 75
RF5040	**Bachelor Belles** Ind 1908	150 - 250
RF5050	**A Checked Love Affair** NY 1903	40 - 60
RF5060	**Cowardice Court** (G.B. McCutcheon) NY 1906	30 - 50
RF5070	**The Day of the Dog** NY 1904	40 - 60
RF5080	**A Dream of Fair Women** NY 1907	100 - 150
RF5090	**The Harrison Fisher Book** NY 1907	125 - 200
RF5100	**Hiawatha** Ind 1906	75 - 125
RF5120	**The Little Gift Book** NY 1913	125 - 200
RF5130	**Maiden's Fair** NY 1914	75 - 125
RF5140	**Their Heart's Desire** NY 1909	75 - 125

Gág, Wanda

RG1510	**The Funny Thing** NY 1929, DJ	100 - 150
RG1520	**Growing Pains** NY 1940, DJ	75 - 125
RG1530	**Millions of Cats** (1st book illustrated) NY 1928, DJ	150 - 250
	w/o DJ	50 - 75
RG1531	NY 1928, 250 cys, signed engraving	700 - 1000
RG1540	**Tales From Grimm** NY 1936, DJ	75 - 125
	w/o DJ	50 - 75

RD8641 (w/o DJ)   RD8641 (frontispiece)

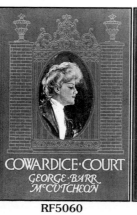

RF2510   RF5060   RF5070   RG1530

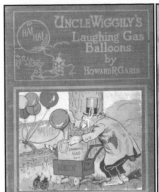

RG2410

Color Plate from RG5810

RG6010

RG7061

RG7121

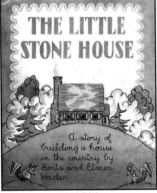

RH3810

RG7420 (w/o DJ)

RG7505

RG8050

RH1530

Garis, Howard R.

RG2410	Uncle Wiggily series, Platt & Munk, 1920s, all titles (20-25 total), cl, each	20 - 30
RG2430	Uncle Wiggly series, Platt & Munk, 1930s, **Uncle Wiggly's Travels, Uncle Wiggly's Airship**, etc, all titles, cl w/DJ, each	40 - 60
	w/o DJ	15 - 25

Gauguin, Paul

RG3050	Avante et Apres Leipzig 1918, 100 cys, wrappers	300 - 500
RG3060	Intimate Journals of… NY 1921, 990 cys	200 - 300
RG3062	Lon 1923, 530 cys	200 - 300
RG3070	**Letters to Ambroise Vollard & Andre Fontainas** (John Rewald) SF 1943, 250 cys	700 - 1000
RG3080	Noa Noa Munich 1926, 320 cys	2000 - 3000

Gibson, Charles Dana

RG5010	**80 Drawings of the Weaker Sex** NY 1903	100 - 150
RG5020	**Americans** NY 1903	100 - 150
RG5030	**College Girls** NY 1895	50 - 75
RG5040	**Pictures of People** NY 1896	125 - 200

Gibson, Eva

RG5110	**Zauberlinda the Wise Witch** Chi (1901)	75 - 125

Goble, Warwick

RG5810	**Stories from the Pentamerone** Lon 1911	150 - 250

Gorey, Edward

RG6010	**Cobweb Castle** (Jan Wahl) NY 1968, DJ	40 - 60

Goya

RG6510	**Goya: Engravings and Lithographs** (Tomas Harris) Oxford 1964, 2 vol, DJs	500 - 700

Greenaway, Kate

RG7010	**The Almanac for 1887** Lon 1887	125 - 200
RG7020	**The Almanac for 1897** Lon 1897	125 - 200
RG7030	**April Baby's Book of Tunes** NY 1900	100 - 150
RG7040	**Greenaway's Babies** Akron 1907	50 - 75
RG7050	**Kate Greenaway's Alphabet** Lon 1885	125 - 200
RG7060	**Kate Greenaway's Birthday Book for Children** Lon 1880	150 - 250
RG7061	Lon (1940s), DJ	40 - 60
RG7070	**Kate Greenaway's Book of Games** Lon 1889	125 - 200
RG7080	**Kate Greenaway's Pictures** Lon 1921, DJ	150 - 250
RG7090	**The Language of Flowers** Lon 1884	125 - 200
RG7100	**The Little Folks Painting Book** Lon 1879	200 - 300
RG7110	**Marigold Garden** Lon 1885	125 - 200
RG7120	**Mother Goose** Lon 1881	150 - 250
RG7121	Lon (1930s), DJ	50 - 75
RG7130	**The Pied Piper of Hamelin** Lon 1888	100 - 150
RG7140	**Under the Window** Lon 1878	200 - 300

Gross, Milt

RG7410	**Famous Fimmales** Garden City 1928, DJ	50 - 75
RG7420	**Nize Baby** NY 1926, DJ	50 - 75
	w/o DJ	20 - 30

Grosz, George

RG7500	**30 Drawings & Watercolors** NY 1944, DJ	200 - 300
RG7505	**1001 Afternoons in New York** (Ben Hecht) NY 1941, DJ	75 - 125
RG7510	**Drawings** NY 1944, DJ	200 - 300
RG7520	**Ecce Homo** NY 1966, DJ	125 - 200
RG7530	**A Little Yes and A Big No** NY 1946, DJ	200 - 300

Gruelle, Johnny

P.F. Volland is the first edition publisher.

RG8010	**The Cheery Scarecrow** Joliet 1929, box	100 - 150
	w/o box	50 - 75
RG8020	**Eddie the Elephant** Chi 1921, box	75 - 125
	w/o box	50 - 75
RG8030	**The Funny Little Book** Chi 1917, box	100 - 150
	w/o box	75 - 125
RG8040	**The Little Brown Bear** Chi 1920	50 - 75
RG8050	**The Magical Land of Noom** Chi 1922	200 - 300
RG8052	Chi (1920s), Donahue reprint	75 - 125
RG8060	**Marcella, A Raggedy Ann Story** Chi 1929	40 - 60
RG8070	**Raggedy Andy Stories** Joliet 1920, box	100 - 150
	w/o box	50 - 75
RG8080	**Raggedy Ann in the Deep Woods** Joliet 1930, box	100 - 150
RG8090	**Wooden Willie** Joliet 1927, box	75 - 125
	w/o box	40 - 60

Guttman, Bessie Pease

RG9010	**Alice in Wonderland** NY 1907	50 - 75
RG9020	**A Child's Garden of Verses** NY 1905	40 - 60
RG9030	**Through the Looking Glass** NY 1909	50 - 75

Hader, Berta & Elmer

RH1510	**Good Little Dog** NY 1930	50 - 75
RH1520	**Jamaica Johnny** NY 1935, DJ	40 - 60
RH1530	**The Little Stone House** NY 1944, DJ	30 - 50
RH1540	**The Ugly Duckling** NY 1927, DJ	40 - 60

Hassam, Childe
RH2010 **Catalog of Etchings and Dry Points of Childe Hassam** NY 1925, 400 cys, signed etching   1200 - 1800

Hockney, David
RH3350 **David Hockney** (Nikos Stangos) NY 1976, DJ   50 - 75
RH3360 **Paper Pools** Lon 1980, 1000 cys, separate print in folder   1200 - 1800

Holling, Holling C. (Clancy)
RH3810 **The Book of Cowboys** NY 1936, DJ   20 - 30
RH3820 **The Book of Indians** NY 1935, DJ   25 - 35
     w/o DJ   15 - 20
RH3830 **Minn of the Mississippi** Bos 1951, DJ   25 - 35
RH3840 **Paddle to the Sea** Bos 1941, DJ   25 - 35
RH3850 **Tree in the Trail** Bos 1942, DJ   25 - 35

Homer, Winslow
RH4510 **The Life and Works of Winslow Homer** (Gordon Hendricks) NY 1979, DJ   100 - 150
RH4520 **Winslow Homer** (Albert Gardner) NY 1961, DJ   30 - 50

Hood, George
RH4710 **Tales from Washington Irving's Traveller** Phil 1913   50 - 75

Hopper, Edward
RH5010 **Edward Hopper** (Lloyd Goodrich) NY 1971, DJ   75 - 125

Humphrey, Maud
Mother of movie star Humphrey Bogart, she also made very collectible chromo-lithographic prints of children.
RH7510 **Baby Sweethearts** NY 1890   300 - 500
RH7520 **Baby's Record** NY 1898   100 - 150
RH7530 **Bonnie Little People** NY 1890   250 - 350
RH7540 **The Book of Fairy Tales** NY 1892   300 - 500
RH7550 **The Book of Pets** NY 1893   200 - 300
RH7560 **Children of the Revolution** NY 1900   200 - 300
RH7570 **Favorite Rhymes from Mother Goose** NY 1891   250 - 350
RH7580 **Gallant Little Patriots** NY 1899   200 - 300
RH7590 **Golf Girl** NY 1899   300 - 500
RH7600 **Jingles and Rhymes** NY 1894   200 - 300
RH7610 **Light Princess** NY 1893   75 - 125
RH7620 **Little Colonial Dame** NY 1898   100 - 150
RH7630 **Little Heroes & Heroines** NY 1899   200 - 300
RH7640 **Littlest Ones** NY 1898   200 - 300
RH7650 **Poems by Dobson, Locker and Praed** NY 1892   250 - 350
RH7660 **Rosebud Stories** NY 1906   75 - 125
RH7670 **Sleepy Time Stories** NY 1900   100 - 150

RH7570

RH7650

Icart, Louis
RI2010 **Icart** (Michael Schessel) NY 1976, DJ   50 - 75

Ingres, L.
RI3510 **Ingres** (Henry Lapauze) Paris 1911   300 - 500

Inness, George
RI4010 **George Inness: The Man and His Art** (Elliott Daingerfield) NY 1911   100 - 150
RI4020 **Life, Art and Letters of George Inness** (George Inness, Jr.) NY 1917   100 - 150

Johns, Jasper
RJ5650 **Jasper Johns** (Max Kozloff) NY 1968, DJ   300 - 500
RJ5660 **Jasper Johns: Prints 1960-1970** (Richard S. Field) NY 1970, DJ   200 - 300
RJ5670 **Technics and Creativity II** NY 1971, wrappers, plastic case, signed litho   300 - 500

Kandinsky, Wassily
RK1050 **Das Graphische Werk** (Hans K. Roethel) Cologne 1970, 150 cys, DJ, slipcase   1500 - 2500
RK1060 **De Blaue Reiter** Munich 1912, 1200 cys   2000 - 3000
RK1070 **Eleven Tableux et Seven Poemes** Amsterdam 1945, 200 cys   1000 - 1500
RK1080 **Kandinsky** (Hans K. Roethel) Ithaca 1982-84, 2 vol, DJs   250 - 350
RK1090 **Poems Without Words** (1st book) Moscow 1903
RK1100 **Tekst Kudozhnika** Moscow 1918   300 - 500
RK1110 **Wassily Kandinsky** (Will Grohman) NY (1958), DJ 150 - 250
RK1120 **Watercolors and Drawings** (Nina Kandinsky) NY (1980s), DJ   50 - 75
RK1130 **Xylographies** Paris 1909, 2 pp text, 5 woodcuts loose in wrappers, index   3000 - 5000

Kane, Paul
RK1410 **Paul Kane's Frontier, Including Wanderings of an Artist Among the Indians** Toronto 1971, 300 cys 400 - 600
RK1411 Austin 1971, 300 cys   400 - 600

Kay, Gertrude
RK2010 **Alice's Adventures in Wonderland** Phil 1923   50 - 75
RK2020 **Through the Cloud Mountain** (Florence Bernard) Phil 1922   75 - 125
RK2030 **When the Sandman Comes** Chi (early 1900s)   40 - 60

Kelly, Ellsworth
RK3010 **Ellsworth Kelly: Drawings, Collages, Prints** (Diane Waldman) Greenwich 1971, DJ   300 - 500

Kelly, Walt
RK3310 **I Go Pogo** NY 1952, wrappers   20 - 30
RK3320 **Pogo Peek-A-Book** NY 1955, wrappers   20 - 30

Kent, Rockwell (also see Modern First Editions)
Illustrated books and magazines as well as architectural catalogs.
RK3810 **All Men Are Enemies** NY 1933   75 - 125
RK3820 **Architec-tonics** (set, includes 1st book illustrated) NY 1914   150 - 250
RK3830 **A Basket of Poses** NY 1924, DJ   100 - 150
RK3840 **Beowulf** NY 1932, DJ   50 - 75
RK3850 **A Birthday Book** NY 1931, 1850 cys   125 - 200
RK3860 **The Bookplates and Marks of Rockwell Kent** NY 1929, 1250 cys, DJ   150 - 250
RK3870 **Canterbury Tales** Garden City 1934, DJ   50 - 75
RK3880 **City Child** NY 1931, DJ   50 - 75
RK3890 **Forty Drawings** Garden City 1936, 1000 cys, box 250 - 350
RK3900 **Greenland Journal** NY 1962, 6 lithographs, box 250 - 350

RH3830

RH4710 (w/o DJ)

RK2020

RK2030

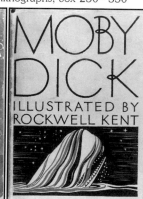
RK3930

RK3950 (w/o DJ)

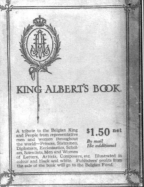
RK4710

RK4860 (w/o DJ)

RK5620

RL1010

RL1640

RL1700 (w/o DJ)

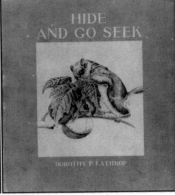
RL1710

RL1800 (frontispiece)

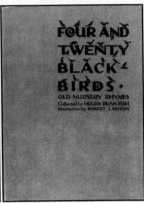
RL2430

RK3910	How I Make a Woodcut Pasadena 1934, 1000 cys	100 - 150
RK3920	Later Bookplates & Marks of Rockwell Kent	
	NY 1937, 1250 cys, DJ	100 - 150
RK3930	Moby Dick NY 1930, DJ	100 - 150
	w/o DJ	40 - 60
RK3940	N. by E. NY 1930, 900 cys, box	250 - 350
RK3941	NY 1930, DJ (1st trade ed)	50 - 75
RK3950	A Northern Christmas NY 1941	50 - 75
RK3960	Paul Bunyan NY 1924, DJ	50 - 75
RK3970	Rockwell Kentia NY 1933, DJ	50 - 75
RK3980	Rollo in Society NY 1922, DJ	75 - 125
RK3990	Salamina NY 1935, DJ	75 - 125
RK4000	This Is My Own NY 1940, DJ	75 - 125
RK4010	Voyaging Southward from the Strait of Magellan	
	NY 1924, 110, signed woodcut	300 - 500
RK4020	NY 1924, DJ (1st trade ed)	125 - 200
RK4030	Wilderness: A Journal of Quiet Adventure in	
	Alaska (author, 1st book illustrated) NY 1920, DJ	200 - 300

King Albert's Book

RK4710	King Albert's Book Lon 1914, DJ (plates by Dulac,	
	Rackham, Parrish, Harrison Fisher & other artists)	50 - 75

Kipling, Rudyard (also see Modern First Editions)

RK4860	Just So Stories NY 1902	75 - 125

Kirk, Maria

RK5010	Alice's Adventures in Wonderland NY 1919	50 - 75
RK5020	At the Back of the North Wind Phil 1910	40 - 60
RK5030	The Child's Rip Van Winkle NY 1908	50 - 75
RK5040	The Favorite Rhymes of Mother Goose NY 1910	40 - 60
RK5050	Heidi Phil 1919	50 - 75
RK5060	Pinocchio Phil 1920	40 - 60
RK5070	The Princess and the Goblin Phil 1907	40 - 60
RK5080	The Secret Garden NY 1911	50 - 75

Klee, Paul

RK5610	Handzeichnungen (Jürgen Glaesemer) Bern	
	1973, 3 vol, DJs	400 - 600
RK5620	Paul Klee (Will Grohmann) NY 1954, DJ	75 - 125
RK5630	Verzeichnis des Graphischen Werkes Von	
	Paul Klee Bern 1963, DJ (limited ed)	1500 - 2500

Klimt, Gustav

RK6100	Fuenfundzwanzig Handzeichnungen Vienna	
	1919, 500 cys	2000 - 3000
RK6110	Gustav Klimt (Fritz Novotny) NY 1968,	
	1250 cys, DJ	250 - 350

RK6120	Gustav Klimt (Fritz Novotny) Bos 1975, DJ	250 - 350

Kriedel, Fritz

RK7510	The Complete Andersen NY 1949, 6 vol, box	150 - 250

Lachman, Harry B.

RL1010	The Magic Image from India (Cornelia Baker)	
	Phil 1909	60 - 80

Lathrop, Dorothy P.

Lathrop's autograph is worth about $50 - 75.

RL1610	Animals of the Bible (1st Caldecott Award Book)	
	NY 1937, DJ	125 - 175
	w/o DJ	30 - 50
RL1620	The Bells and Grass NY 1942, DJ	50 - 75
RL1630	Branches Green NY 1934, DJ	75 - 125
RL1640	The Colt from Moon Mountain NY 1941, DJ	100 - 150
RL1650	Crossings: A Fairy Play NY 1923, DJ	75 - 125
RL1660	Down-Adown-Derry Lon 1922, DJ	100 - 150
RL1662	NY 1922, DJ	75 - 125
RL1670	Fairy Circus NY 1931, DJ	100 - 150
	w/o DJ	50 - 75
RL1680	Fierce Face NY 1936, DJ	50 - 75
RL1690	The Forgotten Daughter NY 1933, DJ	100 - 150
	w/o DJ	30 - 50
RL1700	The Grateful Elephant New Haven 1923, DJ	75 - 125
RL1710	Hide and Go Seek NY 1938, DJ	50 - 75
RL1720	Hitty NY 1929, DJ	75 - 125
RL1730	The Light Princess NY 1926, DJ	75 - 125
RL1740	Little Boy Lost NY 1920, DJ	100 - 150
RL1750	The Little Mermaid NY 1939, DJ	100 - 150
RL1760	The Little White Goat NY 1933, DJ	75 - 125
	w/o DJ	30 - 50
RL1770	The Lost Merry-Go-Round NY 1934, DJ	75 - 125
RL1780	Mr. Bumps and His Monkey NY 1942, DJ	75 - 125
RL1790	Presents for Lupe NY 1940, DJ	50 - 75
RL1800	Stars To-Night NY 1930, DJ	75 - 125
	w/o DJ	25 - 35
RL1810	Who Goes There? NY 1935, DJ	50 - 75

Laurencin, Marie

RL2100	Eventail Paris 1922, 335 cys	2000 - 3000
RL2110	Recueil de 32 Planches Paris 1928	5000 - 7000

Lawson, Robert

RL2410	Aesop's Fables NY 1941, slipcase	30 - 50
RL2420	Ben and Me Bos 1939, DJ	50 - 75
RL2430	Four and Twenty Blackbirds NY 1937, DJ	100 - 150
	w/o DJ	50 - 75

RL2440	**Mr. Twigg's Mistake** Bos 1947, DJ	50 - 75
RL2450	**Pilgrim's Progress** NY 1939, DJ	50 - 75
RL2460	**Poo Poo and the Dragons** Bos 1942, DJ	100 - 150
RL2470	**Rabbit Hill** NY 1944, DJ	50 - 75
	w/o DJ	30 - 50
RL2480	**The Tough Winter** NY 1954, DJ	50 - 75
	w/o DJ	30 - 50
RL2490	**The Unicorn with Silver Shoes** NY 1957, DJ	50 - 75

Le Corbusier

RL4310	**L'Art Decoratif D'Aujourd'Hul** Paris (1920s)	500 - 700
RL4320	**Oeuvre Complete** Zurich 1973-77, 8 vol, DJs	300 - 500
RL4330	**Poeme de L'Angle Droit** Paris 1955, 250 cys	7000 - 10000
RL4340	**Vers une Architecture** Paris (1920s)	500 - 700

Le Mair, H. Willebeek

RL4610	**The Child's Corner** Phil 1915, DJ	125 - 200
RL4620	**A Gallery of Children** Lon 1925, 500 cys	400 - 600
RL4621	Phil 1925, DJ	150 - 250
RL4630	**Old Dutch Nursery Rhymes** Phil 1917, DJ	150 - 250
RL4640	**Our Old Nursery Rhymes** Phil 1911, DJ	200 - 300
	w/o DJ	100 - 150

Legrand, Louis

RL4910	**Louis Legrand** (Camille Mauclair) Paris (1910), wrappers	300 - 500

Lenski, Lois

RL5210	**Arabella and Her Aunts** NY 1932, DJ	100 - 150
	w/o DJ	50 - 75
RL5220	**The Book of Enchanted Tales** NY 1928, DJ	100 - 150
RL5230	**The Golden Age** NY 1921, DJ	100 - 150
RL5235	**The Little Engine That Could** NY 1930, DJ	150 - 250
RL5240	**The Little Fire Engine** NY 1946, DJ	75 - 125

Lentz, Harold B.

RL5350	**The "Pop-Up" Mother Goose** NY 1934	100 - 150

Lewis, Morris

RL5650	**Morris Lewis** (Michael Fried) NY 1979, DJ	100 - 150

Lichtenstein, Roy

RL6500	**Roy Lichtenstein** (Diane Waldman) NY 1971, DJ	300 - 500
RL6510	**Roy Lichtenstein 1970-1980** (Jack Cowart) NY 1981, slipcase	200 - 300
RL6520	**Roy Lichtenstein: Drawings and Prints** (Diane Waldman) NY 1970, DJ	150 - 250

Low, Loretta

RL7210	**A Woodland Party** NY 1913	75 - 125

Maillol, Aristide

RM1010	**Maillol** (John Rewald) Lon 1939, DJ	100 - 150
RM1020	**The Woodcuts** (John Rewald) NY 1943, 550 cys	100 - 150
RM1030	**Woodcuts** (John Rewald) NY 1951, DJ	100 - 150

Manet, Edouard

RM1410	**Edouard Manet** (Jean Harris) NY 1970	300 - 500
RM1420	**Edouard Manet** (Denis Rouart) Paris 1975, 2 vol, DJs	2000 - 3000
RM1430	**Letters with Aquarelles** NY (1940s), 345 cys	300 - 500
RM1440	**Manet and the French Impressionists** (Théodore Duret) Lon 1910	1200 - 1800

Marge (of Little Lulu)

RM1710	**King Kojo** Phil (1938), 8 plates, red cl	300 - 500

Marin, John

RM1810	**John Marin: Drawings and Watercolors** NY 1950, 425 cys, portfolio	250 - 350

Marini, Marino

RM2110	**The Complete Works of...** (Patrick Waldberg) NY 1970, DJ	50 - 75
RM2120	**Images** Berlin 1970, 100 cys, signed, slipcase	300 - 500
RM2130	**Marino Marini** (Edward Trier) NY 1961, DJ	75 - 125

Mars, E. & M. H. Squires

RM2410	**A Childs Garden of Verses** NY 1900	150 - 250
RM2420	**The Lovable Tales of Janey & Josey & Joe** NY 1902	100 - 150
RM2422	NY 1904	40 - 60

Marsh, Reginald

RM2710	**Reginald Marsh** (Lloyd Goodrich) NY 1980, DJ	100 - 150
RM2720	**Reginald Marsh - The Prints** (Norman Sasowsky) NY (1976), DJ	100 - 150

Matisse, Henri

RM3010	**Cinquante Dessins** Paris 1920	3000 - 5000
RM3020	**De La Couleur** Paris 1945 (Verve 13)	200 - 300
RM3030	**Dernieres Oeuvres** Paris 1958 (Verve 35/36)	300 - 500
RM3040	**Dessins: Themes et Variations** Paris 1943, 920 cys	300 - 500
RM3050	**Henri Matisse** (John Jacobus) NY 1972, DJ	50 - 75
RM3060	**Henri Matisse: A Novel** (Louis Aragon) NY 1972, 2 vol, box	200 - 300
RM3070	**Jazz** Paris 1947, 100 cys, separate portfolio	100000 - 150000
	book alone	40000 - 60000
RM3072	250 cys, folded prints	75000 - 125000
RM3074	NY 1983, DJ, box (1st trade ed, facsimile of 250 cy ed)	300 - 500
RM3090	**The Last Works of Matisse** NY 1958 (American ed of Verve 35/36)	300 - 500
RM3100	**Matisse: His Art and His Public** (Alfred H. Barr) NY 1951, 495, cys, DJ, slipcase	800 - 1200
RM3110	**Pierre a Feu** Paris 1947, 49 cys	2000 - 3000
RM3120	**Portraits** Monte Carlo 1954	200 - 300
RM3122	Monte Carlo 1955, 500 cys	300 - 500
MJ42322	**Ulysses** see James Joyce in Modern First Edtions	
RM3140	**Vence 1944-48** Paris 1948 (Verve 21/22)	300 - 500

Maybank, Thomas

RM3250	**Teddy and Trots in Wonderland** (Agnes Herbertson) NY (about 1890)	75 - 125

McDougall, Walt

RM4010	**The Rambillicus Book** Phil 1903	200 - 300

McIntire, Mr. Samuel

RM4310	**Mr. Samuel McIntire, Carver, The Architect of Salem** (Fiske Kimball) Portland, ME 1940, 675 cys	150 - 250

Meteyard, Sidney N.

RM5010	**The Golden Legend** (Henry Wadsworth Longfellow) NY (early 1900s)	75 - 125

RL2470   **RL2490**   **RL7210**

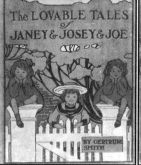

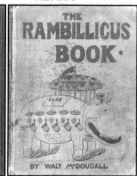

RL4640   **RL5350**   **RM2422**   **RM3250**   **RM4010**

RM6835	RM6841 (Vol. 1)	RM6855	RM8510 (w/o DJ)	RN2010 (w/o DJ)	RN2030 (w/o DJ)

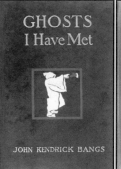

RN2320	RN2612 (w/o DJ)	RN2620	RN4030 (w/o DJ)	RN4040	RP1010 (w/o DJ)

Michael, A. C.
RM6010 **A Christmas Carol** Lon 1911, DJ — 150 - 225
w/o DJ — 50 - 75

Michelangelo
RM6210 **La Plafond de la Sixtine** Paris 1931, 180 cys — 300 - 500
RM6220 **Michelangelo the Painter** (Valerio Marini) Milan 1964, DJ — 75 - 125

Millar, H. R.
RM6510 **The Book of Dragons** (E. Nesbit) Lon 1900 — 150 - 250

Milne, A. A. (see Modern First Editions)

Miró, Joan
RM6810 **Drawings and Lithographs in the Collection of Juan de Juanes** Greenwich (1960), 738 cys, signed litho — 500 - 700
RM6820 **Homage** (G. D. San Lazzaro) NY 1976, DJ — 100 - 150
RM6830 **The Indelible Miró** (Yvon Taillandier) NY 1972, DJ — 300 - 500
RM6835 **Joan Miró Life and Work** (Jacques Dupin) NY (1970s), DJ — 300 - 500
RM6840 **Joan Miró Lithographies** (Jacques Dupin) Paris 1972, 4 vol, DJs — 1000 - 1500
RM6841 NY 1972, 4 vol, DJs — 1000 - 1500
RM6850 **Loiseal Solaire, Loiseal Lunaire Enticelles** Paris 1967, 150 cys — 800 - 1200
RM6855 **Miró** (Clement Greenberg) NY 1948, DJ — 100 - 150
RM6860 **Miró** (Margit Rowell) NY 1970, DJ, slipcase — 100 - 150
RM6870 **Peintures Sur Cartons** (Jacques Dupin) Paris 1965, 150 cys — 1000 - 1500
RM6880 **Scriptures** (A. Balthazar & Jacques Dupin) Paris 1970, 150 cys — 800 - 1200

Modigliani, Amedeo
RM7210 **Amedeo Modigliani** (Alfred Werner) NY 1967, DJ — 50 - 75
RM7220 **Amadeo Modigliani Dessins et Sculptures** (Ambrogio Ceroni) Milan 1965 — 250 - 350
RM7230 **Modigliani** (Franco Russoli) Lon 1959, DJ — 50 - 75

Moe, Louis
RM7510 **The Begging Bear** Phil 1932, DJ — 200 - 300
w/o DJ — 125 - 175

Monet, Claude
RM7810 **Claude Monet** (Diane Kelder) NY 1979, DJ — 50 - 75

Moore, Henry
RM8010 **As the Eye Moves... A Sculpture** (Donald Hall) NY (1970s), DJ — 100 - 150
RM8020 **Catalog of Graphic Works 1931-79** Geneva 1973-80, 3 vol — 300 - 500
RM8030 **Heads, Figures and Ideas** Greenwich 1958, DJ — 200 - 300
RM8040 **Henry Moore** (John Hedgecoe) NY 1968, slipcase — 100 - 150

RM8050 **Henry Moore: Unpublished Drawings** (David Mitchinson) (1970s), DJ — 50 - 75
RM8060 **Sculptures and Drawings 1921-64** Lon 1957-65, 3 vol, DJs — 200 - 300
RM8070 **Sketchbook 1926** Lon 1976, 200 cys — 2000 - 3000
RM8071 NY 1976 (trade ed) — 150 - 250

Moreau, Gustave
RM8310 **Gustave Moreau** (Pierre-Louis Mathieu) Bos 1976, DJ — 100 - 150

Morgan, Ike
RM8510 **The Steps to Nowhere** (Grace Boylan) NY 1910 — 40 - 60

Moses, Grandma
RM8810 **Grandma Moses: American Primitive** (Otto Kallir) NY 1946, DJ — 50 - 75

Motherwell, Robert
RM9110 **The Dada Painters and Poets** NY 1951 — 100 - 150

Mucha, Alphonse
RM9510 **The Point of View** Lon 1905, 250 cys — 300 - 500

Neill, John R. (also see Baumiana & Oziana)
RN2010 **Andersen's Fairy Tales** NY 1923, DJ — 50 - 75
RN2020 **The Curious Cruise of Captain Santa** Chi 1926, DJ — 500 - 800
w/o DJ — 250 - 350
RN2030 **The Raven** Chi 1910 — 150 - 250

Nelson, Emile A.
RN2310 **The Flight Brothers** Chi 1912, DJ — 200 - 300
w/o DJ — 100 - 150
RN2320 **The Magic Aeroplane** Chi 1911, DJ — 200 - 300
w/o DJ — 100 - 150
RN2322 later issue in smaller format — 30 - 50

Newell, Peter
RN2610 **Alice's Adventures in Wonderland** NY 1901 — 75 - 125
RN2612 NY (1930s), DJ — 50 - 75
RN2620 **Ghosts I Have Met** (John Bangs) NY 1898 — 50 - 75
RN2630 **The Hole Book** NY 1908, DJ — 300 - 500
w/o DJ — 150 - 250
RN2640 **House Boat on the Styx** NY 1896 — 40 - 60
RN2650 **The Hunting of the Snark** NY 1903 — 50 - 75
RN2660 **The Rocket Book** NY 1912 — 150 - 250
RN2670 **The Slant Book** NY 1910 — 125 - 200
RN2680 **Topsys & Turveys** NY 1893 — 125 - 200
RN2682 NY 1902 — 75 - 125

Nielsen, Kay
RN4010 **East of the Sun & West of the Moon** NY 1922, DJ — 400 - 600
RN4012 Garden City 1930, DJ — 100 - 150

50

RN4020	**Fairy Tales** Lon 1924, 500 cys, vellum	2500 - 3500
RN4021	Lon 1924 (1st trade ed)	300 - 500
RN4022	NY 1924	200 - 300
RN4030	**Hansel and Gretel** NY (early 1900s)	200 - 300
RN4040	**The Twelve Dancing Princesses** NY (1920s), DJ	250 - 350
	w/o DJ	100 - 150

O'Keefe, Georgia

RO2050	**Georgia O'Keefe** (Lloyd Goodrich) NY 1970, acetate DJ	100 - 150
RO2060	**Georgia O'Keefe** NY 1976, 200 cys	2000 - 3000
RO2061	NY 1976, DJ (trade ed)	150 - 250
RO2070	**The Work of Georgia O'Keefe** NY 1937, 100 cys	2000 - 3000
RO2071	NY 1937, 1050 cys	500 - 700

Olitski, Jules

RO3050	**Jules Olitski** (Kenworth Moffett) NY 1981, DJ	300 - 500

Olmsted, Frederick Law

RO3400	**Frederick Law Olmsted, Landscape Architect 1822-1903** (Frederick Law Olmsted, Jr.) NY 1922-28, 2 vol	250 - 350

Papé, Frank C.

RP1010	**Prince Pimpernel** (Herbert Rix) Bos (early 1900s)	150 - 250
RP1020	**The Revolt of the Angels** (Anatole France) Lon 1924	50 - 75
RP1030	**The Silver Stallion** (James Branch Cabell) NY 1928	75 - 125
RP1040	**Thaïs** (Anatole France) Lon 1916	40 - 60

Parker, Agnes Miller

RP1210	**Down the River** NY 1937, DJ	50 - 75

Parrish, Maxfield

Parrish is the most collected American artist/illustrator; everything he did is collectible. He illustrated stories and advertising for many magazines in the early 1900s: *Ladies Home Journal, Century, Collier's* to name a few. Their price range is $10-150 (depending on size, rarity, etc). His art prints in different sizes in publishers' frames range from $50-500 and oil paintings sell for $20,000-150,000.

RP1310	**Arabian Nights** NY 1909	125 - 175
RP1312	NY 1925	50 - 75
RP1320	**Bolanyo** (1st book illus; illus cover) Chi 1897	300 - 500
RP1325	**The Children's Book** (cover illus only) Bos 1909	50 - 75
RP1330	**Dream Days** NY 1898 (tp date is 1899)	100 - 150
RP1332	NY 1902 (illus by Parrish)	100 - 150
RP1340	**The Emerald Story Book** NY 1915	125 - 175
RP1350	**Free to Serve** NY 1897	100 - 150
RP1360	**Garden of Years** NY 1904	40 - 60
RP1370	**The Golden Age** (Kenneth Grahame) NY 1900	100 - 150
RP1380	**Golden Treasury of Songs and Lyrics** NY 1911	75 - 125
RP1385	**Hiawatha** (cover illus only, interior illus by Frederic Remington) NY 1908	100 - 150

RP1390	**Italian Villas & Their Gardens** NY 1904	125 - 175
RP1410	**The Knave of Hearts** NY 1925, DJ, box	1000 - 1500
	w/o box	800 - 1200
	w/o DJ & box	500 - 700
RP1412	Racine, WI (1930s?), wrappers	300 - 500
RP1420	**The Knickerbocker's History of New York** NY 1900	125 - 175
RP1430	**The Lure of the Garden** NY 1911	75 - 125
	Mother Goose in Prose (see Baumiana & Oziana)	
RP1435	**Maxfield Parrish** (Coy Ludwig) NY 1973, DJ	30 - 50
RP1440	**Peterkin** NY 1912	40 - 60
RP1450	**Poems of Childhood** NY 1904	75 - 125
RP1452	later printings by Scribners	50 - 75
RP1460	**Romantic America** NY 1913	50 - 75
RP1470	**The Ruby Story Book** NY 1916	75 - 125
RP1480	**The Sapphire Story Book** NY (1920s)	50 - 75
RP1490	**The Topaz Story Book** NY (1920s)	50 - 75
RP1500	**The Turquoise Cup** NY 1903	75 - 125
RP1510	**A Wonder Book and Tanglewood Tales** NY 1910, DJ	500 - 700
	w/o DJ	150 - 250

Peat, Fern Bisel

RP2010	**A Christmas Carol** Akron 1929, DJ	40 - 60
RP2020	**Christmas Carols** Akron 1937, DJ	30 - 50
	w/o DJ	20 - 30
RP2030	**JiJi Lou** Akron 1928, DJ	100 - 150
	w/o DJ	50 - 75
RP2040	**Little Black Sambo** Akron 1946	30 - 50
RP2050	**Maxfield Parrish** (Coy Ludwig) NY 1973, DJ	40 - 60
RP2060	**Mother Goose** Akron 1929, DJ	175 - 250
	w/o DJ	75 - 125
RP2080	**Stories Children Like** Akron 1933, DJ	50 - 75
	w/o DJ	30 - 50
RP2090	**The Story of A Happy Doll** Akron 1928, DJ	75 - 125
	w/o DJ	30 - 50
RP2100	**A Wonder-Book** Akron 1929, DJ	75 - 125
	w/o DJ	30 - 50

Peckstein, Max

RP2410	**Reisebilder: Italien-Suedsee** Berlin 1919, 800 cys	1000 - 1500

Pennell, Joseph

RP2710	**Catalog of Etchings** (Louis Wuerth) Bos 1928, 465 cys	700 - 1000
RP2720	**Catalog of the Lithographs of Joseph Pennell** (Louis Wuerth) Bos 1931, 425 cys	700 - 1000

Petersham, Maud & Mishka

RP3010	**Rootabaga Pigeons** (Carl Sandburg) NY 1923, DJ	150 - 250
	w/o DJ	100 - 150

RP1020	**RP1030 (w/o DJ)**	**RP1210**	**RP1320**	**RP1325**	**RP1370**

RP1385	**RP1435**	**RP2020**	**RP2060**	**RP2080**	**RP2090**

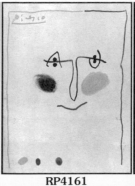

RP2100	RP4060	RP4161	RP4165	RP4170

RP5020 (w/o DJ)	RP5090 (w/o DJ)	RP5130 (w/o DJ)	RP5140 (w/o DJ)	RP9020	RP9030

RP3020 **Rootabaga Stories** (Carl Sandburg) NY 1922, DJ 150 - 250
    w/o DJ 100 - 150
RP3022 later printings w/o DJ 40 - 60

Picasso, Pablo

RP4010 **Autre Chose** (Pierre Benoit) Paris 1956, 35 cys 4000 - 6000
RP4020 **Carnet Catalan** Paris 1958, 500 cys, 2 vol,
    booklet, slipcase 200 - 300
RP4030 **Carnet de la Californie** Paris 1959, 1500 cys 500 - 700
RP4040 **Children's Homage to Picasso** NY 1970, DJ 40 - 60
RP4050 **The Cubist Years 1907-1916** (Pierre Daix)
    Bos 1979, DJ 125 - 200
RP4060 **Goodbye Picasso** (David Douglas Duncan) Lon
    1975, DJ 150 - 250
RP4070 **Les Dé Jeuners** (Douglas Cooper) Paris (1962),
    125 cys, loose in folder 200 - 300
RP4080 **Les Sculptures de Picasso** (Daniel Kahnweiler)
    Paris 1949 100 - 150
RP4090 **Lysistrata** (Aristophanes) NY 1934, 1500 cys,
    glassine DJ, signed by Picasso (Limited Editions
    Club), w/folder & slipcase 2500 - 3500
RP4100 **Pablo Picasso** (William Boeck & Jaime Sabartes)
    NY 1955, DJ 200 - 300
RP4110 **Pablo Picasso** (Christian Zervos) Paris 1957-72,
    26 vol 12000 - 15000
RP4120 **Picasso** (Jean Leymarie) NY 1972, DJ 100 - 150
RP4140 **Picasso 347** NY 1970, 2 vol 200 - 300
RP4150 **Picasso, A Pictorial Biography** (L. G. Buchlein)
    NY 1959, DJ 50 - 75
RP4155 **Picasso as a Book Artist** (Abraham Horodisch)
    Clev 1957, DJ 50 - 75
RP4160 **Picasso at Work** (Roland Penrose) Lon 1965,
    wraparound band, acetate DJ 100 - 150
RP4161 Garden City (1960s) 100 - 150
RP4165 **Picasso Fifty-Five Years of His Graphic Work**
    NY 1965, DJ 50 - 75
RP4170 **Picasso His Recent Drawings 1966-1968**
    (Charles Feld) NY 1969, acetate DJ 75 - 125
RP4180 **Picasso in Antibes** NY 1960, box 100 - 150
RP4190 **Picasso Lithographs** (Fernand Mourlet)
    Bos 1970, DJ 150 - 250
RP4200 **Picasso: Oeuvres de 1895-1972** (Christian
    Zervos) Paris 1943-78, 34 vol 20000 - 30000
RP4210 **Picasso: The Blue and Rose Period 1900-1906**
    (Pierre Daix) NY 1967, DJ 200 - 300
RP4220 **Picasso: The Recent Years 1939-46** (Jean
    Leymarie) NY 1947, 350 cys 2000 - 3000
RP4230 **Picasso Theatre** (Douglas Cooper) NY (1968), DJ 100 - 150
RP4240 **Picasso - Toreros** (Jamie Sabartes) NY (1961), DJ 500 - 700

RP4250 **Picasso's Picassos** (David Douglas Duncan)
    NY 1961, DJ 100 - 150
RP4260 **Picasso's Posters** (Christopher Czwiklitzer)
    NY 1971, DJ 150 - 250
RP4270 **Picasso's World of Children** (Helen Foy) NY
    (1960s), DJ 40 - 60
RP4280 **The Posters of Picasso** (Joseph Foster) NY 1957, DJ 50 - 75
RP4290 **The Sculpture of Picasso** (Roland Penrose) NY
    1967, DJ 40 - 60
RP4300 **The Silent Studio** (David Douglas Duncan) 1976, DJ 50 - 75
RP4310 **Suite of 180 Drawings** NY 1954 (Verve 29/30) 250 - 350

Pogany, Willy

RP5010 **Alice's Adventures in Wonderland** NY 1929, DJ 200 - 300
    w/o DJ 100 - 150
RP5020 **The Blue Lagoon** Lon 1910 125 - 200
RP5030 **Cinderella** NY 1915 150 - 250
RP5040 **Fairy Flowers** NY 1926 150 - 250
RP5050 **The Frenzied Prince** Phil 1943, DJ 75 - 125
RP5060 **Gulliver's Travels** NY 1917, DJ 125 - 200
    w/o DJ 40 - 60
RP5070 **Lohengrin** Lon 1913 150 - 250
RP5080 **Parsifal** Lon 1912 125 - 200
RP5090 **Peterkin** Phil 1940, DJ 100 - 150
    w/o DJ 50 - 75
RP5100 **The Rime of the Ancient Mariner** NY 1910 125 - 200
RP5110 **The Rubaiyat of Omar Khayyam** Lon 1930 40 - 60
RP5120 **Stories to Tell the Littlest Ones** NY 1916, DJ 125 - 175
    w/o DJ 50 - 75
RP5130 **Tannhäuser** (Richard Wagner) NY (early 1900s) 150 - 250
RP5140 **A Wonderbook and Tanglewood Tales**
    Phil nd, DJ 200 - 300
    w/o DJ 100 - 150

Pollock, Jackson

RP5410 **Jackson Pollock** (Bryan Robertson) Lon 1960, DJ 200 - 300
RP5420 **Jackson Pollock: A Catalog Raisonné of Paintings,
    Drawings and Other Works** (Francis Valentine
    O'Connor) New Haven 1978, 4 vol, slipcase 2000 - 3000

Potter, Beatrix

RP5710 **Cecily Parsley's New Rhymes** Lon 1922 100 - 150
RP5720 **Fairy Caravan** Phil 1929 100 - 150
RP5730 **Ginger and Pickles** Lon 1909 150 - 250
RP5731 NY 1909 100 - 150
RP5740 **The Pie and the Patty Pan** Lon 1905 125 - 200
RP5741 NY 1905 100 - 150
RP5750 **The Roly-Poly Pudding** Lon 1908 200 - 300
RP5760 **The Story of a Fierce Bad Rabbit** Lon 1906 150 - 250
RP5780 **The Story of Miss Moppet** Lon 1906 200 - 300
RP5790 **The Tailor of Gloucester** Lon 1903 200 - 300

RP5800	**The Tale of Benjamin Bunny** Lon 1904	125 - 200
RP5810	**The Tale of Jemima Puddle-Duck** Lon 1908	200 - 300
RP5820	**The Tale of Johnny Town Mouse** Lon 1908	150 - 250
RP5830	**The Tale of Little Pig Robinson** Phil 1930	100 - 150
RP5840	**The Tale of Mr. Tod** Lon 1912	150 - 250
RP5850	**The Tale of Mrs. Tittlemouse** Lon 1910	100 - 150
RP5860	**The Tale of Peter Rabbit** Lon 1901, 250 cys, private printing	8000 - 12000
RP5862	Lon 1902, 200 cys	6000 - 8000
RP5863	Lon 1902 (1st trade ed), "Oct. 1902" "wept" for "shed" p 51	400 - 600
RP5880	**The Tale of Pigling Bland** Lon 1913	100 - 150
RP5890	**The Tale of Squirrel Nut Kin** Lon 1903	200 - 300
RP5900	**The Tale of the Flopsy Bunnies** Lon 1909	200 - 300
RP5910	**The Tale of Timmy Tiptoes** Lon 1911	100 - 150
RP5920	**The Tale of Tom Kitten** Lon 1907	200 - 300
RP5930	**The Tale of Two Bad Mice** Lon 1904	200 - 300

Pyle, Howard (also see Americana)

RP9000	**The Autocrat of the Breakfast Table** Cambridge 1894, 2 vol, 250 cys	250 - 350
RP9001	Bos 1893, 2 vol	50 - 75
RP9010	**The Buccaneers and Marooners of America** Lon 1891	75 - 125
RP9020	**Chivalry** (James Cabell) NY 1909, DJ/box	250 - 350
RP9030	**The First Christmas Tree** (Henry van Dyke) NY 1897	50 - 75
RP9040	**The Flute and Violin** NY 1891	50 - 75
RP9050	**Gallantry** NY 1907	100 - 150
RP9060	**The Garden Behind the Moon** NY 1895	75 - 125
RP9070	**Howard Pyle's Book of Pirates** NY 1921, 50 cys, DJ, box	600 - 800
RP9071	NY 1921, DJ (1st trade ed)	200 - 300
	w/o DJ	100 - 150
RP9080	**Howard Pyle's Book of The American Spirit** NY 1923, 6 cys, orig drawing	1200 - 1800
RP9081	NY 1923, 50 cys, DJ	400 - 600
RP9082	NY 1923, DJ (1st trade ed)	200 - 300
	w/o DJ	100 - 150
RP9090	**In Old New York** NY 1894	50 - 75
RP9100	**The Island of Enchantment** NY 1905	50 - 75
RP9110	**The Lady of Shalott** NY 1881	250 - 350
RP9120	**The Man with the Hoe** NY 1900	100 - 150
RP9130	**Men of Iron** NY 1892, 1st state w/1-1/16" width	75 - 125
RP9132	later printings	30 - 50
RP9140	**The Merry Adventures of Robin Hood** (1st book) NY 1883, stamped lea	300 - 500
RP9141	Lon 1883	150 - 250
RP9142	NY 1929	30 - 50
RP9150	**A Modern Aladdin** NY 1892	75 - 125
RP9160	**The One Hoss Shay** NY 1905	50 - 75
RP9170	**Otto of the Silver Hand** NY 1888	125 - 200
RP9171	Lon 1888	100 - 150
RP9172	NY 1930, DJ	50 - 75
RP9180	**The Ruby of Kishmoor** NY 1908	100 - 150
RP9190	**Saint Joan of Arc** (Twain) NY 1919, DJ	175 - 250
	w/o DJ	100 - 150
RP9200	**Snow-Bound** (Whittier) Bos 1906	50 - 75
RP9210	**The Story of Siegfried** NY 1882	100 - 150
RP9220	**The Story of Sir Launcelot and His Companions** NY 1907, DJ	200 - 300
	w/o DJ	75 - 125
RP9230	**The Story of the Grail** NY 1910	50 - 75
RP9240	**The Story of the Revolution** NY 1898, 2 vol	75 - 125
RP9250	**Twilight Land** NY 1895	50 - 75
RP9260	**Within the Capes** NY 1885	100 - 150

RP9270	**The Wonder Clock** NY 1888	125 - 175
RP9280	**Yankee Doodle** (1st book illus) NY 1881	250 - 350

Rackham, Arthur

Most limited editions are signed. Trade editions without dust jackets are worth about half to two-thirds of copies with jackets.

RR1010	**Aesop's Fables** Lon 1912, 1000 cys	700 - 1000
RR1011	NY 1912, 250 cys	700 - 1000
RR1012	Lon 1912 (1st trade ed)	150 - 250
RR1013	NY 1912 (1st U.S. trade ed)	100 - 150
RR1020	**Alice's Adventures in Wonderland** Lon 1907, 1130 cys	700 - 1000
RR1021	NY 1907, 550 cys	800 - 1200
RR1022	Lon 1907 (1st trade ed)	125 - 175
RR1023	NY 1907 (1st U.S. trade ed)	125 - 175
RR1030	**The Allies Fairy Book** Lon 1916, 525 cys	800 - 1200
RR1031	Lon 1916, DJ (1st trade ed)	150 - 250
	w/o DJ	100 - 150
RR1032	Phil 1916 (1st U.S. trade ed)	75 - 125
RR1040	**The Argonauts of the Amazon** Lon 1901	125 - 175
RR1041	NY 1901	75 - 125
RR1050	**The Arthur Rackham Fairy Book** Lon 1933, 460 cys	1000 - 1500
RR1051	Lon 1933, DJ (1st trade ed)	150 - 250
	w/o DJ	75 - 125
RR1052	Phil 1933, DJ	175 - 225
	w/o DJ	75 - 125
RR1060	**Arthur Rackham's Book of Pictures** Lon 1913, 1030 cys	800 - 1200
RR1061	Lon 1913 (1st trade ed)	200 - 300
RR1062	NY 1913	150 - 250
RR1063	Lon 1927, DJ	150 - 250
RR1070	**The Bee-Blowaways** Lon 1900	100 - 150
RR1080	**The Book of Betty Barber** Lon 1910	250 - 350
RR1090	**The Book of the Queen's Doll House** Lon 1924, 2 vol	200 - 300
RR1100	**The Book of the Titmarsh Club** Lon 1925	100 - 125
RR1110	**Bracebridge Hall or The Humorists** NY 1896, 2 vol	100 - 150
RR1120	**The Castle Inn** Lon 1898	100 - 150
RR1130	**Charles O'Malley, The Irish Dragoon** NY 1897	100 - 150
RR1140	**The Chimes** Lon 1931, 1500 cys, box	300 - 500
RR1150	**A Christmas Carol** Lon 1915, 525 cys	1000 - 1200
RR1151	Lon 1915 (1st trade ed)	125 - 175
RR1152	Phil 1915, DJ	175 - 225
	w/o DJ	100 - 150
RR1160	**Cinderella** Lon 1919, 325 cys	700 - 1000
RR1161	Lon 1919, 525 cys	600 - 800
RR1162	Lon 1919, DJ (1st trade ed)	150 - 250
	w/o DJ	100 - 150

RP9070 (w/o DJ)

RP9082

RP9142 (w/o DJ)

RP9172 (w/o DJ)

RP9180

RP9190

RP9230 (title page)

RR1013 (w/o DJ)

RR1023 (w/o DJ)

RR1163 (w/o DJ)	RR1172	RR1183

RR1352 (w/o DJ)	RR1404 (w/o DJ)	RR1481 (frontispiece)

RR1502	RR1682	RR1692

RR1163	Phil 1919, DJ	125 - 200
	w/o DJ	75 - 125
RR1170	**The Compleat Angler** Lon 1931, 775 cys	800 - 1200
RR1171	Lon 1931, DJ (1st trade ed)	150 - 250
	w/o DJ	100 - 150
RR1172	Phil 1931, DJ	175 - 225
	w/o DJ	75 - 125
RR1180	**Comus** Lon 1921, 50 cys	1200 - 1800
RR1181	Lon 1921, 100 cys	1000 - 1500
RR1182	Lon 1921, 400 cys	600 - 800
RR1183	Lon 1921, DJ (1st trade ed)	125 - 200
	w/o DJ	100 - 150
RR1184	NY 1921, DJ	125 - 200
	w/o DJ	100 - 150
RR1200	**Costume Through the Ages** Lon 1938	100 - 150
RR1210	**A Dish of Apples** Lon 1921, 500 cys	600 - 800
RR1211	Lon 1921, DJ (1st trade ed)	175 - 225
RR1212	NY 1921, DJ	150 - 200
RR1220	**The Dolly Dialogues** Lon 1894, yellow or red wrappers	400 - 600
RR1230	Lon 1894, blue or tan cl	125 - 175
RR1240	**East Coast Scenery** Lon 1899	100 - 150
RR1250	**English Fairy Tales Retold** Lon 1918, 500 cys	700 - 1000
RR1251	Lon 1918 (1st trade ed)	150 - 225
RR1252	NY 1918	125 - 200
RR1260	**Elelina** Lon 1898	125 - 200
RR1270	**A Fairy Book** NY 1923	75 - 125
RR1280	**Fairy Tales of the Brothers Grimm** Lon 1900	150 - 250
RR1282	Lon 1909, 750 cys, vellum	1000 - 1500
RR1283	Lon 1909	300 - 500
RR1284	NY 1909, green bds (1st U. S. ed)	300 - 500
RR1300	**Fairy Tales of Hans Andersen** Lon 1932, 525 cys, vellum	1000 - 1500
RR1301	Lon 1932, DJ (1st trade ed)	200 - 300
	w/o DJ	125 - 200
RR1302	Phil 1932, DJ	200 - 300
	w/o DJ	150 - 225
RR1310	**Fairy Tales Old and New** Lon 1905	75 - 125
RR1320	**Faithful Friends** Lon 1913	175 - 250
RR1330	**The Far Familiar** Lon 1938	100 - 150
RR1340	**Feats on the Fjord** Lon 1899, blue flexible cl	75 - 125
RR1342	Lon 1914, red or green cl	75 - 125
RR1343	NY 1914, red or green cl	75 - 125
RR1350	**Goblin Market** Lon 1933, 410 cys, vellum	700 - 1000
RR1351	Lon 1933, pictorial wraps, DJ	200 - 250
	w/o DJ	125 - 200
RR1352	Phil 1933, red cl, DJ	150 - 250
	w/o DJ	100 - 150

RR1360	**Good Night** NY 1907	300 - 500
RR1370	**The Greek Heroes** Lon 1903, limp green cl	150 - 250
RR1371	Lon 1910, blue cl	125 - 200
RR1380	**The Grey House on the Hill** Lon 1903	100 - 150
RR1390	**The Grey Lady** Lon 1897	100 - 150
RR1400	**Gulliver's Travels** Lon 1900	100 - 150
RR1402	Lon 1909, 750 cys	700 - 1000
RR1403	Lon 1909, DJ (trade ed)	175 - 250
	w/o DJ	100 - 150
RR1404	NY 1909, DJ	175 - 250
	w/o DJ	100 - 150
	Haddon Hall Library - J.M. Dent, any titles from this series (such as *Fly Fishing* by Sir Edward Gray, 1899) are worth:	
RR1410	limited editions, 150 cys	175 - 225
RR1420	trade editions	75 - 125
RR1430	**Hansel and Grethel and Other Tales** Lon 1920	150 - 250
RR1431	NY 1920	150 - 250
RR1440	**Imagina** NY 1914	100 - 150
RR1450	**In the Evening of His Days** Lon 1896	200 - 300
RR1460	**The Ingoldsby Legends** Lon 1898, green cl	125 - 175
RR1462	Lon 1907, 560 cys	1000 - 1500
RR1463	Lon 1907	250 - 350
RR1464	NY 1907	175 - 225
RR1480	**Irish Fairy Tales** Lon 1920, 520 cys, white bds	1000 - 1500
RR1481	Lon 1920	125 - 175
RR1482	NY 1920	100 - 150
RR1500	**The King of the Golden River** Lon 1932, 570 cys, limp vellum	600 - 800
RR1501	Lon 1932, DJ, wrappers	125 - 175
	w/o DJ	75 - 125
RR1502	Phil 1932, DJ	125 - 175
	w/o DJ	75 - 125
RR1510	**Kingdom's Curious** Lon 1905	150 - 250
RR1520	**The Land of Enchantment** Lon 1907	150 - 225
RR1530	**The Legend of Sleepy Hollow** Lon 1938, 375 cys, vellum	1000 - 1500
RR1531	Lon 1928, DJ (1st trade ed)	150 - 250
	w/o DJ	100 - 150
RR1532	Phil 1928, DJ	150 - 250
	w/o DJ	100 - 150
RR1540	**Little Brother and Little Sister** Lon 1917, 525 cys, envelope w/extra plate	1600 - 2200
	w/o envelope	800 - 1200
RR1541	Lon 1917 (1st trade ed)	175- 225
RR1542	NY 1917, in pub box	175 - 225
	w/o box	100 - 150
RR1550	**The Little Folks Fairy Book** Lon 1905	100 - 150
RR1560	**The Little Folks Picture Album in Color** Lon 1904	100 - 150
RR1570	**Littledom Castle and Other Tales** Lon 1903	125 - 175
RR1580	**A London Garland** Lon 1895	125 - 200
RR1590	**The Lonesomest Doll** Bos 1928, DJ	250 - 350
	w/o DJ	125 - 175
RR1600	**A Midsummer-Night's Dream** Lon 1908, 1000 cys, vellum	1000 - 1500
RR1601	Lon 1908 (1st trade ed)	250 - 350
RR1602	NY 1908	175 - 250
RR1604	Lon 1938, 1950 cys	250 - 350
RR1620	**The Money-Spinner** Lon 1896	100 - 150
RR1630	**More Tales of the Stumps** Lon 1902	175 - 225
RR1640	**Mother Goose, The Old Nursery Rhymes** Lon 1913, 1130 cys	1200 - 1800
RR1641	Lon 1913 (1st trade ed)	150 - 225
RR1642	NY 1913	150 - 225

RR1650	**Mysteries of Police and Crime** Lon 1901	
	(special 1st ed)	100 - 150
RR1660	**A New Book of Sense and Nonsense** Lon 1928	75 - 125
RR1670	**The New Fiction and Other Papers** Lon 1895	75 - 125
RR1680	**The Night Before Christmas** Lon 1931, 550 cys	700 - 1000
RR1681	Lon 1931, DJ, wrappers (1st trade ed)	150 - 250
	w/o DJ	100 - 150
RR1682	Phil 1931, DJ	150 - 250
	w/o DJ	100 - 150
RR1690	**Peer Gynt** Lon 1936, 460 cys, box	1000 - 1500
RR1691	Lon 1936, DJ (1st trade ed)	175- 250
	w/o DJ	100 - 150
RR1692	Phil 1936, DJ	175 - 250
	w/o DJ	100 - 150
RR1700	**The Peradventures of Private Pagett** Lon 1904	175 - 250
RR1710	**Peter Pan in Kensington Gardens** Lon 1906,	
	500 cys, vellum	1200 - 1800
RR1701	Lon 1906 (1st trade ed)	300 - 500
RR1702	NY 1906 (1st U.S. trade ed)	300 - 500
RR1704	later printings by Charles Scribners Sons	100 - 175
RR1706	Paris 1907 (French ed)	250 - 350
RR1708	Lon 1912, vellum (deluxe ed)	1200 - 1600
RR1709	Lon 1912	300 - 500
RR1720	**Peter Pan in Kensington Gardens Retold by**	
	May Byron for Little People Lon 1930, DJ	100 - 150
RR1721	NY 1930, DJ	100 - 150
RR1730	**The Peter Pan Portfolio** Lon 1912, 500 cys,	
	green cl w/vellum sp	4000 - 6000
RR1740	**The Pied Piper of Hamelin** Lon 1934, 410 cys,	
	vellum	700 - 1000
RR1741	Lon 1934, DJ, wrappers	150 - 250
	w/o DJ	100 - 150
RR1742	Phil 1934, DJ	150 - 250
	w/o DJ	100 - 150
RR1750	**Poor Cecco** NY 1925, 105 cys	7000 - 10000
RR1751	NY 1925, DJ (1st trade ed)	150 - 200
RR1752	Lon 1925	125 - 175
RR1760	**Puck of Pook's Hill** NY 1906	75 - 125
RR1770	**Queen Mab's Fairy Realm** Lon 1901	200 - 300
RR1780	**The Queen's Gift Book** Lon 1915 (w/plates	
	by Rackham)	40 - 60
RR1790	**The Rainbow Book** Lon 1909	125 - 175
RR1800	**Red Pottage** Lon 1904, tan wrappers	400 - 600
RR1810	**The Rhinegold and the Valkyrie** Lon 1910,	
	1150 cys, vellum	700 - 1000
RR1811	Lon 1910 (1st trade ed)	150 - 250
RR1812	NY 1910	125 - 175
RR1820	**Rip Van Winkle** Lon 1905, 250 cys, vellum	1500 - 2200
RR1821	Lon 1905 (1st trade ed)	300 - 500
RR1822	NY 1905	250 - 350
RR1824	Paris 1906, 200 cys (1st French ed)	500 - 700
RR1825	Leipzig 1906, green wrappers (1st German ed)	300 - 500
RR1827	Lon 1916	150 - 200
RR1828	NY 1916	125 - 175
RR1840	**River and Rainbow** Lon 1934, wrappers	100 - 150
RR1850	**A Road to Fairyland** Lon 1926	75 - 125
RR1852	NY 1927, DJ	75 - 125
RR1860	**The Romance of King Arthur and His Knights**	
	of the Round Table Lon 1917, 500 cys	800 - 1200
RR1861	Lon 1917 (1st trade ed)	150 - 250
RR1862	NY 1917	125 - 200
RR1864	NY 1926, DJ	75 - 125
RR1880	**Siegfried and the Twilight of the Gods**	
	Lon 1911, 1150 cys, slipcase	1000 - 1500

RR1881	Paris 1911, 390 cys (1st French ed)	700 - 1000
RR1882	Lon 1911 (1st trade ed)	150 - 250
RR1883	NY 1911	125 - 175
RR1890	**The Sketchbook of Geoffrey Crayon, Gent**	
	NY 1894, 2 vol	75 - 125
RR1891	NY 1894, 2 vol, DJs (Van Tassel ed)	125 - 175
RR1893	NY 1895, 2 vol, 175 sets	200 - 300
RR1900	**The Sleeping Beauty** Lon 1920, 625 cys,	
	white bds	700 - 1000
RR1901	Lon 1920, DJ	150 - 250
RR1902	Phil 1920, DJ	125 - 175
RR1910	**Snickerty Nick** NY 1919	100 - 150
RR1920	**Snickerty Nick and the Giant** LA 1935, DJ	75 - 125
RR1930	**Snowdrop and Other Tales** Lon 1920	125 - 175
RR1931	NY 1920	125 - 200
RR1933	Paris 1922, 1300 cys (French ed)	200 - 300
RR1940	**Some British Ballads** Lon 1919, 575 cys	700 - 1000
RR1941	Lon 1919	125 - 175
RR1942	NY 1919, box	250 - 350
	w/o box	100 - 150
RR1943	Paris 1919, 1300 cys (French ed)	200 - 300
RR1950	**The Springtide of Life, Poems of Childhood**	
	Lon 1918, 765 cys	700 - 1000
RR1951	Lon 1918, DJ	150 - 250
RR1952	NY 1918, DJ	150 - 225
RR1960	**Stories of King Arthur** Lon 1918	150 - 250
RR1970	**Sunrise-Land, Rambles in Eastern England**	
	Lon 1894	200 - 250
RR1980	**The Surprizing Adventures of Tuppy and Tue**	
	Lon 1904	175 - 250
RR1990	**Tales From Shakespeare** Lon 1899	75 - 125
RR1992	Lon 1909, 750 cys	700 - 1000
RR1993	Lon 1909, DJ	200 - 275
RR1994	NY 1909, DJ	200 - 275
	w/o DJ	75 - 125
RR2010	**Tales of a Traveler** NY 1895, 2 vol	75 - 125
RR2020	**Tales of Mystery and Imagination** Lon 1935,	
	460 cys, vellum	1000 - 1500
RR2021	Lon 1935, DJ	200 - 300
	w/o DJ	125 - 200
RR2022	Phil 1935, DJ	200 - 300
	w/o DJ	125 - 200
RR2030	**The Tempest** Lon 1926, 520 cys, white bds	1000 - 1500
RR2031	Lon 1926, DJ (1st trade ed)	225 - 275
RR2032	NY 1926, DJ	225 - 275
	w/o DJ	125 - 175
RR2040	**Through a Glass Lightly** Lon 1897	150 - 225
RR2050	**To the Other Side** Lon 1893, wrappers	300 - 500

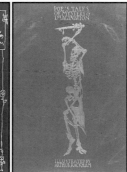

RR1820   **RR1860 (detail of color plate)**

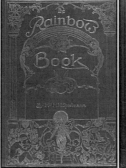

RR1770 (w/o DJ)   **RR1790 (w/o DJ)**   **RR1883 (w/o DJ)**   **RR1902 (w/o DJ)**   **RR1994 (w/o DJ)**   **RR2022 (w/o DJ)**

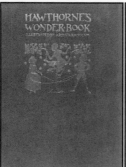

| RR2102 | RR2162 (w/o DJ) | RR2440 (w/o DJ) | RS4110 | RS4130 | RR6080 |

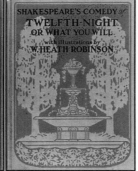

| RR6150 (w/o DJ) | RR6250 (w/o DJ) | RR6370 (w/o DJ) |

RR4030	Rembrandt Paintings (Horst Gerson) NY 1968, DJ	50 - 75
RR4040	Rembrandt: The Complete Etchings (K. G. Boon) NY 1970s), DJ	50 - 75
RR4050	Rembrandt's Etchings True and False (George Biörklund) Stockholm 1955, DJ	500 - 700

Remington, Frederic (also see Americana)
Remington illustrated over 200 books.

RR4310	An Apache Princess NY 1903	50 - 75
RR4320	The Aztec Treasure House NY 1890	150 - 250
RR4330	The Book of the American Indian NY 1923, DJ	200 - 300
	w/o DJ	100 - 150
RR4332	NY 1927, DJ	125 - 200
RR4340	Cuba in War Time NY 1897	50 - 75
RR4350	Daughter of the Souix NY 1903, DJ	200 - 300
RR4360	Frederic Remington Artist of the Old West (Harold McCracken) Phil 1947, DJ	75 - 125
RR4370	John Ermine of the Yellowstone NY 1902	100 - 150
RR4380	Remington's Own West (Harold McCracken) NY 1960, 167 cys, cowhide bound, box	600 - 800
RR4381	NY 1960, DJ (1st trade ed)	50 - 75
RR4390	The Song of Hiawatha (H.W. Longfellow) Bos 1891, 250 cys, vellum	600 - 800
RR4391	Bos 1891 (1st trade ed)	100 - 150
RR4393	Bos 1908	100 - 150
RR4400	Sundown Leflare NY 1899	50 - 75

Rivera, Diego
| RR5010 | Frescoes NY 1933 | 500 - 700 |

Robinson, Charles
RR6010	Adventures of Odysseus Lon 1900	100 - 150
RR6020	Aesop's Fables Lon 1895	100 - 150
RR6030	Alice's Adventures in Wonderland Lon 1910	100 - 150
RR6040	The Big Book of Fables Lon 1912	200 - 300
RR6050	The Big Book of Fairy Tales Lon 1911	200 - 300
RR6060	The Big Book of Nursery Rhymes Lon 1911	150 - 250
RR6070	A Child's Christmas Lon 1906	150 - 250
RR6080	A Child's Garden of Verses (Stevenson) Lon 1896	100 - 150
RR6090	Fairy Tales from Hans Christian Andersen Lon 1899	150 - 250
RR6100	The Happy Prince Lon 1924, DJ	100 - 150
RR6110	Lullaby Land Lon 1898	50 - 75
RR6120	Peacock Pie Lon 1913	100 - 150
RR6130	Rip Van Winkle NY 1914	75 - 125
RR6140	The Secret Garden Lon 1911	100 - 150
RR6150	The Sensitive Plant Lon 1911	125 - 200
RR6160	Songs and Sonnets of William Shakespeare Phil 1915	150 - 250
RR6170	The True Annals of Fairyland Lon 1900	100 - 150

Robinson, T. H.
| RR6250 | The Swiss Family Robinson NY (1920s) | 30 - 50 |

Robinson, W. Heath
RR6310	Arabian Nights Entertainments Lon 1899 (w/other illus)	100 - 150
RR6320	The Book of the Goblins Lon 1934	125 - 200
RR6330	Midsummer Nights Dream Lon 1911	200 - 300
RR6340	Old Time Stories Lon 1921	150 - 250
RR6350	The Song of the English Lon 1909	100 - 150
RR6351	NY 1909	100 - 150
RR6360	Swiss Family Robinson NY 1920, DJ	75 - 125
	w/o DJ	50 - 75
RR6370	Twelfth-Night or What You Will NY (1920'), DJ	150 - 250
	w/o DJ	75 - 125
RR6380	Uncle Lubin Lon 1902	200 - 300
RR6390	The Water-Babies Bos 1915, box	200 - 300
	w/o box	100 - 150

RR2060	Two Old Ladies, Two Foolish Fairies and a Tom Cat Lon 1897	200 - 300
RR2070	Two Years Before the Mast Lon 1904	75 - 125
RR2080	Undine Lon 1909, 1000 cys	700 - 1000
RR2081	Lon 1909 (1st trade ed)	150 - 250
RR2082	NY 1909, DJ, gray bds	175 - 250
RR2084	Paris 1912, 390 cys	800 - 1200
RR2086	Paris 1913	150 - 225
RR2100	The Vicar of Wakefield Lon 1929, 775 cys, vellum	800 - 1200
RR2101	Lon 1929, DJ (1st trade ed)	150 - 250
RR2102	Phil 1929, DJ	125 - 200
RR2110	Where Flies the Flag Lon 1904	125 - 200
RR2120	Where the Blue Begins Lon 1925, 175 cys, box	1200 - 1800
RR2121	Lon 1925, DJ (1st trade ed)	150 - 250
RR2122	NY 1925, DJ	125 - 175
RR2130	The Wind in the Willows NY 1940, 2020 cys, box	1000 - 1500
RR2131	NY 1940, slipcase (1st trade ed)	50 - 75
RR2133	Lon 1951, 500 cys, white calf box	700 - 1000
RR2134	Lon 1951, DJ	100 - 150
RR2136	Lon 1964, calf	300 - 500
RR2150	The Windmill Lon 1923	50 - 75
RR2151	NY 1923, 500 cys	125 - 200
RR2160	A Wonder Book for Girls and Boys Lon 1922, 600 cys, box	800 - 1200
RR2161	Lon 1922, DJ (1st trade ed)	200 - 300
RR2162	NY 1922, DJ	200 - 300
	w/o DJ	100 - 150
RR2170	A World in a Garden Lon 1899	50 - 75
RR2180	The Zankiwank and the Bletherwitch Lon 1896	500 - 700
RR2181	NY 1896 (1st U.S. ed)	300 - 500

Rae, John
RR2410	American Indian Fairy Tales Chi 1921	40 - 60
RR2420	Granny Goose Chi 1926	100 - 150
RR2430	Grimm's Animal Stories NY 1911	100 - 150
RR2440	The New Adventures of "Alice" Chi 1917	100 - 150
RR2450	Reynard the Fox Chi 1925	40 - 60

Raphael (Raphael Sanzio)
| RR2710 | Raphael, The Complete Works of NY 1969, DJ | 100 - 150 |

Rauschenberg, Robert
| RR3010 | Rauschenberg (Andrew Force) NY 1969, DJ | 800 - 1200 |

Rembrandt
RR4010	The Drawings of Rembrandt (Otto Benesch) Lon 1954-57, 6 vol	400 - 600
RR4012	Lon 1973, 6 vol	250 - 350
RR4020	Paintings From the Soviet Museums Leningrad 1975, slipcase	50 - 75

Rockwell, Norman

This profuse magazine illustrator is very collectible.

RR6610	**The Adventures of Huckleberry Finn** NY 1940, slipcase	30 - 50
RR6620	**The Adventures of Tom Sawyer** NY 1936, slipcase	30 - 50
RR6630	**Norman Rockwell** (Thomas Rockwell) NY 1960, DJ	30 - 50
RR6640	**Norman Rockwell** (Laurie Moffatt) Stockbridge 1986, 2 vol, slipcase	100 - 150
RR6650	**Norman Rockwell: Artist and Illustrator** (Thomas S. Buechner) NY 1970, DJ	150 - 200
RR6660	**Norman Rockwell Illustrator** (Arthur Guptill) NY 1946, DJ	50 - 75
RR6670	**One Issue** Curtis Pub. Co., NY 1919 (Salesman's sample of *Saturday Evening Post* bound in book form w/color frontis by Rockwell)	40 - 60
RR6680	**The Secret Play** NY 1915, DJ	200 - 300
RR6690	**Tell Me Why Stories** NY 1912	200 - 300

Rodin, Auguste

RR6750	**Rodin** (Ludwig Goldscheider) Lon 1964, DJ	30 - 50

Rombola, John

RR6810	**Rombola by Rombola** NY 1965, DJ	40 - 60

Ross, Penny

RR6910	**Loraine and the Little People** NY 1915	40 - 60

Rouault, Georges

RR7210	**Cirque de L'Etoile Filante** Paris 1938, 280 cys	1000 - 1500
RR7220	**Divertissement** Paris 1943, 1270 cys, wrappers, 15 color plates	300 - 500
RR7230	**Oeuvre Grave** Monte Carlo 1978, 2 vol	300 - 500
RR7240	**Stella Vespertina** Paris 1947, 2000 cys, wrappers, 12 color plates	300 - 500
RR7250	**Visages** Bos 1969, 450 cys	300 - 500

Rountree, Harry

RR7510	**Stories from Grimm's Fairy Tales** NY 1900	50 - 75
RR7520	**The Wonderful Isles** Bos (early 1900s)	125 - 200

Rowlandson, Thomas

RR7810	**His Drawings and Watercolors** (A. P. Oppe) Lon 1923, 200 cys	150 - 250
RR7820	**The Watercolor Drawings of Thomas Rowlandson** (Arthur Heintzelman) NY 1947, DJ	50 - 75

Ruscha, Edward

RR9010	**Crackers** Hollywood 1969, DJ	100 - 150
RR9020	**Every Building on the Sunset Strip** LA 1966, aluminum foil DJ, slipcase	100 - 150

Russell, Charles M. (also see Americana)

RR9310	**The Charles M. Russell Book** (Harold McCracken) NY 1957, DJ	50 - 75

Saint-Gaudens, Augustus

RS1010	**Augustus Saint-Gaudens** (Royal Cortissoz) Bos 1908	200 - 300
RS1020	**Reminiscences** (Royal Cortissoz) NY 1913, 2 vol	100 - 150

Samaras, Lucas

RS1310	**Lucas Samaras** (Kim Levin) NY 1975, DJ	100 - 150

Sarg, Tony

RS1610	**Tony Sarg's Book for Children** NY 1924	40 - 60

Sargent, John Singer

RS1910	**John Singer Sargent** (Richard Ormond) NY 1970, DJ	100 - 150

Schaeffer, Mead

RS3010	**The Count of Monte Cristo** NY 1928, DJ	50 - 75
RS3020	**Cruise of the Cachalot** NY 1926, DJ	75 - 125
RS3030	**Lorna Doone** NY 1930, DJ	50 - 75
	w/o DJ	30 - 50
RS3040	**Moby Dick** NY 1934, DJ	75 - 125
	w/o DJ	40 - 60
RS3050	**Omoo** NY 1924, DJ	75 - 125
	w/o DJ	30 - 50
RS3060	**Tom Cringle's Log** (Michael Scott) NY 1927, DJ	75 - 125
	w/o DJ	30 - 50
RS3070	**Typee** NY 1923, DJ	75 - 125
	w/o DJ	30 - 50
RS3080	**Wings of the Morning** NY 1924, DJ	40 - 60
RS3090	**Wreck of the Grosvenor** NY 1923, DJ	50 - 75

Schoonover, Frank E.

RS3310	**The Arctic Stowaways** Chi 1917, DJ	75 - 125
RS3320	**Blackbeard the Buccaneer** Phil 1922, DJ	75 - 125
	w/o DJ	50 - 75
RS3330	**The Boy Captive of Old Deerfield** Bos 1929, DJ	50 - 75
	w/o DJ	30 - 50
RS3340	**Flamingo Feather** NY 1915, DJ	125 - 200
	w/o DJ	50 - 75
RS3350	**Ivanhoe** NY 1922, DJ	100 - 150
	w/o DJ	40 - 60
RS3360	**Joan of Arc** Phil 1918, DJ	75 - 125
	w/o DJ	30 - 50
RS3370	**Lafayette** Phil 1921, DJ	75 - 125
	w/o DJ	40 - 60
RS3380	**Questions of the Desert** Bos 1925	40 - 60
RS3390	**With Cortes in Mexico** Phil 1917	30 - 50
RS3400	**With Cortes the Conqueror** (V. Watson) Phil 1917	40 - 60
RS3410	**Yankee Ships in Pirate Waters** Garden City 1931, DJ	50 - 75

Seuss, Dr.

Add $200 - 300 for any 1930s-1940s books signed by Seuss.

RS3710	**The 500 Hats of Bartholomew Cubbins** NY 1938, DJ	100 - 150
	w/o DJ	40 - 60
RS3720	**And to Think That I Saw It on Mulberry Street** (1st book) NY 1937, DJ	250 - 350
	w/o DJ	100 - 150

RR6670 (frontispiece)

RR6750

RR6810

RR6810 (w/o DJ)

RR6910 (w/o DJ)

RR7820

RS3060 (frontispiece ant title page)

RS3360

RS3400 (w/o DJ)

RS3710

RS3910

RS4120

RS4140

RS5100 (w/o DJ)

RS 5120 (w/o DJ)

RS5230

RS5250

RS5340

RS5410

RT2010 (w/o DJ)

Shahn, Ben
RS3910 **Ecclesiastes** NY 1971, DJ   50 - 75

Sheeler, Charles
RS4010 **Charles Sheeler** (Constance Rourke) NY 1938, DJ 100 - 150

Shepard, Ernest H.
RS4110 **Fourteen Songs from When We Were Very Young** (Milne) NY 1925, DJ   50 - 75
RS4120 **Playtime & Company** NY 1925, DJ   20 - 30
RS4130 **When We Were Very Young** (Milne) NY 1927, DJ 100 - 150
RS4140 **The Wind in the Willows** NY 1933, DJ   20 - 30

Sloan, John
RS4510 **John Sloan's Prints** (Peter Morse) New Haven 1969, 150 cys, signed print   300 - 500

Smith, Jessie Willcox
One of the most collected children's book illustrators, she also did numerous illustrations for magazines of the early 1900s: *Ladies Home Journal*, *Colliers*, *Good Housekeeping*, etc. Some color plates from magazines bring $20 and more.

RS5010 **At the Back of the North Wind** Phil 1919, DJ   150 - 225
    w/o DJ   50 - 75
RS5012 Phil 1920, DJ   125 - 200
RS5020 **The Bed Time Book** NY 1907   175 - 250
RS5030 **Billy Boy** NY 1906   75 - 125
RS5040 **The Book of the Child** NY 1902 (other illus by Green)   100 - 150
RS5050 **Boys and Girls of Bookland** NY 1923, DJ   175 - 250
    w/o DJ   100 - 150
RS5052 Phil 1924, DJ   100 - 150
    w/o DJ   50 - 75
RS5060 **Brenda, Her School and Her Club** Bos 1900   100 - 150
RS5070 **Brenda's Summer at Rockley** Bos 1901   100 - 150
RS5080 **A Child's Book of Country Stories** NY 1925   75 - 125
RS5090 **A Child's Book of Modern Stories** NY 1920   100 - 150
RS5100 **A Child's Book of Old Verses** NY 1910, DJ   300 - 500
    w/o DJ   150 - 250
RS5103 NY 1935   50 - 75
RS5110 **A Child's Book of Stories** NY 1911   125 - 175
RS5112 NY 1920   50 - 75
RS5120 **A Child's Garden of Verses** NY 1905   100 - 150
RS5130 **A Child's Prayer** Phil 1925   100 - 150
RS5140 **A Child's Stamp Book of Old Verses Pictured by Jessie Willcox Smith** NY 1915   75 - 125
RS5150 **The Children of Dickens** NY 1926, DJ   125 - 175
    w/o DJ   50 - 75
RS5152 NY 1933, DJ   75 - 125

    w/o DJ   40 - 60
RS5160 **The Chronicles of Rhoda** NY 1909   50 - 75
RS5170 **Dicken's Children** NY 1912   50 - 75
RS5180 **Dream Blocks** NY 1908   200 - 300
RS5190 **Evangeline: A Tale of Acadia** NY 1897   150 - 250
RS5200 **The Everyday Fairy Book** NY 1915   150 - 250
RS5202 NY 1921   125 - 200
RS5210 **The Five Senses** NY 1911   100 - 150
RS5220 **The Head of a Hundred** Bos 1897   50 - 75
RS5222 Bos 1900   50 - 75
RS5230 **Heidi** Phil 1922, DJ   150 - 225
    w/o DJ   50 - 75
RS5240 **In the Closed Room** NY 1904   100 - 150
RS5250 **The Jessie Willcox Smith Mother Goose** NY 1914 150 - 250
RS5260 **Kitchen Fun - A Cookbook for Children** Clev 1932 (cover illus)   40 - 60
RS5270 **A Little Child's Book of Stories** NY 1922   100 - 150
RS5280 **The Little Mother Goose** NY 1915   100 - 150
RS5282 NY 1918   75 - 125
RS5290 **Little Women** Bos 1915   75 - 125
RS5292 Bos 1928, DJ   50 - 75
    w/o DJ   30 - 50
RS5300 **Mistress Goodhope** Chi 1902   150 - 250
RS5310 **The Now-A-Days Fairy Book** NY 1911   175 - 250
RS5320 **An Old Fashioned Girl** Bos 1902   100 - 150
    Bos 1915   50 - 75
RS5330 **The Princess and the Goblin** Phil 1920   100 - 150
    Phil 1921   75 - 125
RS5340 **Rhymes of Real Children** NY 1903   175 - 250
RS5350 **The Seven Ages of Childhood** NY 1909   175 - 250
RS5360 **Sonny's Father** NY 1910   40 - 60
RS5370 **Tales and Sketches** Bos 1900 (1 b&w plate, vol 16 of complete writings of N. Hawthorne Old Manse ed) 30 - 50
RS5380 **Truth Dexter** Bos 1905   20 - 30
RS5390 **'Twas the Night Before Christmas** Bos 1912   50 - 75
RS5400 **A Very Little Child's Book of Stories** NY 1923 100 - 150
RS5410 **The Water-Babies** NY 1916   150 - 250
RS5413 Garden City 1937   50 - 75
RS5420 **The Way to Wonderland** Lon 1917   175 - 250
RS5421 NY 1917   175 - 250
RS5430 **When Christmas Comes Around** NY 1915   50 - 75
RS5440 **The Young Puritans** Bos 1899   50 - 75

Soyer, Raphael
RS6010 **Raphael Soyer** (Lloyd Goodrich) NY 1972, DJ   150 - 250

Strothman, F.
RS7010 **Over the Nonsense Road** (Lucille Gulliver) NY 1910 40 - 60

Stuart, Gilbert
RS7310 **Gilbert Stuart** (Lawrence Park) NY 1926, 4 vol   500 - 700
RS7320 **Gilbert Stuart's Portraits of George Washington**
(Mantle Fielding) Phil 1923, 350 cys   250 - 350

Szyk, Arthur
RS9510 **The New Order** NY 1941, DJ   100 - 150
RS9520 **The Rubaiyat of Omar Khayyam** NY 1946, slipcase 30 - 50

Tenggren, Gustaf
RT2010 **Dickey Byrd** (Woodruff) Springfield 1928, DJ   700 - 1000
    w/o DJ   250 - 350
RT2020 **The Good Dog Book** Bos 1924, DJ   75 - 125
RT2030 **Heidi** Bos 1923   50 - 75
RT2040 **Mother Goose** Bos 1940   75 - 125
RT2050 **The Red Fairy Book** Phil 1924   75 - 125
RT2060 **Stories of the Magic World** Springfield 1933   200 - 300
RT2070 **The Wonder Book and Tanglewood Tales**
Bos 1923, DJ   150 - 250

Thirty
RT3210 **Thirty Favorite Paintings** NY 1908, portfolio of
prints by Parrish, Remington, J.W. Smith, H.
Fisher, C. E. Christy, & others   75 - 125

Toulouse-Lautrec, Henri De
RT5300 **Henri de Toulouse-Lautrec: Dessins Estampes,**
Affiches (Maurice Joyant) Paris 1927, wrappers   300 - 500
RT5310 **Lautrec by Lautrec** (P. Huisman) NY 1964, DJ   75 - 125
RT5320 **Le Roi Chevalier** (Maurice Joyant) Paris 1909 2000 - 3000
RT5330 **Toulouse-Lautrec et Son Oeuvre** (M. G. Dortu)
NY 1971, 6 vol   800 - 1200
RT5340 **Toulouse-Lautrec Feuilles D'Etudes**
(J. P. Crespelle) Paris 1962, 600 cys   150   250
RT5350 **Toulouse-Lautrec His Complete Lithographs**
and Drypoints (Jean Adhemar) NY (1965), DJ   100 - 150

Tudor, Tasha
RT8510 **A is For Annabelle** NY 1954, DJ   100 - 150
RT8520 **Alexander the Gander** NY 1939, DJ   175 - 275
RT8530 **Becky's Birthday** NY 1960, DJ   50 - 75
RT8540 **A Child's Garden of Verses** NY 1947, DJ   100 - 150
    w/o DJ   40 - 60
RT8550 **The County Fair** NY 1940, DJ   150 - 250
    w/o DJ   50 - 100
RT8560 **Dorkas Porkus** Lon 1942, DJ   75 - 125
    w/o DJ   30 - 50
RT8570 **Fairy Tales** NY 1945, DJ   100 - 150
RT8580 **First Delights** NY 1966, DJ   50 - 75
RT8590 **Jackanapes** NY 1948, DJ   50 - 75
RT8600 **Linsey Woolsey** NY 1946, DJ   150 - 250
RT8610 **Little Women** NY 1969, DJ   100 - 150
RT8620 **Mother Goose** NY 1944, DJ   40 - 60
RT8630 **Pumpkin Moonshine** (1st book) NY 1938, DJ   350 - 500
    w/o DJ   125 - 175

RT8640 **The Real Diary of a Real Boy** Peterboro 1967, DJ 50 - 75
RT8650 **Snow Before Christmas** NY 1941, DJ   150 - 250
    w/o DJ   75 - 125
RT8660 **The White Goose** NY 1943, DJ   100 - 150
    w/o DJ   50 - 75
RT8662   later printings in DJ   30 - 50
RT8670 **Wings from the Wind** Phil 1964, DJ   50 - 75

Van Gogh, Vincent
RV1510 **The Complete Letters of...** Greenwich 1955, 3 vol 200 - 300
RV1512   NY 1958, 100 cys, leatherbound   400 - 600
RV1514   later editions   150 - 200
RV1520 **Van Gogh in Arles** (Ronald Pickvance) NY 1984, DJ 50 - 75
RV1530 **Vincent by Himself** (Bruce Bernard) NY 1985, DJ   50 - 75
RV1540 **Vincent Van Gogh: The Complete Works on**
Paper, Catalog Raisonné (J. B. De La Faille)
SF 1992, 2 vol, DJs   150 - 250
RV1550 **The Works of Vincent Van Gogh**
(J. B. De La Faille) NY 1970, DJ   75 - 125

Vasarely, Victor
RV2510 **Vasarely** Paris 1965, DJ, w/inserted portfolio
of prints   100 - 150

Vassos, John
RV3010 **Ballad of Reading Gaol** NY 1938, DJ   75 - 125
    w/o DJ   30 - 50
RV3020 **Salome** NY 1927, DJ   75 - 125

Verve
    This art magazine was published between 1937 and 1960 by Teriade, a French art publisher. Simultaneously published in New York and Paris with English and French texts, it was devoted to individual contemporary artists and medieval illuminated manuscripts. Among the artists illustrating cover and contents were Picasso, Matisse, Chagall, Bonnard and Braque. Prices are for magazines in very good to fine condition.
RV5001 **#1**, 1937, cover by Matisse   250 - 400
RV5002 **#2**, 1938, cover by Braque   200 - 300
RV5003 **#3**, 1938, cover by Bonnard   200 - 300
RV5004 **#4**, 1938, cover by Rouault   200 - 300
RV5005 **#5/6**, 1939, cover by Maillol   125 - 200

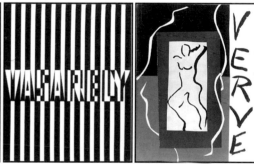

	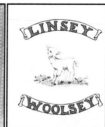	
RT8670	RV2510	RV5001

RT8520	RT8550	RT8560	RT8560 (w/o DJ)	RT8600	RT8630	RT8650

  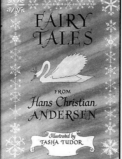   

RT8530	RT8540	RT8570	RT8580	RT8590	RT8610

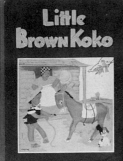

| RV5040 | RV5040 (cover of issue #2) | RW1010 | RW1550 | RW1700 | RW4010 |

RV5007	#7, 1940, illuminated manuscripts	75 - 125
RV5008	#8, 1940, cover by Matisse	200 - 300
RV5009	#9, 1943, illuminated manuscripts	75 - 125
RV5010	#10, 1943, illuminated manuscripts	75 - 125
RV5011	#11, 1945, illuminated manuscripts	75 - 125
RV5012	#12, 1945, illuminated manuscripts	75 - 125
RV5013	#13, 1945, cover by Matisse	150 - 250
RV5014	#14/15, 1946, illuminated manuscripts	75 - 125
RV5016	#16, 1946, illuminated manuscripts	75 - 125
RV5017	#17/18, 1947, cover by Bonnard	300 - 500
RV5019	#19/20, 1948, cover by Picasso	300 - 500
RV5021	#21/22, 1948, cover by Matisse	300 - 500
RV5023	#23, 1949, cover by Matisse	200 - 350
RV5024	#24, 1950, cover by Chagall	200 - 300
RV5025	#25/26, 1951, cover by Picasso	300 - 500
RV5027	#27/28, 1952, cover by Braque	300 - 500
RV5029	#29/30, 1954, cover by Picasso	250 - 350
RV5031	#31/32, 1955, cover by Braque	300 - 500
RV5033	#33/34, 1956, cover by Chagall	4000 - 6000
RV5035	#35/36, 1958, cover by Matisse	300 - 500
RV5037	#37/38, 1960, cover by Chagall	4000 - 6000
RV5040	#2, 3, 4: 3 issues specially bound by Teriade, NY (1930s)	800 - 1200

Wagstaff, Dorothy
RW1010 **Stories of Little Brown Koko** (Blanche Hunt)
Chi 1940, DJ ..... 50 - 75
w/o DJ ..... 30 - 50

Wain, Louis
RW1210 **The Cat Scouts** Lon 1912 ..... 200 - 300
RW1220 **Cats at School** Lon 1911 ..... 200 - 300
RW1230 **Claws and Paws** Lon 1904 ..... 200 - 300

Ward, Lynd
RW1510 **The Cat Who Went to Heaven** NY 1931 ..... 50 - 75
RW1520 **God's Man** NY 1929, DJ ..... 75 - 125
RW1530 **Impassioned Clay** Lon 1931, DJ ..... 75 - 125
RW1540 **Johnny Tremain** Bos 1943, DJ ..... 40 - 60
RW1550 **Vertigo** NY 1937, DJ ..... 100 - 150

Warhol, Andy
RW1700 **A** NY 1968 (Grove Press Pocketbook 1st printing) ..... 75 - 125
RW1710 **Andy Warhol** (John Coplans) NY ..... 50 - 75
RW1720 **Andy Warhol** Malmö, Sweden, 1968 (catalog) ..... 100 - 150
RW1730 **Andy Warhol** (Rainer Crone) NY 1970 ..... 400 - 600
RW1740 **Andy Warhol Das Graphische Werk 1962-1980**
(Hermann Wunsche) wrappers ..... 100 - 150
RW1750 **Andy Warhol's Index Book** NY 1967, 3-D plastic
mounted on cover, 7 pop-ups, phonograph record,
sheet of labels, balloon ..... 300 - 500
signed ..... 700 - 1000
RW1760 **A Gold Book** NY 1957, 100 cys ..... 3000 - 5000
RW1770 **Holy Cats** ("Andy Warhol's Mother") (1954),
20 mounted prints ..... 2000 - 3000
RW1780 **Portraits of the 70's** (Robert Rosennblum)
NY 1979, 200 cys, signed, slipcase ..... 250 - 350
RW1790 **Vanishing Animals** (Kurt Benirischke) NY
1986, DJ ..... 700 - 1000
RW1800 **Wild Raspberries** NY 1959 ..... 5000 - 7000

Whistler, James McNeil
RW2900 **The Etched Work of Whistler** (Campbell
Dodgson) NY 1910, 400 cys, 3 portfolios ..... 1500 - 2500
RW2910 **The Etchings of...** (Campbell Dodgson) Lon 1922 ..... 200 - 300
RW2920 **James McNeil Whistler** (Denys Sutton) Lon
1966, DJ ..... 75 - 125

RW2930 **The Lithographs by...** (Thomas Way) NY 1914,
400 cys ..... 500 - 700

Williams, Garth
RW4010 **Miss Bianca a Fantasy** Lon 1962, DJ ..... 40 - 60

Winter, Milo
RW4410 **The Aesop for Children** Chi 1919 ..... 100 - 150

Wright, Alan
RW5510 **Professor Philanderpan** Lon 1904 ..... 50 - 75

Wright, Frank Lloyd
RW5710 **An American Architecture** NY 1955, DJ ..... 100 - 150
RW5720 **Architecture and Modern Life** NY 1937, DJ ..... 200 - 300
RW5730 **An Autobiography** NY 1932, DJ ..... 300 - 500
RW5740 **Buildings, Plans and Designs** NY 1963, portfolio ..... 700 - 1000
RW5750 **Drawings for a Living Architecture**
NY 1959, DJ ..... 1000 - 1500
RW5760 **The Drawings of Frank Lloyd Wright** NY 1962, DJ ..... 75 - 125
RW5770 **Frank Lloyd Wright** NY 1943, DJ ..... 100 - 150
RW5780 **The Future of Architecture** NY 1953, DJ ..... 100 - 150
RW5790 **Genius and Mobocracy** NY 1949, DJ ..... 75 - 125
RW5800 **In the Nature of Materials** NY 1942, DJ ..... 100 - 150
RW5810 **The Japanese Print** Chi 1912, orange
wrappers ..... 2000 - 3000
RW5820 **The Life-Work of the American Architect: Frank
Lloyd Wright** Santpoort, Holland 1925 ..... 700 - 1000
RW5830 **The Living City** NY 1958, DJ ..... 100 - 150
RW5840 **Modern Architecture** Princeton 1931 ..... 400 - 500
RW5850 **The Natural House** NY 1954, DJ ..... 300 - 500
RW5860 **Studies and Executed Buildings** Berlin 1910,
2 vol ..... 3000 - 5000
RW5870 **A Testament** NY 1957, DJ ..... 100 - 150
RW5880 **The Work of Frank Lloyd Wright** NY 1965, slipcase ..... 250 - 350
RW5890 **Writings and Buildings** NY 1960, DJ ..... 50 - 75

Wyeth, Andrew
RW7010 **Andrew Wyeth** (Richard Meryman) Bos 1968, DJ ..... 200 - 300
RW7020 **Christina's World** Bos 1982, DJ ..... 75 - 125
RW7030 **Four Seasons** NY 1972, w/separate portfolio
of prints ..... 150 - 250
RW7040 **Wyeth at Kuerners** (Betsy James Wyeth) Bos
1976, DJ ..... 75 - 125

Wyeth, N. C. (Newell Convers)
Many of Wyeth's illustrated books were published by Charles
Scribners & Sons as part of the "Scribner's Illustrated Classics"
series. He also did magazine illustrating and designed many dust
jackets.
RW7310 **Adventures of Tom Sawyer** Phil 1931, DJ
(DJ & paste-on by Wyeth) ..... 50 - 75
RW7320 **Anthony Adverse** (Allen) NY 1934, 2 vol, slipcase ..... 75 - 125
RW7330 **Arizona Nights** NY 1907 ..... 50 - 75
RW7340 **Bar 20** NY 1907 ..... 50 - 75
RW7350 **Beth Norvell** (Randall Parrish) Chi 1907 ..... 30 - 50
RW7360 **The Black Arrow** NY 1916, DJ ..... 100 - 150
w/o DJ ..... 50 - 75
RW7362 NY 1924, DJ ..... 75 - 125
RW7370 **Blair's Attic** NY 1929, DJ ..... 50 - 75
w/o DJ ..... 20 - 30
RW7380 **The Bounty Trilogy** Bos 1940, DJ ..... 50 - 75
RW7390 **The Boy's King Arthur** NY 1917, DJ ..... 100 - 150
w/o DJ ..... 50 - 75
RW7392 NY 1924, DJ ..... 75 - 125
RW7400 **Boys of St. Timothy's** NY 1904 ..... 50 - 75
RW7410 **Captain Blood** Bos 1922, DJ ..... 50 - 75
RW7420 **Captain Horatio Hornblower** Bos 1939, DJ ..... 75 - 125
w/o DJ ..... 30 - 50

RW7430	**Cease Firing** Bos 1912, DJ, 500 cys, uncut	250 - 350
RW7431	Bos 1912, DJ (1st trade ed)	75 - 125
	w/o DJ	30 - 50
RW7440	**The Challenge** Ind 1906	40 - 60
RW7450	**The Children's Longfellow** Bos 1908	50 - 75
RW7460	**The Courtship of Miles Standish** NY 1920, DJ	200 - 300
	w/o DJ	75 - 125
RW7470	**David Balfour** NY 1924, DJ	200 - 300
	w/o DJ	100 - 150
RW7472	NY 1933, DJ	75 - 125
	w/o DJ	30 - 50
RW7480	**The Deerslayer** NY 1925, DJ, pict cl	125 - 175
	w/o DJ	50 - 75
RW7485	**Discovery** Bos 1937	30 - 50
RW7490	**Drums** NY 1928, DJ	125 - 200
	w/o DJ	50 - 75
RW7491	NY 1928, 525 cys, box	300 - 500
RW7500	**The Great West** NY 1916	75 - 125
RW7510	**The Guardian** Bos 1912 (frontis by Wyeth)	40 - 60
RW7520	**Hans Brinker or The Silver Skates** Garden City 1932, DJ	50 - 75
	w/o DJ	25 - 35
RW7530	**Jingle Bob** NY 1930, DJ	125 - 175
	w/o DJ	50 - 75
RW7540	**The Journals of Bronson Alcott** Bos 1938, DJ	75 - 125
	w/o DJ	30 - 50
RW7550	**Kidnapped** NY 1913, DJ	100 - 150
	w/o DJ	50 - 75
RW7552	NY 1933, DJ	75 - 125
	w/o DJ	25 - 35
RW7560	**Langford of the Three Bars** Chi 1907	50 - 75
RW7570	**The Last of the Mohicans** (Cooper) NY 1919, DJ	125 - 200
	w/o DJ	50 - 75
RW7580	**Legends of Charlemagne** NY 1924, DJ	200 - 300
	w/o DJ	75 - 125
RW7590	**Letters of a Woman Homesteader** NY 1914, DJ	100 - 150
	w/o DJ	40 - 60
RW7600	**Little Shepherd of Kingdom Come** NY 1931, DJ	100 - 150
	w/o DJ	75 - 125
RW7601	NY 1931, DJ, pict cl	125 - 175
	w/o DJ	75 - 125
RW7610	**The Long Roll** NY 1911, DJ	150 - 225
	w/o DJ	75 - 125
RW7620	**Men of Concord** NY 1936, DJ, box	150 - 250
	w/DJ only	75 - 125
	w/o DJ or box	50 - 75
RW7630	**Michael Strogoff** NY 1927, DJ	150 - 250
	w/o DJ	75 - 125

RW7640	**The Militants** NY 1907	50 - 75
RW7650	**The Mysterious Island** NY 1918, DJ	125 - 175
	w/o DJ	50 - 75
RW7660	**The Mysterious Stranger** (Twain) NY 1916, DJ	200 - 300
	w/o DJ	100 - 150
RW7670	**Nan of Music Mountain** NY 1916, DJ	100 - 150
	w/o DJ	25 - 35
RW7680	**The Odyssey of Homer** NY 1929, 550 cys, cellophane DJ, box	400 - 600
RW7681	NY 1929, cellophane DJ, slipcase	250 - 350
RW7682	NY 1929, DJ, pict cl (1st trade ed)	100 - 150
	w/o DJ	50 - 75
RW7690	**The Oregon Trail** (Parkman) Bos 1925, 975 cys, slipcase (Wyeth-Remington ed)	400 - 600
RW7691	Bos 1925, DJ (1st trade ed)	100 - 150
	w/o DJ	30 - 50
RW7700	**The Parables of Jesus** (S. Parkes Cadman) Phil 1931, DJ, pict cl	700 - 1000
	w/o DJ	300 - 500
RW7710	**The Pike County Ballads** NY 1912, w/box	175 - 250
	w/o box	100 - 150
RW7720	**Poems of American Patriotism** NY 1922, DJ	125 - 175
	w/o DJ	75 - 125
RW7730	**Ramona** Bos 1939, DJ	75 - 125
	w/o DJ	30 - 50
RW7740	**The Red Keep** Bos 1938, DJ	125 - 200
	w/o DJ	75 - 125
RW7750	**Rip Van Winkle** Phil 1931, DJ	150 - 250
	w/o DJ	75 - 125
RW7760	**The Riverman** NY 1908, pict cl	50 - 75
RW7770	**Robin Hood** Phil 1917, DJ	150 - 250
	w/o DJ	50 - 75

RW4410 (w/o DJ)

RW7320 (slipcase and cover)

RW7350

RW7390

RW7460 (w/o DJ)

RW7480

RW7490 (w/o DJ)

RW7570 (w/o DJ)

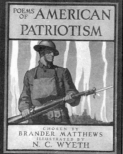

RW7630 (w/o DJ)

RW7691 (w/o DJ)

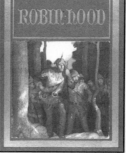

RW7720 (w/o DJ)

RW7770 (w/o DJ)

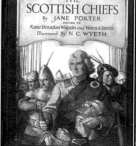

RW7810 (w/o DJ)

RW7880 (w/o DJ)

RW7780	**Robinson Crusoe** NY 1920, DJ	150 - 225
	w/o DJ	75 - 125
RW7790	**Sally Castleton the Southerner** Phil 1913	50 - 75
RW7800	**The Sampo** NY 1912	40 - 60
RW7810	**The Scottish Chiefs** NY 1921, DJ, pict cl	125 - 200
	w/o DJ	50 - 75
RW7820	**The Song of Hiawatha** Lon 1911 (w/other illus)	50 - 75
RW7830	**Susanna & Sue** NY 1909, DJ	100 - 150
	w/o DJ	25 - 35
RW7840	**The Throwback** NY 1906	40 - 60
RW7850	**Treasure Island** NY 1911, DJ, pict cl	175 - 250
	w/o DJ	75 - 125
RW7852	NY 1921, DJ	100 - 150
	w/o DJ	50 - 75
RW7860	**Trending into Maine** Bos 1938, 1075 cys, slipcase	300 - 500
RW7861	Bos 1938, DJ (1st trade ed)	75 - 125
RW7870	**War** Ind 1913, DJ	75 - 125
RW7880	**Westward Ho!** (Kingsley) NY 1920, DJ, pict cl	200 - 300
	w/o DJ	75 - 125
RW7890	**Whispering Smith** NY 1906, DJ	100 - 150
	w/o DJ	30 - 50
RW7900	**The White Company** NY 1922, DJ, pict cl	200 - 300
	w/o DJ	75 - 125
RW7910	**The Witch** Bos 1914, DJ	75 - 125
	w/o DJ	30 - 50
RW7920	**The Yearling** (M. K. Rawlings) NY 1939, DJ	75 - 125
	w/o DJ	30 - 50

AVIATION

During the 19th century, aviation was confined to non-rigid inflatable balloons. Although a few books were published about the adventures of balloonists like the Montgolfier Brothers (1783 flight), Henri Giffard (1852 Paris flight) and Civil War observation balloonists, most aviation books were technical in nature. They offered little more than discussions about the theories of flight, as in *Bird Flight as The Basis of Aviation* by Otto Lilienthal (1889). Even the Wright Brothers' early books were purely technical pamphlets about machine-powered gliders. It was not until World War I that pilots began to write about their adventures. Among better known titles are Lt. Eddie Rickenbacker's *Fighting The Flying Circus* (1919) and *Contact!* by Charles Codman (1937). Personal narratives were commonly written by American, British, German, Canadian and Australian combat pilots.

Exciting novels with aviation themes were published during the early 1900s. William Faulkner's *Pylon* (1935) about air racing or Rudyard Kipling's *With The Night Mail* (1909) on airships crossing the Atlantic are two good examples. Many novels were written by combat pilots; *War Birds* (1926) was authored by U.S. pilot Elliott Springs. Juvenile novels abounded with colorful covers depicting young men hanging from flimsy craft tossing bombs at ships and shooting at German aces.

After World War I, many flyers turned to exploration. *Our Polar Flight* (1925) describes the Amundsen-Ellsworth expedition of 1925 to the North Pole in two Dornier-Wal flying boats. *Discovery* (1935), written by Admiral Richard Byrd, recounts his second Antarctic expedition in 1933 employing a Curtiss-Wright Condor powered by two Wright-Cyclone engines.

Trans-Atlantic, trans-Pacific, and around-the-world flights were first made in the 1920s and 1930s. Charles Lindbergh piloted the first solo flight across the Atlantic in the Wright-Whirlwind-powered Spirit of St. Louis. He wrote several books relating his adventure and numerous volumes were published about this famous flyer.

The most valuable aviation books are the early technical reports, aviation annuals, World War I and II aviation unit histories, aircraft histories, and first editions in dust jacket written by great pilots. Reports on aviation experiments and designs by the Wright Brothers, James Means, Charles Burgess, Robert Goddard, Gustave Eiffel and others may be worth one hundred to several thousand dollars. Initial issues of the aviation annuals *All the Worlds Airships*, first published in 1907, and *Aircraft Annual*, which first appeared in 1919 may bring seventy-five

to several hundred dollars. Several World War I Air Force unit histories have been published; *The Lafayette Flying Corps* (1920) by James Norman Hall is worth $1500. World War II unit histories are more numerous. Some were privately printed and a large number were published by the U.S. Air Force. These can be worth up to several hundred dollars. A good example is *History of the 64th Fighter Wing 1942-1945* (1945) by Harlan Campbell ($500). Early aviation histories are also rare and valuable. These include *New England Aviators 1914-1918* (1919) by Lawrence Lowell ($600), *The World in the Air* (1930, 500 sets) by Francis Trevelyan Miller ($800), *Fighting the Flying Circus* (1919) by Eddie Rickenbacker ($150 in jacket) and *The Red Battle Flyer* (1918) by the German ace Captain Manfred Von Richthofen ($250 in jacket). Of course, any book autographed by a flyer is worth more. Orville and Wilbur Wright (at least $1000), American aviatrix Amelia Earhart (at least $200) and test pilot General Chuck Yeager (at least $30) show how much value a signature can add.

Count Zeppelin, who had experience during the Civil War using observation balloons, had built a giant, cigar-shaped airship. The first flight of the 420-foot long craft was in 1900. Since then, collectors have avidly bought photos, stamps, sheet music, prints, books and anything else pertaining to giant airships. One of the most common books, *The Story of the Airship* by Hugh Allen (1931), is still worth $35. Books about the Navy dirigibles Akron and Shenandoah, the Graf-Zeppelin and the infamous Hindenburg disaster are highly collectible.

Books on specific aircraft like the World War I British Sopwith Camel and German Fokkers, Igor Sikorsky's helicopter, World War II fighters and bombers (including weaponry and camouflage markings), jet aircraft and commercial airliners have all been published. These also have a strong following among aviation collectors.

For most pre-1920 aviation books, dust jackets are so rare collectors usually are satisfied to have a copy without them. A jacketless book's value should not be less than 50% to 75% of the value in jacket. The exceptions are very common titles from the early 1900s in which the presence of a jacket doesn't make a lot of difference. Juvenile aviation novels from around the turn of the century are usually not worth more than $10-15 without a jacket. With a jacket these books may be worth an extra $10-15 at most. Many technical books and annuals never had jackets. Instruction manuals for specific engines and planes were normally jacketless.

One field of aviation-book collecting not heavily covered in this guide is the numerous catalogs and brochures published by aviation companies. Obviously, the very early catalogs published by the Wright Aircraft Co. or The Curtiss Aircraft Company are exceedingly rare and may be worth several hundred dollars. But later catalogs by small private aviation firms may be worth only a few dollars.

Many of the fiction and non-fiction titles of the 1920s-1940s were reprinted in later editions by Grosset & Dunlap and A.L. Burt. Books by these publishers are still collectible but not worth nearly as much as the original publications.

The listings are alphabetical by author or editor. See specific listings for the U.S. Air Force, *Jane's All the Worlds Airships*, *Aviation Annual* and aviation company names.

Abbot, C. G.
AV0400	**The 1914 Tests of the Langley "Aerodrome"** Wash 1942, pub #3699, wrappers	75 - 125

Abbot, Willis J.
AV0420	**Aircraft and Submarines** NY 1918, DJ	75 - 125
	w/o DJ	50 - 75

Ackworth, Marion
AV0440	**The Great Delusion: A Study of Aircraft in Peace and War** NY 1927	40 - 60

Aircraft Annual (1st edited by Howard Mingos)
AV0459	New York (1919 to present) 1919	100 - 150
AV0460	1920-1930	75 - 125

AV0471	1931-1945, DJ	50 - 75
AV0486	1946-1952, DJ	30 - 50
AV0493	later editions, DJ	20 - 40
	later editions, w/o DJ	15 - 30

Aircraft in Profile
AV0520	Garden City 1965-1975, 14 vol, DJs	300 - 500
	each vol	30 - 50

Aircraft of the Fighting Powers
AV0540	Leicester 1941-1944, 5 vol	200 - 300
	each vol	40 - 60

Alexander, Jean
AV0560	Russian Aircraft Since 1940 Lon 1975, DJ	50 - 75

Allen, Hugh
AV0580	The Story of the Airship Akron 1931	25 - 35

Allen, Richard
AV0600	Revolution in the Sky Brattleboro 1967, DJ	50 - 75

Amundsen Roald
AV0620	First Crossing of the Polar Sea NY 1927, DJ	125 - 250
AV0625	My Life as an Explorer Garden City 1928, DJ	75 - 125
AV0630	The Northwest Passage Lon 1908, 2 vol	300 - 500
AV0635	Our Polar Flight NY 1925, DJ	125 - 250
AV0640	The South Pole NY 1913, 2 vol	300 - 500

Andree, S. A.
AV0660	Andree's Story: The Complete Record of His Polar Flight 1897 NY 1930, DJ	30 - 50

Andrews, Charles
AV0680	Vickers Aircraft Since 1908 Lon 1969, DJ	50 - 75

Andrews, Frank A.
AV0700	Dirigible NY 1931, DJ (photoplay)	30 - 50

Angle, Glenn D.
AV0720	Airplane Engine Encyclopedia Dayton 1921	50 - 75

Archibald, Norman
AV0741	Heaven High - Hell Deep 1917-1918 NY 1935, DJ, 1st state w/paper lbl on sp	100 - 150
AV0742	2nd state w/o lbl	75 - 125

Arnold, Henry H. (Major General H. H.)
AV0760	Global Mission NY 1949, DJ	30 - 50
AV0765	Winged Warfare NY 1941, DJ	40 - 60

Arthur, Reginald
AV0780	Contact! Careers of U.S. Naval Aviators Wash 1967	100 - 150

Babbitt, George F.
AV0800	Norman Prince Bos 1917, DJ	200 - 300

Babington-Smith, Constance
AV0820	Air Spy NY 1957, DJ	30 - 50

Bacon, Gertrude
AV0840	The Record of an Aeronaut Lon 1907	100 - 150

Bacon, J. M.
AV0860	The Dominion of the Air Phil 1903	125 - 200

Baldridge, C. Leroy
AV0880	"I Was There" With the Yanks on the Western Front 1917-1919 NY 1919, DJ	100 - 150

Barbas, Bernard
AV0900	Planes of Luftwaffe Aces Melbourne 1985, 2 vol	75 - 125

Barber, H.
AV0920	The Aeroplane Speaks NY 1917	50 - 75

Baring, Maurice
AV0940	R.F.C. H.Q. 1914-1918 Lon 1920, DJ	100 - 150

Barnes, Christopher H.
AV0960	Bristol Aircraft Since 1910 Lon 1964, DJ	50 - 75
AV0965	Shorts Aircraft Since 1900 Lon 1967, DJ	50 - 75

Barnwell, F. S. and W. H. Sayers
AV0980	Aeroplane Design: And a Simple Explanation of Inherent Stability NY 1917	100 - 150

Baroni, George (editor)
AV1000	The Pyramiders 1980	50 - 75

Bartlett, Robert M.
AV1020	Sky Pioneer: The Story of Igor I. Sikorsky NY 1947, DJ	30 - 50

Batten, Jean
AV1040	My Life Lon 1939, DJ	100 - 150

Beamish, Richard J.
AV1060	The Boy's Story of Lindbergh the Lone Eagle Chi 1928, DJ	50 - 75
	w/o DJ	20 - 30

Beaubois, Henry
AV1080	Airships: Yesterday, Today and Tomorrow NY 1976, DJ	75 - 125

Beck, Henry
AV1100	Bridge Busters Clev 1946	200 - 300

Bedell, Fredrick
AV1120	The Airplane NY 1924	50 - 75

Bellah, James Warner
AV1140	Gods of Yesterday NY 1928, DJ	150 - 250
	w/o DJ	75 - 125

Bethuys, G. (Georges Espittallier)
AV1160	Les Aerostiers Militaries Paris 1889	200 - 300

Biddle, Major Charles J.
AV1180	The Way of the Eagle NY 1919, DJ	100 - 150
	w/o DJ	50 - 75

Bingham, Hiram
AV1200	An Explorer in the Air Service New Haven 1920	125 - 250

Bishop, Major William A.
AV1220	Winged Peace NY 1944, DJ	30 - 50
AV1225	Winged Warfare Lon 1918, DJ	200 - 300
AV1226	NY 1918, DJ	100 - 150

Blair, Omar D.
AV1260	The Tuskegee Experience Dallas 1982	75 - 125

Bludworth, Francis T.
AV1280	The Battle of Eastleigh, England USNAF 1918 NY 1919	200 - 300

Blue, Allan G.
AV1300	The B-24 Liberator NY 1975, DJ	30 - 50

Boelcke, Oswald
AV1320	An Aviator's Field Book NY 1917	150 - 250

Boggs, Charles
AV1340	Marine Aviation in the Philippines Wash 1951	50 - 75

AV0400

AV0460

AV1060

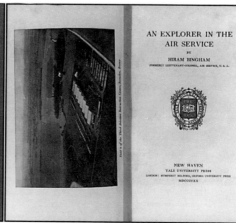

AV1200 (frontispiece and title page

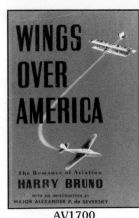
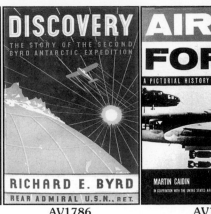

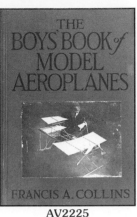

AV1700	AV1786	AV1860	AV1865	AV2225

Bölcke, Oswald
AV1360 An Aviator's Field Book NY 1917, DJ   150 - 250

Bond, R. Russell
AV1380 Inventions of the Great War NY 1919, DJ   50 - 75

Bordeaux, Henry
AV1400 Georges Guynemer: Knight of the Air
         New Haven 1918   75 - 125

Bott, Alan
AV1420 An Airman's Outings Lon 1917, DJ   150 - 250
         w/o DJ   75 - 125
AV1425 Cavalry of the Clouds Garden City 1918, DJ   100 - 150
AV1430 Eastern Nights and Flights Garden City 1919, DJ 100 - 150
         w/o DJ   50 - 75

Bowen, Robert Sidney
AV1460 They Flew to Fame Racine 1963   30 - 50

Bowers, Peter M.
AV1480 Boeing Aircraft Since 1916 Lon 1966, DJ   50 - 75

Bowman, Martin
AV1500 Fields of Little America Cambridge 1983, DJ   50 - 75

Bowyer, Michael
AV1520 Fighting Colours: RAF Fighter Camouflage and
         Markings 1937-1969 Lon 1969, DJ   40 - 60

Boyne, Walter J.
AV1540 The Aircraft Treasures of Silver Hill NY 1983, DJ 20 - 30

Brandly, Raymond
AV1560 Waco Airplanes 1979, wrappers   40 - 60

Brimm, Daniel
AV1600 Aircraft Engine Maintenance NY 1939   20 - 30

Brogden, Stanley
AV1620 The History of Australian Aviation Melbourne
         1960, DJ   30 - 50

Brown, Don L.
AV1640 Miles Aircraft Since 1925 Lon 1970, DJ   50 - 75

Brown, K. S.
AV1660 United States Army and Air Force Fighters
         1916-1961 Letchworth 1961, DJ   50 - 75

Bruce, J. M. (John M.)
AV1680 British Aero Planes 1914-18 Lon 1969, DJ   100 - 150
AV1685 War Planes of the First World War: Fighters
         Lon 1965-1972, 5 vol, DJs   75 - 125
         each vol   20 - 30

Bruno, Harry
AV1700 Wings Over America NY 1942, DJ   30 - 50

Buchanan, A. R. (editor)
AV1720 The Navy's Air War NY 1946, DJ   50 - 75

Burgess, Charles P.
AV1740 Airship Design NY 1927   75 - 125

Burrows, William E.
AV1760 Richthofen: A True History of the Red Baron
         Lon 1970, DJ   30 - 50

Byrd, Richard E. (Admiral)
AV1780 Alone NY 1938, DJ   50 - 75
AV1785 Discovery NY 1935, 500 cys   200 - 300
AV1786 NY 1935, DJ (1st trade ed)   50 - 75
AV1790 Little America NY 1930, DJ   50 - 75
AV1795 Skyward NY 1928, DJ, w/frontis por   75 - 125

Bytebier, Hugo T.
AV1820 The Curtiss D-12 Aero Engine Wash 1972,
         wrappers   30 - 50

Cable, Boyd
AV1840 Air Men O'War Lon 1918, DJ   100 - 150

Caidin, Martin
AV1860 Air Force NY 1957, DJ   30 - 50
AV1865 Rockets and Missiles: Past and Future
         NY 1954, DJ   20 - 30

Campbell, Captain George F.
AV1880 A Soldier of the Sky Chi 1918, DJ   200 - 300

Campbell, Harlan S.
AV1900 History of the 64th Fighter Wing 1942-1945
         Tubingen 1945, DJ   300 - 500

Cardigan, Lord
AV1920 Amateur Pilot Lon 1933, DJ   50 - 75

Casey, Louis S.
AV1940 The First Nonstop Coast-to-Coast Flight
         Wash 1964, wrappers   30 - 50

Cassidy, Carl
AV1960 A History of the 775th Bombardment Squadron
         Iowa 1982, 300 cys   100 - 150

Chamberlain, Clarence D.
AV1980 Record Flights Phil 1928, DJ   200 - 300

Chandler, Charles
AV2000 How Our Army Grew Wings: Airmen and
         Aircraft Before 1914 NY 1943, DJ   50 - 75

Chapman, Victor
AV2020 Victor Chapman's Letters From France NY 1917 50 - 75

Charnley, Mitchell V.
AV2040 The Boy's Life of the Wright Brothers NY 1928 30 - 50

Chennault, Anna
AV2060 Chennault and the Flying Tigers NY 1963, DJ   30 - 50

Christienne, Charles
AV2080 A History of French Military Aviation Wash
         1986, DJ   50 - 75

Clarke, Covington
AV2100 Aces Up Chi 1929, DJ   50 - 75

Cobb, Frank
AV2120 Battling the Clouds Chi 1927, DJ   30 - 50

Cobham, Alan
AV2140 Twenty Thousand Miles in a Flying Boat
         Lon 1930, DJ   40 - 60

Cobianchi, Mario
AV2160 Pionieri Dell 'Aviazione in Italia Rome 1943,
         wrappers   100 - 150

Codman, Charles
AV2180 Contact Bos 1937, DJ   40 - 60

Collins, A. Frederick
AV2200 Aviation and All About It NY 1929, DJ   50 - 75
AV2205 How to Fly NY 1917, DJ   50 - 75

Collins, Francis A.
AV2220 The Air Man NY 1917, DJ   75 - 125
AV2225 The Boys' Book of Model Aeroplanes NY 1910   50 - 75

Collins, Jimmy
AV2240 Test Pilot Garden City 1935, DJ   40 - 60

Combs, Harry
AV2250 Kill Devil Hill Bos 1979, DJ   20 - 30

"Contact" (Captain Alan Bott)
AV2260 An Airman's Outings Edinburgh 1917, DJ   100 - 150
    w/o DJ   30 - 50
AV2265 Cavalry of the Clouds Garden City 1918, DJ   75 - 125
    w/o DJ   30 - 50

Coppens De Houthulst, Willy
AV2280 Days on the Wing Lon, nd (1920s)   75 - 125

Corbett-Smith, A.
AV2300 Riders of the Air Lon 1923   100 - 150

Corrigan, Douglas ("Wrong Way")
AV2320 That's My Story NY 1938, DJ   50 - 75

Coxwell, Henry
AV2340 My Life and Balloon Experiences Lon 1887   125 - 200

Craig, Berry
AV2360 Marine Corps Aviation Paducah 1989, 1000 cys   50 - 75

Crossfield, A. Scott
AV2380 Always Another Dawn: The Story of a Rocket
    Test Pilot Clev 1960, DJ   50 - 75

Cuneo, John
AV2400 Winged Mars Harrisburg 1942, 2 vol   100 - 150

Curry, Manfred
AV2420 Beauty of Flight NY, nd (1930s), DJ   75 - 125

Curtiss, Glen & Curtiss Aeroplane and Motor Corp.
AV2440 The Curtiss Aviation Book NY 1912   125 - 200
AV2445 The Curtiss Standard JN4-D Military Tractor
    Handbook Buffalo 1918 (aviation engine)   300 - 500

David, Evan John
AV2460 Aircraft NY 1919, DJ   50 - 75

Davis, W. Jefferson
AV2480 The World's Wings NY 1927   75 - 125

Davy, M. J. B.
AV2500 Handbook of the Collections Illustrating
    Aeronautics Lon 1934   40 - 60

De Chant, John A.
AV2520 Devilbirds NY 1947, DJ   50 - 75

De Wet, Oloff
AV2540 The Patrol is Ended NY 1938, DJ   50 - 75

DeHan, Richard
AV2560 That Which Hath Wings NY 1918   30 - 50

Dichman, Ernest W.
AV2580 This Aviation Business NY 1929, DJ   100 - 150

Dickey, Philip
AV2600 The Liberty Engine 1918-1942 Wash 1968   30 - 50

Dixie, Lt. Commander A. E.
AV2620 Air Navigation For Flight Officers NY 1917   100 - 150
AV2621 NY 1917, later issues w/all-black illus   50 - 75

Donahue, Arthur
AV2640 Tally-Ho! Yankee in a Spitfire NY 1941, DJ   40 - 60

Dorman, Geoffrey
AV2660 Fifty Years Fly Past From Wright Brothers to
    Comet Lon 1951, DJ   40 - 60

Duke, Neville
AV2680 Neville Duke's Book of Flying Lon 1954, DJ   40 - 60
AV2685 "Sound Barrier", The Story of High-Speed Flight
    NY 1955, DJ   40 - 60

DuPre, Flint O.
AV2700 U.S. Air Force Biographical Dictionary
    NY 1965, DJ   50 - 75

Duval, G. R.
AV2720 British Flying-Boats and Amphibians 1909-1952
    Lon 1966, DJ   50 - 75

Dyke, A. L.
AV2740 Dyke's Aircraft Engine Instructor Chi 1929   50 - 75

Earhart, Amelia
AV2760 20 Hours 40 Minutes NY 1928, DJ   75 - 125
    signed cy   200 - 300
AV2765 The Fun of It NY 1932, DJ   50 - 75
AV2770 Last Flight NY 1937, DJ   50 - 75

Eiffel, Alexandre Gustave
AV2800 Recherches Experimentales Sur La Resistance
    De L'Air Paris 1907   400 - 600

Ellington - 1918
AV2820 Houston 1918   200 - 300

Ellis, Frank H.
AV2840 Canada's Flying Heritage Toronto 1954, DJ   50 - 75

Emde, Heiner
AV2860 Conquerors of the Air NY 1968, DJ   125 - 200

Every, Dale
AV2880 Charles Lindbergh: His Life NY 1927, DJ   50 - 75
    w/o DJ   30 - 50

Fahey, James
AV2900 U.S. Army Aircraft 1908-1946 NY 1946, wrappers 20 - 30

Fallon, Capt. David
AV2920 The Big Flight NY 1918, DJ   100 - 150

Farre, Lt. Henry
AV2940 Sky Fighters of France Bos 1919   300 - 500

Ferris, Richard
AV2960 How It Flies NY 1910   150 - 250

Fife, George Buchanan
AV2980 Lindbergh the Lone Eagle NY 1930s (A.L.
    Burt reprint), red cloth   15 - 25

Fischer, L.
AV3000 Graf Zeppelin, Sein Leben Sein Werk
    Munich 1929   150 - 250

Fokker, Anthony H. G. & Bruce Gould
AV3020 Flying Dutchman: The Life of Anthony Fokker
    NY 1931, DJ   150 - 250

Fonck, Rene
AV3040 Ace of Aces Garden City 1967, DJ   20 - 30

Foxworth, Thomas G.
AV3060 The Speed Seekers NY 1974, DJ   100 - 150

Francillon, Rene J.
AV3080 Japanese Aircraft of the Pacific War NY 1970, DJ 50 - 75
AV3085 Lockheed Aircraft Since 1913 Annapolis 1987, DJ   30 - 50

Francis, Devon
AV3100 Mr. Piper and His Cubs Ames, IA 1973, DJ   50 - 75

Frantz, Harry (editor)
AV3120 DZ Europe Ind 1946   250 - 350

Fraser, Chelsea
AV3140 Heroes of the Air NY 1927, DJ   40 - 60
    w/o DJ   20 - 30

Freeny, William A.
AV3160 The First Three Hundred Hell's Angels
    Lon 1944, wrappers   75 - 125

French, Joseph Lewis (editor)
AV3180 Aces of the Air Springfield 1930, DJ   75 -125

Freudenthal, Elsbeth E.
AV3200 The Aviation Business NY 1940, DJ   30 - 50
AV3205 Flight into History: The Wright Brothers and
    the Air Age Norman 1949, DJ   40 - 60

Friedman, Norman
AV3220 U.S. Aircraft Carriers Annapolis 1985, DJ   40 - 60

Fry, Garry L.
AV3240 Escort to Berlin: The 4th Fighter Group in
    WWII NY 1980, DJ   50 - 75

65

AV2250

AV3140

AV3310   AV3920   AV4810

Galland, Adolf
AV3260 The First and the Last: The German Fighter
Force in World War II Lon 1955, DJ   100 - 150
AV3262 NY 1957, DJ   40 - 60

Gann, Ernest K.
AV3280 In the Company of Eagles NY 1965, DJ   20 - 30

Genet, Edmond Charles
AV3300 Memorial on the Upward Forces of Fluids
Albany 1825, printed bds, 6 plates, folding
table (1st book on aeronautics printed in U.S.)   4000 - 6000

Gentry, Viola
AV3310 Hangar Flying (np, private printing) 550 cys, signed   40 - 60

George, Lloyd and James Gilman
AV3320 Air, Men and Wings NY 1929, DJ   30 - 50

Gibbons, Floyd
AV3340 The Red Knight of Germany Garden City 1927, DJ   75 - 125
AV3341 Garden City 1927, DJ (Star Books reprint)   50 - 75
AV3342 Garden City, DJ (Sun Dial Press reprint)   30 - 50

Gillison, Douglas
AV3360 Royal Australian Air Force 1939-1942
Canberra 1962, DJ   75 - 125

Glaisher, James and others
AV3380 Travels in the Air Lon 1871   300 - 500'
AV3385 Voyages Aeriens Paris 1870   150 - 250

Glines, Carroll V.
AV3400 Doolittle's Tokyo Raiders Princeton 1964, DJ   40 - 60

Goddard, Robert H.
AV3420 A Method of Reaching Extreme Altitudes
Wash 1919, wrappers, pub #2540   3000 - 5000
AV3425 The Papers of Robert H. Goddard NY 1970,
3 vol, box   150 - 250

Goldberg, Alfred (editor)
AV3440 A History of the United States Air Force
1907-1957 Princeton 1957   30 - 50

Goulding, James
AV3460 Camouflage & Markings: R.A.F. Fighter
Command, Northern Europe 1936 to 1945
Garden City 1971, DJ   50 - 75

Grace, Dick
AV3480 Squadron of Death Garden City 1929, DJ   50 - 75

Grahame-White, Claude
AV3500 Aircraft in the Great War Chi 1915   75 - 125
AV3505 The Story of the Aeroplane Bos 1911   200 - 300

Gray, George
AV3520 Frontiers of Flight NY 1948, DJ   30 - 50

Gray, Peter
AV3540 German Aircraft of the First World War
Lon 1962, DJ   50 - 75

Green, William
AV3560 The Air Forces of the World Lon 1958, DJ   50 - 75
AV3565 The Aircraft of the World Garden City 1954, DJ   30 - 50
AV3570 Famous Bombers of the Second World War
Garden City 1960, 2 vol, DJs   40 - 60
AV3575 Famous Fighters of the Second World War
NY 1957, 2 vol, DJs   40 - 60
AV3580 The Jet Aircraft of the World Garden City 1955, DJ   30 - 50
AV3585 The Observer's Book of Aircraft Lon 1967-68,
3 vol, DJs   40 - 60

AV3590 War Planes of the Second World War Garden
City 1967, 10 vol, DJs   150 - 250
AV3595 War Planes of the Third Reich Garden City
1970, DJ   50 - 75

Greenlaw, Olga S.
AV3610 The Lady and the Tigers NY 1943, DJ   50 - 75

Gregory, H. F.
AV3620 Anything a Horse Can Do: The Story of the
Helicopter NY 1944, DJ   30 - 50

Grinnell-Milne, Duncan
AV3640 Wind in the Wires Lon   50 - 75

Gunston, Bill (editor)
AV3660 The Illustrated History of Fighters nd (1970s)   20 - 30

Gurney, Gene
AV3680 Five Down and Glory NY 1958, DJ   30 - 50
AV3685 Flying Aces of WWI NY 1971, wrappers   20 - 30

Guthman, Ensign L. C. (editor)
AV3700 Aeronautics Aircraft Spotters Handbook NY 1943   50 - 75

Haddow, G. W.
AV3720 The German Giants: The Story of the R-Planes,
1914-1919 Lon 1962, DJ   75 - 125

Hadingham, Evan
AV3740 The Fighting Tri-Planes NY 1969, DJ   40 - 60

Hall, Lt. Bert
AV3760 "En L'Air" NY 1918, DJ   150 - 250
AV3765 One Man's War NY 1929, DJ   100 - 150

Hall, Grover M.
AV3780 1,000 Destroyed: The Life and Times of the
4th Fighter Group Montgomery 1946, DJ   200 - 300

Hall, James Norman
AV3800 Flying With Chaucer Bos 1930, DJ   100 - 150
AV3805 High Adventure: A Narrative of Air Fighting
in France Bos 1918, DJ   100 - 150
AV3810 Kitchener's Mob Bos 1916, DJ   150 - 250
AV3815 The Lafayette Flying Corps Bos 1920, 2 vol   1000 - 1500
AV3820 My Island Home Bos 1952, DJ   40 - 60

Hamlin, Benson
AV3840 Flight Testing NY 1946, DJ   40 - 60

Handley-Page
AV3860 Handley-Page - Forty Years on...1909-1948
Lon 1949   50 - 75

Harper, Harry
AV3880 Riders of the Sky Lon 1936, DJ   100 - 150

Harriman, H. H. (editor)
AV3900 Akron and U.S.S. Akron, World's Largest
Airship Akron 1931   40 - 60

Hart, Moss
AV3920 Winged Victory Clev 1944, DJ (movie ed)   20 - 30

Hartney, Lt. Col. Harloo E.
AV3940 Up and At 'Em Harrisburg 1940, DJ   100 - 150

Hastings, H. D.
AV3960 War Planes in Battle Dress 1914-1918 NY 1963   50 - 75

Haugland, Vern
AV3980 The AAF Against Japan NY 1948, DJ   50 - 75

Hawker, Muriel
AV4000 H.G. Hawker, Airman Lon 1922   50 - 75

Haydon, F. Stansbury
AV4020 Aeronautics in the Union and Confederate
Armies Balt 1941   150 - 250

Hearne, R. P.
AV4040 Zeppelins and Super Zeppelins Lon 1916   50 - 75

Hegener, Henri
AV4060 Fokker: The Man and the Aircraft LA 1962, DJ   75 - 125

Heinkel, Ernst
AV4080 HE 1,000 Lon 1957, DJ   40 - 60
AV4085 Stormy Life NY 1956, DJ   30 - 50

Hennessy, Juliette A.
AV4100 The United States Army Air Arm, April 1861
to April 1917 Atlanta 1958, 500 cys, wrappers   75 - 125

Herring, Bob (editor)
AV4120 From Dobodura to Okinawa San Angelo 1946   250 - 350

Hess, William
AV4140 **Pacific Sweep** NY 1974, DJ 50 - 75
Hewlett, Mrs. Maurice
AV4160 **Our Flying Men** Kettering, Eng, nd (1920s) 50 - 75
Highham, Robin
AV4180 **The British Air Ship 1906-1931** Lon 1961, DJ 40 - 60
Hildebrandt, A.
AV4200 **Airships Past and Present** Lon 1908 100 - 150
Hobbs, Leonard
AV4220 **The Wright Brothers' Engines and Their Design**
Wash 1971, wrappers 20 - 30
Hoehling, A. A.
AV4240 **Who Destroyed the Hindenburg?** Lon 1962, DJ 20 - 30
Holland, Rupert Sargent
AV4260 **Historic Airships** Phil 1928 100 - 150
Hubler, Richard G.
AV4280 **Flying Leathernecks** Garden City 1944, DJ 30 - 50
Hull, Robert
AV4300 **September Champions** Harrisburg 1979, DJ 30 - 50
Hymoff, Edward
AV4320 **The First Marine Aircraft Wing, Vietnam**
NY 1969, DJ 200 - 300
Ind, Allison
AV4340 **Bataan** NY 1944, DJ 50 - 75
Insone, Alfred
AV4360 **Earlybirds: Air Transport Memories 1919-1924**
Lon 1938, DJ 40 - 60
Jablonski, Edward
AV4380 **An Illustrated History of Air Power in the**
Second World War NY 1971, 4 vol 100 - 150
AV4390 **Seawings** Garden City 1972, DJ 40 - 60
Jackman, W. J.
AV4420 **Flying Machines** Chi 1910 50 - 75
Jackson, Aubrey Joseph
AV4440 **Avro Aircraft Since 1908** Lon 1965, DJ 50 - 75
AV4445 **Blackburn Aircraft Since 1909** Lon 1962, DJ 50 - 75
AV4450 **British Civil Aircraft 1919-1959** Lon 1959,
2 vol, DJs 75 - 125
AV4455 **de Havilland Aircraft Since 1915** Lon 1962, DJ 50 - 75
Jackson, Robert
AV4480 **The Jet Age** NY 1980, DJ 20 - 30
Jacobs, A. M.
AV4500 **Knights of the Wing** NY 1928, DJ 50 - 75
James, Derek N.
AV4520 **Gloster Aircraft Since 1917** Lon 1971, DJ 50 - 75
Jane, John Thomas Frederick (editor)
AV4540 **Jane's All the World's Aircraft** Lon 1919 300 - 500
AV4542 1920-1925 250 - 350
AV4548 1926-1940 200 - 300
AV4564 1941-1961 150 - 250
AV4585 later editions 75 - 150
AV4610 **Jane's All the World's Airships** Lon 1909 400 - 600
AV4612 1910-1918 300 - 500
Jauneaud, Marcel
AV4640 **L'Evolution De L'Aeronautique** Paris 1923,
wrappers 100 - 150
Jenson, Paul (editor)
AV4660 **The Fireside Book of Flying Stories** NY 1951, DJ 15 - 25
Johnson, Charles
AV4680 **The History of the Hell Hawks** Anaheim
1975, DJ 100 - 150
Johnson, Owen
AV4700 **Arrows of the Almighty** NY 1901 75 - 125
AV4705 **The Spirit of France** Bos 1916 75 - 125
Johnson, Wayne G.
AV4740 **Chennault's Flying Tigers** Dallas 1983, 2 vol 150 - 250
Jones, Henry A.
AV4760 **Over the Balkans and South Russia** Lon 1923 200 - 300
Jones, James Ira
AV4780 **Tiger Squadron** Lon 1955, DJ 40 - 60

Jones, Lloyd
AV4800 **U.S. Fighters: 1925-1980s** Fallbrook 1975 50 - 75
Jordanoff, Assan
AV4810 **Your Wings** NY 1936, DJ 30 - 50
AV4812 later printings, DJ 20 - 30
Joubert De La Ferte, Philip
AV4820 **Rocket** NY 1957, DJ 30 - 50
Junger, Ernest (editor)
AV4840 **Luftfahrt 1st Not!** Berlin 1928 100 - 150
Juptner, Joseph P.
AV4860 **U.S. Civil Aircraft** Fallbrook 1962 9 vol, DJs 200 - 300
Kaappen, Theodore MacFarlane
AV4880 **Wings of War** NY 1920 75 - 125
Keith, C. H.
AV4900 **Flying Years** Lon 1935, DJ 40 - 60
Key, Alexander
AV4920 **The Red Eagle** Joliet, IL 1930 50 - 75
Keyhoe, Donald E.
AV4940 **Flying With Lindbergh** NY 1928, DJ 50 - 75
Kinnert, Reed
AV4960 **American Racing Planes and Historic Air Races**
NY 1952, DJ 50 - 75
Kirchhoff, Arthur
AV4980 **Die Erschliebung Des Luftmeers** Leipzig 1910 100 - 150
Knight, Clayton
AV5000 **Pilot's Luck** Phil 1924, DJ 100 - 150
AV5005 **War Birds** NY 1926, DJ 50 - 75
Koehl, Captain Hermann
AV5040 **The Three Musketeers of the Air** NY 1928, DJ 100 - 150
Lamberton, W. M.
AV5060 **Fighter Aircraft of the 1914-1918 War**
Fallbrook 1964, DJ 50 - 75
AV5065 **Reconnaissance and Bomber Aircraft of the**
1914-1918 War LA 1962, DJ 50 - 75
Lamensdorf, Rolland G.
AV5100 **History of the 31st Fighter Group** Wash 1952 250 - 350
Langley, Samuel
AV5120 **Experiments in Aerodynamics** Wash 1902 150 - 250
AV5125 **Langley Memoir on Mechanical Flight** Wash
1911, wrappers 300 - 500
Lanier, Henry Wysham
AV5160 **The Far Horizon** NY 1933, DJ 50 - 75
Larkins, William T.
AV5180 **U.S. Marine Corps Aircraft 1914-1959**
Concord 1959, DJ 50 - 75
AV5185 **U.S. Navy Aircraft 1921-1941** Concord 1961, DJ 40 - 60
Lawson, Ted W.
AV5220 **Thirty Seconds Over Tokyo** NY 1943, DJ 15 - 25
Lazarus, William C.
AV5240 **Wings in the Sun** Orlando 1951, DJ 50 - 75
Lehmann, Ernst A.
AV5260 **Zeppelin: The Story of Lighter-Than-Air Craft**
Lon 1937, DJ 40 - 60
LeVier, Tony
AV5280 **Pilot** NY 1954, DJ 30 - 50
Lewis, Cecil
AV5300 **Sagittarius Rising** NY 1936, DJ 50 - 75
Lewis, Peter
AV5320 **British Aircraft 1809-1914** Lon 1962, DJ 40 - 60
AV5325 **The British Bomber Since 1914** Lon 1967, DJ 40 - 60
AV5330 **The British Fighter Since 1912** Lon 1965, DJ 40 - 60
Lieberg, Owen S.
AV5360 **The First Air Race** Garden City 1974, DJ 30 - 50
Lilienthal, Otto
AV5380 **Bird Flight as the Basis of Aviation** Lon 1911 300 - 500
AV5385 **Der Vogel Flug Als Grundlage Der Fliege**
Kunst Berlin 1889 1200 - 1800
Lindbergh, Anne Morrow
AV5420 **Listen! The Wind** NY 1938, DJ 30 - 50

| AV5450 (slipcase) | AV5630 | AV5900 |

Lindbergh, Charles A.
AV5440 **The Spirit of St. Louis** NY 1953, limited ed, signed — 300 - 500
AV5441 NY 1953, DJ (1st trade ed) — 20 - 30
AV5450 **We** NY 1927, DJ, slipcase — 50 - 75
  w/o DJ — 20 - 30

Lipsner, Captain Benjamin B.
AV5480 **The Airmail** NY 1951, DJ — 50 - 75

Lloyd, Ian
AV5500 **Rolls Royce: The Merlin At War** Lon 1978, DJ — 50 - 75

Loening, Grover Cleveland
AV5520 **Monoplanes and Biplanes** NY 1911 — 150 - 250

Lougheed, Victor
AV5540 **Aeroplane Designing for Amateurs** Chi 1912 — 75 - 125

Lowell, A. Lawrence
AV5560 **New England Aviators 1914-1918** Bos 1919-20, 2 vol — 400 - 600

Lundborg, Einar
AV5580 **The Arctic Rescue** NY 1929, DJ — 50 - 75

Lundgren, William R.
AV5600 **Across the High Frontier** NY 1955, DJ — 40 - 60

Lundy, Will
AV5620 **History of the 67th Bombardment Squadron** 1984, 150 cys — 150 - 250

Macauley, C. B. F.
AV5630 **The Helicopters Are Coming** NY 1944, DJ (one of the earliest fiction books about helicopters) — 30 - 50

Maitland, E. M.
AV5640 **The Log of H.M.A. R-34 Journey to America and Back** Lon (1920s) DJ — 200 - 300

Maitland, Lt. Lester J.
AV5660 **Knights of the Air** Garden City 1929, DJ — 75 - 125

Manly, Lt. G. B.
AV5680 **Aviation From the Ground Up** Chi 1929, DJ — 75 - 125

Marion, F.
AV5700 **Wonderful Balloon Ascents** NY 1870 — 50 - 75

Marks, Lionel S.
AV5720 **The Airplane Engine** NY 1922 — 50 - 75

Marsh, W. Lockwood
AV5740 **Aeronautical Prints and Drawings** Lon 1924, 100 cys — 1000 - 1500
AV5741 Lon 1924, DJ — 500 - 700

Marshall, Alfred W.
AV5760 **Flying Machines** NY, nd (early 1900s) — 100 - 150

Martin, Eugene
AV5780 **Randy Starr Sky Flyers Series** Akron 1930s (Boys Books fiction about aviation, eg **Randy Starr Above Stormy Seas**) w/DJs — 15 - 25

Mason, Francis K.
AV5800 **The Gloster Gladiator** Lon 1964, DJ — 30 - 50
AV5805 **Hawker Aircraft Since 1920** Lon 1961, DJ — 50 - 75
AV5810 **The Hawker Hurricane** Garden City 1962, DJ — 30 - 50

Mason, Jr., Herbert Molloy
AV5840 **The Lafayette Escadrille** NY 1964, DJ — 50 - 75

Matt, Paul R.
AV5860 **Historical Aviation Album** Temple City 1964-77, 15 vol — 600 - 800
  each vol — 50 - 75

AV5865 **United States Navy and Marine Corps Fighters 1918-1962** Letchworth 1962, DJ — 50 - 75

McAlister, Hugh
AV5900 **The Flight of the Silver Ship** Akron 1930, DJ — 30 - 50
AV5905 **A Viking of the Sky** Akron 1930, DJ — 30 - 50

McClure, Captain Glenn
AV5940 **An Unofficial Pictorial History of the 500th Bombardment Group** Riverside, CA 1946 — 250 - 350

McConnell, James R.
AV5960 **Flying For France: With the American Escadrille at Verdun** Garden City 1917, DJ — 100 - 150
AV5961 NY 1918, DJ — 50 - 75
AV5963 NY 1920s (Grosset & Dunlap reprint) DJ — 30 - 50
  w/o DJ — 15 - 25

McCudden, James Byford
AV5980 **Flying Fury** Lon 1933, DJ — 75 - 125

McMahon, John R.
AV6000 **The Wright Brothers** Bos 1930, DJ — 50 - 75

McMinnies, W. G.
AV6020 **Practical Flying** NY 1918 — 50 - 75

Means, James
AV6040 **Epitome of the Aeronautical Annual** Bos 1910, wrappers — 100 - 150
AV6045 **Manflight** Bos 1891, wrappers — 200 - 300
AV6050 **The Means Control for Flying Machines** Bos 1913, wrappers — 50 - 75

Merricks, K. A.
AV6080 **German Aircraft Markings 1939-1945** NY 1977, DJ — 50 - 75

Merritt, Mary M. (editor)
AV6100 **Curtis Edward Presley 1894-1975** Beckley 1977, DJ — 50 - 75

Michaelis, Ralph
AV6120 **From Bird Cage to Battle Plane** NY 1943, DJ — 30 - 50

Middleton, Edgar C.
AV6140 **Airfare of Today and the Future** Lon 1917 — 75 - 125
AV6145 **Glorious Exploits of the Air** Lon, nd (1917) — 75 - 125
AV6150 **The Great War in the Air** Lon 1920, 2 vol — 100 - 150
AV6155 **The Way of the Air** NY 1917, DJ — 75 - 125

Midlam, Don S.
AV6180 **Flight of the Lucky Lady** Portland 1954, DJ — 30 - 50

Miller, Francis Trevelyan
AV6200 **The World in the Air** NY 1930, 500 cys, 2 vol — 600 - 800

Miller, Ronald
AV6220 **The Technical Development of Modern (Civil) Aviation** Lon 1968, DJ — 50 - 75

Miller, Thomas G.
AV6240 **The Cactus Air Force** NY 1969, DJ — 50 - 75

Mills, Stephen E.
AV6260 **Sourdough Sky** Seattle 1969, DJ — 40 - 60

Mingos, Howard
AV6280 **American Heroes of the War in the Air** (only 1 vol) NY 1943, DJ — 150 - 200
  w/o DJ — 75 - 125

Mitchell, Alan W.
AV6300 **New Zealanders in the Air War** Lon 1945, DJ — 50 - 75

Mitchell, William ("Billy")
AV6320 **Our Air Force** NY 1921, DJ — 200 - 300
AV6325 **Skyways: A Book on Modern Aeronautics** Phil 1930, DJ — 75 - 125
AV6330 **Winged Defense** NY 1925, DJ — 100 - 150

Moench, John O.
AV6360 **Marauder Men** Longwood 1989 — 50 - 75

Mondey, David
AV6380 **Pictorial History of the U.S. Air Force** Lon 1971, DJ — 30 - 50

Monk, F. V. and H. T. Winter
AV6400 **Great Exploits in the Air** Lon, nd (1930s) DJ — 50 - 75

Monks, Noel
AV6420 **Squadrons Up!** NY 1941, DJ — 30 - 50

Morris, Joseph
AV6440 **The German Air Raids on Great Britain 1914-18** Lon, nd (1930s?) — 100 - 150

Morris, Lloyd
AV6460 Ceiling Unlimited NY 1953, DJ   20 - 30
Morrison, Wilbur H.
AV6480 Hellbird's: The Story of the B-29's in Combat
         NY 1960, DJ   40 - 60
Mortane, Jacques
AV6500 Guynemer: The Ace of Aces NY 1918, DJ   100 - 150
AV6505 La Guerre Aerienne Illustree November 1916 -
         October 1917 Paris 1916-17, 2 vol   200 - 300
Mouchotte, Rene
AV6540 The Mouchotte Diaries 1940-43 Lon 1956, DJ   50 - 75
Moulson, Tom
AV6560 The Flying Sword: The Story of 601 Squadron
         Lon 1964, DJ   40 - 60
Mowbray, Jay Henry
AV6580 Thrilling Achievements of "Bird Men" with
         Flying Machines 1911   100 - 150
Munson, Kenneth
AV6600 Aircraft of World War I Lon 1967, DJ   20 - 30
AV6605 Airliners Between the Wars 1919-1939
         NY 1972, DJ   20 - 30
AV6610 Civil Airliners Since 1946 NY 1969, DJ   20 - 30
AV6615 Flying Boats and Seaplanes Since 1910
         NY 1971, DJ   20 - 30
AV6620 Helicopters and Other Rotocraft Since 1907
         Lon 1968, DJ   20 - 30
Musciano, Walter A.
AV6640 Lt. Werner Voss NY 1962, wrappers   20 - 30
Nielsen, Thor
AV6660 The Zeppelin Story Lon 1955, DJ   30 - 50
(no author)
AV6670 Our Flying Navy NY 1944, DJ   30 - 50
Nordhoff, Charles Bernard
AV6680 Falcons of France Bos 1929, DJ   40 - 60
Norman, Aaron
AV6700 The Great Air War (WWI) NY 1968, DJ   50 - 75
Norris, Geoffrey
AV6720 The Royal Flying Corps: A History Lon 1965, DJ 20 - 30
Nowarra, Heinz J.
AV6740 The Focke-Wulf 190 Fallbrook 1965, DJ   50 - 75
AV6745 The Messerschmitt 109 Fallbrook 1966, DJ   50 - 75
AV6750 Russian Civil and Military Aircraft 1884-1969
         Lon 1971, DJ   50 - 75
AV6755 Von Richthofen and the Flying Circus
         Letchworth 1958, DJ   40 - 60
O'Brien, Lt. Paul
AV6780 Outwitting the Hun NY 1918, DJ   75 - 125
         w/o DJ   30 - 50
Ossip, Jerome (editor)
AV6800 509th Pictorial Album Chi 1946   250 - 350
Page, Major Victor M.
AV6820 Airplane Servicing Manual NY 1938, DJ   75 - 125
AV6825 Modern Aircraft NY 1929, DJ   50 - 75
AV6830 Modern Aviation Engines NY 1929, 2 vol, DJs   100 - 150
Paine, Ralph D.
AV6860 The First Yale Unit: A Story of Naval Aviation,
         1916-1919 Cambridge 1925, 2 vol   250 - 350
Palmer, Frederick
AV6880 Danbury Rudd, Aviator NY 1910   40 - 60
Parrish, Randall
AV6900 The Air Pilot Chi 1913, DJ   50 - 75
Parsons, Edwin C.
AV6920 The Great Adventure: The Story of the Lafayette
         Escadrille Garden City 1937, DJ   50 - 75
AV6925 I Flew With the Lafayette Escadrille Ind 1963, DJ 20 - 30
Pellegrino, Charles R. & Joshua Stoff
AV6960 Chariots For Apollo NY 1985, DJ   20 - 30
Pemberton-Billing, N.
AV6980 Air War Portsmouth 1916,. wrappers   100 - 150
Penrose, Harald
AV7000 British Aviation Lon 1967, DJ   50 - 75
Pistole, Larry
AV7020 The Pictorial History of the Flying Tigers
         VA 1981, DJ   75 - 125

Polmar, Norman
AV7040 Aircraft Carriers Garden City 1969, DJ   50 - 75
Porter, Harold
AV7060 Aerial Observation NY 1921   75 - 125
Pritchard, J. Lawrence
AV7080 Sir George Cayley: Inventor of the Airplane
         NY 1962, DJ   30 - 50
Pulitzer, Ralph
AV7100 Over the Front in an Aeroplane NY 1915, DJ   30 - 50
Randers-Pherson, N. H.
AV7120 History of Aviation NY 1944, DJ   20 - 30
Rathbun, John B.
AV7140 Aeroplane Construction and Operation Chi 1919 50 - 75
Rawlings, John
AV7160 Fighter Squadrons of the R.A.F. and Their
         Aircraft Lon 1969, DJ   50 - 75
Reeves, Dache M.
AV7180 Aerial Photographs NY 1927, DJ   50 - 75
Reid, A. Cunningham
AV7200 Planes and Personalities Lon 1920, DJ   50 - 75
Reitsch, Hanna
AV7220 Flying Is My Life NY 1954, DJ   50 - 75
Reynolds, James
AV7240 Wing Commander Paddy Finucane: A Memoir
         NY 1942, limited ed, box   50 - 75
Reynolds, Quentin
AV7260 They Fought for the Sky NY 1957, DJ   20 - 30
Richards, Denis
AV7280 Royal Air Force 1939-1945 Lon 1954-54,
         3 vol, DJs   100 - 150
Richthofen, Captain Manfred
AV7300 The Red Battle Flyer NY 1918, DJ   150 - 250
Rickenbacker, Captain Edward
AV7320 Captain Rickenbacker's Story NY 1943, glassine DJ 50 - 75
AV7325 Fighting the Flying Circus NY 1919, DJ   100 - 150
         signed cy   250 - 350
AV7330 Rickenbacker Englewood Cliffs 1967, DJ   15 - 25
Roberts, Lt. E. M.
AV7360 A Flying Fighter NY 1918, DJ   75 - 125
Robertson, Bruce (editor)
AV7380 Air Aces of the 1914-1918 War LA 1962, DJ   50 - 75
AV7385 Aircraft Camouflage and Markings 1907-1954
         Lon 1966, DJ   50 - 75
AV7390 Aircraft Markings of the World 1912-1967
         Bertfordshire 1967, DJ   40 - 60
AV7395 Bombing Colours: British Bomber Camouflage
         and Markings 1914-1937 Lon 1972, DJ   40 - 60
AV7400 Lancaster: The Story of a Famous Bomber
         Fallbrook 1965, DJ   30 - 50
AV7405 Sopwith: The Man and His Aircraft Letchworth
         1970, DJ   40 - 60
AV7410 Spitfire: The Story of a Famous Fighter
         Letchworth 1960, DJ   40 - 60
Robinson, Derek
AV7440 Goshawk Squadron NY 1972, DJ   20 - 30

AV6670   AV6960

69

AV7940   AV8445

Robinson, Douglas H.
AV7460   The Zeppelin in Combat Lon 1962, DJ   40 - 60

Rolt-Wheeler, Francis
AV7480   The Wonder of War in the Air Bos 1917   100 - 150
AV7485   The World War For Liberty 1919   50 - 75

Roscoe, Theodore
AV7520   On the Seas and in the Skies: A History of
        the U.S. Navy's Air Power NY 1970, DJ   40 - 60

Rosher, Harold
AV7540   In the Royal Naval Air Service Lon 1916, DJ   75 - 125
AV7545   With the Flying Squadron NY 1916, DJ   75 - 125

Roustan-Bek, B.
AV7580   Aerial Russia: The Romance of the Giant
        Aeroplane Lon 1916   250 - 350

Russel, William Muir
AV7600   A Happy Warrior Detroit 1919   150 - 250

Saffern, Eugene
AV7620   The Jug 1946   150 - 250

Saint-Exupery, Antoine De
AV7640   Night Flight NY 1932, DJ   50 - 75

Sakai, Saburo
AV7660   Samurai! NY 1957, DJ   50 - 75

Sanders, C. J.
AV7680   The Book of the C-19 Autogiro Lon 1931   75 - 125

Saunders, Hilary
AV7700   Per Ardua Lon 1945, DJ   50 - 75

Saunders, John Monk
AV7720   Wings NY 1927, DJ   100 - 150

Schick, Ron
AV7740   American Astronaut Photography 1962-1972
        NY 1988, DJ   30 - 50

Schroder, Hans
AV7760   An Airman Remembers Lon 1914, DJ   50 - 75
AV7762   Lon 1933, DJ   30 - 50

Schrotter, Herman Von
AV7780   Hygiene Der Aeronautik und Aviatik Leipzig
        1912, wrappers   150 - 250

Seth, Ronald
AV7800   Lion With Blue Wings Lon 1955, DJ   50 - 75

Shackley, Edward
AV7820   The Gloster Meteor Garden City 1963, DJ   30 - 50

Shamburger, Page
AV7840   Command the Horizon South Brunswick 1968, DJ   30 - 50
AV7845   The Curtiss Hawks Kalamazoo 1972, DJ   50 - 75

Sharp, C. Martin
AV7880   D.H.: An Outline of De Havilland History
        Lon 1960, DJ   50 - 75

Sherman, Frederick
AV7900   Combat Command: The American Aircraft
        Carriers in the Pacific War NY 1950, DJ   75 - 125

Sherman, William C.
AV7920   Air Warfare NY 1926   50 - 75

Shrader, Welman A.
AV7940   Fifty Years of Flight Clev 1953, DJ   50 - 75

Sikorsky, Igor I.
AV7960   The Story of the Winged S NY 1942, DJ   30 - 50

Sinclair, Captain J. A.
AV7980   Airships in Peace and War Lon 1934   100 - 150

Smart, Lawrence L.
AV8000   The Hawks That Guided the Guns 1978   30 - 50

Smith, Robert
AV8020   Staggerwing Media 1967, DJ   150 - 250

Spaight, J. M.
AV8040   Aircraft in War Lon 1914   100 - 150

Sprigg, C.
AV8060   The Airship Lon, nd (1920s)   50 - 75

Springs, Elliott White
AV8080   The Rise and Fall of Carol Banks Garden City
        1931, DJ   50 - 75
AV8085   War Birds NY 1926, 210 cys   200 - 300
AV8086   NY 1926 (1st trade ed), large paper issue   75 - 125
AV8087   NY 1926, DJ (regular ed)   30 - 50

Squier, George Owen
AV8120   Aeronautics in the United States at the Signing
        of the Armistice 1919, wrappers   50 - 75

Steichen, Edward
AV8140   The Blue Ghost NY 1947, DJ   100 - 150

Stevens, James Hay
AV8160   The Shape of the Aeroplane NY 1953, DJ   50 - 75

Stewart, James T. (editor)
AV8180   Air Power: The Decisive Force in Korea
        NY 1957, DJ   50 - 75

Stone, Richard H.
AV8200   Aviation Stories For Boys NY 1936, DJ   30 - 50

Strange, Louis A.
AV8220   Recollections of an Airman Lon 1935   50 - 75

Stroud, John
AV8240   European Transport Aircraft Since 1910
        Lon 1966, DJ   50 - 75

Studley, Lt. Barrett
AV8260   Practical Flight Training NY 1928   50 - 75

Sullivan, Alan
AV8280   Aviation in Canada 1917-1918 Tor 1919   75 - 125

Swanborough, Frederick
AV8300   United States Military Aircraft Since 1909
        Lon 1963, DJ   40 - 60

Sweetman, Bill
AV8320   The Great Book of Modern Warplanes
        NY 1987, DJ   75 - 125

Sweetser, Arthur
AV8340   The American Air Service NY 1919   75 - 125

Talbot, Frederick
AV8360   Aeroplanes and Dirigibles of War Phil 1915   50 - 75

Tallman, Frank
AV8380   Flying the Old Planes Garden City 1973, DJ   30 - 50

Tapper, Oliver
AV8400   Armstrong Whitworth Aircraft Since 1913
        Lon 1973, DJ   50 - 75

Taylor, Harold A.
AV8420   Airspeed Aircraft Since 1931 Lon 1970, DJ   50 - 75
AV8425   Fairey Aircraft Since 1915 Lon 1974, DJ   50 - 75

Taylor, John W. R.
AV8440   Birth Place of Air Power Lon 1958, DJ   30 - 50
AV8445   Combat Aircraft of the World Lon 1969, DJ   30 - 50
AV8450   A Picture History of Flight Lon 1955, DJ   20 - 30

Tennant, Lt. John E.
AV8480   In the Clouds Above Baghdad Lon 1920   150 - 250

Thaden, Louise
AV8500   High, Wide and Frightened NY 1938, DJ   30 - 50

Thayer, Lucien H.
AV8520   America's First Eagles San Jose 1983, DJ   30 - 50

Theiss, Lewis E.
AV8540   Piloting the U.S. Air Mail Bos 1927, DJ   40 - 60

Thetford, Owen G.
AV8560   Aircraft of the 1914-1918 War Leicester 1946, DJ   50 - 75

AV8565 Aircraft of the Royal Air Force 1918-57
         Lon 1957, DJ   50 - 75
AV8570 British Naval Aircraft 1912-58 Lon 1958, DJ 50 - 75
AV8575 Camouflage of 1939-42 Aircraft Lon 1946, DJ 40 - 60
Thomas, Lowell
AV8600 European Skyways Lon 1928, DJ   30 - 50
AV8605 The First World Flight Bos 1925, DJ   30 - 50
Thomas, Rowan T.
AV8620 Born in Battle Phil 1944, DJ   50 - 75
Thompson, Annis G.
AV8640 The Greatest Airlift: The Story of Combat Cargo
         Tokyo 1954   50 - 75
Thompson, Jonathan W.
AV8660 Italian Civil and Military Aircraft 1930-1945
         LA 1963, DJ   50 - 75
Thunderbolt Pilots Association
AV8680 P-47 Thunderbolt: The Jug Dallas 1981   100 - 150
Tinker, F. G.
AV8700 Some Still Live: Experiences of a Fighting
         Plane Pilot in the Spanish War NY 1938, DJ 100 - 150
Tissandier, Gaston
AV8720 Historie Des Balloons et Des Aeronautes
         Celebres Paris 1887   300 - 500
AV8722 Paris 1980 (reprint)   75 - 125
Titler, Dale M.
AV8740 The Day the Red Baron Died NY 1970, DJ   20 - 30
Toland, John
AV8760 Ships in the Sky: The Story of the Great
         Dirigibles NY 1957, DJ   40 - 60
Toliver, Raymond F.
AV8780 The Blond Knight of Germany Garden City
         1970, DJ   40 - 60
AV8785 Fighter Aces NY 1965, DJ   40 - 60
AV8790 Fighter Aces of the Luftwaffe Fallbrook 1977, DJ 30 - 50
AV8795 Fighter Aces of the U.S.A. Fallbrook 1979, DJ   30 - 50
Tomlinson, Lt. D. W.
AV8820 The Sky's the Limit Phil 1930   50 - 75
Tunner, William H.
AV8840 Over The Hump NY 1964, DJ   50 - 75
Turnbull, Archibald D.
AV8860 History of United States Naval Aviation
         New Haven 1949, DJ   50 - 75
Turner, Charles C.
AV8880 My Flying Scrap Book Lon 1918   50 - 75
Turnor, Christopher
AV8900 Astra Castra: Experiments and Adventures
         in the Atmosphere Lon 1965   300 - 500
U.S. War Department
AV8920 Air Corps Field Manual Wash 1941, wrappers 20 - 30
AV8925 Air Service Medical Wash 1919   50 - 75
Udet, Ernst
AV8940 Mein Fliegerleben Berlin 1935, DJ   75 - 125
United States Army Air Force
AV8960 816th Engineer Aviation Battalion Passes
         in Review Munich 1945   75 - 125
AV8965 The 873rd Bombardment Squadron Presents
         Superfort Saga 1945   250 - 350
AV8970 The Earthquakers: Overseas History of the
         12th Bomb Group Wash 1947   150 - 250
AV8975 The History of the 398th Bombardment Group
         San Angelo 1946   200 - 300
AV8980 The History of the 487th Bombardment Group
         San Angelo 1946   300 - 500
AV8990 The History of the Army Air Forces 34th
         Bombardment Group San Angelo 1947   200 - 300
AV9000 The Ninth Air Force Service Command in the
         European Theatre of Operations NY 1945   100 - 150
AV9010 Orange Tails: The Story of the 358th Fighter
         Group Wash (1940s)   300 - 500
AV9020 Pacific Counterblow: The 11th Bombardment
         Group Wash 1945   100 - 150
AV9030 Pilot's Flight Operating Instructions for Army
         Model B-29 Airplanes Wash 1944, 4 vol   150 - 250

AV9040 Resume: 20th Air Force Missions Wash 1969   100 - 150
AV9050 Strike: The Story of the Fighting 17th, South
         Pacific Area 1943-44 Australia 1944   300 - 500
AV9060 Team "B", 325th Air Service Group LA 1946   100 - 150
AV9070 Twelve to One: Fighter Combat Tactics in the
         SWPA; V Fighter Command 1945   250 - 350
AV9080 Wide Wing - A History of the Strategic Air
         Force Headquarters Units in WWII 1946   100 - 150
Veil, Charles
AV9100 Adventure's A Wench NY 1934, DJ   75 - 125
Villard, Henry
AV9120 Contact! NY 1968, DJ   20 - 30
von Braun, Wernher
AV9140 History of Rocketry and Space Travel NY 1966, DJ 30 - 50
Wagner, Ray
AV9160 American Combat Planes Garden City 1960, DJ 20 - 30
AV9165 German Combat Planes Garden City 1971, DJ   40 - 60
AV9170 The North American Sabre Garden City 1963, DJ 50 - 75
AV9175 The Soviet Air Force in World War II Garden City
         1973, DJ   30 - 50
Walcott, Stuart
AV9200 Above the French Lines Princeton 1918   100 - 150
Walker, Hugh (editor)
AV9220 391st Bombardment Group History WWII
         1990, wrappers   75 - 125
Walker, Sam
AV9240 Up the Slot Okla Cty 1984   75 - 125
Wallace, Edgar
AV9260 Tam O' the Scouts Bos 1919   50 - 75
Wandry, Ralph
AV9280 Fighter Pilot Mason City, IA 1950   100 - 150
Warren, J. A. Crosby
AV9300 The Flight Testing of Production Aircraft
         Lon 1943, DJ   30 - 50
Waterton, W. A.
AV9320 The Quick and the Dead Lon 1956, DJ   30 - 50
Webster, Charles
AV9340 History of the Second World War: The Strategic
         Air Offensive Against Germany 1939-1945
         Lon 1961, 4 vol   250 - 350
Wellman, Walter
AV9360 The Aerial Age NY 1911   50 - 75
Wellman, William A.
AV9380 Go, Get 'Em! Bos 1918, DJ   75 - 125
         w/o DJ   50 - 75
West, James E.
AV9400 The Lone Scout of the Sky Phil 1928, DJ   50 - 75
Westervelt, George Conrad
AV9420 The Triumph of the NC's Garden City 1920   100 - 150
Whelan, Russell
AV9440 The Flying Tigers NY 1942   30 - 50
Whitehouse, Arch
AV9460 The Fledgling NY 1964, DJ   20 - 30
AV9465 The Years of the Sky Kings NY 1959, DJ   30 - 50
AV9470 The Zeppelin Fighters Garden City 1966, DJ 30 - 50
Widmer, Emil J.
AV9500 Military Observation Balloons NY 1917   100 - 150
Wilkins, George H.
AV9520 Flying the Arctic NY 1928   30 - 50
Winchester, Clarence (editor)
AV9540 Flying Men & Their Machines Lon 1916   150 - 250
AV9545 Wonders of World Aviation Lon, nd (early
         1900s), 2 vol   75 - 125
Winston, Robert A.
AV9580 Dive Bomber NY 1939, DJ   40 - 60
AV9585 Fighting Squadron NY 1946, DJ   50 - 75
Wise, John
AV9620 A System of Aeronautics Phil 1850   1000 - 1500
Wood, Eric
AV9640 Thrilling Deeds of British Airmen Lon 1917 100 - 150
Woodhouse, Henry
AV9660 Textbook of Naval Aeronautics NY 1917   100 - 150

AV9780	AV9785	AV9820

Woodward, Houston
AV9680 **A Year For France, War Letters of Houston Woodward** New Haven 1919   200 - 300

Woolnough, Lt. Col. John
AV9700 **The 8th Air Force Album** Hollywood 1978   75 - 125
AV9705 **Attlebridge Diaries** San Angelo 1979   75 - 125

Wright, Gail
AV9740 **832nd Engineer Aviation Battalion History** 1945   75 - 125

Wright, Jack Morris
AV9760 **A Poet of the Air** Bos 1918   100 - 150

Wright, Orville
AV9780 **Orville Wright Dinner** Dayton, Jul 17, 1918, wrappers   50 - 75
AV9785 **Stability of Aëroplanes** Bos 1914, wrappers   150 - 250

Wright, Wilbur
AV9820 **Experiments and Observations in Soaring Flight** Dayton, Aug 1903, wrappers   300 - 500
AV9830 **The Papers of Wilbur and Orville Wright** NY 1953, 2 vol, DJs   200 - 300
AV9840 **Some Aeronautical Experiments** Chi 1901 (Journal of Western Society of Engineers reprint), wrappers   5000 - 7000
AV9842 Wash 1902, Smithsonian 1902 Annual Report w/article, entire vol   50 - 75
AV9844 Wash 1903 (Smithsonian Annual Report for 1902 reprint), wrappers   200 - 300

Young, Barnett
AV9900 **The Story of the Crusaders** Ft. Myers 1988, DJ   50 - 75

Young, John
AV9930 **The Aviation Paintings of John Young** Lon 1990   75 - 125

Zweng, Charles A.
AV9960 **Flying the Omni Range** North Hollywood 1952, DJ   20 - 30

BASEBALL

Baseball collectibles are among the hottest commodities in the 1990s. This category includes histories, team yearbooks, guide books, biographies and fiction. Most collectors concentrate on yearbooks and guides. Any team yearbook from the late 1940s to the early 1950s is worth at least $50. The New York Yankees' first official yearbook for 1950 is worth $300-500. Guide books include Spaldings, Reach, Street & Smith and many others. Nineteenth-century guides are very scarce and command premium prices. Beadles, Spaldings and others may be worth hundreds depending on condition. The main problem with these early guides is they were printed on cheap paper in thin paper wrappers. This, combined with excessive handling, contributes to most copies being found in rough condition.

Early team histories are very desirable and are among the most valuable baseball books. *Baseball in Cincinnati* (1907 edition) by Harry Ellard is worth $1000-1500 in fine condition. Even in poor condition it may still bring $200-300. Biographies and autobiographies of famous players like Roger Maris, Sandy Koufax, Lou Gehrig and Honus Wagner are valuable, especially if in the original dust jackets.

Early baseball fiction from the late 1800s through the early 1900s is highly collectible. Juvenile fiction by Christy Mathewson like *Catcher Craig* (NY 1915) is worth $200-300 in dust jacket.

No collection is complete without some of the team histories published by G.P. Putnam in the 1950s-1960s. The first printing of *The Hot Stove League* by Tom Meany ($100-150 in DJ) and *The Baltimore Orioles* by Frank Lieb (NY 1955) ($50 - 75 in DJ) are two examples.

Naturally any book autographed by a player is worth more. Add at least $1000 to a book signed by Babe Ruth.

Many of these books were worth a small fraction of their current value ten to fifteen years ago. Their rise has been meteoric. For instance, a 1919 World Series guide book could be bought for $100 in the late-1970s; by 1993 it was worth over $1000. Any of the guides from the 1800s, which could have been purchased for as little as $10 at one time, can now bring hundreds in fine condition. Books about Willie Mays and Mickey Mantle, published in the 1950s and originally costing several dollars, are sometimes worth over $100.

Condition is very important in collecting these books. Just like baseball cards, any defects may lower the value considerably. Any baseball book published after 1960 that's missing its dust jacket is going to be worth only a fraction of a copy in jacket. Jackets on books from the early 1900s are very rare. (Some were published without jackets.) Harry Ellard's book *Baseball in Cincinnati* could be worth over $3000 if a copy in its original jacket were ever found. Many from the late 1800s and early 1900s are still valuable without the jacket.

The following prices are for first printings. Many were reprinted by Grosset & Dunlap and A. L. Burt, and some post-1960 books were republished by book clubs. These reprints are worth much less.

Biography & History (alphabetical by author or title)

Adler, Bill
BB0200 **Love Letters to the Mets** NY 1965, DJ   20 - 30

Allen, Lee
BB0230 **100 Years of Baseball** NY 1950, DJ   50 - 75
BB0235 **The American League Story** NY 1962, DJ   40 - 60
BB0240 **The Cincinnati Reds** NY 1948, DJ   50 - 75
     w/o DJ   20 - 30
BB0245 **The Giants and the Dodgers** NY 1964, DJ   50 - 75
     w/o DJ   20 - 30
BB0250 **The Hot Stove League** NY 1955, DJ   100 - 150
     w/o DJ   50 - 75
BB0255 **Kings of the Diamond** NY 1965, DJ   20 - 30
BB0260 **The National League Story** NY 1961, DJ   40 - 60
BB0265 **The World Series** NY 1969, DJ   20 - 30

Angell, Roger
BB0290 **The Summer Game** NY 1972, DJ   40 - 60

Anonymous
BB0320 **How To Play Baseball** NY 1913   75 - 125

Anson, Adrian C.
BB0350 **A Ball Player's Career** Chi 1900   250 - 350

Ashenback, Edward
BB0380 **Humor Among the Minors** NY 1911, DJ   150 - 250
     w/o DJ   100 - 150

Asinof, Eliot
BB0410 **Eight Men Out** NY 1963, DJ   50 - 75

"Aunt Carrie" (compiler)
BB0440 **Popular Pastimes For Field and Fireside** NY 1867 (includes baseball chapter w/1865 rules)   200 - 300

Axelson, Gustaf W.
BB0470 **"Commy": The Life Story of Charles A. Comiskey** Chi 1919   150 - 250

Barber, Red
BB0500 **Rhubarb in a Catbird Seat** NY 1961, DJ   40 - 60
BB0502   NY 1968, DJ   20 - 30
BB0510 **The Rhubarb Patch** NY 1954, wrappers   20 - 30
BB0515 **When All Hell Broke Loose in Baseball** NY 1962, DJ   30 - 50

Barrow, Edward
BB0540 **My Fifty Years in Baseball** NY 1951, DJ   40 - 60

Bartlett, Arthur
BB0570 **Baseball and Mr. Spalding** NY 1951, DJ   30 - 50

Baseball Immortals, Hall of Fame Series
BB0600 **Biographies of Famous Players** Cooperstown,
NY 1953 & 1961
BB0605 **Lou Gehrig** 1953, wrappers — 25 - 35
BB0610 **Babe Ruth** 1953, wrappers — 25 - 35
BB0615 **Ty Cobb** 1953, wrappers — 25 - 35
BB0620 **Dizzy Dean** 1959, wrappers — 25 - 35
BB0625 **Honus Wagner** 1961, wrappers — 25 - 35
BB0630 **Christy Mathewson** 1961, wrappers — 25 - 35

Beale, Morris
BB0660 **The Washington Senators** Wash 1947, DJ — 100 - 150

Bonner, M. G.
BB0690 **The Big Baseball Book For Boys** NY 1931, DJ — 40 - 60

Boswell, Thomas
BB0720 **How Life Imitates the World Series** NY 1982, DJ — 30 - 50

Bouton, Jim
BB0750 **Ball Four** NY 1970, DJ — 20 - 30

Braathen, Sverre
BB0780 **Ty Cobb - Idol of Baseball Fandom** NY 1928 — 500 - 700

Brashler, William
BB0810 **Josh Gibson** NY 1978, DJ — 75 - 125

Bready, James
BB0840 **The Home Team** 1959 — 75 - 125

Brosnan, Jim
BB0870 **The Long Season** NY 1960, DJ — 30 - 50
BB0875 **Pennant Race** NY 1962, DJ — 20 - 30

Brown, Warren
BB0900 **Chicago Cubs** NY 1946, DJ — 50 - 75
BB0905 **The Chicago White Sox** NY 1952, DJ — 50 - 75

Chadwick, Henry
BB0930 **Baseball** NY 1888, wrappers — 1000 - 1500
BB0935 **Chadwick's Baseball Manual** Lon (1880s) — 1200 - 1800
BB0940 **The Game of Baseball; How To Learn It, How
To Play It, and How To Teach It** NY 1868
(1st clothbound baseball book, extremely rare) — 3000 - 5000

Church, Seymour
BB0970 **Baseball 1845-1871** SF 1902 — 300 - 500
BB0972 Princeton 1974, DJ — 20 - 30

Clark, John
BB1000 **Constitution of the Olympic Ball Club of
Philadelphia** Phil 1838 — 3000 - 5000

Claudy, C. H.
BB1030 **The Battle of Baseball** NY 1912 — 150 - 250

Cobb, Ty
BB1060 **My Record in Baseball: The True Record**
NY 1961, DJ — 40 - 60

Cobbledick, Gordon
BB1090 **Don't Knock the Rock** NY 1966, DJ — 30 - 50

Cochrane, Mickey
BB1120 **Baseball - The Fan's Game** NY 1939 — 50 - 75

Collett, Ritter
BB1150 **The Cincinnati Reds** Virginia Beach 1976, DJ — 30 - 50

Collins, J. F. (cartoonist)
BB1180 **The "Garry" A Book of Humorous Cartoons,
Pickings From the Diamond by Collins** Cinti
1904, 105 cartoon plates, cloth (very rare, was
given away as promotion by Cinti hat store) — 500 - 700

Conigliaro, Tony
BB1200 **Seeing It Through** NY 1970, DJ — 20 - 30

Cook, Earnshaw
BB1230 **Percentage Baseball** Balt 1964, DJ — 30 - 50

Cox, William
BB1260 **The Mets Will Win the Pennant** NY 1964, DJ — 30 - 50

Daniel, Dan
BB1290 **Babe Ruth - Idol of the American Boy** NY 1930 — 40 - 60

Dansig, Allison
BB1320 **The History of Baseball** NY 1959, DJ — 75 - 125

Delaney, Ed
BB1350 **Bobby Shantz** NY 1953, DJ — 40 - 60

DiMaggio, Joe
BB1380 **Lucky To Be a Yankee** Rudolph Field 1946 — 50 - 75

Durant, John
BB1410 **The Dodgers, An Illustrated History** NY 1948, DJ — 50 - 75
w/o DJ — 20 - 30
BB1420 **The Story of Baseball** NY 1947, DJ — 50 - 75
w/o DJ — 20 - 30
BB1430 **The Yankees, An Illustrated History** NY 1949, DJ — 50 - 75
w/o DJ — 20 - 30

Eckel, J. C.
BB1460 **Universal Baseball Guide** NY 1890 — 1000 - 1500

Einstein, Charles
BB1500 **Coast to Coast Giant** NY 1963, DJ — 30 - 50
BB1510 **The Fireside Book of Baseball** NY 1956, DJ — 50 - 75
BB1512 NY 1958, DJ — 50 - 75
BB1514 NY 1968, DJ — 75 - 125
BB1516 NY 1987, DJ — 20 - 30
BB1518 later printings — 30 - 50

Ellard, Harry
BB1550 **Baseball in Cincinnati** Cinti 1907, 52 glossy
plates, 500 cys, white CL — 800 - 1200
BB1552 Cinti 1908, 62 glossy plates, blue CL (rough cys
missing plates worth much less) — 600 - 900
BB1554 Cinti 1987 — 30 - 50

Evans, William G.
BB1590 **How to Umpire by Billy Evans** NY 1920 — 40 - 60
BB1592 **Umpiring From the Inside** 1947 (privately printed) — 75 - 125

Evers, John J.
BB1630 **Touching Second** Chi 1910 — 75 - 125

Farrell, James T.
BB1660 **My Baseball Dairy** NY 1957, DJ — 30 - 50

Feller, Bob
BB1690 **How to Improve Your Baseball** 1952 (Motorola
Promo) — 30 - 50
BB1695 **Strikeout Story** NY 1947, DJ — 30 - 50

Finch, Robert L.
BB1720 **The Story of Minor League Baseball** Col 1953, DJ — 50 - 75

Fitzgerald, Ed (editor)
BB1750 **The Book of Major League Baseball Clubs**
NY 1952, 2 vol, box — 50 - 75

Fleming, G. H.
BB1780 **The Dizziest Season** NY 1984, DJ — 20 - 30
BB1785 **The Unforgettable Season** NY 1981, DJ — 20 - 30

Fonesca, Lew
BB1810 **How to Pitch Baseball** Chi 1942, DJ — 30 - 50

Franklin, Lewis
BB1840 **The Cleveland Indians** NY 1949, DJ — 50 - 75

Gerlach, Larry R.
BB1870 **The Men in Blue** NY 1980, DJ — 30 - 50

BB0240

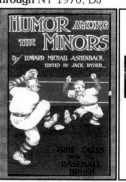
BB0380 (w/o DJ)

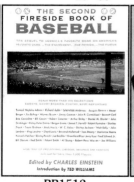
BB1512

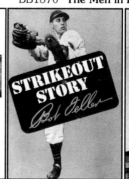
BB1695

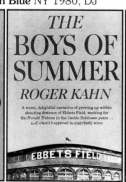
BB2510

BB2840

Graham, Frank
BB1900 Baseball Extra NY 1954, DJ   20 - 30
BB1905 **The Brooklyn Dodgers: An Informal History**
        NY 1945, DJ   50 - 75
        w/o DJ   25 - 35
BB1907 NY 1948, DJ   40 - 60
BB1915 **Casey Stengel** NY 1958, DJ   20 - 30
BB2000 **Lou Gehrig: A Quiet Hero** NY 1942, DJ   30 - 50
        w/o DJ   15 - 25
BB2002 later printings, same year, DJ   20 - 30
BB2010 **The New York Giants** NY 1952, DJ   75 - 125
        w/o DJ   30 - 50
BB2015 **The New York Yankees: An Informal History**
        NY 1948, DJ   75 - 125
        w/o DJ   30 - 50
BB2017 NY 1958, DJ   40 - 60
        w/o DJ   15 - 25
Grobani, Anton
BB2050 **Guide to Baseball Literature** Detroit 1975   75 - 125
Gutkind, Lee
BB2080 **The Best Seat in Baseball But You Have**
        to Stand NY 1975, DJ   30 - 50
Hano, Arnold
BB2110 **A Day in the Bleachers** NY 1955, DJ   40 - 60
Harris, Stanley "Bucky"
BB2140 **Baseball - How To Play It** NY 1925, DJ   75 - 125
BB2145 **Playing the Game** NY 1925, DJ (pub Stokes)   75 - 125
BB2147 NY 1925, DJ (Grosset & Dunlap reprint)   30 - 50
Henderson, Robert
BB2180 **Ball, Bat and Bishop** NY 1947, DJ   75 - 125
Heward, Bill
BB2210 **Some Are Called Clowns** NY 1974, DJ   20 - 30
Higbe, Kirby
BB2240 **The High Hard One** NY 1967, DJ   30 - 50
Hirshberg, Al
BB2270 **The Braves, the Pick and the Shovel** Bos 1948, DJ 50 - 75
BB2275 **The Red Sox, the Bean and the Cod** Bos 1947, DJ 75 - 125
Holway, John B.
BB2300 **Black Ball Stars** Westport 1988, DJ   20 - 30
BB2305 **Voices From the Great Black Baseball**
        Leagues NY 1975, DJ   75 - 125
Honig, Donald
BB2330 **Baseball America** NY 1982, DJ   20 - 30
BB2335 **Baseball in the 30's** NY 1989, DJ   20 - 30
BB2340 **Baseball in the 50's** NY 1987, DJ   20 - 30
BB2345 **Baseball When the Grass Was Real** NY 1975, DJ 20 - 30
BB2350 **Mays, Mantle, Snider** NY 1987, DJ   20 - 30
BB2355 **October Heroes** NY 1979, DJ   15 - 25
Hornsby, Rogers
BB2380 **My Kind of Baseball** NY 1953, DJ   30 - 50
BB2385 **My War With Baseball** NY 1962, DJ   30 - 50
Johnson, Harold "Speed" (editor)
  Also see **Who's Who in Major League Baseball** under **Guides and**
Year Books.
BB2420 **Who's Who in Major League Baseball** Chi
        1933, DJ (one of the finest baseball histories)   600 - 800
        w/o DJ   300 - 500
Kaese, Harold
BB2450 **The Boston Braves** NY 1948, DJ   50 - 75
BB2455 **The Milwaukee Braves** NY 1954, DJ   50 - 75
Kahn, James M.
BB2480 **The Umpire Story** NY 1953, DJ   40 - 60
Kahn, Roger
BB2510 **The Boys of Summer** NY 1972, DJ   30 - 50
BB2511 later printings   15 - 20
Kalinsky, George
BB2540 **The Ball Parks** NY 1975, DJ   75 - 125
Kaufman, Louis, Barbara Fitzgerald & Tom Sewell
BB2550 **Moe Berg Athlete, Scholar...Spy** Bos 1974, DJ 20 - 30
Kennedy, MacLean
BB2570 **The Great Teams of Baseball** NY 1929   150 - 250
King, Joe
BB2600 **The San Francisco Giants** Englewood Cliffs
        1958, DJ   20 - 30

Kinnaird, Clark
BB2630 **Big League Baseball** 1951 (Avon Paperback)   30 - 50
Kirk, William
BB2660 **Right Off the Bat** NY 1911   100 - 150
Knowles, Richard G.
BB2690 **Baseball** Lon 1896, wrappers   1000 - 1500
Koppett, Leonard
BB2720 **The New York Mets** NY 1970, DJ   30 - 50
Koufax, Sandy
BB2750 **Koufax** NY 1966, DJ   20 - 30
Lanigan, Ernest
BB2780 **The Baseball Cyclopedia** NY 1922-33, issued
        annually, each year   50 - 75
Lewis, Allen
BB2810 **The Philadelphia Phillies** NY 1982, DJ   40 - 60
Lewis, Franklin
BB2840 **The Cleveland Indians** NY 1949, DJ   50 - 75
Libby, Bill and Vida Blue
BB2870 **Vida, His Own Story** NY 1972, DJ   15 - 25
Lieb, Frederick
BB2900 **The Baltimore Orioles** NY 1955, DJ   50 - 75
BB2905 **The Boston Red Sox** NY 1947, DJ   50 - 75
BB2910 **Connie Mack: Grand Old Man of Baseball**
        NY 1945, DJ   50 - 75
BB2915 **The Detroit Tigers** NY 1946, DJ   50 - 75
BB2920 **The Philadelphia Phillies** NY 1953, DJ   100 - 150
BB2925 **The Pittsburgh Pirates** NY 1948, DJ   50 - 75
BB2930 **The St. Louis Cardinals** NY 1944, DJ   50 - 75
Liss, Howard
BB2960 **The Mickey Mantle Album** NY 1966, DJ   75 - 125
BB2965 **The Sandy Koufax Album** NY 1966, DJ   30 - 50
BB2970 **The Willie Mays Album** NY 1966, DJ   75 - 125
Luhrs, Victor
BB3000 **The Great Baseball Mystery: The 1919 World**
        Series South Brunswick 1966, DJ   50 - 75
Mack, Connie
BB3030 **Connie Macks Baseball Book** NY 1950, DJ   30 - 50
BB3035 **My 66 Years in the Big Leagues** Phil 1950, DJ 50 - 75
Mantle, Mickey
BB3060 **Education of a Baseball Player** NY 1967, DJ   15 - 25
BB3065 **The Mick** NY 1985, DJ   15 - 25
BB3070 **The Quality of Courage** NY 1964, DJ   20 - 30
Maris, Roger
BB3100 **Roger Maris at Bat** NY 1962, DJ   50 - 75
Mathewson, Christy
BB3130 **Pitching in a Pinch** NY 1912, DJ   400 - 600
        w/o DJ   200 - 300
Mays, Willie
BB3160 **Born To Play Ball** NY 1955, DJ   50 - 75
BB3165 **Say Hey** NY 1988, DJ   15 - 25
McAuley, Ed
BB3190 **Bob Lemon - The Work Horse** NY 1951   30 - 50
McCallum, John
BB3220 **The Tiger Wore Spikes** NY 1956, DJ   30 - 50
BB3225 **Ty Cobb** NY 1975, DJ   15 - 25
McGraw, John
BB3250 **How to Play Baseball** NY 1914 (claims 32
        photos but only 31)   100 - 150
BB3255 **My Thirty Years in Baseball** NY 1923, DJ   300 - 500
        w/o DJ   150 - 200
McGraw, Mrs. John J. (Blanche)
BB3280 **The Real McGraw** NY 1953, DJ   50 - 75
Meany, Tom
  Prices are for first printings with DJs. Books without DJs or Grosset
& Dunlap reprints with DJs are worth half.
BB3310 **Baseball's Greatest Hitters** NY 1950, DJ   50 - 75
BB3315 **Baseball's Greatest Pitchers** NY 1915, DJ   30 - 50
BB3320 **Baseball's Greatest Teams** NY 1949, DJ   30 - 50
BB3323 **The Hot Stove League** NY 1955, DJ   100 - 150
        w/o DJ   50 - 75
BB3325 **The Incredible Giants** NY 1955, DJ   30 - 50
BB3330 **Joe DiMaggio - Yankee Clipper** NY 1951, wrappers 30 - 50
BB3335 **Milwaukee's Miracle Braves** NY 1954, DJ   30 - 50
BB3340 **Ted Williams - Hitting Unlimited** NY 1951, wrappers 30 - 50

BB3345 The Yankee Story NY 1960, DJ	30 - 50	

Moreland, George
BB3370 Balldom: The Britannica of Baseball NY 1914 125 - 200

Morse, Jacob C.
BB3400 Sphere and Ash Bos 1988 (1st baseball history) 500 - 700

Mosedale, John
BB3430 The Greatest of All NY 1974, DJ 30 - 50

Musial, Stan
BB3460 How the Majors Play Baseball (Rawling's
       promo) 1952, wrappers 15 - 20
BB3465 The Man Stan Musial:...Then and Now
       St. Louis 1977, DJ 30 - 50
       signed 75 - 100

Obojski, Robert
BB3520 Bush League: A History of Minor League
       Baseball NY 1975, DJ 30 - 50

Orem, Preston D.
BB3550 Baseball 1845-1891 From the Newspaper
       Accounts Altadena, CA 1961, 11 vol (vol 1:
       1845-1881; vol 2-11: 1882-1891), each vol 50 - 75

Paige, Satchel
BB3580 Maybe I'll Pitch Forever NY 1962, DJ 40 - 60

Palmer, Harry Clay
BB3610 Athletic Sports in America, England and
       Australia Phil 1889 (mostly about baseball
       w/color & b&w plates) 600 - 800
BB3615 Baseball: The National Game of the
       Americans Chi 1888, wrappers 300 - 500

Patten, William (editor)
BB3640 The Book of Baseball: The National Game
       From the Earliest Days to the Present
       NY 1911, folio/pict. bds. 250 - 400

Paxton, Harry
BB3670 The Whiz Kids Phil 1950, DJ 100 - 150

Perry, Gaylord
BB3700 Me and the Spitter NY 1974, DJ 20 - 30

Peterson, Robert W.
BB3730 Only the Ball Was White Englewood Cliffs
       1970, DJ 125 - 200

Piersall, Jim
BB3760 Fear Strikes Out NY 1955, DJ 20 - 30
       signed 40 - 60

Pinelli, Babe
BB3790 Babe Pinelli Phil 1952, DJ 30 - 50

Plimpton, George
BB3820 Out of My League NY 1961, DJ 20 - 30

Pope, Edwin
BB3850 Ted Williams - The Golden Year 1957
       NY 1970, DJ 30 - 50

Povich, Shirley
BB3880 The Washington Senators NY 1954, DJ 75 - 125

Reichler, Joseph (editor)
BB3910 The Baseball Encyclopedia NY 1969-1988
       (issued every several years) 20 - 30
BB3915 The Game and the Glory NY 1976, DJ 20 - 30

Richter, Francis
BB3940 A Brief History of Baseball Phil 1909 500 - 700
BB3945 Richter's History and Records of Baseball, The
       American Nations Chief Sport Phil 1914 300 - 500

Rickey, Branch
BB3970 The American Diamond NY 1965, DJ 100 - 150

Ritter, Lawrence S.
BB4000 The 100 Greatest Baseball Players of All Time
       NY 1981, DJ 20 - 30
BB4005 The Babe - A Life in Pictures Bos 1988, DJ 30 - 50
BB4010 The Glory of Their Times NY 1966, DJ 20 - 30
BB4015 The Image of Their Greatness NY 1979, DJ 20 - 30

Robinson, Jackie
BB4040 Baseball Has Done It NY 1964, DJ 20 - 30
BB4045 My Own Story NY 1948, DJ 150 - 200

Roeder, Bill
BB4070 Jackie Robinson NY 1950, DJ 40 - 60

Rogosin, Donn
BB4100 Invisible Men: Life in Baseball's Negro
       Leagues NY 1983, DJ 30 - 50

Rose, Pete
BB4130 Charlie Hustle NY 1975, DJ 20 - 30
BB4135 The Pete Rose Story NY 1970, DJ 15 - 25
       signed 30 - 50

Ruth, Babe (George Herman)
BB4160 The Babe Ruth Story NY 1948, DJ 50 - 75
BB4170 Babe Ruth's Own Book of Baseball NY 1928, DJ 200 - 300
       w/o DJ 50 - 75
BB4171 NY 1928, DJ (A.L. Burt reprint) 100 - 150
       w/o DJ 20 - 30
       signed +1000

Ruth, Mrs. Babe
BB4190 The Babe and I NY 1959, DJ 30 - 50

Ryan, Nolan
BB4220 Throwing Heat NY 1988, DJ 20 - 30

Schact, Al
BB4250 Clowning Through Baseball NY 1941, DJ 30 - 50
BB4255 My Own Particular Screwball NY 1955, DJ 20 - 30

Schoor, Gene
BB4280 Christy Mathewson NY 1953, DJ 30 - 50
BB4290 Mickey Mantle NY 1958, DJ 50 - 75
BB4295 Roy Campanella NY 1959, DJ 30 - 50

Seaver, Tom
BB4330 The Perfect Game NY 1970, DJ 20 - 30

Seymour, Harold
BB4360 Baseball, The Early Years NY 1960, DJ 75 - 125

Shannon, Bill
BB4390 The Ball Parks NY 1975, DJ (considered the
       best history of baseball stadiums) 125 - 200

Shannon, Mike
BB4420 Diamond Classics: Essays on the 100 of the Best
       Baseball Books Ever Published Jefferson, NC 1989 20 - 30

Silverman, Al
BB4450 Joe DiMaggio - The Golden Year 1941
       NY 1969, DJ 30 - 50

Smelser, Marshall
BB4480 The Life That Ruth Built NY 1975, DJ 50 - 75

Smith, Ira L.
BB4510 Baseball's Famous First Basemen NY 1956, DJ 30 - 50
BB4515 Baseball's Famous Outfielders NY 1955, DJ 30 - 50
BB4520 Baseball's Famous Pitchers NY 1954, DJ 30 - 50

Spalding, A. G. (Alfred G.)
BB4550 Baseball - America's National Game NY 1911 300 - 500

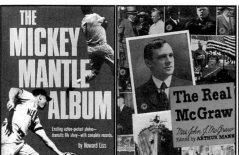

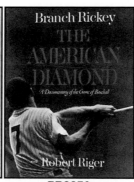
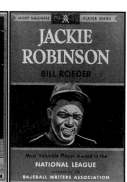

BB2960	BB3280	BB3640	BB3970	BB4005	BB4070

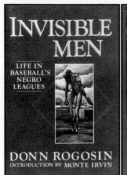
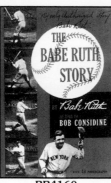
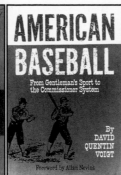

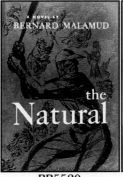

BB4100	BB4160	BB4700	BB5200 (w/o DJ)	BB5520	BB6830

Spink, Alfred E.
BB4580 The National Game St. Louis 1910   300 - 500

Suehsdorf, A. D.
BB4610 The Great American Baseball Scrapbook
NY 1978, DJ   30 - 50

Treat, Roger
BB4640 Walter Johnson NY 1948, DJ   100 - 150

Veeck, Bill
BB4670 Hustler's Handbook NY 1965, DJ   50 - 75
BB4675 Veeck as in Wreck NY 1962, DJ   30 - 50

Voigt, David Quentin
BB4700 American Baseball, Vol I Norman 1966, DJ   50 - 75
BB4705 American Baseball, Vol II Norman 1970, DJ   50 - 75
BB4710 American Baseball, Vol III Norman 1983, DJ   40 - 60

Wardlaw, Charles
BB4740 Fundamentals of Baseball NY 1924   50 - 75

White, Sol
BB4770 Sol White's Official Baseball Guide 1907
(pub H. Walter Schlichter), wrappers w/cover
title **History of Colored Baseball** (1st history
of black baseball, very rare)   2000 - 3000
BB4772 NY 1984, limited ed reprint   100 - 150

Whitehead, Charles
BB4800 A Man and His Diamonds Vantage Press 1980, DJ 75 - 125

Whiting, Robert
BB4830 The Chrysanthemum and the Bat: Baseball
Samurai Style NY 1977, DJ   50 - 75

Young, A. S. "Doc"
BB4860 Great Negro Baseball Stars NY 1953, DJ   75 - 125

Fiction (alphabetical by author)

Barbour, Ralph Henry
Wrote about 25 baseball books
BB5000 Double Play NY 1909, DJ   50 - 75
BB5005 Squeeze Play NY 1931, DJ   30 - 50

Brashler, William
BB5020 The Bingo Long Traveling All Stars and
Motor Kings NY 1973, DJ   30 - 50

Brooks, Noah
BB5040 Our Baseball Club (1st fiction book entirely
about baseball) NY 1884   800 - 1200
BB5042 NY 1896   200 - 300
BB5050 The Fairpoint Nine NY 1880   200 - 300
BB5052 NY 1898   75 - 125

Chadwick, Lester
Pseud. for Edward Stratemeyer; wrote about 12 "Baseball Joe" novels.
BB5080 Baseball Joe on the School Nine, 1912 NY 1912 50 - 75
BB5085 Baseball Joe, Saving the League NY 1923, DJ   40 - 60

Chance, Frank
BB5120 The Bride and the Pennant Bos 1910, wrappers
(author was major league player)   200 - 300

Coffin, Tristram
BB5140 The Old Ball Game: Baseball in Folklore
and Fiction NY 1971, DJ   30 - 50

Coover, Robert
BB5160 The Universal Baseball Association, Inc.
J. Henry Prop. NY 1968, DJ   75 - 125

Dawson, Elmer
BB5180 Larry's Speed Ball NY (1920s) Grosset &
Dunlap, DJ   30 - 50

BB5185 other titles of Buck & Larry Baseball Stories, w/DJ   30 - 50

Duffield, J. W.
Wrote Bert Wilson series: Bert Wilson, Wireless Operator, etc.
BB5200 Bert Wilson's Fadeaway Ball NY 1913   20 - 30

Everett, William
BB5220 Changing Base Bos 1868 (1st fiction book
w/baseball chapter)   1200 - 1800

Greenberg, Eric Rolfe
BB5240 The Celebrant NY 1983, DJ   40 - 60

Grey, Zane (also see Modern First Editions)
BB5260 The Red-Headed Outfield and Other
Stories NY 1920, DJ   75 - 125
w/o DJ   30 - 50
BB5262 NY 1920, DJ (Grosset & Dunlap reprint)   20 - 30
BB5270 The Shortstop NY 1909, DJ   125 - 200
BB5272 NY 1909, DJ (Grosset & Dunlap reprint)   50 - 75
BB5280 The Young Pitcher NY 1911, DJ   100 - 150
BB5282 NY 1911, DJ (Grosset & Dunlap reprint)   30 - 50

Harris, Mark
BB5310 Bang the Drum Slowly NY 1956, DJ   50 - 75
BB5315 The Southpaw Ind 1953, DJ   50 - 75
BB5320 A Ticket For A Seamstitch NY 1957, DJ   50 - 75

Heyliger, William
Wrote about 14 titles; used pseud. Hawley Williams for some books.
BB5340 Bartley, Fisherman Pitcher NY 1911   50 - 75
BB5345 Bean Ball Bill, and Other Stories NY 1920, DJ   50 - 75

Jenks, George
BB5380 Double Curve Dan, The Pitcher Detective
NY 1888, wrappers (Beadle dime novel)   100 - 150

Johnson, Owen
BB5400 The Humming Bird NY 1910, DJ   100 - 150
BB5402 NY 1938, DJ   20 - 30

Kinsella, W. P.
BB5440 The Iowa Baseball Confederacy Bos 1986, DJ   20 - 30
BB5450 Shoeless Joe Bos 1982, DJ   50 - 75

Lardner, Ring W.
BB5480 You Know Me, Al: A Busher's Letters NY
1916, DJ   175 - 250

Lawson, Thomas W.
BB5500 The Krank Bos 1888   150 - 250

Malamud, Bernard
BB5520 The Natural NY 1952, DJ (1st printing)   200 - 300

Mathewson, Christy
Add $1,000 for books with Mathewson's signature.
BB5540 Catcher Craig NY 1915, DJ   200 - 300
BB5542 NY 1915, DJ (Grosset & Dunlap reprint)   50 - 75
BB5550 Pitcher Pollack NY 1914, DJ   200 - 300
BB5552 NY 1914, DJ (Grosset & Dunlap reprint)   50 - 75
BB5560 Second Base Sloan NY 1917, DJ   200 - 300
BB5562 NY 1917, DJ (Grosset & Dunlap reprint)   30 - 50
BB5570 Won in the Ninth R.J. Bodner Co. 1910   200 - 300

Overton, Mark
BB5600 Jack Winters Baseball Team NY 1919   50 - 75

Rice, Damon
BB5620 Season's Past NY 1976, DJ   50 - 75

Rosen, R. D.
BB5640 Strike Three, You're Dead NY 1984, DJ   20 - 30

Ruth, Babe
BB5660 The Home Run King or How Pep Pindar
Won His Title NY 1920   200 - 300

Sherman, Harold
BB5680 Bases Full NY 1928, DJ   30 - 50

Smith, H. Allen
BB5700 Rhubarb Garden City 1946, DJ   20 - 30

Standish, Burt L.
BB5720 Brick King, Backstop NY 1914, DJ   50 - 75
BB5725 Frank Merriwell's Baseball Victory NY 1899,
      wrappers   50 - 75
BB5730 Lefty Locke, Pitcher Manager NY 1915, DJ 50 - 75
BB5735 The Man on First NY 1920, DJ   50 - 75

Standish, Winn
BB5760 Jack Lorimar's Champions NY 1907   50 - 75

Tunis, John R.
BB5780 The Keystone Kids NY 1943, DJ   30 - 50
BB5785 The Kid From Tomkinsville NY 1940, DJ 30 - 50

Wallop, Douglas
BB5820 The Year the Yankees Lost the Pennant
      NY 1954, DJ   30 - 50

Woodley, Richard
BB5840 The Bad News Bears NY 1976, DJ   20 - 30

Guide Books (alphabetical by title)

All Star Programs (guides)
Prices are for guides in very good to fine condition.

BB6010	1933	1500 - 2000
BB6012	1934	1000 - 1500
BB6015	1935-1940	800 - 1200
BB6020	1941-1945	400 - 600
BB6025	1946-1950	250 - 350
BB6030	1951-1952	150 - 250
BB6035	1953	250 - 350
BB6040	1954-1958	150 - 250
BB6045	1959-1960	75 - 125
BB6050	1961	250 - 350
BB6055	1962-1966	75 - 125
BB6060	1967	125 - 200
BB6062	1968	75 - 125
BB6064	1969	50 - 75
BB6066	1970-1971	100 - 150
BB6070	1972	20 - 30
BB6072	1973	100 - 150
BB6074	1974	20 - 30
BB6076	1975	30 - 50
BB6080	1976-1978	20 - 30
BB6084	1979-1980	15 - 25
BB6086	1981	10 - 15
BB6088	1982	15 - 25
BB6090	1983-	10 - 15

American League Red Book
Published annually since 1943.

BB6120	1943-1950	30 - 50
BB6130	1951-1960	15 - 25
BB6140	1961-1970	12 - 20
BB6150	1971-1980	8 - 12
BB6160	1981-	8 - 10

Beadle's Dime Baseball Player
Issued annually 1860-1881. Edited by Henry Chadwick and published by Beadle & Co. Very rare, any copy in fine condition should be worth at least $250, especially earlier editions.

BB6200	1860	500 - 700
BB6202	1861-1865	300 - 500
BB6210	1866-1870	250 - 350
BB6218	1871-1880	150 - 250

Famous Slugger Yearbooks
Published annually by Hillerich & Bradsby 1940-1978.

BB6240	1940-1950	25 - 35
BB6251	1951-1960	15 - 25
BB6261	1961-1970	10 - 15
BB6271	1971-1978	5 - 12

Lajoie's Official Baseball Guide
Published by American League Publishing Co., 1906-1908, and edited by Napoleon Lajoie.

BB6290	1906-1908, wrappers, fine condition	200 - 300

Little Red Book of Baseball
Published by Spalding 1926-1971.

BB6310	1926	30 - 40

BB6312	1927-1929	25 - 35
BB6316	1930-1935	25 - 30
BB6324	1936-1940	20 - 25
BB6331	1941-1950	15 - 20
BB6341	1951-1960	8 - 12
BB6351	1961-1971	6 - 8

National League Green Book
Published annually since 1934.

BB6380	1934-1940	50 - 75
BB6388	1941-1950	30 - 50
BB6401	1951-1960	20 - 30
BB6411	1961-1970	10 - 15
BB6421	1971-1980	7 - 12
BB6431	1981-	7 - 10

Official Baseball Annual
Issued annually 1952-1968 and 1970-1978 by Dell Publishing Co, NY. Also known as the **Dell Baseball Annual** or the **Dell Sports Baseball.**

BB6460	1952-1960	20 - 30
BB6470	1961-1970	15 - 25
BB6480	1971-1978	7 - 12

The Reach Official Baseball Guide
Issued annually in wrappers 1883-1939. Prices are for books in very good to fine condition.

BB6500	1883	300 - 500
BB6502	1884-1886	250 - 350
BB6506	1887-1890	150 - 250
BB6511	1891-1900	125 - 200
BB6521	1901-1920	100 - 150
BB6541	1921-1930	75 - 125
BB6551	1931-1939	50 - 75

Spalding's Official Baseball Guide
Issued annually in wrappers by A.G. Spalding & Brothers, Chi, 1876-1939. Prices are for very good to fine condition.

BB6580	1876	500 - 700
BB6582	1877	400 - 600
BB6584	1878-1880	300 - 500
BB6588	1881-1890	250 - 350
BB6601	1891-1900	200 - 300
BB6611	1901-1920	125 - 175
BB6631	1921-1930	100 - 150
BB6641	1931-1939	50 - 75

True's Baseball Yearbook
Published by *True Magazine*, Fawcett Publications, 1950-1972.

BB6670	1950	30 - 40
BB6671	1951-1960	20 - 30
BB6681	1961-1972	10 - 20

Who's Who in Baseball
Published in 1912 and since 1916. First publisher was Baseball Magazine 1912-1957, then Who's Who in Baseball Magazine Co.

BB6710	1912	75 - 125
BB6714	1916-1920	50 - 75
BB6721	1921-1940	30 - 50
BB6741	1941-1960	20 - 30
BB6761	1961-1970	15 - 25
BB6771	1971-1980	7 - 12
BB6781	1981-	5 - 10

Who's Who in Major League Baseball
Published in 1933 and 1935-1952. Edited in 1933 and 1935-1937 by Harold "Speed" Johnson. Edited by John Carmichal 1938-1952.

BB6810	1933, DJ	600 - 800
	w/o DJ	300 - 500
BB6814	1935-1939	75 - 125
BB6820	1940-1949	50 - 75
BB6830	1950-1952	40 - 60

World Series Programs (guides)
Prices are for very good to fine condition.

BB6903	1903	2000 - 3000
BB6905	1905-1917	800 - 1200
BB6918	1918-1919	1000 - 1500
BB6920	1920-1929	500 - 700
BB6930	1930-1939	300 - 500
BB6940	1940-1944	250 - 350
BB6945	1945-1949	125 - 200
BB6950	1950-1959	100 - 150
BB6960	1960-1969	75 - 125
BB6970	1970-1979	20 - 30
BB6980	1980-	10 - 20

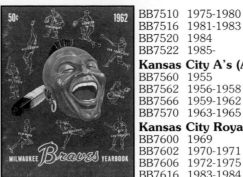

BB7570   BB8580   BB8834

Team Yearbooks (alphabetical by team name)
American League
Baltimore Orioles
BB7010	1954-1960	150 - 200
BB7016	1961	100 - 125
BB7018	1962-1968	40 - 60
BB7024	1969	30 - 50
BB7026	1970	50 - 75
BB7028	1971	30 - 50
BB7030	1972-1974	15 - 20
BB7040	1979-	8 - 15

Boston Red Sox
BB7110	1951	175 - 225
BB7112	1952	100 - 150
BB7116	1955	75 - 125
BB7118	1956-1960	50 - 75
BB7122	1961-1966	30 - 40
BB7124	1967	75 - 100
BB7126	1968-1969	30 - 40
BB7130	1970-1974	20 - 30
BB7136	1975	30 - 40
BB7138	1976-1980	10 - 15
BB7144	1981-1985	8 - 12
BB7150	1986	10 - 15
BB7152	1987-	5 - 12

California Angels
BB7210	1966	30 - 40
BB7212	1967	25 - 35
BB7230	1983-1984	8 - 12
BB7234	1985	10 - 15

Chicago White Sox
BB7270	1948-1950	75 - 125
BB7274	1951	150 - 200
BB7276	1952-1955	100 - 125
BB7280	1956-1958	50 - 75
BB7284	1959	100 - 125
BB7286	1960-1964	30 - 50
BB7290	1965-1969	15 - 25
BB7294	1970	20 - 30
BB7306	1982	8 - 12
BB7308	1983	15 - 20
BB7310	1984	8 - 12
BB7316	1990	8 - 12

Cleveland Indians
BB7350	1948	75 - 125
BB7352	1949-1952	40 - 60
BB7356	1953-1954	50 - 75
BB7358	1955	100 - 125
BB7360	1956-1958	50 - 75
BB7364	1959	100 - 125
BB7366	1960-1964	50 - 75
BB7372	1965-1969	40 - 60
BB7376	1970-1979	15 - 20
BB7386	1980-	6 - 12

Detroit Tigers
BB7460	1934	300 - 500
BB7482	1955	200 - 250
BB7484	1956-1958	100 - 150
BB7488	1959-1960	75 - 125
BB7492	1961-1962	50 - 75
BB7496	1963-1967	40 - 60
BB7502	1968	75 - 125
BB7504	1969-1974	30 - 50

BB7510	1975-1980	10 - 15
BB7516	1981-1983	8 - 12
BB7520	1984	20 - 30
BB7522	1985-	5 - 12

Kansas City A's (Athletics)
BB7560	1955	175 - 225
BB7562	1956-1958	125 - 175
BB7566	1959-1962	50 - 75
BB7570	1963-1965	30 - 40

Kansas City Royals
BB7600	1969	75 - 125
BB7602	1970-1971	20 - 30
BB7606	1972-1975	10 - 15
BB7616	1983-1984	8 - 12
BB7618	1985	20 - 30
BB7620	1986-	5 - 15

Los Angeles Angels
BB7650	1962	100 - 150
BB7652	1963	75 - 125
BB7654	1964	50 - 75
BB7656	1965	40 - 60

Milwaukee Brewers
BB7700	1970	75 - 100
BB7702	1971	15 - 20
BB7712	1980-1981	10 - 15
BB7714	1982	20 - 30
BB7716	1983-1985	10 - 12
BB7720	1986-	5 - 12

Minnesota Twins
BB7750	1961	200 - 300
BB7752	1962	50 - 75
BB7754	1963-1964	30 - 40
BB7756	1965	50 - 75
BB7758	1966-1969	25 - 35
BB7762	1970-1979	10 - 15
BB7772	1980-1982	8 - 12
BB7776	1985	10 - 15
BB7778	1986	10 - 15
BB7780	1987-	5 - 12

New York Yankees
BB7810	1950 (official)	300 - 500
BB7812	1951	175 - 225
BB7814	1952	200 - 250
BB7816	1953-1954	100 - 150
BB7818	1955 (official)	200 - 250
BB7820	1955-1956	150 - 200
BB7822	1957-1964	75 - 100
BB7832	1965-1966	50 - 75
BB7834	1967-1970	30 - 50
BB7840	1971-1977	20 - 30
BB7848	1978-1980	15 - 25
BB7852	1981-	5 - 12

Oakland A's (Athletics)
BB7900	1968	75 - 125
BB7902	1969	50 - 75
BB7904	1970-1971	30 - 40
BB7906	1972-1975	20 - 30
BB7912	1976-1977	10 - 15
BB7916	1978-1979	15 - 20
BB7918	1980	10 - 15
BB7920	1982-1983	8 - 12

Philadelphia A's (Athletics)
BB7950	1949	100 - 125
BB7952	1950	100 - 125
BB7954	1951-1952	75 - 100
BB7958	1953	40 - 60
BB7960	1954	50 - 75

St. Louis Browns
BB7980	1950	300 - 500
BB7982	1951	250 - 350
BB7984	1952	250 - 350

Seattle Mariners
BB8000	1977	30 - 50
BB8002	1978-1980	20 - 30
BB8006	1981-	5 - 15

Seattle Pilots
BB8040	1969	150 - 250

Texas Rangers

BB8060	1976	30 - 40
BB8062	1977	10 - 15
BB8064	1978-1980	8 - 12
BB8068	1981-	5 - 12

Toronto Blue Jays

BB8100	1977	30 - 50
BB8104	1979	10 - 15
BB8106	1980-	7 - 12

Washington Senators

BB8140	1947	200 - 300
BB8144	1950	100 - 150
BB8146	1951-1952	75 - 125
BB8148	1953	30 - 50
BB8150	1954	50 - 75
BB8152	1955	75 - 100
BB8158	1959	
BB8160	1961	150 - 200
BB8162	1962-1963	40 - 60
BB8166	1964-1967	30 - 40
BB8170	1968-1971	20 - 30

National League

Atlanta Braves

BB8300	1966	30 - 50
BB8302	1967-1969	15 - 20
BB8306	1970-1975	10 - 15
BB8312	1976-1980	8 - 12
BB8318	1981-	5 - 12

Boston Braves

BB8360	1946	200 - 300
BB8362	1947	150 - 200
BB8364	1950	150 - 200
BB8366	1951	150 - 200
BB8368	1952	175 - 225

Brooklyn Dodgers

BB8400	1940	300 - 500
BB8402	1941-1942	250 - 350
BB8408	1946	200 - 300
BB8410	1947	125 - 200
BB8414	1949-1951	250 - 350
BB8418	1952	150 - 250
BB8420	1953-1954	125 - 200
BB8424	1955	150 - 250
BB8426	1956-1957	100 - 175

Chicago Cubs

BB8450	1934	250 - 350
BB8466	1948	100 - 150
BB8468	1949-1953	75 - 125
BB8474	1954-1957	50 - 75
BB8478	1958-1968	20 - 30
BB8480	1969-1972	15 - 20
BB8484	1973-1980	5 - 10
BB8494	1981-	4 - 8

Cincinnati Reds

BB8540	1919	500 - 700
BB8570	1946	250 - 350
BB8572	1947	250 - 350
BB8574	1948	250 - 350
BB8576	1949	
BB8578	1951-1952	100 - 125
BB8580	1953-1955	75 - 100
BB8584	1956-1958	50 - 75
BB8588	1959-1962	40 - 60
BB8592	1963	75 - 100
BB8594	1964-1969	30 - 50
BB8600	1970-1974	20 - 30
BB8606	1975-1976	15 - 25
BB8608	1977-1980	8 - 12
BB8612	1981-	5 - 12

Houston Astros

BB8660	1964	50 - 75
BB8662	1965	40 - 60
BB8664	1966	20 - 30
BB8666	1967-1970	10 - 15
BB8672	1971-1980	8 - 12
BB8684	1981-	5 - 12

Houston Colt 45's

BB8720	1962	150 - 250

BB8722	1963	50 - 75

Los Angeles Dodgers

BB8740	1958	150 - 200
BB8742	1959	75 - 100
BB8744	1960-1963	40 - 60
BB8750	1964-1966	20 - 30
BB8754	1967-1971	15 - 20
BB8760	1972-1974	10 - 15
BB8764	1975-1980	8 - 12
BB8772	1981-	5 - 12

Milwaukee Braves

BB8820	1953	150 - 200
BB8822	1954	200 - 250
BB8824	1955	100 - 125
BB8826	1956	100 - 125
BB8828	1957	
BB8830	1958	100 - 125
BB8832	1959	75 - 100
BB8834	1960-1965	30 - 50

Montreal Expos

BB8850	1969	100 - 150
BB8852	1970	50 - 75
BB8854	1971-1972	30 - 40
BB8856	1973-1978	10 - 15
BB8862	1979-1980	12 - 20
BB8866	1981-	5 - 15

New York Giants

BB8900	1947	150 - 200
BB8904	1951	125 - 175
BB8906	1952	100 - 125
BB8908	1953	75 - 100
BB8910	1954	100 - 150
BB8912	1955-1957	75 - 100

New York Mets

BB8940	1962	200 - 300
BB8942	1963	125 - 200
BB8944	1964	50 - 75
BB8946	1965-1968	30 - 50
BB8952	1969	75 - 125
BB8954	1970	30 - 50
BB8956	1971-1980	15 - 25
BB8968	1981-	5 - 15

Philadelphia Phillies

BB9010	1949	150 - 200
BB9012	1950	125 - 200
BB9014	1951-1952	75 - 125
BB9018	1953	40 - 60
BB9020	1954-1959	50 - 75
BB9026	1960-1967	30 - 50
BB9034	1968-1970	20 - 30
BB9038	1971-1980	12 - 20
BB9050	1981-	5 - 12

Pittsburgh Pirates

BB9110	1914	400 - 600
BB9150	1951	150 - 200
BB9152	1952	125 - 175
BB9154	1953	100 - 150
BB9156	1954-1960	50 - 75
BB9164	1961-1966	30 - 50
BB9170	1967-1971	20 - 30
BB9176	1972-1980	10 - 15
BB9186	1981-	5 - 12

St. Louis Cardinals

BB9300	1950	75 - 125
BB9302	1951	150 - 250
BB9304	1952	100 - 150
BB9306	1953-1957	50 - 75
BB9312	1958-1963	40 - 60
BB9320	1964	50 - 75
BB9322	1965-1968	40 - 60
BB9328	1969-1971	20 - 30
BB9332	1972-1978	12 - 20
BB9340	1979-1982	8 - 12
BB9346	1983-	5 - 12

San Diego Padres

BB9410	1969	75 - 125
BB9412	1970-1976	12 - 20
BB9420	1977-1980	8 - 15
BB9426	1981-	5 - 12

San Francisco Giants

BB9510	1958	50 - 75
BB9512	1959	30 - 50
BB9514	1960-1961	20 - 30
BB9518	1962	30 - 50
BB9520	1963-1968	20 - 30
BB9528	1969-1970	12 - 20
BB9531	1971-1980	8 - 15
BB9544	1981-	5 - 12

BAUMIANA & OZIANA

"Baumiana" means all books by L. Frank Baum, including books written under pseudonyms Laura Bancroft, Capt. Hugh Fitzgerald, Floyd Akers, and others. "Oziana" includes all books from the Oz series or with Oz in the title. These were written by Baum, John R. Neill, Ruth Plumly Thompson, and Jack Snow.

L. Frank Baum was born in Chittengo, New York. As a youngster he had many odd jobs including selling his father's axle grease, "Baum's Castorine Oil." He later ventured into newspaper and magazine writing. Baum's first published book, *The Book of Hamburgs* (Hartford 1886), was about poultry. He also wrote for a Chicago newspaper and a "Show Window" advertising magazine.

Baum always enjoyed telling stories to children. Many of these were the groundwork for his books. The origin of the word "Oz" is said to have come from a storytelling session. A little girl suddenly asked "Where is this place?" Baum happened to glance at his file cabinet, noticed the lower file label "O - Z" and quickly replied "Oz."

Baum's first fantasy book was *Mother Goose in Prose*. Illustrated by the then unknown artist Maxfield Parrish, it thus became Parrish's first illustrated book. While in Chicago, Baum joined a "Men's Club." There he met his best-known illustrator, W.W. Denslow.

The Wonderful Wizard of Oz was Baum's first Oz book. Today it's one of the most famous and valuable children's books. An estimated 100,000 copies of the first edition (Chi 1900) were sold. Few have survived; only a small number have the original dust jacket intact. A copy in partial dust jacket recently sold for over $20,000.

Oz books are notorious for being in rough shape. Obviously handled with zeal by children, an early edition is difficult to find in fine condition. Even copies in good condition with only minor wear are usually worth only a fourth to a half the same copy in fine condition. A good example is the first edition first issue of *The Wonderful Wizard of Oz*: a fine copy may be worth over $10,000 while a good copy may be worth only $2,000. A copy in poor condition with heavy soiling and missing pages might be hard to sell for $200. This wide range applies to all of Baum's books. Dust jackets on pre-1910 books are very rare. In some cases no copy of certain titles has ever been found in jacket. Thus a first-edition first-issue copy of *The Wonderful Wizard of Oz* in complete dust jacket might be worth over $50,000.

Many of Baum's early (pre-1920) editions are hybrids made of "points" from various editions, states, and issues. The reason is simple: printers and binders often saved parts from previously-printed books and mixed them with parts from newer printings. This would be very confusing to bibliographers, except Baum signed and dated many of his early books. From his dates it's easy to determine what "points" came first. The first edition first issue of *The Wonderful Wizard of Oz* has many points as well as three binding states. A book with mixed points is worth less than a copy with all the title's earliest points.

Prices are for books without dust jackets unless otherwise stated.

Anonymous & Pseudonymous Titles
Akers, Floyd
BA0511 **The Boy Fortune Hunters in Alaska** Reilly & Britton, Chi (1908), 1st ed: 291 pp, 8vo, 3 b&w plates, lt brown cl stamped in black, white & cream, (reprint of *Sam Steele's Adventures on Land and Sea*, 1st ed under new title) 200 - 300

BA0522 Reilly & Britton, Chi (1908), 2nd ed
BA0531 **The Boy Fortune Hunters in China** Reilly & Britton Chi (1909), 1st ed, 1st state: 325 pp, 8vo, b&w frontis, brown pict cl stamped in black, white & cream, p 325 ends w/title *The Boy Fortune Hunters in Egypt* 200 - 350
BA0532 Chi (1909), 1st ed, 2nd state: cover stamped in black, orange & green, p 325 ends w/title *The Boy Fortune Hunters in Yucatan*
BA0542 **The Boy Fortune Hunters in Egypt** Reilly & Britton, Chi (1908), 1st ed, 2nd state: 291 pp, 8vo, 3 plates, brown pict cl stamped in black, white & cream, p 291 ends w/title *Very Rich Indeed* 150- 250
BA0544 Reilly & Britton, Chi (1908), 1st ed, 2nd state: 1 b&w frontis plate, p 291 ends w/title *The Boy Fortune Hunters in China* 100 - 175
BA0553 Reilly & Britton, Chi (1908), 3rd state: cover stamped in black, orange & green, p 291 ends w/title *The Boy Fortune Hunters in Yucatan* 100 - 175
BA0561 **The Boy Fortune Hunters in Panama** Reilly & Britton, Chi (1908), 1st ed: lt brown pict cl stamped in black, white & cream, 5 color plates (reprint of *Sam Steele's Adventures in Panama*) 200 - 350
BA0562 Chi (1908), 1st ed, 2nd state, b&w frontis, 2 pp. ads at end 150 - 225
BA0563 Chi (1908), 1st ed, 3rd state, p 310 lists titles thru *The Boy Fortune Hunters in Yucatan*, cover stamped in black, orange & green 125 - 200
BA0564 Chi (1908), 1st ed, 4th state: p 310 lists 6 *Aunt Jane's Nieces* titles 125 - 200
BA0581 **The Boy Fortune Hunters in Yucatan** Reilly & Britton, Chi (1910), 1st ed: 343 pp, b&w frontis, 8 vo, tan pict cl stamped in black, orange & green 250 - 450
BA0591 **The Boy Fortune Hunters in the South Seas** Reilly & Britton, Chi (1911), 1st ed: 263 pp, 8vo, b&w frontis, tan pict cl stamped in black, orange & green, 2 states exist: ads in back for *Aunt Jane's Nieces* & *The Aeroplane Boys*, either state 300 - 600
BA0610 **One** b&w illus, p 271 lists titles thru *The Boy Fortune Hunters in China* 150 - 225
BA0613 Reilly & Britton, Chi (1908), 3rd ed, 2nd state binding, cl cover stamped in black, orange & green, lists titles thru *The Boy Fortune Hunters in the Yucatan* 125 - 200

Anonymous
BA1101 **The Last Egyptian** Edward Stern & Co., Phil 1908, 1st ed: 287 pp, 8 color plates, 8vo, dark blue cl w/sp stamped in white, pict p-o cl w/pub name at bottom, 1st issue w/o printer's slug on cr page 175 - 275
BA1112 Phil 1908, 2nd ed: "Press of..." printer's slug on cr page 150 - 225
BA1123 Phil 1908, 3rd ed: "Third Printing" on cr page 150 - 250

Bancroft, Laura
BA2101 **Babes in Birdland, A Fairy Tale** Reilly & Britton, Chi (1911), 1st ed of this title: reprint of *Policeman Blue Jay*, pict bds, green cl sp, (also see Non-Oz Titles) 200 - 275
BA2121 **Policeman Blue Jay** Reilly & Britton, Chi (1907), 1st ed: 116 pp, 8vo, illus by Wright, pict bds, cl sp 700 - 1200
BA2211 **Twinkle and Chubbins: Their Astonishing Adventures in Nature's Fairyland** Reilly & Britton, Chi (1911), 1st ed: reprint of **The Twinkle Tales** series in 1 vol, yellow cl stamped in red, green & black (ink bleed thru on text illus is common) 450 - 650

  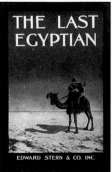

BA0562 (w/o DJ)   BA0581 (w/o DJ)   BA1101 (w/o DJ)

BA2222 Chi 1911, 2nd ed: printed on heavier paper 400 - 600
BA2310 **The Twinkle Tales** (series) Reilly & Britton, Chi (1906), **First Editions**: series of children's books in uniform bindings: **Mr. Woodchuck, Bandit Jim Crow, Prairie-Dog Town, Prince Mudturtle, Sugar-Loaf Mountain** & **Twinkle's Enchantment**, text illus by Maginel Enright, tan cl stamped in variety of colors, red end pprs, each 200 - 300
BA2322 Chi 1906, 2nd ed: bound in white bds, white end pprs, each 125 - 175
BA2333 The Reilly & Lee Co., Chi (1906), 3rd ed: like 2nd ed w/name of later pub, each 100 - 150

Cooke, John Estes
BA3101 **Tamawaca Folks, A Summer Comedy** The Tamawaca Press, USA (1907), 1st ed: 185 pp, 8vo, pp edges uncut, gray cl stamped in blue-green & white (satire about people vacationing at Macatawa, MI) 1500 - 2500
BA3120 modern reprints in cl or wrappers 10 - 25

Fitzgerald, Capt. Hugh
BA4100 **Sam Steele's Adventures in Panama** Reilly & Britton, (1907), 310 pp, 8vo, green pict cl stamped in gold, lt blue, red, white & dark green 350 - 600
BA4121 **Sam Steele's Adventures on Land and Sea** Reilly & Britton, Chi (1906), 1st ed, 1st issue: 271 pp, 8vo, 5 plates, red cl stamped in gold 250 - 450
BA4132 Chi (1906), 2nd issue, blue cl stamped in gold, black, white & lt blue 150 - 250

Metcalf, Susanne
BA6001 **Annabel: A Novel for Young Folks** Reilly & Britton, Chi (1906), 1st ed, 1st issue, 1st state: 231 pp, 8vo, gray cl stamped in gold, 6 plates 500 - 750
BA6022 Chi (1906), 1st issue, 2nd state: blue cl w/white stamping 400 - 600
BA6032 Chi (1906), 2nd issue, 2nd state: 16-pp signatures w/last 8 pp, 6 b&w plates, sp imprint "Reilly and Britton" 250 - 400
BA6042 Reilly & Britton, Chi (1912), 2nd ed: 213 pp, 8vo, 3 plates, lt green pict cl stamped in black, white & peach 200 - 300

Staunton, Schuyler
BA7201 **Daughters of Destiny** Reilly & Britton, Chi (1906), 1st ed, 1st state: 319 pp, 8vo, 8 color plates, dark green cl, pict p-o above author & title on front cover 250 - 400
BA7212 Chi (1906), 2nd state: pict p-o on front cover between title & author's name 200 - 350
BA7222 Reilly & Britton, Chi (1912), 2nd ed: 1 plate (b&w frontis), dark red cl stamped in white w/no pict p-o 100 - 150
BA7261 **The Fate of a Crown** Reilly & Britton, Chi 1905, 1st ed, 1st state: 306 pp, 8vo, 6 b&w illus, red pict cl stamped in black, white & gold 200 - 300

BA7272 Chi 1905, 1st ed, 2nd state: 301 pp, plates included in page numbering 125 - 200
BA7282 Reilly & Britton, Chi (1912), 2nd ed: 291 pp, 8vo, 1 plate (frontis), red cl stamped in white, w/DJ 250 - 400
w/o DJ 100 - 150

Van Dyne, Edith
Later books under this pseudonym exist but were actually written by Emma Speed Sampson.
BA8301 **Aunt Jane's Nieces** Reilly & Britton, Chi (1906), 1st ed: 325 pp, 8vo, 6 plates, lt green cl stamped in gold & dark green w/oval pict p-o 75 - 125
BA8312 Reilly & Britton, Chi (1907), 2nd ed: 7-11/16" x 5-1/4" page size, olive green cl w/ornate floral design & "bow" stamped in gold & purple 50 - 75
BA8323 Chi (1907), 3rd ed: lt tan cl stamped in dark green & purple, 1 b&w plate (frontis), p 327 has ad for 9th ed of *The Girl Graduate* 30 - 50
BA8330 later printings w/ads for later titles or no ads, pict p-o 5 - 15
BA8371 **Aunt Jane's Nieces Abroad** Reilly & Britton, Chi (1906), 1st ed, 1st state binding: 347 pp, 8vo, 5 b&w plates, olive green cl stamped in gold & purple, sp imprint "The Reilly & Britton Co." 100 - 150
BA8382 Chi (1906), 1st ed, 2nd state: lt tan cl w/dark green stamping, sp imprint "Reilly & Britton" 50 - 75
BA8390 later printings w/b&w frontis & ads for later series titles or no titles 5 - 15
BA8392 later printing w/pict cl, w/DJ 35 - 45
BA8431 **Aunt Jane's Nieces and Uncle John** Reilly & Britton, Chi (1911), 1st ed: b&w frontis, tan pict cl stamped in green & purple, ads list titles thru *Uncle John* 30 - 50
BA8440 later printings w/later titles in ads 5 - 15
BA8481 **Aunt Jane's Nieces at Millville** Reilly & Britton, Chi (1908), 1st ed: b&w frontis, tan pict cl stamped in green & purple 30 - 50
BA8490 later printings w/p 306 listing later series titles 5 - 15
BA8531 **Aunt Jane's Nieces at Work** Reilly & Britton, Chi (1909), 1st ed: b&w frontis, lt tan pict cl, p 299 has "The End" at end of text, DJ 50 - 75
w/o DJ 30 - 50
BA8540 later printings w/p 299 listing later titles, DJ 30 - 50
w/o DJ 5 - 15
BA8581 **Aunt Jane's Nieces in Society** Reilly & Britton, Chi (1910), 1st ed: b&w frontis, tan pict cl stamped in green & purple, lists ads for series thru *In Society* 30 - 50
BA8590 later printings w/later titles listed on back of half-title 5 - 15
BA8630 **Aunt Jane's Nieces in the Red Cross** Reilly & Britton, Chi (1915) 30 - 50
BA8640 Reilly & Britton, Chi (1918), revised ed 30 - 50

BA2101   **BA2310 (w/o Dust Jackets, not shown: Mr. Woodchuck)**

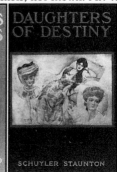
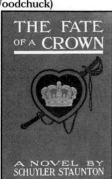

BA2121 (w/o DJ)   BA3101 (w/o DJ)   BA4100 (w/o DJ)   BA4121 (w/o DJ)   BA7212 (w/o DJ)   BA7261 (w/o DJ)   BA7282

| BA8390 | BA8851 | BA9160 | BN1252 | BN1320 | BN1401 |

BA8650   later printings by Reilly & Lee, DJ   30 - 50
          w/o DJ   10 - 20
BA8700 **Aunt Jane's Nieces on the Ranch** Reilly & Britton, Chi
          (1913), b&w frontis, tan pict cl stamped in green &
          purple, half-title back lists series thru *On the Ranch*   30 - 50
BA8710 later printings   5 - 15
BA8750 **Aunt Jane's Nieces on Vacation** Reilly & Britton,
          Chi (1912), b&w frontis, lt tan pict cl stamped in
          green & purple, ad lists titles thru *On Vacation*   30 - 50
BA8760 later printings w/later titles in ads   5 - 15
BA8800 **Aunt Jane's Nieces Out West** Reilly & Britton,
          Chi (1914), 316 pp, 8vo, b&w frontis, tan pict cl
          stamped in green & purple   30 - 50
BA8810 later printings by Reilly & Lee   5 - 15
BA8851 **The Flying Girl** Reilly & Britton, Chi (1911), 1st
          ed, 1st issue: 232 pp, 8vo, 4 plates, red pict cl
          stamped in white & black w/sp lettering & cover
          title stamped in white, DJ   500 - 800
          w/o DJ   150 - 225
BA8862 Reilly & Britton, Chi (1911), 1st ed, 2nd issue: cover
          lettering stamped in black   125 - 200
BA8911 **The Flying Girl and Her Chum** Reilly & Britton,
          Chi (1912), 1st ed, 1st issue: 313 pp, 8vo, 4 plates,
          red cl stamped in black & white w/sp lettering &
          cover title stamped in white   150 - 250
BA8922 Chi (1912), 2nd issue w/sp lettering & cover title
          stamped in black   125 - 200
BA8961 **Mary Louise** Reilly & Britton, Chi (1916), 1st ed,
          1st issue: 267 pp, 8vo, illus by J. Allen St. John,
          b&w frontis, lt blue cl stamped in blind, dark blue
          & white, white & dark blue cover title   40 - 60
BA8972 Chi 1916, 2nd issue: dark blue cover title   15 - 20
BA9010 **Mary Louise Adopts a Soldier** Reilly & Lee, Chi (1919),
          b&w frontis, lt blue cl stamped in dark blue, DJ   30 - 50
          w/o DJ   20 - 30
BA9020 Chi (1919), blue-gray cl   20 - 30
BA9060 **Mary Louise and the Liberty Girls** Reilly & Britton,
          Chi (1918), DJ   40 - 60
          w/o DJ   20 - 35
BA9070 later printings by Reilly & Lee   10 - 15
BA9111 **Mary Louise in the Country** Reilly & Britton, Chi
          (1916), 1st ed, 1st issue: 284 pp, 8vo, b&w frontis,
          lt blue cl stamped in blind, dark blue & white,
          white & dark blue cover title   25 - 35
BA9122 2nd issue: dark blue cover title   10 - 15
BA9160 **Mary Louise Solves a Mystery** Reilly & Britton,
          Chi (1917), DJ   40 - 60
          w/o DJ   20 - 30
BA9170 later printings by Reilly & Lee   10 - 15

Non-Oz Titles

   This section lists non-Oz titles under Baum's name. Prices
are for copies without dust jacket. In many cases no dust jackets
have been found.

BN0800 **American Fairy Tales** Geo. M. Hill, Chi 1901,
          8vo, 205 pp, illus by Ike Morgan, Harry Kennedy
          & N.P. Hall, cl covers w/red flowers   500 - 800
BN0802 cl covers w/green flowers   500 - 800
BN0850 **The Army Alphabet** Geo. M. Hill, Chi 1900,
          pictorial bds, blue cl sp, illus by Kennedy, 4to   600 - 1000
BN1000 **Babes in Birdland** Reilly & Britton, Chi (about 1917),
          2nd ed: 116 pp, 8vo, green cl sp, (also see Laura
          Bancroft under Baum pseudonymous titles)   175 - 225

BN1012 Reilly & Britton, Chi (about 1917), 2nd ed, 2nd
          state: "Laura Bancroft" stamped on brown cl sp   175 - 225
BN1060 **Baum's American Fairy Tales** Ind 1908, 16 color plates
          by George Kerr, large 8vo, blue cl w/pictorial p-o   250 - 450
BN1070 Ind (1920), no pub ads, 8 color plates, lt blue-green
          cl w/pict p-o, 223 pp   150 - 250
BN1100 **Baum's Own Book for Children** Reilly & Britton,
          Chi (1912), 8vo, 196 pp, reprint of *The Juvenile
          Speaker*, color pict p-o over bds, tan cl sp, no ads   350 - 600
BN1110 Chi (1912), variant w/original pages from *The
          Juvenile Speaker* w/ads in back   350 - 600
BN1140 **The Book of Hamburgs** (1st book) Hartford
          1886   1200 - 1800
BN1170 **Christmas Stocking Series** Reilly & Britton, Chi 1905,
          child's storybooks, each w/intro by L. Frank Baum:
          **The Night Before Christmas, Cinderella and
          Sleeping Beauty, The Story of Little Black
          Sambo, Fairy Tales from Grimm, Fairy Tales
          from Anderson, Animal ABC** each volume   75 - 125
BN1178 set of 6 in original publisher's bookcase   1500 - 2500
BN1180 later edition revised (1911), red paper bds, this set's
          color pict cover *Animal ABC* replaced by *Peter
          Rabbit*, each vol   50 - 75
BN1182 set of 6 vol in original publisher's "trunk"   600 - 1000
BN1240 **The Daring Twins** Reilly & Britton, Chi (1911),
          8vo, illus by Batchelder, dark blue pict cl w/cover
          design by Frank Hazenplug   200 - 300
BN1252 2nd state binding of lt blue-gray cl, cover design
          by Joseph Nuyttens   150 - 250
BN1300 **Dot and Tot of Merryland** Geo. M. Hill, Chi
          1901, illus by W.W. Denslow, yellow cl   700 - 1000
BN1310 Bobbs-Merrill, Ind 1903, no ads, pict lt gray cl   250 - 400
BN1320 M.A. Donahue, Chi 1913 green or gray cl   125 - 200
BN1330 Bobbs-Merrill, Ind 1920, blank end pprs, red cl.
          w/cover p-o in black, blue & yellow, DJ   300 - 500
          w/o DJ   100 - 150
BN1340 Bobbs-Merrill, Ind (1924), illus printed in black &
          green only   75 - 125
BN1401 **The Enchanted Island of Yew** Bobbs-Merrill, Ind
          (1903), 1st state, 8 color plates by Fanny Cory, 242 pp,
          grey pict cl, orange & black pict end pprs, printer's
          imprint (Braunworth & Co.) appears below
          cr notice, illus on p 238 printed upside down,
          orange-black tp, orange-black text   250 - 400
BN1422 Ind (1903), 2nd state, no printer's imprint on cr
          page, p 238 illus right side up, some copies have
          lt blue end pprs   150 - 250
BN1432 Robert Drummond Co., Ind (1904?), 2nd ed, tp &
          text printed only in black, most text illus deleted,
          printer's slug on cr page, cys w/both lt blue
          & orange-black end pprs   100 - 150
BN1443 M.A. Donahue, Chi (1913), 3rd ed, blank
          end pprs, no printers slug, either gray or blue cl   75 - 125
BN1453 M.A. Donahue, Chi (1913), 3rd ed, blank end
          pprs, no printer's slug, either gray or blued cl   75 - 125
BN1464 Bobbs-Merrill, Ind (1920), 4th ed, blank end pprs, 8
          plates in orange-black, blue or brown cl, pict p-o   75 - 125
BN1511 **Father Goose His Book** Geo. M. Hill, Chi (1899),
          1st ed: color text illus by Denslow, hand lettered by
          Ralph Seymour, 4to, 106 unnumbered pp, color pict
          bds, no later printings stated on cr page (most cys
          poor w/spine torn, etc; rare in fine condition)   400 - 600
BN1520 poor copies   100 - 150
BN1530 Geo. M. Hill, Chi (1899-1902?), 5 later printings   200 - 350

BN1540 Bobbs-Merrill, Ind 1903, similar to Hill printings 125 - 200
BN1550 M.A. Donahue, (1913), last printing of this title 100 - 150
BN1560 **Father Goose's Year Book** Reilly & Britton, Chi
(1907), gr cl, color pict p-o 250 - 350
BN1570 Reilly & Britton, Chi (1907), gr limp swede, cover
title in gold (pub gift binding) 300 - 500
BN1651 **John Dough and the Cherub** Reilly & Britton, Chi
(1906) 1st ed, 1st issue: color illus by John R. Neill,
8 vol, 315 pp plus advertising p, tan pict cl stamped
in black, brown & red, pub name at foot of sp "The
Reilly & Britton Co.", misprint "cage" for "cave" line
10 p 275, detachable contest blank preceding p 9 450 - 700
w/o contest blank 300 - 500
BN1662 2nd issue: misprint corrected, w/contest blank 250 - 350
w/o contest blank 150 - 250
BN1673 3rd issue: no contest blank, rear cover w/o picture,
pub imprint on sp: "Reilly & Britton" 100 - 150
BN1684 4th issue: cover stamped in black, yellow-green &
red, sp imprint: "Reilly & Britton" 75 - 125
BN1692 Reilly & Lee, Chi (1920), 2nd ed: b&w text illus,
12 color plates, color pict p-o, ad page precedes
tp, ads thru *Glinda of Oz* 75 - 125
BN1703 Reilly & Lee, Chi (1930), 3rd ed: same as 2nd ed
except 1 color plates (frontis), no ads 50 - 75
BN1750 **L. Frank Baum's Juvenile Speaker** Reilly & Britton,
Chi (1910), illus various artists, tan cl stamped in
red, white & black 500 - 800
BN1801 **The Life and Adventures of Santa Claus** Bowen
Merrill Co., Ind (1902), 1st ed, 1st issue: 20 color
plates, 8vo, 206 pp, section headings "Book First,"
"Book Second" & "Book Third" 200 - 400
BN1812 Bowen-Merrill, Ind (1902), 2nd issue: 12 color
plates, added text illus, section headings "Youth,"
"Manhood" & "Old Age" 150 - 300
BN1822 Bobbs-Merrill, Ind (1902), 2nd ed: full-page
text illus p 207 150 - 300
BN1833 M.A. Donahue & Co, Chi (1913), 3rd ed: 12
plates in 2 colors only 125 - 200
BN1843 3rd ed, 2nd state: only 8 color plates 75 - 125
BN1854 Bobbs-Merrill, Ind (1920), 4th ed: 8 plates in
2 colors, gr cl w/pict p-o of Santa & Knook 75 - 150
BN1901 **The Magical Monarch of Mo** Bobbs-Merrill, Ind (1903),
1st ed, 1st state: 12 color plates by Frank Verbeck,
8vo, 237 pp., lt blue cl w/pict p-o, 2-color tp,
"Braunworth" printer's slug on cr page in serified
type, p 121 "The Wizard" hand-lettered caption in
perfect type or shows only slight damage to "D,"
lt blue pict end pprs 250 - 400
BN1912 1st ed, 2nd state: "Braunworth" printer's slug in unserified
type, p 121 "The Wizard" caption damaged 150 - 250
BN1923 1st ed, 3rd state: orange-black pict end pprs 100 - 150
BN1932 M.A. Donahue, Chi (1913), 2nd ed, 1st state:
tp only in black, 12 color plates 75 - 125
BN1942 2nd ed, 2nd state: only 8 color plates 50 - 75
BN1953 Bobbs-Merrill, Ind (1920), 3rd ed: black only tp,
8 color plates, dark blue cl w/pict p-o 75 - 125
BN1960 Bobbs-Merrill, Ind (1947), DJ, Evelyn Copelman illus 50 - 75
w/o DJ 30 - 50
BN2011 **The Master Key** Bowen-Merrill, Ind (1901), 1st ed,
1st state: 12 color plates by Cory, 8vo, olive green
cl, "The Bowen-Merrill Company" on cr page
1-21/32" long, book made of 8-page signatures 300 - 500
BN2022 Bowen-Merrill, Ind (1901), 1st ed, 2nd state: 1st
signature 8 pp, rest 16 pp 150 - 250

BN2033 Bowen-Merrill, Ind (1901), 1st ed, 3rd state: "The
Bowen-Merrill Company" on cr page 1-25/32" long,
1st signature 8 pp, rest 16 pp, tan or olive green cl 150 - 250
catalogue price of only known copy in DJ 8500
BN2101 **Mother Goose in Prose** Way & Williams, Chi 1897,
1st ed, 1st state: 268 pp, 4to, 12 plates by Parrish,
16-pp signatures w/last two 8 pp & 4 pp 4000 - 6000
BN2112 1st ed, 2nd state: 272 pp, 16-pp signatures 3000 - 5000
BN2122 Geo. M. Hill, Chi 1901, 2nd ed: 12 plates by
Parrish, red cl w/new cover design 700 - 1000
BN2133 Bobbs-Merrill, Ind 1905, 3rd ed: 12 plates by
Parrish, brown cl w/"Goose" on sp 300 - 500
BN2144 Bobbs-Merrill, Ind (1920s), 4th ed: 12 plates by
Parrish, green cl w/pict p-o cover, plates printed
in red, pale yellow field 200 - 300
BN2200 **The Navy Alphabet** Geo. M. Hill, Chi 1900, 4to,
color pict bds, blue cl sp, text illus by Harry
Kennedy (very scarce in fine condition, but not so
desirable to collectors because of simple text) 600 - 1000
BN2251 **A New Wonderland** (R.H. Russell) NY 1900, 1st ed,
1st state: 190 pp, 16 color plates & tp by Verbeck,
4to, orange-lt gray end pprs, pict, bds, unprinted
green cl sp 1500 - 2500
BN2262 (R.H. Russell) NY 1900, 2nd state, lt gray cl w/title on
sp, blank end pprs, many cys lack frontis (error?) 1200 - 2000
BN2401 **Phoebe Daring** Reilly & Britton, Chi (1912), 1st ed,
1st state: 298 pp, 8vo, 4 plates by Nuyttens, lt
blue-gray cl stamped in black, cream & orange
to yellow shading 150 - 250
BN2412 Reilly & Britton (1912), 1st ed, 2nd state, lt blue-
gray cl stamped in dark blue 75 - 125
BN2551 **Queen ZIXI of IX** Century Co., NY 1905, 1st ed,
1st state: 303 pp, 16 color plates by Frank Richardson,
8vo, lt green pict cl stamped in dark green & red,
16-pp signatures w/last 12 pp, front & rear end pprs
inserted, text illus pp 169-236 terracotta/black 300 - 500
BN2562 Century Co., NY 1905, 1st ed, 2nd state: 16 pp
signatures only, rear end pprs part of last signature;
text illus pp 169-184 turquoise/black, pp 185-220
terracotta/black, pp 221-236 turquoise/black 250 - 350
BN2572 Century Co., NY 1915, 2nd ed: black text illus, all
plates b&w & part of signatures, 16-pp signatures
w/inserted end pprs, blank rear cover 150 - 250
BN2580 Century Co., NY 1919, 1920, 1922: later
impressions similar to 1915 ed 125 - 200
BN3051 **The Sea Fairies** Reilly-Britton, Chi (1911), 1st ed,
1st state: 240 pp, 12 color plates by John R. Neill,
pict color end pprs, 8vo, lt green cl w/pict p-o
showing 3 heads rising from sea 250 - 350

BN1801 (w/o DJ)   BN1901 (w/o DJ)   BN2011 (w/o DJ)

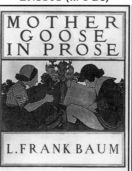

BN1511 (w/o DJ)   BN1560 (w/o DJ)   BN1651 (w/o DJ)   BN2112 (w/o DJ)   BN2122 (w/o DJ)   BN2401 (w/o DJ)

| BN3151 | BO1011 | BO1411 | BO1611 | BO1811 | BO2011 |

| BO2210 | BO2210 | BO2611 |

BN3062   Chi (1911), 1st ed, 2nd state: pict p-o of "Trot"
holding sea horse   150 - 250

BN3072   Reilly & Lee, Chi (1920), 2nd ed: ads list titles
through "Glinda of Oz," blank end pprs, different
cl colors, pict p-o of "Trot" & "Mermaid Queen"   150 - 250

BN3083   Reilly & Lee, Chi (1930), 3rd ed: 1 color plate,
no pub ads   75 - 125

BN3151   **Sky Island** Reilly & Britton, Chi (1912), 1st ed:
12 color plates by Neill, red cl   200 - 375

BN3162   Reilly & Lee, Chi (1920), 2nd ed: pub ads list thru
"Glinda of Oz," blank end pprs   150 - 250

BN3173   Reilly & Lee, Chi (1930), 3rd ed: 1 color plate
(frontis), no ads   100 - 150

BN3251   **The Songs of Father Goose** Geo. M. Hill, Chi
1900, 1st ed: 84 pp, illus by Denslow, songs by
Alberta Hall, 4to, pict bds, red cl sp   350 - 600

BN3260   Geo. M. Hill, Chi 1900, set of 4 song folios issued
concurrently w/hardbound ed, pict wrappers, each   100 - 200

BN3272   Bobbs-Merrill, Ind (1909), 2nd ed: 83 pp, "copyright
1909" notice, "Instructions for Giving a Father
Goose Entertainment" page at end deleted   200 - 400

BN3283   Bobbs-Merrill, Ind (1920), 3rd ed: "1909" cr notice,
pict p-o is Father Goose standing, no cl sp   150 - 300

BN3294   Bobbs-Merrill, Ind (1952), 4th ed: 83 pp, "reprinted
1952" on cr page   100 - 150

BN3310   "The Songs of Father Goose" song sheet inserts in
early 1900s Sunday newspaper supplements, each   25 - 75

BN4601   **The Woggle-Bug Book** Reilly & Britton, Chi 1905,
1st ed, 1st state: 48 pp, 4to, linen-back color pict
wrappers, blue "stippled" background on cover   800 - 1250

BN4612   Chi 1905, 2nd state: pale yellow background
on cover   700 - 1000

Oz Titles

This section includes the works of L. Frank Baum, Ruth Plumly
Thompson, John R. Neill and Jack Snow. The author's name is in
parenthesis. Listings are alphabetical by title.

BO1011   **The Cowardly Lion of Oz** (Thompson)
Reilly & Lee, Chi (1923), 1st ed, 1st issue: 12
color plates, gr cl, 16-pp signatures w/last 8 pp,
plates on stock coated on printed side, publisher's
name has "&" instead of "**&**" on sp   250 - 400

BO1020   1930s reprint w/12 color plates, DJ   100 - 175
     w/o DJ   30 - 50

BO1030   post-1935 reprint w/no color plates, DJ   50 - 75

BO1211   **Dorothy and the Wizard of Oz** (Baum) Reilly & Britton,
Chi (1908), 1st ed, 1st state: 16 color plates, 256 pp,

half-title back lists 3 titles, "The End" on p 257, lt blue
cl w/p-o, sp imprint "The Reilly and Britton Co."   500 - 800

BO1411   **The Emerald City of Oz** (Baum) Reilly & Britton,
Chi (1910), 1st ed, 1st state: 16 color plates, blue
cl w/picture of wagon pulled by "sawhorse",
"ownership" page verso lists 5 titles   350 - 650
     w/DJ   7000 - 10000

BO1422   1st ed, 2nd state: 12 color plates, girl behind wall cover
picture, ads list titles thru *The Lost Princess of Oz*   75 - 125
     w/DJ   250 - 350

BO1611   **Glinda of Oz** (Baum) Reilly & Lee, Chi (1920), 1st ed:
12 color plates, half-title verso lists titles thru *Glinda*   300 - 500

BO1620   later printings in 1920   100 - 150

BO1630   1930s reprint w/12 color plates   75 - 125

BO1640   post-1935 reprint w/no color plates, DJ   100 - 150
     w/o DJ   50 - 75

BO1811   **Handy Mandy in Oz** (Thompson) Reilly & Lee,
Chi 1937, 1st ed: b&w plates, 16-pp signatures   300 - 500
     w/DJ   700 - 1000

BO2011   **Jack Pumpkinhead of Oz** (Thompson) Reilly &
Lee, Chi (1929), 1st ed: 12 color plates, gray cl
w/p-o, earliest cys have "r" in "morning" p 116,
line 1 in undamaged type   200 - 350

BO2020   1930s reprint w/no color plates   50 - 75

BO2210   **The Little Wizard Series** (Baum) Reilly & Britton,
Chi (1913), 6 small books, each 29 pp w/text illus
& pict bds: **The Cowardly Lion and the Hungry
Tiger, Little Dorothy and Toto, Jack Pumpkinhead
and the Sawhorse, The Scarecrow and the Tin
Woodman, Tiktok and the Nome King, Ozma
and the Little Wizard**, each   125 - 200

BO2611   **Little Wizard Stories of Oz** Reilly & Britton,
Chi (1914), 1st ed, 1st state: color text illus, yellow
cl w/p-o, printed on smooth paper, 1" thick   250 - 400

BO2811   **The Lost Princess of Oz** (Baum) Reilly & Britton,
Chi (1917), 1st ed: 12 color plates, lt blue cl, verso
of ownership leaf lists titles thru this title   300 - 650

BO2820   later printings w/12 color plates, DJ   200 - 400
     w/o DJ   100 - 150

BO2830   later printings w/no color plates   50 - 75

BO3011   **The Magic of Oz** (Baum) Reilly & Lee, (1919) 1st ed: 12
color plates, ads list thru *The Tin Woodman of Oz*   300 - 500

BO3020   later printings w/12 color plates   100 - 150

BO3030   post 1935 printings w/no color plates   50 - 75

BO3211   **The Magical Mimics in Oz** (Snow) Reilly & Lee, Chi
(1946), 1st ed, 1st issue: b&w plates, gray cl, white stock
paper, 1-1/16" to 1-3/16" thick, 2 DJ variations   300 - 600
     w/o DJ   200 - 300

BO3222   2nd issue: lt gray stock paper, book is 7-8" thick   75 - 125

BO3611   **The Marvelous Land of Oz** (Baum) Reilly & Britton,
Chi 1904, 1st ed, 1st issue, 1st state: 16 color plates,
lt gr or red cl, front cover title stamped in blue only,
cr page w/o "Published, July, 1904", p 4 box 6-1/4"
tall, p 22 illus Mombi threatening to turn Tip into
statue, Mombi putting Jack in stable p 27, Tip
picture p 82, Jin Jur picture p 158   600 - 1000
(An inscribed copy recently sold for 16,500.)

BO3622   Chi 1904, 1st ed, 1st issue, 2nd state: red cl,
cover title is blue outlined in silver   400 - 750

BO3810   **The New Wizard of Oz** (Baum) Bobbs-Merrill, Ind (1925),
8 silent-film stills, gr cl stamped in lavender, DJ   250 - 350
     w/o DJ   125 - 200

BO4011   **Ozma of Oz** (Baum) Reilly & Britton, Chi (1907),

1st ed, 1st state: color text illus, half-title back lists
2 titles, p 11 line 5 of author's note has "O" in
"Ozma", color illus p 221, color pict end pprs,
tan cl stamped in black, red, blue & yellow,
"The Reilly & Britton Co." sp imprint   500 - 800
(An inscribed cy recently sold for $18,700.)
BO4020 Reilly & Lee, Chi (post 1918 ed)   100 - 150
BO4211 **The Patchwork Girl of Oz** Reilly & Britton, Chi
(1913), 1st ed, 1st issue: color text illus, gr pict cl,
"Reilly & Britton" sp imprint, p 343 ad for 5
titles, p 35 "Chap. Three" overlapping text   700 - 1000
BO4222 Chi (1913), 1st ed, 2nd issue: overlap corrected   350 - 600
BO4411 **Rinkitink in Oz** Reilly & Britton, Chi (1916),
1st ed: 12 color plates, lt gr cl, no pub ads   400 - 750
BO4420 later editions w/12 color plates   100 - 150
BO4430 post 1935 edition w/no color plates   50 - 75
BO4811 **The Road to Oz** (Baum) Reilly & Britton, Chi (1909),
1st ed, 1st state: no color illus, printed on tinted paper:
pp 1-32 off-white, 33-64 lavender, 65-96 gray, 97-
128 lt blue, 129-160 salmon, 161-192 tan, 193-
256 lt gr, 257-264 tan; p 32 line 4 "Toto on" & p
121 # in perfect type, p 129 has page # & caption,
"Reilly & Britton" on sp in lower & upper case   250 - 500
BO4820 later printings on white stock, only in gr pict cl   75 - 125
BO5011 **The Royal Book of Oz** (Thompson) Reilly & Lee,
Chi (1921), 1st ed: 12 color plates, gray pict cl,
plates printed on stock coated on 1 side, plates
face p 126, 143, 174, 207; "scarecorws" on plate
facing p 255 caption, Baum credited as author   250 - 400
BO5020 later printings w/12 color plates   10 - 175
BO5030 post 1935 printings w/no color plates   50 - 75
BO5411 **The Scarecrow of Oz** (Baum) Reilly & Britton,
Chi (1915), 1st ed: 12 color plates, gr pict cl,
half-title verso lists titles thru this, DJ   2000 - 3000
  w/o DJ   400 - 600
BO5420 later printings w/12 color plates, DJ   200 - 400
  w/o DJ   100 - 150
BO5430 post 1935 printing w/no color plates   50 - 75
BO5811 **The Silver Princess in Oz** (Thompson) Reilly &
Lee, Chi (1938), 1st ed, 1st state: b&w illus, pict
cl, 16-pp signatures, cover title printed in silver,
small illus on sp, 1st state DJ   500 - 800
  in later DJ   350 - 500
  w/o DJ   250 - 400
BO5820 later printings w/32-pp signatures, DJ   150 - 250
  w/o DJ   75 - 125
BO6011 **Tiktok of Oz** (Baum) Reilly & Britton, Chi (1914),
1st ed, 1st state: 12 color plates, blue cl w/p-o,
"Reilly & Britton" sp imprint, sp has double-rule
lines head & foot, half-title verso lists 6 Oz titles   400 - 750

BO6022 Chi (1914) 1st ed, 2nd state: sp lacks double-rule
lines, ads list thru *The Lost Princess of Oz*   100 - 150
BO6210 **The Tin Woodman of Oz** (Baum) Reilly & Britton, Chi
(1918), 1st ed: 12 color plates, red cl w/p-o, DJ 2000 - 3000
  w/o DJ   400 - 750
BO6220 Reilly & Lee, Chi (1920s), 12 color plates   100 - 150
BO6230 post-1935 printing w/o color plates   50 - 75
BO6611 **The Visitors From Oz** Reilly & Lee, Chi (1960),
1st ed: DJ   100 - 150
  w/o DJ   50 - 75
BO6811 **The Wishing Horse of Oz** (Thompson) Reilly
& Lee, Chi (1935), 1st ed: 12 color plates, cl
w/p-o, blank end pprs, 1st issue DJ   800 - 1200
  later DJ   600 - 800
  w/o DJ   350 - 600
BO6820 later printings w/no color plates, DJ   125 - 175
  w/o DJ   75 - 125
BO7010 **The Wizard of Oz** Hutchinson & Co., Lon (1926),
English reprint of *The Wonderful Wizard of Oz*   125 - 175
BO7020 Bobbs-Merrill, Ind (1939), movie ed reprint of
The Wonderful Wizard of Oz, 8 color plates,
green-black stamped cl, DJ   200 - 300
  w/o DJ   75 - 125
BO7211 **The Wonder City of Oz** (John R. Neill) Reilly &
Lee, Chi (1940), 1st ed: b&w illus, cl w/p-o, 16
pp signatures, p 292-293 illus printed correctly   75 - 125
BO7220 later printings w/32-pp signatures   200 - 300
BO7611 **The Wonderful Wizard of Oz** (Baum) Geo. M. Hill,
Chi 1900, 1st ed, 1st issue: 24 color plates, lt gr cl
stamped in red & gr, p 2 w/pub ad in box, p 14 line
1 "low wail on", p 81 4th line from bottom "peices",
p 227 line 1 "while Tin Woodman", end-of-book
colophon set in 11 lines & in box, plate facing p 34
has 2 dark blue spots on moon, plate facing p 92 has
red horizon, perfect type on last lines p 100 & 186;
several variations of pub imprint on sp: stamped in
gr w/"Co" in ordinary type (earliest state), stamped
in red w/"Co" in ordinary type, stamped in red
w/large "C" encircling "O" in "Co"; "c" usually
found on later cys   7000 - 12000
(Cy w/partial DJ recently brought over $20,000. Inscribed
cy w/o DJ recently brought over $39,000. Cy w/DJ in fine
condition might bring $50,000.)
BO7632 Chi 1900, 1st ed, 2nd issue: p 2 w/pub ad w/o
box, p 14 line 1 "low wail of...", p 81 4th line
from bottom "pieces", p 14 line 1 "white the
woodman", colophon in 13 lines w/o box,
sp usually stamped in red w/large "C"   1500 - 2500
(Hybrid cys w/mixed points exist. Ask expert to identify &
evaluate these or any "Hill" editions.)

BO3011 (w/o DJ)

BO3211

BO3622 (w/o DJ)

BO3810 (w/o DJ)

BO4211 (w/o DJ)

BO5011 (w/o DJ)

BO6811

BO7010 (w/o DJ)

BO7020

BO7020 (w/o DJ)

BO7211 (w/o DJ)

BO7611 (w/o DJ)

BIRDS (ORNITHOLOGY)

Bird books are among the most published natural-history books. Since Mark Catesby's *The Natural History of Carolina, Florida and the Bahama Islands* (1730s) and John James Audubon's *The Birds of America* (1830s), color-plate bird books have been favored by collectors of natural-history books and prints. The introduction of color photography and photo-mechanical processes in the late 1800s helped create a flourishing business in bird books. By being affordable to most people, these new books competed successfully with the lavish hand coloring and chromolithography of the nineteenth century.

Bird books are divided into four main categories:

a. Birds of a particular region: *Birds of Kansas, Birds of Liberia*, etc.

b. Books about a particular scientific order, genus or species of bird. For example, a book about the order *Passeriformes*, such as flycatchers, larks, and swallows; or a book about a particular genus and species such as *Tree Swallows*.

c. General books: *Bird Life and Bird Lore* by Reginald Smith, Lon. 1905.

d. Technical books about how birds fly, lay eggs, nest, etc.: *North American Bird Eggs* by Chester Reed, NY 1904.

Of the over 9,000 known species of birds in the world, every one has been described in a book or pamphlet, including all known extinct birds (Archaeopteryx, Hesperornis, etc.) and the recently extinct (Dodo, Great Auk, Ivory Billed Woodpecker, etc.)

The main sources for bird literature are state universities, The Smithsonian Institution, National Audubon Society, bird clubs, and almost every major publisher.

Some of the most collectible bird illustrators of the 20th century are Roger Tory Peterson (field guides), Louis Agassiz Fuertes (illustrator for National Geographic magazine), Frances Lee Jacques, Alan Brooks, Robert Bateman and George Miksch Sutton.

Bird books published in England, France, Germany, and Japan are very collectible, especially the more scarce titles from the late 1800s-early 1900s. These are frequently illustrated with hand-colored and chromolithographic plates and are the most expensive.

The following list is arranged alphabetically by author, editor, and illustrator. Lacking the dust jacket (if it has one) deducts 10-20% from the value for most titles. The exception is a book over $100 which has a pictorial cover by a well-known artist. Lack of a jacket in this case may drop the value 30% or more.

Alexander, W. B.
BR0100 Birds of the Ocean NY 1928, DJ   30 - 50
Ali, Salim
BR0120 Handbook of Birds of India and Pakistan
        Delhi 1987   100 - 150
Allen, Arthur A.
BR0140 American Bird Biographies Ithaca 1934, DJ 30 - 50
Allen, Robert
BR0160 Birds of the Caribbean NY 1961, DJ   50 - 75
BR0165 The Flame Birds NY 1947, DJ   25 - 50
BR0170 The Flamingos NY 1956   25 - 50
BR0175 On the Trail of Vanishing Birds NY 1957, DJ 25 - 50
BR0180 The Roseate Spoonbill NY 1942   25 - 50
BR0185 The Whooping Crane NY 1942   25 - 50
Atherton, Loren G.
BR0210 Dakota Birds Pierre, SD 1925, DJ   50 - 75
Audubon, John James (also see Artists & Illustrators)
BR0230 The Art of Audubon NY 1979, DJ   25 - 50
BR0235 Audubon Birds of America NY 1978, DJ   15 - 25
BR0240 The Birds of America NY 1942, DJ   25 - 50
BR0245 The Birds of America NY 1966, DJ   50 - 75
BR0250 The Birds of America NY 1981, DJ   200 - 300
BR0255 Birds of America Johnson Reprint Co, NY
        (1970s) facsimile edition of original double
        elephant folio set (4 vol) by John James Audubon,
        original published price $5400, 250 cys   8000 - 12000
BR0260 The Original Water-Colour Paintings by John
        James Audubon for the Birds of America
        NY 1966, 2 vol, slipcase   250 - 350

Austin, Oliver
BR0280 Birds of the World NY 1961, DJ   50 - 75
Austing, G. Ronald
BR0300 The World of the Great Horned Owl Phil 1966, DJ 30 - 50
BR0305 The World of the Red Tailed Hawk Phil 1964, DJ 30 - 50
Baerg, W. J.
BR0330 Birds of Arkansas Fayetteville 1951   30 - 50
Bailey, Alfred
BR0350 Birds of Colorado Denver 1965, DJ, 2 vol 150 - 250
Bailey, Florence Among
BR0370 The Birds in the Grand Canyon Country
        Wash 1939   30 - 50
BR0375 Birds of New Mexico Albu 1928   150 - 250
BR0380 Handbook of Birds of the Western United
        States NY 1902, DJ   50 - 75
Bailey, Harold
BR0400 The Birds of Florida Balt 1925, DJ   100 - 150
BR0405 The Birds of Virginia Lynchburg 1913   75 - 125
Baird, S. F.
BR0430 A History of North American Birds Bos 1875,
        3 vol   100 - 150
BR0432 Bos 1905, 3 vol   200 - 300
Bannerman, David
BR0460 The Birds of Balearics Lon 1983, DJ   50 - 75
BR0465 The Birds of Cyprus Edinburgh 1958, DJ   150 - 250
BR0470 The Birds of the Maltese Archipelago Malta
        1976, DJ   50 - 75
Barbour, Thomas
BR0490 Cuban Ornithology Cambridge 1943, DJ   50 - 75
Barrows, Walter
BR0510 Michigan Bird Life Lansing 1912, VG   50 - 75
Barrus, Clara
BR0530 The Life and Letters of John Burroughs
        NY 1925, 2 vol   50 - 75
Bateman, Robert
BR0550 The Art of Robert Bateman NY 1981, DJ   50 - 75
BR0555 The World of Robert Bateman Tor 1985, DJ 50 - 75
Beal, F. E. L.
BR0580 The Birds of California Wash 1907 & 1910, 2 vol 30 - 50
Beebe, C. William
BR0600 Adventures with Beebe NY 1955, DJ   20 - 30
BR0605 The Bird NY 1906, DJ   20 - 40
BR0610 Edge of the Jungle NY 1921, DJ   20 - 30
BR0615 Galapagos: Worlds End NY 1924, DJ   50 - 75
BR0620 High Jungle NY 1949, DJ   20 - 30
BR0625 A Naturalists Life of New York Lon 1954, DJ 20 - 30
BR0630 Pheasant Jungles NY 1932, DJ   30 - 50
BR0635 Pheasants - Their Lives and Homes NY 1926,
        DJ, 2 vol   150 - 250
BR0640 Tropical Wildlife in British Guiana NY 1917, DJ 50 - 75
BR0645 Two Bird-Lovers in Mexico NY 1905, DJ,
        1st issue w/Charles M. Beebe on cover   800 - 1200
BR0646 NY 1905, later issues   100 - 300
Beehler
BR0670 Birds of New Guinea Princeton 1986, DJ   100 - 150
Bellrose, Frank
BR0690 Ducks, Geese & Swans of North America
        Harrisburg 1976, DJ   30 - 50
Benoire, Charles
BR0710 Life Histories of North American Birds
        Wash 1895   100 - 150

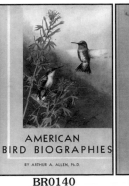

BR0100   BR0140   BR0646 (w/o DJ)

Bent, Arthur C.
BR0730 Life Histories of North American Birds
        Wash 1910-68, 21 vol (complete)   750 - 1500
BR0731 Individual volumes   25 - 75

Berger, Andrew
BR0750 Hawaiian Bird Life Honolulu 1974, DJ   30 - 50

Binford, Lawrence
BR0770 Birds of Western North America NY 1974, DJ 30 - 50

Bishop, Richard
BR0790 Bishop's Birds Phil 1936, 1050 cys   200 - 300
BR0791 Phil 1936, 125 cys   300 - 500

Blake, Emmet
BR0810 Manual of Neotropical Birds Chi 1977, DJ 100 - 150

Blome, Richard
BR0830 Hawking or Falconry Lon 1929, 650 cys   300 - 500

Bohlen, H. David
BR0850 The Birds of Illinois Bloomington 1989, DJ 50 - 75

Bonhote, J. Lewis
BR0870 Birds of Britain Lon 1927, DJ   30 - 50

Boynton, Mary Fuertes
BR0890 Louis Agassiz Fuertes NY 1956, DJ   30 - 50

Bramwell, Martyn
BR0910 The World Atlas of Birds NY 1974, DJ   30 - 50

Brandt, Herbert
BR0930 Alaska Bird Trails Clev 1943, DJ   150 - 250
BR0935 Arizona and Its Bird Life Clev 1951, DJ 150 - 250
BR0940 Texas Bird Adventures Clev 1940, DJ   150 - 250

Brasher, Rex
BR0960 Birds and Trees of North America
        Kent 1930s, 12 vol, 500 cys   15000 - 25000
BR0965 Birds and Trees of North America
        NY 1961, 4 vol   300 - 500

Bridges, Fidelia
BR0980 Familiar Birds NY 1889   50 - 75

Brown, David
BR1000 Arizona Wetlands and Waterfowl Tucson 1985, DJ 25 - 50

Brown, Leslie
BR1020 African Birds of Prey Bos 1971, DJ   25 - 50
BR1025 Birds of Africa Bos 1982, DJ   100 - 150
BR1030 Birds of the African Bush Lon 1975, DJ   25 - 50
BR1035 Eagles NY 1970, DJ   20 - 30
BR1040 Eagles, Hawks and Falcons of the World
        NY 1968, slipcase   150 - 250
BR1045 Eagles of the World NY 1979, DJ   50 - 75

Bull, John
BR1070 Birds of New York State NY 1974, DJ   50 - 75

Bump, Gardiner
BR1090 The Ruffed Grouse NY 1947, DJ   50 - 75

Bunn, D. S.
BR1100 The Barn Owl Vermilion, SD 1982   30 - 50

Burgess, Thornton W.
BR1110 The Burgess Bird Book for Children Bos 1920, DJ 20 - 30

Burleigh, Thomas D.
BR1120 Birds of Idaho Caldwell 1972, DJ   25 - 50
BR1125 Georgia Birds Norman 1958, DJ   50 - 75

Burroughs, John
BR1140 Works of John Burroughs Bos 1924, 23 vol 100 - 150

Burton, John
BR1150 Owls of the World Dover 1984   30 - 50

Butler, Arthur
BR1160 Foreign Finches in Captivity Lon 1894   3000 - 5000
BR1161 Lon 1899   800 - 1200

Caoe, Tom J.
BR1170 The Falcons of the World Ithaca 1982, DJ 50 - 75

Chapman, Frank M.
BR1180 Bird Life NY 1913, DJ   25 - 50
BR1185 Bird Studies with a Camera NY 1900, DJ   50 - 75
BR1190 Camps and Cruises of an Ornithologist
        NY 1908, DJ   75 - 125
BR1195 Essays in South American Ornigeography
        NY 1978   75 - 125
BR1200 Handbook of Birds of Eastern North America
        NY 1895   50 - 75
BR1201 NY 1912, DJ   40 - 60
BR1203 NY 1937, DJ   20 - 30
BR1210 Our Winter Birds NY 1919, DJ   20 - 30

Ching, Raymond
BR1220 New Zealand Birds Auckland 1986, DJ   50 - 75
BR1225 Studies and Sketches of a Bird Painter
        Melbourne 1981, DJ   150 - 250

Clancey, P. A.
BR1240 The Birds of Natal and Zululand Edinburgh
        1964, DJ   100 - 150

Clarke, Herbert
BR1250 Birds of the West South Brunswick 1976, DJ 30 - 50

Coles, Charles
BR1260 Game Birds NY 1983, DJ   75 - 125

Cooper, William T.
BR1270 The Birds of Paradise and Bower Birds
        Bos 1979, DJ   200 - 300
BR1275 A Portfolio of Australian Birds Sydney 1968, DJ 50 - 75

Coves, Elliott
BR1290 Birds of the Colorado Valley Wash 1878   100 - 150
BR1295 Key to North American Birds Bos 1903, 2 vol 100 - 150

Craighead, Frank
BR1310 Hawks in the Hand Bos 1939, DJ   50 - 75
BR1315 Hawks, Owls, and Wildlife Harrisburg 1956, DJ 30 - 50

Cramp, Stanley
BR1330 Handbook of Birds of Europe, the Middle East
        and No. Africa Oxford 1978-85, 4 vol   300 - 500

Crawshay, Richard
BR1340 The Birds of Tierra Del Feugo Lon 1947,
        300 cys   1000 1500

Daff, Lily A.
BR1350 An Album of New Zealand Birds Wellington
        1974, DJ   50 - 75

Daglish, Eric
BR1360 Birds of the British Isles Lon 1948, DJ   75 - 125

Davie, Oliver
BR1370 An Egg Check List of North American Birds
        Col 1885   50 - 75

Davis, Henry
BR1380 The American Wild Turkey Georgetown 1949, DJ 25 - 50

Dawson, William
BR1390 The Birds of California San Diego 1923, 4 vol 600 - 800
BR1395 The Birds of Ohio Col 1903, 2 vol   100 - 150
BR1400 The Birds of Washington Seattle 1909, 2 vol,
        200 cys   500 - 700

BR0890

BR0930

BR1110 (w/o DJ)

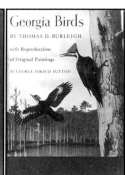
BR1125

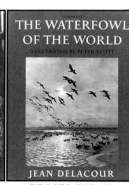
BR1450 (Vol. 1)

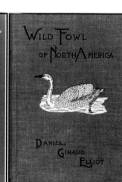
BR1786

De Schauewsee, Rodolphe
BR1410 Guide to the Birds of South America
Wynnewood 1970, DJ   150 - 250
BR1415 Guide to the Birds of Venezuela Princeton
1978, DJ   75 - 125

DeKeyser, Pierre
BR1430 Les Oiseaux de l'Ouest Africain Dakau
1966-68, 3 vol   300 - 500

Delacour, Jean
BR1440 Birds of Malaysia NY 1947, DJ   75 - 125
BR1445 Birds of the Philippines NY 1946, DJ   75 - 125
BR1450 The Waterfowl of the World Lon 1965, 4 vol   300 - 500

Dement'ev, Georgii
BR1460 Birds of the Soviet Union Jerusalem 1966-70,
6 vol   300 - 500

Des Courtilz, Jean
BR1470 Pageantry of Tropical Birds Lon 1960, DJ   100 - 150

Dewar, Douglas
BR1480 Birds of An Indian Village Lon 1921, DJ   200 - 300
BR1485 Game Birds Lon 1928, 50 cys   500 - 700

Dickey, Donald
BR1500 The Birds of El Salvador Chi 1938, DJ   50 - 75

Dickey, Florence
BR1510 Familiar Birds of the Pacific Southwest
Stanford 1935, DJ   75 - 125

Dixon, Charles
BR1530 The Bird Life of London Lon 1909, DJ   125 - 250
BR1535 British Sea Birds Lon 1896   125 - 250
BR1540 Lost and Vanishing Birds Lon 1898   125 - 250

Dresser, Henry
BR1560 Eggs of the Birds of Europe Lon 1910, 2 vol   2000 - 3000
BR1565 A History of the Birds of Europe
Lon 1871-96, 9 vol   5000 - 7000

Dugmore, Arthur
BR1580 Bird Homes NY 1902   25 - 50

Durango, Sigfrid
BR1600 Les Oiseaux Paris 1957   150 - 250

Eaton, Elton
BR1620 Birds of New York Albany 1910-14, 2 vol   100 - 150

Eckert, Allan
BR1640 The Owls of North America NY 1974   75 - 125
BR1645 The Wading Birds of North America NY 1981, DJ   50 - 75

Eckstein, Gustav
BR1660 Canary NY 1936, DJ   25 - 50

Eckstorm, Fannie
BR1680 The Woodpeckers Bos 1901   50 - 75

Edey, Maitland
BR1700 American Water Birds NY 1941, DJ   25 - 50

Edminster, Frank
BR1720 American Game Birds NY 1954, DJ   25 - 50

Edwards, Ernest
BR1740 A Coded List of Birds of the World Sweet Briar,
VA 1974, 1000 cys   50 - 75
BR1745 Finding Birds in Mexico Sweet Briar 1968   25 - 50

Eliot, Willard
BR1760 Birds of the Pacific Coast NY 1923, DJ   75 - 125

Elliot, Daniel
BR1780 North America Shore Birds NY 1895, 100 cys   300 - 500
BR1781 NY 1895 (1st trade ed)   75 - 125
BR1785 The Wild Fowl of the United States and British
Possessions NY 1898, 100 cys   300 - 500
BR1786 NY 1898 (1st trade ed)   75 - 125

Fennessy, Rena
BR1800 Birds of East Africa Nairobi 1980   75 - 125

Fichter, George
BR1820 Birds of Florida Miami 1971   25 - 50

Finley, William
BR1840 American Birds Photographed and Studied
From Life NY 1907   75 - 125

Fletcher, Thomas
BR1860 Birds of An Indian Garden Calcutta 1936   300 - 500

Forbes, Henry Ogg
BR1880 A Naturalist's Wanderings in the Eastern
Archipelago NY 1885   200 - 300

Forbush, Edward
BR1900 Birds of Massachusetts Norwood, MA 1925-29,
3 vol   150 - 250
BR1905 A History of Game Birds, Wild-Fowl and Shore
Birds of Massachusetts Bos 1912   50 - 75
BR1910 Natural History of the Birds of Eastern and
Central North America Bos 1939, DJ   50 - 75

Forshaw, Joseph
BR1930 Parrots of the World Garden City 1973   25 - 50

French, John C.
BR1950 The Passenger Pigeon in Pennsylvania
Altoona, PA 1919   75 - 125

French, Richard
BR1970 A Guide to the Birds of Trinidad and Tobago
Wynnewood 1973, DJ   50 - 75

Gabrielson, Ira
BR1990 The Birds of Alaska Harrisburg 1959, DJ   100 - 150

Gallagher, Michael
BR2010 The Birds of Oman Lon 1980, 500 cys   400 - 600

Gentry, Thomas
BR2030 The House Sparrow Phil 1878   200 - 300
BR2035 Nests and Eggs of Birds of the United States
Phil 1882   300 - 500

Gilliard, Ernest
BR2050 Birds of Paradise and Bower Birds Lon 1969   75 - 125

Glenister, Archibald
BR2070 The Birds of the Malay Peninsula, Singapore
and Perang Lon 1951, DJ   25 - 50

Godfrey, William
BR2090 The Birds of Canada Ottawa 1966   25 - 50

Goodman, Steven M. & Peter L. Meininger (editors)
BR2110 The Birds of Egypt Oxford 1989, DJ   40 - 60

Goodrich, Arthur
BR2130 Birds in Kansas Topeka 1946   25 - 50

Goodwin, Derek
BR2150 Crows of the World Ithaca 1976, DJ   25 - 50

Gordon, Seton P.
BR2170 Days with the Golden Eagle Lon 1927, DJ   25 - 50

Goss, Nathaniel S.
BR2190 History of the Birds of Kansas Topeka 1891   75 - 125

Gould, John
BR2210 Birds of Asia NY 1969, DJ   25 - 50
BR2215 Birds of Australia Lon 1967, DJ   25 - 50
BR2220 Birds of Europe Lon 1966, DJ   25 - 50
BR2225 Birds of New Guinea NY 1970, DJ   25 - 50
BR2230 Birds of South America Lon 1972, DJ   25 - 50
BR2235 John Gould's Birds NY 1981, DJ   50 - 75

Grave, Benjamin
BR2250 The Birds of Wyoming Laramie 1913   125 - 250

Greaves, R. H.
BR2270 Sixty Common Birds of the Nile Delta Cairo 1936   50 - 75

Green, Charlotte
BR2290 Birds of the South Chapel Hill 1933   20 - 30

Greene, William T.
BR2310 The Amateurs Aviary of Foreign Birds Lon 1883   150 - 250
BR2315 Birds of the British Empire Lon 1898   300 - 500
BR2320 British Birds for Cages and Aviaries Lon 1899   150 - 250
BR2325 Parrots in Captivity Lon 1884-87, 3 vol   3000 - 5000

Grieve, Symington
BR2340 The Great Auk Lon 1885   200 - 300

Grinnell, Joseph
BR2360 Checklist of California Birds Santa Clara 1902   75 - 125
BR2365 The Game Birds of California Berkeley 1918, DJ   125 - 250

Griscom, Ludlow
BR2380 The Birds of Concord Cambridge 1949, DJ   25 - 50
BR2385 Birds of the New York City Region NY 1923   30 - 50
BR2390 The Warblers of America NY 1957, DJ   30 - 50
BR2392 NY 1979, DJ   20 - 30

Gromme, Owen J.
BR2410 Birds of Wisconsin Madison 1963, DJ   50 - 75

Groser, Horace
BR2430 The Book of Birds Bos 1911   25 - 50

Grossman, Mary
BR2450 Birds of Prey of the World NY 1964, DJ   50 - 75

Gruson, Edward
BR2470 Checklist of the World's Birds NY 1976, DJ   20 - 30
Gyldenstolpe, Nils
BR2490 The Bird Fauna of Rio Juruá in Western Brazil
　　　　Stockholm 1945   75 - 125
Hachisuka, Masauji
BR2510 The Birds of the Philippine Islands
　　　　Lon 1931-35, 2 vol   800 - 1200
BR2515 The Dodo and Kindred Birds Lon 1953, 485 cys 300 - 500
BR2520 A Handbook of the Birds of Iceland Lon 1927 200 - 300
Hagerbaumer, David
BR2540 Selected American Game Birds Caldwell 1972, DJ 30 - 50
Hall, Henry
BR2560 A Gathering of Shore Birds NY 1960, DJ   50 - 75
Hancock, James & Hugh Elliott
BR2580 The Herons of the World Lon 1978, DJ   75 - 125
Hanzák, Jan
BR2600 The Illustrated Encyclopedia of Birds Lon 1977, DJ 25 - 50
Harris, Harry
BR2620 Birds of the Kansas City Region St. Louis 1919,
　　　　2 vol   125 - 200
Harrison, Colin
BR2640 A Field Guide to the Nests, Eggs, and Nestlings
　　　　of North American Birds Lon 1978, DJ   25 - 50
Harrison, Hal H.
BR2660 A Field Guide to Birds' Nests Bos 1975, DJ   15 - 25
Hatch, Philo
BR2680 Notes of the Birds of Minnesota Minn 1892   100 - 150
Hausman, Leon
BR2700 Field Book of Eastern Birds NY 1946, DJ   15 - 25
BR2705 The Illustrated Encyclopedia of American Birds
　　　　NY 1944, DJ   25 - 50
Hazelton, William
BR2720 Ducking Days Chi 1918, DJ   75 - 125
Headstrom, Birger
BR2740 Bird's Nests NY 1961, DJ   15 - 25
BR2745 Birds Nests of the West NY 1951, DJ   25 - 50
BR2750 A Complete Field Guide to Nests in the United
　　　　States NY 1970, DJ   25 - 50
Heilmann, Gerhard
BR2770 The Origin of Birds NY 1927, DJ   25 - 50
Heilner, Van Campen
BR2790 A Book on Duck Shooting NY 1940, DJ   50 - 75
BR2791 NY 1947, DJ   25 - 50
BR2795 Our American Game Birds NY 1946, DJ   25 - 50
Heinroth, Oskar
BR2810 Die Vogel Mitteleuropas in Allen Lebens...
　　　　Berlin 1926-31, 4 vol   500 - 700
Heintzelman, Donald
BR2830 Autumn Hawk Flights New Brunswick 1975, DJ 25 50
BR2835 Hawks and Owls of North America NY 1979, DJ 25 - 50
BR2840 The Migrations of Hawks Bloomington 1986, DJ 25 - 50
Hellmayr, Carl
BR2860 The Birds of Chile Chi 1932   75 - 125
Henry, George
BR2880 A Guide to the Birds of Ceylon NY 1955, DJ 75 - 125
BR2882 Sri Lanka 1978, DJ   50 - 75
BR2895 Coloured Plates of the Birds of Ceylon
　　　　Columbo 1927-35, 4 vol   300 - 500
Henshaw, Henry
BR2910 Birds of the Hawaiian Islands Honolulu 1902 125 - 250
Herklots, Geoffrey
BR2930 The Birds of Trinidad and Tobago Lon 1961, DJ 30 - 50
BR2935 Hong Kong Birds Hong Kong 1953   50 - 75
Herrick, Francis
BR2950 The American Eagle NY 1934   50 - 75
BR2955 The Home Life of Wild Birds NY 1901   50 - 75
Hickey, Joseph
BR2970 A Guide to Bird Watching NY 1943, DJ   15 - 25
Hicks, James
BR2990 The Encyclopedia of Poultry Lon 1935   25 - 50
Hightower, John
BR3010 Pheasant Hunting NY 1946, DJ, 350 cys   125 - 250

Hill, Norman
BR3030 The Birds of Cape Cod, Massachusetts
　　　　NY 1965, DJ   25 - 50
Hochbaum, Hans
BR3050 The Canvasback on a Prairie Marsh Wash 1944 50 - 75
Hoffmann, Ralph
BR3070 Birds of the Pacific States Bos 1927, DJ   25 - 50
BR3075 A Guide to the Birds of New England Bos 1904 75 - 125
Horne, George
BR3090 Pheasant Keeping for Amateurs Lon 1887   100 - 150
Horsbrugh, Boyd
BR3110 The Game Birds and Water-Fowl of South
　　　　Africa Lon 1912   800 - 1200
House, Charles
BR3130 Canaries Phil 1923   25 - 50
Howard, Henry
BR3150 The British Warblers Lon 1907-14, 2 vol   500 - 700
BR3155 Territory in Bird Life Lon 1920   100 - 150
Howard, Richard
BR3170 A Complete Checklist of the Birds of the World
　　　　NY 1980, DJ   25 - 50
Howe, Reginald
BR3190 The Birds of Massachusetts Cambridge 1901,
　　　　500 cys   200 - 300
BR3195 The Birds of Rhode Island Cambridge 1899   75 - 125
BR3200 "Every Bird"; A Guide to the Identification of the
　　　　Birds of the Woodland, Beach and Ocean Bos 1896 50 - 75
BR3205 On the Bird's Highway Bos 1899   50 - 75
Howell, Arthur
BR3220 Birds of Alabama Montgomery 1924   75 - 125
BR3225 Birds of Arkansas Wash 1911   30 - 50
BR3230 Florida Bird Life NY 1932   100 - 150
Hudson, William H.
BR3250 Adventures Among Birds NY 1920   75 - 125
BR3255 Birds and Man NY 1901   300 - 500
BR3260 Birds in London Lon 1898   200 - 300
BR3265 Birds in Town and Village NY 1920   75 - 125
BR3270 Birds of La Plata Lon 1920, DJ   150 - 250
BR3275 British Birds Lon 1895   300 - 500
BR3277 NY 1902   125 - 250
BR3280 Rare, Vanishing & Lost British Birds NY 1923, DJ 75 - 125
Hume, Allan
BR3300 The Game Birds of India, Burmah, and Ceylon
　　　　Calcutta 1879-81, 3 vol   300 - 500
BR3305 The Nests and Eggs of Indian Birds
　　　　Lon 1889-90, 3 vol   300 - 500
Huntington, Dwight
BR3320 Our Feathered Game NY 1903   200 - 300
Imhof, Thomas
BR3340 Alabama Birds Montgomery 1962, DJ   75 - 125
Irby, Leonard
BR3360 The Ornithology of the Straits of Gibraltar
　　　　Lon 1895   200 - 300
Iredale, Tom
BR3380 Birds of New Guinea Melbourne 1956, 2 vol   400 - 600
BR3385 Birds of Paradise Melbourne 1950   300 - 500
Ives, Paul
BR3400 Domestic Geese and Ducks NY 1947, DJ   50 - 75
Jackson, Christine
BR3420 Bird Illustrators Lon 1975   50 - 75

BR2110　　　　　BR2580　　　　　BR2660

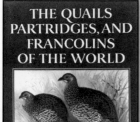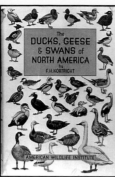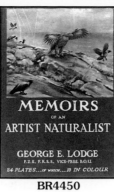

BR3565	BR4110	BR4450

Jackson, John
BR3440 The Birds of Kenya Colony and the Uganda
Protectorate Lon 1938   150 - 250
BR3445 Notes on the Game Birds of Kenya and Uganda
Lon 1926   75 - 125
Japp, Alexander
BR3460 Our Common Cuckoo Lon 1899   125 - 250
Jewett, Stanley
BR3480 Birds of Washington State Seattle 1953   75 - 125
Job, Herbert
BR3500 Among the Waterfowl NY 1902   20 - 30
BR3505 How to Study Birds NY 1910   20 - 30
BR3510 Propagation of Wild Birds Garden City 1915   25 - 50
BR3515 The Sport of Bird Study Winsted 1908   25 - 50
BR3520 Wild Wings Lon 1905   25 - 50
BR3521   NY 1905   25 - 50
Johnsgard, Paul A.
BR3540 Birds of the Great Plains Lon 1979, DJ   30 - 50
BR3545 Cranes of the World Bloomington 1983, DJ   50 - 75
BR3550 Ducks, Geese and Swans of the World Lincoln
1978, DJ   50 - 75
BR3555 Grouse and Quails of North America Lincoln
1973, DJ   50 - 75
BR3560 North American Owls Wash 1988, DJ   50 - 75
BR3565 The Quails, Partridges, and Francolins of the
World NY 1988, DJ   40 - 60
BR3570 Waterfowl of North America Bloomington 1975, DJ 50 - 75
Johnson, Alfredo
BR3590 The Birds of Chile Buenos Aires 1965-67, 2 vol 200 - 300
Johnston, Israel
BR3610 Birds of West Virginia Charleston 1923   25 - 50
Johnston, Richard
BR3630 The Breeding Birds of Kansas Lawrence 1964   25 - 50
Jones, Howard E.
BR3650 Illustrations of the Nests and Eggs of Birds of Ohio
Circleville, OH 1886, 2 vol (one of the rarest & most
sought-after American color plate books)   20000 - 30000
Jones, Lynds
BR3670 The Birds of Ohio Columbus 1903   75 - 125
Jordan, Denham
BR3690 The Wild Fowl and Sea Fowl of Great Britain
Lon 1895   300 - 500
Kearton, Cherry
BR3710 The Island of Penguins Lon 1930   75 - 125
Kearton, Richard
BR3730 The Adventures of Cock Robin and His Mate
Lon 1909   75 - 125
BR3735 Birds Nests, Eggs and Egg Collecting Lon 1896 75 - 125
BR3740 British Birds Nests Lon 1895   75 - 125
Keeler, Charles
BR3760 Bird Notes Afield, Essays on Birds of the
Pacific Coast SF 1907   150 - 250
BR3765 Evolution of the Colors of North American
Land Birds SF 1893   150 - 250
Kennedy, P. G.
BR3780 The Birds of Ireland Edinburgh 1954, DJ   50 - 75
Keyser, Leander
BR3800 Birds of the Rockies Chi 1902   25 - 50
BR3805 In Bird Land Chi 1894   25 - 50

King, Ben
BR3820 A Field Guide to the Birds of South East Asia
Bos 1975, DJ   30 - 50
King, Warren B.
BR3840 Endangered Birds of the World Wash 1979   25 - 50
Kirkman, Frederick
BR3860 The British Bird Book Lon 1911-13, 4 vol   200 - 300
BR3865 British Birds Lon 1941, DJ   50 - 75
BR3870 British Sporting Birds Lon 1924   75 - 125
Kirkwood, F. C.
BR3890 A List of the Birds of Maryland Balt 1895   50 - 75
Knight, Charles
BR3910 The Book of the Golden Eagle Lon 1927, DJ   75 - 125
Knight, John A.
BR3930 Ruffed Grouse NY 1947, DJ, 210 cys   150 - 250
BR3935 Woodcock NY 1944, DJ, 275 cys   150 - 250
Knight, Ora W.
BR3950 The Birds of Maine Bangor 1908   75 - 125
Knight, Wilbur C.
BR3970 The Birds of Wyoming Laramie 1902   75 - 125
Kobayashi, Keisuke
BR3990 Birds of Japan Osaka 1956   300 - 500
BR3995 The Eggs of Japanese Birds Rokko 1932-40,
3 vol   300 - 500
Kortright, F. H.
BR4110 The Ducks, Geese & Swans of North America
Wash 1943, DJ   25 - 50
Krider, John
BR4130 Forty Years Notes of a Field Ornithologist
Phil 1879   200 - 300
Kuroda, Nagamichi
BR4150 Birds of the Island of Java Tokyo 1933-36, 2 vol 200 - 300
Land, Hugh C.
BR4170 Birds of Guatemala Wynnewood 1970, DJ   25 - 50
Langille, James
BR4190 Our Birds in Their Haunts: A Popular Treatise on
the Birds of Eastern North America Bos 1884   75 - 125
Lansdowne, James
BR4210 Birds of the Eastern Forests Bos 1968-70,
2 vol, DJs   125 - 250
BR4215 Birds of the Northern Forests Bos 1966,
2 vol, DJs   125 - 250
BR4220 Birds of the West Coast Bos 1976-80 2 vol, DJs 100 - 150
Larrison, Earl
BR4240 Washington Birds Seattle 1968   50 - 75
Latham, Roger
BR4260 Complete Book of the Wild Turkey Harrisburg 1956 50 - 75
Laycock, George
BR4280 The Bird Watcher's Bible Garden City 1976, DJ 20 - 30
Lea, John
BR4300 The Romance of Bird Life Lon 1917, DJ   25 - 50
Leach, John
BR4320 An Australian Bird Book Melbourne 1912   25 - 50
Levi, Wendell
BR4340 Encyclopedia of Pigeon Breeds Jersey City
1965, DJ   20 - 30
BR4345 The Pigeon Columbia 1941   30 - 50
Ligon, James S.
BR4360 New Mexico Birds Albu 1961, DJ   50 - 75
Lilford, Thomas
BR4380 Coloured Figures of the Birds of the British
Islands Lon 1891-97, 7 vol   5000 - 8000
Linsdale, Jean
BR4400 The Birds of Nevada Berkeley 1936   75 - 125
Lockley, Ronald
BR4420 Birds of the Sea Lon 1945   15 - 25
BR4425 Puffins Lon 1953, DJ   20 - 30
Lodge, George E.
BR4450 Memoirs of an Artist Naturalist Lon 1946, DJ 75 - 125
Lodge, Reginald
BR4470 Bird Hunting Through Wild Europe Lon 1908, DJ 75 - 125
Long, William
BR4490 Fowls of the Air Bos 1901   25 - 50

Low, Rosemary
BR4510 Amazon Parrots Lon 1978, 400 cys   3000 - 5000
BR4515 Parrots and Cockatoos Lon 1978, 60 cys   2000 - 3000
BR4520 The Parrots of South America Lon 1972   3000 - 5000
Lowery, George
BR4540 Louisiana Birds Baton Rouge 1955, DJ   40 - 60
Lucas, Arthur
BR4560 The Birds of Australia Melbourne 1911   75 - 125
Lydekker, Richard
BR4580 The Sportsmans British Bird Book Lon 1908 125 - 250
Lysaught, Averil
BR4600 The Book of Birds: Five Centuries of Bird
        Illustration Lon 1975, DJ   50 - 75
Mabrant, Rene
BR4620 Faune de L'equateur Africain Francais Paris 1949 75 - 125
MacDonald, James
BR4640 Birds of Australia Lon 1973, DJ   75 - 125
MacDonald, Malcolm
BR4660 The Birds of Brewery Creek NY 1947, DJ   50 - 75
MacKworth-Praed, C. W.
BR4680 Birds of Eastern and North Eastern Africa
        Lon 1957, 2 vol   200 - 300
BR4685 Birds of West Central and Western Africa
        Lon 1970-73, 2 vol   200 - 300
Macoun, John
BR4710 Catalog of Canadian Birds Ottawa 1909   75 - 125
MacPherson, H. B.
BR4730 The Home Life of the Golden Eagle Lon 1909   75 - 125
MacPherson, Hugh
BR4750 The Birds of Cumberland Carlisle 1886   300 - 500
BR4755 The Grouse Lon 1894   300 - 500
BR4760 The Partridge Lon 1893, 157 cys   300 - 500
BR4765 The Pheasant Lon 1895, 157 cys   300 - 500
Madoc, G. C.
BR4780 Malayan Birds Kuala Lumpur 1956   125 - 200
Malcolm, George
BR4800 Grouse and Grouse Moors Lon 1910   50 - 75
Marples, George
BR4820 Sea Terns Lon 1934, DJ   50 - 75
Marsh, Othniel
BR4840 Odontornithes: A Monograph on the Extinct
        Toothed Birds of North America Wash 1880   300 - 500
Mathews, Ferdinand
BR4860 Field Book of Wild Birds and Their Music
        NY 1921, DJ   25 - 50
BR4862 NY 1967, DJ   15 - 25
Mathews, Gregory
BR4880 The Birds of Australia Lon 1910-27 12 vol,
        225 cys   8000 - 12000
BR4885 The Birds of Australia Lon 1925   300 - 500
BR4890 The Birds of Norfolk Lon 1928, 2 vol,
        225 cys   8000 - 12000
BR4895 A Supplement to the Birds of Norfolk
        Lon 1936   2000 - 3000
May, John
BR4920 The Hawks of North America NY 1935   75 - 125
Maynard, Charles
BR4940 The Birds of Eastern North America
        Newtonville 1881   2000 - 3000
BR4945 Directory to the Birds of Eastern North America
        West Newton 1907   200 - 300
BR4950 Eggs of North American Birds Bos 1890   300 - 500
BR4955 Hand Book of Sparrows, Finches of New
        England Newtonville 1896   300 - 500
BR4960 Illustrations and Descriptions of the Birds
        of the Bahamas Bos 1895   1000 - 1500
Maynard, Lucy
BR4980 The Birds of Washington and Vicinity Wash 1898 25 - 50
Mayr, Ernst
BR5000 Birds of the Southwest Pacific NY 1945, DJ   20 - 30
McClure, Howe E.
BR5020 Migration and Survival of the Birds of Asia
        Bangkok 1974   50 - 75
McCoy, Joseph
BR5040 The Hunt For the Whooping Cranes NY 1966, DJ 50 - 75

McIlwraith, Thomas
BR5060 The Birds of Ontario Lon 1894   100 - 150
McIntyre, Dugald
BR5080 Wild Life of the Highlands Lon 1936, DJ   25 - 50
McKenny, Margaret
BR5100 Birds in the Garden Minneapolis 1939, DJ   25 - 50
McNeillie, Andrew
BR5120 Guide to the Pigeons of the World Oxford 1976, DJ 25 - 50
Meinertzhagen, Richard
BR5140 Birds of Arabia Edinburgh 1954   300 - 500
Menaboni, Athos
BR5160 Birds by Athos and Sara Menaboni NY 1950, DJ 40 - 60
Mengel, Robert
BR5180 The Birds of Kentucky Anchorage, KY 1965   30 - 50
Mershon, W. B.
BR5200 The Passenger Pigeon NY 1907, DJ   50 - 75
Meyer, Adolf B.
BR5220 The Birds of Celebes Berlin 1898   2000 - 3000
Millais, John G.
BR5240 British Diving Ducks Lon 1913, 2 vol, 450 cys 1000 - 1500
BR5245 Game Birds Lon 1892   400 - 600
BR5250 The Natural History of British Game Birds
        Lon 1909, 550 cys   1000 - 1500
BR5255 The Natural History of British Surface-Feeding
        Ducks NY 1902, 600 cys   1000 - 1500
BR5260 The Wild Fowler in Scotland Lon 1901   125 - 250
Miller, Harriet
BR5280 A Bird Lover in the West Bos 1894   50 - 75
BR5285 The First Book of Birds Bos 1901   50 - 75
BR5290 Upon the Tree Tops Bos 1899   50 - 75
BR5295 With the Birds in Maine Bos 1904   75 - 125
Milne, Lorus
BR5320 North American Birds Englewood Cliffs 1969, DJ 20 - 30
Minot, Henry Davis
BR5340 The Land Birds and Game Birds of New
        England Bos 1877   150 - 250
Montagu, George
BR5360 A Dictionary of British Birds Lon 1880s   200 - 300
Montes de Oca, Rafael
BR5380 Hummingbirds and Orchids of Mexico Mexico
        City 1963   75 - 125
Moreau, Reginald
BR5400 The Bird Faunas of Africa and its Islands
        NY 1966, DJ   75 - 125
Morris, Frank
BR5420 Birds of Prey of Australia Melbourne 1973,
        500 cys   500 - 700
BR5425 Finches of Australia Melbourne 1976, 350 cys 300 - 500
BR5430 Pigeons and Doves of Australia Melbourne
        1975, 500 cys   300 - 500
Muirhead, George
BR5450 The Birds of Berwickshire Edinburgh 1889-95,
        2 vol, 100 cys   200 - 300
Mulsant, Martiag
BR5470 Histoire Naturelle Des Oiseaux-Mouches
        Lyon 1876-77, 4 vol, atlas   8000 - 12000
Murphy, Robert C.
BR5490 Bird Islands of Peru NY 1925, DJ   75 - 125
BR5495 Land Birds of America NY 1953   50 - 75
BR5500 Oceanic Birds of South America NY 1936,
        2 vol, 1200 cys   300 - 500
Murphy, Robert W.
BR5520 The Peregrine Falcon Bos 1964, DJ   50 - 75
Murray, David
BR5540 Birds Through the Year Lon 1938, 175 cys   200 - 300
Murray, James
BR5560 The Avi Fauna of British India Lon 1887-90,
        2 vol   800 - 1200
Nash, C. W.
BR5580 Check List of the Birds of Ontario Toronto 1900 75 - 125
Naumberg, Elsie
BR5600 The Birds of Matto Grosso, Brazil NY 1930, DJ 200 - 300
Nehrling, Henry
BR5620 Our Native Birds of Song and Beauty Milwaukee
        1893-96, 2 vol   200 - 300

| BR6287 | BR6310 | BR6490 |

Nelson, Bryan
BR5640 Galapagos: Islands of Birds Lon 1968, DJ   20 - 30
Newton, Ian
BR5660 Finches Lon 1972   25 - 50
Nicholl, Archibald
BR5680 Fifty Years of Birdwatching Lon 1955, DJ   15 - 25
Nichols, John
BR5700 Birds of Marsh and Mere Lon 1926   150 - 250
Nicholson, Edward
BR5720 The Art of Birdwatching Lon 1931, DJ   15 - 25
BR5725 Birds and Men Lon 1951, DJ   25 - 50
BR5730 Birds in England Lon 1926, DJ   25 - 50
BR5735 Songs of Wild Birds Lon 1943, DJ   50 - 75
Nicoll, Michael
BR5760 Birds of Egypt Lon 1930, 2 vol   400 - 600
BR5765 Handlist of the Birds of Egypt Cairo 1919   100 - 150
(no author)
BR5780 Louisiana Birds Baton Rouge 1931   50 - 75
Nobel, Headley
BR5800 A List of European Birds Lon 1898   200 - 300
Norman, Harry
BR5820 Aviaries, Birdrooms, & Cages Lon 1920   150 - 250
Nuttall, Thomas
BR5840 A Popular Handbook of the Ornithology of
        Eastern North America Bos 1896, 2 vol   50 - 75
Oberholser, Harry C.
BR5860 The Bird Life of Louisiana New Orleans 1938   50 - 75
BR5865 The Bird Life of Texas Austin 1974, 2 vol, slipcase 125 - 250
Ogilvie, Malcolm
BR5890 Wild Geese Vermillion 1978   30 - 50
BR5895 The Winter Birds NY 1976, DJ   20 - 30
Over, William H.
BR5920 Birds of South Dakota Vermillion 1921   100 - 150
Owen, Myrfyn
BR5940 Wild Geese of the World Lon 1980, DJ   25 - 50
BR5945 Wildfowl of Europe Lon 1977, DJ   25 - 50
Page, Wesley T.
BR5970 Aviaries and Aviary Life Ashbourne 1912   75 - 125
Palmer, Ralph S.
BR5990 Handbook of North America Birds New Haven
        1962-76, 3 vol, DJs   200 - 300
BR5991 Wash 1988, 2 vol, DJs   100 - 150
Paquet, Rene
BR6010 Ornithologie du Val de Metz Paris 1899,
        200 cys   2000 - 3000
Paris, Paul
BR6030 Oiseaux Paris 1921   200 - 300
Parmalee, Alice
BR6050 All the Birds of the Bible NY 1959, DJ   50 - 75
Paterson, Andrew
BR6070 Birds of the Bahamas Brattleboro 1972, DJ   15 - 25
Patten, Charles
BR6090 The Aquatic Birds of Great Britain and Ireland
        Lon 1906   200 - 300
Patterson, Robert
BR6110 The Sage Grouse in Wyoming Denver 1952   75 - 125
Payne-Gallwey, Sir Ralph
BR6130 The Book of Duck Decoys Lon 1886   300 - 500
BR6135 The Fowler in Ireland Lon 1992   75 - 125

Paynter, Raymond
BR6150 The Ornithogeography of the Yucatan Peninsula
        New Haven 1955   75 - 125
Paz, Uzi
BR6170 The Birds of Israel Lexington 1987, DJ   30 - 50
Pearson, Thomas G.
BR6190 The Bird Study Book Garden City 1917   50 - 75
BR6195 Birds of North Carolina Raleigh 1919   75 - 125
BR6200 Portraits and Habits of Our Birds NY 1920-21,
        2 vol   30 - 50
BR6205 Stories of Bird Life Richmond 1901   50 - 75
BR6210 Tales From Birdland Yonkers, NY 1925   20 - 30
Peters, Harold
BR6230 The Birds of Newfoundland Bos 1951   50 - 75
Peters, James Lee
BR6250 Checklist of Birds of the World Cambridge
        1934-79, 14 vol   800 - 1200
        (many volumes reprinted later)
Peterson, Roger Tory
BR6270 The Bird Watchers Anthology NY 1957, 750 cys, DJ 100 - 150
BR6275 Birds Over America NY 1948, DJ   100 - 150
BR6280 A Field Guide to Mexican Birds Bos 1973, DJ   25 - 50
BR6285 A Field Guide to the Birds Bos 1934, DJ   50 - 75
BR6286 Bos 1939, DJ   25 - 50
BR6287 Bos 1947, DJ   20 - 30
BR6289 many later reprints, DJ   10 - 25
BR6295 A Field Guide to the Birds East of the Rockies
        Bos 1980, DJ   15 - 25
BR6300 A Field Guide to the Birds of Britain and Europe
        Bos 1954, DJ   25 - 50
BR6305 A Field Guide to the Birds of Texas Bos 1963, DJ 100 - 150
BR6310 A Field Guide to Western Birds Bos 1941, DJ   25 - 50
BR6311 Bos 1969, DJ   15 - 25
BR6315 How to Know the Birds Bos 1949, DJ   20 - 30
BR6320 Penguins Bos 1979, DJ   25 - 50
Pettingill, Olin
BR6340 The American Woodcock Bos 1936, DJ   50 - 75
BR6345 The Bird Watchers America NY 1965, DJ   25 - 50
BR6350 A Guide to Bird Finding East of the Mississippi
        NY 1951, DJ   20 - 30
BR6351 NY 1977, DJ   15 - 25
BR6355 A Guide to Bird Finding West of the Mississippi
        NY 1953, DJ   30 - 50
BR6356 NY 1981, DJ   20 - 30
Phillips, John C.
BR6380 American Waterfowl Bos 1930, DJ   75 - 125
BR6385 A Natural History of the Ducks Cambridge
        1922-26, 4 vol   2000 - 3000
BR6386 NY 1986 2 vol, DJs   125 - 250
Phillips, William
BR6400 Birds of Ceylon Columbo 1949-61, 4 vol   300 - 500
Pike, Oliver
BR6420 Bird Biographies NY 1915, DJ   50 - 75
BR6425 The Nightingale Lon 1932, DJ   50 - 75
Pizzey, Graham
BR6440 A Field Guide to the Birds of Australia
        Sydney 1980, DJ   75 - 125
Porter, Gene Stratton (also see Modern First Editions)
BR6460 Homing with the Birds NY 1919, DJ   300 - 500
BR6461 NY 1920, DJ   150 - 250
BR6462 Lon 1919, DJ   150 - 250
BR6470 Music of the Wild Cinti 1910, Deluxe Ed,
        50 cys, signed   600 - 800
BR6471 Cinti 1910, DJ   300 - 500
BR6472 NY 1910, DJ   200 - 300
BR6473 Lon 1910, DJ   150 - 250
BR6480 The Song of the Cardinal Ind 1903, DJ   250 - 350
BR6481 Ind 1906, DJ   75 - 125
BR6482 Lon 1913, DJ   50 - 75
BR6483 NY 1915, DJ   50 - 75
BR6485 later editions   10 - 30
BR6490 What I Have Done With Birds Ind 1907, slipcase 200 - 300
Pough, Richard
BR6510 Audubon Bird Guide: All the Birds of Eastern
        and Central North America Garden City 1953, DJ 20 - 30
BR6515 Audubon Bird Guide: Eastern Land Birds
        Garden City 1946, DJ   20 - 30

BR6520	Audubon Land Bird Guide Garden City 1949, DJ	20 - 30
BR6525	Audubon Water Bird Guide Garden City 1951, DJ	20 - 30
BR6530	Audubon Western Bird Guide Garden City 1957, DJ	20 - 30

Poynting, Frank
BR6550 Eggs of British Birds Lon 1895-96   800 - 1200

Priest, Cecil D.
BR6570 The Birds of Southern Rhodesia Lon 1933-36,
4 vol   200 - 300

Priestley, Mary
BR6590 A Book of Birds NY 1938, DJ   30 - 50

Prozesky, O. P. M.
BR6610 A Field Guide to the Birds of Southern Africa
Lon 1970, DJ   100 - 150

Prynne, Michael
BR6630 Egg-Shells Lon 1963, DJ   75 - 125

Quarles, Emmet
BR6650 American Pheasant Breeding and Shooting
Wilmington 1916, DJ   100 - 150

Queeny, Edgar
BR6670 Prairie Wings NY 1946, DJ   50 - 75

Rand, Austin L.
BR6690 American Water and Game Birds NY 1956, DJ   50 - 75
BR6695 Birds From Liberia Chi 1951   50 - 75
BR6700 Birds From Nepal Chi 1957   50 - 75
BR6705 Birds of the Philippine Islands Chi 1960   50 - 75
BR6710 Handbook of New Guinea Birds Lon 1967, DJ   50 - 75

Reed, Chester
BR6730 American Game Birds Garden City 1912, DJ   75 - 125
BR6735 The Bird Book NY 1916, DJ   50 - 75
BR6740 Birds of Eastern North America NY 1912, DJ   25 - 50
BR6745 North American Birds Eggs NY 1904, DJ   50 - 75

Reilly, Edgar
BR6760 The Audubon Illustrated Handbook of American
Birds NY 1968, DJ   25 - 50

Rich, Walter
BR6780 Feathered Game of the North East NY 1907   75 - 125

Richards, Harriet
BR6800 Baby Bird Finder Bos 1904-06, 2 vol   100 - 150

Richmond, William
BR6820 England's Birds Lon 1936, DJ   25 - 50

Ridgely, Robert
BR6840 A Guide to the Birds of Panama Princeton
1976, DJ   25 - 50

Ridgway, Robert
BR6860 The Birds of North and Middle America
Wash 1901-19, 11 vol   300 - 500
BR6865 Color Standards and Color Nomenclature
Wash 1912   200 - 300
BR6870 The Hummingbirds Wash 1891   30 - 50
BR6875 A Manual of North American Birds Phil 1887   200 - 300

Riley, Joseph
BR6910 Birds of the Bahama Islands NY 1905   75 - 125

Ripley, Sidney
BR6930 Rails of the World Toronto 1977, DJ   100 - 150
BR6931 Bos 1977, DJ   100 - 150
BR6935 Trail of the Money Bird Lon 1947, DJ   25 - 50

Robert, Leo Paul
BR6960 Les Oiseaux de Chez Novs Neuchatel 1933   200 - 300

Roberts, Austin
BR6980 The Birds of South Africa Lon 1940, DJ   50 - 75

Roberts, Thomas S.
BR7000 Bird Portraits in Color Minn 1934, DJ   30 - 50
BR7002 Minn 1960, DJ   30 - 50
BR7005 The Birds of Minnesota Minn 1932, 2 vol   150 - 250

Robinson, Herbert
BR7020 The Birds of the Malay Peninsula
Lon 1927-76, 5 vol   2000 - 3000

Robinson, John H.
BR7040 A Text Book For Poultry Keepers Bos 1904   25 - 50

Robson, John
BR7060 Canaries, Hybrids and British Birds in Cage
and Aviary Lon 1911   75 - 125

Rothschild, Lionel
BR7080 Extinct Birds Lon 1907   50 - 75

Rourke, Constance
BR7100 Audubon NY 1936, DJ   20 - 30

Rue, Leonard
BR7120 Pictorial Guide to the Birds of North America
NY 1970, DJ   20 - 30

Ruthven, John
BR7140 Top Flight: Speed Index to Waterfowl of
North America Milwaukee 1965, DJ   25 - 50

Sage, John Hall
BR7160 The Birds of Connecticut Hartford 1913   100 - 150

Salmon, Julien
BR7180 Les Oiseaux Paris, early 1900s, 2 vol   200 - 300

Salt, Walter
BR7200 The Birds of Alberta Edmonton 1976   50 - 75

Samuels, E. A.
BR7220 Our Northern and Eastern Birds NY 1883   250 - 350

Sandys, Edwyn
BR7240 Upland Game Birds NY 1924, DJ   30 - 50

Sanford, Leonard
BR7260 The Waterfowl Family NY 1903   30 - 50

Sass, Herbert
BR7280 On the Wings of a Bird Garden City 1929, DJ   25 - 50

Saunders, Aretas
BR7300 Bird Song Albany 1929, DJ   25 - 50
BR7305 A Guide to Bird Songs NY 1935   20 - 30
BR7310 The Lives of Wild Birds Garden City 1954, DJ   25 - 50

Saunders, Howard
BR7330 An Illustrated Manual of British Birds Lon 1889 200 - 300

Saunders, Richard
BR7350 Flashing Wings Toronto 1947   50 - 75

Schorger, Arlie
BR7370 The Passenger Pigeon Madison 1955, DJ   30 - 50
BR7375 The Wild Turkey Norman 1966, DJ   30 - 50

Sclater, Philip L.
BR7390 Argentine Ornithology Lon 1888-89, 2 vol,
200 cys   2000 - 3000

Sclater, William L.
BR7410 A History of the Birds of Colorado Lon 1912, DJ 125   200

Scott, Bob
BR7430 The Birdwatcher's Key... Lon 1976, DJ   20 - 30

Scott, Peter
BR7450 A Coloured Key to the Wildfowl of the World
NY 1961, DJ   20 - 30
BR7451 NY 1977, DJ   15 - 20
BR7455 The Swans Lon 1972, DJ   25 - 50
BR7460 A Thousand Geese Lon 1953, DJ   30 - 50
BR7465 Wildfowl of the British Isles Lon 1957, DJ   50 - 75

Scott, William
BR7490 Bird Studies: An Account of the Land Birds of
Eastern North America NY 1898   50 - 75
BR7495 The Story of a Bird Lover NY 1903   25 - 50

Seebohm, Henry
BR7520 The Birds of Siberia Lon 1901   150 - 250
BR7525 The Birds of the Japanese Empire Lon 1890   300 - 500
BR7530 Colored Figures of Eggs of British Birds
Sheffield 1896   300 - 500
BR7535 A History of British Birds Lon 1884-96, 4 vol 2000 - 3000

Seiden, Rudolph
BR7560 Poultry Handbook NY 1947, DJ   25 - 50

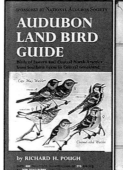

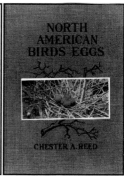

BR6520   BR6590   BR6745 (w/o DJ)

| BR7220 | BR7900 | BR7900 (frontispiece and title page) | BR8130 | BR8135 |

Seigne, John
BR7580 A Bird Watchers Note Book Lon 1930, DJ   25 - 50

Selous, Edmund
BR7600 Beautiful Birds Lon 1901   50 - 75
BR7605 Bird Life Glimpses Lon 1905   50 - 75
BR7610 Bird Watching Lon 1901   50 - 75
BR7620 Realities of Bird Life Lon 1927, DJ   50 - 75

Serle, William
BR7640 A Field Guide to the Birds of West Africa
Lon 1977, DJ   50 - 75

Serventy, Dominic
BR7660 A Handbook of the Birds of Western Australia
Perth 1951, DJ   50 - 75

Seth-Smith, David
BR7680 Parrakeets Lon 1903   50 - 75

Seton, Ernest Thompson
BR7700 The Birds of Manitoba Wash 1891   50 - 75

Shakespeare, Joseph
BR7720 The Bantams Down-To-Date Sellersville 1925   30 - 50

Sheldon, William
BR7740 The Book of the American Woodcock
Amherst 1967, DJ   25 - 50

Shelley, George E.
BR7760 The Birds of Africa Lon 1896-1912, 7 vol   3000 - 5000

Shiras, George
BR7780 Hunting Wildlife with Camera and Flashlight
Wash 1936   20 - 30

Shoffner, Charles
BR7800 The Bird Book NY 1929, DJ   20 - 30

Shortt, Angus
BR7820 Sports Afield Treasury of Waterfowl
Englewood Cliffs 1957, DJ   50 - 75

Shortt, Terence
BR7840 Wild Birds of the Americas Bos 1977, DJ   20 - 30

Shriner, Charles
BR7860 The Birds of New Jersey Paterson 1896   75 - 125

Silloway, Perley
BR7880 Sketches of Some Common Birds Cinti 1897   100 - 150

Simmons, Albert D.
BR7900 Wing Shots NY 1936, 950 cys   200 - 300

Skead, Cuthbert
BR7920 The Sun Birds of Southern Africa Cape Town
1967   75 - 125

Skinner, Milton
BR7940 The Birds of the Yellowstone National Park
Syracuse 1926   50 - 75

Skutch, Alexander
BR7960 A Bird Watcher's Adventures in Tropical
America Austin 1977, DJ   25 - 50
BR7965 Life Histories of Central American Birds
Berkeley 1954-69, 3 vol   75 - 125
BR7970 Parent Birds and Their Young Austin 1976, DJ   50 - 75
BR7975 Studies of Tropical American Birds Cambridge 1972 25 - 50

Slater, Peter
BR8000 A Field Guide to Australian Birds: Non-Passerines
Adelaide 1970, 2 vol, DJs   50 - 75
BR8005 A Field Guide to Australian Birds: Passerines
Wynnewood 1975, DJ   25 - 50

Slud, Paul
BR8030 The Birds of Costa Rica NY 1964   30 - 50

Small, Arnold
BR8050 The Birds of California NY 1974, DJ   25 - 50

Smith, Lawrence
BR8070 American Game Preserve Shooting NY 1933   25 - 50

Smith, Page
BR8090 The Chicken Book Bos 1975, DJ   25 - 50

Smith, Reginald
BR8110 Bird Life and Bird Lore Lon 1905   50 - 75

Smythies, Bertram
BR8130 The Birds of Borneo Edinburgh 1960, DJ   200 - 300
BR8135 The Birds of Burma Edinburgh 1953, DJ   150 - 250
BR8140 The Birds of Burmah Rangoon 1940   200 - 300

Snodgrass, Robert
BR8160 Birds Wash 1904   20 - 30

Snow, David
BR8180 The Cotingas Ithaca 1982, DJ   50 - 75
BR8185 A Study of Blackbirds Lon 1958, DJ   50 - 75

Snyder, Dorothy
BR8200 The Birds of Guyana Salem 1966   50 - 75

Snyder, Lester
BR8220 Ontario Birds Toronto 1951, DJ   50 - 75

Sowls, Lyle
BR8240 Prairie Ducks Harrisburg 1955, DJ   50 - 75

Sparks, John
BR8260 Owls NY 1970, DJ   25 - 50
BR8265 Penguins Newton Abbot 1967   25 - 50

Spiller, Burton
BR8290 Grouse Feathers NY 1935, 950 cys   150 - 250
BR8295 More Grouse Feathers NY 1938, 950 cys   150 - 250

Sprunt, Jr., Alexander
BR8320 Florida Bird Life NY 1954, DJ   50 - 75
BR8325 North American Birds of Prey NY 1955, DJ   20 - 30
BR8330 South Carolina Bird Life Columbia 1949, DJ   50 - 75

Spruyt, Cornelius
BR8350 Toy Pigeons Assen 1927   75 - 125

Stark, Arthur
BR8370 The Birds of South Africa Lon 1900-1906,
4 vol   1500 - 2500

Starling, Alfred
BR8390 Enjoying Indiana Birds Bloomington 1978, DJ   25 - 50

Sterns, Winfrid
BR8410 New England Bird Life Bos 1881-83, 2 vol   75 - 125
BR8411 Bos 1883-85, 2 vol   75 - 125
BR8414 Bos 1894, 2 vol   75 - 125

Stewart, Robert
BR8440 Birds of Maryland Wash 1958   100 - 150

Stokes, Donald
BR8460 A Guide to the Behavior of Common Birds
Bos 1979, DJ   25 - 50

Stone, Witmer
BR8480 Bird Studies at Old Cape May Phil 1937, 2 vol 150 - 250
BR8485 The Birds of Eastern Pennsylvania and New
Jersey Phil 1894   100 - 150
BR8490 The Birds of New Jersey Trenton 1908   50 - 75

Stonham, Charles
BR8510 The Birds of the British Islands Lon 1906-11,
5 vol   2000 - 3000

Stout, Gardner
BR8530 The Shorebirds of North America NY 1967,
350 cys   300 - 500

Studer, Jacob H.
BR8550 The Birds of North America NY 1895 300 - 500
BR8555 Studer's Popular Ornithology Col 1878, 2 vol 400 - 600
BR8556 Columbus 1897, 2 vol 200 - 300
BR8557 Barre, MA 1977 50 - 75

Sturgis, Bertha
BR8580 Field Book of the Birds of the Panama Canal
Zone NY 1928 75 - 125

Sumner, Lowell
BR8600 Birds and Mammals of the Sierra Nevada
Berkeley 1953, DJ 75 - 125

Sutton, George Miksch
BR8620 Birds in the Wilderness NY 1936, DJ 50 - 75
BR8625 An Introduction to the Birds of Pennsylvania
Harrisburg 1928, DJ 50 - 75
BR8630 Mexican Birds Norman 1951, DJ 75 - 125
BR8635 Oklahoma Birds Norman 1967, DJ 75 - 125
BR8640 Portraits of Mexican Birds Norman 1975, DJ 150 - 250

Swann, Harry
BR8660 A Dictionary of English and Folk-Names of
British Birds Lon 1913, DJ 75 - 125

Swaysland, Walter
BR8680 Familiar Wild Birds Lon 1883-89, 4 vol 125 - 250
BR8682 Lon 1901, 4 vol 75 - 125

Takatsukasa, Nobuske
BR8700 The Birds of Nippon Lon 1932-39, 7 parts
in 4 vol 2000 - 3000
BR8702 Tokyo 1967 300 - 500

Taverner, Percy
BR8720 Birds of Canada Toronto 1938, DJ 75 - 125
BR8725 Birds of Eastern Canada Ottawa 1919 75 - 125
BR8730 Birds of Western Canada Ottawa 1926 75 - 125

Terres, John K.
BR8750 The Audubon Society Encyclopedia of North
American Birds NY 1980, DJ 25 - 50

Theuriet, Andre
BR8770 Nos Oiseaux Paris 1880s, 50 cys 3000 - 5000
BR8771 Paris, 1880s, later edition 300 - 500

Thomsen, Peter
BR8790 The Birds of Tunisia Copenhagen 1979, DJ 50 - 75

Thomson, Arthur
BR8810 A New Dictionary of Birds Lon 1964, DJ 25 - 50

Thorburn, Archibald
BR8830 British Birds Lon 1915-16, 4 vol 800 - 1200
BR8832 Lon 1967 75 - 125
BR8833 Woodstock 1976 75 - 125
BR8840 Game Birds Lon 1923, 155 cys 800 - 1200

Thoreau, Henry David
BR8860 Notes on New England Birds Bos 1910 50 - 75

Todd, Frank
BR8880 Waterfowl; Ducks, Geese & Swans of the
World NY 1979, DJ 25 - 50

Todd, Walter
BR8900 The Birds of the Isle of Pines Pittsburgh 1916 75 - 125
BR8910 Birds of the Labrador Peninsula Toronto 1963, DJ 50 - 75
BR8920 Birds of Western Pennsylvania Pittsburgh 1940 75 - 125

Tordoff, Harrison
BR8940 Checklist of the Birds of Kansas Lawrence 1956 50 - 75

Townsend, Charles
BR8960 The Birds of Essex County, Massachusetts
Cambridge 1905 75 - 125
BR8965 Birds of Labrador Bos 1907 75 - 125

Trumbull, Gordon
BR8980 Names and Portraits of Birds Which Interest
Gunners NY 1888 200 - 300

Tufts, Robie, W.
BR9000 The Birds of Nova Scotia Halifax 1961 50 - 75

Turner, Angela
BR9020 Swallows & Martins Bos 1989, DJ 30 - 50

Turner, William
BR9040 Turner on Birds Cambridge 1903 (reprint of
1544 ed) 100 - 150

Twining, Francis
BR9060 Bird Watching in the West Portland 1931, DJ 50 - 75

Udvardy, Miklos
BR9080 The Audubon Society Field Guide to North
American Birds, Western Region NY 1977 50 - 75

Urban, Emil
BR9100 Birds From Coahuila, Mexico Lawrence 1959 50 - 75

Ussher, Richard
BR9120 The Birds of Ireland Lon 1900 150 - 250

Van Pelt Lechner, A. A.
BR9140 "Oologia Neerlandica" The Hague 1910-13,
2 vol 800 - 1200

Van Wormer, Joe
BR9160 The World of the Canada Goose Phil 1968, DJ 50 - 75

Vaucher, Charles
BR9180 Sea Birds Edinburgh 1960 50 - 75

Vaurie, Charles
BR9200 The Birds of Palearctic Fauna Lon 1959 25 - 50
BR9205 Tibet and Its Birds Lon 1972, DJ 75 - 125

Vennor, Henry
BR9220 Our Birds of Prey Montreal 1876 300 - 500

Verner, William
BR9240 My Life Among the Wild Birds in Spain Lon 1909 50 - 75

Vesey-Fitzgerald, Brian
BR9260 British Game Lon 1946, DJ 25 - 50

Walker, Lewis
BR9280 The Book of Owls NY 1974, DJ 20 - 30

Walkinshaw, Lawrence
BR9300 Cranes of the World NY 1973, DJ 20 - 30

Wallace, Robert
BR9320 British Cage Birds Lon 1887 150 - 250

Walters, Michael
BR9340 The Complete Birds of the World Newton Abbot
1980 50 - 75

Warren, Benjamin
BR9360 Report on the Birds of Pennsylvania Harrisburg
1890 100 - 150

Watson, George
BR9380 Birds of the Antarctic and Sub-Antarctic
Wash 1975 50 - 75

Wayne, Arthur
BR9400 Birds of South Carolina Charleston 1910 100 - 150

Weir, Harrison
BR9420 The Poultry Book NY 1909 25 - 50

Wetmore, Alexander
BR9440 The Birds of Haiti Wash 1931 50 -75
BR9445 The Birds of Porto Rico NY 1927 50 - 75
BR9450 Birds of the Past in North America Wash 1929 50 - 75
BR9455 Observations on the Birds of Argentina,
Paraguay, Uraguay and Chile Wash 1926 50 - 75
BR9460 Song and Garden Birds of North America
Wash 1964 25 - 50
BR9465 Water, Prey and Game Birds of North America
Wash 1965 25 - 50

Wheaton, John
BR9480 Report on the Birds of Ohio Columbus 1879 50 - 75

Wheelock, Irene
BR9500 Birds of California Chi 1904 100 - 150
BR9505 Nestlings of Forest and Marsh Chi 1902 75 - 125

Whistler, Hugh
BR9520 Popular Handbook of Indian Birds Lon 1928 300 - 500

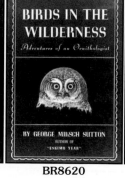

BR8325   BR8620   BR8771

Wicks, John
BR9540 Bird Paradise Phil 1914, DJ   25 - 50
Widmann, Otto
BR9560 A Preliminary Catalog of the Birds of Missouri
            St. Louis 1907   100 - 150
Wildash, Philip
BR9580 Birds of South Vietnam Rutland 1968, DJ   75 - 125
Wilder, George
BR9600 Birds of Northeastern China Peking 1938   100 - 150
Willcox, Mary
BR9620 Pocket Guide to Common Land Birds of New
            England Bos 1895   75 - 125
Williams, Arthur
BR9640 Birds of the Cleveland Region Clev 1950   50 - 75
Wilson, Scott
BR9660 Aves Hawaiienses: The Birds of the Sandwich
            Islands Lon 1890-1899   3000 - 5000
Wing, Leonard
BR9680 Natural History of Birds NY 1956, DJ   50 - 75
Wintle, Ernest
BR9700 The Birds of Montreal Montreal 1896   100 - 150
Wood, Casey
BR9720 The Fundus Oculi of Birds Chi 1917   200 - 300
Wood, Norman
BR9740 The Birds of Michigan Ann Arbor 1951   50 - 75
Woodruff, Frank
BR9760 The Birds of the Chicago Area Chi 1907   50 - 75
Worcester, Dean
BR9780 Contributions to Philippine Ornithology
            Wash 1898   100 - 150
Wright, Horace
BR9800 Birds of the Boston Public Garden Bos 1909   50 - 75
Wright, Mabel
BR9820 Bird Craft NY 1895   100 - 150
BR9825 Citizen Bird NY 1897   100 - 150
Wright, R. G.
BR9840 The Ducks of India Lon 1925   150 - 250
Wyatt, Claude
BR9860 British Birds Lon 1894-99, 2 vol   3000 - 5000
Wyman, Luther
BR9880 Field Book of Birds of the South Western
            United States Bos1925   100 - 150

BOOKS ABOUT BOOKS

This category deals with books themselves, their history and art. It includes a wide range of topics, and most used and antiquarian book dealers have an ample supply of examples on hand. Many are very collectible and valuable, even though over 90% were published during the 20th century.

The following topics and examples fall into this category:

1. Bibliographies: *American First Editions* by Merle Johnson (NY 1936); *Bibliography of Crime Fiction 1749-1975* by Allen Hubin, Del Mar (CA 1979).

2. History: *The Western Book Trade* by Walter Sutton (Col 1961); *A History of McGuffey Readers* by Henry Vail (Clev 1911).

3. Typography (the art of printing): *The Art of the Printer* by Stanley Morison (Lon 1925); *The Book: The Story of Printing and Bookmaking* by Douglas McMurtrie (NY 1937).

4. Papermaking: *Old Papermaking* by Dard Hunter (Chillicothe 1923).

5. Binding: *Rod for the Back of the Binder* Lakeside Press (Chi 1929).

6. Collecting: numerous titles by A. Edward Newton, A.S.W. Rosenbach, John Winterich, William D. Orcutt and many others. These are written from a collectors' or rare-book dealers' viewpoint and detail their personal adventures.

7. Facsimile imprints: books printed to resemble great historical books like *The Gutenberg Bible*, rare early American imprints, and illuminated manuscripts from the 1200s to the 1500s. Some are very expensive because of the involved process of duplicating the original printing, coloring, and paper composition.

8. Private press, auction and dealers catalogs: too numerous to mention, these are beyond the scope of this guide. Hundreds of dealers, auctioneers and presses published large, lavishly-illustrated catalogs from the 1880s to the 1940s. They are worth anywhere from ten to several hundred dollars.

9. Price guides: out-of-print guides are valuable as reference tools. Van Allen Bradley's *Handbook of Values* ran through several revised editions from the 1960s to 1982-83; are all in demand. Other price guides by Wright Howes and William Targ are also collectible.

10. Trade catalogs: profusely illustrated, fine catalogs of printers, papermakers, and so forth which came from the early 1900s. Many have mounted samples of printing, paper-making, and bindings. Some are very scarce because they were only given to salesmen and book dealers.

Listings are arranged alphabetically by author or editor.

Adams, Bess Porter
BK0100 About Books and Children NY 1957, DJ   20 - 30
Adams, Frederick B.
BK0140 Radical Literature in America Stamford 1939,
            650 cys, box   100 - 150
Albion, Robert B.
BK0180 Maritime and Naval History An Annotated
            Bibliog Mystic, CT 1955   30 - 50
Allan, P. B. M.
BK0220 The Book Hunter At Home NY 1922, DJ   30 - 50
Allen, Gay Wilson (editor)
BK0260 Collected Writings of Walt Whitman
            NY 1961-69, 9 vol, DJs   150 - 250
American Book - Prices Current
An annual volume published for the book trade since 1895, ABPC is a yearly compilation of prices realized by major auction houses in the U.S. and Great Britain for autographs, books, maps, and prints. Also issued in five-year installments, it's expensive new. Used copies have only minor interest and are usually worth $20-40 for pre-1970 annuals. The five-year volumes can be worth more and may bring $50 and up. Used volumes from the 1980s-1990s may run from $75 to 125.
BK0300 Vols 1-80, 1895-1975   1000 - 1500
Anderson, Frank J.
BK0400 Private Presswork NY 1977, DJ   20 - 30
Arber, Agnes
BK0440 Herbals, Their Origin and Evolution Cambridge
            1953   150 - 250
Armitage, Merle
BK0480 Notes on Modern Printing NY 1945, DJ   30 - 50
Bagrow, Leo
BK0520 History of Cartography Cambridge 1964   50 - 75
Banta, R. E.
BK0560 Indiana Authors and Their Books 1816-1916
            Crawfordsville 1949, 2 vol   50 - 75
Beach, Sylvia
BK0580 Shakespeare and Company NY 1959, DJ   40 - 60
Belnap, George N.
BK0600 Oregon Imprints 1845-70 Eugene 1968   40 - 60
Benét, William Rose
BK0640 The Reader's Encyclopedia NY 1948, 2 vol   50 - 75
Bennett, Paul
BK0680 Books and Printing Clev 1951, DJ   30 - 50

BK0100   BK0400   BK0580

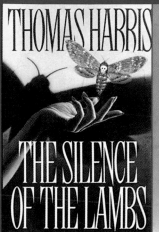

THOMAS HARRIS

THE SILENCE OF THE LAMBS

Native Son

by RICHARD WRIGHT

FLASHMAN

From the Flashman Papers 1839-1842

EDITED AND ARRANGED BY George MacDonald Fraser

The Lime Pit

JONATHAN VALIN

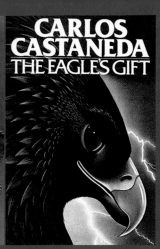

CARLOS CASTANEDA THE EAGLE'S GIFT

THE BEAN TREES

A NOVEL BY BARBARA KINGSOLVER

The Collector

JOHN FOWLES

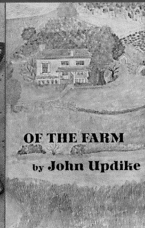

OF THE FARM

by John Updike

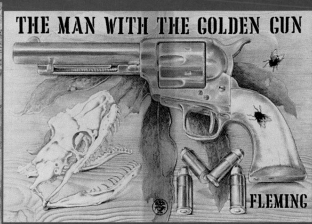

THE MAN WITH THE GOLDEN GUN

FLEMING

WALTER MOSLEY

DEVIL IN A BLUE DRESS

A NOVEL

TOM WOLFE

FROM BAUHAUS TO OUR HOUSE

THEIR ISLAND HOME

by Jules Verne Author of Twenty Thousand Leagues under the Sea.

The Later Adventures of the Swiss Family Robinson

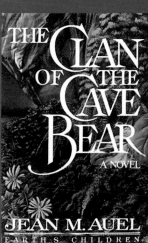

THE CLAN OF THE CAVE BEAR

A NOVEL

JEAN M. AUEL

EARTH'S CHILDREN

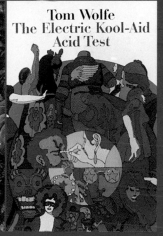

Tom Wolfe
The Electric Kool-Aid Acid Test

CITY

by CLIFFORD SIMAK

A New Science Fiction Novel of the future

Edited, with an Introduction and Notes, by ANDRE NORTON

Space Service

Thrilling science-fiction tales by Theodore R. Cogswell, Gordon R. Dickson, H. B. Fyfe, Raymond Z. Gallun, Edward I. Robb, C. M. Kornbluth, Walt Sheldon, and J. A. Winter, M.D.

The Snow Queen Joan D.Vinge

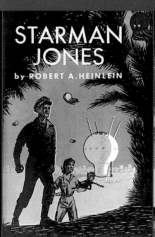

STARMAN JONES

by ROBERT A. HEINLEIN

CARSON OF VENUS

EDGAR RICE BURROUGHS

The Time Machine

CANARY IN A CAT HOUSE
Off the top of his head—the short, wild fantasies of one of America's most imaginative young writers, the author of Player Piano and The Sirens of Titan. KURT VONNEGUT, JR.

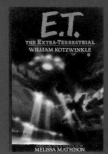
E.T.
THE EXTRA-TERRESTRIAL
WILLIAM KOTZWINKLE
MELISSA MATHISON

NOW WE ARE SIX
BY A.A. MILNE
Decorations by E.H. SHEPARD

STAND ON ZANZIBAR
A NOVEL BY JOHN BRUNNER

SPRAGUE de CAMP's New ANTHOLOGY
6 STORIES from the brightest sun of American Science Fiction

WILLIAM IRISH
A cheap and evil girl sets a hopped-up killer against a city.
MARIHUANA

THE CASE OF THE CAUTIOUS COQUETTE
A PERRY MASON STORY
ERLE STANLEY GARDNER

The Shining by Stephen King
A new novel by the author of CARRIE and 'SALEM'S LOT

THE SWORD IS DRAWN
BY ANDRE NORTON

The Boy Who Made Dragonfly
by Tony Hillerman
Illustrated by Laszlo Kubinyi

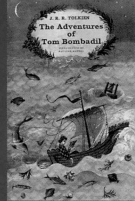
J.R.R. TOLKIEN
The Adventures of Tom Bombadil

WELCOME TO AMERICA IN 2025 WHEN THE BEST MEN DON'T RUN FOR PRESIDENT. THEY RUN FOR THEIR LIVES.
THE RUNNING MAN
RICHARD BACHMAN

pebble in the sky
isaac asimov

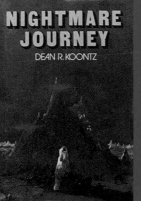
NIGHTMARE JOURNEY
DEAN R. KOONTZ

FLANDRY
POUL ANDERSON

MARTIANS GO HOME
FREDRIC BROWN

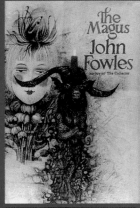
The Magus
John Fowles
author of 'The Collector'

CRY TO HEAVEN
A novel by ANNE RICE

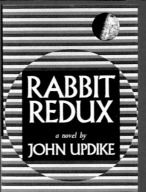
RABBIT REDUX
a novel by JOHN UPDIKE

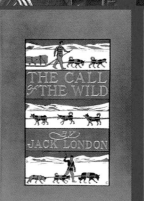
THE CALL OF THE WILD
JACK LONDON

NINE PRINCES IN AMBER
ROGER ZELAZNY
DOUBLEDAY SCIENCE FICTION

Cannery Row
JOHN STEINBECK

ELLERY QUEEN
CAT of MANY TAILS

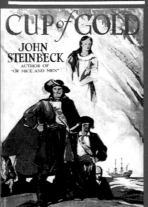
CUP of GOLD
JOHN STEINBECK
AUTHOR OF "OF MICE AND MEN"

THE Dream Merchants
A NOVEL
BY
Harold Robbins
AUTHOR OF Never Love a Stranger

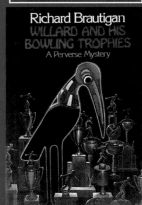
Richard Brautigan
WILLARD AND HIS BOWLING TROPHIES
A Perverse Mystery

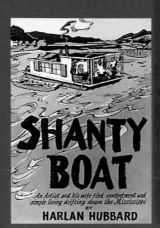

SHANTY BOAT
An Artist and his wife find contentment and simple living drifting down the Mississippi
BY
HARLAN HUBBARD

The Book of the American Indian
Written by Hamlin Garland

Pictured by Frederic Remington
Harper & Brothers Established 1817

AMERICAN INDIANS

FIRST FAMILIES OF THE SOUTHWEST

RED CLOUD'S BUCKSKIN WAR SHIRT ORNAMENTED WITH HUMAN SCALPS AND BEADS, BEADED LEGGINGS AND MOCCASINS.

CASEY JONES

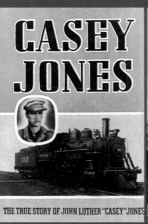

THE TRUE STORY OF JOHN LUTHER "CASEY" JONES

A GHOST TOWN ON THE Yellowstone
ELLIOT PAUL

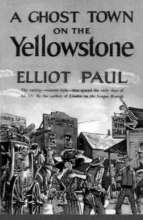

THE MAD BOOTHS OF MARYLAND

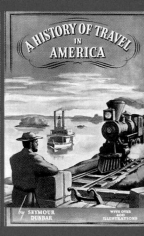

STANLEY KIMMEL

A HISTORY OF TRAVEL IN AMERICA

by SEYMOUR DUNBAR
WITH OVER 400 ILLUSTRATIONS

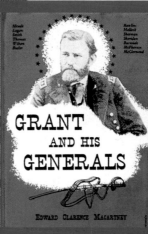

GRANT AND HIS GENERALS

EDWARD CLARENCE MACARTNEY

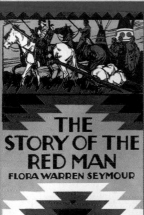

THE STORY OF THE RED MAN
FLORA WARREN SEYMOUR

SCHOOLCRAFT'S EXPEDITION TO LAKE ITASCA
The Discovery of the Source of the Mississippi

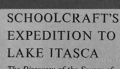

Edited by PHILIP P. MASON

This Reckless Breed of Men
The Trappers and Fur Traders of the Southwest

ROBERT GLASS CLELAND
author of *FROM WILDERNESS TO EMPIRE*
Alfred A. Knopf: Publisher · New York

STEAMBOAT DAYS
BY FRED ERVING DAYTON
The History of the Steamboat in America

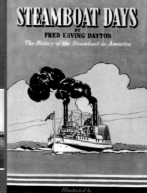

Illustrated by
JOHN WOLCOTT ADAMS

The Orphan Brigade
The Kentucky Confederates Who Couldn't Go Home

WILLIAM C. DAVIS Author of *BATTLE AT BULL RUN*

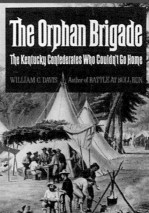

TALES OF THE MISSISSIPPI

Ray Samuel
Leonard V. Huber
Warren C. Ogden

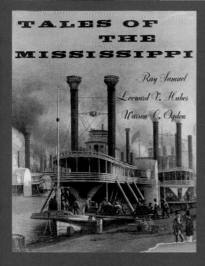

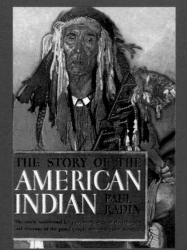

THE STORY OF THE AMERICAN INDIAN PAUL RADIN

A NEW ROMANTIC BIOGRAPHY

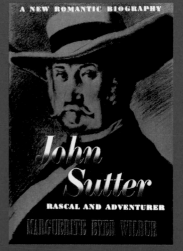

John Sutter
RASCAL AND ADVENTURER
MARGUERITE EYER WILBUR

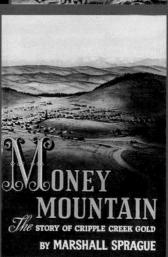

MONEY MOUNTAIN
The STORY OF CRIPPLE CREEK GOLD
BY MARSHALL SPRAGUE

THE
ODYSSEY
OF
HOMER

Green Willow and other
Japanese Fairy Tales

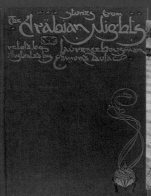

Stories from
The Arabian Nights
retold by Laurence Housman
illustrated by Edmund Dulac

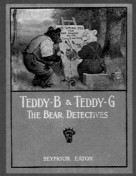

THE BEGGING BEAR

DREAM BLOCKS
AILEEN CLEVELAND HIGGINS
WITH ILLUSTRATIONS
BY JESSIE WILLCOX SMITH

Teddy-B & Teddy-G
The Bear Detectives

SEYMOUR EATON

THE FLIGHT BROTHERS

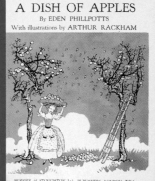

THE PARABLES OF JESUS

JIJI LOU

THE PIED PIPER
of HAMELIN
ROBERT BROWNING

ILLUSTRATED BY
ARTHUR RACKHAM

BOYS AND GIRLS OF BOOKLAND
NORA ARCHIBALD SMITH

JESSIE WILLCOX SMITH

THE FRENZIED
PRINCE
HEROIC STORIES OF ANCIENT IRELAND

Told by PÁDRAIC COLUM
Illustrated by WILLY POGÁNY

A DISH OF APPLES
By EDEN PHILLPOTTS
With illustrations by ARTHUR RACKHAM

HODDER & STOUGHTON Ltd, PUBLISHERS, LONDON, E.C.4

PALMER COX'S
QUEER
PEOPLE

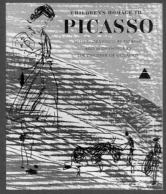

CHILDREN'S HOMAGE TO
PICASSO
WITH 12 DRAWINGS BY PICASSO
AND 12 DRAWINGS BY
THE CHILDREN OF VALLAURIS

A WONDER BOOK
AND TANGLEWOOD TALES
NATHANIEL HAWTHORNE
ILLUSTRATED BY MAXFIELD PARRISH

THE WONDERFUL
ISLES

BY S.H.HAMER
ILLUSTRATED BY
HARRY ROUNTREE.

A CHRISTMAS CAROL

ECCE HOMO BY GEORGE GROSZ

WITH AN INTRODUCTION BY HENRY MILLER

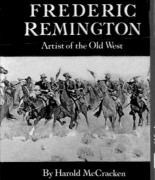

FREDERIC
REMINGTON
Artist of the Old West

By Harold McCracken
With over 80 reproductions, including 32 in full color

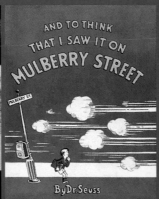

AND TO THINK
THAT I SAW IT ON
MULBERRY STREET

By Dr. Seuss

The MYSTERIOUS
STRANGER · by
MARK TWAIN

FRANK
LLOYD
WRIGHT

THE FUTURE OF
ARCHITECTURE

PUMPKIN MOONSHINE
TASHA TUDOR

THE COUNTY FAIR
BY TASHA TUDOR

DORCAS PORKUS
BY TASHA TUDOR

Little Black Sambo

SNOW BEFORE CHRISTMAS

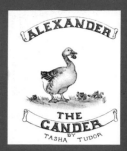

ALEXANDER THE GANDER
BY TASHA TUDOR

UNCLE WIGGILY'S TRAVELS
HOWARD R. GARIS

THE LITTLE ENGINE THAT COULD

BREAKDOWN
A NOVEL BY JOHN BRATBY

DAVID BALFOUR
By ROBERT LOUIS STEVENSON
Illustrated by N. C. WYETH
CHARLES SCRIBNER'S SONS · NEW YORK

Alice's Adventures in Wonderland
by Lewis Carroll
PETER NEWELL EDITION

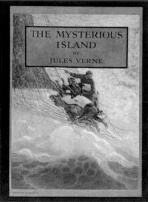

THE MYSTERIOUS ISLAND BY JULES VERNE

ALICE'S ADVENTURES IN WONDERLAND
LEWIS CARROLL

ANIMALS OF THE BIBLE

THE SECRET GARDEN
FRANCES HODGSON BURNETT

The Pike County Ballads
by John Hay

RIP VAN WINKLE

The Tough Winter
by Robert Lawson
by the author of Rabbit Hill

MAXFIELD PARRISH
BY COY LUDWIG

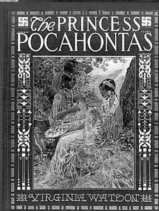

The PRINCESS POCAHONTAS
VIRGINIA WATSON

Illustrated by HOWARD CHANDLER CHRISTY
WHEN SHE WAS ABOUT SIXTEEN
JAMES WHITCOMB RILEY

The Boy's King Arthur
Edited for boys by SIDNEY LANIER
CHARLES SCRIBNER'S SONS · NEW YORK

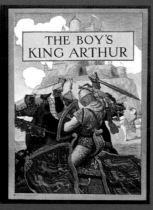

THE BOY'S KING ARTHUR

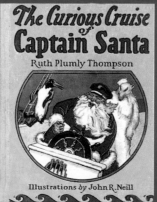

The Curious Cruise of Captain Santa
Ruth Plumly Thompson
Illustrations by John R. Neill

THE WIND IN THE WILLOWS
Kenneth Grahame
ILLUSTRATED BY Tasha Tudor

SAINT JOAN OF ARC by MARK TWAIN

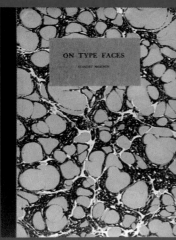

ON TYPE FACES

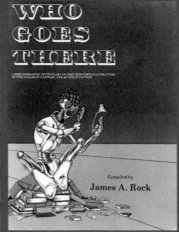

WHO GOES THERE

A BIBLIOGRAPHIC DICTIONARY OF PSEUDONYMOUS LITERATURE
IN THE FIELD OF FANTASY AND SCIENCE FICTION

Compiled by
James A. Rock

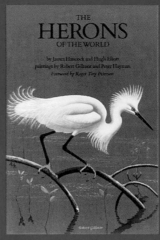

THE HERONS
OF THE WORLD

by James Hancock and Hugh Elliott
paintings by Robert Gillmor and Peter Hayman
Foreword by Roger Tory Peterson

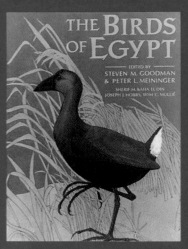

THE BIRDS OF EGYPT

EDITED BY
STEVEN M. GOODMAN
& PETER L. MEININGER

SHERIF M. BAHA EL DIN
JOSEPH J. HOBBS, WIM C. MULLIE

AMERICA and her ALMANACS

Wit, Wisdom & Weather 1639-1970

Almanack 1733

by Robb Sagendorph

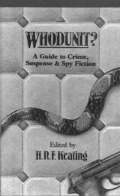

WHODUNIT?
A Guide to Crime,
Suspense & Spy Fiction

Edited by
H.R.F. Keating

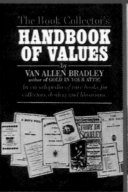

The Book Collector's
HANDBOOK OF VALUES

by
VAN ALLEN BRADLEY
author of GOLD IN YOUR ATTIC

An encyclopedia of rare books for
collectors, dealers and librarians.

The Birds of BORNEO

by
BERTRAM E. SMYTHIES

André Giacomelli

Nos Oiseaux

Compositions
de
F. Giacomelli

Ch. Tallandier
Éditeur

Our FLYING NAVY

THE MACMILLAN COMPANY

YOUR WINGS

by
JORDANOFF

NEW EDITION
The Standard Book on Flying
the World Over

NX-211

"WE"
NX-211

The famous flier's own
story of his life and —
his Transatlantic flight,
together with his views
on the future of aviation.

By
CHARLES A. LINDBERGH

THE HELICOPTERS ARE COMING

C·B·F· MACAULEY

the FLIGHT OF the SILVER SHIP

ROCKETS and MISSILES : PAST

and FUTURE

MARTIN CAIDIN

THE BOY'S STORY OF LINDBERGH THE LONE EAGLE

CLEAN LIVING   PREPAREDNESS

COURAGE

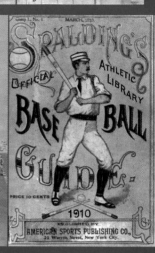

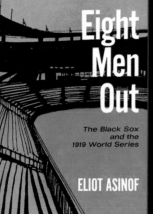

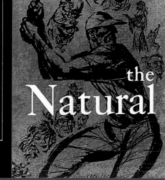

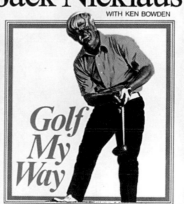

PRINCE MUDTURTLE

LAURA BANCROFT

THE LAST EGYPTIAN

EDWARD STERN & CO. INC.

LITTLE WIZARD Stories of OZ

BY L. FRANK BAUM

The Magical Mimics IN OZ

JACK SNOW

THE ROYAL BOOK OF OZ

By L. FRANK BAUM

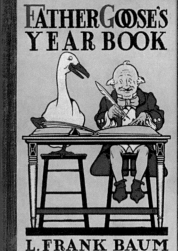

FATHER GOOSE'S YEAR BOOK

L. FRANK BAUM

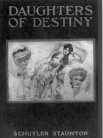

DAUGHTERS OF DESTINY

SCHUYLER STAUNTON

The FLYING GIRL

By Edith Van Dyne
Author of Aunt Jane's Nieces

The WISHING HORSE OF OZ

by Ruth Plumly Thompson Founded on and continuing the famous Oz stories by L. Frank Baum Illustrated by Jno R. Neill

THE EMERALD CITY OF OZ

The MAGIC of OZ

By L. Frank Baum

Illustrated by John R. Neill

MOTHER GOOSE IN PROSE

L. FRANK BAUM

The DARING TWINS

L. Frank Baum

JOHN DOUGH AND THE CHERUB

L. FRANK BAUM

PHOEBE DARING

by L. Frank Baum

OZMA OF OZ

L. FRANK BAUM

The SILVER PRINCESS OZ

By Ruth Plumly Thompson

L. Frank Baum

THE VICTORY MARCH

THE MYSTERY OF THE TREASURE CHEST

This book was prepared at the suggestion of the U.S. Treasury Department. It contains an officially approved album for United States Savings Stamps and war Savings Stamps.

WALT DISNEY

A RANDOM HOUSE BOOK

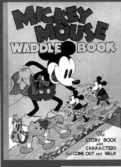

MICKEY MOUSE WADDLE BOOK

The STORY BOOK with CHARACTERS that COME OUT and WALK

MICKEY MOUSE

by WALT DISNEY

BOOK NO. 2

DAVID McKAY CO. PUBLISHERS Philadelphia

'THREE LITTLE PIGS'

WHO'S AFRAID OF THE BIG BAD WOLF?

from the WALT DISNEY SILLY SYMPHONY ILLUSTRATED in COLOR

WALT DISNEY'S box of SIX Pinocchio BOOKS

for Reading · Coloring · Playing

MICKEY MOUSE presents his SILLY SYMPHONIES BABES IN THE WOODS KING NEPTUNE with POP-UP ILLUSTRATIONS

THE MICKEY MOUSE FIRE BRIGADE

by WALT DISNEY

MICKEY MOUSE in King Arthur's Court with POP-UP ILLUSTRATIONS

WALT DISNEY'S FANTASIA

by DEEMS TAYLOR

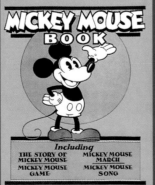

MICKEY MOUSE BOOK

Including THE STORY OF MICKEY MOUSE MICKEY MOUSE GAME MICKEY MOUSE MARCH MICKEY MOUSE SONG

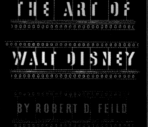

THE ART OF WALT DISNEY

BY ROBERT D. FEILD

MICKEY MOUSE MAGAZINE

A Fun-Book for Boys and Girls to Read to Grown-ups

Bennett, Whitman
BK0720 A Practical Guide to American Book Collecting
(1663-1940) NY 1941, limited ed 50 - 75
BK0730 A Practical Guide to American Nineteenth
Century Color Plate Books NY 1949 75 - 125

Blades, William
BK0770 The Biography and Typography of William
Caxton, England's First Printer Lon 1882 75 - 125
BK0780 The Enemies of Books Lon 1896 150 - 250
BK0790 The Pentateuch of Printing Chi 1891 75 - 125

Blanck, Jacob
BK0830 Bibliography of American Literature New Haven
1955-73, 6 vol 300 - 500
BK0840 Harry Castlemon: Boy's Own Author NY 1941,
750 cys 100 - 150
BK0850 Peter Parley to Penrod NY 1938, 500 cys 125 - 200
BK0852 NY 1956 75 - 125

Bland, David
BK0890 A History of Book Illustration Clev 1958, DJ 30 - 50

Bliss, Douglas P.
BK0930 A History of Wood Engraving Lon 1928 50 - 75

Bolton, Theodore
BK0970 American Book Illustrators NY 1938, 1000 cys 200 - 300

Bookman's Price Index (BPI)
Annual volume listing offerings of major dealers in the U.S. The first
volume began in 1946.
BK1010 1940s-1970s 30 - 50
BK1050 1980s 60 - 90

Bradley, Van Allen
BK1090 Book Collector's Handbook of Values
NY 1972-73 ed, DJ 40 - 60
BK1095 1978-79 ed, DJ 50 - 75
BK1100 1982-83 ed, DJ 75 - 125
BK1110 Gold in Your Attic NY 1958, DJ 40 - 60
BK1111 NY 1958 (paperback ed) 5 - 10
BK1120 More Gold in Your Attic NY 1961, DJ 30 - 50

Bradley, Will
BK1150 The Delectable Art of Printing np (American
Type Founders Co.) 1904, wrappers 200 - 300

Briggs, Asa
BK1190 Essays in the History of Publishing NY 1974, DJ 20 - 30

Brigham, Clarence
BK1230 History and Bibliography of American Newspapers
1690-1820 Worcester 1947, 2 vol 300 - 500
BK1240 Paul Revere's Engravings Worcester 1954, DJ 200 - 300

Briquet, C. M.
BK1280 Les Filigranes: Dictionnaire Historique Des
Marques Du Papier NY 1966, 4 vol 400 - 600

Broadfoot, Tom
BK1320 Civil War Books Wilmington 1978 40 - 60

Browne, Irving
BK1360 Ballads of a Book Worm East Aurora 1899,
850 cys 75 - 125

Brussel, I. R.
BK1400 Anglo-American First Editions 1826-1900:
East to West Lon 1935, 2 vol, 500 cys 200 - 300

Burke, W. J.
BK1440 American Authors and Books 1640 to the
Present Day NY 1943, DJ 30 - 50

Campbell, John F.
BK1480 History and Biblig. of the New American
Practical Navigator Salem 1964 30 - 50

Canson Et Montgolfier
BK1520 (French Paper Catalog) NY 1925, 500 cys 100 - 150

Carter, John
BK1560 ABC For Book Collectors NY 1952, DJ 20 - 30
BK1570 Binding Variants in English Publishing
1820-1900 Lon 1932, 500 cys 200 - 300
BK1580 An Enquiry into the Nature of Certain
Nineteenth C. Pamphlets Lon 1934 150 - 250
BK1590 Printing and the Mind of Man Lon 1963, DJ 150 - 250
BK1592 Lon 1967, DJ 100 - 150
BK1593 NY 1967, DJ 100 - 150
BK1596 Munich 1983, DJ 50 - 75

Caxton, William
BK1640 The Metamorphoses of Ovid NY 1968, 2 vol,
box (facsimile of 1480 manuscript by Caxton) 500 - 700

Churchill, W. A.
BK1680 Watermarks in Paper in Holland, France & Etc.
Amsterdam 1965 200 - 300

Clark, Thomas D.
BK1720 Travels in the Old South: A Bibliog. Norman
1969, 3 vol 150 - 250

Cobden-Sanderson, Thomas James
BK1760 Cobden-Sanderson the Master Printer
Harper Woods 1969, 329 cys 500 - 700
BK1770 The Ideal Book Hammersmith 1900, 300 cys 300 - 500

The Colophon
BK1810 The Colophon: A Book Collectors Quarterly
1930s, each 30 - 50
BK1820 1940s-1950s, each 15 - 30

Cosenza, Mario
BK1860 Biog. & Bibliog. Dict. of Italian Printers & Etc.
Bos 1968 150 - 250

Coyle, William
BK1900 Ohio Authors and Their Books 1796-1950
Clev 1962 50 - 75

Craig, Maurice
BK1940 Irish Bookbindings 1600-1800 Lon 1954, DJ 200 - 300

Currier & Ives
BK1980 An Alphabetical List of 5,735 Titles of N. Currier
and Currier & Ives Prints NY 1930, 1001 cys 50 - 75

Cutler, B. D. & Villa Stiles
BK2020 Modern British Authors: Their First Editions
NY 1930, 1050 cys 100 - 150

Dance, S. Peter
BK2060 The Art of Natural History Woodstock 1978, DJ 50 - 75

Darrell, R. D.
BK2100 Schirmer's Guide to Books on Music and
Musicians NY 1951 30 - 50

Davenport, Cyril
BK2130 Roger Payne, English Bookbinder of the
Eighteenth Century Chi 1929, 250 cys, slipcase 500 - 700
BK2140 Samuel Mearne: Binder to Charles II Chi 1906,
252 cys 600 - 800

Davies, H. W. (Hugh William)
BK2180 Devices of the Early Printers 1457-1560
Lon 1935 100 - 150

Dearden, Robert
BK2220 The Guiding Light on the Great Highway
Phil (1920s) 50 - 75
BK2230 An Original Leaf From the Bible of the
Revolution SF 1930, 580 cys, orig leaf, slipcase 200 - 300

DeHalsalle, Henry
BK2260 The Romance of Modern First Editions
Phil 1931, DJ 30 - 50

DeRicci, Seymour
BK2290 English Collectors of Books & Manuscripts
1950-1930 Bloomington 1960, DJ 20 - 30

Derrydale Press
BK2320 A Decade of American Sporting Books and
Prints 1927-1937 NY 1937, 950 cys 200 - 300

Deuel, Leo
BK2350 Testaments of Time NY 1965, DJ 20 - 30

BK1090 BK1110 BK1590

105

| BK2060 | BK2520 (w/o DJ) | BK2552 |

DeVinne, T. L. (Theodore Low)
BK2380 The First Editor: Aldus Pius Manutius
NY 1983, 250 cys, slipcase 125 - 200
BK2385 The Invention of Printing NY 1876 300 - 500
BK2390 Notable Printers of Italy During the Fifteenth
Century NY 1910, 300 cys 125 - 200
BK2395 The Plantin-Moretus Museum SF 1929,
425 cys, slipcase 125 - 200
BK2400 The Practice of Typography NY 1900-1904,
4 vol 150 - 250

Dichter, Harry
BK2430 Early American Sheet Music: Its Lure and
Lore 1768-1889 NY 1941 150 - 250

Diehl, Edith
BK2460 Bookbinding: Its Background and Technique
NY 1946, 2 vol, box 150 - 250

Dill & Collins Catalog
BK2490 Some Examples of the Work of American
Designers Phil 1918 150 - 250

Dixson, Zella Allen
BK2520 Concerning Book-Plates - A Handbook For
Collectors Chi 1903 50 - 75

Dobie, J. Frank (also see Americana)
BK2550 Guide to Life and Literature of the Southwest
Dallas 1943, wrappers 75 - 125
BK2552 Dallas 1952, DJ or wrappers 50 - 75

Dodgson, Campbell
BK2580 Stephen Gooden: A Iconography of the
Engravings Lon 1944, 500 cys 100 - 150

Doves Press
BK2610 Catalog Raisonne of Books Printed & Published
1900-1916 Hammersmith 1916, 150 cys 300 - 500
BK2615 Catalog Raisonne of Books Printed & Published
at the Doves Press Hammersmith 1908, 300 cys,
8 pp 125 - 200

Duff, E. G.
BK2650 Handlist of Books Printed by London Printers
1501-1556 Lon 1913 125 - 200

Durling, Richard
BK2680 A Catalog of Sixteenth Century Printed Books in
the National Library of Medicine Bethesda 1967 50 - 75

Dwiggins, W. A.
BK2710 22 Printers' Marks and Seals NY 1929, 350 cys 125 - 200

Dykes, Jeff
BK2740 Fifty Great Western Illustrators Flagstaff 1975, DJ 50 - 75

Eames, Wilberforce
BK2770 Bibliog. Notes on Eliot's Indian Bible & Etc.
Wash 1890, wrappers 200 - 300

Eckel, John C.
BK2800 Charles Dickens NY 1932, 750 cys 100 - 150
BK2810 The First Editions of the Writings of Charles
Dickens Lon 1913, 250 cys 250 - 350

Ege, Otto F.
BK2840 Pre-Alphabet Days Balt 1923 30 - 50

Emich, Karl
BK2870 German Book-Plates: An Illustrated Handbook
Lon 1901 100 - 150

Fay, Bernard
BK2900 Notes on the American Press at the End of the
Eighteenth Century NY 1927, 325 cys, box 150 - 250

Ferguson, John
BK2930 Bibliotheca Chemica Glasgow 1904, 2 vol 300 - 500
BK2932 Lon 1954, 2 vol 100 - 150

Fite, Emerson D.
BK2970 A Book of Old Maps Cambridge 1926 125 - 200

Fletcher, F. Morley
BK3000 Wood Block Printing Lon 1916 100 - 150

Ford, Worthington
BK3030 The Boston Book Market, 1679-1700
Bos 1917, 151 cys 150 - 250

Fraxi, Pisanus
BK3060 Bibliog. of Prohibited Books NY 1962, 3 vol 125 - 200

Friend, Leon
BK3090 Graphic Design NY 1936 30 - 50

Gallup, Donald
BK3120 Ezra Pound Lon 1963, DJ 100 - 150

Garcia, Rojo D.
BK3150 Catalogo de Incunables de la Biblioteca
Nacional Madrid 1945 150 - 250

Garnett, Richard & Goose Edmund
BK3180 English Literature NY 1935, 2 vol 50 - 75

George, M. Dorothy
BK3210 Hogarth to Cruikshank NY 1967 50 - 75

Golden Cockerel Press
BK3240 Cockalorum: A Bibliography of the Press
Golden Cockerel Press 1950, DJ 75 - 125

Goodrich, Lloyd
BK3270 The Graphic Art of Winslow Homer Wash 1968 50 - 75

Goudy, Frederick W.
BK3300 Typologia LA 1940, 300 cys, acetate DJ, slipcase 300 - 500

Grabhorn, Jane
BK3330 A California Gold Rush Miscellany SF 1934,
550 cys 150 - 250
BK3340 The Complete Jane Grabhorn SF 1968,
400 cys, prospectus laid in 200 - 300

Grabhorn Press
BK3370 Bibliog. of the Grabhorn Press 1957-1966 &
Grabhorn - Hoyem 1966-1973 SF 1977,
225 cys, prospectus laid in 500 - 700

Graesse, J. G. T.
BK3400 Tresor de Livres Rares et Precieux Milan 1950,
8 vol 400 - 600

Grand-Carteret, John
BK3430 L'Histoire, La Vie, Les Moeurs et La Curiosite
Par L'Image Paris 1927-28, 5 vol 400 - 600
BK3440 Vieux Papiers, Vielles Images Paris 1896,
wrappers 300 - 500

Gress, Walter B.
BK3470 Advanced Typography Wash 1931 50 - 75

Gumuchian & Cie (publisher)
BK3500 Les Livres de L'Enfance Du XV au XIX Siecle
Paris 1930, wrappers, 2 vol, 900 cys 400 - 600

Halkett, Samuel & John Laing
BK3530 Dictionary of Anonymous and Pseudonymous
English Literature Edinburgh 1926-32, 6 vol, DJs 600 - 900
BK3537 Edinburgh 1934, vol 7, DJ 100 - 150
BK3538 Edinburgh 1956, vol 8, DJ 100 - 150
BK3539 Edinburgh 1962, vol 9, DJ 100 - 150

Haller, Margaret
BK3570 The Book Collectors Fact Book NY 1976, DJ 20 - 30

Hardie, Martin
BK3600 English Coloured Books Lon 1906 150 - 250

Hargrave, Catherine Perry
BK3630 A History of Playing Cards Bos 1930, DJ 250 - 350

Harrsen, Meta
BK3660 Illuminated Manuscripts NY 1958, 850 cys, box 50 - 75

Hatton, Thomas and Arthur H. Cleaver
BK3690 Charles Dickens Lon 1933, DJ, 750 cys 300 - 500

Hayn, Hugo
BK3720 Bibliotheca Germanorum Erotica & Curiosa
Main 1968, 9 vol 200 - 300

Hazlitt, W. C.
BK3750 Confessions of a Collector Lon 1897 50 - 75

BK3755 Old Cookery Books and Ancient Cuisine
       Lon 1886   75 - 125
Heal, Sir Ambrose
BK3790 The English Writing Masters and Their Copy
       Books Hildesheim 1962   200 - 300
Heartman, C. F.
BK3820 Edgar Allen Poe Hattiesburg 1943   100 - 150
Herbert, J. A.
BK3850 Illuminated Manuscripts NY 1911   100 - 150
Herdeg, Walter (editor)
BK3880 Art in the Watermark Zurich 1952   125 - 200
Hiatt, Charles
BK3910 Picture Posters Lon 1895   150 - 250
Higginson, Fred H.
BK3940 Robert Graves: A Bibliography Lon 1966, DJ 100 - 150
Hind, Arthur M.
BK3970 A History of Engraving & Etching From the
       15th Century to the Year 1914 Lon 1923   125 - 200
BK3975 An Introduction to the History of the Woodcut
       Lon 1935, 2 vol   200 - 300
BK3980 A Short History of Engraving and Etching
       Lon 1908   75 - 125
BK3982 Bos 1911   50 - 75
Hobson, Anthony
BK4010 Great Libraries NY 1970, DJ   100 - 150
BK4020 Humanists and Bookbinders Cambridge 1989, DJ 100 - 150
Hobson, G. D.
BK4050 Bindings in Cambridge Libraries Cambridge
       1929, 230 cys   1000 - 1500
BK4055 Blind-Stamped Panels in the English Book-Trade
       c. 1485-1555 Lon 1944, wrappers   100 - 150
BK4060 English Binding Before 1500 Cambridge 1929,
       500 cys   300 - 500'
BK4070 Thirty Bindings Lon 1926, 600 cys   300 - 500
Hogben, Lancelot
BK4100 From Cave Painting to Comic Strip NY 1949, DJ 20 - 30
Holden, John A.
BK4130 The Bookman's Glossary NY 1931, DJ   30 - 50
Holmes, R. R.
BK4160 Specimens of Royal Fine and Historical
       Bookbinding Lon 1893   1000 - 1500
Holmes, Thomas J.
BK4190 Cotton Mather: A Bibliography of His Works
       Cambridge 1940, 3 vol, 500 sets   250 - 350
BK4192 Newton 1974, 3 vol, 500 sets   100 - 150
BK4200 Increase Mather: His Works Clev 1930, 250 cys,
       DJ, slipcase   100 - 150
BK4202 Clev 1931 500 cys, 2 vol   150 - 250
BK4210 The Mather Literature Clev 1927, 250 cys   100 - 150
Horblit, Harrison D.
BK4240 One Hundred Books Famous in Science
       NY 1964, 1000 cys, box   500 - 700
Hortetler, John
BK4270 Annotated Bibliog. on the Amish Scottsdale 1951,
       wrappers   30 - 50
Howes, Wright
BK4300 "USiana" 1700-1950 NY 1954   75 - 125
BK4302 NY 1962   75 - 125
BK4304 NY 1964   75 - 125
Hubin, Allen
BK4340 The Bibliography of Crime Fiction 1749-1975
       San Diego 1979   30 - 50
Hudson, Derek
BK4370 Arthur Rackham: His Life and Work Lon 1960, DJ 75 - 125
Hunter, Dard
BK4400 Before Life Began, 1883-1923 Clev 1941,
       219 cys, box   500 - 700
BK4410 Chinese Ceremonial Paper Chillicothe 1937,
       125 cys   6000 - 8000
BK4415 The Life Work of Dard Hunter Chillicothe
       1981-83, 50 cys, 2 vol   5000 - 7000
BK4420 The Literature of Papermaking 1390-1800
       Chillicothe 1925, 190 cys   5000 - 7000
BK4430 My Life With Paper NY 1958, DJ, prospectus 150 - 250
BK4435 Old Papermaking Chillicothe 1923, 200 cys 2500 - 3500

BK4440 Old Papermaking in China and Japan
       Chillicothe 1932, 200 cys, box   3000 - 5000
BK4450 Paper Making by Hand in America Chillicothe
       1950, 210 cys   6000 - 8000
BK4455 Papermaking by Hand in India NY 1939,
       370 cys, box   2000 - 3000
BK4460 Papermaking in Indo-China Chillicothe 1947,
       182 cys   5000 - 7000
BK4465 Papermaking in Pioneer America Phil 1952, DJ 100 - 150
BK4470 Papermaking in Southern Siam Chillicothe
       1938, 115 cys   5000 - 7000
BK4475 A Papermaking Pilgrimage to Japan, Korea
       and China NY 1936, 370 cys, box   3000 - 5000
BK4480 Papermaking: The History and Technique of
       an Ancient Craft NY 1943, DJ   100 - 150
BK4485 Papermaking Through Eighteen Centuries
       NY 1930, DJ   200 - 300
BK4490 Primitive Papermaking Chillicothe 1927,
       200 cys   6000 - 8000
BK4500 A Specimen of Type Cambridge 1940, 100 cys 500 - 700
Jackson, Holbrook
BK4530 The Anatomy of Bibliomania Lon 1930,
       1000 sets, 2 vol   125 - 200
James, Philip
BK4560 Children's Books of Yesterday Lon 1933   50 - 75
Jenkins, John H. (also see Americana)
BK4590 Basic Texas Books Austin 1981   200 - 300
BK4600 Cracker Barrel Chronicles: A Bibliog. of Texas
       Town and Country Histories Austin 1965,
       15 cys, box   300 - 500
BK4601 Austin 1965 (1st trade ed)   75 - 125
BK4610 Most Remarkable Texas Book 64 cys   300 - 500
BK4615 Papers of the Texas Revolution 1835-1836
       Austin 1973, 10 vol   300 - 500
BK4620 Patriotic Songs and Poems of Early Texas
       Austin 1966, wrappers   20 - 30
Jillson, Willard Rouse
BK4650 Rare Kentucky Books 1776-1926 Louisville 1939 75 - 125
Johnson, Henry Lewis
BK4680 Gutenberg and the Book of Books NY 1932,
       750 cys, slipcase   250 - 350
BK4685 Historic Design in Printing Bos 1923, folding case 75 - 125
BK4690 Printing Type Specimens Bos 1924   75 - 125
Johnson, Merle
BK4720 American First Editions NY 1928, 1000 cys 150 - 250
BK4722 NY 1932   50 - 75
BK4724 NY 1936   50 - 75
BK4730 A Bibliography of the Works of Mark Twain
       NY 1910, 500 cys   100 - 150
BK4732 NY 1935   150 - 250
BK4740 High Spots of American Literature NY 1929,
       750 cys   100 - 150
Johnston, Edward
BK4770 Writing, Illuminating & Lettering Lon 1913 50 - 75
Joline, Adrian
BK4800 At the Library Table Bos 1910   30 - 50
BK4805 Diversions of a Book Lover NY 1903   30 - 50
Jolly, David C.
BK4830 Antique Maps, Sea Charts, City Views & Etc. Price
       Guide and Collectors Handbook Brookline 1983 20 - 30
Kaser, David
BK4860 Messrs. Carey & Lea of Philadelphia Phil 1950 40 - 60
Keating, H. R. F.
BK4890 Whodunit? NY 1982, DJ   20 - 30

Keynes, Geoffrey
BK4920 Bibliog. of Rupert Brooke Lon 1959, DJ   50 - 75
BK4925 Bibliog. of Siegfried Sassoon Lon 1962, DJ   50 - 75
BK4930 Bibliotheca Bibliographici Lon 1964, 500 cys   150 - 250
BK4940 Jane Austin: A Bibliog. Lon 1929, 875 cys, DJ 150 - 250
BK4950 William Blakes Illuminated Books NY 1953,
         400 cys   75 - 125
Kithredge, George L.
BK4980 The Old Farmer and His Almanack
         Cambridge 1920   40 - 60
Kraus, Hans P.
BK5010 The Cradle of Printing NY 1954-71   125 - 200
BK5020 Sir Francis Drake: A Pictorial Biography
         Amsterdam 1970   150 - 250
Kubler, George
BK5050 A New History of Stereotyping NY 1941   30 - 50
Lakeside Press
BK5080 Extra Binding at the Lakeside Press Chi 1925   50 - 75
BK5085 A Rod for the Back of the Binder Chi 1929   50 - 75
Lang, Andrew
BK5120 Books and Bookmen NY 1886   30 - 50
BK5125 The Library Lon 1892   30 - 50
Latimore, Sarah B.
BK5160 Arthur Rackham LA 1936, 550 cys, box   300 - 500
Le Clert, Louis
BK5190 Le Papier Paris 1926, 675 cys, wrappers   800 - 1200
Lehmann-Haupt, Hellmut
BK5220 Gutenberg and the Master of Playing Cards
         NY 1966 (folding chart in pocket)   75 - 125
BK5230 Two Essays on the Decretum of Gratian
         LA 1971, 193 cys, orig leaf laid in, slipcase 800 - 1200
Lewis, John
BK5260 Printed Ephemera Lon 1962, DJ   20 - 30
Livingston, Flora
BK5290 Rudyard Kipling NY 1927, DJ   50 - 75
Livingston, Luther S.
BK5320 Franklin and His Press at Passy NY 1914, 300 cys 150 - 250
Locke, Harold
BK5350 Sir Arthur Conan Doyle Tunbridge Wells 1928   200 - 300
Loring, Rosamond B.
BK5380 Decorated Book Papers Cambridge 1942,
         250 cys, box   500 - 700
Lowman, Al
BK5410 Printing Arts in Texas 1975, 395 cys   100 - 150
MacLean, David
BK5440 Gene Stratton-Porter Decatur 1976, wrappers   15 - 25
Magee, David (Grabhorn Press)
BK5470 Bibliography of the Grabhorn Press 1940-1956
         SF 1957, 225 cys   1000 - 1500
BK5480 Catalog of Some 500 Examples of the Printing
         of Edwin & Robert Grabhorn 1917-1960
         SF 1960, wrappers   150 - 250
BK5490 The Hundredth Book SF 1958, 400 cys, DJ   300 - 500
Mahony, Bertha and others
BK5520 Illustrators of Childrens Books 1744-1945
         Bos 1947   100 - 150
BK5522 Bos 1961   50 - 75
BK5524 Bos 1970   30 - 50
Mandeville, Mildred (compiler)
BK5560 The Used Book Price Guide Kenmore, WA 1972,
         5 year ed, 2 vol   50 - 75
Marks, Hayward
BK5590 Proofs of Some Early Nineteenth-Century
         Woodblocks For Tea and Tobacco Papers
         Kensington 1948, 50 cys   400 - 600
Mason, John
BK5620 More Papers Hand Made by John Mason
         NY 1966   200 - 300
Massey, Linton R.
BK5650 William Faulkner: "Man Working", 1919-1962
         Charlottesville 1968   50 - 75
McKay, George L. (compiler)
BK5680 Catalog of a Collection of Writings By and
         About Robert Louis Stevenson New Haven
         1951-64, 6 vol, 500 sets   300 - 500

McMurtrie, Douglas C.
BK5710 Alphabets NY 1926, DJ   100 - 150
BK5715 American Type Design in the 20th C. Chi 1924   100 - 150
BK5720 The Beginnings of Printing in Arizona Chi 1937 100 - 150
BK5725 The Beginnings of Printing in Chicago Chi 1931,
         160 cys   200 - 300
BK5730 The Beginnings of Printing in Utah Chi 1931,
         160 cys   200 - 300
BK5735 Bibliog. of Mississippi Imprints 1798-1830
         Beauvoir Community, MS 1945   150 - 250
BK5740 Bibliography of Chicago Imprints 1835-50
         Chi 1944, 200 cys   150 - 250
BK5745 The Book: The Story of Printing and
         Bookmaking NY 1937   150 - 250
BK5750 Checklist of Kentucky Imprints Louisville 1939,
         2 vol   150 - 250
BK5760 Early Printing in Colorado Denver 1935, 250 cys 150 - 250
BK5765 Early Printing in Michigan Chi 1931, 250 cys   125 - 200
BK5770 Early Printing in New Orleans 1764-1810
         New Orleans 1929, 410 cys   125 - 200
BK5775 Early Printing in Tennessee Chi 1933, 900 cys 100 - 150
BK5780 Early Printing in Wisconsin Seattle 1931, 300 cys 125 - 200
BK5785 Early Printing in Wyoming Hattiesburg 1943   100 - 150
BK5790 Eighteenth Century North Carolina Imprints
         1749-1800 Chapel Hill 1938, 200 cys, DJ   150 - 250
BK5795 The First Printers of Chicago Chi 1927, 250 cys 125 - 200
BK5796 650 cys   100 - 150
BK5800 The First Twelve Years of Printing in N. Carolina
         Raleigh 1933   100 - 150
BK5805 The Golden Book Chi 1927, 220 cys   200 - 300
BK5806 Chi 1927, DJ (1st trade ed)   50 - 75
BK5815 Gutenberg Documents NY 1941, 900 cys   150 - 250
BK5820 A History of Printing in the United States
         NY 1936 (vol 2 only)   125 - 200
BK5825 Indiana Imprints 1804-1849 Ind 1937   100 - 150
BK5830 Jotham Meeker: Pioneer Printer of Kansas
         Chi 1930, 650 cys   100 - 150
BK5835 Louisiana Imprints 1768-1810 Hattiesburg
         1942, 99 cys   125 - 200
BK5840 Montana Imprints 1864-1880 Chi 1937   150 - 250
BK5845 New York Printing Chi 1928, 240 cys   125 - 200
BK5850 Pioneer Printing in Ohio Cinti 1943   100 - 150
BK5855 Pioneer Printing in Texas Austin 1932, 200 cys,
         wrappers   200 - 300
BK5865 Short Title Check List of Books, Pamphlets
         and Broadsides Printed in Florida 17-1760
         Jacksonville 1937   100 - 150
BK5870 Sketches of Louisville and its Environs
         Louisville 1919   100 - 150
Meine, Franklin J. (editor)
BK5900 The Crockett Almanacs Chi 1955   100 - 150
Meriwether, James
BK5930 William Faulkner: A Checklist Princeton 1957,
         wrappers   15 - 25
Merryweather, F. S.
BK5960 Bibliomania in the Middle Ages Lon 1933   75 - 125
Middleton, Richard C.
BK5990 A History of English Craft Bookbinding
         Technique Lon 1978   100 - 150
Miller, Bertha Mahony & Elinor Whitney Field
BK6020 Caldecott Medal Books: 1938-1957 Bos 1957, DJ 30 - 50
Miner, L.
BK6050 Our Rude Forefathers Cedar Rapids 1937   50 - 75
Moran, James
BK6080 The Double Crown Club: A History of Fifty
         Years Lon 1974, 500 cys   100 - 150
BK6090 Heraldic Influence on Early Printers' Devices
         Leeds 1978, 475 cys   100 - 150
Mores, Edward Rowe
BK6120 A Dissertation Upon English Typographical
         Founders and Foundries NY 1924, 250 cys   100 - 150
Morison, Stanley
BK6155 The Art of the Printer Lon 1925, DJ   300 - 500
BK6165 Eustachio Celebrino da Udene Paris 1929,
         175 cys   800 - 1200
BK6170 Four Centuries of Fine Printing Lon 1924, 990 cys 500 - 700
BK6172 NY 1960, DJ   40 - 60

BK6180 **German Incunabula in the British Museum** Lon 1928, 398 cys 500 - 700
BK6190 **Modern Fine Printing** Lon 1925, 650 cys 300 - 500
BK6191 Lon 1925, 1000 cys 200 - 300
BK6195 **A Newly Discovered Treatise on Classic Letter Design** Paris 1927, 350 cys, box 500 - 700
BK6200 **On Type Faces** Westminster, 750 cys 250 - 350
BK6210 **The Typographic Book 1450-1935** Lon 1963, DJ, box 150 - 250

Morris, William
BK6240 **Note by William Morris in Founding the Kelmscott Press** Lon 1898, 525 cys 1500 - 2500
BK6245 **Printing: An Essay** Park Ridge, IL 1903 300 - 500
BK6250 **Some Hints on Pattern Designing** Lon 1899 200 - 300

Morse, W. S.
BK6280 **Howard Pyle** Wilmington 1921, 500 cys 75 - 125

Mortimer, Ruth
BK6310 **French 16th Century Books** Cambridge 1964, 2 vol, box 200 - 300
BK6320 **Italian 16th Century Books** Cambridge 1974, 2 vol, box 200 - 300

Mueller, Hans
BK6350 **Woodcuts and Wood Engravings** NY 1939, DJ 75 - 125

Muir, Percy H.
BK6380 **Points, 1866-1934** Lon 1934, 750 cys 100 - 150
BK6385 **Points, 1874-1930** Lon 1931, 500 cys 100 - 150

Mullins, John
BK6420 **Indiana Incunabula** Ind 1988, 90 cys, wrappers 30 - 50
BK6422 10 cys, cloth 75 - 125

Mumey, Nolie (also see Americana)
BK6450 **A Study of Rare Books** Denver 1930, 1000 cys 300 - 500

Muscatine, Charles
BK6480 **The Book of Geoffrey Chaucer** SF 1963, 450 cys 200 - 300

Neuburg, Victor
BK6510 **The Penny Histories** NY 1969, DJ 20 - 30

Newton, A. Edward
BK6540 **The Amenities of Book Collecting** Bos 1918, DJ, errata slip 100 - 150
BK6541 Bos 1918-1920s (later editions) 30 - 50
BK6550 **Derby Day and Other Adventures** Bos 1934, 1129 cys, box 100 - 150
BK6551 Bos 1934, DJ (1st trade ed) 30 - 50
BK6555 **End Papers** Bos 1933, 1351 cys, box 100 - 150
BK6556 Bos 1933, DJ (1st trade ed) 30 - 50
BK6560 **The Greatest Book in the World** Bos 1925, 470 cys 125 - 200
BK6561 Bos 1925, DJ (1st trade ed) 30 - 50
BK6570 **A Magnificent Farce** Bos 1921, 265 cys, box 200 - 300
BK6571 Bos 1921, DJ (1st trade ed) 60 - 90
BK6575 **On Books and Business** NY 1930, 325 cys 100 - 150
BK6580 **Rare Books, Original Drawings & Etc. For Public Sale** NY 1941 (3 vol sales catalog of Newton's collection) 50 - 75
BK6585 **This Book Collecting Game** Bos 1928, 990 cys 75 - 125
BK6586 Bos 1928, DJ (1st trade ed) 30 - 50
BK6590 **Thomas Hardy: Novelist or Poet** 1920, 950 cys 100 - 150

(no author)
BK6620 **Die Bilderhandschrift des Hamburgischen Stadtrechts Von 1497 & Etc** Hamburg 1917, 260 cys (facsimile of illuminated manuscript) 300 - 500
BK6650 **Liber Librorum, 1955** Stockholm 1956, 500 sets, 42 leaves, folder 300 - 500
BK6670 **Lorsch Gospels** NY 1967, 1000 cys, pamphlet (cy of 810 AD manuscript) 300 - 500

Norman, D. C. (Don Cleveland)
BK6700 **The 500th Anniversary Pictorial Census of the Gutenberg Bible** Chi 1961, 985 cys, slipcase 300 - 500

Oldham, J. Basil
BK6730 **Blind Panels of English Binders** Cambridge 1958, DJ 100 - 150

Olivier, Eugene
BK6770 **Manuel de L'Amateur de Relivres Armoriees Francaises** Paris 1924-1938, 1025 sets, 30 vol 1000 - 1500

Orcutt, William Dana
BK6800 **The Book in Italy** NY 1928, 750 cys, DJ 125 - 200
BK6801 NY 1928, DJ (1st trade ed) 40 - 60
BK6810 **In Quest of the Perfect Book** Bos 1926, 365 cys, DJ 20 - 30
BK6811 Bos 1926, DJ (1st trade ed) 50 - 75
BK6815 **The Kingdom of Books** Bos 1927, 475 cys, box 150 - 250
BK6816 Bos 1927, DJ (1st trade ed) 40 - 60
BK6825 **The Magic of the Book** NY 1930, 375 cys, DJ 200 - 300
BK6826 NY 1930, DJ (1st trade ed) 50 - 75
BK6830 **The Manual of Linotype Typography** Brooklyn 1923 100 - 150

Osler, Sir William
BK6860 **Bibliotheca Osleriana** Oxford 1929 300 - 500
BK6865 **Incunabula Medica** Lon 1923 800 - 1200

Osley, A. S.
BK6890 **Calligraphy and Paleography** NY 1966, DJ 40 - 60

Oswald, John
BK6920 **Printing in the Americas** NY 1968 30 - 50

Paine, A. B.
BK6950 **Thomas Nast** NY 1904 50 - 75

Parrish, M. L.
BK6980 **Charles Kingsley and Thomas Hughes** Lon 1936, 150 cys 100 - 150
BK6985 **Victorian Lady Novelists** Lon 1933, 150 cys 100 - 150

Pearson, Edmund
BK7020 **Books in Black or Red** NY 1923 40 - 60

Pearson, Edwin
BK7050 **Banbury Chapbooks and Nursery Toy Book Literature** Lon 1890, 50 cys 250 - 350

Perkins, P. D. and Ione
BK7080 **Lafcadio Hearn: A Bibliography of His Writings** Kenkyuska 1934 300 - 500

Peters, Fred J.
BK7110 **Railroad, Indian and Pioneer Prints, Clipper Ship Prints, Sporting Prints** NY 1930, 3 vol, box 300 - 500

Peters, Harry T.
BK7140 **America on Stone** Garden City 1931, 751 cys, box 1200 - 1800
BK7145 **Currier & Ives: Print Makers to the American People** Garden City 1931, 2 vol, 501 cys, slipcases 500 - 700

Peterson, L. G. (editor)
BK7180 **Illustrated Price Catalog of Old Books Wanted** Chi (1930s) 20 - 30

Pforzheimer, Carl H.
BK7210 **English Literature 1475-1700** NY 1940, 3 vol, 150 cys 3000 - 5000

Philip, James
BK7240 **Children's Books of Yesterday** Lon 1933 30 - 50

Phillips, P. Lee
BK7270 **A List of Geographical Atlases in the Library of Congress** Wash 1909-20, 4 vol 300 - 500
BK7275 **A List of Maps of America in the Library of Congress** Wash 1901 200 - 300

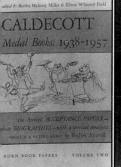

BK6020

BK6200

BK6571

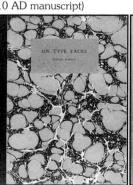

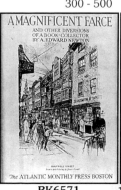

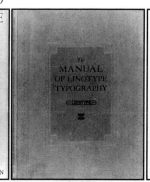

BK6830

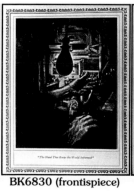

BK6830 (frontispiece)

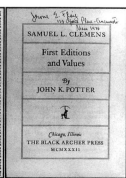

BK7500 (title page)

BK7830 (wrapper)	BK8040	BK8810

Pilling, James Constantine
BK7310 Bibliog. of the Algonquian Languages Wash 1891 150 - 250

Plomer, Henry R.
BK7340 A Dictionary of the Printers and Booksellers
Who Were at Work in (Britain) 1668-1725
Oxford 1922   125 - 200
BK7345 English Printers' Ornaments Lon 1924   100 - 150
BK7350 Wynkyn De Worde & His Contemporaries
Lon 1925   75 - 125

Pollard, Alfred W.
BK7380 Cobden-Sanderson and the Doves Press
SF 1929, 27 cys   3000 - 5000
BK7385 An Essay on Colophons Chi 1905, 252 cys, box 250 - 350
BK7390 Fine Books Lon 1912, DJ   125 - 200
BK7395 Last Words on the History of the Title-Page
Lon 1891, 260 cys   200 - 300
BK7405 Records of the English Bible Lon 1911   200 - 300
BK7410 Shakespeare Folios and Quartos Lon 1909   200 - 350

Poortenaar, Jan
BK7440 The Art of the Book Phil   100 - 150

Portalis, Baron Roger (editor)
BK7470 Researches Concerning Jean Grolier NY 1907,
300 cys, box   400 - 600

Potter, John K.
BK7500 Samuel L. Clemens First Editions and Values
Chi 1932, 500 cys   100 - 150

Powell, G. H.
BK7530 Excursions in Libraria NY 1896   50 - 75

Raines, C. W.
BK7560 A Bibliog. of Texas Austin 1896   250 - 350
BK7562 Austin 1934, slipcase   100 - 150
BK7564 Houston 1955, 500 cys, box   100 - 150

Ramage, Robert H.
BK7600 The History of Envelopes NY 1952   20 - 30

Ransom, Will
BK7630 Private Presses and Their Books NY 1929,
1200 cys, DJ   300 - 500
BK7632 NY 1963, DJ   30 - 50

Reed, Talbot
BK7670 A History of the Old English Letter Foundries
Lon 1887   250 - 350
BK7672 Lon 1952, DJ   100 - 150

Reese, William
BK7700 Nichols Collection of Custerian and Army in
the West Bryan 1975, wrappers   50 - 75
BK7710 Six Score Austin 1976   150 - 250

Rieger, Paul
BK7740 The Upper Ohio Valley: A Bibliog. & Price
Guide Balt 1983   30 - 50

Robertson, John W.
BK7770 Edgar Allan Poe: Bibliography of His Writings
SF 1934, 350 cys, 2 vol   300 - 500

Robinson, Charles N.
BK7800 Old Naval Prints, Their Artists and Engravers
Lon 1924, DJ   300 - 500

Rock, James A.
BK7830 Who Goes There Bloomington 1979, wrappers   30 - 50

Rosenbach, A. S. W.
BK7865 The All Embracing Dr. Franklin Phil 1932,
198 cys   200 - 300

BK7870 An American Jewish Bibliography Phil 1926   125 - 200
BK7875 A Book Hunter's Holiday Bos 1936, 760 cys   150 - 250
BK7880 Books and Bidders: The Adventures of a
Bibliophile Bos 1927, 760 cys, slipcase   200 - 300
BK7881 Bos 1927, DJ (1st trade ed)   50 - 75
BK7890 Early American Children's Books Portland
1933, 88 cys, box   1000 - 1500
BK7891 585 cys, box   500 - 700
BK7893 NY 1966, DJ   50 - 75

Rottensteiner, Frank
BK7920 The Science Fiction Book Lon 1975, wrappers   20 - 30

Rouveyre, Edouard
BK7950 Connaissances Necessaires a un Bibliophile
Paris 1899, 10 vol   200 - 300

Russo, A. J. and D. R.
BK7980 James Whitcomb Riley Ind 1944, 2 vol   50 - 75

Sadleir, Michael
BK8010 Excursions in Victorian Bibliography Lon 1922   50 - 75
BK8015 XIX Century Fiction Cambridge 1951, 1025 cys,
2 vol, DJs   300 - 500

Sagendorph, Robb
BK8040 America and Her Almanacs Bos 1970, DJ   20 - 30

Sawyer, Charles J.
BK8070 English Books, 1475-1900 Westminster 1927,
2000 cys, 2 vol   200 - 300

Senefelder, Alois
BK8100 The Invention of Lithography NY 1911   75 - 125

Shadwell, Wendy J.
BK8130 American Printmaking Wash 1969   50 - 75

Shaffer, Ellen
BK8160 The Nuremberg Chronicle LA 1950, 300 cys,
orig 1497 leaf   250 - 350

Simon, Oliver
BK8190 Printing of Today NY 1928   50 - 75

Skelton, R. A.
BK8220 The Vinland Map and the Tartar Relation
New Haven 1966, DJ   50 - 75

Slater, J. H.
BK8250 How to Collect Books Lon 1905   30 - 50

Slocum, J. J. and Herbert Cahoon
BK8280 James Joyce Lon 1957, DJ   100 - 150

Smith, Harry B.
BK8320 First Nights and First Editions Bos 1931,
260 cys, DJ   200 - 300
BK8325 A Sentimental Library NY 1914, DJ   300 - 500

Sparling, H. Halliday
BK8360 The Kelmscott Press and William Morris,
Master Craftsman Lon 1924   75 - 125

Sparrow, Ruth A.
BK8390 Milestones of Science: Epochal Books
Buffalo 1972, 2000 cys   100 - 150

Spielmann, M. H.
BK8420 Kate Greenaway Lon 1905   100 - 150

Spiller, Robert E. (editor)
BK8450 James Fenimore Cooper NY 1934, 500 cys   75 - 125
BK8455 Literary History of the United States NY 1962, DJ 30 - 50

Spoerri, J. F.
BK8490 James Joyce Chi 1948, 60 cys, wrappers   150 - 250

Staff, Frank
BK8520 The Valentine and its Origins NY 1969, DJ   30 - 50

Starrett, Vincent
BK8550 All About Mother Goose Glen Rock 1930,
275 cys, DJ   250 - 350
BK8555 Ambrose Bierce: A Bibliography Phil 1929,
45 cys   125 - 200
BK8560 Arthur Machen Chi 1918, 250 cys   300 - 500
BK8565 Books Alive NY 1940, DJ   75 - 125
BK8570 Et Cetera: A Collector's Scrap Book Chi 1924,
625 cys   125 - 200
BK8575 Flame and Dust Chi 1924, 450 cys, DJ   125 - 200
BK8585 Penny Wise and Book Foolish NY 1929,
300 cys, box   200 - 300
BK8590 Persons From Porlock Chi 1933, wrappers,
300 cys   200 - 300

Stephenson, J. N.
BK8620 Pulp and Paper Manufacture NY 1950, 3 vol   30 - 50
Stern, Madeleine
BK8650 Imprints on History: Book Publishers and American Frontiers Bloomington 1956   20 - 30
Stevens-Nelson Catalog
BK8680 Specimens: A Stevens-Nelson Paper Catalog NY (1950s), box   200 - 300
Stillwell, Margaret Bingham
BK8710 Incunabula and Americana, 1450-1800 NY 1931   100 - 150
Stokes, I. N. Phelps
BK8740 American Historical Prints NY 1932   500 - 700
Streeter, Thomas W.
BK8770 Bibliography of Texas 1794-1845 Cambridge 1955, 3 vol, DJs, 600 sets   300 - 500
BK8780 The Celebrated Collection of Americana NY 1966-70 (Parke-Bernet Catalog) 8 vol   300 - 500
Sutton, Walter
BK8810 The Western Book Trade Col 1961, DJ   30 - 50
Symons, A. J. A.
BK8840 Nonesuch Century Lon 1936, 750 cys   1000 - 1500
Tapley, Harriet S.
BK8870 Salem Imprints 1768-1825 Salem 1927   75 - 125
Targ, William (editor)
BK8900 Bibliophile in the Nursery Clev 1957, DJ   100 - 150
BK8910 Bouillabaise For Collectors Clev 1955, DJ   50 - 75
BK8920 Carrousel For Bibliophiles NY 1947, DJ   50 - 75
BK8925 Hearn: First Editions and Values Chi 1934, 550 cys   100 - 150
BK8930 Modern English First Editions and Their Prices Chi 1931, 500 cys   50 - 75
BK8940 Ten Thousand Rare Books and Their Prices Chi 1941   50 - 75
Thomas, Alan G.
BK8970 Great Books and Book Collectors Lon 1975, DJ   20 - 30
Thomas, Isaiah
BK9000 The History of Printing in America; with A Biography of Printers & An Account of Newspapers Barre, MA 1970, box   75 - 125
BK9002 Barre, MA 1972, 1950 cys, orig leaf laid in   250 - 350
Tomkinson, G. S.
BK9040 A Select Bibliog. of the Principal Printing Presses Lon 1928   200 - 300
Tooley, R. V.
BK9075 English Books with Coloured Plates 1790 to 1860 Lon 1954   100 - 150
BK9077 NY 1973, DJ   50 - 75
BK9085 Maps and Map Makers Lon 1949, DJ   75 - 125
BK9090 Some English Books with Coloured Plates Lon 1935   75 - 125
Tuer, Andrew W.
BK9120 History of the Horn-Book Lon 1896, 2 vol, 7 facsimile Horn Books   1000 - 1500
BK9124 Lon 1897, 2 vol, 3 facsimile Horn Books   800 - 1200
BK9130 Pages and Pictures From Forgotten Children's Books Lon 1898-99   200 - 300
Twyman, Michael
BK9160 Printing 1770-1970 Lon 1970, DJ   40 - 60
Tyler, Moses Coit
BK9190 A History of American Literature NY 1879, 2 vol   125 - 200
Updike, D. B. (Daniel Berkeley)
BK9220 Notes on the Merrymount Press and its Work Cambridge 1934, 500 cys   125 - 200
BK9225 Printing Types: Their History, Forms, and Use Cambridge 1937, 2 vol, DJs   100 - 150
Uzanne, Octave
BK9250 The Book Hunter in Paris Lon 1893   125 - 200
Vail, Henry H.
BK9280 A History of the McGuffey Readers Clev 1910, 300 cys   75 - 125
Von Hagen, Victor Wolfgang
BK9310 The Aztec and Maya Papermakers NY 1943, 220 cys   400 - 600

BK9311 NY 1944 (1st trade ed)   50 - 75
Wade, Allan
BK9340 A Bibliography of the Writings of William Butler Yeats Lon 1951, DJ   75 - 125
Wagner, Henry R.
BK9370 The Plains and the Rockies: A Bibliography of Original Narratives of Travel and Adventure, 1800-1865 SF 1921   125 - 200
BK9372 Col 1953   75 - 125
Wakeman, Geoffrey
BK9400 English Hand Made Papers Suitable For Book Work Loughborough 1972, 75 cys   400 - 600
BK9410 Twentieth Century English Vat Paper Mills Loughborough, 102 cys   200 - 300
Warner, Sir George
BK9440 Illuminated Manuscripts Oxford 1920   200 - 300
Wegelin, Oscar
BK9470 Early American Fiction 1774-1830 NY 1929   50 - 75
BK9475 Early American Poetry, 1650-1820 NY 1930   50 - 75
West, Herbert F.
BK9510 Modern Book Collecting Bos 1936, DJ   30 - 50
Wheat, Carl I.
BK9540 Books of the Gold Rush SF 1949, 500 cys   300 - 500
BK9545 Mapping the Trans-Mississippi West SF 1957-63, 6 vol, 1000 sets   2000 - 3000
BK9550 The Maps of the California Gold Region 1848-57 SF 1942, 300 cys   1500 - 2500
BK9555 The Pioneer Press of California Oakland 1948, 450 cys   300 - 500
Williams, Sidney
BK9580 Lewis Carroll Lon 1924, 700 cys   75 - 125
Winship, George Parker
BK9610 The First American Bible Bos 1929, 157 cys, orig leaf laid in   600 - 800
BK9615 The Merrymount Press of Boston Vienna 1929, 350 cys   200 - 300
BK9620 William Caxton Lon 1909, 15 cys, vellum   500 - 700
BK9621 54 cys   300 - 500
BK9622 246 cys   150 - 250
Winterich, John T.
BK9650 Early American Books & Printing Bos 1935, DJ   50 - 75
BK9655 A Primer of Book Collecting Bos 1936, DJ   30 - 50
BK9657 NY 1966, DJ   15 - 25
Wise, Thomas J.
BK9690 A Byron Library Lon 1928, 200 cys   100 - 150
BK9695 Letters to John Henry Wrenn: A Further Inquiry into the Guilt of Certain Nineteenth-Century Forgers NY 1944   100 - 150
Wolf, Edwin
BK9720 John Rosenbach Clev 1960, 250 cys, box   250 - 350
BK9721 Clev 1960, DJ (1st trade ed)   100 - 150
Wolfe, Richard
BK9750 The Role of the Mann Family of Dedham, Mass. in the Marbling of Paper in 19th Century America Chestnut Hill 1981   50 - 75

BK8900

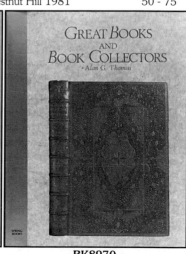
BK8970

Worthington, Greville
BK9780　**A Bibliog. of the Waverley Novels** Lon 1931,
　　　　500 cys　　　　　　　　　　　　　　　150 - 250
Wright, Lyle H.
BK9810　**American Fiction, 1774-1900** San Marino
　　　　1948-65-66, 3 vol, DJs　　　　　　　125 - 200
Wroth, Lawrence C.
BK9840　**The Colonial Printer** NY 1931, 300 cys　200 - 300
BK9850　**The Early Cartography of the Pacific** NY 1934,
　　　　100 cys　　　　　　　　　　　　　300 - 500
Zapf, Hermann and J. W. Stauffacher
BK9880　**Hunt Roman: The Birth of a Type** Pittsburgh
　　　　1965, 750 cys　　　　　　　　　　　50 - 75

DISNEYANA

Disneyana means any products, advertising or original art created by Walt Disney or his company since the early 1920s. This includes books.

Walt Disney organized one of the first animation studios. He was responsible for many animation breakthroughs, including the first cartoon with synchronized sound, first color cartoon, and first full-length animated feature.

Most of the books published in Disney's name are about his animated characters and their films. Later he did some live-action movies like *20,000 Leagues Under the Sea* with some books as spin-offs.

Thousands of titles have been published since 1930. Most are inexpensive, but some are very valuable. The most valuable are from the first decade of Disney publishing. This includes the first book, *Mickey Mouse Book - Hello Everybody* (Bibo & Lang 1930) and the "pop-up" *Mickey Mouse Waddle Book* (Blue Ribbon Books 1934) in which punch-out Mickey and Minnie figures walk down a folding ramp (notoriously rare with the figures unused).

Disney's publishers in the 1930s were David McKay (*Mickey Mouse Book #1*, the 2nd Disney book), Whitman (*Mickey Mouse Series #1*, the third Disney book), Blue Ribbon Books ("pop-ups"), and Saalfield (large coloring and story books). Later came Grosset & Dunlap (G & D in the listings), Simon & Schuster, Random House, and D. C. Heath. The first book about a Disney film is *Fantasia* (Random House 1940).

Any book signed by Walt Disney is worth at least $200 more. If it includes a sketch, it's worth as least $2000, even though Walt did virtually no animation himself.

Most books come without dust jackets. They either have pictorial boards, stiff paper wrappers, or are "linen like" (reinforced). For books with dust jackets, the difference in price can be astronomical. *Fantasia* without a jacket is worth about $100; with a jacket it can command up to $800.

For more information, see *Tomart's Illustrated Disneyana Catalogs and Price Guides*.

Art, Animation & Reference

This category includes "coffee table" books, catalogs, biographies, histories, everything associated with The Walt Disney Company. Usually, these are profusely illustrated with scenes from films, original story board sketches, and celluloid artwork. Some have photos of studio interiors, Walt, and his employees. Regarding catalogs, the earliest are the most valuable.

DI0200　**American Heritage** — Vol 14, No 3, Apr 1968　20 - 30
DI0250　**Animated Features** 1980, Abbeville　　　　10 - 15
DI0300　**The Art of Animation** NY 1958, DJ　　　300 - 500
DI0350　**The Art of the Little Mermaid** (Sotheby's auction
　　　　catalog)　　　　　　　　　　　　　　40 - 60
DI0400　**The Art of Walt Disney** NY 1942, DJ　　250 - 500
　　　　w/o DJ　　　　　　　　　　　　　　75 - 125
DI0450　**The Art of Walt Disney** (C. Finch) NY 1973, acetate
　　　　DJ w/high-relief figure of Mickey Mouse on cover 100 - 150
　　　　w/o DJ　　　　　　　　　　　　　　40 - 60
DI0452　NY 1984, DJ　　　　　　　　　　　　40 - 60
DI0500　**The Art of Who Framed Roger Rabbit** (Sotheby's
　　　　auction catalog) 1989　　　　　　　　50 - 75

DI0600　Christmas toy catalogs 1930 to present, especially
　　　　ones from 1933-39 depicting Disneyana　　15 - 100
DI0650　**Cartoon Collectibles** 1984, Doubleday　　15 - 25
DI0700　**A Celebration of Comic Art and Memorabilia**
　　　　1975, Hawthorn, DJ　　　　　　　　　40 - 60
DI0750　**Character Toys and Collectibles** 1984, Collectors
　　　　Book　　　　　　　　　　　　　　　15 - 25
DI0800　**Disney Animation - The Illusion of Life** NY 1981 300 - 500
DI0850　**Disney Dons Dogtags** 1992, Abbeville, DJ　15 - 25
DI0900　**The Disney Studio Story** 1988, Crown Publishers Inc. 25 - 50
DI0950　**The Disney Touch** 1991, Irwin　　　　　10 - 15
DI1000　**The Disney Version** 1968, Simon and Schuster　10 - 15
DI1050　**Disney's World** 1985, Stein and Day　　　10 - 15
DI1100　**Disneyana** (Cecil Munsey) NY 1974, DJ　75 - 115
DI1200　**Disneyland: Inside Story** 1987, Abrams　25 - 50
DI1225　**Dispatch From Disney's** 1942, Disney, Burbank　75 - 200
DI1250　**Donald Duck** 1978, Abbeville　　　　　15 - 25
DI1300　**Donald Duck** 1979, Harmony　　　　　10 - 25
DI1350　**Donald Duck - 50 Years of Happy Frustration**
　　　　1984, HP　　　　　　　　　　　　　15 - 25
DI1400　**Donald Duck and His Nephews** 1983, Abbeville　10 - 15
DI1430　**Fantasia** NY 1940, DJ　　　　　　　600 - 950
　　　　w/o DJ　　　　　　　　　　　　　100 - 175
DI1450　**The Fine Art of Walt Disney's Donald Duck**
　　　　(Carl Barks) 1981　　　　　　　　　800 - 1200
DI1500　**Goofy** 1979, Abbeville　　　　　　　10 - 15
DI1550　**He Drew as He Pleased** (Albert Hurter) NY
　　　　1948, DJ　　　　　　　　　　　　100 - 150
DI1600　**Justice For Disney** Dayton, 1992, DJ, 1000 cys　75 - 125
DI1650　Mail order catalogs 1930 to present　　　15 - 100
DI1700　**The Man Behind the Magic** 1991, Viking　12 - 20
DI1750　Manufacturer catalogs and sales sheets　　15 - 100
DI1800　**Mickey Mouse** 1978, Abbeville　　　　10 - 15
DI1850　**Mickey Mouse Club Scrapbook** 1975, Grosset
　　　　& Dunlap　　　　　　　　　　　　10 - 15
DI1900　**Mickey Mouse - Fifty Happy Years** 1977, Harmony 10 - 25
DI1950　**Mickey Mouse in Color** w/picture disc & Barks' art 300 - 500
DI2000　**Mickey Mouse Memorabilia** 1986, Abrams　40 - 50
DI2050　**The New Mickey Mouse Club Book** 1977, G & D 10 - 15
DI2150　**Snow White Sketch Book** Lon 1938, DJ　700 - 1000
DI2200　**Storming the Magic Kingdom** 1987, Knopf　15 - 20
DI2250　**The Story of Walt Disney** 1957, Holt　　30 - 50
DI2350　**Treasures of Disney Animation Art** 1982　100 - 200
DI2400　**Uncle Scrooge** 1979, Abbeville　　　　15 - 25
DI2450　**Uncle Scrooge in Color** (Carl Barks) w/photo　600 - 800
　　　　w/o photo　　　　　　　　　　　400 - 600
DI2500　**Walt Disney - An American Original** 1976, S & S 20 - 40
DI2550　**Walt Disney and Assorted Other Characters**
　　　　1988, Harmony Books　　　　　　　50 - 75
DI2600　**Walt Disney Magician of the Movies** 1966,
　　　　Grosset & Dunlap　　　　　　　　　20 - 30
DI2650　**Walt Disney's Bambi** 1990, w/flip book　25 - 40
DI2700　**Walt Disney's Fantasia** 1983, DJ　　　20 - 40
DI2750　**Walt Disney's Uncle Scrooge McDuck: His Life
　　　　and Times** 1981　　　　　　　　　600 - 800
DI2800　**Window On Main Street**, 1991, Laughter
　　　　hardbound (limited to 500)　　　　　30 - 50
DI2850　**Wisdom** — Vol 32, 1959　　　　　　20 - 30

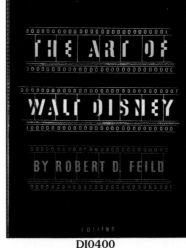

DI0400

DI1225

Big Little Books, Big Big Books, Better Little Books, Wee Little Books & Penny Books

These novelty books were usually printed on pulp paper and had very colorful pictorial boards. Most Big Little Books were published by Whitman (Racine, WI) during the 1930s and 1940s, although the line was revived in the 1960s. In the 30s, the books sold for 10 cents and were all a standard size (about 4" x 4-3/4"). Big Little Books were called Better Little Books after 1938. They feature an immense collection of cartoon and comic-strip characters. Mickey Mouse and Donald Duck were the most published with about 50 titles between them. Big Big Books, Wee Little Books, and Penny Books are the same idea put into an extra large or very small format.

Big Little Books

DI3020	Donald Duck Hunting for Trouble 1938, #1478	20 - 30
DI3030	Mickey Mouse 1933, #717	125 - 200
DI3040	Mickey Mouse 1933, new cover, #717	75 - 125
DI3050	Mickey Mouse and Bobo the Elephant 1935, #1160	40 - 60
DI3060	Mickey Mouse and Pluto the Racer 1936, #1128	40 - 60
DI3070	Mickey Mouse and the Bat Bandit 1935, #1153	25 - 40
DI3071	1935, different soft cover, no #	40 - 60
DI3080	Mickey Mouse and the Sacred Jewel 1936, #1187	40 - 60
DI3090	Mickey Mouse in Blaggard Castle 1934, #726	40 - 60
DI3100	Mickey Mouse in the Race for Riches 1938, #1476	20 - 30
DI3110	Mickey Mouse Presents a Walt Disney Silly Symphony 1934, #756	40 - 60
DI3120	Mickey Mouse Presents Walt Disney's Silly Symphonies Stories 1936, #1111	50 - 75
DI3130	Mickey Mouse Runs His Own Newspaper 1937, #1409	50 - 75
DI3140	Mickey Mouse Sails For Treasure Island 1933, #750	40 - 60
DI3145	Mickey Mouse Sails For Treasure Island 1935, Kolynos giveaway, 2 versions	50 - 75
DI3150	Mickey Mouse the Detective 1934, #1139	40 - 60
	soft cover	50 - 75
DI3160	Mickey Mouse the Mail Pilot 1933, #731	40 - 60
DI3161	soft cover, larger size	40 - 60
DI3162	soft cover, American Gas giveaway, 1933	50 - 75
DI3170	Pluto the Pup 1938, #1467	20 - 30
DI3180	Silly Symphony Featuring Donald Duck 1937, #1169	50 - 75
DI3190	Silly Symphony Featuring Donald Duck and His Misadventures 1937, #1441	40 - 60
DI3200	Snow White and the Seven Dwarfs 1938, #1460	30 - 50

Better Little Books

DI3410	Donald Duck Gets Fed Up 1940, #1462	25 - 40
DI3420	Donald Duck Says: Such Luck! 1941, #1424	25 - 40
DI3430	Donald Forgets to Duck 1939, #1434	20 - 30
DI3440	Mickey Mouse and the Pirate Submarine 1939, #1463	25 - 40
DI3450	Mickey Mouse and the Seven Ghosts 1940, #1475	25 - 40
DI3460	Mickey Mouse in the Foreign Legion 1940, #1428	20 - 30
DI3470	Mickey Mouse on Sky Island 1941, #1417	25 - 40
DI3480	Pinocchio and Jiminy Cricket 1940, #1435	30 - 50
DI3490	Such a Life! Says: Donald Duck 1939, #1404	20 - 30

New Better Little Book Series with Flip Movies

DI3610	Bambi's Children 1943, #1497 (no flip movie)	30 - 50
DI3620	Donald Duck Headed For Trouble 1942, #1430	20 - 30
DI3630	Donald Duck Off the Beam! 1943, #1438	20 - 30
DI3640	Donald Duck Sees Stars 1941, #1422	20 - 30
DI3650	Dumbo: Only His Ears Grew! 1941, #1400	30 - 50
DI3660	Mickey Mouse and the Dude Ranch Bandit 1943, #1471	20 - 30
DI3670	Mickey Mouse and the Magic Lamp 1942, #1429	20 - 30
	Mickey Mouse in the Treasure Hunt 1941, #1401	20 - 30
DI3680	Walt Disney's Bambi 1942, #1469	20 - 30

New Whitman Numbering Series Begins — Some Disney titles in the previous 1400 series reappear with fewer pages. Flip movies were dropped in new titles.

DI3710	Brer Rabbit 1947, #1426	20 - 30
DI3720	Donald Duck and Ghost Morgan's Treasure 1946, #1411	25 - 40
DI3730	Donald Duck and the Green Serpent 1947, #1432	25 - 40
DI3740	Donald Duck in Volcano Valley 1949, #1457	25 - 40
DI3750	Donald Duck is Here Again 1944, #1484	15 - 25
DI3760	Donald Duck Lays Down the Law 1948, #1449	25 - 40
DI3770	Donald Duck Up In the Air 1945, #1486 (Barks)	30 - 50
DI3780	Mickey Mouse and the Desert Palace 1948, #1451	20 - 30
DI3790	Mickey Mouse and the Lazy Daisy Mystery 1947, #1433	15 - 25
DI3800	Mickey Mouse and the 'Lectro Box 1946, #1413	20 - 30
DI3810	Mickey Mouse and the Stolen Jewels 1949, #1464	20 - 30
DI3820	Mickey Mouse Bellboy Detective 1945, #1483	15 - 25
DI3830	Mickey Mouse in the World of Tomorrow 1948, #1444	15 - 25
DI3840	Mickey Mouse on the Cave-Man Island 1944, #1499	15 - 25
DI3850	Thumper and the Seven Dwarfs 1944, #1409	50 - 75

New Better Little Book Series

DI3910	Brer Rabbit 1949, #704	15 - 20
DI3920	Cinderella and the Magic Wand 1950, #711	12 - 20
DI3930	Donald Duck and the Mystery of the Double X 1949, #705	25 - 40
DI3940	Mickey Mouse on the Haunted Island 1950, #708	15 - 25

Tall Book Series

DI4010	Mickey's Dog Pluto 1937 - 1943, #532	20 - 30

Big Big Books

DI4110	The Story of Mickey Mouse and the Smugglers 1935, #4062, two cover versions available	15 - 90

Wee Little Books

DI4210	Mickey Mouse and Tanglefoot	15 - 25
DI4220	Mickey Mouse at the Carnival	15 - 25
DI4230	Mickey Mouse Will Not Quit	15 - 25
DI4240	Mickey Mouse Wins the Race	15 - 25
DI4250	Mickey Mouse's Misfortune	15 - 25
DI4260	Mickey Mouse's Up Hill Fight	15 - 25
DI4270	Boxed set of 6 books, 1934, #512	200 - 300

Penny Book Series 1938-39

DI4410	Brave Little Tailor	20 - 30
DI4420	Donald Duck's Cousin Gus	20 - 30
DI4430	Donald's Better Self	20 - 30
DI4440	Donald's Lucky Day	20 - 30
DI4450	Farmyard Symphony	20 - 30
DI4460	Goofy and Wilbur	20 - 30
DI4470	Mickey's Gold Rush	20 - 30
DI4480	Pluto at the Society Dog Show	20 - 30
DI4490	The Practical Pig	20 - 30
DI4500	The Ugly Duckling	20 - 30

DI1430

DI2150

DI3030   DI3040   DI3090   DI3160

DI3430   DI3480   DI3440   DI3470

DI4810   DI4840   DI4860   DI4870

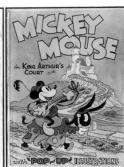

DI5210   DI5220   DI5230

Dell Fast Action

Dell published a series of hard-cover comic books known as *Dell Fast Action* in the 1930s and 1940s.

DI4810	**Donald Duck and the Ducklings** 1938	50 - 75
DI4820	**Donald Duck Out of Luck** 1940	25 - 40
DI4830	**Donald Duck Takes It on the Chin** 1941	40 - 60
DI4840	**Dumbo the Flying Elephant** 1941, #10	40 - 60
DI4850	**Mickey Mouse and Pluto** 1942, #16	40 - 60
DI4860	**Mickey Mouse in the Sheriff of Nugget Gulch** 1938	50 - 75
DI4870	**Mickey Mouse with Goofy and Mickey's Nephews** 1938	50 - 75
DI4880	**Pinocchio and Jiminy Cricket** 1940	40 - 60

Mickey Mouse Magazines

These magazines were first used as promotional items, then sold later. They proved very successful. They had pictorial paper wrappers.

Mickey Mouse Weekly

DI5001	vol I #1, Summer 1935	400 - 1000
DI5002	vol I #2, Oct 1935	200 - 600
DI5003	vol I, #3-12	75 - 300
DI5013	vol II, #1-12	70 - 250
DI5025	vol III, #1-12	50 - 175
DI5037	vol IV, #1-12	45 - 150
DI5049	vol V, #1-8	40 - 125
DI5057	vol V, #9 (1st comic book size)	75 - 300
DI5058	vol V, #10-11	60 - 275
DI5060	vol V, #12 (change to comic book format, became *Walt Disney's Comics & Stories* #1 w/next issue)	200 - 750

Pop-Up & Mechanical

This category includes some of the most hotly sought after children's and Disney books. With parts that move, these books excite toy collectors as well as bibliophiles. During the 1930s, Blue Ribbon Books published many "pop-ups" and most came with dust jackets. Jackets are rare and it is uncommon to find the books in fine condition because the delicate moving parts are either torn or missing. These listings are arranged by year.

DI5210	**Pop-up Mickey Mouse** 1933	200 - 325
DI5220	**Pop-up Minnie Mouse** 1933	200 - 325
DI5230	**Mickey Mouse in King Arthur's Court** 1933, DJ	450 - 950
DI5240	**Silly Symphonies Pop-up** 1933, DJ	350 - 700

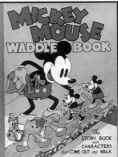

DI5240   DI5260   DI5260 (back)

DI5250	**Pop-up Mickey Mouse in Ye Olden Days** 1934	200 - 400
DI5260	**Mickey Mouse Waddle Book** 1934, complete, unpunched	2000 - 3000
DI5270	**Mickey Mouse Waddle Book** 1934, complete, w/punched Waddles	700 - 1000
DI5280	**The Victory March** 1942, Random House	100 - 150
DI5290	**Cinderella Puppet Show** 1949, Golden	50 - 75
DI5300	**Fun-filled Visit to Walt Disney World** 1972, Hallmark	10 - 15
DI5310	**Bambi's Big Day** 1976	10 - 15
DI5320	**Snow White's Party** 1976	10 - 15
DI5330	**Pinocchio and the Puppet Theater** 1976	10 - 15
DI5340	**Mickey Mouse and the Martian Mix-up** 1978	10 - 15
DI5350	**The Black Hole** 1979	10 - 15
DI5360	**Bambi Gets Lost** 1979	10 - 15

DI5280   DI6010

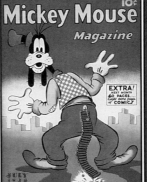

DI5001   DI5002   DI5025   DI5037   DI5057

DI5370	Goofy and the Chimp 1979	10 - 15
DI5380	Donald Duck and the Chipmunks 1980	10 - 15
DI5390	Mickey's Lucky Day 1980	10 - 15

Story

Story books are among the earliest and most abundant of Walt Disney's books. The first book, *Mickey Mouse Book - Hello Everybody* (Bilbo & Lang 1930) is a story book. Main publishers were Whitman and David McKay. These books tell a story, often set to rhyme, about Disney characters. Usually every page or every other page is illustrated with cartoon characters with the accompanying text either beneath the cartoon or on the facing page. The covers are usually brightly-colored boards and some books had jackets. *A Mickey Mouse ABC Story* (Whitman 1936) is set to rhyme with the first letter of a key word matching the letters of the alphabet. Mickey, Goofy, Clarabelle and many other cartoon characters are playing in a band. The illustrations are in black and red.

Whitman also published "linen like" story books. These books are oversized with very colorful covers. They were printed on a heavy, very durable paper similar to children's books of the 1800s which were made from real linen. These books are identified with the abbreviation "LL."

| DI6010 | Mickey Mouse Book ("Hello Everybody"), Bibo and Lang, 1930 | 500 - 700 |
| DI6011 | 2nd version has slight changes | 300 - 500 |

1931 (McKay)

DI6110	The Adventures of Mickey Mouse - Book 1 hard or soft cover	200 - 300
DI6120	Mickey Mouse Illustrated Movie Stories	200 - 300
DI6130	Mickey Mouse Illustrated Movie Stories Canada	
DI6140	Mickey Mouse - Series No. 1	200 - 450
DI6150	Mickey Mouse Story Book hard or soft cover	75 - 125
DI6151	Mickey Mouse Stories (#2)	75 - 125

1932 (McKay)

| DI6210 | The Adventures of Mickey Mouse - Book 2 | 150 - 250 |
| DI6220 | Mickey Mouse - Book No. 2 | 150 - 300 |

1933 (McKay unless otherwise noted)

DI6310	Mickey Mouse Whitman #948	75 - 150
DI6320	Mickey Mouse - Book No. 3	200 - 300
DI6330	The Three Little Pigs Blue Ribbon	100 - 150
DI6340	Who's Afraid of the Big Bad Wolf?	25 - 50

1934 (McKay unless otherwise noted)

DI6410	The Big Bad Wolf and Little Red Riding Hood Blue Ribbon	100 - 150
DI6420	Little Red Riding Hood and the Big Bad Wolf	50 - 75
DI6430	Mickey Mouse - Book No. 4	150 - 250

DI6440	Mickey Mouse in Giantland	75 - 125
DI6445	Mickey Mouse Library & Toy - Boxed	300 - 500
DI6450	Mickey Mouse Movie Stories - Book 2	200 - 350
DI6460	Mickey Mouse Stories - Book 2 hard or soft cover	75 - 125
DI6470	Peculiar Penguins	40 - 60
DI6480	The Wise Little Hen	75 - 125

DI6220   DI6330

DI6510   DI6540

DI6550   DI6570

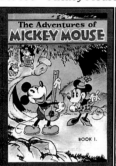
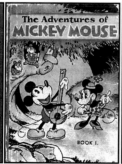

DI6110 (hardcover)   DI6110 (softcover)   DI6120   DI6150 (hardcover)   DI6150 (softcover)   DI6151

DI6210   DI6340   DI6420   DI6440   DI6470   DI6640

DI6500

DI6790

DI7000

DI7010

DI7015

1935 (McKay unless otherwise noted. McKay version has titles on spine.)

DI6500	**Donald Duck** (1st Donald Duck book) Whitman, #978, LL	300 - 500
DI6510	**The Robber Kitten**	50 - 75
DI6520	**The Robber Kitten** Whitman, No #	50 - 75
DI6530	**The Three Orphan Kittens**	50 - 75
DI6540	**The Three Orphan Kittens** Whitman, No #	50 - 75
DI6550	**The Tortoise and the Hare**	50 - 75
DI6560	**The Tortoise and the Hare** Whitman	50 - 75
DI6570	**The Wise Little Hen**	60 - 90
DI6580	**The Wise Little Hen** Whitman, No #	

1936 (Whitman unless otherwise noted)

DI6600	**Donald Duck** G & D	70 - 100
DI6610	**Elmer Elephant** McKay	50 - 100
DI6620	**Forty Big Pages of Mickey Mouse** #945	75 - 125
DI6630	**Mickey Mouse** (Stand Out Book), #841	75 - 125
DI6640	**A Mickey Mouse ABC Story** #921	50 - 90
DI6650	**A Mickey Mouse Alphabet Book** #936	50 - 90
DI6660	**Mickey Mouse and his Friends** #904, LL	100 - 150
DI6670	**Mickey Mouse and His Horse Tanglefoot** McKay	75 - 175
DI6680	**Mickey Mouse and Pluto the Pup** #2028	60 - 90
DI6690	**Mickey Mouse Crusoe** #711	75 - 125
DI6700	**The Mickey Mouse Fire Brigade** #2029	60 - 115
DI6710	**Mickey Mouse in Pigmyland** #711	50 - 75

1937 (Whitman unless otherwise noted)

DI6750	**The Country Cousin** McKay	50 - 75
DI6760	**Donald Duck and His Friends** #507	50 - 75
DI6770	**Donald Duck Has His Ups and Downs** #1077	50 - 90
DI6775	**The Golden Touch**	40 - 75
DI6780	**Hiawatha** McKay	50 - 75
DI6790	**Mickey Mouse** (reprints *Good Housekeeping* pp) #973, LL	75 - 125
DI6800	**Mickey Mouse and Donald Duck Gag Book** #886	60 - 90
DI6810	**Mickey Mouse and His Friends** Nelson	40 - 75
DI6820	**Mickey Mouse and His Friends Wait for the County Fair** #883	50 - 75
DI6830	**Mickey Mouse and Mother Goose** #411	50 - 100
DI6840	**Mickey Mouse, Donald Duck and All Their Pals** #887	60 - 90
DI6850	**Mickey Mouse Has a Busy Day** #1077	50 - 75
DI6860	**Mickey Mouse Presents Walt Disney's Nursery Stories**	40 - 75
DI6870	**Mickey's Magic Hat Cookie Carnival** #1077	40 - 60
DI6880	**Pluto and the Puppy** G & D	50 - 75
DI6885	**Pluto the Pup** #894, LL	50 - 75
DI6890	**Snow White and the Seven Dwarfs** Harper	75 - 150
DI6900	**Snow White and the Seven Dwarfs** G & D	75 - 125
DI6901	Reprinted as an art book for 50th anniversary of Snow White, Abrams	
DI6910	**Snow White and the Seven Dwarfs** McKay	60 - 90
DI6920	**Walt Disney Annual** #4001	125 - 200
DI6930	**The Wise Little Hen** #888	50 - 75
DI6940	**The Wise Little Hen** #888, LL	30 - 50

1938 (Whitman unless otherwise noted)

DI7000	**Animals from Snow White and the Seven Dwarfs** #922, LL	50 - 75
DI7005	**Brave Little Tailor** #972	50 - 75
DI7010	**Clock Cleaners** #947, LL	60 - 90
DI7015	**Dopey — He Don't Talk None** #955, LL	50 - 75
DI7020	**Edgar Bergen's Charlie McCarthy Meets Walt Disney's Snow White** #986	50 - 75
DI7025	**Elmer Elephant** #948, LL	50 - 75
DI7030	**The Famous Movie Story of Walt Disney's Snow White and the Seven Dwarfs** (K.K. Publications)	30 - 50
DI7040	**Famous Seven Dwarfs** #933, LL	75 - 125
DI7042	**Famous Seven Dwarfs** #944	30 - 50
DI7060	**Ferdinand the Bull** #842	25 - 40
DI7065	**Ferdinand the Bull** #903, LL	25 - 40
DI7070	**Ferdinand the Bull** (Dell)	25 - 40
DI7080	**Forest Friends from Snow White** G & D	25 - 40
DI7085	**Hiawatha** #924, LL	30 - 50
DI7090	**Mickey Mouse Alphabet** #889, LL	50 - 75
DI7100	**Mickey Mouse Has a Party** #798	40 - 75
DI7110	**Mickey Mouse in Numberland** #745	50 - 75
DI7120	**Mickey Mouse the Boat Builder** G & D	40 - 75
DI7130	**Snow White and the Seven Dwarfs** G & D	50 - 75
DI7140	**Snow White and the Seven Dwarfs** #714	30 - 50
DI7150	**Snow White and the Seven Dwarfs** #927	30 - 50
DI7160	**Snow White and the Seven Dwarfs** #777	30 - 50
DI7162	**Snow White and the Seven Dwarfs** #925, LL	40 - 60
DI7164	**Snow White and the Seven Dwarfs** #927, LL	40 - 60
DI7168	**Snow White and the Seven Dwarfs from the Famous Movie Story** no #	
DI7170	**The Story of Bashful** #1044	25 - 40
DI7180	**The Story of Doc** #1044	25 - 40
DI7190	**The Story of Dopey** #1044	25 - 40
DI7200	**The Story of Grumpy** #1044	25 - 40
DI7210	**The Story of Happy** #1044	25 - 40
DI7220	**The Story of Sleepy** #1044	25 - 40
DI7230	**The Story of Sneezy** #1044	25 - 40
DI7240	**The Story of Snow White** #1044	25 - 40
DI7250	**Story of Clarabelle Cow** #1066	20 - 30
DI7260	**Story of Dippy the Goof** #1066	20 - 30
DI7270	**Story of Donald Duck** #1066	20 - 30
DI7280	**Story of Mickey Mouse** #1066	20 - 30
DI7290	**Story of Minnie Mouse** #1066	20 - 30
DI7300	**Story of Pluto the Pup** #1066	20 - 30
DI7310	**Toby Tortoise and the Hare** #928, LL	30 - 50

1939 (Whitman unless otherwise noted)

DI7410	**Brave Little Tailor** #1058	25 - 40
DI7420	**Donald Duck and His Friends** Heath	20 - 30
DI7430	**Donald's Lucky Day** #897	30 - 50
DI7440	**The Farmyard Symphony** #1058	25 - 40
DI7450	**Little Pig's Picnic and Other Stories** Heath	20 - 30
DI7460	**The Mickey Mouse Box** #2146, includes **Brave Little Tailor**, **Mother Pluto**, **The Practical Pig**, **Timid Elmer**, and **The Ugly Duckling**, set	200 - 350
DI7470	**Mickey Never Fails** Heath	25 - 40
DI7480	**Mother Pluto** #1058	25 - 40

DI6680

DI6700

DI7570

DI7490	**Pinocchio** Dell	25 - 40
DI7500	**The Practical Pig** #1058	25 - 40
DI7510	**School Days in Disneyville** Heath	20 - 30
DI7520	**Timid Elmer** #1058	20 - 30
DI7530	**The Ugly Duckling** Lippincott	50 - 75
DI7540	**The Ugly Duckling** #1058	20 - 30
DI7550	**Walt Disney Tells the Story of Pinocchio** #556	30 - 50
DI7560	**Walt Disney's Version of Pinocchio** G & D	30 - 50
DI7570	**Walt Disney's Version of Pinocchio** Random House	50 - 75
DI7580	**Walt Disney's Version of Pinocchio** Cocomalt	15 - 25
DI7590	**Walt Disney's Version of Pinocchio** #709	15 - 25
DI7600	**Walt Disney's Version of Pinocchio** #6880	15 - 25
1940	**(Whitman unless otherwise noted)**	
DI7650	**Ave Maria** Random House	30 - 50
DI7660	**The Blue Fairy** #1059	20 - 30
DI7670	**Dance of the Hours** Harper	50 - 75
DI7680	**Donald Duck and His Nephews** Heath	20 - 30
DI7690	**Donald's Penguin** Garden City	40 - 75
DI7700	**Figaro and Cleo** #1059	20 - 30
DI7710	**Figaro and Cleo** Random House	20 - 30
DI7720	**Geppetto** #1059	20 - 30
DI7730	**Heath Teachers Guide**	20 - 30
DI7740	**Here They Are** Heath	20 - 40
DI7750	**Honest John and Giddy** Random House	20 - 30
DI7760	**J. Worthington Foulfellow and Gideon** #1059	20 - 30
DI7770	**Jiminy Cricket** #1059	20 - 30
DI7780	**Jiminy Cricket** Random House	20 - 30
DI7790	**The Nutcracker Suite from WD Fantasia** Little, Brown	40 - 60
DI7800	**Pastoral from Walt Disney's Fantasia** Harper	40 - 60
DI7810	**Pinocchio** #846	15 - 25
DI7815	**Pinocchio** #1039, LL	25 - 40
DI7820	**Pinocchio** #1059	20 - 30
DI7822	**Pinocchio** #1061, LL	25 - 40
DI7824	**Pinocchio** #6881, LL	25 - 40
DI7826	**Pinocchio** Heath	20 - 30
DI7830	**Pinocchio Picture Book** G & D	40 - 60
DI7840	**Pinocchio Picture Book** #849	30 - 50
DI7850	**The Practical Pig** Garden City	50 - 75
DI7860	**The Sorcerer's Apprentice** G & D	50 - 75
DI7870	**Stories from Walt Disney's Fantasia** Random House	50 - 75
DI7875	**Story Paint Book Series** #2035 (6, all have #1059), set in box	50 - 75
DI7880	**The Walt Disney Parade** Garden City	100 - 175
DI7890	**Walt Disney's Version of Pinocchio** 24 pages	20 - 30
DI7900	**Water Babies Circus and Other Stories** Heath	15 - 25
1941	**(Whitman unless otherwise noted)**	
DI8000	**Baby Weems** Doubleday	60 - 90
DI8010	**Bambi** Simon & Schuster	20 - 30
DI8020	**Dumbo of the Circus** Garden City	40 - 60
DI8030	**Dumbo of the Circus** K.K. Publications	25 - 40
DI8040	**Dumbo the Flying Elephant**	25 - 40
DI8050	**Dumbo - The Story of the Little Elephant with Big Ears** Disney, distributed by Winkler & Ramen	25 - 40
DI8060	**The Life of Donald Duck** Random House	75 - 125
DI8070	**The Story of Casey, Jr.** Garden City	40 - 60
DI8080	**Story of the Reluctant Dragon** Garden City	50 - 75
DI8090	**The Story of Timothy's House** Garden City	40 - 60
1942	**(Whitman unless otherwise noted)**	
DI8140	**Bambi** G & D	15 - 25
DI8150	**Bambi Picture Book** #930, LL	25 - 40
DI8160	**Bambi Story Book** #725	20 - 30
DI8165	**Bambi Story Book** Racine 1942, wrappers	50 - 75
DI8170	**Dumbo - The Story of the Flying Elephant** #710	25 - 40
DI8180	**Thumper** G & D	12 - 20
1943		
DI8250	**Donald Duck in the High Andes** G & D	20 - 30
DI8260	**The Gremlins** Random House	50 - 75
DI8270	**Pedro - The Story of a Little Airplane** G & D	20 - 30
1944		
DI8400	**Bambi** Heath	20 - 30
DI8410	**The Cold-Blooded Penguin** NY 1944, DJ	50 - 75
	w/o DJ	25 - 40
DI8420	**Mickey Sees the U.S.A.** Heath	20 - 30
DI8430	**The Three Caballeros** Random House	50 - 75
1945		
DI8500	**Donald Duck Sees South America** Heath	15 - 25
DI8510	**Funny Stories About Donald and Mickey** Whitman #714	20 - 30
1946		
DI8600	**Brer Rabbit Rides the Fox** G & D	12 - 20
DI8610	**The Wonderful Tar Baby** G & D	12 - 20
1948		
DI8660	**Dumbo of the Circus** Heath	50 - 100

GOLF

Golf originated in Scotland in the 1400s and was played in America as early as the late 1700s. Printed matter was almost non-existent until the 19th century. One exception was the rules of "Goff" or Golf published in *Hoyles Games* in the early 1800s. The only other book mentioning golf is a long poem printed in paper wraps entitled *The Goff* by Thomas Mathison. It was published in 1743 and reprinted in 1763 and 1793.

George F. Carnegie wrote *Golfiana, or Niceties Connected with the Game of Golf,* published in 1833. Then in 1857 "Keen Hand" Farnie authored the first golf instructor, *The Golfers Manual.* The earliest Golf Club histories were published in the late 1800s. In 1895, James Lee wrote the first book about American golf entitled *Golf in America.*

Collectible golf books encompass a broad range of subjects. They include instructionals, club histories, players' biographies/autobiographies, golf-course architecture, golf-course care, tournament histories, pictorials and bound volumes of prints, humor, novels, poetry, essays, and golf-equipment technology and history.

The most published books are instructionals. These are usually written by professional golfers. Bobby Jones, Henry Cotton, Gary Player, Arnold Palmer, and Jack Nicklaus are among the most prolific instructional authors.

Biographies and autobiographies are also popular and are most often penned by club pros and tournament winners.

The most expensive golf books tend to be from the 19th and

DI7790   DI7875

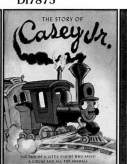  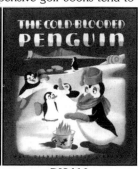 

DI7560   DI8070   DI8090   DI8410   GN0200

early 20th centuries, partly because they are so scarce. These include club histories, golf course architecture, annuals, instructors, biographies, and pictorials.

Fiction from the early 1900s is very collectible. A good example is the mystery writer Herbert Adams. A prolific writer, Adams wrote about ten murder mysteries with golf themes.

Dust jackets from the late 1800s and early 1900s are very scarce. Many golf books of this vintage didn't have jackets and most (especially annuals and instructionals) were bound in stiff wrappers.

Any book signed by a famous golfer is worth more than an unsigned copy. Add about $200 for Bobby Jones. Charles "Chick" Evans' signed books are worth about $50 - 75 more. The great contemporary golfers like Jack Nicklaus, Arnold Palmer, Sam Snead, and Cary Middlecoff signed many books. Their signatures enhance a book by $10-25.

The following listings are alphabetical by author or editor; a few are by title.

Non-Fiction

Aikman, George (G. A.)
GN0050 **Pen and Pencil Sketches on the Game of Golf**
Edinburgh 1888   400 - 600
GN0060 **A Round of the Links: Views of the Golf
Greens of Scotland** Edinburgh 1893   1000 - 1500

Aitchison, Thomas
GN0080 **Reminiscences of the Old Bruntsfield Link
Golf Club 1866-1874** (Edinburgh) 1902   400 - 600

Allen, Peter
GN0110 **Play the Best Courses** Lon 1973, DJ   50 - 75

Allerton, Mark (also see Fiction, Humor & Poetry)
GN0130 **Golf Faults Remedied** Lon (1911), wrappers   100 - 150
GN0140 **Golf Made Easy** Lon 1910, wrappers   100 - 150

Alliss, Percy
GN0170 **Better Golf** Lon 1926, DJ   30 - 50

Armour, Tommy (1927 U.S. Open Champion)
GN0190 **How to Play Your Best Golf** NY 1953, DJ   15 - 25
GN0200 **How to Play Your Best Golf all the Time**
NY 1953, DJ   15 - 25
GN0210 **Round of Golf with Tommy Armour** NY 1959, DJ   15 - 25
GN0220 **Tommy Armour's A.B.C.'s of Golf** NY 1967, DJ   15 - 25

Bailey, C. W.
GN0245 **The Brain and Golf** Lon 1923   100 - 150
GN0246 Lon 1924   50 - 75
GN0247 Bos 1924   50 - 75

Balfour, James
GN0280 **Reminiscences of Golf on St. Andrews Links**
Edinburgh 1887, wrappers   1200 - 1800

Balfour, Stuart
GN0300 **Golf** NY (1893; Spalding Athletic Library; 1st golf
book published in America), wrappers   300 - 500

Bantock, Miles
GN0320 **On Many Greens: A Book of Golf and Golfers**
NY 1901   300 - 500

Barnes, James M. (1921 U.S. Open Champion)
GN0340 **A Guide to Good Golf** NY 1925, DJ   20 - 30
GN0350 **Picture Analysis of Golf Strokes** Phil 1919, DJ   50 - 75

Barton, Pam
GN0380 **A Stroke a Hole** Lon 1937, DJ   30 - 50

Bateman, H. M. (Henry Mayo)
GN0400 **Adventures at Golf** Lon (1923)   50 - 75

Bauer, Aleck
GN0420 **Hazards: The Essential Elements in a Golf
Course...** Chi 1913   300 - 500

Baxter, Peter
GN0440 **Golf in Perth and Perthshire** Perth 1899   500 - 700

Beldam, George W.
GN0460 **Golf Faults Illustrated** Lon (1905)   50 - 75
GN0470 **Golfing Illustrated** Lon 1908, wrappers   50 - 75
GN0480 **Great Golfers** Lon 1904   100 - 150
GN0490 **The World's Champion Golfers** Lon (1924),
wrappers   50 - 75

Bennett, Andrew
GN0510 **The Book of St. Andrew Links** St. Andrews
1898, 1000 cys, wrappers   700 - 1000

Benson, E. F. (editor)
GN0530 **A Book of Golf** Lon 1903   50 - 75

Berg, Patty (1946 U.S. Women's Open Champion)
GN0550 **Golf** NY 1941, DJ   30 - 50
GN0560 **Golf For Women Illustrated** Lon 1951, DJ   20 - 30
GN0570 **Golf Illustrated** NY 1950, DJ   20 - 30

Berkeley, Earl of
GN0590 **Sound Golf** Lon 1936   40 - 60

Bisher, Fruman
GN0610 **Augusta Revisited** Birmingham 1976, DJ   50 - 75

Blogh, Arthur
GN0620 **Crotchets and Foibles** Lon 1903   50 - 75

Bovis, John L.
GN0640 **The "It" of Golf** Cinti (1927)   30 - 50

Braid, James (British Open Champion for many years)
GN0660 **Advanced Golf** Lon 1908   300 - 500
GN0661 Phil 1908   250 - 350
GN0670 **Golf Guide and How to Play Golf** Lon 1906,
wrappers (Spalding Athletic Library)   50 - 75
GN0672 NY 1907, wrappers   50 - 75

Breeden, Marshall
GN0700 **U.S. Golfers and Our California Links** LA (1923)   50 - 75

Broadbent, W. F.
GN0720 **Golf** Lon 1937, wrappers   20 - 30

Brown, George S.
GN0740 **First Steps to Golf** Lon 1913   50 - 75
GN0742 NY (1913-14)   50 - 75

Brown, Innis
GN0760 **How to Play Golf** NY 1931, wrappers (Spalding
Athletic Library)   30 - 50

Brown, James
GN0780 **Songs of Golf** St. Andrews 1902   150 - 250

Brown, John Arthur
GN0790 **Short History of Pine Valley** Clementon 1963,
slipcase   50 - 75

Brown, William G.
GN0820 **Golf** Bos 1902   100 - 150

Browne, Tom
GN0840 **That Game of Golf and Some Other Sketches**
Lon 1902   200 - 300

Browning, Robert H. K. (also Fiction, Humor & Poetry)
GN0860 **Golf with Seven Clubs** Lon 1950, DJ   20 - 30
GN0870 **The Golfer's Catechism** Lon 1935, DJ   30 - 50
GN0880 **A History of Golf: The Royal and Ancient Game**
Lon 1955, DJ   150 - 250
GN0890 **Moments with Golfing Masters** Lon 1932, DJ   50 - 75
GN0900 **Super Golf** Lon 1919   100 - 150

Burke, Jack (1956 U.S. Masters Champion)
GN0930 **The Natural Way to Better Golf** Garden City
1954, DJ   20 - 30

Butler, W. Meredith
GN0960 **The Golfer's Manual** Lon (1907)   150 - 250
GN0961 Phil 1907   100 - 150

"Calamo Currente"
GN0990 **Half Hours with an Old Golfer** Lon 1895   200 - 300
GN0992 Lon 1897   100 - 150

Campbell, Sir Guy
GN1020 **Golf at Prince's and Deal** Lon (1950)   75 - 125

Cavanagh, Walter
GN1050 **The Art of Golf** 1928, wrappers   50 - 75

Chambers, Charles
GN1080 **Golfing...** Edinburgh 1887   400 - 600
GN1082 Edinburgh 1891   200 - 300

Chambers, Robert
GN1110 **A Few Rambling Remarks on Golf** Edinburgh
1862, wrappers   3000 - 5000
GN1120 **Gymnastics, Golf and Curling** Edinburgh
1866, wrappers   700 - 1000

Chattell, C. C.
GN1150 **The Golfer's Guide** 1908 Chi 1908   100 - 150

Clapcott, C. B.
GN1180 The History of Handicapping (1924), wrappers 300 - 500
GN1190 The Rules of the Ten Oldest Golf Clubs From
            1754-1848 Edinburgh 1935, 500 cys   300 - 500
Clark, Robert
GN1230 Golf: A Royal and Ancient Game Edinburgh
            1875, 50 cys   1500 - 2500
GN1231 200 cys   1000 - 1500
GN1233 Lon 1893   700 - 1000
GN1235 Lon 1899   400 - 600
Clement, Joe
GN1270 Classic Golf Clubs Jackson 1980   30 - 50
Cochran, Alastair
GN1300 Search for the Perfect Golf Swing Lon 1968, DJ 20 - 30
Collett, Glenna
GN1330 Golf for Young Players Bos 1926, DJ   75 - 125
GN1340 Ladies in the Rough NY 1928, DJ   75 - 125
"The Colonel"
GN1370 Golfing by Numbers Lon 1927   30 - 50
Colt, Harry
GN1400 Some Essays on Golf Course Architecture
            NY 1920   400 - 600
Colville, George M.
GN1430 Five Open Champions and the Musselburgh
            Golf Story Musselburgh 1890   500 - 700
Cornish, Geoffrey S. & Ronald E. Whitten
GN1460 The Golf Course NY 1981, DJ   50 - 75
Cotton, T. Henry (British, French, Belgian Open
    Champion, golf-course architect)
GN1490 Golf Lon 1931   50 - 75
GN1500 Golf: A Pictorial History Lon 1975, DJ   30 - 50
GN1510 Golfing in Scotland at 100 Holiday Resorts
            Lon (1936), DJ   30 - 50
GN1520 Henry Cotton's Guide to Golf in the British Isles
            1961, DJ   30 - 50
GN1530 Hints on Play with Steel Shafts Lon 1934   50 - 75
GN1540 My Golfing Album Lon 1959, DJ   50 - 75
GN1550 My Swing Lon 1952, DJ   30 - 50
GN1560 The Picture Story of the Golf Game Lon (1965), DJ 50 - 75
GN1570 Play Better Golf Lon 1973, DJ   15 - 25
GN1580 Study the Golf Game with Henry Cotton
            Lon 1964, DJ   30 - 50
Cox, Charles (editor)
        Spalding's Official Golf Guide NY 1897-1942,
        wrappers, issued annually from 1897 to 1942
GN1617 1897   300 - 500
GN1618 1898-1900   200 - 350
GN1621 1901-1910   100 - 200
GN1631 1911-1920   75 - 125
GN1641 1921-1932   40 - 75
GN1653 1933-1942   30 - 50
Cox, Leo (editor)
GN1690 Fraser's International Golf Year Book
            NY 1923 1932 (annual), each   30 - 50
Cundell, John
GN1720 Rules of the Thistle Golf Club with Some Historical
            Accounts Relative to the Progress of the Game of Golf
            in Scotland Edinburgh 1824 (1st golf history) 5000 - 7000
Cunningham, Andrew S.
GN1750 The Golf Clubs Around Largo Bay Leven 1909 200 - 300
GN1760 Lundin Links, Upper & Lower Largo and Leven
            Portobello 1913, wrappers   200 - 300

Dante, Jim and Leo Diegel
GN1790 The Nine Bad Shots of Golf NY 1947, DJ   15 - 25
Darwin, Bernard (grandson of scientist Charles Darwin)
GN1820 British Golf Lon 1946, DJ   20 - 30
GN1830 A Friendly Round Lon 1922, DJ   50 - 75
GN1840 Golf Between the Two Wars Lon 1944, DJ   30 - 50
GN1850 The Golf Courses of Great Britain Lon 1925, DJ 125 - 200
GN1860 The Golf Courses of the British Isles Lon 1910 300 - 500
GN1870 A Golfer's Gallery of Old Masters Lon 1920
            (art print portfolio)   500 - 700
GN1880 Golfing By-Paths Lon 1946, DJ   30 - 50
GN1890 Green Memories Lon (1928), DJ   50 - 75
GN1900 Hints on Golf Lon (1912)   150 - 250
GN1910 A History of Golf in Britain Lon 1952, DJ   125 - 200
GN1920 James Braid Lon 1952, DJ   50 - 75
GN1930 Out of the Rough Lon (1932), DJ   50 - 75
GN1940 A Round of Golf on the London & North
            Eastern Railway York (1924), wrappers   75 - 125
GN1950 Rubs of the Green Lon 1936, DJ   50 - 75
GN1960 Tee Shots and Others Lon 1911   100 - 150
GN1970 The World That Fred Made Lon 1955, DJ   30 - 50
Davis, William H.
GN2000 100 Greatest Golf Courses - And Then Some
            Norwalk 1982, DJ   30 - 50
GN2010 Great Golf Courses of the World NY 1974, DJ   40 - 60
Demaret, Jimmy (3 time U.S. Masters Champion)
GN2040 My Partner, Ben Hogan NY 1954, DJ   20 - 30
Dobereiner, Peter
GN2070 The Book of Golf Disasters NY 1983, DJ   20 - 30
GN2080 The Glorious World of Golf NY 1973, DJ   30 - 50
GN2090 Golf Explained NY 1977, DJ   20 - 30
Duke of Beaufort (see Horace Hutchinson)
Duncan, George (British, Irish & French Open Champion)
GN2130 Golf at the Gallop Lon 1951, DJ   20 - 30
GN2140 Golf for Women Lon (1907)   100 - 150
GN2150 Present Day Golf Lon 1921, DJ   50 - 75
GN2151 NY 1921, DJ (1st American Ed)   50 - 75
Dunn, John Duncan
GN2180 ABC of Golf NY 1916   50 - 75
GN2190 Natural Golf NY 1931, slipcase   75 - 125
Dunn, Seymour
GN2210 Golf Fundamentals Lake Placid 1922   150 - 250
East, Victor
GN2240 Better Golf in 5 Minutes Englewood Cliffs 1956, DJ 20 - 30
Edgar, J. Douglas
GN2270 The Gate to Golf Wash 1920, deluxe ed, box,
            rubber "gate"   250 - 350
GN2271 Wash 1920 (trade ed)   100 - 150
Evans, Charles Jr. ("Chick"; 1916 U.S. Open champion)
GN2300 The Chick Evans Golf Book Chi 1921, 999 cys,
            signed   700 - 1000
GN2301 Chi 1921 (trade ed)   100 - 150
GN2310 Chick Evans' Golf Secrets NY (1922), wrappers 100 - 150
GN2320 Ida Broke NY 1929, DJ   50 - 75
GN2330 Tee, Fairway and Green NY 1926, DJ   50 - 75
Everhard, H. S. C.
GN2360 Golf: In Theory and Practice Lon 1896   150 - 250
GN2362 Lon 1901   100 - 150
GN2364 Lon 1910   75 - 125
GN2370 A History of the Royal and Ancient Golf Club,
            St. Andrews, From 1754-1900 Edinburgh
            1907 (1st history of St. Andrews)   800 - 1200

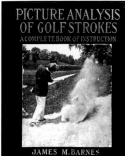
GN0350 (w/o DJ)

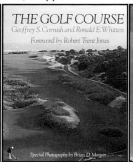
GN1460

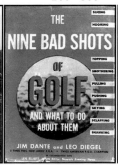
GN1790

GN2010

GN2190 (slipcover)

GN2760

Fall, R. G.
GN2400 **History of Golf at the Cape** Cape Town 1918,
wrappers 300 - 500
Farnie, Henry (see "A Keen Hand")
Ferguson, J. C.
GN2430 **The Royal and Ancient Game of Golf** Dumfries
1908, wrappers 100 - 150
Fitzpatrick, H. L.
GN2460 **Golf Don'ts** NY 1900 150 - 250
Flaherty, Thomas
GN2490 **The Masters** NY 1961, DJ 20 - 30
Forgan, Robert
GN2520 **The Golfer's Handbook** Cupar 1881 300 - 500
Forrest, James
GN2550 **The Basis of the Golf** Swing Lon 1925, DJ 30 - 50
GN2560 other titles by same author 30 - 50
Fulford, Harry
GN2590 **Golf's Little Ironies** Lon 1919 50 - 75
Gibson, Nevin H.
GN2620 **Encyclopedia of Golf** NY 1958, DJ 30 - 50
GN2622 NY 1964, DJ 20 - 30
GN2630 **Pictorial History of Golf** NY 1968, DJ 30 - 50
Golf Digest
GN2660 Various titles by this publisher, most are in $10-30 range.
Gordon, John
GN2690 **Understandable Golf** Buffalo (1920s) 30 - 50
The Gorham Manufacturing Co.
GN2720 **The Gorham Golf Book** NY 1903, 500 cys 500 - 700
Graffis, Herb (editor)
GN2750 **Esquire's World of Golf** NY 1965, DJ 20 - 30
GN2760 **The PGA** NY 1975, DJ 30 - 50
Greene, Kell
GN2790 **The Golf Swing of Bobby Jones** 50 - 75
Griffiths, E. M.
GN2820 **With Club and Caddie** Lon 1909 100 - 150
Grimsley, Will
GN2850 **Golf: Its History, People and Events**
Englewood Cliffs 1966, DJ 40 - 60
Hackbarth, John C.
GN2880 **The Discipline System of Golf** Madison 1928 30 - 50
GN2890 **The Key to Better Golf** Madison 1929 30 - 50
Hagan, Walter (The "Haid"; U.S., British Open Champion)
GN2920 **The Walter Hagan Story** NY 1956, DJ 50 - 75
GN2922 NY 1978, DJ 15 - 20
Hamilton, David
GN2960 **Early Golf at Edinburgh** Glasgow 1988, 300 cys 50 - 75
Hammond, Daryn
GN2990 **The Golf Swing: The Ernest Jones Method**
NY 1921 30 - 50
Hare, Burnham
GN3020 **Golfing Swing Simplified** Lon (early 1900s) 50 - 75
Harris, Robert
GN3050 **Sixty Years of Golf** Lon 1953, DJ 50 - 75
Haultain, Arnold
GN3080 **The Mystery of Golf** Bos 1908, deluxe ed, box 700 - 1000
GN3081 Bos 1908 (trade ed) 200 - 300
GN3083 NY 1910 100 - 150
GN3085 NY 1912 100 - 150
GN3088 NY 1965, slipcase 30 - 50
Hecker, Genevieve
GN3120 **Golf for Women** NY 1902 150 - 250
Helme, Eleanor
GN3150 **After the Ball** Lon 1931, DJ 100 - 150
Henderson, Ian
GN3180 **Golf in the Making** Yorkshire 1979, DJ 20 - 30
Hengel, Steven J. H. Van
GN3210 **Early Golf** Amsterdam 1982 30 - 50
Herd, Alexander
GN3240 **My Golfing Life** Lon 1923, DJ 100 - 150
Hillinthorn, Gerald
GN3270 **Your First Game of Golf** Lon 1891, wrappers 300 - 500
Hilton, Harold
GN3300 **Modern Golf** NY 1913 100 - 150

GN3310 **My Golfing Reminiscences** Lon 1907 200 - 300
GN3320 **The Royal and Ancient Game of Golf**
Lon 1912, 900 cys 1000 - 1500
GN3321 Lon 1912 (trade ed) 300 - 500
Historical Gossip (George Robb)
GN3350 **Historical Gossip About Golf and Golfers by a**
Golfer "Far and Sure" Edinburgh 1863, wrappers
(one of earliest golf histories) 3000 - 5000
Hogan, Ben (U.S. Open Champion 1948-50, 51, 53)
GN3380 **The Complete Guide to Golf** Ind 1955, DJ 20 - 30
GN3390 **The Modern Fundamentals of Golf** NY 1957,
deluxe ed, box 75 - 125
GN3391 NY 1957, DJ (trade ed) 20 - 30
GN3400 **Power Golf** NY 1948, DJ 30 - 50
Hooper, R. W. (editor)
GN3430 **The Game of Golf in East Africa** Nairobi 1953 125 - 200
Hopkinson, Cecil
GN3460 **Collecting Golf Books 1743-1938** Lon 1938 300 - 500
GN3462 Lon 1980 30 - 50
Houghton, George
Wrote about 40 books on golf, most are in the $15-25 range.
GN3500 **An Addict in Bunkerland** Lon 1962, DJ 15 - 25
GN3510 **Confessions of a Golf Addict** Lon 1959, DJ 15 - 25
GN3520 **Golf Addict Among the Irish** Lon 1967, DJ 10 - 15
GN3530 **Golf Addict Visits the USA** Lon 1955, wrappers 15 - 25
Hughes, Henry
GN3560 **Golf for the Late Beginner** Lon (1911) 40 - 60
Hughes, W. E.
GN3590 **Chronicles of the Blackheath Golfers** Lon 1897
(1st history of a golf club) 500 - 700
Hunter, Robert
GN3620 **The Links** NY 1926, DJ 300 - 500
Hutchinson, Horace (also see Fiction, Humor & Poetry;
1886 and 1887 British Amateur Champion)
GN3650 **Aspects of Golf** Bristol 1900, wrappers 150 - 250
GN3660 **The Book of Golf and Golfers** Lon 1899 150 - 250
GN3670 **Fifty Years of Golf** Lon 1919 150 - 250
GN3680 **Golf** Lon 1890 (Badminton Library of Sports) 200 - 300
GN3682 many later editions 50 - 150
GN3690 **Golf: A Complete History of the Game** Phil 1900
GN3700 **Golf Greens and Greenkeeping** Lon 1906 300 - 500
GN3710 **Golfing: The Oval Series of Games** Lon 1893 150 - 250
GN3720 **Hints on the Game of Golf** Edinburgh 1886 300 - 500
GN3730 **The New Book of Golf** Lon 1912 100 - 150
"Ignotus"
GN3760 **Golf in a Nutshell** Lon 1919 50 - 75
GN3761 NY 1919 50 - 75
Ito, Cho
GN3790 **Golfer's Treasures** Lon 1925 300 - 500
Johnston, Alastair
GN3820 **The Clapcott Papers** Edinburgh 1985, slipcase 75 - 125
Jones, Robert T. ("Bobby"; U.S., British Open Champion)
GN3850 **Bobby Jones on Golf** NY 1930, DJ 50 - 75
GN3852 NY 1966, DJ 20 - 30
GN3860 **Bobby Jones on the Basic Golf Swing**
Garden City 1969, DJ 30 - 50
GN3870 **Down the Fairway** NY 1927, DJ 75 - 125
GN3871 Lon 1927, DJ 75 - 125
GN3872 NY 1927, 300 cys, signed 800 - 1200
GN3880 **How to Play Golf** NY 1929 40 - 60
GN3890 **My Twelve Most Difficult Shots** NY 1927 100 - 150
GN3900 **Rights and Wrongs of Golf** NY 1936, wrappers 40 - 60
GN3910 **Short Cuts to Par Golf** NY 1931 40 - 60
Jones, Robert Trent
GN3940 **Golf Course Architecture** NY 1936 150 - 250
Keeler, O. B.
GN3970 **A Boy's Life of Bobby Jones** NY 1931, DJ 50 - 75
"A Keen Hand" (Henry B. Farnie)
GN4000 **The Golfer's Manual; Being an Historical and**
Descriptive Account of the National Game in
Scotland Cupar: Whitehead and Orr, 1857 (1st
golf instruction book) 3000 - 5000
GN4002 Cupar 1862 2000 - 3000
GN4004 St. Andrews (1870) 2000 - 3000
GN4006 Lon 1947, 750 cys 500 - 700

Kennedy, Patrick
GN4040 **Golf Club Trademarks American 1898-1930**
    South Burlington 1984, DJ   30 - 50

Kerr, Rev. John
GN4070 **The Golf Book of East Lothian** Edinburgh
    1896, 250 cys, large paper   700 - 1000
GN4071 500 cys   500 - 700

Kingzett, C. T.
GN4110 **The Evolution of the Rubbercored Golf Ball**
    Lon 1904   150 - 250

Kirkaldy, Andrew
GN4140 **Fifty Years of Golf: My Memories** Lon 1921   75 - 125
GN4141 NY 1921   75 - 125

Leach, Henry
GN4170 **Great Golfers in the Making** Lon 1907 150 - 250
GN4180 **The Happy Golfer** Lon 1914 150 - 250
GN4190 **Letters of a Modern Golfer to His Grandfather**
    Lon 1910   100 - 150
GN4200 **The Spirit of the Links** Lon 1907 100 - 150

Lee, James P.
GN4230 **Golf and Golfing: A Practical Manual** NY 1895 200 - 300
GN4240 **Golf in America** NY 1895 (1st book about
    American Golf)   400 - 600

Lees, Peter W.
GN4270 **Care of the Greens** NY 1918 100 - 150

Leigh-Bennett, E. P.
GN4300 **Some Friendly Fairways** Lon 1930 40 - 60
GN4310 **Southern Golf** Lon 1935 40 - 60

Leitch, Cecil
GN4340 **Golf:** Lon 1922 40 - 60
GN4350 **Golf for Girls** Lon 1911 100 - 150
GN4360 **Golf Simplified** Lon 1924 30 - 50

Lema, Tony
GN4390 **Golfer's Gold** Bos 1964, DJ 20 - 30

Leng, John
GN4420 **Leng's Golfer's Manual** Dundee 1907 250 - 350

Life Magazine
GN4450 **Fore! Life's Book for Golfers** NY 1900 300 - 500

Locke, Bobby
GN4480 **Bobby Locke on Golf** NY 1954, DJ 20 - 30

Lockyer, Sir Joseph Norman
GN4510 **The Rules of Golf: Being the St. Andrews
    Rules for the Game** Lon 1896 300 - 500

Longhurst, Henry
GN4540 **Golf** Lon 1937, DJ 30 - 50
GN4550 **Golf Mixture** Lon 1952, DJ 30 - 50
GN4560 **Round in Sixty-Eight** Lon 1953, DJ 30 - 50

Lopez, Nancy
GN4590 **Education of a Woman Golfer** NY 1979, DJ 15 - 25

Loring, Phillip Quincy
GN4620 **Rhymes of a Duffer** Portland 1914 50 - 75

Low, John Laing
GN4650 **F.G. Tait: A Record...** Lon (1900) (1st golf
    biography)   300 - 500
GN4660 **Nisbet's Golf Year Book** Lon, published annually
    1905-1914, 10 vol, each vol 50 - 75

MacArthur, Charles
GN4690 **The Golfer's Annual for 1869-70** Ayr 1870,
    wrappers   300 - 500

MacBeth, James Currie
GN4720 **Golf From A to Z** Lon 1935, DJ 20 - 30

MacDonald, Charles
    Considered the first American golf course architect.
GN4750 **Scotland's Gift; Golf Reminiscences 1872-1927**
    NY 1928, 260 cys, box 500 - 700
GN4751 NY 1928, DJ (1st trade ed) 250 - 350

MacDonald, Robert G.
GN4780 **Golf** Chi 1927, DJ 30 - 50
GN4790 **Golf at a Glance** Chi 1931 20 - 30
GN4800 **How to Improve Your Golf** Chi 1952, wrappers 15 - 25

MacKenzie, Dr. Alister (golf course architect)
    Helped design Augusta National with "Bobby" Jones.
GN4830 **Dr. MacKenzie's Golf Architecture** Droitwich 1982 50 - 75
GN4840 **Golf Architecture** Lon 1920, DJ 200 - 300

MacKern, Mrs. Louis
GN4870 **Our Lady of the Green** Lon 1899 200 - 300

MacLean, G. A.
GN4900 **Golf Through the Ages** LA 1923 30 - 50

MacLennon, R. J.
GN4930 **Golf at Gleneagles** Glasgow (1928) 100 - 150

MacPherson, Duncan
GN4960 **Golf Simplified** Chi 1936 15 - 25

Maltby, Ralph
GN4990 **Golf Club Design** Newark 1974 30 - 50

Martin, H. B. (Harry Brownlaw)
GN5020 **Fifty Years of American Golf** NY 1936, DJ 200 - 300
GN5022 NY 1966, box 50 - 75
GN5030 **Golf Yarns** NY 1913 40 - 60
GN5040 **St. Andrews (New York) Golf Club 1888-1938**
    NY 1938, 500 cys 250 - 350

Martin, John Stuart
GN5070 **The Curious History of the Golf Ball** NY 1968, DJ 40 - 60
GN5071 NY 1968, 500 cys, box 300 - 500

Mathieson, Donald
GN5110 **Golfer's Handbook** Edinburgh 1898-1910 250 - 350
GN5120 1911-1925 150 - 250
GN5130 1926-1930 100 - 150
GN5140 1931-1941 50 - 75

Maughan, William Charles
GN5170 **Picturesque Musselburgh and its Golf Links**
    Paisley (1906), wrappers 400 - 600

McAlister, Alexander
GN5200 **The Eternal Verities of Golf** Greensboro (1911),
    wrappers   125 - 200

McAndrew, J.
GN5230 **Golfing: Step by Step** Glasgow (1910) 75 - 125

McBain, J.
GN5260 **Golf: Dean's Champion Handbook** Lon 1897 150 - 250

McCullough, J.
GN5290 **Golf: Practical Hints and the Rules** Lon 1899,
    wrappers   200 - 300

McMurtrie, J. (editor)
GN5320 **The Golfer's Guide** Glasgow 1902 100 - 150
GN5322 Glasgow 1903 75 - 125

McPherson, Rev. J. G.
GN5360 **Golf and Golfers; Past and Present**
    Edinburgh 1891 300 - 500

McSpadden, Joseph Walker
GN5390 **How to Play Golf** NY (1907) 100 - 150

Metz, Dick (Richard Carleton)
GN5420 **The Secret to Par Golf** NY 1940, DJ 30 - 50

Metzger, Sol
GN5450 **Putting Analyzed** NY 1929, DJ 30 - 50

Middlecoff, Cary
GN5480 **Advanced Golf** Englewood Cliffs 1957, DJ 15 - 25
GN5490 **Golf Doctor** NY 1950, DJ 15 - 25

Miller, Rev. T. D.
GN5530 **Famous Scottish Links and Other Golfing
    Papers** Edinburgh 1911 400 - 600
GN5540 **History of Royal Perth Golfing Society**
    Perth 1935 200 - 300

Mitchell, Abe and J. Martin
GN5570 **Down to Scratch** Lon 1933 30 - 50
GN5580 **Essentials of Golf** Lon 1927, DJ 20 - 30
GN5590 **Length on the Links** Lon 1935, DJ 30 - 50

Montague, William Kelly
GN5630 **The Golf of Our Fathers** Duluth 1952 125 - 200

Moran, Frank
GN5650 **Golfer's Gallery** Edinburgh 1946, DJ 20 - 30

Morrison, Alex J.
GN5680 **Pocket Guide to Better Golf** NY 1934, DJ 20 - 30

Morrison, J. S. F. (John Stanton Fleming)
GN5710 **Around Golf** Lon 1939, DJ 30 - 50

Murdoch, Joseph
GN5740 **Library of Golf 1743-1966** Detroit 1968 40 - 60

Murray, Dr. C. M.
GN5770 **Greenskeeping in South Africa** Cape Town
    1932, wrappers 100 - 150

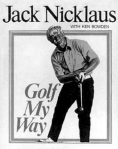

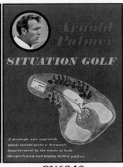
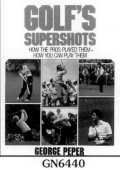
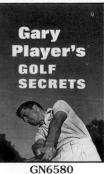

GN5830	GN5980	GN5990	GN6340	GN6440	GN6580

Musser, H. Burton
GN5800 **Turf Management** NY 1950, DJ — 30 - 50

Nelson, Byron (1939 U.S. Open Champion)
GN5830 **Winning Golf** NY 1946, DJ — 20 - 30
GN5832 Lon 1947, DJ — 20 - 30

Newman, Joseph
GN5870 **Official Golf Guide of America for 1900**
Garden City 1900 — 300 - 500
GN5880 **Official Golf Guide to the United Kingdom 1903-1904** Lon 1903 — 300 - 500

"Niblick" (Charles Stedman Hanks)
Niblick is an old golf term for a club with a heavy iron head for lofting balls out of a cart track.
GN5910 **Hints to Golfers** Bos 1902 — 100 - 150
GN5920 later editions — 50 - 75

Nichols, Bobby
GN5950 **Never Say Never: The Psychology of Winning Golf** NY 1965, DJ — 15 - 20

Nicklaus, Jack (U.S. Open, British Open & U.S. Masters champion)
GN5980 **Golf My Way** NY 1974, DJ — 10 - 15
GN5990 **The Greatest Game of All: My Life in Golf**
NY 1969, DJ — 10 - 15
GN6000 **Jack Nicklaus' Lesson Tee** NY 1977, DJ — 10 - 15
GN6010 **Jack Nicklaus' Playing Lesson** NY 1977, DJ — 10 - 15
GN6020 **Jack Nicklaus, The Full Swing** NY 1984, DJ — 10 - 15
GN6030 **My 55 Ways to Lower Your Golf Score**
NY 1964, DJ — 15 - 25
GN6040 **On and Off the Fairway** NY 1978, DJ — 10 - 15
GN6050 **Take a Tip From Me** NY 1968, DJ — 15 - 20
GN6060 **Winning Golf** NY 1969, DJ — 15 - 20

Norman, Greg
GN6090 **Greg Norman: My Story** Lon 1983, DJ — 20 - 30

Norval, Ronald
GN6120 **King of the Links: The Story of Bobby Locke**
Cape Town (1951) — 40 - 60

"Old Golfer" (L. Everage)
GN6150 **Golf on a New Principle: Iron Clubs Superceded**
Bournemouth 1897 — 150 - 250

"Old Player" (Col. W. E. Riordan)
GN6180 **Golf and How to Play It** Lon 1905 — 100 - 150
GN6182 Lon 1912 — 75 - 125

Olman, John and Morton
GN6210 **The Encyclopedia of Golf Collectibles**
Florence 1985 — 20 - 30

Ouimet, Francis
GN6240 **A Game of Golf: A Book of Reminiscences**
NY 1932, 550 cys — 250 - 350
GN6241 NY 1932, DJ (1st trade ed) — 50 - 75
GN6250 **Golf Facts For Young People** NY 1921 — 50 - 75

Oyler, T. H.
GN6280 **The Golfer's Glossary** Maidstone (1920), wrappers — 75 - 125

Palmer, Arnold
GN6310 **Arnold Palmer's Golf Book: Hit It Hard**
NY 1961, DJ — 15 - 25
GN6320 **My Game and Yours** NY 1965, DJ — 15 - 25
GN6330 **Portrait of a Professional Golfer** South
Norwalk 1964 — 40 - 60
GN6340 **Situation Golf** NY 1970, DJ — 20 - 30

Park, Jr., Willie
GN6370 **The Art of Putting** Edinburgh 1920 — 150 - 250

GN6380 **The Game of Golf** Lon 1896 (1st instructor
written by a professional golfer) — 300 - 500

Parrish, Samuel L.
GN6410 **Some Facts, Reflections and Personal
Reminiscences & Etc.** NY 1923, wrappers — 75 - 125

Peper, George
GN6440 **Golf's Supershots** NY 1982, DJ — 20 - 30

Peter, H. Thomas
GN6470 **Reminiscences of Golf and Golfers** Edinburgh
1890, wrappers — 300 - 500

Pickworth, H. O. and John Reeve
GN6500 **Golf, 'The Pickworth Way'** Sydney 1949 (photos
reversed for left handers) — 30 - 50

Piper, Charles V. and Russell A. Oakley
GN6530 **Turf For Golf Courses** NY 1917 — 40 - 60
GN6532 NY 1919 — 30 - 50

Player, Gary
GN6570 **Gary Player's Golf Class** Lon 1967, DJ — 10 - 15
GN6580 **Gary Player's Golf Secrets** Englewood Cliffs
1962, DJ — 15 - 25
GN6590 **Golf Tips From Gary Player** Lon 1967, DJ — 10 - 15

Plimpton, George
GN6630 **The Bogey Man** NY 1968, DJ — 15 - 25

Pole-Soppitt, Capt. H. A.
GN6660 **The Eastern Counties Golf Links Guide**
Suffolk 1893 — 125 - 200

Pollock, William H.
GN6690 **You, The Golfer** Milwaukee (1937) — 40 - 60

Prain, Eric M.
GN6720 **The Oxford and Cambridge Golfing Society
1898-1948** Lon 1949 — 40 - 60

Price, Charles
GN6750 **The American Golfer** (editor) NY 1964, DJ — 30 - 50
GN6760 **The Carolina Low Country: Birth Place of
American Golf, 1786** NY 1980, DJ — 20 - 30
GN6770 **The World of Golf** NY 1962, DJ — 30 - 50

Professional Golfers Association of America
GN6800 **Official Tournament Record** Dunedin, FL,
1941, wrappers (1st PGA Guide) — 50 - 75
GN6810 **Tournament Player Catalog** Dunedin, FL,
1959-1963, 5 vol, wrappers, each — 15 - 25

Pulver, P. C.
GN6840 **American Annual Golf Guide** NY, issued
annually 1916-1932, 1916 — 50 - 75
GN6842 1917-1920 — 40 - 60
GN6850 1921-1932 — 30 - 50

Ray, Edward
GN6880 **Driving, Approaching and Putting** Lon 1922 — 30 - 50
GN6881 NY 1922 — 30 - 50
GN6890 **Inland Golf** Lon 1915 — 100 - 150
GN6891 NY 1915 — 100 - 150

Read, Opie
GN6930 **Opie Read on Golf** Chi (1925) — 50 - 75

Reid, William F. J. I.
GN6960 **Golfing Reminiscences the Growth of the
Game 1887-1925** Edinburgh 1925 — 100 - 150

Revell, Alexander H.
GN6990 **Pro and Con of Golf** Chi 1915 — 50 - 75

Revolta, Johnny
GN7020 **Johnny Revolta's Short Cuts to Good Golf**
NY 1949, DJ — 15 - 25

Rice, Grantland
GN7050 The Bobby Jones Story: From the Writings
of O.B. Keeler Atlanta 1953, DJ   40 - 60
GN7060 The Duffer's Handbook of Golf NY 1926,
500 cys   250 - 350
GN7061 NY 1926, DJ (1st trade ed)   40 - 60

Richardson, W. D.
GN7090 Golfer's Year Book NY 1930-33   30 - 50
GN7096 NY 1938-40   20 - 30

Robb, George (also see Historical Gossip)
GN7130 Manual of the Bruntsfield Links Edinburgh 1867 800 - 1200
GN7132 Edinburgh 1868   700 - 1000

Robbie, J. Cameron
GN7160 The Chronicle of the Royal Golfing Society of
Edinburgh 1735-1935 Edinburgh 1936   100 - 150

Roberts, Henry
GN7190 The Green Book of Golf SF (1914)   40 - 60

Robertson, A. J.
GN7220 The ABC of Golf Lon (1904)   75 - 125

Robertson, Mrs. Gordon
GN7250 Hints to Lady Golfers Lon 1909   50 - 75

Robertson, James K.
GN7280 St. Andrews: Home of Golf St. Andrews 1967   40 - 60

Robinson, W. Heath
GN7310 Humors of Golf Lon 1923   30 - 50
GN7311 NY 1923   30 - 50

Rose, William Ganson
GN7340 Cut Down That Score: The Psychology of Golf
Cleveland 1925   50 - 75

Ryan, Joseph E. G.
GN7370 Golfer's Green Book Chi 1901   100 - 150
GN7372 Chi 1902   75 - 125
GN7374 Chi 1903   75 - 125

Salmond, D. S.
GN7410 Reminiscences of Arbroath and St. Andrews
Arbroath 1905   200 - 300

Salmond, Dr. J. B.
GN7440 Story of the R. & A. Lon 1956, DJ   40 - 60

Sarazen, Gene
GN7470 Gene Sarazen's Commonsense Golf Tips Chi 1924 40 - 60
GN7480 Thirty Years of Championship Golf NY 1950, DJ 75 - 125

Saxe, John Godfrey
GN7510 The Jones' Golf Swing and Other Suggestions
NY (1948)   20 - 30

Schon, Leslie
GN7540 The Psychology of Golf Lon 1922   30 - 50
GN7541 NY 1922   30 - 50

Schrite, J. Ellsworth
GN7570 Divots for Dubs Fernwood, PA 1934   20 - 30

"Scot" (F. A. Bald)
GN7600 Consistent Golf, or How to Become a
Champion Lon (1934)   40 - 60

Scott and Sons, O. M.
GN7630 The Putting Greens Marysville 1931, wrappers   30 - 50
GN7640 The Seeding and Care of Golf Courses
Marysville 1922   40 - 60

Senat, Prosper L.
GN7670 Through the Greens and Golfer's Yearbook
Phil 1898, wrappers   200 - 300

Servos, Lancelot C.
GN7700 Practical Instruction in Golf Bos 1905   100 - 150

Seton-Karr, Sir Henry
GN7730 Golf: Greening's Useful Handbook Series
Lon 1907, wrappers   150 - 250

Seymour, Bert
GN7760 All About Golf Lon 1924   40 - 60

Shelly, Warner
GN7790 Pine Valley Golf Club, A Chronicle Clementon
1982   50 - 75

Shepherd, Jr., James
GN7820 Golf Shots Hyannis, MA, 1924   30 - 50

Simpson, Sir Walter
GN7850 The Art of Golf Edinburgh 1887 (1st use of
photographs to demonstrate technique)   600 - 800

Smith, Alex
GN7880 Lessons in Golf NY 1907   100 - 150

Smith, Charles
GN7910 The Aberdeen Golfers Lon 1909, 150 cys   300 - 500

Smith, Garden C.
GN7940 Golf Lon 1897   125 - 200
GN7950 Side Lights on Golf Lon (1907)   100 - 150
GN7960 The World of Golf: The Isthmian Library
Lon 1898   125 - 200

Smith, J. S. K. (Joseph Stanley Kellet)
GN7990 The Foundations of Golf Lon 1925   30 - 50
GN7992 NY 1926   30 - 50

Smith, Robert Howie
GN8030 The Golfer's Year Book For 1866 Ayr 1867
(1st golf annual)   1000 - 1500

Snead, Sam (1949, 1952, 1954 U.S. Masters Champion)
GN8060 How to Hit a Golf Ball From Any Sort of Lie
Garden City 1950, wrappers   15- 25
GN8070 How to Play Golf Garden City 1946, DJ   20 - 30
GN8080 Natural Golf NY 1953, DJ   20 - 30
GN8090 Sam Snead on Golf NY 1961, DJ   15 - 20
GN8100 Sam Snead's Quick Way to Better Golf
NY 1938, wrappers   30 - 50

Soutar, Daniel G.
GN8130 The Australian Golfer Sydney 1906   125 - 200

Southern California Golf Association
GN8160 The History of Golf in Southern California
LA 1925, wrappers   75 - 125

Spalding, Anthony
GN8190 Golf for Beginners Lon (1935), wrappers   20 - 30

Springman, J. F.
GN8220 The Beauty of Pebble Beach Phil 1964   100 - 150
GN8230 The Many Faces of the American Golf Course
Camden (1963)   30 - 50

Stancliffe (Stanley Clifford; also Fiction, Humor & Poetry)
GN8260 The Autobiography of a Caddy-Bag Lon 1924   40 - 60
GN8270 Golf Do's and Don'ts Lon 1902   40 - 60

Stark, A.
GN8300 Physical Training for Golfers St. Andrews
(1937), wrappers   30 - 50

Steel, Donald
GN8330 Encyclopedia of Golf NY 1975, DJ   30 - 50

Stewart, James Lindsey
GN8360 Golfiana Miscellanea Glasgow 1887   400 - 600

Stoddard, William Leavitt
GN8390 The New Golfer's Almanac Bos 1909   40 - 60

Stringer, Mabel E.
GN8420 Golfing Reminiscences Lon 1924   100 - 150

GN6630

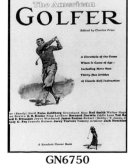
GN6750

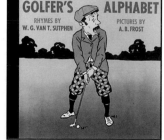
GN8450

GN9820

GF4112

Sutphen, W. G. van T.
GN8450 The Golfer's Alphabet Rutland 1967
        (facsimile reprint)   30 - 50
Sutton, Martin A. F.
GN8480 Golf Courses: Design, Construction and
        Upkeep Lon 1933   300 - 500
Sutton, Martin H. F.
GN8510 Book of the Links: A Symposium on Golf
        Lon 1912   300 - 500
GN8520 Layout and Upkeep of Golf Courses and
        Putting Greens Lon (1906)   300 - 500
Sweny, Harry Roy
GN8550 Keep Your Eye on the Ball and Your Right Knee Stiff
        Albany 1898 (2nd instructor published in U.S.)   100 - 150
Taylor, Bert Leston
GN8580 A Line O'Gowf or Two NY 1923, DJ   30 - 50
Taylor, Dawson
GN8610 The Masters South Brunswick 1973   50 - 75
Taylor, J. H. (John Henry)
GN8640 Golf, My Life's Work Lon 1943, DJ   75 - 125
GN8650 Taylor on Golf Lon 1902   100 - 150
GN8651 NY 1902   100 - 150
Taylor, Joshua
GN8680 The Art of Golf Lon (1913)   150 - 250
GN8690 The Lure of the Links Lon 1920   75 - 125
Thomas, George C.
GN8730 Golf Course Architecture in America LA 1927 300 - 500
Thompson, W. J.
GN8760 Common Sense Golf Toronto 1923   30 - 50
Thomson, James
GN8790 Hit 'Em a Mile NY 1940, wrappers   20 - 30
Tolley, Cyril J. H.
GN8820 The Modern Golfer Glasgow 1924   30 - 50
GN8821 NY 1924   30 - 50
Travers, Jerome D. (1915 U.S. Open Champion)
GN8850 The Fifth Estate: Thirty Years of Golf
        NY 1926, DJ   75 - 125
GN8860 Travers' Golf Book NY 1913   75 - 125
GN8870 The Winning Shot NY 1915   100 - 150
Travis, Walter
GN8900 The Art of Putting Lon 1904, wrappers   75 - 125
GN8910 Practical Golf NY 1901   75 - 125
Tripp, William A.
GN8940 The Geometry of Golf NY 1960   30 - 50
Triscott, C. Pette
GN8970 Golf in Six Lessons Lon 1924   30 - 50
GN8972 Phil (1925)   30 - 50
Tufts, Richard S.
GN9000 The Scottish Invasion Pinehurst 1962   50 - 75
Tulloch, W. W.
GN9030 The Life and Times of Tom Morris Lon 1982
        (reprint of 1908 book)   100 - 150
GN9040 The Life of Tom Morris Lon 1908   300 - 500
Turgeon, A. J.
GN9070 Turf Grass Management 1980   30 - 50
Uzzell, Thomas H.
GN9100 Golf in the World's Oldest Mountains
        Murray Bay (1926)   100 - 150
Vaile, P. A.
GN9130 Golf on the Green NY 1915   50 - 75
GN9140 How to Learn Golf NY 1922, wrappers   30 - 50
GN9150 The Illustrated Rules of Golf and the Etiquette
        of the Game Chi 1919   50 - 75
GN9160 Modern Golf Lon 1909   50 - 75
GN9170 The New Golf NY 1916   40 - 60
GN9180 Putting Made Easy Chi (1935)   40 - 60
GN9190 The Short Game Chi 1929, wrappers   20 - 30
GN9200 The Soul of Golf Lon 1912   50 - 75
Vander Meulen, John M.
GN9230 Getting Out of the Rough NY 1926, DJ   20 - 30
Vardon, Harry
GN9260 The Complete Golfer Lon 1905   200 - 300
GN9261 NY 1905 (1st American ed)   200 - 300
GN9270 The Gist of Golf Lon 1922   40 - 60

GN9271 NY 1922   40 - 60
GN9280 How to Play Golf Lon 1912   40 - 60
GN9290 My Golfing Life Lon 1933, DJ   75 - 125
GN9300 Success at Golf Lon (1912)   75 - 125
Venturi, Ken
GN9330 Comeback: The Ken Venturi Story NY 1966, DJ 15 - 25
GN9340 Venturi Analysis NY 1981, DJ   15 - 25
"Victim" (D. W. C. Falls)
GN9370 An A.B.C. of Golf 1898, wrappers   300 - 500
W. E. F. (Walter E. Fairlie)
GN9400 The Old Course of St. Andrews: Plans, with
        Names of Holes and Bunkers St. Andrews
        (1908), wrappers (1st book about St. Andrews) 125 - 200
Webb, Warren H.
GN9430 Lessons in Golf Lon 1907   100 - 150
Wendehack, Clifford C.
GN9460 Golf and Country Clubs NY 1929   100 - 150
GN9470 Recent Golf and Country Clubs in America NY 200 - 300
Wethered, H. N. & Tom Simpson (golf course architects)
GN9500 The Architectural Side of Golf Lon 1929, DJ 300 - 500
GN9510 Design for Golf Lon 1952   40 - 60
GN9520 The Perfect Golfer Lon 1931   75 - 125
Wethered, Roger
GN9550 Golf From Two Sides Lon 1922   30 - 50
Whigham, H. J.
GN9580 How to Play Golf Chi 1897 (1st instructor
        published in U.S. & 1st to use action photos) 200 - 300
White, Jack
GN9610 Easier Golf Lon 1924   30 - 50
GN9620 Putting Lon 1921   30 - 50
Whitlatch, Marshall
GN9650 Golf for Beginners and Others NY 1910   50 - 75
Whitton, Ivo
GN9680 Golf Melbourne 1937, wrappers   30 - 50
Williams, Lewis
GN9710 Golf Without Tears 1904   30 - 50
Wilson, Enid
GN9740 A Gallery of Woman Golfers Lon 1961, DJ   30 - 50
Wind, Herbert Warren
GN9770 The Complete Golfer NY 1954, DJ   30 - 50
GN9780 Following Through Lon 1986, DJ   30 - 50
GN9790 Herbert Warren Wind's Golf Book NY 1971, DJ 50 - 75
GN9800 On Tour with Harry Sprague NY 1960, DJ   20 - 30
GN9810 The Story of American Golf NY 1948, DJ   100 - 150
GN9812 NY 1956, DJ   75 - 125
GN9814 NY 1975, DJ   20 - 30
GN9820 Tips From the Top NY 1955, DJ   20 - 30
Wood, Harry B.
GN9850 Golfing Curios and "The Like" Lon 1910   400 - 600
GN9852 Lon 1911, 150 cys   500 - 700
Wright, Harry
GN9880 A Short History of Golf in Mexico and the
        Mexico City Country Club NY 1938   200 - 300
Youmans, Thomas Grant
GN9910 Play Golf with Greater Ease Columbus 1939, DJ 20 - 30
Zaharias, Mildred "Babe"
GN9940 Championship Golf NY 1948, DJ   20 - 30
GN9950 This Life I've Led: My Autobiography NY 1956, DJ 20 - 30

Fiction, Humor & Poetry
Adams, Herbert (Jonathan Gray)
    Wrote about 60 mystery novels; those listed below have a golf theme. They are worth half without the dust jackets.
GF0400 Body in the Bunker Lon 1935, DJ   50 - 75
GF0401 Bos 1935, DJ   50 - 75
GF0410 Death off the Fairway Lon 1936, DJ   50 - 75
GF0420 Death on the First Tee Lon 1957, DJ   20 - 30
GF0430 The Golf House Murder Bos 1933, DJ   50 - 75
GF0440 The Nineteenth Hole Mystery Lon 1939, DJ   50 - 75
GF0450 The Perfect Round: Tales of the Links
        Lon 1927, DJ   75 - 125
GF0460 The Secret of Bogey House Lon 1924, DJ   50 - 75
GF0462 Bos 1925, DJ   40 - 60
Allerton, Mark (also see Non-Fiction)
GF0610 The Girl on the Green Lon 1914   200 - 300

Andre, Richard
GF0710   Colonel Bogey's Sketch Book Lon 1897, bds   300 - 500
GF0720   Golf Plays and Recitations Lon 1903   150 - 250
Anonymous
GF0810   Poems on Golf Edinburgh 1867   1500 - 2500
GF2220   Shakespeare on Golf (see W. A. Knight)   200 - 300
Boynton, H. W.
GF0910   The Golfer's Rubaiyat Chi 1901   200 - 300
GF0912   Lon 1903   100 - 150
Briggs, Clare
GF1010   Golf: The Book of a Thousand Chuckles Chi 1916   50 - 75
Brown, Kenneth
GF1110   Putter Perkins Bos 1923, DJ   40 - 60
Browning, Robert H. K. (also see Non-Fiction)
GF1210   The Stymie: A Miscellany of Golfing Humor
            and Wit Glasgow 1910, wrappers   100 - 150
Camp, Walter
GF1310   Drives and Putts: A Book of Golf Stories
            Bos 1899   200 - 300
Carnegie, George Fullerton
GF1410   Golfiana or Niceties Connected with the Game
            of Golf Edinburgh 1833 (2nd book about golf)   3000 - 5000
GF1412   Edinburgh 1842   2500 - 3500
Frome, David
GF1510   Murder on the Sixth Hole Lon 1931, DJ   40 - 60
Gault, William Campbell
GF1610   The Long Green NY 1965, DJ   20 - 30
Graves, Charles
GF1660   Candid Caddies Lon 1935, DJ   40 - 60
Hall, Holworthy
GF1710   Dormie One and Other Golf Stories NY 1917, DJ   75 - 125
Hutchinson, Horace (also see Non-Fiction)
GF1810   Bert Edward, the Golf Caddie Lon 1903   100 - 150
GF1820   A Golfing Pilgrim on Many Links NY 1898   250 - 350
J. A. C. K. (J. McCullough)
GF1910   Golf in the Year 2000 Lon 1892   300 - 500
GF1914   Cinti 1984   20 - 30
Keene, Francis Bowler
GF2010   Lyrics of the Links NY 1923   40 - 60
Kennard, Mrs. Edward
GF2110   The Golf Lunatic and His Cycling Wife Lon 1902   100 - 150
GF2120   The Sorrows of a Golfer's Wife Lon 1896   125 - 200
Knight, William Angus (also see "Novice")
GF2210   On the Links Edinburgh 1889   200 - 300
GF2220   Shakespeare on Golf Edinburgh 1885   200 - 300
GF2230   Stories of Golf Lon 1894   150 - 250
Knox, Edmund
GF2280   Mr. Punch on the Links NY 1929   30 - 50
Lang, Andrew
GF2340   A Batch of Golfing Papers Lon 1892   100 - 150
MacNamara, Dr. T. J.
GF2410   The Gentle Golfer Bristol 1905, wrappers   100 - 150
"Marietta"
GF2510   Six Golfing Stories Dublin 1905, wrappers   100 - 150
Mathison, Thomas
GF2610   The Goff, An Heroi-Comical Poem in Three
            Cantos Edinburgh 1743, wrappers (1st book
            about golf)   15000 - 25000
GF2612   Edinburgh 1763   10000 - 15000
GF2614   Edinburgh 1793   3000 - 5000
"A Member" (Dr. Stone)
GF2710   The Duffer's Golf Club Papers Montrose 1891,
            wrappers   125 - 200
Murphy, Michael
GF2760   Golf in the Kingdom NY 1972, DJ   30 - 50
Myers, Edward
GF2810   Experiences of a Caddy Phil (1927)   75 - 125
"Novice" (William Angus Knight)
GF2910   On the Links, Being Golfing Stories by Various Hands
            with Shakespeare on Golf Edinburgh 1889   200 - 300
"Orion" (W. W. Tulloch)
GF3010   Lost and Won, or, Fresh Golfing Pastures
            Glasgow 1883   200 - 300

Peck, Samuel Minturn
GF3110   The Golf Girl NY 1899   250 - 350
Peille, Pentland
GF3210   Clanbrae: A Golfing Idyll Edinburgh 1908   40 - 60
Punch
GF3310   The Funny Side of Golf From the Pages of
            Punch Lon 1909   100 - 150
GF3320   Mr. Punch's Golf Stories Lon (1909)   100 - 150
R. A. S.
GF3410   The Links: An Auld Kirk Allegory Edinburgh
            (1895), wrappers   200 - 300
Ralston, W.
GF3510   North Again, Golfing This Time Edinburgh
            (1894), wrappers   150 - 250
Reynolds, Frank
GF3610   The Frank Reynold's Golf Book: Drawings
            From "Punch" Lon 1932   50 - 75
GF3611   NY 1932   50 - 75
Rice, Grantland
GF3660   Duffer's Handbook of Golf NY 1926, DJ   50 - 75
Ricornus, C. A. P. (William D. Moffat)
GF3710   The Goat Club Golf Book NY 1911   75 - 125
Risk, Robert K.
GF3810   Songs of the Links Edinburgh 1904   100 - 150
Rowland, Ralph
GF3910   The Humours of Golf: 24 Pen Etchings of the
            Royal and Ancient Game Lon 1903   150 - 250
Sabin, Edwin L. (also see Americana)
GF4010   The Magic Mashie and Other Golfish Stories
            NY 1902   50 - 75
Santee, Ross (also see Americana)
GF4110   The Bar X Golf Course NY (1933), DJ   40 - 60
GF4112   Flagstaff 1971, DJ   15 - 25
Scholz, Jackson
GF4210   Fairway Challenge NY 1964, DJ   15 - 20
Scollard, Clinton
GF4310   The Epic of Golf Bos 1923, DJ   75 - 125
Shaw, Joseph T.
GF4410   Out of the Rough NY 1934, DJ   75 - 125
Shotte, Cleeke (John Hogben)
GF4510   The Golf Craze: Sketches and Rhymes
            Edinburgh (1905)   150 - 250
Simpson, Harold
GF4610   Seven Stages of Golf, and Other Golf Stories
            in Pictures and Verse Lon 1909   300 - 500
Simpson, S. R.
GF4710   A Green Crop (1937)   40 - 60
Smith, Everett
GF4760   Synonym Golf NY 1931, DJ   30 - 50
Somerville, John
GF4810   A Foursome at Rye Rye 1898, wrappers   200 - 300
"Stancliffe" (also see Non-Fiction)
GF4910   An Astounding Golf Match Lon 1944   50 - 75
Steele, Chester
GF5000   The Golf Course Mystery Cleveland 1919, DJ   75 - 125
Stewart, T. Ross
GF5110   Lays of the Links: A Score of Parodies
            Edinburgh 1895   200 - 300
Stobart, M. A.
GF5210   Won at the Last Hole A Golfing Romance
            Lon 1893 (1st golf novel)   200 - 300
Sutphen, W. G. van T.
GF5310   The Golfer's Alphabet NY 1898   300 - 500
GF5312   Rutland 1967   30 - 50
GF5320   The Golficide and Other Tales of the Fair Green
            NY 1898 (1st golf fiction published in U.S.)   200 - 300
GF5330   The Nineteenth Hole: Being Tales of the Fair
            Green NY 1901   150 - 250
Taylor, Arthur V.
GF5510   Origines Golfianae Newark 1912, box   125 - 200
Thomson, John
GF5610   Golfing and Other Poems and Songs Glasgow
            1893, 50 cys   500 - 700
GF5611   Glasgow 1893 (1st trade ed)   250 - 350

Tillinghast, A. W. (golf course architect)
GF5710 **Cobble Valley Golf Yarns and Other Sketches**
Phil (1915)   250 - 350
GF5720 **The Mutt and Other Golf Stories** 1925   200 - 300

Triefus, Paul
GF5810 **The Most Excellent Historie of MacHamlet & Etc**
Lon 1922   50 - 75

Twaddler, A.
GF5910 **Golf Twaddle** Edinburgh 1897, wrappers   100 - 150

Tyner, Frederick D.
GF6010 **The Golfer's Dream** Minn 1936   20 - 30

Van Loan, Charles E.
GF6110 **Fore: Golf Stories** NY 1918

Verbeck, Frank
GF6210 **A Handbook of Golf For Bears** NY 1900   300 - 500

Watson, A. Campbell
GF6310 **Podson's Golfing Year** Edinburgh (1930) 40 - 60

Weibling, W. Hastings
GF6410 **Fore: The Call of the Links** Bos 1909   100 - 150
GF6420 **Locker Room Ballads** NY 1925, DJ   75 - 125
GF6430 **On and Off the Links** Hamilton 1921, wrappers 40 - 60

West, Henry L.
GF6610 **Lyrics of the Links** NY 1921   40 - 60

Wheatley, Vera
GF6710 **Mixed Foursomes: A Saga of Golf** Lon 1936 40 - 60

White, Stewart Edward
GF6810 **The Shepper-Newfounder** NY 1931, 1st printing
in DJ   50 - 75

Wild, Payson Sibley
GF6910 **The Links of Ancient Rome & Etc** Chi 1912,
wrappers   75 - 125

Wodehouse, P. G. (also see Modern First Editions)
GF7000 **Divots** Lon 1927, DJ   50 - 75
GF7010 **The Golf Omnibus** Lon 1973, DJ   30 - 50
GF7020 **The Heart of a Goof** Lon 1926, DJ   50 - 75
GF7030 **Wodehouse on Golf** Lon 1940, DJ   50 - 75

MODERN FIRST EDITIONS

A modern first edition is the first appearance in print by a contemporary literary author. The work can be any novel, story, poetry, play or essay created to be sold to the public. Such nineteenth century authors as Edgar Allen Poe, Herman Melville and Nathaniel Hawthorne are not recent enough to be in this category, but Mark Twain, Jules Verne, and Sir Arthur Conan Doyle are deemed so.

First editions have a greater number of collectors than almost any other category of book collecting. In fact, they have been collected for hundreds of years. For instance, collectors in the 1600s were buying the first editions of Francis Bacon and William Shakespeare.

Modern first collectibles also include books printed from original manuscripts that were not intended to be sold publicly. These include galleys, proofs, advance review copies, and salesmen's samples or "dummies." Proofs are uncorrected printed manuscripts; they're usually bound in plain wrappers. Galleys are a book's printed pages done on long sheets with several pages per sheet. Advance review copies precede a book's release. They are normally bound in stiff paper instead of cloth. Most are pictorial, but some have a synopsis of the book printed on the front cover. Proofs, galleys and advance review copies may be worth 1-1/2 to 5 times what the first published edition is worth, depending on the rarity and collectibility of the title and author. Salesmen's samples or "dummies" are shortened versions of a book, usually with an advertising flyer and blank pages in the back for itinerant book salesmen to record buyers' names and addresses. This was a popular way to sell books from the late 1800s up to the 1940s. For many modern firsts, there are no known examples of salesmen's samples, proofs, etc. This is especially true for books published in the early 1900s. Thus, when an already highly desirable book appears on the market in some unique, never-before-seen form, the price can easily "go through the roof." A proof or

advance review copy of *Gone with The Wind* by Margaret Mitchell could exceed $10,000, even though the first edition in first state dust jacket is worth only $2,000.

Naturally, the rarest and most desirable form of a highly collectible book is the author's original handwritten or typed manuscript. The original manuscript for *Gone with The Wind* could exceed $300,000 if offered at auction.

Signed modern firsts are always worth more than unsigned copies. Any book signed by Jack London is worth at least $200-300 more, based on the autograph's value. If it's an inscribed, rare first edition in dust jacket, it may be worth thousands more. Signed limited editions are frequently the true first edition, appearing before the first "trade" edition. Limited editions are printed in small numbers (1,500 or less). William Faulkner's limited editions are usually 300 to 1,000 copies. Each copy of a limited modern first is usually signed by the author.

The printed or pictorial dust jacket is of utmost importance in determining a modern first's value. The dust jacket is an integral part of the book and in most cases makes a collector's book worth far more. Examples include all major American and British authors from the late 1800s up to the present. Dust jackets from the turn of the century are frequently very rare or non-existent. For many late authors (1950s on up), their first editions are almost unsalable without one.

Condition is critical. Collectors are usually more selective and discriminating about the condition of modern firsts than just about any other type of book. Covers and dust jackets that are torn, stained or faded are invariably worth much less than those in pristine condition. In some fields of book collecting, such as Americana and children's books, a small amount of wear is acceptable because the books were often heavily used. But a modern first must look like it just came off the rack or out of the shipping box to command a premium price. Some modern firsts are so desirable that grades of fair to good will still bring a sizeable price. But for common literature, anything less than good condition is reading material only. Ex-library copies may be worth no more than a fraction of copies in fine condition. Even if a modern first is fine otherwise, the presence of a card pocket, library stamp or other detracting "ex-lib" features can severely reduce the value. A fine first edition first issue copy of F. Scott Fitzgerald's *The Great Gatsby* is worth $7,000-10,000 in dust jacket, but an ex-library copy with the dust jacket pasted to the cover, library stamps, a discard stamp, and a card pocket might be hard to sell for $300. Any novel published after 1980 in ex-library condition is reading material to most collectors. The book must also have all original parts: dust jacket (if it has one) or such other possible parts as slipcase, box, errata slip, paper band, etc.

MA0911

Abbey, Edward
MA0080 **Desert Solitaire** NY 1968, DJ   200 - 300
MA0090 **Fire on the Mountain** NY 1962, DJ   300 - 500
MA0100 **Jonathan Troy** (1st book) NY 1954, DJ   200 - 300
MA0110 **The Monkey Wrench Gang** Phil 1975, DJ   200 - 250
MA0120 **Slick Rock** SF 1971, DJ   200 - 300
MA0130 **Vox Clementis in Deserto** SF 1989, 250 cys,
DJ, slipcase   100 - 150

Ackerley, J. R.
MA0210 **My Dog Tulip** Lon 1956, DJ   75 - 125
MA0220 **The Prisoners of War** (1st book) Lon 1925, DJ 200 - 300

Ackroyd, Peter
MA0310 **The Great Fire of London** Lon 1982, DJ   150 - 250
MA0320 **London Lickpenny** (1st book) Lon 1973,
26 cys, wrappers   150 - 250

Adams, Henry
MA0410 **The Education of Henry Adams** Wash 1907,
100 cys, slipcase   2000 - 3000
MA0412 Bos 1918, DJ   150 - 250

MA0414 NY 1942 1500 cys, slipcase 75 - 125

Adams, Richard
MA0510 **The Plague Dogs** Lon 1977, DJ 50 - 75
MA0520 **Watership Down** Lon 1972, DJ 500 - 700
    signed 1000 - 1500
MA0522 NY 1972 (1st American ed) DJ 75 - 125

Addams, Charles
MA0610 **Drawn and Quartered** (1st book) NY 1942, DJ 75 - 100
MA0620 **Homebodies** NY 1954, DJ 50 - 75

Ade, George
MA0710 **Artie** (1st book) Chi 1896 75 - 125
MA0720 **Circus Days** Akron 1903, DJ 50 - 75
MA0730 **Fables in Slang** Chi 1900, DJ 100 - 150
MA0740 **Stories of the Streets and of the Town**
    Chi 1941, 500 cys 50 - 100
MA0750 **The Sultan of Sulu** NY 1903, wrappers 75 - 125

Agee, James
MA0911 **A Death in the Family** NY 1957, DJ, 1st issue
    w/tp printed in blue 150 - 200
MA0912 2nd issue 30 - 50
MA0913 NY 1957, wrappers (advance review cy) 300 - 500
MA0920 **Four Early Stories** West Branch 1964,
    285 cys, glassine DJ 200 - 300
MA0930 **Let Us Now Praise Famous Men** Bos 1941, DJ 300 - 500
MA0931 Bos 1960, DJ 30 - 50
MA0940 **The Morning Watch** Rome 1950, wrappers 300 - 500
MA0941 Bos 1951, DJ (1st American ed) 100 - 150
MA0950 **Permit Me Voyage** (1st book) New Haven
    1934, DJ 500 - 700

Aiken, Conrad
MA1100 **Blue Voyage** NY 1927, DJ 150 - 250
MA1110 **Bring! Bring!** NY 1925, DJ 100 - 150
MA1120 **The Charnel Rose, Senlin** Bos 1918, DJ 150 - 250
MA1131 **The Coming Forth By Day of Osiris Jones**
    NY 1931, DJ, 1st issue: "The Music" in
    capital letters on p.37 150 - 200
MA1132 later printings, DJ 20 - 40
MA1140 **Costumes By Eros** NY 1928, 2,005 cys, DJ 100 - 150
MA1150 **Earth Triumphant and Other Tales in Verse**
    (1st book) NY 1914, DJ 200 - 300
MA1160 **Great Circle** NY 1933, DJ 250 - 350
MA1170 **The House of Dust: A Symphony** Bos 1916, DJ 200 - 300
MA1180 **The Jig of Forslin** Bos 1916, DJ 200 - 300
MA1190 **Nocturne of Remembered Spring** Bos 1917, DJ 250 - 350
MA1200 **Preludes For Memnon** NY 1931, DJ 150 - 250
MA1210 **Priapus and the Pool** Cambridge 1922, 425 cys 250 - 350
MA1211 Cambridge 1922, 50 cys 300 - 500
MA1213 NY 1925 (1st trade ed) 75 - 125
MA1220 **Punch: The Immortal Liar** NY 1921, DJ 200 - 300
MA1230 **Scepticisms** NY 1919, DJ 150 - 250
MA1240 **Selected Poems** NY 1929, 210 cys signed, box 300 - 500
MA1241 NY 1929, DJ (trade ed) 75 - 125
MA1250 **Thee** NY 1967, 100 cys, box 300 - 500
MA1260 **Time in the Rock** NY 1936, DJ 125 - 250
MA1270 **Turns and Movies and Other Tales in Verse**
    Bos 1916 200 - 300

Albee, Edward
MA1410 **The American Dream** NY 1961, DJ 75 - 125
MA1420 **A Delicate Balance** NY 1966, DJ 50 - 100
MA1430 **Everything in the Garden** NY 1968, DJ 50 - 100
MA1440 **Tiny Alice** NY 1965, DJ 50 - 100
MA1442 Lon 1966, DJ 20 - 30
MA1450 **Who's Afraid of Virginia Woolf** NY 1962, DJ 100 - 150
MA1460 **The Zoo Story, The Death of Bessie Smith,**
    The Sandbox (1st book) NY 1960, DJ 150 - 200

Aldington, Richard
MA1610 **All Men Are Enemies** Lon 1933, 110 cys 150 - 250
MA1620 **At All Costs** Lon 1930, 275 cys 75 - 125
MA1621 Lon 1930, DJ (trade ed) 75 - 125
MA1630 **The Colonel's Daughter** Lon 1931, 210 cys 150 - 250
MA1640 **Death of a Hero** Lon 1929, DJ 150 - 200
MA1642 Paris 1930, 2 vol, 300 cys 500 - 700
MA1650 **The Eaten Heart** Lon 1933, DJ 150 - 200
MA1660 **Fifty Romance Lyric Poems** NY 1928, 9 cys 400 - 600
MA1661 NY 1928, 900 cys 75 - 125
MA1670 **A Fool i' the Forest** Lon 1925, DJ 150 - 250
MA1680 **Images** (1st book) Lon 1915, DJ 200 - 300
MA1690 **Images of War** Lon 1919 120 cys 150 - 250

MA1691 Lon 1919, 50 cys 250 - 350
MA1700 **Images - Old and New** Bos 1916 200 - 300
MA1710 **Last Straws** Paris 1930, 200 cys 300 - 500
MA1720 **Love and the Luxembourg** NY 1930, 475 cys 100 - 150
MA1730 **The Love of Myrrhine and Konallis** Chi 1926,
    150 cys 250 - 350
MA1740 **Stepping Heavenward** Florence, Italy 1931,
    808 cys, box, DJ 100 - 150
MA1741 Lon 1931, DJ (trade ed) 50 - 75

Aldiss, Brian W.
MA1910 **Barefoot in the Head** NY 1969, DJ 75 - 125
MA1920 **The Billion-Year Spree** NY 1973, DJ 75 - 125
MA1930 **The Bright Fount Diaries** (1st book) Lon 1955, DJ 100 - 150
MA1940 **Gray Beard** NY 1964, DJ 75 - 125
MA1950 **Non-Stop** Lon 1958, DJ 200 - 300
MA1960 **Starship** NY 1959, DJ 100 - 150

Algren, Nelson
MA2110 **The Devil's Stocking** NY 1983, DJ 40 - 60
MA2120 **The Man With the Golden Arm** NY 1949, DJ 200 - 300
MA2130 **The Neon Wilderness** NY 1947, w/1st state DJ 100 - 150
MA2140 **Never Come Morning** NY 1942, DJ 200 - 300
MA2150 **Somebody in Boots** (1st book) NY 1935, DJ 1000 - 1200
MA2160 **A Walk on the Wild Side** NY 1956, DJ 200 - 300
MA2170 **Who Lost An American** NY 1963, DJ 100 - 150

Allen, Gracie
MA2310 **How to Become President** (1st book) NY 1947, DJ 75 - 125

Allen, Hervey
MA2410 **Anthony Adverse** NY 1933, DJ, 1st issue
    w/errors: "Xaxier" for "Xavier" line 6,
    p 352; "ship" for "shop" line 18, p 1086 150 - 250
MA2411 Later printings same year 25 - 75
MA2413 NY 1937 3 vol, 1500 cys 150 - 200
MA2421 **Ballads of the Border** (1st book) El Paso 1916,
    1st state w/author's name misspelled on cr page 600 - 800
MA2430 **The Bride of Huitzil** NY 1922, 350 cys 125 - 250
MA2440 **Carolina Chansons** NY 1922, DJ 125 - 250
MA2450 **Israfel:...** NY 1926, DJ 2 vol, 1st state w/wine
    glass on table in illus facing p 529 150 - 250
MA2451 NY 1926, 250 cys 300 - 500
MA2460 **Toward the Flame** NY 1926, DJ, w/pub
    monogram on cr page 150 - 250
MA2470 **Wampum and Old Gold** New Haven 1921,
    500 cys 150 - 250

Allen, James Lane
    Kentucky author, wrote about 30 books, all collectible, most $15 - 40.
MA2610 **Aftermath** NY 1896, 1st state w/o ads for Aftermath 50 - 75
MA2620 **The Blue Grass Region of Kentucky** NY 1892 75 - 125
MA2630 **Flute and Violin** (1st book) NY 1891, w/1st
    state measuring 1-1/16" across top 150 - 200
MA2640 **A Kentucky Cardinal** NY 1895, 1st state w/o
    ad for Aftermath 50 - 75
MA2650 **The Reign of Law: A Tale of the Kentucky Hemp**
    Fields NY 1900, 1st state w/illus in photogravure 50 - 75

Allen, Woody
MA2810 **Don't Drink the Water** (1st book) NY 1967 wrappers 30 - 50
MA2811 NY 1967 DJ 50 - 75
MA2820 **The Floating Light Bulb** NY 1982 DJ 50 - 75
MA2830 **Without Features** NY 1975, DJ 75 - 100

Amis, Kingsley
MA3010 **Bright November** (1st book) Lon 1947 200 - 300
MA3020 **The Darkwater Hall Mystery** Edinburgh
    1978, 15 cys 500 - 700
MA3030 **I Like It Here** NY 1958, DJ 75 - 125
MA3040 **The James Bond Dossier** NY 1965, DJ 20 - 30
MA3050 **Lucky Jim** Lon 1953, DJ 800 - 1200
MA3051 NY 1954 (1st American ed) DJ 300 - 500
MA3060 **New Maps of Hell** NY 1960, DJ 50 - 75
MA3070 **The Old Devils** Lon 1966, 250 cys, glassine DJ 100 - 150
MA3080 **That Uncertain Feeling** Lon 1955, DJ 200 - 300

Amis, Martin
MA3210 **Dead Babies** Lon 1975, DJ 300 - 500
MA3220 **The Rachel Papers** (1st book) Lon 1973, DJ 300 - 500
MA3221 NY 1974 (1st American ed) 100 - 150
MA3230 **Success** Lon 1978, DJ 100 - 150

Ammons, A. R.
MA3410 **Expressions of Sea Level** Col 1963, DJ 75 - 125
MA3420 **Ommateum: With Doxology** (1st book)
    Phil 1955 700 - 1000

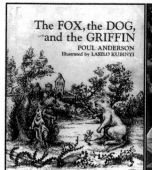

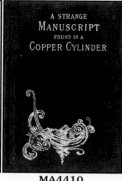

| MA3730 | MA3750 | MA3760 | MA3910 | MA4410 | MA5250 |

Anderson, Maxwell
MA3510	**Valley Forge** Wash 1934, 200 cys	100 - 150
MA3520	**You Who Have Dreams** (1st book) NY 1925, DJ, 25 cys, signed	200 - 300
MA3521	975 cys	40 - 60

Anderson, Poul
MA3700	**Brainwave** NY 1969, DJ	100 - 150
MA3710	**Broken Sword** NY 1954, DJ	100 - 150
MA3720	**The Enemy Stars** Phil 1959, DJ	100 - 150
MA3730	**The Fox, the Dog, and the Griffin** Garden City 1966, DJ	250 - 400
MA3740	**The High Crusade** NY 1960, DJ	250 - 350
MA3742	NY 1974, DJ	100 - 150
MA3750	**Star Ways** NY 1956, DJ	100 - 150
MA3760	**Three Hearts and Three Lions** NY 1961, DJ	200 - 300
MA3770	**Twilight World** NY 1961, DJ	200 - 300
MA3780	**Vault of the Ages** (1st book) Phil 1952	75 - 125
MA3790	**Virgin Planet** NY 1959, DJ	100 - 150

Anderson, Poul and Gordon Dickson
MA3910	**Earthman's Burden** NY 1947, DJ	40 - 60

Anderson, Sherwood
MA4010	**Alice and the Lost Novel** Lon 1929, 500 cys, DJ	150 - 250
MA4020	**Beyond Desire** NY 1932, 165 cys	150 - 250
MA4021	NY 1932, DJ (1st trade ed)	100 - 150
MA4030	**Dark Laughter** NY 1925, 330 cys, box	200 - 300
MA4031	NY 1925, 20 cys, box	400 - 500
MA4040	**Death in the Woods** NY 1933, DJ	125 - 250
MA4050	**Dreiser** 1940s?, Harvest Press, 50 cys	300 - 500
MA4061	**Hello Towns!** NY 1929, 1st issue: "fingers" misspelled line 30, p 35	150 - 200
MA4071	**Horses and Men** NY 1923, DJ, 1st issue w/orange top edge	200 - 300
MA4072	2nd issue w/plain top edge	100 - 150
MA4081	**Many Marriages** NY 1923, DJ, 1st issue w/orange top edge	200 - 300
MA4082	2nd issue w/plain top edge	100 - 150
MA4090	**Marching Men** NY 1917, DJ	300 - 500
MA4100	**Mid-American Chants** NY 1918, DJ	500 - 700
MA4110	**The Modern Writer** SF 1925, 950 cys, box	150 - 250
MA4111	SF 1925, 50 cys, vellum	400 - 600
MA4120	**Nearer the Grass Roots** SF 1929, 500 cys	300 - 500
MA4130	**A New Testament** NY 1927, 265 cys, slipcase	300 - 500
MA4131	NY 1927, DJ (1st trade ed)	75 - 125
MA4140	**No Swank** Phil 1934, 50 cys, signed	300 - 500
MA4141	Phil 1934, 950 cys	150 - 200
MA4150	**Perhaps Women** NY 1931, DJ	200 - 300
MA4161	**Poor White** NY 1920, DJ, 1st state w/blue top edge	200 - 300
MA4162	2nd state w/plain top edge	100 - 150
MA4163	Lon 1921, DJ (1st English ed)	150 - 250
MA4170	**Puzzled America** NY 1935, DJ	150 - 250
MA4180	**Sherwood Anderson's Notebook** NY 1926, 225 cys, box	200 - 300
MA4181	NY 1926, DJ (1st trade ed)	75 - 150
MA4191	**A Story Teller's Story** NY 1924, 1st issue w/yellow top edge	200 - 300
MA4200	**Tar: A Midwest Childhood** NY 1926, 330 cys	200 - 300
MA4201	NY 1926, 20 cys	300 - 400
MA4202	NY 1926, DJ (1st trade ed)	100 - 150
MA4211	**The Triumph of the Egg** NY 1921, DJ, 1st issue w/yellow top edge	100 - 150
MA4213	Chi 1932	50 - 75
MA4220	**Windy McPherson's Son** (1st book) NY 1916, DJ	300 - 500

MA4231	**Winesburg, Ohio** NY 1919, DJ, 1st state w/yellow top edge	2000 - 3000
MA4232	2nd state w/orange top edge	1000 - 1500

Anon (James De Mille)
MA4410	**A Strange Manuscript found in a Copper Cylinder** NY 1888	50 - 75

Antonius, Brother (William Everson)
MA4510	**A Canticle to the Waterbirds** Berkeley 1968, 200 cys	200 - 300
MA4511	Berkeley 1968, wrappers (1st trade ed)	25 - 50
MA4520	**The Last Crusade** Berkeley 1969, 165 cys, acetate DJ	200 - 300
MA4530	**These Are the Ravens** San Leandro 1935	300 - 500
MA4540	**Who is She That Looketh Forth as the Morning** Santa Barbara 1972, 250 cys, acetate DJ	150 - 200

Apollinaire, Guillaume
MA4710	**Alcools** Paris 1913, wrappers, slipcase	4000 - 6000
MA4720	**Calligrammes: Poemes de La Paix et de La Guerre** Paris 1918	1200 - 1800

Arlen, Michael
MA4810	**The Green Hat** Lon 1924, DJ	150 - 250
MA4820	**The London Venture** (1st book) Lon 1920, DJ, erratum on p 19	200 - 300
MA4821	NY 1920, DJ (1st American ed)	50 - 75

Ashbery, John
MA4910	**The New Spirit** NY 1970, 65 cys	200 - 300
MA4911	NY 1970, 100 cys	100 - 150
MA4920	**Some Trees** New Haven 1956, 851 cys, DJ	200 - 300
MA4930	**Sunrise in Suburbia** NY 1968 100 cys, wrappers	200 - 300
MA4931	NY 1968, 26 cys, wrappers	300 - 500
MA4940	**Turandot and Other Poems** (1st book) NY 1953, 300 cys	600 - 800

Asimov, Isaac
Scientist and author of many science books.
MA5110	**3 by Asimov** NY 1981, 250 cys	100 - 150
MA5120	**The Caves of Steel** NY 1954, DJ	150 - 200
MA5130	**The Currents of Space** NY 1952, DJ	75 - 125
MA5140	**The Death Dealers** (Avon Paperback) NY 1958	25 - 50
MA5150	**The End of Eternity** NY 1955, DJ	150 - 200
MA5160	**Fantastic Voyage** Bos 1966, DJ	100 - 150
MA5170	**Foundation** NY 1951, DJ	200 - 300
MA5180	**Foundation and Earth** NY 1986, 300 cys	200 - 300
MA5190	**Foundation and Empire** NY 1952, DJ	200 - 300
MA5200	**The Foundation Series** Gnome Press NY 1951-53, 3 vol, DJs	500 - 700
MA5210	**I, Robot** NY 1950, DJ	400 - 600
MA5220	**More Tales of the Black Widowers** NY 1976, DJ	25 - 50
MA5230	**Murder at the ABA** NY 1976, DJ	25 - 50
MA5240	**Opus 100** Bos 1969, DJ	25 - 50
MA5250	**Pebble in the Sky** (1st book) NY 1950, DJ	200 - 300
MA5260	**Prelude to Foundation** NY 1988, 500 cys, slipcase	150 - 250
MA5270	**The Robots of Dawn** Huntington Woods 1983, DJ	150 - 200
MA5280	**Second Foundation** NY 1953, DJ	200 - 300

Atherton, Gertrude
Wrote about 40 novels.
MA5410	**Black Oxen** NY 1923, 250 cys	100 - 150
MA5411	NY 1923, DJ (1st trade ed)	25 - 50
MA5420	**The Conqueror** NY 1902, DJ, 1st state w/page numerals on p 546 in upper left	200 - 300
MA5430	**The Splendid Idle Forties** NY 1902, DJ	100 - 150
MA5440	**What Dreams May Come** (1st book) Lon 1889, under pseud Frank Lin	100 - 150

Attaway, William
MA5610 **Blood on the Forge** Garden City 1941, DJ 250 - 350
Atwood, Margaret
MA5710 **Cat's Eye** Lon 1989, DJ 30 - 40
MA5720 **Double Persephone** (1st book) Tor 1961,
    wrappers 800 - 1200
MA5730 **The Edible Woman** Bos 1969, DJ 75 - 125
MA5740 **The Handmaid's Tale** Bos 1986, DJ 30 - 50
MA5750 **The Journals of Susanna Moodie** Tor 1970, DJ 75 - 100
MA5760 **Lady Oracle** NY 1976, DJ 30 - 50
MA5770 **Life Before Man** Tor 1979, DJ 30 - 50
MA5780 **Surfacing** Tor 1972, DJ 100 - 150
Auchincloss, Louis (Andrew Lee)
MA5940 **The Book Class** Bos 1984, DJ 15 - 25
MA5950 **The Golden Calves** Bos 1988, DJ 15 - 25
MA5960 **The Great World and Timothy Colt** NY 1956, DJ 50 - 75
MA5970 **The Indifferent Children** (1st book) NY 1947,
    DJ, under pseud Andrew Lee 100 - 150
MA5980 **The Injustice Collectors** Bos 1950, DJ 100 - 150
MA5990 **Tales of Manhattan** Bos 1967, DJ 30 - 50
Auden, W. H. (Hugh Wystan)
MA6110 **The Age of Anxiety** NY 1947, DJ 150 - 250
MA6111 Lon 1948, DJ 75 - 125
MA6120 **Another Time** NY 1940, DJ 200 - 300
MA6130 **The Ascent of F6** Lon 1936, DJ 150 - 250
MA6141 **The Collected Poetry** NY 1945, DJ,
    1st state w/tp in green & black 250 - 350
MA6150 **Collected Shorter Poems 1930-44** Lon 1950, DJ 125 - 250
MA6160 **Collected Shorter Poems 1927-57** Lon 1966, DJ 75 - 125
MA6170 **The Dance of Death** Lon 1933, DJ 150 - 250
MA6180 **The Dog Beneath...** Lon 1935, DJ 150 - 250
MA6181 NY 1935, DJ (1st American ed) 125 - 250
MA6190 **The Double Man** NY 1941, DJ 200 - 300
MA6200 **The Enchafed Flood** NY 1950, DJ 100 - 150
MA6210 **Epithalamion** Princeton 1939, composed of
    1 folded sheet of 4 pp 500 - 700
MA6220 **Five Poems** Cedar Falls 1984, 100 cys 200 - 300
MA6230 **For The Time Being** NY 1944, DJ 125 - 250
MA6232 Lon 1945, DJ (1st English ed) 150 - 250
MA6240 **Homage to Clio** Lon 1960, DJ 75 - 125
MA6250 **Letters From Iceland** Lon 1937, DJ 250 - 350
MA6260 **Look Stranger!** Lon 1936, DJ 200 - 300
MA6270 **Louise MacNeice** Lon 1963, 250 cys 150 - 200
MA6280 **Marginalia** Ibex Press, Cambridge 1966, 150 cys 250 - 350
MA6281 Cambridge 1966, 26 lettered cys 300 - 500
MA6290 **New Year Letter** Lon 1941 100 - 150
MA6300 **On The Frontier** Lon 1938, DJ 200 - 300
MA6310 **On This Island** NY 1937, DJ 200 - 300
MA6320 **The Orators** Lon 1932, DJ, 1000 cys 250 - 350
MA6330 **Our Hunting Fathers** Cambridge 1935, 22 cys 1000 - 1500
MA6331 Cambridge 1935, 5 cys, Incudine paper 2000 - 3000
MA6340 **Poem Bryn Mawr** 1933, wrappers, 5 cys,
    Fabriano paper 2500 - 3500
MA6341 5 cys, Kelmscott paper 2500 - 3500
MA6350 **Poems** (1st book) Hampstead 1928 8000 - 12000
MA6360 **Poems** (Frognal & Oxford) 1928, 45 cys 12000 - 18000
MA6362 Cinti 1964, 500 cys 50 - 75
MA6370 **Poems** Lon 1930, tissue DJ, slipcase 400 - 600
MA6371 Lon 1933, DJ 200 - 300
MA6372 NY 1934, DJ 100 - 150
MA6380 **Selected Poems** Lon 1938, DJ 200 - 300
MA6382 Lon 1968, DJ 40 - 60
MA6390 **The Shield of Achilles** NY 1955, DJ 125 - 250
MA6391 Lon 1955, DJ (1st English ed) 100 - 150

MA6400 **Some Poems** Lon 1940, DJ 125 - 250
MA6410 **Sonnet** Cambridge 1935, 22 cys, wrappers 1500 - 2000
MA6420 **Spain** Lon 1937, wrappers 100 - 150
MA6430 **Three Songs...** NY 1941, 250 cys 300 - 500
MA6440 **Three Unpublished Poems** NY 1986, 220 cys,
    Arches paper 300 - 500
MA6450 **Two Songs** NY 1968, 100 cys 200 - 300
Auel, Jean M.
MA6610 **The Clan of the Cave Bear** (1st book) NY 1980, DJ 50 - 75
MA6620 **The Mammoth Hunters** NY 1985, DJ 20 - 30
MA6630 **The Plains of Passage** NY 1990, DJ 20 - 30
MA6640 **The Valley of the Horses** NY, 1982, DJ 50 - 75
Bacheller, Irving
    Wrote about 40 novels. Most are mildly collectible at $15-30.
MB0060 **Eben Holden** Bos 1900, DJ, 1st issue reads
    on line 13, p 400 "go to fur" 100 - 150
MB0070 **The Master of Silence** (1st book) NY 1892 75 - 125
Bachman, Richard (see Stephen King)
Bailey, J. O.
MB0150 **Pilgrims Through Space and Time** NY 1947, DJ 150 - 200
Baldwin, James
MB0210 **Blues for Mister Charlie** NY 1964, DJ 50 - 75
MB0220 **Gilvanni's Room** NY 1956, DJ 100 - 150
MB0230 **Go Tell It on the Mountain** (1st book) NY
    1953, DJ 300 - 500
MB0232 Lon 1954, DJ 100 - 150
MB0240 **Gypsy and Other Poems** 1989, 331 cys,
    original etching 1000 - 1500
MB0250 **If Beale Street Could Talk** NY 1974, 250 cys, box 150 - 250
MB0260 **No Name in the Street** NY 1972, DJ 50 - 75
MB0270 **Nothing Personal** NY 1964, illus by Ayedon, box 200 - 300
MB0280 **Tell Me How Long the Trains Been Gone**
    NY 1968, DJ 100 - 150
Ballard, J. G.
MB0350 **The Atrocity Exhibition** Lon 1970, DJ 200 - 300
MB0360 **The Burning World** Lon 1965, DJ 200 - 300
MB0370 **The Crystal World** Lon 1966, DJ 200 - 300
MB0371 NY 1966, DJ (1st American ed) 100 - 150
MB0380 **The Drowned World and The Wind**
    From Nowhere Lon 1962, DJ 200 - 300
MB0390 **The Four Dimensional Nightmare** Lon 1963, DJ 300 - 500
Balmer, Edwin
MB0440 **Flying Death** NY 1927, DJ 125 - 150
Bangs, John Kendrick
RN2620 **Ghosts I Have Met** see Peter Newell in Artists & Illustrators
MB0490 **Peeps at People** NY 1899 40 - 60
Banks, Iain
MB0540 **The Wasp Factory** Lon 1984, DJ 100 - 150
Bannerman, Helen
    Author of *Little Black Sambo*; wrote many other children's books
that are lesser known but collectible.
MB0610 **Pat and the Spider** NY 1905 125 - 250
MB0615 **Sambo and the Twins** NY 1936 75 - 125
MB0620 **Story of Little Black Mingo** NY 1901 125 - 250
MB0625 **Story of Little Black Quasha** NY 1908 125 - 250
MB0630 **The Story of Little Black Sambo** Grant
    Richards Pub, Lon 1899, green cl 6000 - 8000
MB0631 NY Frederick Stokes & Co, 1901?
    (1st American ed) Pict, bds 800 - 1200
MB0633 NY 1905 Barse & Hopkins Pub 125 - 250
    This book has gone through numerous printings since 1905. Price
range is $25-125, depending on illustrator, size, etc.

MA5610

MA5730

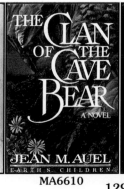
MA6610

MB0210

MB0440

MB0490

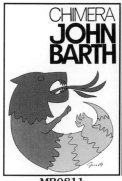

MB0811	MB1240	MB1250

MB0640	**Story of Little Kettle-Head** NY 1904	125 - 250
MB0645	**Story of the Teasing Monkey** NY 1907	125 - 250

Barrie, Sir James
MB0700	**The Admirable Crichton** Lon 1914	125 - 250
MB0701	500 cys, vellum	300 - 500
MB0705	**The Author** Cinti 1925, 20 cys, wrappers	400 - 600
MB0710	**Better Dead** (1st book) Lon 1888, wrappers	500 - 700
MB0715	**The Greenwood Hat...** Lon 1930, 550 cys, box	150 - 250
MB0720	**The Ladies Shakespeare** Lon 1925, 25 cys	200 - 300
MB0725	**The Little White Bird** Lon 1902, DJ	200 - 300
MB0730	**The Novels, Tales and Sketches** NY 1912, 12 vol	300 - 500
MB0735	**Peter and Wendy** Lon 1911, DJ	1500 - 2500
MB0736	NY 1911, DJ (1st American ed)	1500 - 2500
MB0740	**Peter Pan in Kensington Gardens** Lon 1906, 500 cys, illus by Arthur Rackham	2000 - 3000
MB0741	Lon 1906, DJ (trade ed)	400 - 600
MB0742	NY 1906, DJ (1st American ed)	300 - 500
MB0743	NY 1907, DJ	150 - 250
MB0744	Lon 1907, DJ	150 - 250
MB0745	later editions in DJ	75 - 125
MB0746	later editions w/o DJ	50 - 75
MB0750	**Quality Street** Lon 1913, 1000 cys on vellum	300 - 400
MB0751	Lon 1910 (trade ed)	100 - 150
MB0760	**Walker** London NY 1907	100 - 150
MB0765	**The Works** Lon 1930, 1000 sets, 10 vol	300 - 400
MB0766	NY 1929, 1030 sets, 14 vol	500 - 700

Barth, John
MB0810	**Chimera** NY 1972, 300 cys, box	100 - 150
MB0811	NY 1972, DJ (1st trade ed)	50 - 75
MB0815	**The End of the Road** NY 1958, DJ	300 - 400
MB0817	Lon 1962	150 - 200
MB0825	**The Floating Opera** (1st book) NY 1956, DJ	200 - 300
MB0827	Lon 1968, DJ	20 - 30
MB0835	**Giles Goat-Boy** NY 1966, 250 cys, box	200 - 300
MB0836	NY 1966, DJ (1st trade ed)	50 - 75
MB0845	**The Last Voyage of Somebody the Sailor** Bos 1991, DJ	20 - 30
MB0850	**Lost in the Fun House** NY 1968, 250 cys, box	200 - 300
MB0851	NY 1968, DJ (trade edition)	50 - 75
MB0860	**Sabbatical** NY 1982, DJ	20 - 30
MB0865	**The Sot-Weed Factor** NY 1960, DJ	200 - 300
MB0866	Lon 1961, DJ (1st English ed)	50 - 75

Barthelme, Frederick
MB0900	**Forty Stories** NY 1987, DJ	20 - 30
MB0905	**Great Days** NY 1979, DJ	40 - 60
MB0910	**Second Marriage** NY 1984, DJ	20 - 30
MB0920	**Tracer** NY 1985, DJ	20 - 30

Bass, Rick
MB0970	**Oil Notes** Bos 1989, DJ	20 - 30
MB0980	**The Watch Stories** NY 1989, DJ	20 - 30

Basshe, Emjo
MB1020	**Doomsday Circus** NY 1938, DJ	75 - 100
MB1030	**Earth** NY 1927, DJ	75 - 125

Bates, H. E.
MB1090	**The Last Bread: A Play in One Act** (1st book) Lon 1926	150 - 200

Baum, L. Frank (See Baumania & Oziana)
Baum, Vicki
MB1150	**The Mustard Seed** NY 1953, DJ	30 - 50
MB1160	**The Weeping Wood** NY 1943, DJ	40 - 60

Beagle, Peter S.
MB1240	**A Fine and Private Place** NY 1960, DJ	200 - 300

MB1250	**The Last Unicorn** NY 1968, DJ	75 - 125

Beckett, Samuel (1969 Nobel Laureate)
MB1330	**All Strange Away** NY 1976, 200 cys, box	700 - 1000
MB1331	26 lettered cys	1500 - 2000
MB1340	**All That Fall: A Play** NY 1957, 100 cys, box	300 - 500
MB1341	Lon 1957, wrappers (1st English ed)	100 - 150
MB1350	**Beginning To End** NY 1988, 300 cys, box	200 - 300
MB1360	**Come and Go: Dramaticule** Lon 1967, 100 cys, box	300 - 500
MB1370	**Comment C'est** Paris 1961, 100 cys, tissue DJ	500 - 700
MB1380	**Drunken Boat** Reading, PA 1976, 100 cys, signed	200 - 300
MB1381	Reading, PA 1976, 200 cys, unsigned	100 - 150
MB1390	**Echo's Bones and Other Precipitates** Paris 1935 25 cys on vellum	2000 - 3000
MB1391	Paris 1935 250 cys	800 - 1200
MB1400	**En Attendant Godot** Paris 1952, 35 cys	8000 - 12000
MB1401	Paris 1952, wrappers (1st trade ed)	300 - 500
MB1410	**End Game** Lon 1958, DJ	1000 - 1500
MB1412	NY 1958 100 cys, signed	1000 - 1500
	unsigned	500 - 700
MB1420	**How It Is** Lon 1964, 2 vol, 100 cys, box	300 - 500
MB1430	**Ill Seen Ill Said** Northridge 1982, 299 cys	150 - 250
MB1440	**The Lost Ones** Lon 1972, 200 cys, box	300 - 400
MB1450	**Malone Dies** NY 1956, 500 cys, tissue DJ	250 - 350
MB1451	Lon 1958, DJ (1st English ed)	150 - 250
MB1453	Paris 1951 titled "Malone Meurt"	
MB1454	tissue DJ	150 - 250
MB1460	**Molloy** Paris 1951, 500 cys	300 - 500
MB1462	Paris 1955, wrappers	150 - 200
MB1463	NY 1955, DJ	150 - 200
MB1470	**More Pricks Than Kicks** Lon 1934, DJ	1000 - 1500
MB1472	Lon 1970, 100 cys, box	400 - 600
MB1480	**Murphy** Lon 1938, DJ	4000 - 6000
MB1490	**The Negress in the Brothel** Lon 1989, 24 cys, etching, box	200 - 300
MB1491	Lon 1989, 100 cys, lithograph, box	150 - 250
MB1500	**The North** Lon 1972, 137 cys, box	1000 - 1500
MB1510	**No's Knife** Lon 1967, 100 cys, slipcase	400 - 600
MB1520	**Our Exagmination Round His Factification For Incamination of Work in Progress** (1st book) Paris 1929, 96 cys, wrappers	3000 - 5000
MB1530	**Poems in English** Lon 1961, 100 cys	800 - 1200
MB1540	**Proust** Lon 1931	500 - 700
MB1541	Paris 1931	500 - 700
MB1543	NY 1957, 250 cys	300 - 500
MB1550	**Sans** Paris 1972, 550 cys	200 - 300
MB1560	**The Unnamable** NY 1978, 26 cys	500 - 700
MB1561	100 cys	300 - 500
MB1562	NY 1978 (advance review cy)	200 - 300
MB1570	**Waiting For Godot** Paris 1952, 59 cys	600 - 800
MB1572	NY 1954, DJ (1st American ed)	200 - 300
MB1573	Lon 1956, DJ	150 - 200
MB1580	**Watt** Paris 1953, 25 cys, wrappers	1200 - 1800
MB1581	Paris 1953 (1st trade ed)	300 - 500
MB1583	NY 1959, DJ (1st American ed)	100 - 150
MB1590	**Whoroscope** Paris 1930, 100 cys, signed	2000 - 3000
MB1591	200 cys, unsigned	1000 - 1500

Beecher, John
MB1680	**And I Will Be Heard** (1st book) NY 1940	50 - 100
MB1690	**Here I Stand** NY 1941, 100 signed cys, DJ	150 - 200

Beer, Thomas
MB1770	**The Fair Rewards** (1st book) NY 1922, advance issue, 100 cys	200 - 300
MB1771	NY 1922 (1st ed), DJ	150 - 200
MB1780	**Hanna** NY 1929, 250 cys, DJ	150 - 200
MB1781	1st trade ed, DJ	25 - 50
MB1790	**The Mauve Decade** NY 1926, 150 cys	200 - 300
MB1791	NY 1926, 15 cys	500 - 700
MB1792	NY 1926, DJ (1st trade ed)	50 - 75

Beerbohm, Max (see Artists & Illustrators)
Behan, Brendan
MB1880	**The Hostage** Lon 1958	
MB1881	NY 1958, 26 lettered cys w/o DJ	300 - 500
MB1882	NY 1958, DJ (1st trade ed)	50 - 75
MB1890	**The Quare Fellow** (1st book) Lon 1956, DJ	150 - 200
MB1891	NY 1956, 100 cys, DJ	100 - 150

Belloc, Hillaire
MB1950	**Cautionary Tales For Children** Lon 1908, DJ	150 - 250

MB1955	**The Free Press** Lon 1918, DJ	75 - 125
MB1960	**The Highway and Its Vehicles** Lon 1926, 1250 cys	150 - 200
MB1965	**New Cautionary Tales** Lon 1930, 110 signed cys	200 - 300
MB1970	**Pongo and The Bull** Lon 1910, DJ	200 - 300
MB1975	**The Praise of Wine** Lon 1931, wrappers	200 - 300
MB1985	**Verse** Lon 1954	75 - 125
MB1990	**Verses and Sonnets** (1st book) Lon 1896	400 - 600

Bellow, Saul (1976 Nobel Laureate)

MB2031	**The Adventures of Augie March** NY 1953, 1st issue w/orange top edge & DJ w/o reviews	150 - 200
MB2032	2nd issue w/top edge unstained & Wolff imprint DJ	50 - 75
MB2040	**Dangling Man** (1st book) NY 1944, DJ	500 - 700
MB2042	Lon 1946, DJ	200 - 300
MB2051	**Henderson the Rain King** NY 1959, DJ, 1st issue w/yellow top edge	100 - 150
MB2052	Lon 1959, DJ (1st English ed)	50 - 75
MB2060	**Herzog** NY 1964, DJ	150 - 200
MB2070	**More Die of Heartbreak** NY 1987, DJ	25 - 50
MB2080	**Mr. Sammler's Planet** Lon 1970, DJ	25 - 50
MB2090	**Seize the Day** NY 1956, DJ	100 - 150
MB2100	**A Silver Dish** NY 1979, 300 cys, DJ	150 - 200
MB2110	**The Victim** NY 1947, DJ	100 - 150

Bemelmans, Ludwig

MB2200	**The Donkey Inside** NY 1941, 175 cys, box	200 - 300
MB2210	**Father Dear Father** NY 1953, 150 cys, original drawing, box	300 - 400
MB2220	**Hansi** (1st book) NY 1934, DJ	200 - 300
MB2230	**Hotel Splendide** NY 1941, 245 cys, box	200 - 300
MB2240	**Now I Lay Me Down to Sleep** NY 1943, 400 cys, box	200 - 300

Benchley, Robert

MB2310	**20,000 Leagues Under the Sea, or David Copperfield** NY 1928, DJ	150 - 200
MB2320	**No Poems** NY 1932, DJ	150 - 200
MB2330	**Of All Things** (1st Book) NY 1921, DJ	200 - 300
MB2331	Lon 1922, DJ	100 - 150

Benet, Stephen Vincent

MB2400	**Ballad of William Sycamore** New Haven 1923, 500 cys	200 - 300
MB2405	**Ballads and Poems: 1915-1930** NY 1931, 201 cys, box	200 - 300
MB2406	NY 1931, DJ (1st trade ed)	50 - 75
MB2410	**The Beginning of Wisdom** NY 1921, DJ	150 - 250
MB2415	**A Book of Americans** NY 1933, 125 cys, box	150 - 200
MB2416	NY 1933, DJ (1st trade edition) 1st printing w/publishing monogram on cr page	50 - 75
MB2417	later issues	20 - 30
MB2425	**Burning City** NY 1936, 275 cys, glassine DJ, box	150 - 250
MB2426	NY 1936, DJ (1st trade ed)	75 - 125
MB2435	**The Devil and Daniel Webster**, Weston, VT 1937, 700 cys, box	250 - 350
MB2436	NY 1937, DJ (1st trade ed)	50 - 75
MB2445	**The Drug Shop...** New Haven 1917, 100 cys, wrappers	500 - 700
MB2450	**Five Men and Pompey** (1st book) Bos 1915, purple wrappers	300 - 500
MB2451	brown wrappers	200 - 300
MB2455	**John Brown's Body** NY 1928, 201 cys, signed, box	250 - 350
MB2456	NY 1928, DJ (1st trade ed)	50 - 75
MB2457	NY 1948 (Limited Editions Club) 1500 cys	75 - 125
MB2458	NY 1980 (BOMC) DJ, box	100 - 150
MB2465	**King David** NY 1923, 350 cys	200 - 300
MB2470	**Nightmare At Noon** NY 1940, 1st state w/publishing monogram on cr page	250 - 350
MB2475	**A Portrait and A Poem** Paris 1934, 50 cys	500 - 700
MB2480	**Tiger Joy** NY 1925, DJ	200 - 300
MB2485	**Tuesday, Nov 5th, 1940** NY 1941, 50 cys	300 - 500
MB2490	**Young Adventure** New Haven 1918, DJ, 1st ed, reads "Sept. 1918" on cr page	300 - 500

Benét, William Rose

MB2540	**The Burglar of the Zodiac** New Haven 1918, DJ	200 - 300
MB2545	**The Dust Which Is God** NY 1941, 246 cys	200 - 300
MB2550	**Harlem and Other Poems** Lon 1935, DJ	150 - 200
MB2560	**Merchants From Cathay** (1st book) NY 1913, DJ	300 - 500

Bennett, Arnold E.

MB2640	**Anna of the Five Towns** Lon 1902	150 - 250

MB2650	**The Bright Island** Lon 1924, 200 cys	200 - 300
MB2655	**Buried Alive** Oxford 1987, 385 cys, box	400 - 600
MB2665	**Clayhanger** Lon 1910, DJ	200 - 300
MB2670	**The Clayhanger Family** Lon 1925, 200 cys	250 - 350
MB2680	**Don Juan De Marana** Lon 1923, 100 cys, DJ	500 - 700
MB2681	Lon 1923, 1000 cys, DJ	150 - 250
MB2690	**Elsie and the Child** Lon 1929, 100 cys	700 - 1000
MB2691	Lon 1929, 750 cys	400 - 600
MB2700	**From the Log of the Velsa** Lon 1920, 110 cys	300 - 500
MB2710	**Hilda Lessways** Lon 1911, DJ	250 - 350
MB2715	**Imperial Palace** Lon 1930, 2 vol, 100 cys	300 - 500
MB2720	**Journal 1929** Lon 1930, 75 cys	250 - 350
MB2725	**The Loot of Cities** Lon 1904, 200 cys	300 - 500
MB2730	**A Man From the North** (1st book) Lon 1898, 1st issue w/ads dated 1897	300 - 500
MB2735	**Mr. Prohack** Lon 1922, DJ	150 - 250
MB2740	**The Old Wives' Tales** Lon 1908, 1500 cys, 2 vol	300 - 500
MB2742	Lon 1927 2 vol, 500 cys	200 - 300
MB2744	NY 1941 2 vol, DJs	50 - 75
MB2750	**These Twain** Lon 1915, DJ	150 - 250
MB2755	**Things That Interested Me...** Burslem, Eng 1906, 100 cys	250 - 350
MB2757	Lon 1921, DJ	100 - 150
MB2759	Lon 1926, DJ	100 - 150
MB2770	**Venus Rising From The Sea** Lon 1931, 350 cys	500 - 700

Benson, R. H.

MB2850	**The Light Invisible** (1st book) Lon 1903, DJ	50 - 75

Berry, Wendell

MB2930	**An Eastward Look** Berkeley 1974, 350 cys, wrappers	30 - 40

Berryman, John

MB3000	**The Dispossessed** NY 1948, DJ	200 - 300
MB3010	**The Freedom of the Poet** NY 1976, DJ	30 - 40
MB3020	**His Thoughts Made Pockets...** Pawlet, VT 1958, 26 lettered cys	700 - 1000
MB3030	**Homage to Mistress Bradstreet** NY 1956, DJ	150 - 250
MB3040	**Love and Fame** NY 1970 250 cys, box	200 - 300
MB3041	NY 1970, DJ (1st trade ed)	50 - 75
MB3050	**Poems** (1st book) Norfolk 1942, blue wrappers w/DJ	50 - 100
MB3051	Norfolk 1942 500 cys	200 - 300
MB3060	**Stephen Crane** NY 1950, DJ	100 - 150

Bester, Alfred

MB3130	**The Demolished Man** (1st book) Chi 1953, DJ	150 - 250
MB3131	Lon 1953, DJ (1st English ed)	50 - 75
MB3140	**Tiger! Tiger!** Lon 1956, DJ	150 - 250

Betjeman, John

MB3210	**Metro Land** Lon 1977, 220 cys, box	200 - 300
MB3221	**Mount Zion** (1st book) Lon 1931, 1st state w/blue & gold cover	300 - 500
MB3222	2nd state w/striped cover	200 - 300

Bierce, Ambrose

MB3300	**Battle Sketches** Lon 1930, 350 cys, box	150 - 200
MB3305	**Collected Works** NY 1909-12, 12 vol	700 - 1000
MB3310	**The Cynic's Word Book** NY 1906, 1st state w/o frontis	200 - 300
MB3315	**Fantastic Fables** NY 1899, 1st printing w/"Anna Fuller" heading for ads in back	300 - 500
MB3316	2nd printing w/"New Fiction" heading for ads in back	200 - 300
MB3320	**A Horseman in the Sky** SF 1920, 400 cys	200 - 300
MB3325	**In the Midst of Life** Lon 1892	150 - 250
MB3326	NY 1898	75 - 125
MB3335	**The Letters of Ambrose Bierce** SF 1922, 415 cys	200 - 300
MB3340	**My Favorite Murder** NY 1916, wrappers	250 - 350
MB3345	**The Shadow on the Dial...** SF 1909, DJ	250 - 350
MB3350	**Shapes of Clay** SF 1903, 1st issue w/reversed lines on p 71 beginning "We've nothing..."	300 - 500
MB3355	**Tales of Soldiers and Civilians** SF 1891	400 - 600
	signed cy	700 - 1000
MB3357	NY 1943, box	75 - 125
MB3365	**Ten Tales** Lon 1925, DJ	150 - 250
MB3370	**Write It Right** NY 1909, DJ, 1st issue, 5-3/4"x3"	250 - 350
MB3372	SF 1971, 400 cys, box	100 - 150

Biggers, Earl Derr

MB3420	**The Agony Column** Ind 1916, DJ	50 - 75
MB3425	**Behind That Curtain** Ind 1928, DJ	50 - 100
MB3430	**The Black Camel** Ind 1929, DJ	75 - 125
MB3435	**Charlie Chan Carries On** Ind 1930, DJ	75 - 125

MB4880	MB5630	MB6140

MB3440 **The Chinese Parrot** Ind 1926, DJ 75 - 125
MB3445 **Earl Derr Biggers Tells Ten Stories** Ind 1933, DJ 50 - 75
MB3450 **The House Without a Key** IN 1925, DJ 50 - 100
MB3455 **If You're Only Human** (1st book) Ind 1912, DJ 125 - 250
MB3460 **Keeper of the Keys** Ind 1930, DJ 50 - 75
MB3465 **Seven Keys to Baldpate** Ind 1913, DJ 75 - 125

Bishop, Elizabeth
MB3510 **The Complete Poems** NY 1969, DJ 50 - 75
MB3515 **North & South** (1st book) Bos 1946, DJ 300 - 500
MB3520 **Poems** Lon 1956, DJ 100 - 150
MB3525 **Questions of Travel** NY 1956, DJ 100 - 150

Blackmur, R. P. (Richard Palmer)
MB3610 **The Expense of Greatness** NY 1940 30 - 50
MB3620 **From Jordan's Delight** NY 1937, DJ 50 - 75
MB3630 **The Good European & Other Poems**
 Cummington, MA 1947, 40 cys 150 - 250
MB3640 **The Second World** Cummington, MA
 1942, 300 cys 150 - 250
MB3650 **T.S. Eliot** (1st book) Cambridge 1928 100 - 150

Blackwood, Algeron
MB3710 **The Empty House and Other Ghost Stories**
 (1st book) Lon 1906, DJ 200 - 300
MB3712 NY 1917, DJ 75 - 100
MB3720 **Incredible Adventures** Lon 1914, DJ 150 - 200
MB3730 **Julius Le Vallon** NY 1916, DJ 200 - 300
MB3740 **The Lost Valley** NY 1914, 500 cys 200 - 300

Blish, James
MB3820 **A Case of Conscience** Lon 1959, DJ 150 - 250
MB3830 **The Star Dwellers** NY 1965, DJ 100 - 150

Bloch, Robert
MB3910 **Blood Runs Cold** NY 1961, DJ 50 - 75
MB3920 **The Dead Beat** NY 1960, DJ 50 - 75
MB3930 **The Eighth Stage of Fandom** Chi 1962, DJ 50 - 75
MB3940 **The Opener of the Way** (1st book)
 Sauk City, WI 1945, DJ 200 - 250
MB3950 **Psycho** NY 1959, DJ 250 - 350
MB3960 **Sea Kissed** Lon 1945, wrappers 200 - 300

Blunden, Edmund C.
MB4040 **Poems 1913 and 1914** (1st book)
 Horsham 1914, 100 cys 200 - 300

Bly, Robert
MB4100 **The Kabir Book** Bos 1977, DJ 30 - 40
MB4110 **The Lions Tale and Eyes** (1st book)
 Madison 1962, DJ 100 - 150
MB4120 **Mirabai Versions** NY 1980, 210 cys 200 - 300
MB4121 NY 1980, 10 cys, hand colored, signed 600 - 800
MB4122 NY 1980, DJ (1st trade ed) 30 - 40
MB4130 **Silence in the Snowy Fields** Middleton 1962 50 - 100
MB4140 **Visiting Emily Dickinson's Grave**
 Madison 1979, 200 cys 150 - 200

Bodenheim, Maxwell
MB4210 **Crazy Man** NY 1923, DJ 50 - 75
MB4220 **Duke Herring** NY 1931, DJ 50 - 75
MB4231 **Minna and Myself** (1st book) NY 1918, DJ,
 1st issue w/"Master - Posner" on p 67 75 - 100
MB4240 **The Sardonic Arm** Chi 1923, 575 cys 75 - 125

Bogan, Louise
MB4320 **Body of This Death: Poems** (1st book)
 NY 1923, DJ 200 - 300
MB4330 **Dark Summer** NY 1929, DJ 150 - 200
MB4340 **Poems and New Poems** NY 1941, DJ 75 - 125
MB4350 **The Sleeping Fury** NY 1937, DJ 75 - 125

Bond, Nelson
MB4430 **Exiles of Time** Phil 1949, 112 cys, box 75 - 125
MB4440 **Mr. Mergenthwirker's Lobblies and Other**
 Fantastic Tales (1st book) NY 1946, DJ 75 - 100
MB4450 **Nightmares and Daydreams** Sauk City 1968, DJ 50 - 100
MB4460 **The Thirty First of February** NY 1949,
 112 cys, box 100 - 150
MB4461 NY 1949, DJ (1st trade ed) 25 - 50

Bontemps, Arna W.
MB4540 **Black Thunder** NY 1936, DJ 150 - 250
MB4550 **God Sends Sunday** (1st book) NY 1931, DJ 200 - 300

Boulle, Pierre
MB4630 **The Bridge Over the River Kwai** (1st book),
 Lon 1954, DJ 100 - 150
MB4631 NY 1954, DJ (1st American ed) 50 - 75

Bowen, Elizabeth
MB4710 **Ann Lee's and Other Stories** Lon 1926, DJ 100 - 150
MB4711 NY 1927, DJ (1st American ed) 50 - 75
MB4720 **The Death of the Heart** Lon 1938, DJ 100 - 150
MB4730 **Encounters** (1st book) Lon 1923, DJ 800 - 1000
MB4740 **Seven Winters** Dublin 1942, 450 cys, box 250 - 350

Bowles, Jane
MB4810 **Two Serious Ladies** (1st book) NY 1943, DJ 300 - 500
MB4811 Lon 1965, DJ 50 - 75

Bowles, Paul
MB4880 **The Delicate Prey and Other Stories**
 NY 1950, DJ 50 - 75
MB4890 **Let It Come Down** NY 1952, DJ 100 - 150
MB5000 **The Sheltering Sky** (1st novel) Lon 1949, DJ 200 - 300
MB5001 NY 1949, DJ (1st American ed) 150 - 200
MB5010 **Two Poems** (1st book) NY 1934, DJ 600 - 800
MB5020 **Up Above the World** NY 1966, DJ 30 - 50
MB5030 **Yallah** Zurich 1956, DJ 50 - 75
MB5032 NY 1957, DJ (1st American ed) 20 - 30

Boyd, James
MB5100 **Drums** (1st book) NY-Lon 1925, DJ 200 - 300
MB5101 NY 1928, 525 cys, DJ 100 - 150

Boyd, William
MB5170 **A Good Man in Africa** (1st book) Lon 1981, DJ 125 - 250
MB5171 NY 1981, DJ (1st American ed) 25 - 50
MB5180 **The New Confessions** NY 1988, DJ 50 - 75

Boyle, Kay
MB5260 **The Crazy Hunter** NY 1940, DJ 200 - 300
MB5270 **Fifty Stories** NY 1980, DJ 25 - 50
MB5280 **The First Lover and Other Stories** NY 1933 200 - 300
MB5290 **Gentlemen, I Address You Privately** NY 1933 200 - 300
MB5300 **Monday Night** NY 1938 100 - 150
MB5310 **Plagued by the Nightingale** NY 1931, DJ 150 - 250
MB5311 Lon 1931, DJ 150 - 250
MB5320 **Short Stories** (1st book) Paris 1929, 15 cys
 on Japan paper 1000 - 1200
MB5321 150 cys, box 400 - 600
MB5322 20 cys on Arches paper 800 - 1200
MB5330 **A Statement** NY 1932, 175 cys 250 - 350
MB5340 **The Underground Woman** NY 1975, DJ 100 - 150
MB5350 **Wedding Day and Other Stories** NY 1930,
 DJ, photo laid in 150 - 200
MB5360 **The White Horses of Vienna** NY 1936, DJ 150 - 250
MB5370 **Year Before Last** NY 1932, DJ 200 - 300

Brackett, Leigh
MB5450 **Silent Partner** NY 1969, DJ 50 - 75

Bradbury, Malcolm
MB5530 **Eating People Is Wrong** (1st book) Lon 1959, DJ 125 - 250

Bradbury, Ray
MB5610 **The Anthem Sprinters and Other Antics**
 NY 1963, DJ 150 - 250
MB5620 **Dandelion Wine** Lon 1957, DJ 150 - 250
MB5630 **Dark Carnival** (1st book) Sauk City 1947, DJ 600 - 800
MB5631 Lon 1948, DJ (1st English ed) 250 - 350
MB5640 **Fahrenheit 451** NY 1953, DJ 300 - 500
MB5641 NY 1953 (Ballantine Paperback) 50 - 75
MB5642 Lon 1954, 200 cys, asbestos covers 1000 - 1500
MB5650 **The Golden Apples of the Sun** NY 1953, DJ 150 - 250
MB5660 **I Sing the Body Electric** NY 1969, DJ 75 - 125
MB5670 **The Illustrated Man** NY 1951, DJ 250 - 350
MB5680 **Long After Midnight** NY 1976, DJ 50 - 75
MB5690 **The Machineries of Joy** NY 1964, DJ 200 - 300

MB5700	**The Martian Chronicles** NY 1950, DJ	300 - 500
MB5702	NY 1974, slipcase	125 - 250
MB5710	**A Medicine for the Melancholy** NY 1959, DJ	150 - 250
MB5720	**The October Country** NY 1955, DJ	300 - 500
MB5730	**The Silver Locusts** Lon 1951, DJ	250 - 350
MB5740	**Something Wicked This Way Comes** Lon 1963, DJ	250 - 350
MB5750	**Switch On The Night** NY 1955, DJ	150 - 250
MB5760	**When Elephants Last in the Door Yard Bloomed** Lon 1975, DJ	50 - 75

Bradford, Roark

MB5840	**How Come Christmas** NY 1930, 1400 cys	75 - 125
MB5842	NY 1934, DJ (1st trade ed)	50 - 75
MB5850	**John Henry** NY 1931, DJ	50 - 75
MB5851	NY 1931 (Literary Guild Reprint) DJ	20 - 30
MB5860	**Kingdom Coming** NY 1933, DJ	50 - 75
MB5870	**Ol' King David an' the Philistines** NY 1930, DJ	50 - 75
MB5880	**Ol' Man Adam and His Chillun** (1st book) NY 1928, DJ	100 - 150
MB5890	**This Side Jordan** NY 1929, DJ	50 - 75

Braine, John

MB5970	**Life at the Top** Lon 1962, DJ	30 - 40
MB5980	**Room at the Top** (1st book) Lon 1957, DJ w/wraparound band	100 - 150
MB5981	Bos 1957, DJ (1st American ed)	25 - 50

Braithwaite, William S.

MB6040	**Lyrics of Life and Love** (1st book) Bos 1904, 500 cys, DJ	150 - 200

Bramah, Ernest

MB6120	**English Farming and Why I Turned It Up** (1st book) Lon 1894	200 - 300
MB6130	**The Eyes of Max Carrados** Lon 1923, DJ	300 - 500
MB6140	**Kai Lung Unrolls His Mat** Garden City 1928, DJ	100 - 150
	w/o DJ	20 - 30
MB6150	**Kai Lung's Golden Hours** Lon 1924, 250 cys	250 - 350
MB6160	**Max Carrados** Lon 1914, DJ	300 - 500
MB6170	**The Mirror of Kong Ho** NY 1930, DJ	150 - 250
MB6180	**The Transmutation of Ling** Lon 1911, 500 cys	300 - 500
MB6190	**The Wallet of Kai Lung** Lon 1900, DJ, 1st issue: 1-1/2" across	150 - 200
MB6192	Lon 1923, 200 cys	200 - 300

Brautigan, Richard

MB6300	**A Confederate General From Big Sur** NY 1964, DJ	100 - 150
MB6310	**Dreaming of Babylon** NY 1977, DJ	50 - 75
MB6320	**Four New Poets** SF 1957 (Anthology; 1st appearance of Brautigan)	100 - 150
MB6330	**The Galilee Hitch-Hiker** SF 1958	100 - 150
MB6340	**The Hawkline Monster** NY 1974, DJ	30 - 50
MB6350	**In Watermelon Sugar** SF 1968, 50 signed cys	200 - 300
MB6360	**Lay the Marble Tea** SF 1959	150 - 200
MB6370	**The Octopus Frontier** SF 1960	125 - 250
MB6380	**The Pill Versus the Springhill Mine Disaster** SF 1968, 50 cys	200 - 300
MB6390	**Please Plant This Book** SF 1968	200 - 300
MB6400	**The Return of the Rivers** (1st book) SF 1958	1000 - 1200
MB6410	**Rommel Drives On Deep Into Egypt** NY 1970, DJ	50 - 75
MB6420	**So The Wind Won't Blow It Away** NY 1982, DJ	20 - 30
MB6430	**Sombrero Fallout** NY 1976, DJ	30 - 50
MB6440	**The Tokyo-Montana Express** NY 1980, DJ	30 - 50
MB6450	**Willard and His Bowling Trophies** NY 1975, DJ	40 - 60

Breton, Andre

MB6540	**Nadja** Paris 1928, 100 cys, slipcase	4000 - 6000

Bridges, Robert

MB6620	**Eros and Psyche, A Poem** Newton, Wales 1935, 300 cys, slipcase	1500 - 2500
MB6621	Newton, Wales 1935, 15 cys	3000 - 5000
MB6630	**The Influence of the Audience** NY 1926, 100 cys, box	200 - 300
MB6640	**The Tapestry** Lon 1925, 150 cys, box	500 - 700
MB6650	**The Testament of Beauty** Oxford 1929, 50 cys	300 - 500
MB6651	NY 1929, 250 cys	150 - 250

Bromfield, Louis

MB6740	**Awake and Rehearse** NY 1929, 500 cys, box	100 - 150
MB6750	**Early Autumn** NY 1926, DJ (Pulitzer Prize 1927)	50 - 100
MB6760	**The Farm** NY 1933, DJ	50 - 100
MB6770	**A Good Woman** NY 1927, DJ	50 - 100
MB6780	**The Green Bay Tree** (1st book) NY 1924, DJ	200 - 300

MB6790	**Possession** NY 1925, DJ	50 - 75

Brooke, Rupert

MB6870	**1914 and Other Poems** Lon 1915, DJ	800 - 1200
MB6871	NY 1915, 87 cys	500 - 700
MB6880	**"1914": Five Sonnets** Lon 1915 w/envelope	300 - 500
MB6890	**Collected Poems** NY 1915, 100 cys	1000 - 1500
MB6892	Lon 1919, 13 cys on vellum	3000 - 5000
MB6900	**Lithuania: A Drama in One Act** Chi 1915	300 - 500
MB6910	**Poems** Lon 1911, 100 cys	2000 - 3000
MB6920	**The Pyramids** (1st book) Rugby 1904, wrappers	7000 - 10000

Brooks, Gwendolyn

MB7000	**Annie Allen** NY 1949, DJ	100 - 150
MB7010	**The Bean Eaters** NY 1960, DJ	75 - 125
MB7020	**Bronzeville Boys and Girls** NY 1956, DJ	100 - 150
MB7030	**Family Pictures** Detroit 1970, DJ	50 - 75
MB7040	**Maud Martha** NY 1953, DJ	100 - 150
MB7050	**Report From Part One** Detroit 1972, DJ	25 - 50
MB7060	**A Street in Bronzeville** (1st book) NY 1945	200 - 300

Broun, Heywood

MB7140	**The Catacombs** NY 1965, DJ	75 - 100

Brown, Bob

MB7210	**Demonics** Cagnes-Sur-Mer, France 1931	500 - 700
MB7220	**Let There Be Beer** NY 1932, DJ	100 - 150
MB7230	**Readies For Bob Brown's Machine** Cagnes-Sur-Mer, France 1931	500 - 700
MB7240	**The Remarkable Adventures of Christopher Poe** (1st book) Chi 1913, DJ	300 - 500
MB7250	**Words** Paris 1931, 150 cys	300 - 500

Brown, Fredric

MB7340	**The Fabulous Clipjoint** (1st book) NY 1947, DJ	200 - 300
MB7350	**Martians, Go Home** NY 1955, DJ	200 - 300

Brown, Rosellen

MB7430	**Civil Wars** NY 1984, DJ	20 - 30

Brunner, John

MB7510	**Galactic Storm** Lon 1952, wrappers, under pseud Gill Hunt	100 - 150
MB7530	**Stand on Zanzibar** NY 1968, DJ	200 - 300

Buck, Pearl (1938 Nobel Laureate)

MB7600	**East Wind: West Wind** NY 1930, DJ	300 - 500
MB7610	**The Exile** NY 1936, DJ	50 - 100
MB7620	**The First Wife** NY 1933, DJ	50 - 100
MB7630	**The Good Earth** NY 1931, DJ, 1st issue w/"flees" instead of "fleas" on line 17, p 100	2000 - 3000
MB7631	NY 1931 (advance review cy)	800 - 1200
MB7632	NY 1938 (pocket book reprint)	10 - 20
MB7633	later issues	50 - 150
MB7640	**A House Divided** NY 1935, DJ	75 - 125
MB7650	**Sons** NY 1932, 371 cys, box	150 - 200

Bukowski, Charles

MB7710	**At Terror Street and Agony Way** LA 1968, 75 cys w/original illus	200 - 300
MB7720	**Cold Dogs in the Courtyard** Chi 1965, 500 cys	100 - 150
MB7730	**Crucifix in a Death Hand** NY 1965, wrappers	100 - 150
MB7740	**The Curtains Are Waving** LA 1967, 125 cys	200 - 300
MB7750	**The Days Run Away Like Wild Horses Over The Hills** LA 1969, 250 cys, acetate DJ	200 - 300
MB7760	**Flower, Fist and Bestial Wail** (1st book) Eureka 1959, wrappers	300 - 500
MB7770	**Poems Written Before Jumping Out of an 8 Story Window** Berkeley 1968, ppr wraps	75 - 100

MB6450   MB7350   MB7530

133

MB8730	**MB8780**	**MC0345**

MB7780	**Post Office** LA 1971 250 cys, acetate DJ	150 - 200
MB7781	LA 1971, 50 cys	300 - 500
MB7790	**Septuagenarian Stew** Santa Rosa 1990, 1000 cys, acetate DJ	30 - 50
MB7800	**War All the Time Poems 1981-84** Santa Barbara 1984, 400 cys, acetate DJ	75 - 100

Bunting, Basil

MB7910	**Brigg Flatts** Lon 1966 100 cys, DJ	200 - 300
MB7920	**Collected Poems** Lon 1968, DJ, 150 cys w/numbered silkscreen	200 - 300
MB7930	**Descant on Rawthey's Madrigal** Lexington 1968, 25 cys	200 - 300
MB7940	**First Book of Odes** Lon, 125 cys	200 - 300
MB7950	**Loquitar** Lon 1965 26 cys	200 - 300
MB7951	Lon 1965, 200 cys	75 - 100
MB7952	Lon 1965, 1000 cys	30 - 50
MB7960	**Redimiculum Metallarum** (1st book) Milan 1930, DJ	1800 - 2500
MB7970	**Two Poems** Santa Barbara 1967, 250 cys, signed	100 - 150
	unsigned	50 - 75

Burgess, Anthony

MB8100	**Beds in the East** Lon 1959, DJ	150 - 250
MB8110	**A Clockwork Orange** Lon 1962, DJ	200 - 300
MB8112	NY 1963, DJ	125 - 200
MB8120	**Devil of a State** Lon 1961, DJ	150 - 250
MB8130	**The Doctor is Sick** Lon 1960, DJ	150 - 250
MB8131	NY 1960, DJ	50 - 75
MB8140	**Earthly Powers** NY 1980, DJ	20 - 30
MB8150	**The Enemy in the Blanket** Lon 1958, DJ	150 - 250
MB8160	**Honey For The Bears** Lon 1963, DJ	150 - 200
MB8162	NY 1964, DJ	50 - 100
MB8170	**Nothing Like The Sun** Lon 1964, DJ	150 - 200
MB8171	NY 1964, DJ	50 - 100
MB8180	**The Right to an Answer** Lon 1960, DJ	150 - 250
MB8182	NY 1961, DJ	75 - 125
MB8190	**Time For a Tiger** (1st book) Lon 1956, DJ	300 - 500
MB8200	**A Vision of Battlements** Lon 1964, 1st issue DJ w/Pagram illus	100 - 150
MB8202	NY 1965, DJ	30 - 50
MB8210	**Will and Testament** Verona 1977, 96 cys, wood box	2000 - 3000

Burke, James Lee

MB8310	**Heaven's Prisoners** NY 1988, DJ	30 - 50
MB8320	**The Neon Rain** (1st novel) NY 1987, DJ	40 - 60

Burnett, Frances Hodgson

MB8410	**The Secret Garden** NY 1911, pictorial cover	125 - 175
	plain cream cl	50 - 75

Burnett, W. R. (William Riley)

MB8510	**Little Caesar** (1st book) NY 1929	500 - 700

Burnett, Whit

MB8610	**The Maker of Signs** (1st book) NY 1934, DJ	50 - 75

Burroughs, Edgar Rice

MB8700	**At the Earth's Core** Chi 1922, DJ	1500 - 2500
	w/o DJ	125 - 250
MB8710	**Back in the Stone Age** Tarzana 1937, DJ	300 - 500
MB8720	**The Beasts of Tarzan** Chi 1916, DJ	3000 - 5000
	w/o DJ	200 - 300
MB8730	**Carson of Venus** Tarzana, CA, 1939, DJ	300 - 500
MB8740	**The Chessmen of Mars** Chi 1922, DJ	1000 - 1500
	w/o DJ	100 - 150
MB8750	**The Eternal Lover** Chi 1925, DJ	700 - 1000
MB8760	**A Fighting Man of Mars** NY 1931, DJ	800 - 1200
	w/o DJ	100 - 150

MB8770	**The Girl From Hollywood** NY 1923, DJ, 1st state w/green print on cover	300 - 500
MB8780	**Jungle Girl** Lon 1933, DJ	125 - 200
MB8790	**Jungle Tales of Tarzan** Chi 1919, DJ	2000 - 3000
	w/o DJ	200 - 300
MB8800	**The Master Mind of Mars** Chi 1928, DJ	1000 - 1500
	w/o DJ	200 - 300
MB8810	**The Mucker** Chi 1921, DJ	300 - 500
MB8820	**The Outlaw of Torn** Chi 1927	1500 - 2500
MB8830	**A Princess of Mars** Chi 1917, DJ	1500 - 2500
	w/o DJ	200 - 300
MB8840	**The Return of Tarzan** Chi 1915, DJ	3000 - 5000
	w/o DJ	200 - 300
MB8850	**The Son of Tarzan** Chi 1917, DJ	3000 - 5000
	w/o DJ	200 - 300
MB8860	**Tarzan and the Ant Men** Chi 1924, DJ	1200 - 1800
	w/o DJ	150 - 250
MB8870	**Tarzan and the Golden Lion** Chi 1933, DJ	2000 - 3000
	w/o DJ	150 - 250
MB8880	**Tarzan and the Jewels of Opar** Chi 1918, DJ	3000 - 5000
	w/o DJ	200 - 300
MB8890	**Tarzan and the Leopard Men** Tarzana 1935, DJ	300 - 500
MB8900	**Tarzan at the Earth's Core** NY 1930, DJ	800 - 1200
	w/o DJ	100 - 150
MB8910	**Tarzan, Lord of the Jungle** Chi 1928, DJ	2000 - 3000
	w/o DJ	150 - 250
MB8920	**Tarzan of the Apes** (1st book) Chi 1914, DJ, 1st issue w/printer's name on cr page in Old English type	15000 - 25000
	w/o DJ	300 - 500
MB8922	Lon 1917, DJ, w/ ads dated Autumn	300 - 500
MB8923	NY, about 1932, DJ (Grosset & Dunlap reprint)	100 - 150
MB8930	**Tarzan the Untamed** Chi 1920, DJ	2000 - 3000
	w/o DJ	200 - 300
MB8940	**Tarzan Triumphant** Tarzana 1932, DJ	300 - 500
MB8950	**Thuvia, Maid of Mars** Chi 1920, DJ	1200 - 1800
	w/o DJ	100 - 150
MB8960	**The Warlord of Mars** Chi 1919, DJ, 1st issue w/"W.F. Hall" on cr page	2000 - 3000
	w/o DJ	200 - 300

Burroughs, William S.

MB9110	**The Adding Machine** NY 1986, DJ	75 - 100
MB9120	**Ali's Smile** Brighton 1971, 99 cys, lp record	200 - 300
MB9130	**The Book of Breething** Essex 1974, 350 cys	100 - 150
MB9140	**Cities of the Red Night** NY 1981, DJ	30 - 50
MB9150	**Junkie** NY 1953, Ace - D-15 Pocketbook, 1st edition under pseud William Lee	150 - 200
MB9160	**The Last Words of Dutch Schultz** Lon 1970, DJ	50 - 75
MB9170	**The Naked Lunch** Paris 1959, DJ, 1st state w/green border on tp	200 - 300
MB9172	NY 1962, DJ	75 - 125
MB9180	**Nova Express** NY 1964, DJ	50 - 75
MB9190	**Queer** NY 1985. DJ	75 - 125
MB9200	**The Retreat Diaries** NY 1976, 2000 cys, w/poem by Allen Ginsberg	50 - 75
MB9210	**Sinki's Sauna** NY 1982, 500 cys	50 - 75
MB9220	**The Soft Machine** Paris 1961	50 - 75
MB9230	**The Third Mind** NY 1978, DJ	75 - 125
MB9240	**The Ticket That Exploded** Paris 1962, DJ	75 - 125
MB9250	**Time** NY 1965, 100 cys, wrappers	100 - 150
MB9251	NY 1965, wrappers	20 - 30

Butler, Ellis Parker

MB9310	**Philo Gubb: Correspondence School Detective** Bos 1918, DJ	50 - 75
MB9321	**Pigs is Pigs** (1st book) Chi 1905, DJ, 1st state w/author's name on 1st page of text	800 - 1200
MB9323	NY 1906, DJ	20 - 30

Butts, Mary

MB9410	**Armed with Madness** Lon 1928, 100 cys, box	300 - 500
MB9420	**Ashe of Rings** Paris 1925, 100 cys, box	400 - 600
MB9421	Lon 1933 (1st English ed)	200 - 300
MB9430	**The Crystal Cabinet** Lon 1937	250 - 350
MB9440	**Imaginary Letters** Paris 1928, 250 cys, glassine DJ	250 - 350
MB9450	**The Macedonian** Lon 1933	150 - 250
MB9460	**Scenes From the Life of Cleopatra** Lon 1935, DJ	200 - 300
MB9470	**Several Occasions** Lon 1932	150 - 250
MB9480	**Speed the Plow and Other Stories** (1st book) Lon 1923	500 - 700

Byrne, Donn

MB9610	**Blind Raftery and His Wife Hilaria** NY 1924, DJ	100 - 150
MB9620	**Brother Saul** NY 1927, 500 cys, box	150 - 250
MB9630	**The Changeling and Other Stories** NY 1923	100 - 150
MB9640	**Crusade** Bos 1928, 365 cys, box	150 - 250
MB9641	Bos 1928 (1st trade ed) DJ	50 - 75
MB9650	**Destiny Bay** Bos 1928, 365 cys, box	150 - 250
MB9651	Bos 1928, DJ (1st trade ed)	50 - 75
MB9660	**Field of Honor** NY 1929, 500 cys, box	150 - 250
MB9661	NY 1929, DJ (1st trade ed)	50 - 75
MB9670	**The Foolish Matrons** NY 1920, DJ, 1st issue w/"I-U" on cr page	100 - 150
MB9680	**Hangmans House** NY 1926, 350 cys, box	200 - 300
MB9681	NY 1926, DJ (1st trade ed)	50 - 75
MB9690	**Messer Marco Polo** NY 1921, DJ, w/perfect type in word "of" p 10, 2nd to last line	150 - 250
MB9700	**Stories Without Women** (1st book) NY 1915, DJ	150 - 250
MB9710	**The Strangers' Banquet** NY 1919, w/"M-T" on cr page	75 - 125
MB9720	**The Wind Bloweth** NY 1922 w/misprint on P 151, line 20 "mouth of money"	100 - 150

Cabell, James Branch

MC0100	**Ballades From the Hidden Way** NY 1928, 839 cys	100 - 150
MC0101	NY 1928, 8 cys	1000 - 1500
MC0105	**Beyond Life** NY 1919, DJ, w/black cl & "Demi urges" instead of "Démi urges" on tp	150 - 250
MC0110	**Branchiana** Richmond 1907, 147 cys, slipcase	700 - 1000
MC0115	**The Certain Hour** NY 1916, DJ	150 - 250
MC0120	**Chivalry** NY 1909, glassine DJ, box, red cl, green, white, gold printing	250 - 350
MC0125	**The Cords of Vanity** NY 1909, 1st state w/"The" omitted on sp	200 - 300
MC0127	NY 1920, DJ	50 - 75
MC0131	**The Eagles Shadow** (1st book) NY 1904, DJ, 1st issue w/dedication to M.L.P.B.	250 - 350
MC0132	2nd issue dedicated to "Martha Branch"	75 - 125
MC0134	NY 1923, DJ	20 - 30
MC0140	**Gallantry** NY 1907, 1st state w/silver-gray cl, box	200 - 300
MC0145	**Hamlet Had An Uncle** NY 1940, 125 cys, slipcase	300 - 500
MC0151	**Jurgen** NY 1919, DJ, 1st state meas 1-3/8" across top	500 - 700
MC0152	DJ, slipcase	
MC0154	Lon 1949 (Golden Cockerell) 100 cys	800 - 1200
MC0155	Lon 1949 (Golden Cockerell) 400 cys	300 - 500
MC0160	**Ladies and Gentlemen** NY 1934, 153 cys, slipcase	150 - 200
MC0165	**The Line of Love** NY 1905, 1st state w/white & gold printing on cover, glassine DJ	150 - 250
MC0170	**The Majors and Their Marriages** Richmond 1915, wrappers	300 - 500
MC0175	**The Music From Behind the Moon** NY 1926, glassine DJ, slipcase	100 - 150
MC0180	**The Nightmare Has Triplets** Garden City 1937, Doubleday flyer tipped in	200 - 300
MC0185	**The Rivet in Grandfather's Neck** NY 1915, DJ	75 - 125
MC0190	**Smirt** NY 1934, DJ	75 - 125
MC0191	NY 1934, 153 cys, box	250 - 300
MC0195	**Smith** NY 1935, 153 cys, slipcase	150 - 200
MC0200	**Sonnets From Antan** NY 1929, 718 cys	150 - 250
MC0205	**The Soul of Melicent** NY 1913, DJ	250 - 350
MC0210	**Special Delivery** NY 1933, 207 cys, slipcase	150 - 250
MC0215	**Taboo** NY 1921 100 cys	300 - 500
MC0216	NY 1921, 820 cys	75 - 125
MC0220	**The Way of Ecben** NY 1929, 850 cys, glassine DJ, box	150 - 200
MC0221	NY 1929, slipcase	20 - 40

Cain, James M.

MC0310	**The Baby in the Icebox** NY 1981, DJ	20 - 30
MC0315	**Galatea** NY 1953, DJ	200 - 300
MC0320	**The Institute** NY 1976, DJ	20 - 30
MC0325	**Mildred Pierce** NY 1941, DJ	100 - 150
MC0326	NY 1941, wrappers (advance review cy)	250 - 350
MC0330	**The Moth** NY 1948, DJ	250 - 350
MC0335	**Our Government** (1st book) NY 1930, DJ	200 - 300
MC0340	**The Postman Always Rings Twice** NY 1934, DJ	400 - 600
MC0345	**Serenade** NY 1937, DJ	300 - 500

Caldwell, Erskine

MC0410	**All Night Long** NY 1942, DJ	100 - 150
MC0415	**American Earth** NY 1931, DJ, w/letter "A" on cr page	75 - 100
MC0420	**The Bastard** (1st book) NY 1929, 200 cys, signed, glassine DJ	300 - 500
MC0421	NY 1929, 900 cys, unsigned	200 - 300
MC0425	**God's Little Acre** NY 1933, DJ	100 - 150
MC0430	**Gretta** Bos 1955, DJ	30 - 40
MC0435	**Jenny By Nature** NY 1961	25 - 35
MC0440	**Journeyman** NY 1935, 1475 cys, glassine DJ, box	75 - 100
MC0445	**Kneel to the Rising Sun and Other Stories** NY 1935, 300 cys, box	200 - 300
MC0446	NY 1935, DJ (1st trade ed)	50 - 75
MC0450	**Mama's Little Girl** Mount Vernon 1933, 100 cys	300 - 500
MC0455	**A Message For Genevievi** Mount Vernon 1933, 100 cys, wrappers	400 - 600
MC0460	**North of the Danube** NY 1939, DJ	150 - 250
MC0465	**Poor Fool** NY 1930, 1000 cys	100 - 150
MC0470	**Say, Is This the U.S.A.** NY 1941, DJ	100 - 150
MC0475	**Southways** NY 1938, DJ	100 - 150
MC0480	**Tenant Farmer** NY 1935, 1500 cys, wrappers	150 - 200
MC0485	**Tobacco Road** NY 1932, DJ, "A" on cr page	400 - 600
MC0490	**We Are the Living** NY 1933, 250 cys, box	200 - 300
MC0491	NY 1933, DJ (1st trade ed)	100 - 150

Caldwell, Taylor

MC0550	**Dynasty of Death** (1st book) NY 1938, DJ	50 - 75

Calisher, Hortense

MC0610	**In the Absence of Angels** (1st book) Bos 1951, DJ	75 - 125
MC0612	Lon 1953, DJ	50 - 75
MC0620	**Journal From Ellipsia** Bos 1965, DJ	40 - 60
MC0630	**The Railway Police and The Last Trolley Kids** Bos 1966, DJ	30 - 40

Callaghan, Morley

MC0710	**A Native Argosy** NY 1929, DJ	150 - 200
MC0720	**No Man's Meat** Paris 1931, 525 cys, box	300 - 500
MC0730	**Strange Fugitive** (1st book) NY 1928, DJ	200 - 300

Campbell, John W.

MC0810	**The Atomic Story** (1st book) NY 1947	100 - 150
MC0820	**Invaders of the Infinite** Hicksville 1961, DJ	75 - 100
MC0821	Reading 1961, 112 cys	200 - 300
MC0830	**The Mightiest Machine** Providence 1947, DJ	100 - 150

Campbell, Roy

MC0910	**Adamastor: Poems** Lon 1930, 90 cys	300 - 500
MC0911	Lon 1930, 1st issue of trade ed w/name printed twice on DJ	100 - 150
MC0912	later issues	50 - 75
MC0920	**Broken Record** Lon 1934, DJ, 50 cys	400 - 600
MC0925	**Choosing A Mast** Lon 1931, 300 cys	300 - 500
MC0930	**The Flaming Terrapin** (1st book) Lon 1924, DJ	200 - 300
MC0931	NY 1924, DJ	75 - 100
MC0935	**Flowering Reeds: Poems** Lon 1933, 69 cys	400 - 600
MC0936	Lon 1933 (1st trade ed) DJ	150 - 250
MC0940	**The Georgiad** Lon 1931, 150 cys	250 - 350
MC0941	Lon 1931, 20 cys	700 - 1000
MC0945	**The Gum Trees** Lon 1930, 400 cys	200 - 300
MC0950	**Mithraic Emblems** Lon 1936, 30 cys	500 - 700
MC0955	**Poems** Paris 1930, 200 cys	300 - 500
MC0960	**Pomegranates** Lon 1932, 99 cys, glassine DJ	300 - 500
MC0965	**The Wayzgoose** Lon 1928	150 - 250

Camus, Albert (1957 Nobel Laureate)

MC1020	**The Fall** Kentfield 1966, 140 cys	100 - 150
MC1025	**La Peste** Paris 1947, wrappers	700 - 1000
MC1030	**L'Entranger** (1st novel) Paris 1942, wrappers	800 - 1200
MC1035	**The Outsider** Lon 1946	150 - 250
MC1040	**September 15th, 1937** Bronxville 1963, 50 cys	150 - 250
MC1045	**The Stranger** NY 1946, DJ	150 - 250

Capa, Robert

MC1110	**Death in the Making** NY 1938, DJ	150 - 200
MC1120	**Slightly Out of Focus** NY 1947, DJ	50 - 75

Capek, Karel

Coined the word "Robot" for a mechanical man.

MC1210	**The Absolute at Large** Lon 1927, DJ	100 - 150
MC1220	**Krakatit** NY 1925, DJ	200 - 300
MC1230	**The Makropolous Affair** (1st book) Lon 1922	200 - 300

 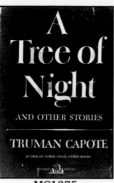 

MC1250	MC1375	MC2160

MC1232	Bos 1925	100 - 150
MC1240	**Tales From Two Pockets** Lon 1932, DJ	50 - 75
MC1250	**War With the Newts** Lon 1936, DJ	150 - 200

Capote, Truman
MC1310	**Breakfast at Tiffany's** NY 1958, DJ	150 - 200
MC1315	**A Christmas Memory** NY 1966, 600 cys, box	200 - 300
MC1320	**The Grass Harp** NY 1952, DJ	100 - 150
MC1325	**I Remember Grandpa, A Story** Atlanta 1987, DJ	30 - 50
MC1330	**In Cold Blood** NY 1965, 500 cys, glassine DJ	200 - 300
MC1331	NY 1965, DJ (1st trade ed)	20 - 30
MC1340	**Local Color** NY 1950, DJ	200 - 300
MC1341	Lon 1950, 200 cys	200 - 300
MC1345	**Music for Chameleons** NY 1980, 350 cys, box	200 - 300
MC1346	NY 1980, DJ (1st trade ed)	15 - 25
MC1350	**Observations** NY 1959, folio, box	400 - 600
MC1355	**One Christmas** NY 1983, 500 cys, slipcase	150 - 200
MC1360	**Other Voices, Other Rooms** (1st book) NY 1948, DJ	300 - 500
MC1361	Lon 1948, DJ	100 - 150
MC1363	PA 1979 (Franklin Library ed) signed	100 - 150
MC1370	**The Thanksgiving Visitor** NY 1968, 300 cys, box	300 - 500
MC1375	**A Tree of Night** NY 1949, DJ	200 - 300

Carman, Bliss
MC1440	**Ballads and Lyrics** Lon 1902	200 - 300
MC1445	**The Gate of Peace: A Poem** NY 1907, 112 cys	
MC1450	**Low Tide on Grand Pre** (1st book) NY 1893	400 - 600
MC1451	Lon 1893	200 - 300
MC1455	**Poems** NY 1904, 2 vol, 500 cys, box	300 - 500
MC1456	Bos 1905 2 vol, 500 cys, box	200 - 300
MC1460	**The Princess of the Tower** NY 1906, 62 cys	400 - 600
MC1465	**Sappho** Bos 1904, 500 cys	150 - 250
MC1466	50 cys, vellum	700 - 1000
MC1470	**Songs From Vagabondia** Bos 1894	200 - 300
MC1475	**The Vengeance of Noel Brassard** Cambridge 1899, w/misdated tp	300 - 500

Carpenter, Don
MC1550	**Hard Rain Falling** (1st book) NY 1966, DJ	30 - 40

Carr, John Dickson
MC1610	**Death Turns the Tables** NY 1941, DJ	200 - 300
MC1620	**It Walks by Night** (1st book) NY 1930, DJ	700 - 1000

Carter, Angela
MC1710	**Heroes and Villians** Lon 1969, DJ	100 - 150
MC1715	**Honey Buzzard** NY 1966, DJ	50 - 75
MC1720	**Love** Lon 1971, DJ	100 - 150
MC1725	**The Magic Toyshop** Lon 1967, DJ	100 - 150
MC1730	**Shadow Dance** Lon 1966, DJ	125 - 250
MC1735	**Unicorn** (1st book) Leeds 1966, DJ	200 - 300

Carter, Forrest
MC1810	**The Education of Little Tree** NY 1976, DJ	40 - 60
MC1820	**The Rebel Outlaw: Josey Wales** 1973, DJ	75 - 125
MC1822	later title: **Gone to Texas** NY 1975, DJ	50 - 75

Carver, Raymond
MC1910	**Cathedral** NY 1983, DJ	20 - 30
MC1915	**Elephant and Other Stories** Lon 1988, DJ	30 - 50
MC1920	**Fires** Lon 1985, DJ	30 - 50
MC1925	**Ultramarine** NY 1986, DJ	30 - 50
MC1930	**What We Talk About When We Talk About Love** NY 1981, DJ	30 - 50

Cary, Joyce (Arthur)
MC2010	**Aissa Saved** Lon 1932, DJ	400 - 600
MC2020	**The Horse's Mouth** Lon 1944, DJ	200 - 300
MC2030	**Verse** (1st book) Edinburgh 1908	2000 - 3000

Casement, Roger
MC2110	**Some Poems of Roger Casement** Dublin 1918, wrappers	150- 200

Castaneda, Carlos
MC2160	**The Eagle's Gift** NY 1981, DJ	15 - 25
MC2170	**The Teachings of Don Juan** (1st book) Berkeley 1968, DJ	125 - 200

Cather, Willa
MC2211	**Alexander's Bridge** Bos 1912, DJ, 1st issue w/author's middle initial "S" on sp & DJ	300 - 500
MC2212	2nd issue w/o "S" on DJ	150 - 200
MC2213	Lon 1912, DJ	150 - 250
MC2220	**April Twilights** (1st book) Bos 1903	800 - 1200
MC2222	Lon 1924, DJ (1st English ed)	200 - 300
MC2224	NY 1923, 450 cys	300 - 500
MC2230	**Death Comes for the Archbishop** NY 1927, DJ (1st trade ed)	300 - 500
MC2231	NY 1927, 170 cys, box	1000 - 1500
MC2232	NY 1927, 50 cys, box	2000 - 3000
MC2233	Lon 1927, DJ (1st English ed)	150 - 250
MC2235	NY 1929, 170 cys, box	1000 - 1500
MC2240	**The Fear That Walks by Noonday** NY 1931, 30 cys	400 - 600
MC2245	**A Lost Lady** NY 1923, DJ, 1st state in green cl, DJ	200 - 300
MC2246	NY 1923 20 cys, glassine DJ, Box	1500 - 2000
MC2247	NY 1923 200 cys, glassine DJ, box	700 - 1000
MC2248	NY 1923 (advance review cy)	1000 - 1500
MC2255	**Lucy Gayheart** NY 1935, DJ	100 - 150
MC2256	NY 1935, 749 cys, box, DJ	300 - 500
MC2260	**My Antonia** Bos 1918, DJ, 1st issue w/glazed ppr illus	800 - 1200
MC2261	Lon 1919, DJ	200 - 300
MC2265	**My Mortal Enemy** NY 1926, DJ, box	150 - 200
MC2266	NY 1926, 220 cys, DJ, box	700 - 1000
MC2270	**Not Under Forty** NY 1936, DJ	200 - 300
MC2271	NY 1936, DJ, 333 cys, box	300 - 500
MC2275	**The Novels and Stories of Willa Cather** Bos 1937-41, 13 vol, 970 cys, DJ	1200 - 2000
MC2280	**O Pioneers!** Bos 1913, DJ, 1st issue w/last text page tipped in	300 - 500
MC2281	Bos 1913, DJ, 2nd issue in brown cl	200 - 300
MC2285	**Obscure Destinies** NY 1932, DJ	100 - 150
MC2286	NY 1932, DJ, 260 cys, box	300 - 500
MC2290	**One of Ours** NY 1922, DJ	150 - 250
MC2291	NY 1922, 35 cys, box	2000 - 3000
MC2292	NY 1922, 310 cys, box	700 - 1000
MC2293	NY 1922, 2nd printing	50 - 75
MC2300	**The Professor's House** NY 1925, DJ	100 - 150
MC2301	NY 1925, 40 cys, vellum, box	500 - 700
MC2302	NY 1925, 185 cys, box	300 - 500
MC2310	**Sapphira and the Slave Girl** NY 1940, DJ	25 - 50
MC2311	NY 1940, 520 cys, DJ, box	200 - 300
MC2312	NY 1940, DJ (advance review cy)	150 - 200
MC2320	**Shadows on the Rock** NY 1931, DJ	100 - 150
MC2321	NY 1931, 619 cys, DJ, box	300 - 500
MC2322	NY 1931, 199 cys, DJ, box	700 - 1000
MC2330	**The Song of the Lark** Bos 1915, DJ	150 - 250
MC2335	**The Troll Garden** NY 1905, DJ, 1st issue w/McClure Phillips & Co. at bottom of sp	700 - 1000
MC2340	**Youth and the Bright Medusa** NY 1920, DJ	75 - 125
MC2341	NY 1920, 25 cys, DJ	1000 - 1500

Chabon, Michael
MC2410	**A Model World and Other Stories** NY 1991, DJ	30 - 40
MC2420	**The Mysteries of Pittsburgh** (1st book) NY 1988, DJ	30 - 40

Chambers, Robert
Wrote about 100 books; most are $25-75 except rarest and earliest.
MC2510	**Ashes of Empire** NY 1898	100 - 150
MC2515	**Barbarians** NY 1917, DJ	25 - 50
MC2520	**The Flaming Jewel** NY 1922, DJ	25 - 50
MC2525	**In The Quarter** (1st book) NY 1894	150 - 250
MC2530	**The King in Yellow** NY 1895	150 - 200
MC2535	**Quick Action** NY 1914, DJ	25 - 50

Chandler, Raymond
MC2610	**The Big Sleep** (1st book) NY 1939, DJ	7000 - 10000
	w/o DJ	800 - 1200
MC2611	Avon #38 (Pocketbook Reprint 1940s)	50 - 75
MC2613	SF 1986 425 cys, Plexiglass binding, poster	300 - 500

MC2620	**Farewell, My Lovely** NY 1940, DJ	1500 - 2500
MC2625	**The High Window** NY 1942, DJ	800 - 1200
MC2626	NY 1942, wrappers (advance review cy)	3000 - 5000
MC2630	**Killer in the Rain** Lon 1964, DJ	150 - 200
MC2631	Bos 1964, DJ	75 - 100
MC2635	**The Lady in the Lake** NY 1943, DJ	800 - 1200
MC2640	**The Long Goodbye** Lon 1953, DJ	250 - 350
MC2641	Bos 1954, DJ	150 - 200
MC2645	**Playback** Lon 1958, DJ	150 - 250
MC2646	Bos 1958, DJ	75 - 125
MC2650	**The Simple Art of Murder** Bos 1950, DJ	300 - 500
MC2655	**The Smell of Fear** Lon 1965, DJ	150 - 200

Chanslor, Roy
MC2710	**The Ballad of Cat Ballou** Bos 1956, DJ	40 - 60

Charyn, Jerome
MC2810	**Once Upon A Droshky** (1st book) NY 1964, DJ	50 - 75
MC2820	**The Seventh Babe** NY 1979, DJ	25 - 50

Cheever, John
MC2900	**The Brigadier and the Golf Widow** NY 1964, DJ	50 - 75
MC2905	**Bullet Park** NY 1969, DJ	30 - 50
MC2910	**The Enormous Radio** NY 1953, 1st printing w/"1" on cr page	200 - 300
MC2915	**Homage To Shakespeare** Stevenson, CT 1968, 150 cys, DJ	150 - 250
MC2920	**The Housebreaker of Shady Hill** NY 1958, DJ	100 - 125
MC2921	Lon 1958, DJ	75 - 100
MC2925	**Some People, Places, and Things That Will Not Appear In My Next Novel** NY 1961, DJ	150 - 200
MC2930	**The Wapshot Chronicle** NY 1957, DJ	75 - 125
MC2931	Lon 1957, DJ	50 - 75
MC2935	**The Way Some People Live** (1st book) NY 1943, DJ	500 - 700
MC2937	NY 1957, DJ	30 - 50
MC2938	Lon 1957, DJ	30 - 50

Chesnutt, Charles W.
MC3010	**The Conjure Woman** (1st book) Bos 1899, 150 cys	1000 - 1200
MC3011	Bos 1899 (1st trade ed)	200 - 300
MC3015	**Frederick Douglass** Bos 1899	150 - 250
MC3020	**The House Behind The Cedars** Bos 1900	150 - 250
MC3025	**The Wife of His Youth** Bos 1899	150 - 250

Chesterton, G. K. (Gilbert Keith)
MC3110	**The Ballad of the White Horse** Lon 1911, DJ	125 - 250
MC3112	Lon 1928, DJ, illus ed	200 - 300
MC3115	**Charles Dickens Fifty Years After** 1920, wrappers	300 - 500
MC3120	**Chaucer** Lon 1932, DJ	50 - 75
MC3125	**Collected Poems** Lon 1927, 350 cys	250 - 350
MC3130	**The Colored Lands** Lon 1938, DJ	150 - 200
MC3135	**Four Faultless Felons** Lon 1930, DJ	200 - 300
MC3140	**Graybeards at Play: Rhymes and Sketches** (1st book) Lon 1900	400 - 600
MC3145	**The Innocence of Father Brown** Lon 1911, DJ	500 - 700
MC3147	London Lon 1914	300 - 500
MC3150	**Man Alive** Lon 1912, DJ	300 - 500
MC3155	**The Man Who Knew Too Much** NY 1922, DJ	300 - 500
MC3160	**The Man Who Was Thursday** Lon 1908	300 - 500
MC3165	**The Poet and the Lunatics** Lon 1929, DJ	150 - 200
MC3166	NY 1929, DJ (1st American ed)	125 - 175
MC3170	**The Scandal of Father Brown** NY 1935, DJ	200 - 300
MC3171	Lon 1935, DJ (1st English ed)	150 - 250
MC3175	**The Secret of Father Brown** Lon 1927, DJ	200 - 300
MC3180	**The Sword of Wood** Lon 1928, 530 cys, DJ	200 - 300
MC3185	**The Wild Knight and Other Poems** Lon 1900	150 - 250
MC3190	**The Wisdom of Father Brown** Lon 1914, DJ	300 - 500

Cheyney, Peter
MC3250	**Lady, Behave** Lon 1950, DJ	40 - 60
MC3260	**Try Anything Twice** Lon 1948, DJ	40 - 60

Christie, Agatha
Wrote over 100 mystery books 1920-1970s. Her main protagonist is Hercule Poirot. Her books have been reprinted as Pocket Books, many having considerable value.

MC3310	**The ABC Murders** Lon 1936, DJ	300 - 500
MC3311	NY 1936, DJ (1st American ed)	300 - 500
MC3315	**The Adventure of the Christmas Pudding** Lon 1960, DJ	75 - 125
MC3320	**An Autobiography** Lon 1977, DJ	30 - 50
MC3325	**Bertram's Hotel** Lon 1965, DJ	25 - 50

MC3330	**The Big Four** Lon 1927, DJ	500 - 700
MC3331	NY 1927 DJ (1st American ed)	300 - 500
MC3333	NY (early 1940s), (Avon Pocketbook)	50 - 75
MC3340	**The Body in the Library** NY 1942, DJ	200 - 300
MC3341	Lon 1942, DJ (1st English ed)	200 - 300
MC3345	**Cards on the Table** Lon 1936, DJ	300 - 500
MC3346	NY 1937, DJ (1st American ed)	200 - 300
MC3350	**A Caribbean Mystery** Lon 1964, DJ	50 - 75
MC3351	NY 1965, DJ (1st American ed)	20 - 30
MC3355	**Death Comes as the End** NY 1944, DJ	300 - 500
MC3356	Lon 1945, DJ (1st English ed)	200 - 300
MC3360	**Elephants Can Remember** NY 1972, DJ	20 - 30
MC3361	Lon 1972, DJ (1st English ed)	30 - 50
MC3365	**Evil Under The Sun** Lon 1941, DJ	250 - 400
MC3366	NY 1941, DJ (1st American ed)	200 - 300
MC3370	**Hercule Poirot's Christmas** Lon 1938, DJ	300 - 500
MC3375	**Hickory Dickory Dock** Lon 1955, DJ	75 - 125
MC3377	U.S. title: **Hickory Dickory Death** NY 1955, DJ	75 - 125
MC3380	**The Hollow** Lon 1946, DJ	150 - 250
MC3381	NY 1946, DJ (1st American ed)	150 - 250
MC3385	**The Hound of Death** Lon 1933, DJ	300 - 500
MC3390	**The Man in the Brown Suit** Lon 1924, DJ	500 - 700
MC3395	**Murder in Mesopotamia** Lon 1936, DJ	300 - 500
MC3400	**A Murder is Announced** NY 1950, DJ	200 - 300
MC3405	**The Murder of Roger Ackroyd** Lon 1926, DJ	500 - 700
MC3410	**The Mysterious Affair at Styles** (1st book) Lon 1920, DJ	2000 - 3000
MC3411	NY 1920, DJ (1st American ed)	2000 - 3000
MC3415	**Nemesis** Lon 1971, DJ	30 - 50
MC3416	NY 1971, DJ (1st American ed)	30 - 50
MC3420	**Ordeal By Innocence** Lon 1958, DJ	75 - 125
MC3421	NY 1959, DJ (1st American ed)	50 - 75
MC3425	**Parker Pyne Investigates** Lon 1934, DJ	300 - 500
MC3427	U.S. title: **Mr. Parker Pyne: Detective** NY 1934, DJ	300 - 500
MC3430	**A Pocketful of Rye** Lon 1953, DJ	100 - 150
MC3431	NY 1954, DJ (1st American ed)	50 - 75
MC3435	**Poirot Investigates** Lon 1924, DJ	700 - 1000
MC3436	NY 1925, DJ (1st American ed)	300 - 500
MC3440	**Poirot's Early Cases** Lon 1974, DJ	30 - 50
MC3445	**The Regatta Mystery** NY 1939, DJ	200 - 300
MC3450	**The Seven Dials Mystery** Lon 1929, DJ	300 - 500
MC3451	NY 1929, DJ (1st American ed)	300 - 500
MC3455	**Ten Little Niggers** Lon 1939, DJ	500 - 700
MC3457	U.S. title: **And Then There Were None** NY 1940, DJ	200 - 300
MC3460	**The Thirteen Problems** Lon 1932, DJ	500 - 700
MC3462	U.S. title: **The Tuesday Club Murders** NY 1933, DJ	300 - 500

Clancy, Tom
MC3520	**The Hunt For Red October** Annapolis 1984, DJ	600 - 800
MC3530	**Patriot Games** NY 1987, DJ	20 - 30
MC3540	**Red Storm Rising** NY 1986, DJ	20 - 30

Clarke, Arthur C.
Scientist and writer of science books like Isaac Asimov.

MC3610	**2010: Odyssey Two** Huntington Woods 1982, 650 cys, slipcase	100 - 150
MC3611	NY 1982, DJ (1st trade ed)	20 - 30
MC3612	NY 1982 (uncorrected proof - stiff wraps)	100 - 150
MC3615	**Childhood's End** NY 1953, DJ	300 - 500
MC3620	**The City and the Stars** NY 1956, DJ	150 - 200
MC3625	**Earthlight** NY 1955, DJ	200 - 300
MC3630	**Expedition To Earth** NY 1953, DJ	200 - 300
MC3635	**Interplanetary Flight** (1st book) Lon 1950, DJ	100 150

MC2610   MC3333   MC3520

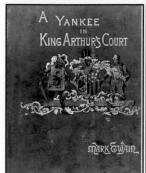  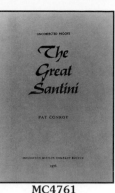

MC3800	MC3825	MC4761

| MC3640 | Reach For Tomorrow NY 1956, DJ | 1000 - 1500 |

Clavell, James
| MC3710 | King Rat (1st book) Bos 1962, DJ | 150 - 250 |
| MC3712 | Lon 1963, DJ (1st English ed) | 100 - 150 |

Clemens, Samuel (Mark Twain)
MC3800	A Connecticut Yankee in King Arthur's Court NY 1889, 1st issue w/"s" before "King" p 59	600 - 800
MC3810	A Dog's Tale NY 1904, 250 cys	
MC3812	Lon 1903, wrappers	500 - 700
MC3815	A Double Barrelled Detective Story NY 1902	150 - 250
MC3816	Lon 1902 (1st English ed)	200 - 300
MC3820	Eve's Diary NY 1906	100 - 150
MC3825	Extract From Captain Stormfield's Visit To Heaven NY 1906, 1st state (3/4" thick)	150 - 200
MC3826	2nd state	75 - 125
MC3827	NY 1909	
MC3830	Extracts From Adam's Diary NY 1904	100 - 150
MC3835	King Leopold's Soliloquy Bos 1905, 1st state w/dark green print	200 - 300
MC3840	The Man That Corrupted Hadleyburg NY 1900	150 - 250
MC3845	My Debut as a Literary Person Hartford 1903, 512 cys	300 - 500
MC3855	The Mysterious Stranger and Other Stories NY 1916, DJ	200 - 300

Clement, Hal
| MC3910 | Mission of Gravity NY 1954, DJ | 100 - 150 |

Clifton, Mark and Frank Riley
| MC4010 | They'd Rather Be Right NY 1957, DJ | 150 - 200 |

Cobb, Irvin S.
Wrote about 50 books; all are mildly collectible, most in $10-20 range.
MC4110	Back Home (1st book) NY 1912, DJ, 1st state w/"Plimpton Press" on cr page	50 - 75
MC4115	Cobb's Anatomy NY 1912, DJ	20 - 30
MC4120	Cobb's Bill of Fare NY 1913, DJ	20 - 30
MC4125	The Escape of Mr. Trimm NY 1913, DJ	30 - 50
MC4130	Old Judge Priest NY 1916, DJ	20 - 30

Cocteau, Jean
| MC4210 | Paris Album 1900-1914 Lon 1956, DJ | 30 - 50 |
| MC4220 | The White Paper By Anonymous Paris 1957, wrappers | 30 - 50 |

Collier, John
MC4310	Green Thoughts Lon 1932, 550 cys	300 - 500
MC4315	His Monkey Wife (1st book) Lon 1930, DJ	300 - 400
MC4316	NY 1931, DJ	200 - 300
MC4320	Pictures in the Fire Lon 1958, DJ	30 - 50
MC4325	Tom's A-Cold Lon 1933, DJ	150 - 250
MC4330	Witch's Money NY 1948, 350 cys, glassine DJ	200 - 300

Comfort, Will Levington
| MC4410 | Apache NY 1931, DJ | 300 - 500 |

Conrad, Joseph
MC4510	Admiralty Paper NY 1925, 93 cys	700 - 1000
MC4515	Almayer's Folly: A Story of an Eastern River (1st book) Lon 1895, 1st issue w/"generosity" mis-spelled on p 110, 2nd to last line	1000 - 1500
MC4516	NY 1895 (1st American ed)	500 - 700
MC4521	The Arrow of Gold: A Story Between Two Notes NY 1919, DJ, 1st issue w/"credentials and apparently" p 5, line 16	1000 - 1500
MC4522	2nd issue w/"credentials and who" p 5, line 16	500 - 700
MC4523	Lon 1919, DJ, 1st issue w/correct heading p 67	300 - 500
MC4524	Lon 1919, DJ, 2nd issue w/incorrect heading p 67, "A" missing	200 - 300

MC4530	The Blackmate Edinburgh 1922, 50 cys	1000 - 1500
MC4535	Chance: A Tale in Two Parts Lon 1914, DJ, 1st issue w/date "1913" on verso of title page	3000 - 5000
MC4536	later issues w/date "1914", DJ	300 - 700
MC4537	NY 1914, DJ (1st American ed)	300 - 500
MC4545	The Children of the Sea NY 1897	300 - 500
MC4550	The Inheritors NY 1901	300 - 500
MC4551	Lon 1901 (1st English ed)	
MC4555	Last Essays Lon 1926, DJ	200 - 300
MC4560	Laughing Anne: A Play Lon 1923, 200 cys, box	500 - 700
MC4565	Lord Jim Edinburgh 1900	300 - 500
MC4566	NY 1900	200 - 300
MC4570	The Mirror of the Sea Lon 1906, dated August, 1906, DJ	300 - 500
MC4571	NY 1906, DJ (1st American ed)	200 - 300
MC4575	The Nigger of the Narcissus Lon 1898, 1st issue w/"H" of Heinemann in larger type than other letters at bottom of spine	400 - 600
MC4576	2nd issue w/correct size	200 - 300
MC4581	Nostromo: A Tale of the Seaboard Lon 1904, 1st issue w/478 pp	300 - 500
MC4582	2nd issue w/480 pp	200 - 300
MC4583	NY 1904 (1st American ed)	150 - 200
MC4585	NY 1961 (Limited Editions Club) Box	100 - 150
MC4590	An Outcast of the Islands Lon 1896, 1st issue w/"absolution" instead of "ablution" on line 12, p 110	700 - 1000
MC4591	2nd issue corrected	300 - 500
MC4592	NY 1896, wrappers	700 - 1000
MC4593	NY 1896, clothbound	200 - 300
MC4600	The Rescue: A Romance of the Shallows Garden City 1920, DJ	300 - 500
MC4601	Lon 1920 (advance review cy)	1000 - 1500
MC4602	Lon 1920 DJ (1st English ed)	300 - 500
MC4610	The Rover Lon 1923, DJ	250 - 350
MC4611	NY 1923, DJ, 377 cys, box	1000 - 1500
MC4612	NY 1923, DJ (1st trade edition)	300 - 500
MC4620	The Secret Agent: A Drama in Three Acts Lon 1923, 1000 cys, DJ	700 - 1000
MC4621	Lon 1923 (1st trade ed) 1st issue w/40 pp of ads	250 - 350
MC4625	The Secret Agent: A Simple Tale Lon 1907, 1st issue w/misprint on p 117 "anarchist activity was be be apprehended"	1000 - 1500
MC4626	NY 1907	200 - 300
MC4631	A Set of Six Lon 1908, 1st issue w/ads dated "February"	500 - 700
MC4632	2nd issue w/ads dated "June"	300 - 500
MC4635	The Shadow Line: A Confession Lon 1917, 1st issue w/18 pp of ads	250 - 350
MC4640	Some Reminiscences NY 1912, DJ	200 - 300
MC4645	Suspense NY 1925, 377 cys, DJ	400 - 600
MC4646	NY 1925, DJ (1st trade ed)	200 - 300
MC4647	Lon 1925, DJ (1st English ed)	200 - 300
MC4655	Tales of Hearsay Lon 1925, DJ	200 - 300
MC4656	Garden City 1925, DJ	150 - 250
MC4660	Tales of the Sea Lon 1919, 25 cys	2000 - 3000
MC4665	Twixt Land and Sea Tales Lon 1912, DJ, 1st issue has "secret" instead of "seven" as part of cover title	1000 - 1500
MC4666	2nd issue w/misprint corrected	400 - 600
MC4667	NY 1912, DJ (1st American ed)	200 - 400
MC4675	Typhoon NY 1902, DJ, 1st issue w/4 pp of ads	500 - 700
MC4680	Typhoon and Other Stories Lon 1903 DJ	300 - 500
MC4685	Under Western Eyes Lon 1911, DJ, 1st issue w/September ads	200 - 300
MC4690	Victory: An Island Tale NY 1915, DJ	300 - 500
MC4691	Lon 1915, DJ w/35 pp of ads	200 - 300
MC4700	Within the Tides: Tales Lon 1915, DJ	300 - 500
MC4710	Youth: A Narrative and Two Other Stories Edinburgh 1902, 1st issue w/October 2 ads, DJ	700 - 1000
MC4711	NY 1902 (1st American ed)	200 - 300
MC4713	Kentfield, CA 1959, 140 cys, box	700 - 1000

Conroy, Pat
MC4760	The Great Santini Bos 1976, DJ	75 - 100
MC4761	Bos 1976 (uncorrected proof - still wraps)	100 - 150
MC4770	The Water is Wide Bos 1972, DJ	250 - 400

Cook, Robin
| MC4810 | Brain NY 1981, DJ | 20 - 30 |
| MC4815 | Coma NY 1977, DJ | 20 - 30 |

MC4820 **Fever** NY 1982, DJ		15 - 25
MC4825 **God Player** NY 1983, DJ		15 - 25
MC4830 **Harmful Intent** NY 1990, DJ		15 - 25
MC4835 **Mind Bend** NY 1985, DJ		15 - 25
MC4840 **Mutation** NY 1989, DJ		15 - 25
MC4845 **Outbreak** NY 1987, DJ		15 - 25
MC4850 **Public Parts and Private Places** NY 1967, DJ		30 - 50
MC4855 **Sphinx** NY 1979, DJ		20 - 30

Cooper, Madison
MC4920 **Sironia, Texas** (1st book) NY 1952, DJ   50 - 75

Coppard, A. E. (Alfred Edgar)
MC5010 **Adam and Eve and Pinch Me** (1st book)
     NY 1921, 160 cys   300 - 400
MC5011 NY 1921, 340 cys   150 - 200
MC5012 NY 1922, 350 cys   100 - 150
MC5020 **The Black Dog** Lon 1923   100 - 150
MC5025 **Cherry Ripe: Poems** Monmouthshire 1935,
     10 cys   700 - 1000
MC5026 150 cys   200 - 300
MC5030 **Pink Furniture** Lon 1930, 260 cys, DJ   250 - 350
MC5035 **Silver Circus** Lon 1928, 125 cys   200 - 300
MC5040 **Yokohama Garland and Other Poems**
     Phil 1926, 500 cys, box   200 - 300

Corle, Edwin
MC5110 **Burro Alley** NY 1946, 1500 cys, DJ   75 - 100
MC5120 **Coarse Gold** NY 1952, 1000 cys, DJ   50 - 75

Corso, Gregory
MC5210 **10 Times A Poem** 1971, 20 cys ,
     w/holograph poem   300 - 500
MC5215 **Ankh** NY 1971, 100 cys, wrappers   150 - 250
MC5220 **Gasoline** SF 1958, wrappers   150 - 200
MC5225 **Hitting The Big 5-0** NY 1983, 100 cys   50 - 75
MC5230 **The Riverside Interviews** Lon 1982   30 - 40
MC5235 **The Vestal Lady on Brattle** (1st book)
     Cambridge 1955, 250 cys   200 - 300

Coward, Noel
MC5310 **I'll Leave It To You** (1st book) Lon 1920, wrappers 200 - 300
MC5320 **Point Valaine** NY 1935, DJ   30 - 40
MC5330 **This Happy Breed** NY 1947, DJ   20 - 30

Cozzens, James Gould
MC5410 **By Love Possessed** NY 1957, DJ   30 - 40
MC5415 **Cock Pit** NY 1928, DJ   100 - 150
MC5420 **Confusion** (1st book) Bos 1924, DJ   500 - 700
MC5425 **S.S. San Pedro** NY 1931, DJ   50 - 75

Crane, Hart
MC5510 **The Bridge** Paris 1930, 200 cys,
     glassine DJ, box   2000 - 3000
MC5511 Paris 1930 (advance review cy)   3000 - 5000
MC5512 Paris 1930 50 cys, glassine DJ, slipcase   3000 - 5000
MC5513 Paris 1930, 8 cys   8000 - 12000
MC5514 NY 1930, DJ (1st trade ed)   300 - 500
MC5516 NY 1981, 2000 cys, slipcase   100 - 150
MC5521 **The Collected Poems of Hart Crane** NY 1933,
     1st issue w/"Liveright Inc., Publishers" on sp, DJ 250 - 350
MC5522 2nd issue w/"Liveright Publishing Corporation"
     on sp, DJ   150 - 200
MC5523 NY 1933, DJ, 50 cys   700 - 1000
MC5530 **Two Letters: Hart Crane** Brooklyn Heights,
     1934, 50 cys   700 - 1000
MC5535 **Voyages** NY 1957, 975 cys, wrappers   300 - 500
MC5541 **White Buildings** (1st book) NY 1926, DJ,
     1st issue w/"Allen Tate" misspelled   2000 - 3000
MC5542 2nd issue w/ correct spelling   1000 - 1500
MC5543 Paris 1930, DJ   500 - 700

Crawford, F. Marion
MC5610 **Man Overboard** NY 1903, DJ   75 - 100

Creeley, Robert
MC5710 **5 Numbers** NY 1968, 170 cys   200 - 300
MC5715 **All That is Lovely in Men** Asheville 1955, 200 cys
MC5720 **Away** LA 1976, 200 cys   100 - 150
MC5725 **The Charm** Mt. Horeb 1967, 250 cys   250 - 350
MC5730 **Day Book** NY 1972, DJ   25 - 50
MC5735 **Divisions and Other Early Poems** Mt. Horeb
     1968, 110 cys   150 - 200
MC5740 **For Love, Poems 1950-1960** NY 1962, DJ   150 - 250
MC5745 **A Form of Women** Poems, NY 1959, DJ   150 - 250
MC5750 **The Gold Diggers** Mallorca 1954   150 - 250
MC5752 NY 1965 (1st American ed)   75 - 125

MC5755 **Hello** NZ 1976   50 - 75
MC5760 **The Immoral Proposition** Baden 1953, 200 cys,
     wrappers, envelope   300 - 500
MC5765 **Island** NY 1963, wrappers   100 - 150
MC5770 **The Kind of Act Of** Mallorca 1953   300 - 500
MC5775 **Le Fou** (1st book) Columbus 1952, DJ   500 - 700
MC5780 **Pieces** LA 1968, 250 cys   150 - 250
MC5785 **Poems 1950-1965** Lon 1966, 100 cys, slipcase 250 - 350
MC5790 **A Sight** Lon 1967 50 cys, signed   300 - 500
MC5791 Lon 1967, 50 cys, unsigned   200 - 300
MC5795 **The Whip** Worcester 1957, 100 cys   300 - 500

Crews, Harry
MC6110 **The Gospel Singer** (1st book) NY 1968, DJ   200 - 300
MC6120 **The Knockout Artist** NY 1988, DJ   20 - 30
MC6130 **Naked in Garden Hills** NY 1969, DJ   150 - 250

Crichton, Michael
MC6210 **The Andromeda Strain** NY 1969, DJ   20 - 30
MC6215 **Congo** NY 1980, DJ   15 - 25
MC6220 **Eaters of the Dead** NY 1976, DJ   20 - 30
MC6225 **Five Patients** NY 1970, DJ   20 - 30
MC6230 **The Great Train Robbery** NY 1975, DJ   20 - 30
MC6235 **Jurassic Park** NY 1990, DJ   40 - 60
MC6240 **The Terminal Man** NY 1972, DJ   20 - 30

Crofts, Freeman Wills
MC6310 **The Cask** (1st book) Lon 1920, DJ, 1st state
     w/2 pp of ads dated Spring, 1920   1500 - 2000
MC6320 **The Groote Park Murder** Lon 1923, DJ   300 - 500
MC6330 **The Pit-Prop Syndicate** Lon 1922, DJ   300 - 500

Crosby, Caresse
MC6410 **Crosses of Gold** (1st book) Paris 1925   800 - 1000
MC6411 Exeter 1925   150 - 200

Crosby, Harry
   Owned the Black Sun Press.
MC6510 **Anthology** (1st book) Paris 1924, wrappers   600 - 800
MC6515 **Chariot of the Sun** Paris 1931, 500 cys, wrappers 300 - 500
MC6520 **Mad Queen: Tirades** Paris 1929, 20 cys   1000 - 1500
MC6525 **Shadows of the Sun** Paris 1929, 44 cys,
     glassine DJ   800 - 1200
MC6530 **Sleeping Together: A Book of Dreams**
     Paris 1931, 500 cys   300 - 500
MC6535 **Torch Bearer** Paris 1931, 500 cys   300 - 500
MC6540 **Transit of Venus** Paris 1928, 44 cys, wrappers 1000 - 1500
MC6541 Paris 1928, 200 cys, glassine DJ, box   250 - 350
MC6543 Paris 1931, 500 cys, glassine DJ, box   200 - 300

Crowder, Henry
MC6710 **Henry Music** (1st book) Paris 1930, 100 cys,
     tissue DJ   2000 - 3000

Crowe, Cameron
MC6810 **Fast Times At Ridgemont High** (1st book)
     NY 1981, DJ   20 - 30

Crowley, Aleister
MC6910 **Ahab and Other Poems** Lon 1903   300 - 500
MC6915 **Moonchild: A Prologue** Lon 1929, DJ   200 - 300
MC6920 **Olla: An Anthology of Sixty Years of Song**
     Lon 1946, 500 cys, DJ   200 - 300
MC6925 **Songs of the Spirit** Lon 1898, 50 cys   600 - 800
MC6930 **The Soul of Osiris** Lon 1901   300 - 500
MC6935 **The Stratagem and Other Stories** Lon 1929, DJ 200 - 300

Crumley, James
MC7010 **One To Count Cadence** (1st book) NY 1969,
     DJ (1st Vietnam war novel)   200 - 300

MC6235   MC7010   MC7125 (w/o DJ)

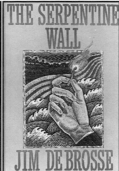

| MC7260 (w/o DJ) | MC7710 | MD1810 |

Cullen, Countee
MC7110 **The Ballad of the Brown Girl** NY 1927,
500 cys, box 200 - 300
MC7115 **The Black Christ and Other Poems** NY 1929,
128 cys, box 250 - 350
MC7116 NY 1929, DJ (1st trade ed) 100 - 150
MC7120 **Caroling Dusk** NY 1927, DJ 150 - 200
MC7125 **Color** (1st book) NY 1925, DJ 200 - 300
MC7130 **On These I Stand** NY 1947, DJ 75 - 100
MC7135 **One Way To Heaven** NY 1932, DJ 100 - 150

cummings, e e (Edward Estlin)
MC7210 **(No Title)** NY 1925, 111 cys, box 700 - 1000
MC7211 NY 1925, 222 cys, box 500 - 700
MC7215 **(No Title)** NY 1930, 491 cys 300 - 500
MC7220 **50 Poems** NY 1940, DJ, 150 cys, glassine DJ 300 - 500
MC7225 **73 Poems** NY 1962, DJ 150 - 250
MC7230 **95 Poems** NY 1958, 300 cys, glassine DJ, box 200 - 300
MC7235 **Anthropos: The Future of Art** NY 1944,
222 cys, DJ, box 300 - 500
MC7240 **Christmas Tree** NY 1928, glassine DJ 700 - 1000
MC7245 **Clopw** NY 1931, 391 cys 800 - 1200
MC7246 NY 1931, DJ (1st trade ed) 200 - 300
MC7250 **Collected Poems** NY 1938, DJ 200 - 300
MC7255 **Complete Poems** Lon 1968, 2 vol, 150 cys,
glassine DJ, box 300 - 500
MC7260 **EIMI** NY 1933, 1381 cys, DJ 700 - 1000
w/o DJ 250 - 350
MC7262 NY 1958, 26 cys 300 - 500
MC7265 **The Enormous Room** (1st book) NY 1922, DJ,
1st issue w/expletive "shit" not inked out on p 219 600 - 800
MC7267 Lon 1928, DJ 300 - 400
MC7270 **Fairy Tales** NY 1950, DJ 75 - 125
MC7275 **Him** NY 1927, 160 cys, box 600 - 800
MC7276 NY 1927, DJ, 1381 cys 250 - 350
MC7280 **I: Six Non Lectures** Cambridge 1953, 350 cys, DJ 300 - 500
MC7281 Cambridge 1953 (1st trade ed) DJ 75 - 125
MC7285 **IS 5** NY 1926, DJ 200 - 300
MC7286 NY 1926, 77 cys, box 500 - 700
MC7290 **No Thanks** NY 1935, 90 cys, DJ, box 400 - 600
MC7291 NY 1935, 9 cys w/manuscript p, vellum 1000 - 1500
MC7292 NY 1935, 900 cys 200 - 300
MC7300 **One Times One** NY 1944, DJ 200 - 300
MC7305 **Poems** NY 1954, DJ 200 - 300
MC7310 **Poems 1905-1962** Lon 1963, 225 cys, DJ 250 - 350
MC7315 **Poesis Scelte** Milan 1958, 1000 cys, wrappers 200 - 300
MC7320 **Santa Clause** NY 1946, 250 cys, glassine DJ 300 - 500
MC7321 NY 1946, DJ (1st trade ed) 75 - 125
MC7325 **Tom: A Ballet** Santa Fe 1935, DJ 250 - 350
MC7330 **Tulips and Chimneys** NY 1923, DJ 300 - 500
MC7332 Mount Vernon 1937, 481 cys, DJ 300 - 500
MC7335 **Viva: Seventy New Poems** NY 1931, 95 cys,
glassine DJ 1000 - 1500
MC7336 NY 1931, DJ (1st trade ed) 300 - 500
MC7340 **XLI Poems** NY 1925, 111 cys 1000 - 1500
MC7341 NY 1925, 222 cys 700 - 1000
MC7342 NY 1925, DJ (1st trade ed) 200 - 300

Cunningham, J. V.
MC7510 **12 Poems in a Yearbook of Stanford Writing**
(1st appearance) Stanford 1932, 150 cys 200 - 300
MC7520 **The Helmsman** (1st book) SF 1942, DJ 400 - 600
MC7521 SF 1942, wrappers 200 - 300

Cunningham, Michael
MC7610 **A Home at the End of the World** (1st book)
NY 1990, DJ 30 - 40

Curwood, James Oliver
MC7710 **The Country Beyond** NY 1922, DJ 30 - 50
MC7720 **The Courage of Captain Plum** (1st book)
Ind 1908, DJ 50 - 75

D., H. (Hilda Doolittle)
MD0110 **Choruses From I Phigeneia In Aulis** (1st book)
Clev 1916, wrappers 1000 - 1500
MD0111 Lon 1916, DJ 200 - 300
MD0120 **Collected Poems** NY 1925 300 - 500
MD0130 **Hedylus** Oxford 1928, 775 cys, DJ 200 - 300
MD0140 **Hippolytus Temporizes** Bos 1927, 550 cys, box 300 - 500
MD0150 **Hymen** NY 1921, wrappers 200 - 300
MD0151 Lon 1921, wrappers 200 - 300
MD0160 **Kora and Ka** Dijon 1934, 100 cys 700 - 1000
MD0170 **Palimpsest** Paris 1926, wrappers 400 - 600
MD0171 Bos 1926, 700 cys, DJ 400 - 600
MD0180 **Red Roses For Bronze** NY 1928, wrappers 100 - 150
MD0190 **Sea Garden: Imagist Poems** Lon 1916, wrappers 300 - 500
MD0191 Bos 1917 100 - 150
MD0200 **Selected Poems** NY 1957, 50 cys 250 - 350
MD0210 **The Tribute and Circe - Two Poems**
Clev 1917, 50 cys 300 - 500
MD0220 **The Usual Star** Lon 1928, 100 cys 400 - 600
MD0230 **The Walls Do Not Fall** NY 1944, DJ 75 - 125
MD0231 Lon 1944, wrappers (1st English ed) 75 - 125

Dahl, Roald
MD0410 **Charlie and the Great Glass Elevator** NY 1972, DJ 30 - 40
MD0420 **The Gremlins** (1st book) NY 1943, DJ 200 - 300
MD0422 Lon 1944, DJ 200 - 300
MD0430 **Kiss Kiss** NY 1960, DJ 30 - 50
MD0440 **My Uncle Oswald** NY 1980, DJ 30 - 40
MD0450 **Over To You** NY 1946, DJ 100 - 150
MD0451 Lon 1946 100 - 150
MD0460 **Rhyme Stew** Lon 1989, DJ 20 - 30
MD0470 **Some Time Never** NY 1948, DJ 75 - 125
MD0480 **Someone Like You** NY 1953, DJ 50 - 75
MD0490 **Switch Bitch** NY 1974, DJ 30 - 40

Dahlberg, Edward
MD0610 **Bottom Dogs** (1st book) Lon 1929, 520 cys, DJ 300 - 500
MD0611 Lon 1929, DJ 50 - 75
MD0613 NY 1930, DJ 200 - 300
MD0620 **Do These Bones Live?** NY 1941, DJ 75 - 100
MD0630 **The Flea of Sodom** Lon 1950, DJ 75 - 100
MD0640 **Kentucky Blue Grass Henry Smith** Clev 1932,
DJ, 10 cys, signed 700 - 1000
MD0641 Clev 1932, 85 cys, unsigned 300 - 500
MD0650 **The Sorrows of Priapus** NY 1957, 150 cys,
signed litho, glassine DJ, box 300 - 500

Darrow, Clarence
MD0810 **Argument in Defense of the Communists**
Chi 1920, wrappers 75 - 125
MD0820 **Resist Not Evil** (1st book) Chi 1903, DJ 200 - 300
MD0830 **The Story of My Life** NY 1932, DJ 200 - 300

Davies, W. H.
MD1010 **The Autobiography of a Super Tramp** Lon 1908 150 - 250
MD1020 **The Lovers Song Book** Newtown 1933, 250 cys 300 - 500
MD1021 18 cys in Morocco 1000 - 1500
MD1030 **Selected Poems** Newtown 1928, 310 cys,
bound by Gregynog Bindery 1500 - 2500
MD1031 other cys in Buckram 300 - 500
MD1040 **The Sorrows of Priapus** NY 1957, 150 cys,
glassine DJ, box w/signed print inserted 300 - 500
MD1050 **The Souls Destroyer** (1st book) Lon 1905,
wrappers 700 - 1000

Davis, Richard Harding
Wrote about 50 novels; most are in $75-125 range with DJ.
MD1210 **The Boy Scout** NY 1914, DJ 75 - 125
MD1212 NY 1917, DJ 30 - 50
MD1215 **Captain Macklin** NY 1902, DJ 50 - 75
MD1220 **In The Fog** NY 1901, DJ 150 - 250
MD1230 **Novels and Stories** NY 1916, 12 vol 300 - 500
MD1240 **Ranson's Folly** NY 1902, 1st state w/p 345
correctly numbered 75 - 125
MD1250 **Real Soldiers of Fortune** NY 1906, DJ 75 - 125

Dawson, Fielding
MD1410 **The Girl With The Pale Cerulean Eyes The Man
With The Gray Hair** NY 1974, wrappers 75 - 100
MD1420 **Krazy Kat/The Unveiling** LA 1969, 1000 cys,
acetate DJ 50 - 75

Day-Lewis, Cecil
MD1610 **Beechen Vigil** (1st book) Lon 1925, wrappers 300 - 500

De Beauvoir, Simone
MD1710 **Force of Circumstance** NY 1965, DJ 30 - 40

De Brosse, Jim
MD1810 **The Serpentine Wall** NY 1988, DJ 50 - 75

De Camp, L. Sprague
MD1910 **Demons and Dinosaurs** Sauk City 1970, DJ 75 - 125
MD1920 **Land of Unreason** NY 1942, DJ 200 - 300
MD1930 **Lest Darkness Fall** NY 1941, DJ 200 - 300
MD1940 **New Anthology** Lon 1953, DJ 100 - 150
MD1950 **Wall of Serpents** NY 1960, DJ 150 - 200

De Camp, L. Sprague and Fletcher Pratt
MD2110 **The Carnelian Cube** NY 1948, DJ 75 - 125
MD2120 **Tales From Gavagan's Bar** NY 1953, DJ 50 - 75

De Chair, Somerset
MD2310 **The Golden Carpet** Lon 1943, 30 cys 500 - 700
MD2311 470 cys 150 - 200

De La Mare, Walter
MD2410 **At First Sight A Novel** NY 1928, 650 cys 150 - 250
MD2420 **Behold, This Dreamer** Lon 1939, 50 cys 250 - 350
MD2430 **Broomsticks and Other Tales** Lon 1925, 278 cys, DJ 100 - 150
MD2431 Lon 1925 (1st trade ed) 25 - 50
MD2440 **A Childs Day: A Book of Rhymes** Lon 1912, DJ 75 - 125
MD2450 **Crossings: A Fairy Play** Lon 1921, 264 cys, box 150 - 250
MD2451 Lon 1921, 56 cys, box 300 - 500
MD2452 Lon 1921, 10 cys, box 500 - 700
MD2460 **Desert Islands and Robinson Crusoe** Lon 1930, 650 cys, DJ 150 - 200
MD2461 Lon 1930, DJ (1st trade ed) 25 - 50
MD2470 **Ding Dong Bell** Lon 1924, 300 cys, DJ 150 - 250
MD2471 Lon 1924, DJ (1st trade ed) 50 - 75
MD2480 **Down-Adown-Derry** Lon 1922, DJ 150 - 250
MD2490 **Flora** Lon 1919, DJ 100 - 150
MD2500 **Henry Brocken** Lon 1904, 1st issue w/o gilt on top edge, DJ 100 - 150
MD2510 **Lispet, Lispett and Vaine** Lon 1923, 200 cys, box 200 - 300
MD2520 **The Listeners and Other Poems** Lon 1912, DJ 75 - 125
MD2530 **The Lord Fish** Lon 1933, 60 cys, DJ, box 300 - 500
MD2540 **Memoirs of a Midget** Lon 1921, 210 cys 300 - 500
MD2541 Lon 1921, DJ (1st trade ed) 200 - 300
MD2550 **Motley and Other Poems** Lon 1918, DJ 75 - 125
MD2560 **On The Edge: Short Stories** Lon 1930, 300 cys, DJ 150 - 250
MD2561 Lon 1930, DJ (1st trade ed) 50 - 75
MD2570 **Peacock Pie: A Book of Rhymes** Lon 1915 200 - 300
MD2572 Lon 1924, 250 cys, DJ 300 - 400
MD2574 Lon 1946, DJ 75 - 100
MD2580 **Poems** Lon 1906
MD2582 Lon 1927, 50 cys 400 - 600
MD2590 **Poems 1901 to 1918** Lon 1920, 2 vol, 210 cys 200 - 300
MD2591 Lon 1920 DJ (1st trade ed) 50 - 75
MD2601 **The Return** Lon 1910, 1st issue w/o ads 200 - 300
MD2602 2nd issue w/8 pp ads 75 - 125
MD2604 Lon 1922, 250 cys 150 - 250
MD2610 **The Riddle and Other Stories** Lon 1923, 310 cys, DJ 150 - 250
MD2620 **Seven Short Stories** Lon 1931, 170 cys, box 200 - 300
MD2630 **Silver** Gaylordsville 1930, 9 cys 300 - 500
MD2640 **Songs of Childhood** (1st book; 1st published in 1902 under pseud Walter Ramal) Lon 1923, 310 cys, DJ 300 - 500

MD2641 Lon 1902 300 - 500
MD2650 **The Sunken Gardens** Lon 1917, 230 cys, box 200 - 300
MD2651 Lon 1917, 20 cys, box 500 - 700
MD2660 **This Year: Next Year** Lon 1937, 100 cys, DJ 200 - 300
MD2671 **The Three Mulla-Mulgars** Lon 1910, DJ, 1st issue w/gilt top 700 - 1000
MD2672 2nd issue w/plain top 300 - 500
MD2674 Lon 1924, 260 cys 300 - 500
MD2680 **Told Again** Oxford 1927, 260 cys, box 200 - 300
MD2690 **Two Tales** Lon 1925, 250 cys, box 200 - 300

De Mille, James (see Anon)

De Vries, Peter
MD2810 **But Who Wakes the Burglar** (1st book) Bos 1940, DJ 150 - 200
MD2820 **The Cats Pajamas and Witches Milk** Bos 1968, DJ 25 - 50
MD2830 **Let Me Count The Ways** Bos 1965, DJ 25 - 50
MD2840 **Reuben, Reuben** Bos 1964, DJ 25 - 50

Del Vecchio, John M.
MD3010 **The 13th Valley** (1st book) NY 1982, DJ 30 - 50

Dell, Floyd
MD3110 **The Briary-Bush** NY 1921, DJ 50 - 75
MD3120 **Moon Calf** NY 1920, DJ 50 - 100
MD3130 **Runaway** NY 1925, 250 cys, box 50 - 100
MD3140 **Women As World Builders** (1st book) Chi 1913, DJ 150 - 200

Derleth, August
MD3310 **Bright Journey** NY 1940, DJ 20 - 30
MD3320 **Collected Poems** NY 1967, DJ 20 - 30
MD3330 **Dark of the Moon** Sauk City 1947, DJ 100 - 150
MD3340 **Death Stalks The Wakely Family** NY 1934 150 - 200
MD3350 **Habitant of Dusk** Bos 1946, 300 cys, DJ 75 - 125
MD3360 **In Re: Sherlock Holmes** Sauk City 1945, DJ 100 - 150
MD3370 **Last Night** Mt. Horeb 1978, 150 cys 200 - 300
MD3380 **The Memoirs of Solar Pons** Sauk City 1951, DJ 100 - 150
MD3390 **The Narracong Riddle** NY 1940, DJ 100 - 150
MD3400 **Not Long For This World** Sauk City 1978, DJ 100 - 150
MD3410 **The Return of Solar Pons** Sauk City 1958, DJ 100 - 150
MD3420 **Someone in the Dark** Sauk City 1941, DJ, 1st state less than 18 cm high 300 - 500
MD3430 **To Remember** (1st book) Vermont 1931, wrappers 200 - 300
MD3440 **The Wind Leans West** NY 1969, DJ 20 - 30

Dexter, Pete
MD3610 **God's Pocket** (1st book) NY 1983, DJ 50 - 75

Dick, Philip K.
MD3710 **Flow My Tears, The Policeman Said** NY 1974, DJ 75 - 100
MD3720 **A Handful of Darkness** (1st book) Lon 1955, DJ, blue boards 500 - 700
 orange boards 300 - 500
MD3730 **The Man in the High Castle** NY 1962, DJ 200 - 300
MD3740 **A Maze of Death** NY 1970, DJ 400 - 600
MD3750 **Necromancer** NY 1962, DJ 100 - 150
MD3760 **Now Wait For Last Year** NY 1966, DJ 200 - 300
MD3780 **The Three Stigmata of Palmer Eldritch** Garden City 1965, DJ 600 - 800
MD3790 **Ubik** NY 1969, DJ 500 - 750

Dickey, James
MD3910 **Babel To Byzantium** NY 1968, DJ 25 - 50
MD3920 **Deliverance** NY 1970, DJ 25 - 50
MD3930 **Drowning With Others** (1st book) Middleton 1962, DJ 200 - 300
MD3931 Middleton 1962, wrappers 100 - 150
MD3940 **Sorties** NY 1971, DJ 30 - 40
MD3950 **Spinning The Crystal Ball** Wash 1967, DJ 30 - 40

MD1940

MD2110

MD2120

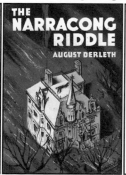
MD3390

MD3610

MD3740

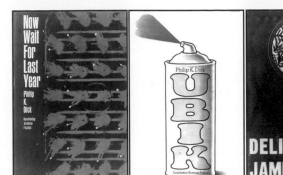

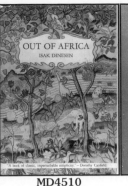

| MD3760 | MD3790 | MD3920 | MD4510 | MD5230 |

MD3960 **Tucky the Hunter** NY 1978, DJ   30 - 40

Dickinson, Emily
MD4110 **Complete Poems** Bos 1924, DJ   100 - 150
MD4120 **Further Poems of Emily Dickinson** Bos 1929,
    465 cys, DJ, box   200 - 300
MD4121 Bos 1929, DJ   100 - 150
MD4130 **Poems** (1st book) Bos 1890, 500 cys   1000 - 1500
MD4131 Lon 1891   300 - 500
MD4133 NY 1952 (Limited Edition Club) slipcase   75 - 100
MD4140 **Poems For Youth** Bos 1934, DJ   75 - 125
MD4150 **The Single Hound: Poems of a Lifetime**
    Bos 1914, DJ, w/pub "Sept. 1914" on cr page   400 - 600
MD4152 Bos 1915, DJ   150 - 200

Dickson, Gordon R.
MD4310 **Necromancer** NY 1962, DJ   100 - 150

Didion, Joan
MD4410 **Slouching Towards Bethlehem** NY 1968, DJ   50 - 75

Dinesen, Isak
MD4510 **Out of Africa** NY 1938, DJ   100 - 150

Dobie, J. Frank (see Americana & Books About Books)

Doctorow, E. L.
MD4610 **Billy Bathgate** NY 1989, DJ   20 - 30
MD4620 **The Book of Daniel** NY 1971, DJ   40 - 60
MD4630 **Lives of the Poets** NY 1984, 350 cys, slipcase   75 - 125
MD4631 NY 1984, DJ (1st trade ed)   20 - 30
MD4640 **Loon Lake** NY 1980, DJ   20 - 30
MD4650 **Ragtime** NY 1975, 150 cys, slipcase   150 - 250
MD4651 NY 1975, DJ (1st trade ed)   20 - 30
MD4660 **Welcome To Hard Times** (1st book) NY 1960, DJ   150 - 250
MD4670 **World's Fair** NY 1985, 300 cys, slipcase   50 - 100
MD4671 NY 1985, DJ (1st trade ed)   20 - 30

Donleavy, J. P.
MD4810 **The Ginger Man** (1st book) Paris 1955, DJ   300 - 500
MD4811 NY 1961 (play ed)   30 - 40

Dos Passos, John
MD4910 **1919** NY 1932, DJ   150 - 200
MD4920 **Airways, Inc.** NY 1928, DJ   75 - 100
MD4930 **The Big Money** NY 1936, DJ   50 - 75
MD4940 **The Garbage Man** NY 1926, DJ   50 - 75
MD4950 **Manhattan Transfer** NY 1925, DJ   75 - 100
MD4960 **One Man's Initiation** (1st book) Lon 1920, DJ,
    1st issue w/broken type, p 32   300 - 500
MD4970 **Orient Express** NY 1927, DJ, w/"M-A" on
    cr page   100 - 150
MD4980 **Three Soldiers** NY 1921, DJ, 1st issue w/"signing"
    for "singing" p 213, line 7 from bottom   700 - 1000
MD4982 NY 1932, DJ   20 - 30

Doyle, Sir Arthur Conan
MD5110 **The Adventures of Sherlock Holmes** Lon
    1892, 1st state w/o street sign letters   2000 - 3000
MD5120 **The Case Book of Sherlock Holmes**
    Lon 1927, DJ   800 - 1200
MD5121 NY 1927, DJ (1st American ed)   700 - 1000
MD5130 **Collected Poems of Sir Arthur Conan Doyle**
    Lon 1922, DJ   200 - 300
MD5140 **The Complete Sherlock Holmes** Lon 1953,
    2 vol, 147 cys, acetate DJ, slipcase   3000 - 5000
MD5150 **The Crime of the Congo** Lon 1910?, DJ   300 - 500
MD5160 **Danger and Other Stories** Lon 1918, DJ   200 - 300
MD5170 **His Last Bow** Lon 1917, DJ   200 - 300
MD5171 NY 1917, DJ   200 - 300
MD5180 **The Hound Of Baskervilles** Lon 1902, DJ   1200 - 1800

MD5181 NY 1902, DJ (1st American ed) 1st issue w/o
    "Pub. 1902" on cr page   800 - 1200
MD5183 SF 1985, 400 cys   300 - 500
MD5190 **The Last Valley** Lon 1911, DJ   200 - 300
MD5200 **The Lost World** Lon 1912, 500 cys   700 - 1000
MD5201 Lon 1912, DJ (1st trade ed)   200 - 300
MD5202 NY 1912, DJ   150 - 200
MD5210 **Maracot Deep or The Lost World Under**
    The Sea Lon 1927, DJ   200 - 300
MD5220 **The Poison Belt** NY 1913   75 - 125
MD5230 **Profile by Gaslight** NY 1944, DJ, anthology
    w/other authors, 1st issue in red bds   100 - 125
MD5240 **The Return of Sherlock Holmes** Lon 1905   600 - 800
MD5241 NY 1905   100 - 150
MD5250 **Round The Fire Stories** Lon 1908, DJ   300 - 500
MD5261 **A Study in Scarlet** (1st book) Lon 1888,
    (Beeton's Christmas Annual) wrappers, 1st
    issue w/"Younger" correct in preface   12000 - 20000
MD5262 2nd issue w/"Youuger" for "Younger"   8000 - 12000
MD5270 **Through The Magic Door** Lon 1907, DJ   200 - 300
MD5280 **Valley of Fear** Lon 1915, DJ   700 - 1000
MD5281 Lon 1915, DJ (colonial ed)   300 - 500
MD5282 NY 1915, DJ (1st American ed)   500 - 800
MD5284 NY 1916, DJ (A. L. Burt reprint)   200 - 300

Dr. Seuss (see Artists & Illustrators under Seuss)

Dreiser, Theodore
MD5410 **An American Tragedy** NY 1925, 2 vol, DJ, box   800 - 1200
MD5411 NY 1925, 795 cys, box   200 - 300
MD5420 **A Book About Myself** NY 1922, DJ   75 - 125
MD5422 NY 1931, DJ   30 - 50
MD5430 **Chains** NY 1927, 440 cys   300 - 500
MD5431 NY 1927, DJ (1st trade ed)   150 - 250
MD5440 **The Color of a Great City** NY 1923, DJ   150 - 250
MD5450 **The Financier** NY 1912, DJ, 1st issue w/pub
    Oct 1912 and "K-M" on cr page   200 - 300
MD5452 NY 1927, DJ   30 - 50
MD5454 NY 1940, DJ   20 - 30
MD5460 **Free and Other Stories** NY 1918, DJ, "B-L"
    monogram on tp   300 - 500
MD5461 Lon 1918, DJ (1st English ed)   250 - 350
MD5470 **A Gallery of Women** NY 1929, 2 vol, 560 cys   200 - 300
MD5480 **The "Genius"** NY 1915, DJ, 1st state w/plain
    top edge   300 - 500
MD5490 **The Hand of the Potter** NY 1918, DJ   150 - 250
MD5500 **Hey, Rub-A-Dub-Dub** NY 1920, DJ   150 - 250
MD5510 **Hoosier Holiday** NY 1916, DJ, 1st state in
    olive spine   150 - 250
MD5520 **Jennie Gerhardt** NY 1922, DJ, 1st state w/blue
    cloth & 1st issue w/"is" for "it" on line 30, p 22   150 - 250
MD5530 **My City** NY 1929, 275 cys   300 - 500
MD5540 **Plays of the Natural and Supernatural** NY 1916,
    DJ, 1st state w/o rear flyleaf   200 - 300
MD5550 **The Seven Arts: Life Art and America**
    NY 1917, DJ   150 - 250
MD5560 **Sister Carrie** (1st book) NY 1900, DJ, red
    buckram   3000 - 5000
MD5561 Lon 1901, DJ (1st English ed)   300 - 500
MD5563 NY 1907, DJ   150 - 250
MD5565 NY 1932, DJ   25 - 50
MD5567 NY 1939, box (Limited Editions Club)   100 - 150
MD5580 **The Titan** NY 1914, DJ, mottled blue cl   150 - 250
MD5590 **Tragic America** NY 1931, DJ   150 - 250
MD5591 NY 1931 (suppressed pre-pub edition containing
    deleted words)   800 - 1200

MD5601	**A Traveler at Forty** NY 1913, DJ, 1st state	
	w/brick-red cloth	200 - 300
MD5602	2nd state w/bright red cl	150 - 250
MD5610	**Twelve Men** NY 1919, DJ	150 - 250

Drury, Allen

MD5710	**Advise and Consent** NY 1959, DJ	25 - 50

Dunbar, Paul Lawrence

Dust jackets for first editions are non-existent or very rare.

MD5810	**Candle-Lightin' Time** NY 1901	150 - 250
MD5820	**Chris'mus is A-Comin'** NY 1907	100 - 150
MD5830	**Complete Poems** NY 1913	75 - 125
MD5840	**The Fanatics** NY 1901	150 - 250
MD5850	**Folks From Dixie** NY 1898	200 - 300
MD5860	**The Heart of Happy Hollow** NY 1904	150 - 250
MD5870	**Howdy, Honey, Howdy** NY 1905	150 - 250
MD5880	**In Old Plantation Days** NY 1903	150 - 250
MD5890	**Joggin' Erlong** NY 1906	150 - 250
MD5900	**Li'l' Gal** NY 1904	150 - 250
MD5910	**The Love of Landry** NY 1900	150 - 250
MD5920	**Lyrics of Love and Laughter** NY 1903	150 - 250
MD5930	**Lyrics of Lowly Life** NY 1896	200 - 300
MD5940	**Lyrics of Sunshine and Sorrow** NY 1905	150 - 250
MD5950	**Lyrics of the Hearthside** NY 1899	200 - 300
MD5960	**Majors and Minors** Toledo 1895, 1000 cys	300 - 500
MD5970	**Oak and Ivy** (1st book) Dayton 1893, 500 cys	1500 - 2000
MD5980	**Poems of Cabin and Field** NY 1899	200 - 300
MD5990	**The Sport of the Gods** NY 1902	150 - 250
MD6000	**The Strength of Gideon** NY 1900	150 - 250
MD6010	**The Uncalled** NY 1898	200 - 300

Duncan, Robert

MD6210	**The Five Songs** La Jolla 1981, 100 cys, DJ	150 - 200
MD6220	**Playtime Pseudo Stein** SF 1969, wrappers	150 - 200

Dunning, John

MD6410	**Booked to Die** NY 1992, DJ	75 - 125

Durrell, Lawrence

MD6610	**Balthazar** Lon 1958, DJ	300 - 500
MD6620	**Clea** Lon 1960, DJ	200 - 300
MD6630	**Justine** Lon 1957, DJ	300 - 500
MD6640	**The Pied Piper of Lovers** (1st novel) Lon 1935, DJ	2000 - 3000
MD6650	**Quaint Fragment** (1st book) Lon 1931, wrappers	8000 - 12000

Dylan, Bob

MD6910	**Tarantula** NY 1971, DJ	40 - 60

Eckert, Allan W.

ME1000	**The Court Martial of Daniel Boone** Bos 1973, DJ	30 - 50
ME1010	**The Great Auk** (1st book) Bos 1963, DJ	75 - 100
ME1020	**Johnny Logan Shawnee Spy** Bos 1983, DJ	20 - 30
ME1030	**Savage Journey** Bos 1979, DJ	40 - 60
ME1040	**A Sorrow in Our Heart The Life of Tecumseh** NY 1992, DJ	30 - 50
ME1050	**Tecumseh** Bos 1974, wrappers	15 - 25
ME1060	**A Time of Terror** Bos 1965, DJ	20 - 30
ME1061	Bos 1965, wrappers	15 - 25
ME1070	**Wild Season** Bos 1967, DJ	20 - 30
ME1080	**Wilderness Empire** Bos 1969, DJ	20 - 30

Eddison, E. R.

ME1210	**The Mezentian Gate** Plaistow 1958, DJ	150 - 250

Eliot, T. S.

ME5010	**After Strange Gods** Lon 1934, DJ	
ME5011	NY 1934, DJ (1st American Ed)	150 - 200
ME5020	**Animula** Lon 1929, wrappers	75 - 125

ME5021	Lon 1929, 4000 cys	250 - 350
ME5030	**Ash-Wednesday** NY 1930, 600 cys, DJ, box	700 - 1000
ME5031	Lon 1930, DJ (1st English ed)	150 - 250
ME5032	NY 1930, DJ (1st trade ed)	150 - 250
ME5040	**Catholic Anthology 1914** (contains poems by Eliot) Lon 1915	300 - 500
ME5050	**The Cocktail Party** Lon 1949, DJ, 1st issue w/"here" for "her" line 1, p 29	100 - 150
ME5060	**Collected Poems 1909-1935** Lon 1936, DJ	700 - 1000
ME5061	NY 1936, DJ (1st American ed)	200 - 300
ME5070	**The Confidential Clerk** Lon 1954, DJ	150 - 250
ME5080	**Dante** Lon 1929, DJ	200 - 300
ME5081	Lon 1929, 125 cys	1000 - 1500
ME5090	**Ezra Pound: His Metric and Poetry** NY 1917, DJ	800 - 1200
ME5100	**The Family Reunion** Lon 1939, DJ	150 - 250
ME5101	NY 1939, DJ (1st American ed)	150 - 250
ME5110	**For Lancelot Andrewes** Lon 1928, DJ	200 - 300
ME5111	NY 1928, DJ (1st American ed)	200 - 300
ME5120	**Four Quartets** NY 1943, DJ	1000 - 1500
ME5130	**Journey of the Magi** Lon 1927, wrappers	300 - 500
ME5131	NY 1927, 27 cys, wrappers	2000 - 3000
ME5140	**The Literary Essays of Ezra Pound** NY 1954, DJ	75 - 125
ME5150	**Murder in the Cathedral** Canterbury 1935, 750 cys	250 - 350
ME5151	Lon 1942, DJ (film ed)	40 - 60
ME5160	**Old Possum's Book of Practical Cats** Lon 1939, DJ	300 - 500
ME5161	NY 1939, DJ (1st American ed)	300 - 500
ME5170	**Poems** Richmond 1919, wrappers, 1st issue w/"capitaux" for "chapitaux" line 11, p 13	4000 - 6000
ME5171	NY 1920, DJ (1st American ed)	300 - 500
ME5180	**Poems, 1909-1925** Lon 1925, 85 cys, glassine DJ	2000 - 3000
ME5181	Lon 1925, DJ (1st trade ed)	250 - 350
ME5183	NY 1932, DJ (1st American ed)	150 - 250
ME5190	**A Practical Possum** Cambridge 1947, 80 cys, wrappers	1000 - 1500
ME5200	**Prufrock and Other Observations** (1st book) Lon 1917, 500 cys, wrappers	5000 - 7000
ME5210	**The Sacred Wood** Lon 1920, DJ, 1st state w/sub-title on front of DJ	400 - 600
ME5220	**Selected Essays 1917-1932** Lon 1932, 115 cys, DJ	1500 - 2000
ME5221	Lon 1932, DJ (1st trade ed)	250 - 350
ME5222	NY 1932, DJ (1st American ed)	200 - 300
ME5230	**A Song For Simeon** Lon 1928, 500 cys	400 - 600
ME5240	**Sweeney Agonistes** Lon 1932, DJ	150 - 250

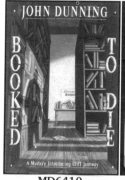

MD6410

MD6910

MD5810

MD5890

MD5900

ME1020

ME1210

ME5410

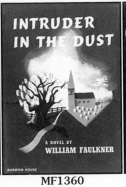
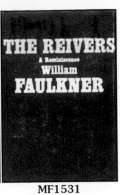

| ME6510 | MF0800 | MF0820 | MF1280 | MF1360 | MF1531 |

ME5250	**T. S. Eliot: The Complete Poems and Plays** NY 1952, DJ	75 - 125
ME5260	**Thoughts After Lambeth** Lon 1931, wrappers	250 - 350
ME5261	Lon 1931, cl, DJ	300 - 500
ME5270	**Triumphal March** Lon 1931, 300 cys	300 - 500
ME5281	**The Waste Land** NY 1922, flexible cl, DJ, 1000 cys, 1st issue w/"mountain" line 339, p 41	3000 - 5000
ME5282	2nd issue w/"mountin" line 339, p 41	2000 - 3000
ME5283	NY 1923, DJ (2nd ed)	300 - 500
ME5284	Richmond 1923 (1st English ed)	1000 - 1500
ME5286	Lon 1961, 300 cys, box	1000 - 1500

Ellison, Harlan
ME5410	**Love Ain't Nothing But Sex Misspelled** NY 1968, DJ	250 - 350

Erdrich, Louise
ME6510	**Tracks** NY 1988, DJ	20 - 30

Fair, A. A. (see Erle Stanley Gardner)

Fairbanks, Douglas
MF0110	**Making Life Worth While** NY 1918	20 - 30

Farmer, Philip Jose
MF0210	**The Adventure of the Peerless Peer** Boulder 1974, DJ	75 - 125
MF0220	**The Dark Design** Berkeley 1977, DJ	25 - 50
MF0230	**Doc Savage** NY 1973, DJ	30 - 50
MF0240	**The Fabulous Riverboat** Lon 1974, DJ	75 - 125
MF0250	**Flesh** NY 1968, DJ	300 - 500
MF0260	**Green Odyssey** (1st book) NY 1957, DJ	1200 - 1500
MF0261	NY 1957, wrappers	75 - 125
MF0270	**To Your Scattered Bodies Go** NY 1971, DJ	400 - 600

Farrell, J. G.
MF0410	**A Girl in the Head** Lon 1967, DJ	200 - 300
MF0420	**A Man From Elsewhere** (1st book) Lon 1963, DJ	125 - 250

Farrell, James T.
MF0610	**Calico Shoes and Other Stories** NY 1934, DJ	150 - 250
MF0620	**Gas House McGinty** NY 1933, DJ	150 - 250
MF0630	**Judgment Day** NY 1935, DJ, 1st issue w/ "thay" for "they" on line 3, p 218	150 - 250
MF0640	**Young Lonigan: A Boyhood in Chicago Streets** (1st book) NY 1932, DJ	200 - 300
MF0650	**The Young Manhood of Studs Lonigan** NY 1934, DJ, 1st issue w/errata slip	200 - 300

Farrow, G. E.
MF0800	**The Missing Prince** Lon 1896	50 - 75
MF0810	**Professor Philanderpan** Lon (early 1900s)	50 - 75
MF0820	**The Wallypug in London** Lon 1898	60 - 90

Fast, Howard
MF0960	**Spartacus** NY 1951, DJ	40 - 60
MF0970	**Two Valleys** (1st book) NY 1933, DJ	200 - 300

Faulkner, William H. (1949 Nobel Laureate)
MF1210	**Absalom Absalom** NY 1936, 300 cys, slipcase	1500 - 2000
MF1211	NY 1936, DJ (1st trade ed)	250 - 350
MF1212	Lon 1936, DJ (1st English ed)	200 - 300
MF1220	**Anthology of Magazine Verse For 1925** Bos 1925, DJ, contains "Lilacs"	700 - 1000
MF1230	**An Anthology of the Younger Poets** Phil 1932, 500 cys (5 poems by Faulkner)	700 - 1000
MF1241	**As I Lay Dying** NY 1930, DJ, 1st issue w/misplaced "I" on p 11	800 - 1200
MF1242	2nd issue w/corrected "I"	200 - 300
MF1250	**Best Short Stories of 1932** NY 1932, contains "Smoke"	200 - 300

MF1260	**Best Short Stories of 1934** NY 1934, contains "Beyond"	200 - 300
MF1270	**Best Short Stories of 1935** NY 1935, contains "Lo!"	200 - 300
MF1280	**Big Woods** NY 1955, DJ	150 - 250
MF1290	**Collected Stories of William Faulkner** NY 1950, DJ	100 - 150
MF1300	**Doctor Martino and Other Stories** NY 1934, DJ, 360 cys, box	700 - 1000
MF1301	NY 1934, DJ (1st trade ed)	200 - 300
MF1302	Lon 1934, DJ (1st English ed)	200 - 300
MF1310	**A Fable** NY 1954, tissue DJ, 1000 cys, box	300 - 500
MF1311	NY 1954, DJ (1st trade ed)	75 - 100
MF1320	**Go Down, Moses and Other Stories** NY 1942, 100 cys, slipcase	1000 - 1500
MF1321	NY 1942, DJ (1st trade ed)	200 - 300
MF1322	Lon 1942, DJ (1st English ed)	200 - 300
MF1330	**A Green Bough** NY 1933, 360 cys w/o DJ	1000 - 1500
MF1331	NY 1933, DJ (1st trade ed)	200 - 350
MF1340	**The Hamlet** NY 1940, 250 cys, cellophane DJ, Box	1000 - 1500
MF1341	NY 1940, DJ (1st trade ed)	200 - 300
MF1350	**Idyll in the Desert** NY 1931, 400 cys, glassine DJ	2000 - 3000
MF1360	**Intruder in the Dust** NY 1948, DJ	150 - 250
MF1362	Lon 1949, DJ (1st English ed)	100 - 150
MF1370	**Jealousy and Episode** Minn 1955, 500 cys	400 - 600
MF1380	**Knights Gambit** NY 1949, DJ	200 - 300
MF1390	**Light in August** NY 1932, DJ, glassine wrapper	700 - 1000
MF1400	**The Mansion** NY 1959, 500 cys, acetate DJ	600 - 800
MF1401	NY 1959 (1st trade ed)	75 - 125
MF1403	Lon 1961	
MF1410	**The Marble Faun** (1st book) Bos 1924, 500 cys, DJ	12000 - 20000
MF1420	**The Marionettes** Charlottesville 1975, 100 cys, box	700 - 1000
MF1421	Charlottesville 1975, 26 cys	1000 - 1500
MF1430	**Mayday** Notre Dame 1977, 150 cys, pamphlet, box	400 - 600
MF1440	**Mirrors of Chartres Street** Minn 1953, 1000 cys, DJ	250 - 350
MF1450	**Miss Zilphia Gant** Dallas 1932, 300 cys, glassine DJ	2000 - 3000
MF1461	**Mosquitoes** NY 1927, 1st state DJ w/Mosquito on cover	1000 - 1500
MF1462	2nd state DJ	400 - 600
MF1470	**New Orleans Sketches** New Brunswick 1958, DJ	50 - 75
MF1471	Tokyo 1955, DJ	200 - 300
MF1480	**Notes on a Horse Thief** Greenville 1950, 975 cys	600 - 1000
MF1491	**O. Henry Memorial Award Prize Stories of 1931** NY 1931, contains "Thrift"	200 - 300
MF1492	(Same anthology title) NY 1932, contains "Turn About"	200 - 300
MF1494	(Same anthology title) NY 1934, contains "Wash"	200 - 300
MF1500	**Ole Miss: The Yearbook of The University of Mississippi** 1919-1920, contains "To a Co-Ed" (Faulkner's college yearbook)	400 - 600
MF1510	**The Portable Faulkner** NY 1946, DJ	150 - 250
MF1520	**Pylon** NY 1935, 310 cys, box	700 - 1000
MF1521	NY 1935, DJ (1st trade ed)	200 - 300
MF1530	**The Reivers** NY 1962, 500 copies, DJ	400 - 600
MF1531	NY 1962, DJ (1st trade ed)	50 - 75

MF1540	**Requiem For A Nun** NY 1951, 750 cys, DJ	400 - 600
MF1541	NY 1951, DJ (1st trade ed)	75 - 125
MF1542	Lon 1953, DJ (1st English ed)	75 - 125
MF1543	NY 1959, DJ (play adaptation)	150 - 250
MF1550	**A Rose For Emily** NY 1945, wrappers	150 - 250
MF1560	**Salma Gundi** Milwaukee 1932, 525 cys,	
	box w/bottom edge untrimmed	2000 - 3000
	w/edge trimmed	1500 - 2500
MF1570	**Sanctuary** NY 1931, w/"first pub 1931"	
	on cr page in grey end papers	1000 - 1500
MF1571	Lon 1931, DJ (1st English ed)	200 - 300
MF1580	**Sartoris** NY 1929, DJ	300 - 500
MF1590	**Sherwood Anderson and Other Famous**	
	Creoles New Orleans 1926, 400 cys	
MF1591	hand-tinted cys	2000 - 3000
MF1592	other cys	500 - 1000
MF1600	**Soldier's Pay** NY 1926, DJ	7000 - 10000
MF1601	Lon 1930, DJ (1st English ed)	700 - 1000
MF1610	**The Sound and The Fury** NY 1929, "First	
	Published 1929" on cr page, DJ	2000 - 3000
MF1612	Lon 1931, DJ (1st English ed)	300 - 500
MF1620	**Story in America: An Anthology** NY 1934,	
	contains "Artist At Home"	150 - 250
MF1630	**These 13** NY 1931, 299 cys, tissue DJ	700 - 1000
MF1631	NY 1931, DJ (1st trade ed)	200 - 300
MF1633	Lon 1933, DJ (1st English ed)	150 - 250
MF1640	**This Earth** NY 1932, 1000 cys, envelope	300 - 500
MF1650	**The Town** NY 1957, 450 cys, acetate DJ	1000 - 1500
MF1651	NY 1957, DJ (1st trade ed)	100 - 150
MF1652	Lon 1958, DJ (1st English ed)	100 - 150
MF1660	**The Unvanquished** NY 1938, 250 cys,	
	glassine DJ	1500 - 2500
MF1661	NY 1938, DJ (1st trade ed)	400 - 600
MF1670	**The Wild Palms** NY 1939, 250 cys, glassine DJ	1500 - 2500
MF1671	NY 1939, DJ (1st trade ed)	400 - 600
MF1672	Lon 1939, DJ (1st English ed)	300 - 500
MF1680	**The Wishing Tree** NY 1964, 500 cys, DJ, box	250 - 350
MF1681	NY 1964, DJ (1st trade ed)	40 - 60

Feist, Raymond E.

MF1910	**Magician** Garden City 1982, DJ	175 - 225

Ferber, Edna

Wrote about 30 books. Common editions are mildly collectible at $15 - 40.

MF2010	**American Beauty** NY 1931, 200 cys	150 - 250
MF2011	NY 1931, DJ (1st trade ed)	25 - 50
MF2020	**Dawn O'Hara: The Girl Who Laughed**	
	(1st book) NY 1911, DJ	100 - 150
MF2030	**Show Boat** NY 1926, 201 cys	250 - 350
MF2031	1000 cys	100 - 150
MF2032	NY 1926, DJ (1st trade ed)	25 - 50
MF2040	**So Big** NY 1924, DJ	75 - 125

Fergusson, Harvey

MF2210	**The Life of Riley** NY 1937, DJ	30 - 50

Ferlinghetti, Lawrence

MF2310	**Back Roads To Far Places** NY 1971, wrappers	15 - 25
MF2320	**Her** Lon 1966, DJ	25 - 50
MF2330	**Landscapes of Living and Dying** NY 1979, DJ	20 - 30
MF2340	**Love in the Days of Rage** NY 1988, DJ	20 - 30
MF2350	**Pictures of the Gone World** (1st book)	
	SF 1955, wrappers w/title band	150 - 250
MF2351	SF 1955, 25 cys	500 - 700
MF2360	**The Secret Meaning of Things** NY 1968,	
	150 cys, box	150 - 250
MF2361	NY 1968, DJ	30 - 50
MF2362	NY 1968, wrappers	20 - 30

Finney, Charles G.

MF2510	**The Circus of Dr. Lao** NY 1935, DJ	200 - 300

Firbank, Ronald

MF2610	**Concerning the Eccentricities of Cardinal**	
	Pirelli Lon 1926, DJ	150 - 200
MF2620	**Inclinations** Lon 1916, DJ	150 - 200
MF2630	**O'Dette D'Antrevernes and A Study in**	
	Temperment (1st book) Lon 1905, wrappers	200 - 300
MF2640	**Prancing Nigger** NY 1924, DJ	150 - 200
MF2650	**The Princess Zoubaroff: A Comedy** Lon 1920,	
	513 cys	150 - 200
MF2660	**Sorrow in Sunlight** Lon 1925, 1000 cys	150 - 200

Fisher, Vardis

MF2910	**Mountain Man** NY 1965, DJ	25 - 50

Fitzgerald, F. Scott

MF3010	**Afternoon of An Author** Princeton 1950,	
	1500 cys, DJ	150 - 250
MF3020	**All the Sad Young Men** NY 1926, DJ, 1st	
	issue w/Scribner seal on cr page & green cl	2000 - 3000
MF3021	NY 1926, DJ, later issues	300 - 500
MF3030	**The Beautiful and the Damned** NY 1922, DJ,	
	1st state w/title in black on DJ, no ads, "March	
	1922" on cr page	3000 - 5000
MF3031	NY 1922, 2nd state DJ w/o title in black	1000 - 1500
MF3040	**A Book of Princeton Verse** Princeton	
	1919, DJ, w/contributions by Fitzgerald	700 - 1000
MF3050	**The Crack-Up** NY 1945, DJ, w/tp in red/black	200 - 300
MF3060	**The Evil Eye** Cinti 1915, DJ	1200 - 1800
MF3070	**Fie! Fie! Fie! Fi-Fi!** Cinti 1914, DJ	1200 - 1800
MF3080	**Flappers and Philosophers** NY 1920, DJ,	
	w/"Pub. Sept. 1920" on cr page	1000 - 1500
MF3090	**The Great Gatsby** NY 1925, DJ, 1st issue	
	w/"sick in tired" for "sickntired" line 9, p 205,	
	in 1st state DJ w/flaps listings books by	
	Fitzgerald & Lardner	7000 - 10000
MF3091	NY 1925, later issues & states w/DJs	1200 - 1800
	w/o DJ	300 - 500
MF3100	**The Pat Hobby Stories** NY 1962, DJ	100 - 150
MF3110	**Safety First** Cinti 1916, DJ	700 - 1000
MF3120	**Tales of the Jazz Age** NY 1922, DJ,	
	w/"Pub. Sept. 1922" on cr page	2000 - 3000
MF3130	**Taps at Reveille** NY 1935, DJ, 1st issue	
	w/"and was" on line 15, p 351	1000 - 1500
MF3140	**Tender Is The Night** NY 1934, DJ, w/"A"	
	on cr page	2000 - 3000
	w/o DJ	200 - 300
MF3143	NY 1982, 2000 cys, slipcase	200 - 300
MF3150	**This Side of Paradise** (1st book) NY 1920,	
	DJ, w/"Pub. April, 1920"	3000 - 5000
	w/o DJ	300 - 500
MF3160	**The Vegetable** NY 1923, DJ, w/"Pub. April,	
	1923" on cr page	1200 - 1800

Fitzgerald, Zelda

MF3310	**Save Me The Waltz** (1st book) NY 1932, DJ	700 - 1000
MF3312	Lon 1953, DJ (1st English ed)	75 - 100

Flanner, Janet

MF3410	**The Cubical City** (1st book) NY 1926, DJ	300 - 500

Fleming, Ian

MF3510	**Casino Royale** (1st book) Lon 1953, DJ	
	(a signed cy brought £5,500 in 1988)	2000 - 3000
MF3511	NY 1954, DJ	300 - 500
MF3520	**Chitty Chitty Bang Bang** Lon 1964, DJ	50 - 75
MF3521	NY 1964, DJ	25 - 50
MF3530	**The Diamond Smugglers** Lon 1957, DJ	300 - 400
MF3531	NY 1957, DJ	50 - 75
MF3540	**Diamonds Are Forever** Lon 1956, DJ	600 - 800
MF3541	NY 1956, DJ	100 - 150
MF3551	**Dr. No** Lon 1958, DJ, 1st state w/o silhouette	
	on cover DJ	250 - 350
MF3552	Lon 1958, DJ, 2nd state	100 - 150
MF3553	NY 1958, DJ	75 - 125
MF3560	**For Your Eyes Only** Lon 1960, DJ	200 - 300
MF3570	**From Russia With Love** Lon 1957, DJ	300 - 500
MF3580	**Goldfinger** Lon 1959, DJ	300 - 500
MF3581	NY 1958, DJ	100 - 150

MF1651   MF1681   MF1910

| MF3600 | MF3620 | MF3621 | MF3630 | MF3670 | MF3910 |

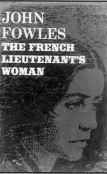

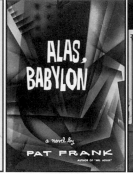

| MF5011 | MF5021 | MF5031 | MF5510 | MF5810 | MF6020 |

MF3590 **Live and Let Die** Lon 1954, DJ   700 - 1000
MF3592 NY 1955, DJ   250 - 350
MF3600 **The Man with the Golden Gun** Lon 1965, DJ   100 - 150
MF3610 **Moonraker** Lon 1955, DJ   800 - 1200
MF3611 NY 1955, DJ (1st American ed)   200 - 300
MF3620 **Octopussy and The Living Daylights** Lon 1966, DJ   50 - 75
MF3621 NY 1966, DJ   30 - 40
MF3630 **On Her Majesty's Secret Service** Lon 1963, DJ, 250 cys   2000 - 3000
MF3640 **The Spy Who Loved Me** Lon 1962, DJ   100 - 150
MF3641 NY 1962, DJ   25 - 50
MF3650 **Thrilling Cities** Lon 1963, DJ   100 - 150
MF3660 **Thunderball** Lon 1961, DJ   150 - 200
MF3670 **You Only Live Twice** Lon 1964, DJ   100 - 150
MF3671 NY 1964, DJ   25 - 50

Fletcher, George U.
MF3910 **The Well of the Unicorn** NY 1948, DJ   100 - 150

Follett, Ken
MF4010 **Eye of the Needle** NY 1978, DJ   30 - 50
MF4020 **The Key To Rebecca** NY 1980, DJ   20 - 30
MF4030 **The Modigliani Scandal** NY 1976, DJ   30 - 50
MF4040 **On Wings of Eagles** NY 1983, DJ   20 - 30
MF4050 **Paper Money** NY 1987, DJ   20 - 30
MF4060 **Triple** NY 1979, DJ   20 - 30

Ford, Paul Leicester
Wrote about 15 books. All are collectible for highly decorative bindings and color plates by Howard Chandler Christy and other artists. The dust jackets are rare or non-existent. Most are $20-50.
MF4210 **The Best Laid Plans** (1st book) Brooklyn 1889, 50 cys   200 - 300
MF4220 **The Great K.&A. Train Robbery** NY 1897   20 - 40
MF4230 **Janice Meredith** NY 1899, 1st state w/L in "leader" on line 22, p 121   50 - 75
MF4240 **Wanted - A Chaperon** NY 1902, DJ   50 - 75
MF4250 **Wanted - A Match Maker** NY 1905, DJ   50 - 75

Forester, C. S.
MF4410 **The African Queen** Bos 1935, DJ   300 - 500
MF4420 **Lieutenant Hornblower** Bos 1952, DJ   50 - 75
MF4430 **Lord Nelson** Ind 1929, DJ   125 - 200
MF4440 **A Pawn Among Kings** (1st book) Lon 1924, DJ   700 - 1000

Forster, E. M.
MF4610 **Aspects of the Novel** Lon 1927, DJ   200 - 300
MF4620 **The Celestial Omnibus** Lon 1911   200 - 300
MF4630 **The Longest Journey** Lon 1907, DJ   300 - 500
MF4640 **A Passage to India** Lon 1924, 200 cys, box   2000 - 3000
MF4642 Lon 1924, DJ (1st trade ed)   300 - 500
MF4650 **A Room with a View** Lon 1908, DJ   300 - 500

MF4661 **Where Angels Fear to Tread** (1st book) Edinburgh 1905, DJ, 1st state w/o this title in the ads   500 - 700
MF4662 2nd state w/title in ads   200 - 300
MF4663 NY 1920, DJ (1st American ed)   125 - 250

Forsyth, Frederick
MF4910 **The Day of the Jackal** (1st book) Lon 1971, DJ   75 - 125

Fowles, John
MF5010 **The Collector** (1st book) Lon 1963, DJ 1st issue w/o pub blurbs on DJ   700 - 1000
MF5011 Bos 1963, DJ (1st American ed)   75 - 125
MF5020 **The French Lieutenant's Woman** Lon 1969, DJ   150 - 250
MF5021 Bos 1969, DJ (1st American ed)   100 - 150
MF5030 **The Magus** Lon 1966, DJ   200 - 300
MF5031 Bos 1965, DJ   100 - 150

Fox, Jr., John
MF5210 **Blue Grass and Rhododendron** NY 1901, DJ   50 - 75
MF5220 **Crittenden** NY 1900 DJ   50 - 75
MF5230 **A Cumberland Vendetta** (1st book) NY 1896   50 - 100
MF5240 **Hell Fer Sartain** NY 1897   40 - 60
MF5250 **A Knight of the Cumberland** NY 1906, DJ   50 - 75
MF5260 **The Little Shepherd of Kingdom Come** NY 1903, DJ, 1st state w/"laugh" for "lap" on line 14, p 61   50 - 100

Francis, Dick
MF5510 **Blood Sport** Lon 1967, DJ   200 - 300
MF5520 **Break In** NY 1986, DJ   20 - 30
MF5530 **Dead Cert** Lon 1962, DJ   300 - 500
MF5531 NY 1962, DJ (1st American ed)   100 - 150
MF5540 **The Edge** NY 1989, DJ   20 - 30
MF5550 **Hot Money** NY 1988, 250 cys, box   75 - 100
MF5560 **Knock Down** NY 1974, DJ   50 - 75
MF5570 **Long Shot** NY 1990, DJ   20 - 30
MF5580 **Risk** NY 1977, DJ   30 - 50
MF5590 **The Sport of Queens** (1st book) Lon 1957, DJ   200 - 300
MF5591 NY 1957, DJ   150 - 200

Frank, Pat
MF5810 **Alas, Babylon** NY 1959, DJ   200 - 250
MF5811 Phil 1959, stiff wraps (advance review cy)   600 - 800

Fraser, George MacDonald
MF6010 **Flash For Freedom!** Lon 1971, DJ   75 - 125
MF6020 **Flashman** (1st book) Lon 1969, DJ   150 - 250
MF6030 **Flashman and the Dragon** Lon 1985, DJ   50 - 75
MF6040 **Flashman and the Mountain of Light** Lon 1990, DJ   25 - 50
MF6050 **Flashman and the Redskins** Lon 1982, DJ   50 - 75
MF6060 **Flashman at the Charge** Lon 1973, DJ   75 - 125
MF6070 **McAuslan in the Rough** Lon 1974, DJ   50 - 75
MF6080 **Mr. American** Lon 1980, DJ   25 - 50

French, Paul (pseud for Isaac Asimov; also see Asimov)

MF6210	**Lucky Starr and the Pirates of the Asteroids** Garden City 1953, DJ	100 - 150
MF6215	4 other books in the Lucky Starr series	100 - 225

Frost, Robert

MF6410	**Away** NY 1958, 185 cys	150 - 250
MF6421	**A Boy's Will** Lon 1913, 1st state: bronze cloth binding	3000 - 5000
MF6422	2nd state: white parchment binding	2000 - 3000
MF6423	3rd state: buff wrappers w/decorated A	700 - 1000
MF6424	4th state: buff wrappers w/plain A	300 - 500
MF6426	NY 1915, 1st issue w/"aind" on last line, p 14	300 - 500
MF6427	NY 1915, 2nd issue w/"and" on last line, p 14	150 - 200
MF6429	NY 1935, DJ	50 - 75
MF6440	**Collected Poems** NY 1930, 1000 cys, DJ	1000 - 1500
MF6441	NY 1930, DJ (1st trade ed)	200 - 300
MF6443	NY 1939, DJ	75 - 125
MF6450	**Complete Poems** NY 1949, 500 cys, DJ	700 - 1000
MF6451	NY 1949, DJ (1st trade ed)	100 - 175
MF6460	**The Complete Poems of Robert Frost** NY 1950, 1500 cys, box	400 - 600
MF6470	**The Cow's in the Corn** Gaylordsville 1929, 91 cys, errata slip	1000 - 1500
MF6480	**Dedication** NY 1961, 250 cys	150 - 250
MF6490	**A Further Range** NY 1936, 803 cys, box	400 - 600
MF6491	NY 1936, DJ (1st trade ed)	75 - 125
MF6492	NY 1936, DJ (BOMC ed)	20 - 30
MF6494	Lon 1937, DJ (1st English ed)	75 - 125
MF6501	**The Gold Hesperidee** Cortland 1935, 1st issue w/"unturned" on 2nd to last line, p 7	300 - 500
MF6502	2nd issue: "turned and carried over" on 2nd to last line, p 7	200 - 300
MF6510	**Greece** Chi 1948, 47 cys, envelope	700 - 1000
MF6520	**Hard Not to be King** NY 1951, 300 cys, DJ	300 - 500
MF6530	**In the Clearing** NY 1962, 1500 cys, box	200 - 300
MF6531	NY 1962, DJ (1st trade ed)	40 - 60
MF6540	**The Lone Striker** NY 1933, envelope, #8 of "Borzoi Chap Books"	150 - 250
MF6550	**The Lovely Shall Be Choosers** NY 1929, 475 cys, wrappers	200 - 300
MF6560	**A Masque of Mercy** NY 1947, 751 cys, box	200 - 300
MF6561	NY 1947, DJ (1st trade ed)	50 - 75
MF6570	**A Masque of Reason** NY 1945, 800 cys, box	200 - 300
MF6571	NY 1945, DJ (1st trade ed)	40 - 60
MF6573	Lon 1949, DJ (1st English ed)	50 - 75
MF6581	**Mountain Interval** NY 1916, DJ, 1st issue: verses 6 & 7, p 88 are identical	300 - 500
MF6582	2nd issue: P 88 verses correct	200 - 300
MF6584	NY 1921, DJ	75 - 125
MF6590	**New Hampshire** NY 1923, 350 cys, glassine DJ, box	700 - 1000
MF6591	NY 1923, DJ (1st trade ed)	50 - 75
MF6592	Lon 1924, DJ (1st English ed)	50 - 75
MF6601	**North of Boston** Lon 1914, 1st state: green buckram w/gold lettering	3000 - 5000
MF6602	2nd state: green buckram w/blind lettering	1500 - 2000
MF6603	3rd state: blue buckram w/black lettering	1500 - 2000
MF6604	4th state: green buckram w/blind rule at top & bottom	800 - 1200
MF6605	NY 1914, DJ (1st American ed)	800 - 1200
MF6607	NY 1915, DJ	300 - 500
MF6620	**Selected Poems** NY 1923, DJ	200 - 300
MF6630	**Steeple Bush** NY 1947, 751 cys, tissue DJ, box	200 - 300
MF6631	NY 1947, DJ (1st trade ed)	50 - 75
MF6640	**Three Poems** Hanover 1935, 125 cys	600 - 800
MF6650	**Twilight** (1st book) Lawrence, MA 1894, 20 pp bound in leather	30000 - 50000
MF6660	**A Way Out** NY 1929, 485 cys, DJ	200 - 300
MF6670	**West Running Brook** NY 1928, 1000 cys, DJ, box	300 - 500
MF6671	NY 1928, DJ (1st trade ed) w/"roams" for "romps" p 38	200 - 300
MF6680	**A Witness Tree** NY 1942, 735 cys, box	250 - 350
MF6681	NY 1942, DJ (1st trade ed)	50 - 75
MF6683	Lon 1943, DJ (1st English ed)	50 - 75
MF6690	**The Wood Pile** NY 1961, DJ	50 - 75
MF6700	**A Young Birch** NY 1946, DJ	75 - 125

Gaines, Ernest

MG0080	**The Autobiography of Miss Jane Pittman** NY 1971, DJ	40 - 60
MG0090	**A Gathering of Old Men** NY 1983, DJ	30 - 50

Gardner, Erle Stanley (A. A. Fair, Carleton Kendrake)

One of the most prolific of mystery writers, Gardner wrote over 100 mystery stories during 1930s-1980s. His most famous character is Perry Mason. His titles usually begin with "The Case of…".

MG0340	**The Case of the Backward Mule** NY 1946, DJ	50 - 75
MG0350	**The Case of the Beautiful Beggar** NY 1965, DJ	20 - 30
MG0360	**The Case of the Calendar Girl** NY 1958, DJ	30 - 50
MG0370	**The Case of the Cautious Coquette** NY 1949, DJ	40 - 60
MG0380	**The Case of the Counterfeit Eye** NY 1935, DJ	150 - 250
MG0381	NY 1936, DJ (Grosset & Dunlap reprint)	20 - 30
MG0390	**The Case of the Curious Bride** NY 1934, DJ	200 - 300
MG0391	NY 1935, DJ (Grosset & Dunlap reprint)	20 - 30
MG0400	**The Case of the Empty Tin** NY 1941, DJ	100 - 150
MG0410	**The Case of the Grinning Gorilla** NY 1952, DJ	30 - 50
MG0420	**The Case of the Howling Dog** NY 1934, DJ	250 - 350
MG0421	NY 1935, DJ (Grosset & Dunlap reprint)	30 - 50
MG0430	**The Case of the Irate Witness** NY 1972, DJ	20 - 30
MG0440	**The Case of the Lucky Legs** NY 1934, DJ	300 - 500
MG0441	NY 1935, DJ (Grosset & Dunlap reprint)	30 - 50
MG0450	**The Case of the Musical Cow** NY 1950, DJ	50 - 75
MG0460	**The Case of the Perjured Parrot** NY 1939, DJ	200 - 300
MG0461	Lon 1939, DJ (1st English ed)	100 -150
MG0470	**The Case of the Singing Skirt** NY 1959, DJ	20 - 30
MG0480	**The Case of the Sulky Girl** NY 1933, DJ	400 - 600
MG0481	NY 1934, DJ (Grosset & Dunlap reprint)	30 - 50
MG0490	**The Case of the Sun Bather's Diary** NY 1955, DJ	30 - 50
MG0500	**The Case of the Velvet Claws** (1st book) NY 1932, DJ	800 - 1200
MG0501	Lon 1933, DJ	400 - 600
MG0502	NY 1934, DJ (Grosset & Dunlap reprint)	50 - 75
MG0510	**Clew of the Forgotten Murder** NY 1935, DJ, under pseud Carleton Kendrake	200 - 300
MG0520	**The D.A. Breaks An Egg** NY 1949, DJ	30 - 50

Gardner, John

MG0710	**The Forms of Fiction** NY 1962	150 - 250
MG0720	**Grendel** NY 1971, DJ	250 - 350
MG0721	Lon 1971, DJ (1st English ed)	75 - 125
MG0730	**Jason and Medea** NY 1973, DJ	75 - 125
MG0740	**The King's Indian** NY 1974, DJ	75 - 125
MG0750	**The Miller's Mule** 1965, mimeographed sheets, bds	1000 - 1500
MG0760	**Nickel Mountain** NY 1973, DJ	75 - 125
MG0770	**The Resurrection** NY 1966, DJ	700 - 100
MG0780	**The Sunlight Dialogues** NY 1972, DJ	75 - 125
MG0790	**The Wreckage of Agathon** NY 1970, DJ	150 - 250

Garland, Hamlin

Wrote over 50 western books from 1890s-1940s. Most are worth $25-75 with DJ.

MF6210   MF6460 (slipcase)   MF6531   **147**   MF6571   MG0080   MG0370

| MG2010 | MG2475 | MG2486 | MG3440 | MG4710 (w/o DJ) |

| MG5211 | MG5260 | MG5280 |

MG0910 **The Book of the American Indian** NY 1923,
    DJ, box   200 - 300
MG0920 **Boy Life on the Prairie** NY 1899   75 - 125
MG0930 **The Captain of the Gray Horse Troop**
    NY 1902, DJ   75 - 125
MG0940 **A Daughter of the Middle Border** NY 1921, DJ   50 - 75
MG0950 **The Forester's Daughter** NY 1914, DJ   50 - 75
MG0960 **The Long Trail** NY 1907, DJ   75 - 125
MG0970 **Main-Travelled Roads** Bos 1891, wrappers
    w/"first thousand"   300 - 500
MG0971 Bos 1891, cl   200 - 300
MG0980 **A Son of the Middle Border** NY 1917, DJ   75 - 125
MG0990 **Under the Wheel** (1st book) Bos 1890   200 - 300

Gernsback, Hugo
MG1510 **Ralph 124 41+** Bos 1925, DJ   2000 - 3000

Gibbons, Floyd
MG2010 **The Red Napoleon** NY 1929, DJ   200 - 300

Gibson, William
MG2210 **Neuromancer** Lon 1984, DJ   150 - 250
MG2212 West Bloomfield 1986, 375 cys   200 - 300
MG2213 West Bloomfield 1986, DJ (1st American trade ed)   50 - 75

Ginsberg, Allen
    A prolific signer of postcards, photographs, posters, and broadsides.
All are collectible.
MG2410 **Allen Verbatim** NY 1974   20 - 40
MG2420 **Ankor Wat** Lon 1969, 100 cys   100 - 150
MG2430 **Bixby Canyon Ocean Path Word Breeze**
    NY 1972, 26 cys   250 - 350
MG2431 NY 1972 wrappers (1st trade ed)   50 - 75
MG2440 **Careless Love** Madison 1978, 280 cys   150 - 250
MG2450 **Empty Mirror: Early Poems** NY 1961   75 - 125
MG2460 **First Blues** NY 1975   20 - 40
MG2470 **The Gates of Wrath** Bolinas 1972, 100 cys   100 - 150
MG2475 **Howl and Other Poems** SF 1956, 1st printing,
    paper wrappers   250 - 350
MG2480 **Howl For Carl Solomon** (1st book) SF 1955,
    50 mimeographed cys   5000 - 7000
MG2481 SF 1956 wrappers (1st trade ed)   250 - 350
MG2482 SF 1971, 275 cys   300 - 500
MG2486 **Iron Horse** SF 1974, wrappers   25 - 35
MG2490 **Kaddish and Other Poems** SF 1961   50 - 75
MG2500 **The Moments Return** SF 1970, 200 cys   100 - 150
MG2510 **New Year Blues** NY 1972, wrappers, 100 cys   100 - 150
MG2511 NY 1972, 26 cys   250 - 350
MG2520 **Notes After an Evening with William Carlos
    Williams** Brooklyn 1960s?, 300 cys   75 - 125
MG2530 **Planet News: 1961-1967** SF 1968, 500 cys, box   150 - 250

MG2540 **Siesta in Xbalba and Return to the States**
    Near Icy Cape, AK, 1956, wrappers,
    56 mimeographed cys   3000 - 5000
MG2550 **T.V. Baby Poems** Lon 1967, DJ, 100 cys   200 - 300
MG2551 Lon 1967, wrappers (1st trade ed)   25 - 50
MG2553 NY 1968, wrappers (1st American ed)   25 - 50

Godwin, Tom
MG3010 **The Survivors** Hicksville 1958, DJ   75 - 100

Golding, William (1983 Nobel Laureate)
MG3210 **Free Fall** Lon 1959, DJ   200 - 300
MG3220 **The Inheritors** Lon 1955, DJ   300 - 500
MG3230 **Lord of the Flies** (1st book) Lon 1954, DJ   800 - 1200
MG3231 NY 1954, DJ (1st American ed)   400 - 600
MG3240 **The Spire** Lon 1964   100 - 150

Goldman, William
MG3410 **Butch Cassidy and the Sundance Kid** NY 1969, DJ 25 - 50
MG3420 **The Hot Rock** NY 1972, DJ   25 - 50
MG3430 **Hype and Glory** NY 1990, DJ   20 - 30
MG3440 **The Princess Bride** NY 1973, DJ   125 - 250
MG3450 **Soldier in the Rain** NY 1960, DJ   30 - 50
MG3460 **The Temple of Gold** (1st book) NY 1957, DJ   100 - 150
MG3470 **Wait Till Next Year** NY 1988, DJ   20 - 30
MG3480 **Your Turn to Curtsy, My Turn to Bow** NY 1958, DJ 50 - 75

Goodman, Paul
MG3710 **The Breakup of Our Camp** Norfolk 1949, DJ   75 - 125
MG3720 **The Facts of Life** NY 1945, DJ   75 - 125
MG3730 **Red Jacket** NY 1955, wrappers   75 - 125
MG3740 **Ten Lyric Poems** (1st book) NY 1934, wrappers   200 - 300

Gordon, Caroline
MG4010 **None Shall Look Back** DJ   50 - 75

Gordon, Rex
MG4110 **Utopia 239** Lon 1955, DJ   75 - 100

Gorey, Edward
MG4410 **The Bug Book** NY 1959, wrappers   200 - 300
MG4420 **The Gilded Bat** NY 1966, DJ   100 - 150
MG4430 **The Listing Attic** NY 1954, DJ   150 - 250
MG4440 **The Unstrung Harp** (1st book) NY 1953, DJ   150 - 250

Gorman, Herbert
MG4710 **A Place Called Dagon** NY 1927, DJ   400 - 600
    w/o DJ   100 - 150

Grafton, Sue
    Currently one of the most collectible detective-mystery writers.
MG5210 **"A" is for Alibi** NY 1982, DJ (1st ed)   1000 - 1500
MG5211 NY 1982, DJ (book club reprint)   20 - 30
MG5220 **"B" is for Burglar** NY 1985, DJ   250 - 350
MG5230 **"C" is for Corpse** NY 1986, DJ   100 - 150
MG5231 NY 1986, wrappers (advance review cy)   150 - 250
MG5240 **"D" is for Deadbeat** NY 1987, DJ   50 - 75
MG5250 **"E" is for Evidence** NY 1988, DJ   30 - 50
MG5260 **"F" is for Fugitive** NY 1989, DJ   20 - 30
MG5270 **"G" is for Gumshoe** NY 1990, DJ   20 - 30
MG5280 **"J" is for Judgment** NY 1993, DJ   20 - 30
MG5290 **Keziah Dane** (1st book) NY 1967, DJ   200 - 300

Graham, Tom (see Sinclair Lewis)

Grahame, Kenneth
MG5501 **Dream Days** NY 1899, 1st issue w/15 pp ads
    dated 1898   300 - 500
MG5502 Lon 1902   200 - 300
MG5504 Lon 1930, 275 cys, box   300 - 500
MG5510 **The Golden Age** Lon 1895   300 - 500
MG5511 Chi 1895 (1st American ed)   200 - 300

MG5513 Lon 1900 — 200 - 300
MG5515 Lon 1928, 275 cys, box — 300 - 500
MG5530 **Pagan Papers** (1st book) Lon 1894, 450 cys — 300 - 500
MG5540 **The Wind in the Willows** Lon 1908, DJ — 8000 - 12000
MG5541 Lon 1908, w/o DJ — 500 - 800
MG5542 NY 1908, DJ (1st American ed) — 500 - 700
MG5544 NY 1913, DJ — 100 - 150
MG5546 Lon 1931, 200 cys, box — 300 - 500
MG5548 NY 1940, 1500 cys, box — 1000 - 1500
MG5550 Lon 1951, 500 cys, box — 1000 - 1500

Graves, Robert
MG5810 **Adam's Rib** Lon 1955, 250 cys, DJ, box — 400 - 600
MG5820 **Beyond Giving Poems** Lon 1969, wrappers,
536 cys — 150 - 250
MG5830 **Country Sentiment** Lon 1920, DJ — 200 - 300
MG5831 NY 1920, DJ (1st American ed) — 100 - 150
MG5840 **Fairies and Fusiliers** Lon 1917, DJ — 500 - 700
MG5850 **Goliath and David** Lon 1916, 200 cys, wrappers — 700 - 1000
MG5860 **I, Claudius** Lon 1934, DJ — 200 - 300
MG5870 **Lawrence and the Arabs** Lon 1927, DJ — 250 - 350
MG5880 **Love Respect** Lon 1965, 250 cys, DJ — 150 - 250
MG5890 **Man Does, Woman Is** Lon 1964, 26 cys,
glassine DJ — 400 - 600
MG5900 **My Head! My Head!** Lon 1925, DJ — 300 - 500
MG5901 NY 1925, DJ (1st American ed) — 200 - 300
MG5910 **Over the Brazier** (1st book) Lon 1916, wrappers — 800 - 1200
MG5911 Lon 1920, DJ — 300 - 500
MG5920 **Poems (1914-1927)** Lon 1927, 115 cys, DJ — 500 - 700
MG5930 **Poems 1926-1930** Lon 1932, DJ — 200 - 300
MG5940 **Poems 1929** Lon 1929, 225 cys — 300 - 500
MG5950 **The Shout** Lon 1929, 530 cys, DJ — 200 - 300
MG5960 **Ten Poems More** Paris 1930, 200 cys, DJ — 500 - 700
MG5970 **Treasure Box** Lon 1919, wrappers, 200 cys — 800 - 1200
MG5980 **Whipperginny** Lon 1923, DJ — 400 - 600
MG5990 NY 1923, DJ (1st American ed) — 200 - 300

Green, Anna Katharine
Wrote about 50 mystery novels in 1870s-1920s. All are collectible.
MG6310 **The Amethyst Box** Ind 1907, DJ — 150 - 200
MG6320 **The Circular Study** NY 1900, DJ, 1st state
w/green/gold stamped cl — 250 - 350
MG6330 **Doctor Izaro** NY 1895 — 150 - 250
MG6340 **The Filigree Ball** Ind 1903, DJ, 1st state: pub
"March, 1903" on cr page w/red printer's slug — 150 - 200
MG6350 **Hand and Ring** NY 1883 — 100 - 150
MG6360 **The Leavenworth Case** (1st book) NY 1878 — 1500 - 2000

Green, Henry
MG6510 **Blindness** (1st book) Lon 1926, DJ — 1000 - 1500
MG6511 NY 1926, DJ (1st American ed) — 200 - 300
MG6520 **Doting** Lon 1952, DJ — 100 - 150
MG6530 **Nothing** Lon 1950, DJ — 100 - 150

Greenaway, Kate (see Artists & Illustrators)

Greene, A. C.
MG6710 **A Personal Country** (1st book) NY 1969, DJ — 50 - 75

Greene, Graham
MG6910 **Babbling April** (1st book) Lon 1925, DJ — 2000 - 3000
MG6920 **Brighton Rock** Lon 1938, DJ — 300 - 500
MG6921 NY 1938, DJ (1st American ed) — 100 - 150
MG6930 **A Burnt Out Case** Lon 1961, DJ — 50 - 75
MG6931 NY 1961, DJ (1st American ed) — 25 - 50
MG6940 **The Confidential Agent** Lon 1939, DJ — 300 - 500
MG6941 NY 1939, DJ (1st American ed) — 100 - 150
MG6950 **A Gun For Sale** Lon 1936, DJ — 300 - 500
MG6960 **Its A Battlefield** Lon 1934, DJ — 400 - 600
MG6961 Garden City 1934, DJ (1st American ed) — 150 - 250
MG6970 **Loser Takes All** Lon 1955, DJ — 75 - 125
MG6980 **The Man Within** Lon 1929, DJ — 800 - 1200
MG6981 Garden City 1929, DJ (1st American ed) — 300 - 500
MG6990 **Nineteen Stories** Lon 1947, DJ — 150 - 250
MG6991 NY 1949, DJ (1st American ed) — 50 - 75
MG7010 **The Orient Express** Garden City 1933, DJ
(1st American ed) — 200 - 300
MG7011 1st pub as **The Stamboul Train** Lon 1932, DJ — 500 - 700
MG7020 **Our Man in Havana** Lon 1958, DJ — 125 - 250
MG7021 NY 1958, DJ (1st American ed) — 50 - 75
MG7030 **Rumour at Nightfall** Lon 1931, DJ — 500 - 700
MG7031 Garden City 1931, DJ (1st American ed) — 200 - 300
MG7040 **The Third Man** Lon 1950, DJ — 300 - 500
MG7041 NY 1950, DJ (1st American ed) — 75 - 125

MG7050 **Travels With My Aunt** Lon 1969, DJ — 50 - 75
MG7051 NY 1970, DJ (1st American ed) — 25 - 50
MG7060 **Twenty One Stories** Lon 1954, DJ — 75 - 125
MG7061 NY 1962, DJ (1st American ed) — 25 - 50

Grey, Zane (also see Baseball - Fiction)
All Grey's western books are collectible. The Grosset & Dunlap
reprints in DJs are worth $10-25.
MG7610 **Arizona Ames** Lon 1931, DJ — 75 - 125
MG7620 **Betty Zane** (1st book) NY 1903 (no DJ) — 500 - 700
MG7630 **The Call of the Canyon** NY 1924, DJ — 100 - 150
MG7640 **Code of the West** Lon 1934, DJ — 75 - 125
MG7650 **The Day of the Beast** NY 1922, DJ — 150 - 250
MG7660 **The Last of the Plainsmen** NY 1908, DJ — 200 - 300
MG7670 **The Light of Western Stars** NY 1914, DJ — 100 - 150
MG7680 **The Rainbow Trail** NY 1915, DJ — 150 - 250
MG7690 **Riders of the Purple Sage** NY 1912, DJ,
w/"Pub. Jan. 1912" on cr page — 250 - 350
MG7700 **Tappan's Burro** NY 1923, DJ — 150 - 250
MG7710 **The Thundering Herd** NY 1925, DJ — 100 - 150

Grimes, Martha
MG8110 **The Anodyne Necklace** Bos 1983, DJ — 75 - 125
MG8120 **The Deer Leap** Bos 1985, DJ — 50 - 75
MG8130 **The Dirty Duck** Bos 1984, DJ — 50 - 75
MG8140 **Help The Poor Struggler** Bos 1985, DJ — 40 - 60
MG8150 **The Man with a Load of Mischief** Bos 1981, DJ — 75 - 125
MG8160 **The Old Contemptibles** Bos 1991, DJ — 20 - 30
MG8161 Bos 1991, wrappers (advance review cy) — 30 - 50

Guthrie, A. B.
MG9010 **Murders at Moon Dance** (1st book) NY 1943, DJ — 300 - 500
MG9020 **The Way West** NY 1949, DJ — 75 - 125

Haley, Alex
MH0110 **Roots** NY 1976, DJ — 30 - 50
signed cy — 100 - 150

Hamilton, Edmond
MH0210 **Battle for the Stars** NY 1961, DJ — 75 - 125
MH0220 **The Haunted Stars** NY 1960, DJ — 75 - 125
MH0230 **The Star Kings** NY 1949, DJ — 100 - 150

Hammett, Dashiell
MH0410 **The Dain Curse** NY 1929, DJ, 1st issue
w/"dopped in" on line 19, p 260 — 3000 - 5000
MH0420 **Farewell My Lovely** NY 1940, DJ — 1200 - 1800
MH0430 **The Glass Key** NY 1931, DJ — 2000 - 3000
MH0440 **The Maltese Falcon** NY 1930, DJ — 3000 - 5000
MH0451 **Red Harvest** (1st book) NY 1929, DJ,
1st state DJ w/o Review of Book — 7000 - 10000
MH0452 2nd state DJ w/Review — 3000 - 5000
MH0460 **Secret Agent X-9** Phil 1934, DJ — 1000 - 1500
MH0471 **The Thin Man** NY 1934, 1st state red DJ — 3000 - 5000
MH0472 2nd state green DJ — 2000 - 3000

Hardy, Thomas
MH0610 **Satires of Circumstance** Lon 1914, DJ — 800 - 1200

Harris, Joel Chandler
MH0800 **Little Mr. Thimblefinger and His Queer Country**
Bos 1894 — 125 - 200
MH0810 **The Tar Baby and Other Rhymes of Uncle
Remus** NY 1904, DJ — 1500 - 2500
w/o DJ — 150 - 250
MH0821 **Uncle Remus: His Songs and His Sayings**
(1st book) NY 1881, 1st issue w/"presumptive"
in last line, p 9 — 2000 - 3000
MH0822 NY 1881, 2nd issue — 800 - 1200
MH0824 NY 1895, 250 cys, signed — 400 - 600

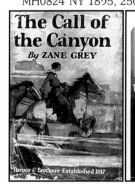

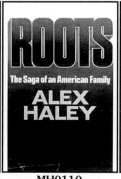

MG7630   MH0110   MH0800

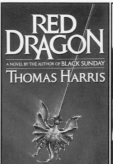
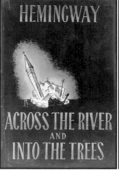

| MH0840 | MH1110 | MH1120 | MH1210 | MH1950 | MH2020 |

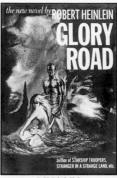

| MH2050 | MH2070 | MH2402 | MH2431 | MH2450 | MH2471 |

MH0830 **Uncle Remus Returns** Bos 1918, DJ 1500 - 2500
w/o DJ 200 - 300
MH0840 **Wally Wanderoon and his Story Telling
Machine** NY 1903 100 - 150

Harris, Thomas
MH1110 **Red Dragon** NY 1981, DJ 50 - 75
MH1120 **The Silence of the Lambs** NY 1988, DJ 40 - 60

Harrison, Harry
MH1210 **Make Room! Make Room!** Garden City 1966, DJ 150 - 200

Healy, Raymond & J. McComas (editors)
MH1310 **Adventures in Time and Space** (anthology)
NY 1946, DJ 100 - 150

Hearn, Lafcadio
MH1410 **Creole Sketches** NY 1924 75 - 125
MH1420 **Fantastics and Other Fancies** Bos 1914, 550 cys 400 - 600
MH1430 **In Ghostly Japan** Bos 1899 150 - 250
MH1440 **Japanese Fairy Tales** Tokyo 1898-1903, 5 vol,
crepe paper 1500 - 2500
MH1441 Tokyo 1898-1903, 5 vol (large paper ed) 1000 - 1500
MH1442 Tokyo 1898-1903, 5 vol (trade ed) 300 - 500
MH1450 **Japanese Lyrics** Bos 1915, wrappers 200 - 300
MH1460 **A Japanese Miscellany** Bos 1901, DJ 200 - 300
MH1470 **Karma** NY 1918, DJ 150 - 250
MH1480 **Kokoro** Bos 1896 125 - 200
MH1490 **Kotto** NY 1902, 1st state w/tp background
upside down 200 - 300
MH1500 **Kwaidan** Bos 1904, DJ 100 - 150
MH1502 NY 1932, silk portfolio 100 - 150
MH1510 **Occidental Gleanings** NY 1925, DJ 75 - 125
MH1520 **The Romance of the Milky Way** Bos 1905 150 - 250
MH1530 **Shadowings** Bos 1900, DJ 300 - 500
MH1540 **Some Chinese Ghosts** Bos 1887 300 - 500
MH1550 **Stray Leaves From Strange Literature**
(1st Book) Bos 1884 700 - 1000

Heinemann, Larry
MH1710 **Close Quarters** (1st book) NY 1977, DJ 50 - 100
MH1720 **Paco's Story** NY 1986, DJ 30 - 50

Heinlein, Robert
MH1910 **Assignment in Eternity** Reading 1953, DJ 150 - 250
MH1911 Reading 1953, 500 cys, DJ 300 - 500
MH1930 **Double Star** Lon 1958, DJ 150 - 250
MH1940 **Friday** NY 1982, 500 cys, slipcase 200 - 300
MH1950 **Glory Road** NY 1963 (book club reprints are
almost identical & difficult to identify w/o DJ) 400 - 500
MH1960 **The Green Hills of Earth** Chi 1951, DJ, 300 cys 500 - 700
MH1970 **I Will Fear No Evil** NY 1970, DJ 100 - 150
MH1980 **Job: A Comedy of Justice** NY 1984, 750 cys,
slipcase 175 - 250

MH1990 **(Juveniles)** most 1st editions in DJ 100 - 200
MH2000 **The Man Who Sold The Moon** Chi 1950, DJ 300 - 500
MH2010 **The Moon is a Harsh Mistress** NY 1964, DJ 500 - 700
MH2020 **The Past Through Tomorrow** NY 1967, DJ 100 - 150
MH2030 **Revolt in 2100** Chi 1953, DJ 300 - 400
MH2040 **Rocket Ship Galileo** (1st book) NY 1947 700 - 1000
MH2050 **Starman Jones** NY 1953, DJ 200 - 250
MH2060 **Starship Troopers** NY 1959, DJ 400 - 600
MH2070 **Stranger in a Strange Land** NY 1961, DJ 800 - 1200
MH2080 **Tomorrow the Stars** NY 1952, DJ 250 - 350
MH2090 **Waldo and Magic Inc.** NY 1950, DJ 200 - 250

Heller, Joseph
MH2210 **Catch-22** NY 1961, DJ 300 - 500
Lon 1962, DJ (1st English ed) 100 - 150

Hemingway, Ernest (1954 Nobel Laureate)
MH2401 **Across the River and Into the Trees** NY 1950,
w/"A" on cr page & DJ w/yellow printing 150 - 200
MH2402 2nd state: DJ w/orange printing 100 - 150
MH2404 Lon 1950, DJ 100 - 150
MH2410 **The Dangerous Summer** NY 1985, DJ 20 - 30
MH2420 **Death in the Afternoon** NY 1932, w/"A" on
cr page, DJ 500 - 700
MH2421 Lon 1932, DJ 200 - 300
MH2431 **A Farewell to Arms** NY 1929, 1st issue
w/o disclaimer: "None of the characters in
this book is a living person.", DJ 5000 - 7000
MH2432 2nd issue w/disclamer, DJ 2000 - 3000
w/o DJ 200 - 300
MH2433 NY 1929, glassine DJ (advance review cy) 2000 - 3000
MH2434 Lon 1929, DJ 200 - 300
MH2435 NY 1929, 510 cys, glassine DJ, signed, box 3000 - 5000
MH2440 **Fiesta** Lon 1927, 1st English ed of **The Sun
Also Rises**, DJ 500 - 700
MH2450 **The Fifth Column and four unpublished stories
of the Spanish Civil War** NY 1969, DJ 40 - 60
MH2460 **The Fifth Column and The First Forty Nine
Stories** NY 1938, "A" on cr page, DJ 300 - 500
MH2461 NY 1938 (advance review cy) 2000 - 3000
MH2471 **For Whom the Bell Tolls** NY 1940, "A" on cr
page, 1st state DJ w/o photog name on back 400 - 600
MH2472 2nd state w/photog name "Arnold" on back 50 - 75
MH2473 later issue in later state DJ 30 - 50
MH2474 NY 1940, advance review cy w/only 6 pp of text 2000 - 3000
MH2475 NY 1940, 15 presentation cys, signed, DJ 4000 - 6000
MH2480 **The Garden of Eden** NY 1965, DJ 20 - 40
MH2481 NY 1965 (advance review cy) 200 - 300
MH2490 **God Rest You Merry Gentlemen** NY 1933,
300 cys, glassine DJ 500 - 700

MH2500 **Green Hills of Africa** NY 1935, DJ, w/"A" on
    cr page   400 - 600
MH2510 **Hemingway the Wild Years** NY 1962, DJ   50 - 75
MH2511 NY, December 1962 (paperback)   30 - 50
MH2520 **Hokum** Sans Souci 1978, 26 lettered cys,
    DJ, slipcase   400 - 600
MH2521 273? numbered cys, DJ, slipcase   200 - 300
MH2530 **In Our Time** NY 1925, DJ   300 - 500
MH2531 Paris 1924, 170 cys   8000 - 12000
    signed cy   20000 - 30000
MH2533 Lon 1926, DJ   200 - 300
MH2534 NY 1930, DJ   150 - 250
MH2536 Paris 1932   200 - 300
MH2550 **Islands in the Stream** NY 1970, DJ   40 - 60
MH2551 Lon 1970, DJ   30 - 40
MH2552 NY 1970 (advance review cy)   400 - 600
MH2560 **Kiki's Memoirs** Paris 1930   200 - 300
MH2570 **Men at War** NY 1942, DJ, w/"A" on cr p   200 - 300
MH2581 **Men Without Women** NY 1927, 1st state
    weighing 15 oz., DJ   400 - 600
    signed cy   7000 - 10000
MH2590 **A Moveable Feast** NY 1964, DJ   40 - 60
MH2591 Lon 1964, DJ   20 - 30
MH2601 **The Old Man and the Sea** NY 1952, w/"A" on
    cr page, 1st state DJ w/o mention of Nobel Prize   200 - 300
MH2602 Lon 1952, DJ   50 - 75
MH2603 NY 1952, presentation cy, before publication,
    signed, glassine DJ   10000 - 15000
MH2605 NY 1960, 1st illus ed, DJ   100 - 150
MH2620 **The Spanish Earth** Clev 1938, w/pictorial
    endpapers, glassine DJ   300 - 500
MH2621 w/plain endpapers, glassine DJ   300 - 500
MH2631 **The Sun Also Rises** NY 1926, 1st issue w/
    "stoppped" for "stopped" line 26, p 181, DJ   15000 - 20000
    signed cy   20000 - 30000
MH2632 2nd issue w/correction, DJ   800 - 1200
MH2640 **Three Stories & Ten Poems** (1st book) Dijon
    1923, 300 cys, blue/gray wrappers   18000 - 25000
MH2650 **To Have and Have Not** NY 1937 "A" on
    cr page, DJ   800 - 1200
MH2651 Lon 1937, DJ   150 - 250
MH2660 **Today Is Friday** Englewood 1926, 300 cys,
    wrappers, envelope   700 - 1000
MH2670 **The Torrents of Spring** NY 1926, DJ   1000 - 1500
    signed   8000 - 12000
MH2672 Paris 1932, wrappers, glassine DJ   400 - 600
MH2673 Lon 1933, DJ   300 - 500
MH2690 **Two Christmas Tales** Berkeley 1959, 1950 cys,
    wrappers   700 - 1000
MH2700 **Winner Take Nothing** NY 1933 "A" on cr
    page, DJ   500 - 700
MH2701 NY 1933 (salesman's sample)   2000 - 3000

Henry, O. (William Sidney Porter)
MH2911 **Cabbages and Kings** (1st book) NY 1904, DJ,
    1st state w/"McClure, Phillips & Co." on sp   400 - 600
MH2920 **The Complete Works of O. Henry** NY 1912,
    12 vol, suede   300 - 500
MH2921 NY 1912, 125 sets, 12 vol, bds   1000 - 1500
MH2931 **The Four Million** NY 1906, DJ, 1st state
    w/"McClure, Phillips & Co." on sp   150 - 250
MH2940 **The Gentle Grafter** NY 1908, DJ   150 - 250
MH2950 **Heart of the West** NY 1907, DJ   300 - 500
MH2960 **Let Me Feel Your Pulse** NY 1910, DJ   150 - 250

MH2971 **Roads of Destiny** NY 1909, DJ, 1st issue
    w/missing "h" line 6, p 9   300 - 500
MH2980 **Rolling Stones** Garden City 1912, DJ   75 - 125
MH2990 **The Trimmed Lamp** NY 1907, DJ   200 - 300
MH3001 **The Voice of the City** NY 1908, DJ, 1st state
    w/"McClure, Phillips & Co." on sp   300 - 500

Henry, Will
MH3110 **I, Tom Horn** Phil 1975, DJ   50 - 75
MH3120 **No Survivors** NY 1950, DJ   150 - 250

Herbert, Frank
MH3310 **The Dragon in the Sea** NY 1956, DJ   200 - 300
MH3321 **Dune** Phil 1965, DJ, 1st state in blue cl   1200 - 1800
MH3330 **Dune Messiah** NY 1969, DJ   150 - 200
MH3340 **Survival and the Atom** (1st book) Santa Rosa
    1950, wrappers   500 - 700

Hergesheimer, Joseph
MH3510 **Balisand** NY 1924, 50 cys, vellum, box   200 - 300
MH3511 NY 1924, 175 cys, rag, box   75 - 125
MH3512 NY 1924, DJ (1st trade ed)   25 - 50
MH3520 **Berlin** NY 1932, 110 cys, box   150 - 250
MH3521 NY 1932, DJ (1st trade ed)   25 - 50
MH3530 **The Bright Shawl** NY 1922, 225 cys, box   75 - 125
MH3540 **Cytherea** NY 1922, 270 cys, DJ   75 - 125
MH3541 NY 1922, 100 cys   75 - 125
MH3550 **Gold and Iron** NY 1918, DJ   50 - 75
MH3560 **The Happy End** NY 1919, 60 cys, DJ   150 - 250
MH3570 **Java Head** NY 1919, 100 cys   75 - 125
MH3580 **The Lay Anthony** (1st book) NY 1914, DJ   75 - 125
MH3590 **The Limestone Tree** NY 1931, 225 cys, DJ, box
MH3600 **Linda Condon** NY 1919, 60 cys   125 - 200
MH3610 **Mountain Blood** NY 1915, DJ   75 - 100
MH3620 **The Party Dress** NY 1930, 60 cys, vellum   150 - 250
MH3621 NY 1930, 225 cys, DJ   75 - 125
MH3622 NY 1930, DJ (1st trade ed)   25 - 50
MH3630 **Sheridan: A Military Narrative** Bos 1931, DJ   75 - 125
MH3640 **Swords and Roses** NY 1929, DJ   50 - 75
MH3651 **The Three Black Pennys** NY 1917, 1st state
    w/medallion on half-title page 2" from bottom   75 - 125
MH3660 **Tropical Winter** NY 1933, 210 cys, DJ, box   125 - 200
MH3661 NY 1933, DJ (1st trade ed)   25 - 50

Hersey, John
MH3910 **A Bell For Adano** NY 1944, DJ   50 - 75
MH3920 **Men on Bataan** (1st book) NY 1942, DJ   100 - 150

Heyward, Du Bose
MH4110 **Angel** NY 1926, DJ   150 - 250
MH4120 **Brass Ankle** NY 1931, 100 cys   200 - 300
MH4121 NY 1931, DJ (1st trade ed)   50 - 75
MH4130 **Carolina Chansons** (1st book) NY 1922, DJ   300 - 500
MH4140 **Jasbo Brown and Selected Poems** NY 1931   200 - 300
MH4150 **Mamba's Daughters** NY 1929   200 - 300
MH4160 **Porgy** NY 1925, DJ   200 - 300
MH4162 NY 1934, DJ (Modern Library ed)   20 - 30
MH4170 **Porgy and Bess: An Opera in Three Acts**
    NY 1935, 250 cys   200 300

Hijuelos, Oscar
MH4310 **The Mambo Kings Play Songs of Love**
    NY 1990, DJ   20 - 30

Hillerman, Tony
One of the more collectible current western U.S. mystery writers, his work involves Navajo Indians. A few books have original drawings by Ernest Franklin. His main protagonist is Lt. Joe Leaphorn.
MH4500 **The Blessing Way** (1st book) NY 1970, DJ   800 - 1200

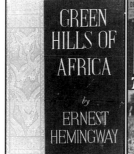
MH2500

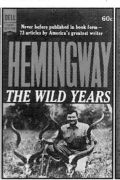
MH2511

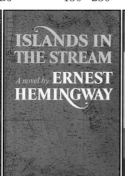
MH2550

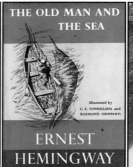
MH2605

MH3321

MH4510

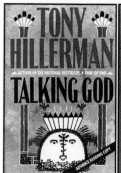
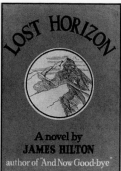

MH4621	MH4830	MH6110	MH6120	MH7210	MI5010

MH4502 NY 1990, DJ, 26 cys   300 - 500
MH4503 NY 1990, DJ, 100 cys   200 - 300
MH4510 **The Boy Who Made Dragonfly** NY 1972, DJ   150 - 250
MH4520 **Coyote Waits** NY 1990, DJ   30 - 50
MH4530 **Dance Hall of the Dead** NY 1973, DJ   250 - 350
MH4540 **The Dark Wind** NY 1982, DJ   75 - 125
MH4550 **The Fly on the Wall** NY 1971, DJ   300 - 500
MH4560 **The Ghost Way** NY 1984, DJ   100 - 150
MH4561 NY 1984, DJ, 300 cys, signed   300 - 500
MH4570 **The Great Taos Bank Robbery** Albu 1973, DJ   100 - 150
MH4580 **Listening Woman** NY 1978, DJ   150 - 250
MH4590 **New Mexico** Portland 1974, DJ   50 - 75
MH4600 **People of Darkness** NY 1980, DJ   150 - 250
MH4610 **Skinwalkers** NY 1986, DJ   50 - 75
MH4620 **Talking God** NY 1989, DJ   50 - 75
MH4621 NY 1989, wrappers (advance review cy)   30 - 50
MH4630 **Talking Mysteries** Albu 1991, DJ, signed   75 - 125
MH4640 **A Thief of Time** NY 1988, DJ   50 - 75
MH4650 **Words, Weather & Wolfmen** NY 1989,
350 cys, DJ   200 - 300

Hilton, James
MH4810 **Catherine Herself** (1st book) Lon 1920, DJ   300 - 500
MH4820 **Goodbye Mr. Chips** Bos 1934, DJ   300 - 500
MH4830 **Lost Horizon** Lon 1933, DJ   400 - 600
MH4831 Lon 1933, wrappers (advance review cy)   1000 - 1500
MH4840 **Random Harvest** Bos 1941, DJ   200 - 300

Hinton, S. E.
MH5010 **The Outsiders** (1st book) NY 1967, DJ,
w/wraparound band   75 - 100

Hjortsberg, William
MH5110 **Alp** (1st book) NY 1969, DJ   30 - 40

Hough, Emerson
Wrote about 40 books.
MH5211 **The Covered Wagon** NY 1922, DJ, 1st issue w/"I"
below last line of text, Table of Contents leaf tipped in   75 - 125
MH5220 **The Girl at the Halfway House** NY 1900   50 - 75
MH5231 **The Mississippi Bubble** Ind 1902, DJ, 1st issue
w/"April" on cr page & "Hough" on sp instead
of "Emerson Hough"   150 - 250
MH5240 **The Singing Mouse Stories** (1st book) NY 1895   200 - 300
MH5250 **The Story of the Cowboy** NY 1897   125 - 250
MH5261 **The Story of the Outlaw** NY 1907, DJ,
1st state w/rule at top of page v.   125 - 250

Housman, A. E.
MH5410 **A Shropshire Lad** (1st book) Lon 1896, 500 cys   1200 - 1800

Howard, Robert E.
MH5510 **Almuric** West Kingston 1975, DJ   50 - 75
MH5520 **Always Comes Evening** Sauk City 1957, DJ   350 - 450
MH5530 **The Coming of Conan** NY 1953, DJ   250 - 350
MH5540 **Conan the Barbarian** NY 1954, DJ   250 - 350
MH5550 **Conan the Conqueror** NY 1950, DJ   250 - 350
MH5560 **The Dark Man and Others** Sauk City 1963, DJ   250 - 350
MH5570 **Great Iron Trail** NY 1962, DJ   75 - 125
MH5580 **King Conan** NY 1953, DJ   250 - 350
MH5590 **Red Shadows** West Kingston 1968   200 - 300
MH5600 **Skull Face and Others** Sauk City 1946, DJ   400 - 600
MH5610 **The Sword of Conan** NY 1952, DJ   250 - 350
MH5620 **Tales of Conan** NY 1955, DJ   200 - 250

Hubbard, Elbert
Founded Roycrofters, an arts & crafts company which produced hand-made books from the late 1800s to the early 1900s. All Roycrofters' books are collectible. Those written by Hubbard were often limited/signed editions. The most valuable are the hand-illuminat-

ed books in fine hand-tooled gold-stamped leather bindings. These usually sell for $100-300. Of lesser value are the signed books in suede bindings, being in the range of $50-150. The unsigned trade editions are much less: $15-50. The William Wise Company reprinted some Roycrofters books in the 1920s-1930s, such as the very common *Elbert Hubbard's Scrapbook*, which is worth about $15.

MH5810 **The City of Tagaste** East Aurora 1900,
940 cys, bds   150 - 250
MH5820 **The Complete Writings** East Aurora 1914,
20 vol, 1000 sets, each vol signed   1500 - 2500
MH5830 **Consecrated Lives** East Aurora 1905, 100 cys,
vellum, levant   200 - 300
MH5831 900 cys, suede   75 - 125
MH5840 **Contemplations** East Aurora 1902, 100 cys,
marbled bds   150 - 250
MH5850 **Jesus of Nazareth** East Aurora 1902?, 10 cys,
full levant (highly polished Morocco)   300 - 500
MH5851 90 cys, 3/4 levant   200 - 300
       Little Journeys to the Homes... East Aurora, late 1800s-early 1900s. A series of biographies about famous people issued in finely bound leather/marbled bds, suede [limp leather] & paper wrappers.
MH5860 cys in fine bindings, usually in limited editions of
100 cys or less, boxed   200 - 350
MH5861 suede cys in limited editions of 950 or less   75 - 150
MH5862 cys in paper wrappers, unsigned, not limited editions   7 - 15
MH5880 biography series titled **To The Homes of Eminent
Painters, To The Homes of American Authors
& To The Homes of Great Scientists** bound
together & issued in suede, not limited   25 - 50.
MH5900 **Little Journey's to the Homes of Eminent Artists**
East Aurora 1902?, 2 vol, 100 cys, 3/4 levant, box   300 - 450
MH5910 **A Message to Garcia** East Aurora 1901?,
1000 cys, suede   50 - 75
MH5920 **Pig Pen Pete** East Aurora 1907, suede   50 - 75
MH5930 **White Hyacinths** East Aurora 1907, suede   30 - 50

Hubbard, Kin
MH6110 **Abe Martin** Ind 1907   40 - 60
MH6120 **Short Furrows by Abe Martin** Ind (early 1900s)   40 - 60

Hubbard, L. Ron
Founder of Scientology; has written 30-40 science fiction novels.
MH6310 **Buckskin Brigade** (1st book) NY 1937, DJ   1500 - 2000
MH6320 **Death's Deputy** F.P.C.I. NY 1948, DJ   200 - 300
MH6331 **Dianetics** NY 1950, DJ, 1st printing   1200 - 1800
    signed cy   2500 - 3500
MH6333 Lon 1951, DJ (1st English ed)   300 - 500
MH6340 **Final Blackout** NY 1948, DJ   200 - 300
MH6350 **The Kingslayer** F.P.C.I. NY 1949, DJ   200 - 300
MH6360 **Triton and the Battle of the Wizards** 1949, DJ   200 - 300

Hughes, Dorothy B.
MH6510 **The Bamboo Blonde** NY 1941, DJ   125 - 250
MH6520 **The Big Barbecue** NY 1949, DJ   50 - 75
MH6530 **The Candy Kid** NY 1950, DJ   50 - 75
MH6540 **The Cross-Eyed Bear** NY 1940, DJ   125 - 250
MH6550 **The Davidian Report** NY 1952, DJ   50 - 75
MH6560 **The Delicate Ape** NY 1944, DJ   75 - 125
MH6570 **Dread Journey** NY 1945, DJ   75 - 125
MH6580 **The Expendable Man** NY 1963, DJ   30 - 50
MH6590 **The Fallen Sparrow** NY 1942, DJ   125 - 250
MH6600 **In a Lonely Place** NY 1947, DJ   200 - 300
MH6610 **Kiss for a Killer** Lon 1954, DJ   75 - 125
MH6620 **The So Blue Marble** NY 1940, DJ   400 - 600

Hughes, Langston (also see Americana)
MH6910 **The Big Sea** NY 1940, DJ   200 - 300
MH6920 **Dear Lovely Death** Amenia 1931, 100 cys   700 - 1000

MH6930	**The Dream Keeper** NY 1932, DJ	700 - 1000
MH6940	**Fine Clothes to the Jew** NY 1927, DJ	500 - 700
MH6950	**I Wonder As I Wander** NY 1956, DJ	100 - 150
MH6961	**Jim Crow's Last Stand** NY 1943, wrappers, 1st issue w/"belt" upside down on contents page	300 - 500
MH6970	**The Panther and the Lash** NY 1967, DJ	50 - 75
MH6980	**Scottsboro Limited** NY 1932, 30 cys	700 - 1000
MH6981	NY 1932 DJ (1st trade ed)	250 - 350
MH6990	**Shakespeare in Harlem** NY 1942, DJ	400 - 600
MH7000	**Simple Speaks His Mind** NY 1950, DJ	150 - 200
MH7010	**The Weary Blues** (1st book) NY 1926, DJ	1500 - 2000

Huie, William B.
MH7110	**The Execution of Private Slovik** NY 1954, DJ	75 - 100

Hunter, Evan
MH7210	**The Blackboard Jungle** NY 1954, DJ	50 - 75

Huxley, Aldous
MH7310	**Antic Hay** Lon 1923, DJ	500 - 700
MH7320	**Brave New World** Lon 1932, 324 cys	2000 - 3000
MH7321	Lon 1932, DJ (1st trade ed)	300 - 500
MH7322	Garden City 1932, DJ (1st American ed)	300 - 500
MH7330	**The Burning Wheel** (1st book) Oxford 1916, wrappers	700 - 1000
MH7340	**Crome Yellow** Lon 1921, DJ, w/top edge stained green	500 - 700
MH7351	**Ends and Means** Lon 1937, DJ, 1st issue DJ w/o reviews	200 - 300
MH7360	**Point Counter Point** Lon 1928, 256 cys	800 - 1200
MH7361	Lon 1928, DJ (1st trade ed)	250 - 350
MH7362	NY 1928, DJ (1st American ed)	150 - 250
MH7370	**Selected Poems** Oxford 1925, DJ	200 - 300
MH7380	**Vulgarity in Literature** Lon 1930, 260 cys	300 - 500
MH7390	**Wheels** Oxford 1917, DJ	500 - 700
MH7400	**Words and Their Meanings** LA 1940, 100 cys, DJ	300 - 500

Irish, William
MI5010	**Marihuana** NY 1941 (Dell #11 pocketbook)	100 - 175

Irving, John
MI6010	**Setting Free the Bears** (1st book) NY 1968, DJ	200 - 300
MI6020	**The Water-Method Man** NY 1972, DJ	150 - 250
MI6030	**The World According to Garp** NY 1978, DJ	100 - 150

Jackson, Shirley
MJ0110	**The Birds Nest** NY 1954, DJ	75 - 125
MJ0120	**Come Along With Me** NY 1968, DJ	25 - 50
MJ0130	**Hangsaman** NY 1951, DJ	100 - 150
MJ0140	**The Haunting of Hill House** NY 1959, DJ	200 - 300
MJ0150	**The Lottery** NY 1949, DJ	150 - 250
MJ0160	**Raising Demons** Lon 1957, DJ	40 - 60
MJ0170	**The Road Through the Wall** (1st book) NY 1948, DJ	150 - 250
MJ0180	**The Sundial** NY 1958, DJ	50 - 75

Jakes, John
MJ0810	**The Texans Ride North** (1st book) Phil 1952, DJ	50 - 75

James, Will
MJ1410	**All in a Day's Riding** NY 1933, DJ, w/"A" on cr page	150 - 250
MJ1420	**Big-Enough** NY 1931, DJ, w/"A" on cr page	200 - 300
MJ1430	**Cow Country** NY 1927, DJ, w/"A" on cr page	200 - 300
MJ1440	**Cowboy's North and South** (1st book) NY 1924, DJ, w/"A" on cr page	150 - 200
MJ1450	**The Drifting Cowboy** NY 1925, DJ, w/"A" on cr page	300 - 500
MJ1460	**Home Ranch** NY 1935, DJ, w/"A" on cr page	100 - 150
MJ1470	**In the Saddle with Uncle Bill** NY 1935, DJ, w/"A" on cr page	200 - 300
MJ1480	**Lone Cowboy** NY 1930, DJ, 150 cys, signed	700 - 1000
MJ1481	NY 1930, DJ (1st trade ed) w/"A" on cr page	200 - 300
MJ1490	**Sand** NY 1929, DJ w/"A" on cr page	150 - 200
MJ1510	**Smoky: The Cowhorse** NY 1926, DJ, w/"A" on cr page	200 - 300
MJ1520	**Sun Up** NY 1931, DJ, w/"A" on cr page	150 - 200
MJ1530	**The Three Mustanger's** NY 1933, DJ, w/"A" on cr page	150 - 250

Jeffers, Robinson
MJ2200	**An Artist** Austin 1928, 96 cys, wrappers	700 - 1000
MJ2210	**Be Angry at the Sun** NY 1941, 100 cys, slipcase	700 - 1000
MJ2211	NY 1941, DJ (1st trade ed)	75 - 125
MJ2220	**The Beaks of Eagles** SF 1936, 135 cys, wrappers	500 - 700

MJ2230	**Californians** NY 1916, DJ	400 - 600
MJ2240	**Cawdor and Other Poems** NY 1928, 375 cys, glassine DJ, slipcase	300 - 500
MJ2241	NY 1928, DJ (1st trade ed)	150 - 250
MJ2250	**Dear Judas and Other Poems** NY 1929, 25 cys, slipcase	800 - 1200
MJ2251	NY 1929, 375 cys, slipcase	300 - 500
MJ2252	NY 1929, DJ (1st trade ed)	150 - 250
MJ2260	**The Double Axe and Other Poems** NY 1948, DJ	400 - 600
MJ2261	NY 1948, w/special page signed	800 - 1200
MJ2262	NY 1948, DJ (1st trade ed)	75 - 125
MJ2270	**Flagons and Apples** LA 1912, 500 cys, slipcase	800 - 1200
MJ2280	**Hunger Field and Other Poems** NY 1954, DJ	75 - 125
MJ2290	**Poems** SF 1928, 10 cys, slipcase	2000 - 3000
MJ2291	SF 1928, 310 cys, slipcase	700 - 1000
MJ2300	**Stars** Pasadena 1930, 72 cys	800 - 1200
MJ2310	**Tamar and Other Poems** NY 1924, 500 cys, slipcase	800 - 1200
MJ2320	**Thurso's Landing** NY 1932, DJ, 200 cys, slipcase	300 - 500
MJ2321	NY 1932, DJ (1st trade ed)	150 - 250
MJ2330	**The Women at Point Sur** NY 1927, 265 cys, glassine DJ	300 - 500

Johnson, Charles
MJ3010	**The Sorcerer's Apprentice** NY 1986, DJ	30 - 40

Joyce, James
MJ4010	**Anna Livia Plurabelle** NY 1928, 800 cys	1000 - 1500
MJ4021	**Chamber Music** Lon 1907, 1st state w/thick laid endpapers	5000 - 7000
	signed	15000 - 20000
MJ4022	2nd state w/thick wove endpapers	1000 - 1500
MJ4023	3rd state w/thin wove translucent endpapers	1000 - 1500
MJ4025	Bos 1918 (1st American ed)	300 - 400
MJ4026	NY 1918, DJ	300 - 400
MJ4028	Lon 1923	200 - 300
MJ4040	**Collected Poems** NY 1936, 750 cys, glassine DJ	400 - 600
MJ4041	50 cys, vellum, signed, tissue DJ, box	2000 - 3000
MJ4042	NY 1937, DJ	200 - 300
MJ4050	**Dubliners** Lon 1914, DJ	15000 - 20000
	signed	20000 - 30000
MJ4052	NY 1916, DJ	400 - 600
MJ4053	NY 1917, DJ	200 - 300
MJ4054	Lon 1922, DJ	200 - 300
MJ4056	NY 1926, DJ (Modern Library ed)	200 - 300
MJ4057	Paris 1926, DJ	200 - 300
MJ4059	NY 1986, 1000 cys, slipcase	500 - 700
MJ4070	**Exiles** Lon 1918, DJ	700 - 1000
MJ4071	NY 1918, DJ	400 - 600
MJ4073	NY 1951, DJ	150 - 250
MJ4080	**Finnegan's Wake** Lon 1939, 425 cys, box	5000 - 7000
MJ4081	Lon 1939, DJ (1st trade ed)	1000 - 1500
MJ4082	NY 1939, DJ	200 - 300
MJ4090	**Haveth Childers Everywhere** Paris 1930, 500 cys, tissue DJ, box	300 - 500
MJ4091	Paris 1930, 100 cys, vellum, box	2000 - 3000
MJ4100	**The Joyce Book** Lon 1933, 500 cys, envelope	1000 - 1500
	w/o envelope	300 - 500
MJ4110	**The Mime of Mick, Nick, and the Maggies** Hague, Netherlands 1934, 1000 cys, box	500 - 700
MJ4111	Hague, Netherlands 1934, 29 cys, box	2000 - 3000
MJ4120	**Our Exagmination Round His Factification for Incamination of Work in Progress** Paris 1929	300 - 500
MJ4121	Paris 1929, 96 cys, wrappers, glassine DJ	3000 - 5000
MJ4130	**Pomes Penyeach** Paris 1927, w/errata slip	300 - 500

MI6010   MI6020   MJ0160

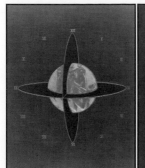 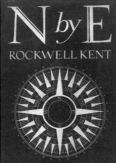   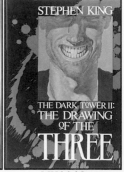

MJ4232   MK0522   MK1111   MK1123   MK1125   MK1142

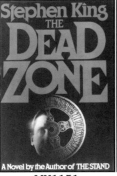     

MK1151   MK1160   MK1170   MK1180 (title page)   MK1210 (slipcase and signature page)   MK1220

MJ4132	Paris 1932, 25 cys, portfolio	30000 - 50000
MJ4133	Paris 1932 (trade ed)	300 - 500
MJ4134	Lon 1932	300 - 500
MJ4150	**A Portrait of the Artist as a Young Man** NY 1916, DJ	7000 - 10000
MJ4151	Lon 1917, DJ	700 - 1000
MJ4153	Lon 1918, DJ	200 - 300
MJ4155	Lon 1924, DJ	50 - 75
MJ4157	NY 1968, slipcase	100 - 150
MJ4170	**Stephen Hero** Lon 1944, DJ	300 - 500
MJ4171	NY 1944, DJ	100 - 150
MJ4180	**Storiella As She Is Syung** Lon 1937, 150 cys, box	3000 - 5000
MJ4181	Lon 1937, 26 cys, signed, box	7000 - 10000
MJ4190	**Tales Told of Shem and Shaun** Paris 1929, 100 cys, vellum, glassine DJ, box	7000 - 10000
MJ4191	Paris 1929, 500 cys, glassine DJ, box	2000 - 3000
MJ4193	Lon 1932, DJ	150 - 200
MJ4200	**Two Essays: "A Forgotten Aspect" and "The Day of the Rabblement"** (1st published writings) Dublin 1901, wrappers	6000 - 8000
MJ4210	**Ulysses** Paris 1922, blue wrappers, 100 cys, Van Gelder paper, signed	30000 - 50000
MJ4211	Paris 1922, 150 cys, Verge d'Arches paper, signed	20000 - 30000
MJ4212	Paris 1922, 750 cys	10000 - 15000
MJ4213	Lon 1922, 2000 cys, errata slip, 4 pp leaflet	3000 - 5000
MJ4214	Paris 1922 Shakespeare Head Press (1st trade ed)	1000 - 1500

(Later printings by Shakespeare Head Press may vary from $100-700, the earlier printings being more valuable. It is rumored the 11th printing was suppressed & is rare.)

MJ4218	Lon 1923, 500 cys	2000 - 3000
MJ4220	Paris 1929, 10 cys, Van Gelder paper	5000 - 7000
MJ4221	Paris 1929, 25 cys, Holland paper	3000 - 5000
MJ4222	Paris 1929, 875 cys, Alfa paper	1200 - 1800
MJ4224	Hamburg 1932, 25 cys, 2 vol, signed	2000 - 3000
MJ4225	Hamburg 1932 (trade ed)	300 - 500
MJ4228	NY 1934, DJ (1st authorized American ed)	600 - 800
MJ4229	NY 1934, 2nd printing	75 - 100
MJ4231	NY 1935, 250 cys, signed by Joyce, illus by Matisse	4000 - 6000
MJ4232	NY 1935, 1500 cys, slipcase, signed by Matisse (Limited Editions Club)	3000 - 5000
MJ4236	Lon 1936, 900 cys, DJ	700 - 1000
MJ4237	Lon 1936, 100 cys, vellum, signed, box	4000 - 6000

Judd, Cyril

MJ6010	**Gunner Cade** NY 1952, DJ	75 - 100

Kafka, Franz

MK0110	**Die Verwand Lung** Leipzig 1915, wrappers	4000 - 6000

Kantor, McKinley

MK0210	**Andersonville** Clev 1955, DJ	75 - 100
MK0220	**Diversay** (1st book) NY 1928, DJ	100 - 150

Kennedy, John F.

MK0310	**Why England Slept** (1st book) NY 1940, DJ	400 - 600
MK0311	Lon 1940, DJ (1st English ed)	200 - 300

Kennedy, William

MK0410	**The Ink Truck** NY 1969, DJ	150 - 250
MK0420	**Ironweed** NY 1983, DJ	30 - 50

Kent, Rockwell (also see Artists & Illustrators)

MK0500	**Elmer Adler** NY 1929, 25 cys	700 - 1000
MK0510	**Greenland Journal** NY 1962, DJ, box	100 - 150
MK0520	**N by E** NY 1930, 100 cys, box	700 - 1000
MK0521	900 cys, box	300 - 500
MK0522	NY 1930, DJ (1st trade ed)	150 - 250
MK0530	**Salamina** NY 1935, DJ	75 - 125

Kerouac, Jack

MK0610	**Beat Road** NY 1982, DJ	20 - 30
MK0620	**Big Sur** NY 1962, DJ	150 - 200
MK0630	**Book of Dreams** SF 1961	
MK0640	**The Dharma Bums** NY 1958, DJ	150 - 250
MK0650	**Dr. Sax** NY 1959, 26 cys, box	1000 - 1500
MK0651	NY 1959, DJ (1st trade ed)	75 - 125
MK0660	**Home at Christmas** NY 1973, 195 cys	100 - 150
MK0670	**Lonesome Traveler** NY 1960, DJ	75 - 100
MK0680	**Not Long Ago Joy Abounded at Christmas** NY 1972, 195 cys	100 - 150
MK0690	**On The Road** NY 1957, DJ	1500 - 2000
MK0691	NY 1957 (Signet: 1st paperback printing)	20 - 30
MK0693	Lon 1958, DJ (1st English ed)	300 - 500
MK0700	**Pull My Daisy** NY 1959, DJ	150 - 250
MK0710	**Scattered Poems** SF 1971	20 - 30
MK0720	**The Town & The City** (1st book) NY 1950, DJ	250 - 350
MK0730	**Two Early Stories** NY 1973, 175 cys	100 - 150
MK0740	**Vanity of Duluoz** NY 1968, DJ	75 - 100
MK0750	**Visions of Cody** NY 1972, DJ	40 - 60

Kesey, Ken

MK0830	**One Flew Over the Cuckoo's Nest** (1st book) NY 1962, DJ	400 - 600
MK0831	Lon 1962, DJ (1st English ed)	75 - 125

Kilmer, Joyce

MK0910	**The Circus and Other Essays** NY 1916, DJ	150 - 250
MK0920	**Main Street and Other Poems** NY 1917, DJ	150 - 250
MK0930	**Summer of Love** (1st book) NY 1911, DJ, 1st issue w/"Baker & Taylor" imprint at foot of sp	200 - 300

MK0940 **Trees and Other Poems** NY 1914, DJ, 1st
state w/o "Printed in USA" on cr page   1200 - 1800

King, Stephen (also pseud Richard Bachman)

MK1050 **Carrie** (1st book) Lon 1974, 1000 cys, DJ   600 - 800
MK1051 NY 1974, DJ   200 - 300
MK1052 NY 1974, DJ (advance review cy)   400 - 600
MK1060 **Christine** West Kingston 1983, 1000 cys, DJ, box   400 - 600
MK1061 NY 1983, DJ   50 - 75
MK1062 NY 1983 (advance review cy)   200 - 300
MK1080 **Cujo** NY 1981, 26 cys, DJ, slipcase   1000 - 1500
MK1081 NY 1981, 750 cys, DJ   400 - 600
MK1082 NY 1981, DJ (1st trade ed)   50 - 75
MK1083 NY 1981 (advance review cy)   200 - 300
MK1084 Lon 1982, DJ   30 - 40
MK1100 **Cycle of the Werewolf** Westland 1983, 7500 cys   100 - 150
MK1110 **Danse Macabre** NY 1981, 15 cys, tissue DJ,
slipcase   2000 - 3000
MK1111 NY 1981, DJ (1st trade ed)   50 - 75
MK1112 NY 1981, DJ (1st trade ed w/o later printing
on DJ flap)   50 - 75
MK1113 NY 1981, 250 cys, slipcase   600 - 800
MK1120 **The Dark Tower: The Gunslinger** West
Kingston 1982, 500 cys, DJ, box   1200 - 1800
MK1121 West Kingston 1982, 35 cys, DJ, box   2000 - 3000
MK1122 West Kingston 1982, 12 cys, DJ, box   3000 - 5000
MK1123 West Kingston 1982, DJ (1st trade ed)   500 - 700
MK1124 West Kingston 1984, DJ   150 - 225
MK1125 NY 1988, wrappers (1st illus ed)   10 - 15
MK1126 NY 1988, DJ   20 - 30
MK1140 **The Dark Tower II: The Drawing of the Three**
West Kingston 1987, 800 cys, box   500 - 700
MK1141 West Kingston 1987, 3000 cys, DJ   100 - 150
MK1142 West Kingston 1987, DJ (1st trade ed)   75 - 125
MK1150 **The Dead Zone** Lon 1979, DJ   150 - 200
MK1151 NY 1979, DJ   50 - 75
MK1160 **Different Seasons** NY 1982, DJ   40 - 60
MK1170 **Dolan's Cadillac** Northridge 1989, 1000 cys   250 - 350
MK1171 Northridge 1989, 250 cys   300 - 500
MK1180 **The Eyes of the Dragon** Lon 1984, 1250 cys, box   500 - 700
MK1181 Bangor, ME, 1984, 1000 cys, slipcase   600 - 800
MK1182 Bangor, ME, 1984, 250 cys, slipcase   1500 - 2500
MK1200 **Fire Starter** Huntington 1980, 750 cys   700 - 1000
MK1210 **Gerald's Game** NY 1992, slipcase (ABA ed)   50 - 75
MK1220 **The Long Walk** (Bachman) NY 1979, wrappers
(New American Library)   100 - 150
MK1230 **Misery** NY 1987, DJ   25 - 50
MK1240 **My Pretty Pony** NY 1988, 250 cys, 9 color
lithos by Barbara Kruger, signed by artist   2000 - 3000

MK1250 **Night Shift** NY 1978, DJ   200 - 300
MK1251 NY 1978, DJ (advance review cy)   800 - 1200
MK1260 **Pet Sematary** NY 1983, DJ   40 - 60
MK1261 NY 1983 (advance review cy) pictorial wrappers   100 - 150
MK1262 NY 1983, 50 cys (advance review cy; photo
offset from typescript)   300 - 500
MK1270 **Rage** (Bachman) NY 1977, wrappers (New
American Library)   100 - 150
MK1280 **Roadwork** (Bachman) NY 1981, paperback   75 - 125
MK1290 **The Running Man** (Bachman) NY 1982, wrappers
(New American Library)   50 - 75
MK1300 **'Salem's Lot** Lon 1975, DJ   400 - 600
MK1301 Garden City 1975, DJ (1st American ed)   500 - 700
MK1310 **The Shining** Lon 1977, DJ   200 - 300
MK1320 **Skeleton Crew** Santa Cruz 1985, DJ, 1000 cys   300 - 400
MK1321 NY 1985, DJ (1st trade ed)   50 - 75
MK1330 **The Stand** NY 1978, DJ   150 - 200
MK1340 **Startling Mystery Stories** #12, 1969 (King
short story)   50 - 75
MK1350 **The Talisman** West Kingston 1984, 1200 cys,
2 vol, slipcase   500 - 800
MK1351 NY 1984, DJ (1st trade ed)   50 - 75
MK1360 **Thinner** (Bachman) NY 1984, wrappers (New
American Library)   50 - 75
MK1370 **Tommy Knockers** NY 1987, DJ   25 - 50

Kingsolver, Barbara

MK1510 **The Bean Trees** (1st book) NY 1988, DJ   50 - 75
MK1511 Lon 1989, DJ   50 - 75

Kipling, Rudyard (also see Artists & Illustrators) (1907 Nobel Laureate)

MK1610 **Barrack Room Ballads** Lon 1892, 30 cys   1000 - 1500
MK1611 Lon 1892, 225 cys   700 - 1000
MK1612 Lon 1892 (1st trade ed)   100 - 150
MK1613 NY 1892 (1st American ed)   100 - 150
MK1620 **The Brushwood Boy** NY 1899   200 - 300
MK1630 **Captains Courageous** Lon 1896, wrappers   2000 - 3000
MK1631 Lon 1897, DJ (1st trade ed)   700 - 1000
MK1632 NY 1897, DJ (1st American ed)   300 - 500
MK1640 **Collected Verse** NY 1907   150 - 250
MK1642 NY 1910, 125 cys   500 - 700
MK1643 NY 1910, 500 cys   300 - 500
MK1650 **The Day's Work** NY 1898   200 - 300
MK1651 Lon 1898 (1st English ed)   200 - 300
MK1660 **A Diversity of Creatures** Lon 1917, DJ   150 - 250
MK1670 **The Five Nations** Lon 1903, 30 cys, vellum   500 - 700
MK1671 NY 1903 (1st American ed)   50 - 75
MK1680 **From Sea to Sea** NY 1899, 2 vol   150 - 250
MK1682 Lon 1900, 2 vol   200 - 300

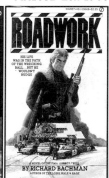

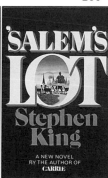

MK1240   MK1261   MK1270   MK1280   MK1290   MK1301

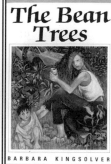

MK1310   MK1330   MK1340   MK1360   MK1510   MK1511

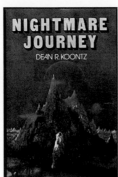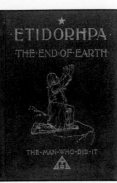

MK3290	MK3530	MK3540	MK3550	ML1710	ML4220

MK1690	The Jungle Book Lon 1894, DJ	300 - 500
MK1691	NY 1894 (1st American ed)	200 - 300
MK1700	Just So Stories For Little Children Lon 1902, DJ	2000 - 3000
MK1711	Kim NY 1901, DJ, 1st issue w/chapter headings for only chapters 8 & 13	700 - 1000
MK1712	Lon 1901, DJ (1st English ed)	300 - 500
MK1720	On Dry-Cow Fishing as a Fine Art Clev 1926, 176 cys	700 - 1000
MK1730	Puck of Pook's Hill Lon 1906	300 - 500
MK1731	NY 1906 (1st American ed)	125 - 175
MK1740	Schoolboy Lyrics (1st book) Lahore 1881, 25 cys, blank wrappers	7000 - 10000
MK1741	25 cys, printer wrappers	5000 - 7000
MK1750	The Second Jungle Book Lon 1895, DJ	300 - 500
MK1760	Songs of the Sea Lon 1927, 500 cys, DJ	300 - 500
MK1770	Stacky & Co. Lon 1899	300 - 500
MK1780	Verse: 1885-1918 Lon 1919, 3 vol	200 - 300
MK1790	With the Night Mail NY 1909, DJ	200 - 300

Knight, Eric

MK2310	Lassie Come-Home Lon 1941, DJ	500 - 700

Knowles, John

MK2610	Indian Summer NY 1966, DJ	30 - 40
MK2620	Morning in Antibes NY 1962, DJ	40 - 60
MK2630	A Separate Peace Lon 1959, DJ	300 - 500
MK2631	NY 1959, DJ	100 - 150

Koontz, Dean R.

MK3200	Bad Place NY 1990	30 - 50
MK3210	Darkfall NY 1984, DJ	50 - 75
MK3220	Door to December Lon	
MK3230	Dragonfly NY 1975, DJ	50 - 75
MK3240	The Eyes of Darkness Arlington Heights 1989, DJ	30 - 50
MK3250	Hanging On NY 1973, DJ	75 - 125
MK3260	House of Thunder Arlington Heights 1988, 450 cys, slipcase	125 - 200
MK3270	The Key to Midnight Arlington Heights 1989, DJ	30 - 50
MK3280	The Mask NY 1988, DJ	50 - 75
MK3281	Lon 1988, DJ (1st English ed)	50 - 75
MK3290	Nightmare Journey NY 1975, DJ	200 - 250
MK3300	Oddkins NY 1988, DJ	30 - 50
MK3310	Phantoms NY 1983, DJ	50 - 75
MK3320	Shattered NY 1973, DJ, under pseud K. R. Dwyer	75 - 125
MK3330	The Wall of Masks NY 1975,DJ, under pseud Brian Coffey	75 - 125

Kotzwinkle, William

MK3520	Doctor Rat NY 1976, DJ	50 - 75
MK3530	Elephant Bangs Train NY 1971, DJ	30 - 50
MK3540	E.T. the Extra-Terrestrial NY 1982, DJ	25 - 35
MK3550	Trouble in Bugland Bos 1983, DJ	50 - 75

Kuttner, Henry

MK4510	Robots Have No Tails NY 1952, DJ	150 - 250

La Farge, Oliver

ML0110	Laughing Boy (1st book) Bos 1929, DJ	75 - 100

L'Amour, Louis

Has written over 100 western books since 1939. Many were released as Bantam Pocket Books. Hardcover first editions have been published in the 1980s.

ML0210	Daybreakers NY 1981, DJ	20 - 30
ML0220	Haunted Mesa NY 1987, DJ	20 - 30
ML0230	Jubal Sackett NY 1985, DJ	20 - 30
ML0240	Smoke From This Alter (1st book) Okla Cty 1939, DJ	200 - 300

Lardner, Ring

ML0410	Bib Ballads (1st book) Chi 1915, 500 cys, box	300 - 500
ML0420	The Big Town Ind 1921, DJ	150 - 250
ML0430	First and Last NY 1934, DJ, w/"A" on cr page	75 - 100
ML0440	Gullible's Travels Ind 1917, DJ	200 - 300
ML0451	How to Write Short Stories NY 1924, DJ, 1st issue w/Scribner seal on cr page	150 - 200
ML0460	Lose with a Smile NY 1933, DJ, w/Scribner seal	100 - 150
ML0470	The Love Nest NY 1925, DJ, w/Scribner seal	200 - 300
ML0480	My Four Weeks in France Ind 1918, DJ	150 - 250
ML0490	Own Your Own Home Ind 1919	100 - 150
ML0500	The Real Dope Ind 1919, DJ	150 - 250
ML0510	Regular Fellows I Have Met Chi, 1919	300 - 500
ML0520	Round Up NY 1919, DJ, w/Scribner seal	150 - 250
ML0530	Say It With Oil NY 1923, DJ	150 - 250
ML0540	The Story of a Wonder Man NY 1927, DJ, w/Scribner seal	200 - 300
ML0550	Symptoms of Being 35 Ind 1921, DJ	150 - 250
ML0561	Treat 'Em Rough Ind 1918, DJ, 1st state w/o poem on p 6	200 - 300
ML0562	2nd state w/poem	100 - 150
ML0570	What Of It? NY 1925, DJ	100 - 150
ML0580	You Know Me Al NY 1916, DJ	150 - 250
ML0590	The Young Immigrunts Ind 1920, DJ	200 - 300

Lawrence, D. H.

ML0700	Aaron's Rod NY 1922, DJ	200 - 300
ML0701	Lon 1922, DJ (1st English ed)	150 - 200
ML0710	Amores: Poems Lon 1916, 16 pp of ads	150 - 250
ML0711	NY 1916 (1st American ed)	100 - 150
ML0720	Apocalypse Florence 1931, 750 cys, DJ	300 - 500
ML0730	Bay: A Book of Poems Westminster 1919, 30 cys, vellum #1-30	2000 - 3000
ML0731	50 cys, cartridge paper #31-80	1500 - 2500
ML0732	120 cys, handmade paper #81-200	800 - 1200
ML0740	Birds, Beasts and Flowers NY 1923, DJ	700 - 1000
ML0741	Lon 1923, DJ (1st English ed)	150 - 250
ML0742	Lon 1930, 30 copies, box	700 - 1000
ML0750	The Boy in the Bush Lon 1924, DJ	200 - 300
ML0760	Collected Poems Lon 1928, 2 vol, 100 cys, DJs	2000 - 3000
ML0761	Lon 1928, DJs (1st trade ed)	200 - 300
ML0763	NY 1929 (1st American ed) box	100 - 150
ML0770	David: A Play Lon 1926, 500 cys, DJ	300 - 500
ML0771	NY 1926, DJ (1st American ed)	100 - 150
ML0780	England, My England and Other Stories NY 1922, DJ	250 - 350
ML0781	Lon 1924, DJ (1st English ed)	150 - 200
ML0790	The Escaped Clock Paris 1929, wrappers, 50 cys	1500 - 2500
ML0791	450 cys, glassine DJ, box	300 - 500
ML0800	Fantasia of the Unconscious NY 1922, DJ	300 - 500
ML0802	Lon 1923, DJ (1st English ed)	200 - 300
ML0810	Fire and Other Poems SF 1940, 300 cys, DJ	500 - 700
ML0830	Glad Ghosts Lon 1926, wrappers, 500 cys	200 - 300
ML0840	Kangaroo Lon 1923, DJ	200 - 300
ML0841	NY 1923, DJ (1st American ed)	100 - 150
ML0860	The Lady Bird Lon 1923, DJ	200 - 300
ML0870	Lady Chatterley's Lover Florence 1928, 1000 cys, DJ	2000 - 3000
ML0871	Florence 1928, wrappers	300 - 500
ML0872	Florence 1928, black cl (pirate)	100 - 150
ML0874	Paris 1950, 100 cys, box	700 - 1000
ML0890	Last Poems Florence 1932, 750 cys, DJ, box	300 - 500
ML0891	Lon 1933, DJ (1st English ed)	100 - 150
ML0892	NY 1933, DJ (1st American ed)	100 - 150

ML0910	**Look! We Have Come Through** Lon 1917, DJ	200 - 300
ML0911	NY 1919, DJ (1st American ed)	100 - 150
ML0921	**The Lost Girl** Lon 1920, 1st issue w/pages 256 & 258 forming part of signatures	500 - 700
ML0922	2nd issue w/pages 256 & 258 tipped in	150 - 250
ML0930	**Love Among The Haystacks** Lon 1930, 1600 cys, DJ	100 - 150
ML0940	**Love Poems and Others** Lon 1913, DJ	700 - 1000
ML0950	**Mornings in Mexico** Lon 1927, DJ	300 - 500
ML0960	**My Skirmish with Jolly Roger** NY 1929, 600 cys, DJ	150 - 250
ML0970	**Nettles** Lon 1930	100 - 150
ML0980	**Pansies** Lon 1929, 500 cys, glassine DJ, slipcase	500 - 700
ML0990	**The Plumed Serpent** Lon 1926, DJ	200 - 300
ML0991	NY 1926, DJ	200 - 300
ML1000	**Pornography and Obscenity** Lon 1930, DJ	150 - 250
ML1010	**The Prussian Officer and Other Stories** Lon 1914, DJ, 1st state w/20 pp of undated ads	300 - 500
ML1020	**The Rainbow** Lon 1915, DJ	300 - 500
ML1030	**Rawdon's Hoof** Lon 1928, 500 cys, DJ	300 - 500
ML1040	**Reflections on the Death of a Porcupine** Phil 1925, 475 cys	200 - 300
ML1050	**Sea and Sardinia** NY 1921, DJ	300 - 500
ML1052	Lon 1923, DJ	200 - 300
ML1060	**Son's and Lovers** Lon 1913, DJ	300 - 500
ML1061	NY 1913, DJ (1st American ed)	200 - 300
ML1070	**St. Mawr** Lon 1925, DJ	150 - 250
ML1071	NY 1925, DJ (1st American ed)	75 - 125
ML1080	**Sun** Lon 1926, 100 cys, wrappers	1500 - 2000
ML1082	Paris 1928, 15 cys, DJ, box	3000 - 5000
ML1083	Paris 1928, 150 cys, DJ, box	800 - 1200
ML1084	Lon 1928, DJ (1st trade ed)	200 - 300
ML1100	**Tortoises** NY 1921, DJ	200 - 300
ML1110	**Touch and Go** Lon 1920, DJ	300 - 500
ML1121	**The Trespasser** Lon 1912, DJ, 1st state blue cl, gold stamped	1000 - 1500
ML1122	NY 1902, DJ (1st American ed)	700 - 1000
ML1131	**The White Peacock** (1st book) NY 1911, DJ, 1st state w/publisher's logo (windmill) blind stamped on back cover	8000 - 12000
ML1132	2nd state w/o windmill	2000 - 3000
ML1133	Lon 1911, DJ (1st English ed) w/windmill	800 - 1200
ML1150	**The Woman Who Rode Away** Lon 1928, DJ	200 - 300
ML1160	**Women in Love** NY 1920, DJ, 1250 cys, signed	3000 - 5000
	unsigned	300 - 500
ML1162	Lon 1921 (1st English ed) 50 cys	3000 - 5000
ML1163	Lon 1921, DJ (1st trade ed)	200 - 300

Lawrence, T. E.

ML1310	**Seven Pillars of Wisdom: A Triumph** Lon 1926, 211 cys	15000 - 25000
ML1311	Lon 1926, 500 cys	3000 - 5000
ML1313	Lon 1935, 750 cys, DJ, box	1000 - 1500
ML1314	Lon 1935, DJ (1st trade ed)	200 - 300
ML1315	Garden City 1935, DJ, box	400 - 600
ML1316	Garden City 1935, DJ, (1st American trade ed)	100 - 150

Le Carre, John

ML1510	**Call for the Dead** (1st book) Lon 1960, DJ	800 - 1200
ML1512	NY 1962, DJ	200 - 300
ML1520	**The Clandestine Muse** Newark 1986, 260 cys, DJ	100 - 150
ML1530	**The Honourable Schoolboy** NY 1977, DJ	50 - 75
ML1540	**The Little Drummer Girl** NY 1983, DJ	20 - 30
ML1550	**The Looking Glass War** Lon 1965, DJ	100 - 150
ML1560	**A Perfect Spy** Lon 1986, DJ	100 - 150
ML1561	NY 1986, DJ (1st American ed)	30 - 50
ML1580	**Smiley's People** NY 1980, DJ	20 - 30

Le Guin, Ursula K.

ML1700	**The Dispossessed** NY 1974, DJ	150 - 250
ML1710	**The Farthest Shore** NY 1972, DJ	100 - 150
ML1720	**The Left Hand of Darkness** NY 1969, DJ	200 - 300
ML1730	**A Wizard of Earth Sea** Berkeley 1968, DJ	400 - 600

Lea, Tom (see Americana)

Lee, Harper

ML1911	**To Kill a Mockingbird** (1st book) Phil 1960, DJ, 1st state w/DJ photo of author by Truman Capote	200 - 300
ML1912	Lon 1960, DJ (1st English ed)	75 - 125

Lee, Vernon

ML2010	**Pope Jacynth & Other Fantastic Tales** Lon 1904, DJ	200 - 300

Lee, William (see William S. Burroughs)

Leiber, Fritz

ML2110	**Conjure, Wife** NY 1953, DJ	200 - 300
ML2120	**Nights Black Agents** (1st book) Sauk City 1947, DJ	150 - 200

Leinster, Murray

ML2210	**Colonial Survey** NY 1957, DJ	150 - 250

Lemay, Alan

ML2310	**Painted Ponies** (1st book) NY 1927, DJ	150 - 250
ML2320	**The Searchers** NY 1954, DJ	100 - 150

Lennon, John

ML2410	**In His Own Write** (1st book) Lon 1964	75 - 125

Leonard, Elmore

ML2510	**Bandits** NY 1987, DJ	30 - 40
ML2520	**The Bounty Hunters** (1st book) Bos 1954, DJ	100 - 150
ML2530	**Cat Chaser** NY 1982,. DJ	30 - 40
ML2540	**The Moonshine War** NY 1969, DJ	75 - 125
ML2550	**Swag** NY 1976, DJ	75 - 125

Leroux, Gaston

ML2710	**Le Fantome de l'Opera** Paris 1910, wrappers	2000 - 3000
ML2720	**The Phantom of the Opera** Ind 1911, DJ	300 - 500

Lessing, Doris

ML2910	**Five Short Novels** Lon 1953, DJ	125 - 250
ML2920	**The Golden Notebook** Lon 1962, DJ	100 - 150
ML2930	**The Grass is Singing** (1st book) Lon 1950, DJ	200 - 300
ML2931	NY 1950, DJ (1st American ed)	100 - 150
ML2950	**Martha Quest** Lon 1952, DJ	100 - 150
ML2970	**Retreat To Innocence** Lon 1956, DJ	100 - 150
ML2980	**This Was the Old Chief's Country** Lon 1951, DJ	200 - 300
ML2981	NY 1951, DJ (1st American ed)	100 - 150

Lewis, Sinclair (1930 Nobel Laureate)

ML3210	**Ann Vickers** NY 1933, DJ	200 - 300
ML3220	**Arrowsmith** NY 1925, 550 cys, glassine DJ, box	500 - 700
ML3221	NY 1925, DJ (1st trade ed)	200 - 300
ML3231	**Babbitt** NY 1922, DJ, 1st issue w/"Purdy" for "Lyte" line 4, p 49	300 - 500
ML3240	**Dodsworth** NY 1929, 500 cys, glassine DJ, box	300 - 500
ML3241	NY 1929, DJ (1st trade ed w/Mar 1929 on cr page)	150 - 250
ML3251	**Elmer Gantry** NY 1927, DJ, 1st issue w/"C" on sp instead of "G"	300 - 500
ML3260	**Free Air** NY 1919, DJ	200 - 300
ML3270	**Gideon Planish** NY 1943, DJ	75 - 125
ML3280	**Hike and the Aeroplane** (1st book) NY 1912, DJ, under pseud Tom Graham	15000 - 25000
ML3290	**The Innocents** NY 1917, DJ, w/"F-R" on cr page	200 - 300
ML3300	**The Job** NY 1917, DJ, w/"B-R" on cr page	150 - 200
ML3320	**Kings Blood Royal** NY 1947, 1050 cys, box	150 - 250
ML3331	**Main Street** NY 1920, DJ, 1st issue w/perfect type on p 387	500 - 700
ML3333	NY 1937, 1500 cys, box	400 - 600
ML3350	**The Man Who Knew Coolidge** NY 1928, DJ	100 - 150
ML3360	**Mantrap** NY 1926, DJ	150 - 250
ML3370	**Our Mr. Wrenn** NY 1914, DJ, w/"M-N" on cr page	200 - 300
ML3380	**The Trail of the Hawk** NY 1915, DJ, w/"H-P" on cr page	250 - 350
ML3381	NY 1915, wrappers (advance review cy)	300 - 500

Lewis, Wyndham

ML3510	**The Apes of God** Lon 1930, 750 cys, DJ	700 - 1000
ML3520	**The Ideal Giant** Lon 1917, 200 cys	700 - 1000
ML3530	**The Red Priest** Lon 1956, DJ	100 - 150
ML3540	**Rotting Hill** Lon 1951, DJ	100 - 150
ML3550	**Self-Condemned** Lon 1954, DJ	100 - 150
ML3560	**Tarr** NY 1918, DJ	300 - 500
ML3561	Lon 1918, DJ (1st English ed)	100 - 150
ML3570	**Timon of Athens** (1st book) Lon 1913, w/portfolio & plates	2000 - 3000

Liebling, A. J.

ML3710	**Back Where I Came From** (1st book) NY 1938, DJ	200 - 300

Lindsay, David

ML3810	**A Voyage to Arcturus** Lon 1920, DJ	600 - 800

Lindsay, Vachel

ML3910	**Adventures While Preaching the Gospel of Beauty** NY 1914	250 - 350
ML3920	**The Candle in the Cabin: A Weaving Together of Script and Singing** NY 1926	100 - 150

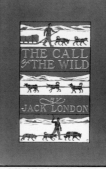
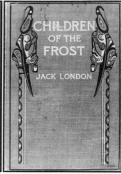

| ML4230 (w/o DJ) | ML4530 (w/o DJ) | ML4540 | ML4561 | ML4571 (w/o DJ) | ML4590 (w/o DJ) |

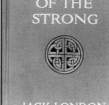

| ML4730 (w/o DJ) | ML4830 (w/o DJ) | ML5020 (w/o DJ) |

ML3930	The Chinese Nightingale and Other Poems NY 1917	300 - 500
ML3940	Collected Poems NY 1923, DJ	150 - 250
ML3950	The Congo and Other Poems NY 1914, DJ	150 - 250
ML3960	General William Booth Enters into Heaven and Other Poems NY 1913, DJ	200 - 300
ML3970	The Golden Whales of California, and Other Rhymes in the American Language NY 1920, DJ	100 - 150
ML3980	A Handy Guide For Beggars NY 1916	100 - 150
ML3990	The Tree of Laughing Bells (1st book) NY 1905, wrappers	2000 - 3000

Lloyd, John Uri

ML4220	Etidorhpa Cinti 1895, limited ed, signed	250 - 350
ML4230	Red-Head NY 1903	75 - 125
ML4240	Stringtown on the Pike NY 1900	20 - 30
ML4250	Warwick of the Knobs NY 1901	15 - 25

Lockridge, Ross

ML4410	Raintree County (only book) Bos 1948	100 - 150

London, Jack

ML4510	The Abysmal Brute NY 1913, DJ, w/"Pub. May, 1913" on cr page	2000 - 3000
	w/o DJ	300 - 500
ML4520	The Acorn Planter NY 1916, DJ	2500 - 3500
ML4530	Adventure NY 1911, DJ	2000 - 3000
	w/o DJ	300 - 500
ML4540	The Assassination Bureau, Ltd. NY 1963, DJ	50 - 75
ML4550	Before Adam NY 1907, DJ, w/"Pub. Feb. 1907" on cr page	1200 - 1800
	w/o DJ	100 - 150
ML4560	Burning Daylight NY 1910, DJ	2000 - 3000
ML4561	NY (early 1900s), DJ, Grosset & Dunlap reprint	30 - 50
ML4571	The Call of the Wild NY 1903, DJ, 1st state binding w/green vertically ribbed cl & pub. "April, 1903" on cr page	2000 - 3000
	w/o DJ	300 - 500
ML4572	Lon 1903, DJ (1st English ed)	500 - 700
ML4574	later printings by MacMillan & Co. w/DJ	25 - 50
ML4575	reprints by Grosset & Dunlap w/DJ	25 - 50
ML4590	Children of the Frost NY 1902, DJ	2000 - 3000
ML4600	The Complete Works NY 1919-20	200 - 300
ML4610	The Cruise of the Dazzler NY 1902, DJ, w/"Pub. Oct. 1902" on cr page	5000 - 7000
	w/o DJ	1000 - 1500
ML4620	The Cruise of the Snark NY 1911, DJ	1500 - 2500
	w/o DJ	200 - 300
ML4630	A Daughter of the Snows Phil 1902, DJ	1500 - 2500
	w/o DJ	250 - 350

ML4640	The Dream of Debs Chi 1909, wrappers	500 - 700
ML4650	Dutch Courage and Other Stories NY 1922, DJ	1500 - 2500
ML4660	The Faith of Men and Other Stories NY 1904, DJ	2000 - 3000
ML4670	The Game NY 1905, DJ, w/rubber stamped notice on cr page	2000 - 3000
ML4680	The God of His Fathers and Other Stories NY 1901, DJ	2000 - 3000
ML4690	Hearts of Three NY 1920, DJ	5000 - 7000
ML4700	The House of Pride and Other Tales of Hawaii NY 1912, DJ	1000 - 1500
ML4720	The Human Drift NY 1917, DJ	1500 - 2500
ML4730	The Iron Heel NY 1908, DJ	2000 - 3000
ML4740	The Jacket Lon 1915, DJ	1000 - 1500
ML4750	Jerry of the Islands NY 1917, DJ, w/"stilled" for "still" line 12, p 173	2000 - 3000
ML4760	John Barleycorn or Alcoholic Memoirs NY 1913, DJ	2000 - 3000
	w/o DJ	200 - 300
ML4762	Lon 1914, DJ	300 - 500
ML4780	The Kempton-Wace Letters NY 1903, DJ	500 - 700
ML4790	The Little Lady of the Big House NY 1916, DJ	2000 - 3000
ML4800	Lost Face NY 1910, DJ	1500 - 2500
ML4810	Love of Life and Other Stories NY 1907, DJ	1500 - 2500
ML4812	Lon 1946, DJ	100 - 150
ML4820	Martin Eden NY 1909, DJ	1200 - 1800
	w/o DJ	200 - 300
ML4830	Michael Brother of Jerry NY 1917, DJ	1000 - 1500
ML4840	Moon Face and Other Stories NY 1906, DJ	1500 - 2500
ML4850	The Mutiny of the Elsinore NY 1914, DJ	800 - 1200
ML4860	The Night-Born NY 1913, DJ	1200 - 1800
ML4870	On the Makaloa Mat NY 1919, DJ	1200 - 1800
ML4880	The People of the Abyss NY 1903, DJ	2000 - 3000
	w/o DJ	200 - 300
ML4890	The Red One NY 1918, DJ	3000 - 5000
	w/o DJ	600 - 800
ML4900	Revolution Chi 1909, DJ	1000 - 1500
ML4910	Revolution and Other Essays NY 1910, DJ	1000 - 1500
ML4920	The Road NY 1907, DJ	1500 - 2500
ML4930	The Scarlet Plague NY 1915, DJ	1000 - 1500
ML4940	Scorn of Women NY 1906, DJ	1500 - 2500
ML4950	The Sea Wolf NY 1904, DJ	5000 - 7000
	w/o DJ	500 - 700
ML4960	Smoke Bellew NY 1912, DJ	1500 - 2500
	w/o DJ	200 - 300
ML4970	A Son of the Sun Garden City 1912, DJ	1000 - 1500
ML4981	The Son of the Wolf (1st book) Bos 1900, DJ, 1st state binding in black cl, silver stamped	3000 - 5000
	w/o DJ	400 - 600
ML4990	South Sea Tales NY 1911, DJ	1200 - 1800
ML5000	The Star Rover NY 1915, DJ	1200 - 1800
ML5020	The Strength of the Strong and Other Pieces NY 1914, DJ	1000 - 1500
ML5030	Tales of the Fish Patrol NY 1905, DJ	2000 - 3000
	w/o DJ	300 - 500
ML5040	Theft NY 1910, DJ	1200 - 1800
ML5050	The Turtles of Tasman NY 1916, DJ	1500 - 2500
ML5060	The Valley of the Moon NY 1913, DJ	1500 - 2500
	w/o DJ	200 - 300
ML5070	War of the Classes NY 1905, DJ	2000 - 3000
	w/o DJ	300 - 500
ML5080	When God Laughs and Other Stories NY 1911, DJ	1500 - 2500
	w/o DJ	200 - 300

ML5091	**White Fang** NY 1906, DJ, 1st issue	
	w/o tp tipped in	1500 - 2500
	w/o DJ	150 - 200
ML5100	**Wonder of Woman: A Smoke Bellew Story**	
	NY 1912, DJ	1200 - 1800
	Grosset & Dunlap reprints of London's books in DJ	30 - 50
	reprints w/o DJ	10 - 20

Lovecraft, H. P.
ML5310	**3 Tales of Horror** Sauk City 1967, DJ	150 - 200
ML5320	**Beyond the Wall of Sleep** Sauk City 1943, DJ	1500 - 2500
ML5330	**The Case of Charles Dexter Ward** Lon 1951, DJ	200 - 300
ML5340	**The Cats of Ulthar** Cassia, FL 1935, DJ	200 - 300
ML5350	**Collected Poems** Sauk City 1963, DJ	150 - 250
ML5360	**The Dark Brotherhood** Sauk City 1966, DJ	150 - 250
ML5370	**Dreams and Fancies** Sauk City 1966, DJ	200 - 300
ML5380	**The Haunter of the Dark** Lon 1951, DJ	
ML5390	**The Lurker at the Threshold** Sauk City 1945, DJ	150 - 200
ML5400	**Marginalia** Sauk City 1944, DJ	200 - 300
ML5410	**The Outsider and Others** Sauk City 1939, DJ	1500 - 2500
ML5420	**The Shadow Over Innsmouth** Everett, PA	
	1936, errata slip, DJ	3000 - 5000
ML5430	**The Shunned House** (1st book) Athol, MA 1928	3000 - 5000
ML5432	Sauk City 1961, DJ	1000 - 1500
ML5450	**Something About Cats and Other Pieces**	
	Sauk City 1949, DJ	150 - 250
ML5460	**Supernatural Horror in Literature** NY 1945	150 - 200

Lowell, Amy
ML5610	**Ballads For Sale** Bos 1927, DJ	75 - 125
ML5620	**Can Grande's Castle** NY 1918, DJ	150 - 250
ML5630	**A Dome of Many-Colored Glass** (1st book)	
	Bos 1912, DJ	200 - 300
ML5640	**East Wind** Bos 1926, DJ	75 - 125
ML5650	**Pictures of the Floating World** NY 1919, DJ	200 - 300

Lowry, Malcolm
ML5810	**Dark as the Grave Wherein My Friend is Laid**	
	NY 1969, DJ	75 - 125
ML5820	**Lunar Caustic** Paris 1963, wrappers	150 - 200
ML5822	Lon 1968, wrappers	150 - 200
ML5850	**Ultramarine** (1st book) Lon 1933, DJ	5000 - 7000
ML5852	Phil 1962, DJ (1st American ed)	100 - 150
ML5860	**Under the Volcanoe** NY 1947, DJ	200 - 300
ML5861	Lon 1947, DJ	150 - 250

Lowry, Robert
ML6010	**Casualty** NY 1946, DJ	75 - 125
ML6020	**Gup 3 Adventures** Cinti 1942, wrappers	50 - 75
ML6030	**Hutton Street** (1st book) Cinti 1940, wrappers	150 - 200
ML6040	**The Journey Out** Bari, Italy, 1945, 250 cys	150 - 200
ML6041	Bari, Italy, 100 cys, unsigned	75 - 100

MacDonald, John D.
MM0110	**The Brass Cupcake** (1st book) NY 1950, DJ	100 - 150
MM0120	**Condominium** NY 1977, DJ	20 - 30
MM0130	**One More Sunday** NY 1984, DJ	20 - 30
MM0140	**Wine of the Dreamer** NY 1951, DJ	100 - 150

MacLeish, Archibald
MM0300	**Class Poem** (1st published writing) New Haven	
	1915, 4 pp leaflet	2000 - 3000
MM0310	**Conquistador** Bos 1932, DJ	200 - 300
MM0312	Lon 1933, DJ	200 - 300
MM0320	**Einstein** Paris 1929, 100 cys, box	250 - 350
MM0321	Paris 1929, 50 cys, vellum, box	300 - 500
MM0330	**The Happy Marriage and Other Poems**	
	Bos 1924, DJ	150 - 250
MM0340	**Land of the Free** NY 1938, DJ	150 - 250
MM0350	**New Found Land** Paris 1930, 100 cys, box	200 - 300
MM0351	Paris 1930, 25 cys, box	300 - 500
MM0352	Bos 1930, 500 cys, box	150 - 250
MM0360	**Nobo Daddy** Cambridge 1926, 50 cys, box	300 - 500
MM0361	Cambridge 1926, 700 cys, box	100 - 150
MM0370	**The Pot of Earth** Cambridge 1925, 100 cys,	
	DJ, box	200 - 300
MM0371	Bos 1925, DJ (1st trade ed)	100 - 150
MM0380	**Public Speech** NY 1936, 275 cys, glassine DJ, box	200 - 300
MM0390	**Songs For A Summer Day** (1st book)	
	New Haven 1913, wrappers	400 - 600
MM0400	**Streets in the Moon** Bos 1926, 60 cys, box	300 - 500
MM0401	Bos 1926, 500 cys, box	100 - 150
MM0410	**Tower of Ivory** New Haven 1917, 750 cys, box	150 - 200
MM0411	New Haven 1917, DJ (1st trade ed)	75 - 125

Mailer, Norman
MM0510	**Advertisements For Myself** NY 1959, DJ	50 - 75
MM0520	**An American Dream** NY 1964, DJ	35 - 50
MM0530	**Barbary Shore** NY 1951, DJ, circled "R" on	
	cr page	75 - 125
MM0540	**Cannon Balls and Christians** NY 1966, DJ	30 - 40
MM0550	**Deaths For The Ladies** NY 1962, DJ	50 - 75
MM0560	**The Deer Park** NY 1955, DJ	50 - 75
MM0570	**Genius and Lust** NY 1976, DJ	20 - 30
MM0580	**Marilyn** NY 1973, limited ed, DJ, box	200 - 300
MM0581	NY 1973, DJ (1st trade ed)	50 - 75
MM0582	NY 1973, DJ (Grosset & Dunlap reprint)	20 - 30
MM0590	**The Naked and the Dead** (1st book) NY 1948,	
	DJ, circled "R" on cr page	300 - 500
MM0592	Lon 1949, 250 cys, box	400 - 600
MM0600	**The White Negro** SF 1957, DJ	50 - 75

Malamud, Bernard
MM0710	**The Fixer** NY 1966, DJ	50 - 75
MM0720	**The Natural** NY 1952, DJ	200 - 300
MM0722	Lon 1963, DJ (1st English ed)	
MM0730	**The Tenants** NY 1971, 250 cys, DJ	200 - 300
MM0731	Lon 1972, DJ (1st English ed)	25 - 50
MM0733	NY 1971, DJ (1st trade ed)	25 - 50

Manfred, Frederick
MM0810	**The Golden Bowl** (1st book) St. Paul 1944, DJ,	
	under pseud Feike Feikema	100 - 150
MM0820	**Lord Grizzly** NY 1954, DJ	75 - 125

Mann, Thomas
MM0910	**The Magic Mountain** NY 1927, 2 vol, 200 cys	800 - 1200

Mansfield, Katharine
MM1010	**The Garden Party and Other Stories** Lon	
	1922, DJ, 1st issue w/"sposition" on last	
	line p 193, 1st state DJ w/blue print	1000 - 1500

Markham, Edwin
MM1110	**California the Wonderful** NY 1914, DJ	75 - 125
MM1120	**Children in Bondage** NY 1914, DJ	75 - 125
MM1130	**The Man with the Hoe** (1st book) SF 1899,	
	wrappers	150 - 200

Marquand, John P.
MM1210	**The Late George Apley** Bos 1937, DJ, 1st issue	
	w/"pretty pearl" 1st line, p 19	100 - 150
MM1220	**The Unspeakable Gentlemen** (1st book) NY 1922,	
	DJ, 1st state w/Scribner's seal on cr page	150 - 200

Marquis, Don
MM1310	**Archy and Mehitabel** NY 1927, DJ	50 - 75
MM1320	**Danny's Own Story** (1st book) NY 1912, DJ	75 - 100

Marx, Groucho
MM1410	**Beds** (1st book) NY 1930, DJ	150 - 200

Masefield, John
MM1510	**Ballads** Lon 1903, wrappers	300 - 500
MM1520	**Salt Water Ballads** (1st book) Lon 1902, 1st	
	issue w/"Grant Richards" imprint on tp	400 - 600

Masters, Edgar Lee
MM1600	**A Book of Verses** (1st book) Chi 1898	300 - 500
MM1610	**The Bread of Idleness: A Play** Chi 1911	150 - 200
MM1620	**Maximillan: A Play** Bos 1902, wrappers	250 - 350
MM1630	**The New Star Chamber and Other Essays**	
	Chi 1904	150 - 200
MM1640	**Spoon River Anthology** NY 1915, DJ, 1st	
	state 7/8" across top	1000 - 1500

Matheson, Richard
MM1710	**Bid Time Return** NY 1975, DJ, 1st state	
	w/white cl sp, tan bds	300 - 500

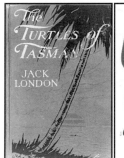  

ML5050 (w/o DJ)   ML6020   MM0510

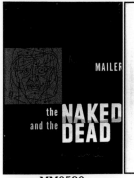

MM0590	MM1710	MM1730

MM1720 **Someone is Bleeding** NY 1953, wrappers 150 - 250
MM1730 **What Dreams May Come** NY 1978, DJ 75 - 100

Maugham, W. Somerset
MM1810 **Ashenden, or the British Agent** Lon 1928, DJ 200 - 300
MM1820 **The Book Bag** Florence 1932, DJ, 725 cys 300 - 500
MM1831 **Cakes and Ale** Lon 1930, DJ, 1st issue w/
"won" instead of "won't" line 14, p 147 300 - 500
MM1832 NY 1930, DJ (1st American ed) 150 - 200
MM1833 Lon 1930, 1000 cys, box 300 - 500
MM1840 **Cosmopolitans: Very Short Stories** Lon 1936, DJ 75 - 125
MM1850 **The Explorer** Lon 1908, DJ 250 - 350
MM1851 NY 1908, DJ (1st American ed) 150 - 250
MM1860 **The Hero** Lon 1901, DJ 300 - 500
MM1870 **The Land of the Blessed Virgin** Lon 1905, DJ 200 - 300
MM1880 **Liza of Lambeth** (1st book) Lon 1897 1500 - 2000
MM1882 Lon 1947, DJ, 1000 cys 200 - 300
MM1890 **The Magician** Lon 1908, DJ 150 - 250
MM1892 NY 1909, DJ 150 - 250
MM1900 **A Man of Honor** Lon 1903, wrappers, 150 cys 1000 - 1500
MM1910 **The Merry-Go-Round** Lon 1904, DJ 200 - 300
MM1921 **The Moon and Sixpence** Lon 1919, DJ,
1st state w/4 pp of ads 250 - 350
MM1922 NY 1919, DJ w/"Maughan" for "Maugham"
on front cover 150 - 250
MM1931 **My South Sea Island** Chi 1936, 1st issue
w/"Sommerset" on tp 700 - 1000
MM1932 2nd issue corrected 300 - 500
MM1941 **Of Human Bondage** NY 1915, DJ, 1st state
w/Geo. H. Doran imprint 800 - 1200
MM1942 Lon 1915, DJ, 1st state w/ads (1st English ed) 300 - 500
MM1944 NY 1936, 751 cys, DJ, box 200 - 300
MM1945 NY 1938, 2 vol 75 - 125
MM1947 Wash 1946, 500 cys 150 - 200
MM1960 **The Razor's Edge** NY 1944, 750 cys, box 250 - 350
MM1961 NY 1944, DJ (1st trade ed) 75 - 125
MM1970 **The Sacred Flame** NY 1928, DJ 150 - 250
MM1971 Lon 1928, DJ (1st English ed) 75 - 125
MM1980 **The Unconquered** NY 1944, 300 cys, DJ 200 - 300
MM1990 **The Unknown** Lon 1920, DJ 150 - 250

McCullers, Carson
MM2110 **The Ballad of the Sad Cafe** Bos 1951, DJ 200 - 300
MM2120 **The Heart is a Lonely Hunter** (1st book)
Bos 1940, DJ 300 - 500
MM2122 Lon 1943, DJ (1st English ed) 200 - 300

McCutcheon, George Barr
MM2200 **Beverly of Graustark** NY 1904, DJ 75 - 125
MM2210 **Brewster's Millions** Chi 1903, DJ, under
pseud Richard Grave 75 - 125
MM2220 **Castle Craneycrow** Chi 1902, DJ 50 - 75
MM2230 **The Day of the Dog** NY 1904, DJ 50 - 75
MM2240 **Graustark** (1st book) Chi 1901, DJ, 1st issue
has "noble" for "lorry" line 6, p 150 150 - 250
MM2250 **The Prince of Graustark** NY 1914, DJ,
w/"Sept., 1914" on cr page 50 - 75

McFee, William
MM2341 **Aliens** Lon 1914, DJ, 1st state w/pub ads at back 75 - 125
MM2351 **Captain Macedoine's Daughter** NY 1920, DJ,
1st state w/yellow stamping on blue cl 75 - 125
MM2360 **Casuals of the Sea** Lon 1916, DJ 50 - 75
MM2371 **An Engineer's Note Book** NY 1921, 1st state
DJ w/"by William McFee" on front cover 75 - 125
MM2380 **Letters From An Ocean Tramp** (1st book)
Lon 1908, DJ 150 - 200

McKay, Claude
MM2510 **Banjo** NY 1929, DJ 300 - 500
MM2520 **Gingertown** NY 1932, DJ 300 - 500
MM2530 **Harlem Shadows** NY 1922, DJ 500 - 700
MM2540 **A Long Way From Home** NY 1937, DJ 300 - 500
MM2550 **Songs of Jamaica** (1st book) Kingston 1912 1200 - 1800
MM2560 **Spring in New Hampshire** Lon 1920, wrappers 300 - 500

McMurtry, Larry
MM2700 **All My Friends are Going to be Starngers** NY
1972, DJ 75 - 125
MM2710 **Horseman, Pass By** (1st book) NY 1961, DJ 800 - 1200
MM2730 **Its Always We Rambled: An Essay on Rodeo**
NY 1974, 300 cys 300 - 500
MM2740 **The Last Picture Show** NY 1966, DJ 200 - 300
MM2750 **Leaving Cheyenne** NY 1963, DJ 200 - 300
MM2760 **Lonesome Dove** NY 1985, DJ 100 - 150
MM2770 **Terms of Endearment** NY 1975, DJ 125 - 200
MM2780 **Texasville** NY 1987, DJ 40 - 60

McPherson, James Alan
MM2910 **Elbow Room** 1978, DJ 20 - 30
MM2920 **Hue and Cry** Bos 1969, DJ 30 - 50

Meltzer, David
MM3010 **The Dark Continent** Berkeley 1967, 31 cys 150 - 200
MM3020 **Luna** LA 1970, 200 cys 75 - 125
MM3030 **Poems** SF 1957, 25 cys, cl 100 - 150
MM3031 5 cys, cl 200 - 300
MM3032 470 cys, wrappers 75 - 125
MM3040 **Ragas** SF 1959, wrappers 25 - 50
MM3050 **Yesod** Lon 1969, 100 cys, glassine DJ 150 - 200

Mencken, H. L.
MM3210 **The American Language** NY 1919, 1500 cys, DJ 100 - 150
MM3211 25 cys, DJ 1500 - 2500
MM3212 NY 1919, DJ (1st trade ed) 30 - 50
MM3220 **The Artist** Bos 1912, DJ 100 - 150
MM3230 **A Book of Burlesques** NY 1916, DJ 75 - 125
MM3240 **Heliogabalus** NY 1920, DJ 100 - 150
MM3251 **In Defence of Women** NY 1918, DJ, 1st issue
w/pub name on tp misspelled "Ppilip" 300 - 500
MM3252 2nd issue corrected 200 - 300
MM3260 **Men Versus the Man** NY 1910, DJ 150 - 250
MM3270 **Prejudices** NY 1919-1927, DJs, 1st to 6th
series limited editions, per vol 150 - 250
MM3280 **Ventures Into Verse** (1st book) Balt 1903,
wrappers 3000 - 5000
MM3290 **What You Should Know About Your Baby**
NY 1910, DJ 150 - 250

Merrill, James
MM3400 **The Black Swan and Other Poems**
Athens 1946, 100 cys 1200 - 1800
MM3410 **First Poems** NY 1951 990 cys, DJ 200 - 300
MM3420 **Jim's Book** (1st book) NY 1942, DJ 3000 - 5000
MM3430 **Short Stories** Pawlet, VT, 1954, 210 cys 250 - 350
MM3440 **Violent Pastoral** Cambridge 1965, 100 cys 250 - 350

Merritt, A.
MM3510 **Burn Witch Burn** NY 1933, DJ 200 - 300
MM3520 **Creep, Shadow!** Garden City 1934, DJ 150 - 200
MM3530 **Dwellers in the Mirage** NY 1932, DJ 300 - 500
MM3540 **The Face in the Abyss** NY 1931, DJ 200 - 300
MM3551 **The Moon Pool** (1st book) NY 1919, DJ,
1st state w/o ad on p 434 200 - 300
MM3561 **The Ship of Ishtar** NY 1926, DJ, 1st state
red cl, yellow stamping 300 - 500

Merton, Thomas
MM3710 **Eighteen Poems** NY 1985, 250 cys, slipcase 200 - 300
MM3720 **Original Child Bomb** NY 1961, 500 cys 150 - 200
MM3721 NY 1961 (1st trade ed) 25 - 50
MM3730 **The Seven-Storey Mountain** NY 1948, DJ 150 - 250
MM3740 **Thirty Poems** (1st book) Norfolk 1944, DJ 200 - 300
MM3750 **The Tower of Babel** Norfolk 1957, 250 cys, box 300 - 500
MM3760 **The Waters of Siloe** NY 1949, DJ 200 - 300
MM3770 **What Are These Wounds?** Milwaukee 1950, DJ 150 - 250

Merwin, W. S.
MM3840 **The Dancing Bears** New Haven 1954, DJ 200 - 300
MM3850 **Green with Beasts** Lon 1956, DJ, wraparound
band 200 - 300
MM3860 **A Mask For Janus** (1st book) New Haven
1952, DJ 300 - 500
MM3870 **Three Poems** NY 1968, 100 cys 250 - 350

Metcalfe, John
MM3930 **The Feasting Dead** Sauk City 1954, DJ   50 - 75
Michener, James
MM4000 **The Bridge at Andau** NY 1957, DJ   25 - 50
MM4010 **The Bridges at Toko-Ri** NY 1953, DJ   75 - 125
MM4020 **Centennial** NY 1974, 500 cys, slipcase   100 - 150
MM4030 **Chesapeake** NY 1978, DJ   30 - 50
MM4040 **The Drifters** NY 1971, DJ   15 - 25
MM4050 **The Floating World** NY 1954, DJ   125 -400
MM4060 **Iberia** NY 1968, 500 cys, box   100 - 150
MM4070 **Poland** NY 1983, DJ   20 - 30
MM4080 **The Quality of Life** Lon 1971, DJ   30 - 50
MM4090 **The Report of the Country Chairman** NY 1961, DJ 30 - 50
MM4100 **Return to Paradise** NY 1951, DJ   75 - 125
MM4110 **The Source** NY 1965, 500 cys, box   125 - 200
MM4111 NY 1965, DJ   20 - 30
MM4120 **Space** NY 1982, DJ   20 - 30
MM4130 **Tales of the South Pacific** (1st book) NY 1947, DJ 200 - 300
MM4132 NY 1950, 1500 cys, box   125 - 200
MM4140 **Texas** NY 1985, DJ   20 - 30

Millay, Edna St. Vincent
MM4310 **The Ballad of the Harp-Weaver** NY 1922,
    75 cys, various colored wrappers   300 - 500
MM4311 425 cys, orange wrappers   150 - 250
MM4320 **The Buck in the Snow** NY 1928, 479 cys, box   200 - 300
MM4321 36 cys, glassine DJ, box   400 - 600
MM4322 NY 1928, DJ (1st trade ed)   50 - 75
MM4323 Lon 1928, DJ (1st English ed)   50 - 75
MM4330 **Conversation at Midnight** NY 1937, 579 cys,
    glassine DJ, box   200 - 300
MM4331 NY 1937, 36 cys, glassine DJ, box   400 - 600
MM4332 NY 1937, DJ (1st trade ed)   50 - 75
MM4340 **Fatal Interview: Sonnets** NY 1931, 479 cys,
    glassine DJ, box   150 - 200
MM4341 36 cys, glassine DJ, box   400 - 600
MM4342 NY 1931, DJ (1st trade ed) w/yellow top edge   50 - 75
MM4350 **A Few Figs From Thistles** NY 1920, wrappers   200 - 300
MM4352 NY 1921, wrappers (w/added material)   75 - 125
MM4360 **The Harp-Weaver and Other Poems**
    NY 1923, DJ   150 - 200
MM4370 **Huntsman, What Quarry** NY 1929, 551 cys, box 200 - 300
MM4380 **The King's Henchman** NY 1927, DJ, 500 cys   150 - 250
MM4381 158 cys, box   200 - 300
MM4382 31 cys   300 - 500
MM4383 NY 1927, DJ (1st trade ed)   50 - 75
MM4390 **The Lamp and the Bell** NY 1921, wrappers   200 - 300
MM4400 **Poems** Lon 1923, DJ   150 - 250
MM4410 **Poems Selected For Young People** NY 1929,
    1050 cys, box   75 - 125
MM4420 **Renascence: (A Poem)** NY 1924, wrappers   300 - 500
MM4431 **Renascence and Other Poems** (1st book) NY 1917,
    1st state black cl w/paper watermarked "Glaslan" 300 - 500
MM4432 2nd state w/paper watermarked "Ingres d'Arches" 200 - 300
MM4433 17 cys, Japan vellum   3000 - 5000
MM4441 **Second April** NY 1921, DJ, 1st state on
    "Glaslan" paper   300 - 500
MM4450 **Wine From These Grapes** NY 1934, 36 cys,
    vellum   700 - 1000
MM4451 NY 1934, DJ (1st trade ed)   50 - 75

Miller, Arthur
MM4610 **After the Fall** NY 1964, 500 cys, box   150 - 200
MM4620 **All My Sons** NY 1947, DJ   200 - 300
MM4630 **Death of a Salesman** NY 1949, DJ   200 - 300
MM4640 **Situation Normal** (1st book) NY 1944, DJ   150 - 250

Miller, Henry
MM4810 **The Air-Conditioned Nightmare** NY 1945, DJ   75 - 125
MM4820 **Aller Retour New York** Paris 1935, 150 cys 1500 - 2000
MM4822 NY 1945, 500 cys   200 - 300
MM4830 **Black Spring** Paris 1936 w/yellow paper band 1200 -1800
MM4831 Paris 1938, wrappers   200 - 300
MM4833 NY 1963, DJ (1st American ed)   50 - 75
MM4840 **The Colossus of Maroussi** SF 1941, 100 cys 800 - 1200
MM4841 SF 1941, DJ (1st trade ed)   75 - 125
MM4851 **The Cosmological Eye** Norfolk 1939, 1st state
    DJ w/white printing   150 - 200
MM4853 Lon 1945, DJ (1st English ed)   75 - 125
MM4860 **Halmet** Santurce, PR, 1939, 2 vol   500 - 700
MM4870 **Into the Night Life** Berkeley 1947, 800 cys, box 800 - 1200
MM4880 **Maurizius Forever** SF 1946, 500 cys   200 - 300
MM4890 **Max and the White Phagocytes** Paris 1938,
    wrappers   500 - 700
MM4900 **Nexus** Paris 1960, wrappers   200 - 300
MM4910 **The Nightmare Notebook** NY 1975, 700 cys 200 - 300
MM4920 **Order and Chaos** New Orleans 1966, 99 cys,
    slipcase   250 - 350
MM4930 **Plexus** Paris 1953, 2 vol, wrappers   300 - 500
MM4940 **Quiet Days in Clichy** Paris 1956, wrappers   300 - 500
MM4950 **Remember to Remember** NY 1947, DJ   100 - 150
MM4960 **Sexus** Paris 1948, 2 vol, wrappers   300 - 500
MM4970 **A Smile at the Foot of the Ladder** NY 1948, DJ 250 - 350
MM4972 SF 1955, 500 cys, glassine DJ   300 - 500
MM4980 **Tropic of Cancer** Paris 1934, w/"pub. Sept.
    1934" on cr page & yellow band, wrappers 4000 - 6000
MM4981 Paris 1935, DJ   800 - 1200
MM4983 NY 1940 (1st American ed)   200 - 300
MM4985 NY 1961, 100 cys   300 - 500
MM4986 NY 1961, DJ (1st trade ed)   75 - 100
MM5000 **Tropic of Capricorn** Paris 1939, w/errata slip,
    wrappers   2000 - 3000
MM5010 **What Are You Going To Do About Alf?**
    Paris 1935, wrappers   1200 - 1800
MM5012 Paris 1938, wrappers   300 - 500
MM5014 Berkeley 1944 (1st American ed)   75 - 100
MM5020 **The Wisdom of the Heart** NY 1941, 1500 cys, DJ 150 - 250
MM5030 **The World of Sex** Chi 1940, 250 cys, DJ   500 - 700
MM5031 NY 1940, DJ   150 - 200

Miller, Jr., Walter M.
MM5210 **A Canticle for Leibowitz** Bos 1960, DJ   500 - 700

Milne, A. A.
MM5350 **A Gallery of Children** Lon 1925, 500 cys, box 500 - 700
MM5360 **The House at Pooh Corner** NY 1928,
    250 cys, box   1500 - 2500
MM5370 **Now We Are Six** Lon 1927, 200 cys, DJ 1200 - 1800
MM5371 Lon 1927, DJ (1st trade ed)   300 - 500
MM5380 **Toad of Toad Hall** Lon 1929, 200 cys, DJ 1500 - 2500
MM5381 Lon 1929, DJ (1st trade ed)   200 - 300
MM5390 **Winnie the Pooh** NY 1926, DJ, illus by
    Ernest Shepard, (1st American trade ed)   300 - 500
    w/o DJ   125 - 200
MM5391 Lon 1926, DJ, 350 cys   1200 - 1800
MM5392 Lon 1926, DJ (1st trade ed)   400 - 600
MM5393 NY 1926, 200 cys, DJ   1000 - 1500

Mitchell, Margaret
MM5511 **Gone With The Wind** (only novel) NY 1936, 1st
    printing w/"Pub. May 1936" on cr page & listing
    no other printings. In 1st state DJ w/"Gone With
    The Wind" listed in 2nd column on back cover 1500 - 2000
    signed   5000 - 7000

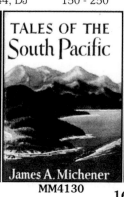

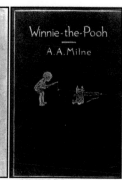
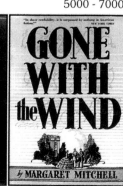

MM2770   MM3930   MM4130   MM5371   MM5390 (w/o DJ)   MM5511

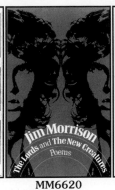

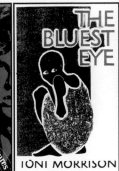

| MM5520 | MM5522 (back cover) | MM6620 | MM6822 | MM6850 | MM7010 |

MM5512 1st printing in 2nd state DJ w/"Gone With The
Wind" listed at top of 1st column   500 - 1000
MM5513 1st printing w/o DJ   125 - 200
MM5514 later printings in 2nd state DJ   300 - 500
MM5515 later printings in gray cl w/o DJ (up to 1940)   15 - 35
MM5516 later printings (up to 1940) in 3rd state DJ
w/"All America is reading Gone With The
Wind" on back cover   50 - 100
MM5518 NY 1939, red cl, DJ, slipcase   200 - 300
MM5519 NY 1939 DJ "Movie Edition" red cl in pictorial DJ   75 - 100
    w/o DJ   25 - 50
MM5520 NY 1939 "Movie Edition" pictorial wrappers w/large
picture of Rhett & Scarlet on front cover, color plates 25 - 40
MM5521 NY 1939, edited by Howard Dietz souvenir guide
(sold at theaters), large format w/many scenes
from movie   50 - 100
MM5522 NY 1939, same as MM5521, special West Coast
version w/Hattie McDaniel's picture (Black maid)
on back cover   200 - 300
MM5523 NY 1940, movie ed w/movie-scene pict p-o on
front cover   50 - 75
MM5524 NY 1940, movie ed w/map p-o on front cover   50 - 75
MM5526 NY 1961, 25 anniversary ed, cl, slipcase   75 - 125
MM5527 NY1965, DJ, deluxe ed illus by Stahl   50 - 75
MM5528 NY 1967, large print ed, 2 vol, slipcase   50 - 75
MM5531 Franklin Library editions: 1981   50 - 75
MM5535 Franklin Library editions: 1985, 1988, 1991   30 - 50

Mo, Timothy
MM5610 **The Monkey King** (1st book) Lon 1978, DJ   200 - 300
MM5620 **Sour Sweet** Lon 1982, DJ   100 - 150

Moore, C. L.
MM5710 **North West of Earth** NY 1952, DJ   100 - 150
MM5720 **Shambleau and Others** NY 1954, DJ   100 - 150

Moore, Marianne
MM5810 **The Absentee** NY 1962, 326 cys   200 - 300
MM5820 **Collected Poems** Lon 1951, DJ   75 - 125
MM5830 **Eight Poems** NY 1963, 195 cys, box   200 - 300
MM5840 **Marriage** NY 1923, 200 cys, wrappers   700 - 1000
MM5850 **Nevertheless** NY 1944, DJ   150 - 250
MM5860 **Observations** NY 1924, DJ   700 - 1000
MM5870 **The Pangolin and Other Verse** Lon 1936,
120 cys, tissue DJ   1500 - 2000
MM5880 **Poems** (1st book) Lon 1921, wrappers   600 - 800
MM5890 **Predilections** NY 1955, DJ   75 - 125
MM5900 **Selected Poems** NY 1935, 1st state DJ
w/#2 price wrappers   700 - 1000
MM5910 **Silence** Cambridge 1965, 25 cys   300 - 500
MM5920 **Tipoo's Tiger** NY 1967, 126 cys   200 - 300
MM5930 **What Are Years** NY 1941, DJ   200 - 300

Morley, Christopher
MM6110 **The Eighth Sin** (1st book) Lon 1912
250 cys, wrappers   1200 - 1500
MM6120 **The Haunted Bookshop** NY 1919, DJ,
1st issue w/"sty" for "styx" line 1, p 100
& p 76 so numbered   250 - 350
MM6130 **Parnassus on Wheels** Garden City 1917,
DJ, 1st issue w/space between Y & ears
for "Years" line 8, p 4   700 - 1000
MM6140 **The Rocking Horse** NY 1919, DJ, 1st state
w/Burns quotation facing tp   300 - 500
MM6150 **Shandygaff** NY 1918, DJ, 1st state binding
of gold stamped dark blue cl   250 - 350

MM6160 **Songs For A Little House** NY 1917, DJ, 1st state
w/"Southwell" quote facing tp   200 - 300
MM6170 **Where the Blue Begins** NY 1922, DJ   200 - 300

Morris, Wright
MM6310 **The Deep Sleep** NY 1953, DJ   150 - 250
MM6320 **The Field of Vision** NY 1956, w/blue/black DJ   150 - 250
MM6330 **The Home Place** NY 1948, DJ   200 - 300
MM6340 **The Inhabitants** NY 1946, DJ   200 - 300
MM6350 **Man and Boy** NY 1951, DJ   150 - 250
MM6360 **The Man Who Was There** NY 1945, DJ   250 - 350
MM6370 **My Uncle Dudley** (1st book) NY 1942, DJ   800 - 1200
MM6380 **The World in the Attic** NY 1949, DJ   200 - 300

Morrison, Arthur
MM6510 **Chronicles of Martin Hewitt** Lon 1895   700 - 1000

Morrison, Jim
MM6610 **The Lords** LA 1969, 100 cys   250 - 350
MM6620 **The Lords and The New Creatures Poems**
NY 1970, DJ   100 - 150
MM6630 **The New Creatures** LA 1969, 100 cys   250 - 350

Morrison, Toni (1993 Nobel Laureate)
MM6810 **Beloved** NY 1988, DJ   20 - 30
MM6820 **The Bluest Eye** (1st book) NY 1970, DJ   400 - 600
MM6822 Lon 1979, DJ (1st English ed)   100 - 150
MM6830 **Jazz** NY 1992, DJ   20 - 30
MM6840 **Sula** NY 1974, DJ   75 - 125
MM6850 **Tar Baby** NY 1981, DJ   50 - 75

Mosley, Walter
MM7010 **Devil in a Blue Dress** NY 1990, DJ   50 - 75

Mulford, Clarence
MM7210 **Bar-20** (1st book) NY 1907, DJ, 1st issue
w/"Blazing Star" in listing of illus   150 - 200
MM7220 **Bar-20 Days** Chi 1911, DJ   75 - 125
MM7230 **Hopalong Cassidy Sees Red** NY 1921, DJ   75 - 125

Mundy, Talbot
MM7410 **The Ivory Trail** Ind 1919, DJ   100 - 150
MM7420 **Queen Cleopatra** Ind 1929, DJ   75 - 125
MM7430 **Rung Ho!** (1st book) NY 1914, DJ   150 - 200
MM7440 **Tros of Samothrace** NY 1934, DJ   75 - 125

Murdoch, Iris
MM7610 **The Bell** Lon 1958, DJ   100 - 150
MM7620 **The Flight From the Enchanter** Lon 1956, DJ   300 - 500
MM7630 **The Italian Girl** Lon 1964, DJ   75 - 125
MM7640 **The Sandcastle** Lon 1957   150 - 250
MM7650 **Under The Net** Lon 1954, DJ   400 - 600

Nabokov, Vladimar
MN0100 **Bend Sinister** NY 1947, DJ   200 - 300
MN0110 **Camera Obscura** (1st book) Lon 1936, DJ   2000 - 3000
MN0120 **Despair** Lon 1937, DJ   800 - 1200
MN0130 **The Eye** NY 1965, DJ   75 - 125
MN0132 Lon 1966, DJ   50 - 75
MN0141 **Lolita** Paris 1955, 2 vol, 1st state w/"900
Francs" on back cover, wrappers   2000 - 3000
MN0142 2nd state   300 - 500
MN0143 Paris 1958, wrappers   75 - 125
MN0144 NY 1955, DJ (1st American ed)   75 - 125
MN0146 Lon 1959, DJ (1st English ed)   75 - 125
MN0150 **Nikolai Gogol** Lon 1947, DJ   125 - 250
MN0160 **Nine Stories** NY 1947, blue wrappers   200 - 300
MN0161 NY 1947 clothbound   800 - 1200
MN0170 **Pale Fire** NY 1962, DJ   150 - 250
MN0171 Lon 1962, DJ   75 - 150

MN0180 **Poems** NY 1959, DJ 200 - 300
MN0181 Lon 1961, DJ 125 - 250
MN0190 **Speak Memory** Lon 1951, DJ 200 - 300
MN0200 **The Waltz Invention** NY 1966, pink DJ 150 - 250
    blue DJ 75 - 125

Naipaul, V. S.
MN0310 **The Mystic Masseur** (1st book) Lon 1957, DJ 200 - 300
MN0312 NY 1959, DJ (1st American ed) 50 - 100

Nash, Ogden
MN0410 **The Cricket of Carador** (1st book) Garden City
    1925, DJ 200 - 300
MN0420 **Hard Lines** NY 1931, DJ 200 - 300

Neihardt, John G.
MN0510 **Black Elk Speaks** NY 1932, DJ 150 - 250
MN0520 **A Bundle of Myrrh** NY 1907, 5 cys 1200 - 1800
MN0521 NY 1907 200 - 300
MN0530 **Collected Poems** NY 1926, DJ, 250 cys 150 - 250
MN0540 **The Dawn Builder** NY 1911, DJ 200 - 300
MN0550 **The Divine Enchantment: A Mystical Poem**
    (1st book) NY 1900 700 - 1000
MN0560 **Indian Tales and Others** NY 1926, DJ 150 - 250
MN0570 **The Lonesome Trail** NY 1907, DJ 150 - 250
MN0580 **Man Song** NY 1909, DJ 150 - 250
MN0590 **The River and I** NY 1910, DJ 150 - 250
MN0600 **The Song of the Indian Wars** NY 1925,
    500 cys, DJ 250 - 350
MN0601 NY 1925, DJ (1st trade ed) 75 - 125

Nemerov, Howard
MN0810 **The Homecoming Game** NY 1957, DJ 75 - 125
MN0820 **The Image and the Law** (1st book) NY 1947, DJ 100 - 150

Nesbit, E.
MN1010 **The Book of Dragons** NY 1901 250 - 350
MN1020 **The Wouldbegoods** NY 1901 100 - 150

Newell, Peter (see Artists & Illustrators)

Nordhoff, Charles and James Norman Hall
MN1210 **Mutiny on the Bounty** Bos, Oct 1932, DJ 125 - 200

Norris, Frank
MN1410 **Blix** NY 1899 200 - 300
MN1420 **Complete Works** NY 1928, 10 vol 250 - 350
MN1430 **A Man's Woman** NY 1900, DJ, red cl 150 - 200
MN1440 **McTeague** NY 1899, w/"moment" as last word
    on p 106 300 - 500
MN1450 **Moran of the Lady Letty** NY 1898 150 - 250
MN1460 **The Octopus** NY 1901, DJ, w/"J.J. Little" on
    cr page 300 - 500
MN1470 **The Pit** NY 1903, bds, ppr label 250 - 350
MN1471 NY 1903, DJ (1st trade ed) 75 - 125
MN1480 **Vandover and the Brute** Garden City 1914 150 - 250
MN1490 **Yvernelle** (1st book) Phil 1892 1200 - 1800

Norton, Andre
MN1810 **At Swords' Points** NY 1954, DJ 100 - 150
MN1820 **Catseye** NY 1961, DJ 150 - 250
MN1830 **Follow the Drum** NY 1942, DJ 200 - 300
MN1840 **Huon of the Horn** NY 1951, DJ 200 - 300
MN1850 **Ice Crown** NY 1970, DJ 50 - 75
MN1860 **Judgment on Janus** NY 1963, DJ 75 - 125
MN1870 **The Prince Commands** (1st book) NY 1934, DJ 400 - 600
MN1880 **Ralestone Luck** NY 1938, DJ 300 - 400
MN1890 **Ride Proud, Rebel!** Clev 1961, DJ 40 - 60
MN1900 **Space Service** Clev 1953, DJ 75 - 125
MN1910 **The Sword Is Drawn** Bos 1944, DJ 100 - 150

Oates, Joyce Carol
MO0100 **Angel of Light** NY 1981, DJ 30 - 50
MO0110 **Bellefleur** NY 1980, DJ 20 - 30
MO0120 **A Bloodsmoor Romance** NY 1982, DJ 30 - 50
MO0130 **By The North Gate** (1st book) NY 1963, DJ 125 - 175
MO0140 **Cupid and Psyche** NY 1970, 200 cys, wrappers 200 - 300
MO0150 **A Garden of Earthly Delights** NY 1967, DJ 75 - 125
MO0160 **The Girl, A Short Story** Cambridge 1974, 300 cys 200 - 300
MO0170 **The Lamb of Abyssalia** Cambridge 1979, 50 cys,
    acetate DJ 200 - 300
MO0180 **Raven's Wing** NY 1986, DJ 30 - 50
MO0190 **Solstice** NY 1985, DJ 20 - 30
MO0200 **Them** NY 1969, DJ 75 - 125
MO0210 **Upon the Sweeping Flood and Other Stories**
    NY 1966, DJ 75 - 125
MO0212 Lon 1973, DJ 50 - 75
MO0220 **With Shuddering Fall** NY 1964, DJ 125 - 175
MO0230 **Women in Love and Other Poems** NY 1968,
    150 cys 200 - 300
MO0240 **Wonderland** NY 1971, DJ 30 - 50
MO0250 **The World According to Garp** NY 1978, DJ 50 - 75

O'Brien, Tim
MO0510 **Going After Cacciato** NY 1978, DJ 150 - 250
MO0520 **If I Die in a Combat Zone** (1st book) NY 1973, DJ 200 - 300
MO0521 Lon 1973, DJ (1st English ed) 75 - 100
MO0530 **Northern Lights** NY 1975, DJ 200 - 300

O'Casey, Sean
MO0810 **Cock-A-Doodle Dandy** Lon 1949, DJ 150 - 250
MO0820 **Drums Under the Window** Lon 1945, DJ 150 - 250
MO0830 **I Knock at the Door** Lon 1939, DJ 150 - 250
MO0840 **The Plough Under the Stars** Lon 1926, DJ 200 - 300
MO0841 NY 1926, DJ 75 - 125
MO0850 **Purple Dust** Lon 1940, DJ 150 - 250
MO0860 **Red Roses To Me** Lon 1942, DJ 150 - 250
MO0870 **Rose and Crown** Lon 1952, DJ 75 - 125
MO0880 **The Story of the Irish Citizen Army** (1st book)
    Lon 1919, gray wrappers (under Gaelic name
    "O'Cathasaigh") 150 - 250
MO0890 **Windfalls** Lon 1934, DJ 150 - 250

O'Connor, Edwin
MO1510 **The Edge of Sadness** NY 1961, DJ 20 - 30
MO1520 **The Oracle** (1st book) NY 1951, DJ 25 - 50

O'Connor, Flannery
MO1710 **The Complete Stories** NY 1971, DJ 125 - 200
MO1720 **A Good Man is Hard to Find** NY 1955, DJ 300 - 500
MO1730 **The Violent Bear It Away** NY 1960, DJ 300 - 500
MO1740 **Wise Blood** (1st book) NY 1952, DJ 700 - 1000

MN1210   MN1810   MN1890

MM7630   MN1010   MN1020   MN1900   MN1910   MO2900

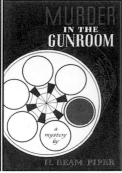

| MP0110 | MP0210 | MP0220 | MP0230 | MP0330 | MP0650 (w/o DJ) |

MO1741 Lon 1952, DJ (1st English ed) 200 - 300

O'Connor, Frank
MO1910 **Guests of the Nation** (1st book) Lon 1931, DJ 200 - 300
MO1920 **A Lament For Art O'Leary** Dublin 1940,
130 cys, DJ 200 - 300
MO1930 **A Picture Book** Dublin 1943, 480 cys, DJ 100 - 150
MO1940 **The Saint and Mary Kate** Lon 1932, DJ 200 - 300
MO1950 **Three Old Brothers and Other Poems**
Lon 1936, DJ 150 - 250
MO1960 **The Wild Birds Nest** Dublin 1932, 250 cys 250 - 350

Odets, Clifford
MO2900 **The Country Girl** NY 1951, DJ 40 - 60
MO2910 **Golden Boy** NY 1937, DJ 50 - 75
MO2920 **Paradise Lost** NY 1936, DJ 50 - 75
MO2930 **Three Plays** (1st book) NY 1935, DJ 75 - 125

O'Flaherty, Liam
MO3210 **The Assassin** Lon 1928, 150 cys 200 - 300
MO3211 Lon 1928, DJ (1st trade ed) 100 - 150
MO3220 **The Black Soul** Lon 1924, DJ 250 - 350
MO3230 **The Child of God** Lon 1926, 100 cys 200 - 300
MO3240 **The Ecstasy of Angus** Lon 1931, 365 cys 200 - 300
MO3250 **The Informer** Lon 1925, DJ 800 - 1200
MO3260 **Red Barbara and Other Stories** NY 1928, 600 cys 150 - 250
MO3270 **Return of the Brute** Lon 1929, DJ 100 - 150
MO3280 **Thy Neighbors Wife** (1st book) Lon 1923, DJ 300 - 500

O'Hara, Frank
MO3610 **A City Winter and Other Poems** (1st book)
NY 1951, 130 cys 700 - 1000
MO3611 NY 1951, 20 cys 1800 - 2500
MO3621 **The Collected Poems of Frank O'Hara**
NY 1971, 1st state DJ w/nude drawing 200 - 300
MO3630 **Odes** NY 1960, 225 cys, acetate DJ 400 - 600

O'Hara, John
MO3810 **Appointment in Samarra** (1st book) NY
1934, DJ, 1st state w/ads on DJ 10000 - 15000
MO3820 **Butterfield 8** NY 1935, DJ 500 - 700
MO3830 **The Doctor's Son** NY 1935, DJ 400 - 600
MO3840 **Hellbox** NY 1947, DJ 250 - 350
MO3850 **Hope of Heaven** NY 1938, DJ 300 - 500
MO3860 **The Instrument** NY 1967, 300 cys, box 200 - 300
MO3861 NY 1967, DJ (1st trade ed) 25 - 50
MO3870 **Pal Joey** NY 1940, DJ 250 - 350
MO3880 **Pipe Night** NY 1945, DJ 300 - 500

Olson, Charles
MO4410 **Call Me Ishmael** (1st book) NY 1947, DJ 200 - 300
MO4420 **The Maximus Poems** NY 1960, 26 cys 300 - 500
MO4421 75 cys 200 - 350
MO4422 NY 1960, wrappers (1st trade ed) 25 - 50
MO4430 **O'Ryan 1 2 3 4 5 6 7 8 9 10** SF 1965, 26 cys 300 - 500
MO4431 SF 1965, wrappers (1st trade ed) 20 - 30
MO4440 **Stocking Cap: A Story** SF 1966, 100 cys,
wrappers 200 - 350
MO4441 SF 1966, wrappers (1st trade ed) 25 - 50

O'Neill, Eugene (1936 Nobel Laureate)
MO5010 **All God's Chillun Got Wings, and Welded**
NY 1924, DJ 150 - 200
MO5020 **Before Breakfast** NY 1916, wrappers 200 - 300
MO5030 **Beyond the Horizon** NY 1920, DJ, 1st state
w/letters on cover 9/16" high 200 - 300
MO5040 **Bound East For Cardiff** NY 1916, wrappers
in "The Provincetown Plays" 200 - 300
MO5050 **Complete Works** NY 1924, 2 vol 300 - 500

MO5060 **The Hairy Ape: Anna Christie: The First Man**
NY 1922, 775 cys, DJ, box 250 - 350
MO5061 NY 1922, DJ (1st trade ed) 75 - 125
MO5070 **The Moon of the Caribees, and Six Other Plays
of the Sea** NY 1919, DJ, 1st state 7/8" thick 200 - 300
MO5080 **Strange Interlude** NY 1928, 775 cys, box 300 - 500
MO5081 NY 1928, DJ (1st trade ed) 100 - 150
MO5090 **Thrist and Other One Act Plays** (1st book)
Bos 1914, DJ 800 - 1200

Orwell, George (Eric Arthur Blair)
MO6010 **Animal Farm** Lon 1945, DJ 300 - 500
MO6011 NY 1946, DJ (1st American ed) 100 - 150
MO6012 NY 1946, wrappers (advance review cy) 300 - 500
MO6020 **Burmese Days** NY 1934, DJ 300 - 500
MO6030 **A Clergyman's Daughter** Lon 1935, DJ 200 - 300
MO6040 **Down and Out in Paris and London** (1st book)
Lon 1933, DJ 2500 - 4000
MO6041 NY 1933, DJ (1st American ed) 800 - 1200
MO6050 **The Lion and the Unicorn** NY 1941, DJ
MO6060 **Nineteen Eighty Four** Lon 1949, DJ 400 - 600
MO6061 NY 1949, DJ, w/1st state DJ, red 150 - 250
MO6062 NY 1949, wrappers (advance review cy) 400 - 600

Owen, Wilfred
MO7010 **Poems** (1st book) Lon 1920, DJ 700 - 1000
MO7011 NY 1921, DJ (1st American ed) 300 - 500
MO7012 Lon 1931, DJ 100 - 150

Owens, Rochelle
MO7210 **Not Be Essence That Cannot Be** (1st book)
NY 1961, wrappers 75 - 100

Ozick, Cynthia
MO8110 **Trust** (1st book) NY 1966, DJ 100 - 150
MO8120 Lon 1966, DJ 50 - 75

Paine, Albert Bigelow
MP0110 **The Great White Way** NY 1901 75 - 125

Parker, Robert
MP0160 **The Godwulf Manuscript** (1st book) Bos 1974, DJ 200 - 300
MP0161 Lon 1974, DJ (1st English ed) 150 - 200

Patchen, Kenneth
MP0210 **Before the Brave** NY 1936, DJ 250 - 350
MP0220 **The Famous Boating Party** NY 1954, DJ 100 - 150
MP0230 **Red Wine and Yellow Hair** NY 1949, DJ 100 - 150

Peake, Mervyn
MP0270 **The Gormenghast Trilogy** Lon 1946, DJ 300 - 500

Piper, H. Beam
MP0310 **Four-Day Planet** NY 1961, DJ 200 - 300
MP0320 **Junkyard Planet** NY 1963, DJ 150 - 250
MP0330 **Murder in the Gunroom** NY 1953, DJ 250 - 350

Plath, Sylvia
MP0410 **Ariel** Lon 1965, DJ 150 - 250
MP0420 **The Bell Jar** Lon 1963, DJ 700 - 1000
MP0430 **The Colossus and Other Poems** (1st book)
Lon 1960, DJ 800 - 1200
MP0431 NY 1962, DJ (1st American ed) 200 - 300

Poole, Ernest
MP0510 **His Family** Chi 1918, DJ 50 - 75
MP0520 **Katharine Breshovsky** (1st book) Chi 1905,
wrappers 100 - 150

Porter, Gene Stratton (also see Birds)
MP0610 **After the Flood** Ind 1911, red cl (came as part
of 12 vol set of several authors' works) 400 - 600
MP0620 **At the Foot of the Rainbow** Outing Co., NY
1907, DJ, yellow cl 50 - 75

	w/o DJ	30 - 50
MP0622	Numerous later printings by Doubleday and Grosset & Dunlap w/DJs	10 - 25
MP0630	**Birds of the Bible** Jennings & Graham, Cinti 1909, slipcase	300 - 500
MP0631	Abington, Cinti 1909, slipcase	150 - 250
MP0633	Lon 1910	150 - 250
MP0640	**Birds of the Limberlost** (very rare) NY 1914, wrappers	1500 - 2500
MP0650	**A Daughter of the Land** Doubleday, NY 1918, DJ	50 - 75
	w/o DJ	30 - 50
MP0652	numerous later eds, various pubs, DJ	8 - 25
MP0660	**The Fire Bird** NY 1922, DJ	400 - 600
MP0661	Lon 1922, DJ	300 - 500
MP0670	**Freckles** Doubleday, NY 1904, DJ	400 - 600
	w/o DJ	200 - 300
MP0672	NY 1914 (illus by Fogarty)	50 - 75
MP0673	numerous later eds, various pubs, DJs	8 - 25
MP0680	**A Girl of the Limberlost** Doubleday, NY 1909, DJ	50 - 75
	w/o DJ	30 - 50
MP0682	numerous later eds, various pubs, DJs	8 - 25
MP0691	**The Harvester** Doubleday, NY 1911, DJ, 1st issue w/o "Pub. Aug. 1911" on cr page	75 - 125
	w/o DJ	50 - 75
MP0692	2nd issue w/"Pub. Aug. 1911" on cr page	50 - 75
	w/o DJ	30 - 50
MP0694	numerous later eds, various pubs, DJs	8 - 25
MP0700	**Her Father's Daughter** Doubleday, NY 1921, DJ	75 - 125
	w/o DJ	30 - 50
MP0701	numerous later eds, various pubs, DJs	8 - 25
MP0710	**Homing with the Birds** Doubleday, NY 1919, DJ	300 - 500
MP0711	Lon 1919, DJ	150 - 250
MP0712	NY 1920, DJ	150 - 250
MP0720	**Jesus of the Emerald** Doubleday, NY 1923, glassine DJ, box	1500 - 2000
MP0721	Lon 1923, glassine DJ, box	1200 - 1500
MP0730	**The Keeper of the Bees** Doubleday, NY 1925, DJ (1st ed stated on cr page)	250 - 350
	w/o DJ	125 - 200
MP0732	numerous later eds, various pubs, DJs	8 - 25
MP0740	**Laddie** Doubleday, NY 1913, DJ	50 - 75
	w/o DJ	30 - 50
MP0742	numerous later eds, various pubs, DJs	8 - 25
MP0750	**Let Us Highly Resolve** NY 1927, DJ (1st ed so stated)	400 - 600
	w/o DJ	200 - 300
MP0751	Lon 1927, DJ	200 - 300
MP0760	**The Magic Garden** Doubleday, NY 1927, DJ (1st ed stated on cr page)	75 - 125
	w/o DJ	50 - 75
MP0761	Lon 1927, DJ	50 - 75
MP0763	numerous later eds, various pubs, DJs	10 - 35
MP0770	**Michael O'Halloran** Doubleday NY 1915, DJ	50 - 75
	w/o DJ	30 - 50
MP0771	Lon 1915, DJ	30 - 60
MP0773	numerous later eds, various pubs, DJs	8 - 25
MP0780	**Morning Face** NY 1916, DJ	200 - 400
	w/o DJ	100 - 150
MP0781	Lon 1916, DJ	150 - 250
MP0790	**Moth's of the Limberlost** NY 1912, DJ, box	250 - 350
MP0791	Lon. 1912, DJ, box	200 - 300
MP0792	NY 1914, DJ	150 - 200
MP0794	Later eds by Doubleday up to 1920, DJs	75 - 125
MP0800	**Music of the Wild** Jennings & Graham, Cinti 1910, DJ	300 - 500
MP0801	Abington, NY 1910, DJ	200 - 300
MP0802	Lon 1910, DJ	150 - 250
MP0810	**The Song of the Cardinal** Ind 1903, DJ	250 - 350
	w/o DJ	150 - 200
MP0811	Ind 1906, DJ	75 - 125
MP0813	Lon 1913, DJ	50 - 75
MP0814	Doubleday, NY 1915, DJ	50 - 75
MP0816	numerous later eds, various pubs, DJs	10 - 30
MP0820	**Tales You Won't Believe** Doubleday NY 1925, DJ	250 - 350
	w/o DJ	100 - 150
MP0822	numerous later eds, various pubs, DJs	15 - 50
MP0830	**What I Have Done With Birds** Ind 1907 DJ	250 - 350
MP0840	**The White Flag** Doubleday, NY 1923, DJ	75 - 100
	w/o DJ	30 - 50
MP0841	Lon 1923, DJ	50 - 75

MP0843	numerous later eds, various pubs, DJs	10 - 25
MP0850	**Wings** NY 1923, wrappers	300 - 500
MP0851	NY 1924, wrappers	200 - 300
MP0852	NY 1924, DJ	200 - 300

Porter, Katharine Anne

MP1010	**A Christmas Story** NY 1967, 500 cys, box	125 - 250
MP1020	**Flowering Judas** NY 1930, 600 cys, glassine DJ	400 - 600
MP1022	NY 1935, DJ (1st trade ed)	150 - 250
MP1030	**Hacienda** NY 1934, 895 cys, errata slip, box	300 - 500
MP1040	**Pale Horse, Pale Rider** NY 1939, DJ	125 - 200

Potter, Beatrix (see Artists & Illustrators)

Pound, Ezra

MP1110	**ABC of Economics** Lon 1933, DJ	300 - 500
MP1120	**ABC of Reading** Lon 1934, DJ	300 - 500
MP1121	New Haven 1934, DJ (1st American ed)	150 - 250
MP1130	**Antheil and the Treatise on Harmony** Paris 1924, 40 cys	800 - 1200
MP1131	560 cys	300 - 500
MP1133	NY 1926, DJ (1st American ed)	150 - 250
MP1134	Chi 1927, DJ	75 - 125
MP1140	**Canto CX** Cambridge 1965, 80 cys, wrappers	150 - 250
MP1150	**Cantos LII - LXXI** Lon 1940, DJ	250 - 350
MP1151	Norfolk 1940, 500 cys w/envelope	200 - 300
MP1160	**Cantos XVII - XXVII** Lon 1928, 70 cys	700 - 1000
MP1170	**Canzoni** Lon 1911, 1000 cys	300 - 500
MP1180	**Canzoni & Ripostes of Ezra Pound** Lon 1913	150 - 250
MP1190	**Carta da Visita** Rome 1942	150 - 250
MP1200	**Des Imagistes: An Anthology** NY 1914, contains 6 poems by Pound	
MP1210	**Diptych Rome - London** Norfolk 1957, 125 cys, box	800 - 1200
MP1211	Lon 1957, 50 cys	600 - 800
MP1220	**A Draft of XXX Cantos** Paris 1930, 200 cys	1500 - 2500
MP1221	10 cys	4000 - 6000
MP1223	NY 1933, DJ (1st American ed)	300 - 500
MP1224	Lon 1933, DJ (1st English ed)	150 - 250
MP1230	**Drafts and Fragments of Cantos CX - CXVII** NY 1967, 100 cys, errata slip, box	800 - 1200
MP1231	NY 1969, 200 cys, errata slip, box	800 - 1200
MP1233	NY 1968, DJ (1st trade ed)	150 - 250
MP1240	**Eleven New Cantos: XXXI - XLI** NY 1934, w/"F-R" on cr page	300 - 500
MP1250	**Exultations** Lon 1909, 1000 cys, box	700 - 1000
MP1260	**The Fifth Decade of Cantos** Lon 1937, DJ	500 - 700
MP1261	NY 1937, DJ, 750 cys	300 - 500
MP1270	**Gaudier-Brzeska: A Memoir** Lon 1916, 450 cys	700 - 1000
MP1271	NY 1916, w/olive green cl	400 - 600
MP1280	**Homage to Sextus Propertius** Lon 1934, DJ, 1000 cys	300 - 500
MP1290	**How to Read** Lon 1931, DJ, red cl, silver stamping	200 - 300
MP1300	**Hugh Selwyn Mauberley** Lon 1920, 165 cys	2000 - 3000
MP1310	**Imaginary Letters** Paris 1930, 300 cys, glassine DJ, box	400 - 600
MP1311	50 cys, vellum, box	800 - 1200
MP1320	**Indiscretions; Or, Une Revue Des Deux Mondes** Paris 1923, 300 cys	1500 - 2500
MP1330	**Instigations** NY 1920, DJ	250 - 350
MP1340	**Jefferson And/Or Mussolini** Lon 1935, DJ	200 - 300
MP1342	NY 1936, DJ (1st American ed)	150 - 200
MP1350	**A Lume Spento** (1st book) Venice 1908, wrappers	18000 - 30000
MP1351	NY 1965, DJ (1st American ed)	75 - 125
MP1360	**Lustra** Lon 1916, 200 cys	1500 - 2500

MP0672   MP0700 (w/o DJ)   MP0740 (w/o DJ)

| | MP2241 | MP4010 | MQ5010 |

MP1361	Lon 1916 (1st trade ed)	200 - 300
MP1363	NY 1917 60 cys, DJ	1000 - 1700
MP1364	NY 1917, DJ (1st American trade ed)	300 - 500
MP1370	**Make It New: Essays** Lon 1934, DJ	300 - 500
MP1371	New Haven 1935, DJ (1st American ed)	200 - 300
MP1380	**'Noh'; Or, Accomplishment** Lon 1916, DJ	250 - 350
MP1381	NY 1917, DJ (1st American ed)	150 - 200
MP1390	**Pavannes and Divisions** NY 1918, DJ, blue cl	250 - 350
	gray cl	150 - 250
MP1400	**Personae** Lon 1909	400 - 600
MP1410	**Personae: The Collected Poems of Ezra Pound** NY 1926, DJ, blue cl	300 - 500
MP1420	**The Pisan Cantos** NY 1948, DJ	150 - 250
MP1421	Lon 1949, DJ (1st English ed)	75 - 125
MP1430	**Poems 1918 - 1921** NY 1921, DJ	300 - 500
MP1440	**Polite Essays** Lon 1937, DJ	300 - 500
MP1442	Norfolk 1940, DJ (1st American ed)	200 - 300
MP1450	**Provenca** Lon 1909, DJ	700 - 1000
MP1451	Bos 1910, DJ, w/brown stamping	400 - 600
MP1452	Bos 1910, DJ, w/green stamping	300 - 500
MP1460	**Quia Pauper Amavi** Lon 1919, 100 cys	1500 - 2500
MP1461	Lon 1919, 500 cys	400 - 600
MP1470	**A Quinzaine For This Yule** Lon 1908, wrappers, 100 cys, "Pollock" imprint	800 - 1200
MP1471	100 cys, "Mathews" imprint	700 - 1000
MP1480	**Redondillas, or Something Like That** NY 1967, DJ, 100 cys	300 - 500
MP1490	**Ripostes** Lon 1912, DJ	300 - 500
MP1491	Bos 1913, DJ (1st American ed)	300 - 500
MP1500	**Selected Poems** Lon 1928, 100 cys	800 - 1200
MP1501	Lon 1928, DJ (1st trade ed)	125 - 200
MP1510	**Sixteen Cantos of Ezra Pound** Paris 1924, 70 cys	2000 - 3000
MP1511	15 cys, "Whatman" paper	3000 - 5000
MP1512	5 cys, vellum	4000 - 6000
MP1514	Lon 1925 retitled **Cantos I - XVI**	250 - 350
MP1520	**The Spirit of Romance** Lon 1910, DJ	250 - 350
MP1521	NY 1910, DJ (1st American ed)	250 - 350
MP1523	Norfolk 1953, DJ	50 - 75
MP1530	**Thrones** Lon 1960, DJ	75 - 100
MP1531	Norfolk 1959, DJ	30 - 50
MP1540	**Umbra** Lon 1920, DJ, 100 cys	400 - 600
MP1541	Lon 1920, DJ (1st trade ed)	150 - 250
MP1550	**Versi Prosaici** Rome 1959, 30 cys, wrappers	1500 - 2000
MP1551	220 cys, wrappers	700 - 1000

Powell, Anthony
MP1710	**The Acceptance World** Lon 1953, DJ	200 - 300
MP1711	NY 1955, DJ (1st American ed)	100 - 150
MP1720	**Afternoon Men** (1st book) Lon 1931, DJ	700 - 1000
MP1721	NY 1932, DJ (1st American ed)	300 - 500
MP1730	**At Lady Molly's** Lon 1957, DJ	150 - 250
MP1740	**A Buyer's Market** Lon 1952, DJ	150 - 250
MP1741	NY 1953, DJ (1st American ed)	100 - 150
MP1750	**Caledonia: A Fragment** Lon 1934, DJ	300 - 500
MP1760	**Casanova's Chinese Restaurant** Lon 1960, DJ	100 - 150
MP1770	**From a View to a Death** Lon 1933, DJ	300 - 500
MP1780	**The Kindly Ones** Lon 1962, DJ	100 - 150
MP1790	**A Question of Upbringing** Lon 1951, DJ	300 - 500
MP1791	NY 1951, DJ (1st American ed)	100 - 150

Powys, John Cowper
MP1910	**Ballads and Other Poems** (1st book) Lon 1893	250 - 350
MP1920	**Confessions of Two Brothers** Rochester 1916, DJ	150 - 250
MP1930	**Poems** Lon 1899	150 - 250

| MP1940 | **Rodmoor: A Romance** NY 1916, DJ | 200 - 300 |

Powys, Llewellyn
MP2010	**A Baker's Dozen** Herrin, IL 1939, 493 cys, box	200 - 300
MP2020	**Now That The Gods Are Dead** NY 1932, 400 cys	200 - 300
MP2030	**Thirteen Worthies** Lon 1923, DJ	150 - 200

Powys, T. F. (Theodore Francis)
MP2110	**Fables** Lon 1929, 750 cys	200 - 300
MP2111	NY 1929, DJ (1st American ed)	75 - 125
MP2120	**Goat Green, or the Better Gift** Lon 1937, 150 cys, box	200 - 300
MP2121	Lon 1937, wrappers	75 - 125
MP2130	**An Interpretation of Genesis** Lon 1929, 490 cys, DJ, box	200 - 300
MP2131	NY 1929, 260 cys, glassine DJ, box	150 - 250
MP2140	**Soliloquies of a Hermit** Lon 1918, DJ	150 - 200
MP2150	**When Thou Wast Naked** Lon 1931, DJ, 500 cys, box	200 - 300

Price, Reynolds
MP2210	**A Generous Man** NY 1966, DJ	100 - 150
MP2220	**Kate Vaiden** NY 1986, DJ	20 - 30
MP2230	**Late Warning** NY 1968, 176 cys, wrappers	200 - 300
MP2241	**A Long and Happy Life** (1st book) NY 1962, 1st state DJ w/green printing	150 - 200
MP2242	Lon 1962, DJ (1st English ed)	75 - 125
MP2250	**The Names and Faces of Heroes** NY 1963, DJ	75 - 125
MP2260	**One Sunday in Late July** (1st book) 1960, 50 cys, wrappers	2000 - 3000

Priestley, J. B.
MP2410	**Angel Pavement** Lon 1930, 1025 cys	200 - 300
MP2420	**Brief Diversions** Cambridge 1922, DJ	250 - 350
MP2430	**The Chapman of Rhymes** (1st book) Lon 1918, wrappers	300 - 500
MP2440	**Faraway** Lon 1932, DJ	150 - 250
MP2450	**The Town Major of Miraucourt** Lon 1930, 525 cys	200 - 300

Purdy, James
MP3210	**63: Dream Palace** NY 1956, wrappers	200 - 300
MP3220	**A Day After The Fair** NY 1977, DJ	50 - 75
MP3230	**Don't Call Me By My Right Name and Other Stories** (1st book) NY 1956, wrappers	200 - 300
MP3240	**An Oyster is a Wealthy Beast** SF 1967, 50 cys, original drawings	300 - 500
MP3241	SF 1967, 200 cys, wrappers	200 - 300
MP3250	**Proud Flesh** Northridge 1980, 50 cys	150 - 250

Puzo, Mario
MP3510	**The Dark Arena** (1st book) NY 1955, DJ	75 - 125
MP3520	**Fools Die** NY 1978, DJ	25 - 50
MP3530	**The Godfather** NY 1969, DJ	125 - 250

Pyle, Howard (see Artists & Illustrators)

Pym, Barbara
MP3710	**Excellent Women** Lon 1952, DJ	200 - 300
MP3720	**A Glass of Blessings** Lon 1961, DJ	300 - 500
MP3730	**Jane and Prudence** Lon 1953, DJ	125 - 250
MP3740	**Less Than Angels** Lon 1955, DJ	125 - 250
MP3750	**No Fond Return of Love** Lon 1961, DJ	125 - 250
MP3760	**Quartet in Autumn** Lon 1977, DJ	75 - 125
MP3770	**Some Tame Gazelle** (1st book) Lon 1950, DJ	200 - 300

Pynchon, Thomas
| MP4010 | **The Crying of Lot 49** Phil 1966, DJ | 200 - 300 |
| MP4020 | **Gravity's Rainbow** NY 1973, DJ | 300 - 500 |

Queen, Ellery (Frederic Dannay & Manfred Lee)
MQ5000	**The Calendar of Crime** Bos 1952, DJ	50 - 75
MQ5010	**Cat of Many Tails** Bos 1949, DJ	50 - 75
MQ5020	**The Chinese Orange Mystery** NY 1934, DJ	150 - 250
MQ5030	**The Devil to Pay** NY 1938, DJ	150 - 250
MQ5040	**The Dutch Show Mystery** NY 1931, DJ	150 - 250
MQ5050	**The Egyptian Cross Mystery** NY 1932, DJ	150 - 250
MQ5060	**Finishing Stroke** NY 1958, DJ	40 - 60
MQ5070	**The Glass Village** Bos 1954, DJ	50 - 75
MQ5080	**Inspector Queen's Own Case: November Song** NY 1956, DJ	40 - 60
MQ5090	**The King is Dead** Bos 1952, DJ	50 - 75
MQ5100	**The Literature of Crime** Bos 1950, DJ	25 - 50
MQ5110	**The Misadventures of Sherlock Holmes** Bos 1944, DJ	300 - 500
MQ5120	**The Origin of Evil** Bos 1951, DJ	50 - 75
MQ5130	**Rogues' Gallery** (editor) Bos 1945, DJ	50 - 75

MQ5132 Bos 1947, DJ (Sun Dial Press reprint)   30 - 50
MQ5140 **The Roman Hat Mystery** (1st book) NY
1929, DJ   1200 - 1800
MQ5150 **The Spanish Cape Mystery** NY 1932, DJ   150 - 250

Rand, Ayn
MR0060 **Atlas Shrugged** NY 1957, DJ   50 - 75

Rawlings, Marjorie Kinnan
MR1010 **South Moon Under** (1st book) NY 1933, DJ   150 - 250
MR1021 **The Yearling** NY 1938, DJ, 1st state w/Scribner's
seal on cr page   150 - 250
MR1022 NY 1939, DJ, 770 cys, box   300 - 500

Remington, Frederic (see Americana; Artists & Illustrators)

Repplier, Agnes
MR1510 **The Fireside Sphinx** Bos 1901   50 - 75

Rice, Anne
MR2000 **Belinda** NY 1986, DJ   30 - 50
MR2010 **Cry To Heaven** NY 1982, DJ   40 - 60
MR2020 **The Feast of All Saints** NY 1979, DJ   75 - 125
MR2030 **Interview with the Vampire** (1st book) NY
1976, DJ   200 - 300
MR2031 NY 1976, DJ (Book Club ed)   40 - 60
MR2040 **The Mummy** NY 1989, DJ   75 - 125
MR2041 Lon 1989, DJ (1st English ed)   75 - 125
MR2050 **Vampire Lestat** NY 1985, DJ   75 - 125
MR2060 **The Witching Hour** NY 1990, DJ   25 - 50

Richmond, Grace S.
MR2150 **Red Pepper Burns** NY 1911, DJ   50 - 75

Richter, Conrad
MR2210 **Brothers of No Kin** (1st book) NY 1924, white DJ   300 - 500
orange DJ   200 - 300

Riley, James Whitcomb
MR2310 **Afterwhiles** Ind 1888   100 - 150
MR2320 **All The Year Round** Ind 1916, DJ   300 - 500
MR2330 **The Apology** New Castle 1915 (privately printed,
signed)   200 - 300
MR2340 **Armazindy** Ind 1894, Cl   50 - 75
MR2341 red silk   100 - 150
MR2350 **The Baby Book** Ind 1913, glassine DJ, box   400 - 600
MR2360 **The Book of Joyous Children** NY 1902, DJ   75 - 100
MR2370 **The Boys of the Old Glee Club** Ind 1907, DJ   75 - 100
MR2381 **Character Sketches, The Boss Girl, A Christmas
Story, and Other Sketches** Ind 1886, 1st issue
w/exclamation point after "sir" on line 5, p 9   200 - 300
MR2382 2nd issue w/o exclamation point   100 - 150
MR2390 **A Child World** Ind 1897, DJ   50 - 75
MR2400 **A Defective Santa Claus** Ind 1904, DJ   50 - 75
MR2410 **Down Around the River and Other Poems**
Ind 1911, DJ   50 - 75
MR2420 **Early Poems** NY 1914, DJ   50 - 75
MR2430 **Flying Islands of the Night** Ind 1892   50 - 75
MR2432 Ind 1913, DJ (illus ed)   150 - 200
MR2440 **Fugitive Pieces** NY 1914, DJ   50 - 75
MR2450 **Green Fields and Running Brooks** Ind 1893   75 - 100
MR2460 **His Pa's Romance** Ind 1903, DJ   50 - 75
MR2470 **Home Again With Me** Ind 1908, DJ   50 - 75
MR2481 **Home-Folks** Ind 1893, 1st state has repeated
caption on p 59   100 - 150
MR2490 **A Hoosier Romance** 1868 NY 1910, DJ   50 - 75
w/o DJ   15 - 25
MR2500 **Morning** Ind 1907, DJ   50 - 75
MR2510 **Neighborly Poems** Ind 1891, under pseud
Benj. F. Johnston   50 - 100
MR2520 **Nye and Riley's Railway Guide** Chi 1888   30 - 50
MR2530 **Old Fashioned Roses** Lon 1888   50 - 75
MR2531 Ind 1889   20 - 35
MR2540 **Old School Day Romances** Ind 1909, DJ   50 - 75
MR2550 **Old Sweetheart of Mine** Ind 1902, glassine
DJ, box   150 - 200
MR2560 **The Old Swimmin'-Hole and 'Leven More
Poems** Ind 1883, under pseud Benj. F. Johnston   800 - 1200
MR2562 many later facsimile cys were done w/minute
variations   20 - 50
MR2570 **Pipes O' Pan at Zekesbury** Ind 1889   50 - 75
MR2580 **Poems Here at Home** NY 1893   50 - 75
MR2590 **The Prayer Perfect and Other Poems** Ind 1912, DJ   50 - 75
MR2600 **Rhymes of Childhood** Ind 1891, w/child's head
on front cover   50 - 75
MR2610 **Riley Child-Dreams** Ind 1898, DJ   50 - 75

w/o DJ   20 - 30
MR2620 **Riley Farm-Rhymes** Ind 1901, DJ   50 - 75
w/o DJ   20 - 30
MR2640 **Riley Love Lyrics** Ind 1899   50 - 75
MR2642 Ind 1921, DJ   75 - 100
w/o DJ   30 - 50
MR2650 **Riley Songs O'Cheer** Ind 1905, DJ   50 - 75
w/o DJ   15 - 25
MR2660 **Rub'aiy'at of Doc Sifers** NY 1897, 100 cys   200 - 300
MR2661 NY 1897, DJ (1st trade ed)   100 - 150
MR2670 **The Runaway Boy** Ind 1908, DJ   75 - 100
w/o DJ   15 - 25
MR2680 **Sketches in Prose and Occasional Verses** Ind 1891   50 - 75
MR2690 **Songs of Home** Ind 1910, DJ   50 - 75
w/o DJ   15 - 25
MR2700 **A Summer's Day and Other Poems** Ind 1911, DJ   50 - 75
MR2710 **While The Heart Beats Young** Ind 1906, DJ   50 - 75
w/o DJ   15 - 25

Robbins, Harold
MR2910 **The Dream Merchants** NY 1949, DJ   30 - 50

Roberts, Elizabeth Madox
MR3010 **A Buried Treasure** NY 1931, 200 cys, box   100 - 150
MR3011 NY 1931, DJ (1st trade ed)   20 - 30
MR3020 **The Great Meadow** NY 1930, 295 cys   100 - 150
MR3021 NY 1931, DJ (1st trade ed)   15 - 25
MR3030 **In The Great Steep's Garden** (1st book)
Colorado Springs 1905, DJ, wrappers   2000 - 3000
MR3040 **My Heart and My Flesh** NY 1927, DJ   75 - 125
MR3051 **The Time of Man** NY 1926, DJ, 1st state
w/title printed in blue   75 - 125
MR3060 **Under the Tree** NY 1922, DJ   150 - 250

Roberts, Kenneth
MR3210 **Arundel** NY 1930, DJ   50 - 75
MR3220 **Europes Morning After** NY 1921, DJ   150 - 250
MR3230 **Lydia Bailey** NY 1947, 1050 cys, box   100 - 150
MR3231 NY 1947, DJ (1st trade ed)   15 - 25
MR3240 **Northwest Passage** NY 1937, 1050 cys, box   200 - 300
MR3241 NY 1937, DJ (1st trade ed)   50 - 75
MR3250 **Oliver Wiswell** NY 1940, 1050 cys, box   100 - 150
MR3251 NY 1940, DJ (1st trade ed)   15 - 25
MR3260 **Panatela** (1st book) Ithaca 1907, wrappers   250 - 350
MR3270 **Sun Hunting** Ind 1922, DJ   100 - 150
MR3280 **Trending Into Maine** Bos 1938, 1075 cys,
slipcase (illus by Wyeth)   300 - 500

Robinson, Edwin Arlington
MR3410 **Avon's Harvest** NY 1921, DJ   75 - 125
MR3420 **Captain Craig** Bos 1902, 125 cys   200 - 300
MR3430 **Cavender's House** NY 1929, 500 cys, box   100 - 150
MR3440 **The Children of the Night** Bos 1897, 500 cys   500 - 700
MR3441 50 cys, vellum   2000 - 3000
MR3450 **Dionysius in Doubt** NY 1925, 350 cys, box   150 - 250
MR3451 NY 1925, DJ (1st trade ed)   50 - 75
MR3460 **Lancelot** NY 1920, 450 cys, box   200 - 300
MR3471 **The Man Against the Sky** NY 1916, DJ,
1st state w/gold top edge   125 - 2000
MR3480 **The Man Who Died Twice** NY 1924,
500 cys, box   100 - 150
MR3481 NY 1924, DJ (1st trade ed)   50 - 75
MR3491 **Merlin** NY 1917, DJ, 1st issue reads "with only
philosophy" on line 8, p 79   150 - 250
MR3501 **The Porcupine** NY 1915, DJ, 1st state w/gold
top edge, errata slip   150 - 250
MR3510 **Roman Bartholow** NY 1923, 750 cys, box   100 - 150

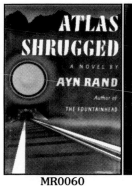

MR0060   MR2010   MR2150 (w/o DJ)

MR2910	MR5510	MS0711

MR3520 **The Three Taverns** NY 1920, DJ   100 - 150
MR3531 **Tristram** NY 1927, DJ, 1st issue reads "rocks"
     for "rooks" p 86   150 - 250
MR3532   NY 1927, 350 cys, box   200 - 300
MR3540 **The Torrent and the Night Before** (1st book)
     Gardiner 1896, blue wrappers   2000 - 3000
MR3542   NY 1928, 110 cys, slipcase   250 - 350
MR3550 **Van Zorn** NY 1914, DJ   100 - 150

Roethke, Theodore
MR3740 **Open House** (1st book) NY 1941, 1000 cys, DJ   700 - 1000
MR3750 **Sequence Sometimes Metaphysical** Iowa City
     1963, 330 cys, box   150 - 250
MR3760 **Words For The Wind** Lon 1957, DJ   100 - 150
MR3761   NY 1958, DJ (1st American ed)   75 - 125

Rossner, Judith
MR3910 **Looking For Mr. Goodbar** NY 1975, DJ   30 - 50

Roth, Philip
MR4010 **Goodbye, Columbus** (1st book) Bos 1959, DJ   200 - 300
MR4011   Lon 1959, DJ (1st English ed)   75 - 125
MR4020 **On The Air** NY 1970, 1500 cys, wrappers   125 - 250
MR4030 **Portnoy's Complaint** NY 1969, 600 cys, DJ, box   125 - 250

Ruark, Robert C.
MR5010 **Grenadine Etching** (1st book) NY 1947, DJ   75 - 125
MR5020 **Grenadine's Spawn** NY 1952, DJ   75 - 125
MR5030 **Horn of the Hunter** Garden City 1953, DJ   100 - 175
MR5040 **The Old Man's Boy Grows Older** NY 1961, DJ   50 - 75

Runyon, Damon
MR5210 **The Tents of Trouble** (1st book) NY 1911, DJ   75 - 125

Russell, Charles M. (see Americana)

Russo, Richard
MR5510 **Mohawk** (1st book) NY 1986, wrappers   20 - 30

Sadleir, Michael
MS0110 **Fanny by Gaslight** Lon 1940, DJ   200 - 300
MS0120 **Hyssop** (1st novel) Lon 1915, DJ   75 - 125
MS0130 **XIX Century Fiction** Cambridge 1951, 2 vol,
     1025 cys   300 - 500

Saint-Exupéry, Antoine de
MS0210 **The Little Prince** NY 1943, DJ, 525 cys   250 - 350
MS0211   NY 1943, DJ (1st trade ed)   50 - 75
MS0220 **Night Flight** (1st book) Paris 1932, wrappers   100 - 150
MS0221   NY 1932, DJ (1st American ed)   75 - 125
MS0230 **Wind, Sand and Stars** NY 1939, 500 cys, box   200 - 300

Saki (H. H. Munro)
MS0310 **Beasts and Super Beasts** Lon 1914   150 - 250
MS0320 **Reginald** Lon 1904   100 - 150
MS0330 **The Westminster Alice** (1st book) Lon 1902,
     wrappers   200 - 300

Salinger, J. D.
MS0411 **The Catcher in the Rye** (1st book) Bos 1951,
     1st state DJ w/o pub slug   700 - 1000
MS0420 **The Kit Book for Soldiers, Sailors, and Marines**
     Chi 1942, includes story "The Hang of It"   100 - 150
MS0430 **Nine Stories** Bos 1953, DJ   300 - 500
MS0441 **Raise High the Roof Beam** Bos 1959, DJ,
     1st issue w/o dedication   300 - 500
MS0442   2nd issue w/dedication page tipped in   75 - 125

Salten, Felix
MS0610 **Bambi** Berlin 1923   1500 - 2500
MS0612   NY 1928, DJ (1st American ed)   200 - 300

Sampson, Joan
MS0710 **The Auctioneer** NY 1976, DJ   40 - 60

MS0711   NY 1976 (advance review cy)   100 - 150

Sandburg, Carl (also see Americana)
MS0910 **Always the Young Strangers** NY 1953,
     600 cys, box   150 - 200
MS0920 **The American Songbag** NY 1927, DJ   75 - 125
MS0931 **Chicago Poems** (1st book) NY 1916, DJ,
     1st state w/ads dated "Mar. 1916"   200 - 300
MS0941 **Cornhuskers** NY 1918, DJ, 1st state w/p 3
     correctly numbered   200 - 300
MS0950 **Early Moon** NY 1930, DJ   150 - 250
MS0960 **Good Morning, America** NY 1928, DJ   75 - 125
MS0970 **In Reckless Ecstasy** (1st book) Galesburg
     1904, pamphlet   7000 - 10000
MS0980 **M'Liss and Louie** LA 1929, 125 cys   250 - 350
MS0990 **The People, Yes** NY 1936, 270 cys, slipcase   250 - 350
MS0991   NY 1936, DJ (1st trade ed)   75 - 125
MS1000 **Poems of the Midwest** Clev 1946, 950 cys, box   125 - 250
MS1010 **Potato Face** NY 1930, DJ   150 - 250
MS1020 **Remembrance Rock** NY 1948, DJ   75 - 125
MS1030 **Rootabaga Pigeons** NY 1923, DJ   200 - 300
MS1040 **Rootabaga Stories** NY 1932, DJ   125 - 250
MS1051 **Slabs of the Sunburnt West** NY 1922, DJ,
     1st issue w/test ending at bottom of P 75   300 - 500
MS1060 **Smoke and Steel** NY 1920, DJ   250 - 350
MS1070 **Steichen, The Photographer** NY 1929,
     925 cys, box   300 - 500

Sandoz, Mari (see Americana)

Saroyan, William
MS1210 **The Beautiful People** NY 1941, DJ   150 - 250
MS1220 **The Darling Young Man** (1st book)   200 - 300
MS1230 **My Name is Aram** NY 1940, DJ   25 - 50

Sassoon, Siegfried
MS1410 **The Counter Attack** Lon 1917, wrappers   250 - 350
MS1420 **The Heart's Journey** NY 1927, 590 cys, DJ   200 - 300
MS1430 **Lingual Exercizes for Advanced Vocabularians:**
     Poems Cambridge 1925, 99 cys   300 - 500
MS1440 **Memoirs of a Fox Hunting Man** Lon 1929, DJ,
     300 cys   150 - 250
MS1450 **Poems** (1st book) Lon 1906, 50 cys, wrappers   2000 - 3000

Sayers, Dorothy L.
MS1610 **In the Teeth of the Evidence and Other Stories**
     NY 1940, DJ   50 - 75
MS1620 **The Nine Tailors** NY 1934, DJ   100 - 150
MS1631 **Whose Body?** (1st book) NY 1923, 1st issue
     w/o "Inc" after publisher   1200 - 1800

Schaefer, Jack
MS1810 **Monte Walsh** Bos 1963, DJ   150 - 250
MS1820 **Shane** (1st book) Bos 1949, DJ   700 - 1000
MS1821   Lon 1963, DJ (1st English ed)   50 - 75

Schmitz, James H.
MS1910 **A Nice Day For Screaming** Phil 1965, DJ   150 - 250
MS1920 **A Tale of Two Clocks** NY 1962, DJ   150 - 250

Schulberg, Budd
MS2010 **The Harder They Fall** NY 1947, DJ   75 - 125

Schulkers, Robert (see Seckatary Hawkins)

Scott, Paul
MS2100 **The Alien Sky** Lon 1953, DJ   100 - 150
MS2110 **The Jewel in the Crown** Lon 1966, DJ   100 - 150
MS2120 **Johnny Sahib** (1st book) Lon 1952, DJ   200 - 300
MS2130 **A Male Child** Lon 1956, DJ   150 - 250
MS2140 **The Mark of the Warrior** Lon 1958, DJ   75 - 125
MS2150 **Staying On** Lon 1977, DJ   75 - 125

Seckatary Hawkins (Robert Schulkers)
The pseudonym for Robert Schulkers, Seckatary Hawkins is the name of the main protagonist for juvenile stories about a boys' club and its adventures. These stories were syndicated by newspapers and became a very popular comic strip in the 1920s and 1930s. A few titles were published as juvenile novels in the 1920s-1940s. Over the past 15 years the books have become highly collectible along with Seckatary Hawkins toys, games, tokens, buttons, and advertising. For copies signed "Seckatary Hawkins" add $75-100.

MS2410 **Adventures in Cuba or The Casanova Treasure**
     (Stewart Kidd) Cinti 1921, DJ   200 - 350
     w/o DJ   75 - 125
MS2420 **The Cazanova Treasure** (Seckatary Hawkins Co.)
     Cinti 1948, DJ   20 - 30
MS2430 **The Chinese Coin** (Robert Schulkers Pub) Cinti
     1926, DJ   175 - 250

	w/o DJ	50 - 75
MS2440	**The Ching Toy** (Robert Schulkers Pub) Cinti 1926, DJ	175 - 250
	w/o DJ	50 - 75
MS2450	**The Ghost of Lake Tapaho** (Ralston Purina premium, probably the rarest book) 1930s, wrappers	300 - 500
MS2460	**The Gray Ghost** (Robert Schulkers Pub) Cinti 1926, DJ	175 - 250
	w/o DJ	50 - 75
MS2470	**The Grey Ghost** (Robert Schulkers Pub) Cinti 1950, DJ	20 - 30
MS2480	**Herman the Fiddler or The Mystery of the Three-Eyed Ape** (Robert Schulkers Pub) Cinti 1930	75 - 125
MS2490	**Knights of the Square Table** (Robert Schulkers Pub) Cinti 1926, DJ	175-250
	w/o DJ	50 - 75
MS2500	**The Red Runners** (Stewart Kidd Co.) Cinti 1922, DJ	200 - 300
	w/o DJ	75 - 125
MS2501	(Robert Schulkers Pub) Cinti 1930, DJ	175 - 250
	w/o DJ	50 - 75
MS2503	(Robert Schulkers Pub) Cinti 1950, DJ, yellow-brown cl stamped in brown	20 - 30
MS2510	**Seckatary Hawkins in Cuba** (D. Appleton & Co.) NY 1925, DJ	100 - 150
	yellow ribbed cl stamped in black, w/o DJ	40 - 60
MS2511	(D. Appleton & Co.) NY 1925, DJ	75 - 125
	orange cl stamped in black, w/o DJ	30 - 50
MS2520	**Stoner's Boy** (Robert Schulkers Pub) Cinti 1926, DJ	175 - 250
	w/o DJ	50 - 75
MS2522	(Seckatary Hawkins Co.) Cinti 1948, DJ	20 - 30
MS2530	**Stormie the Dog Stealer** (D. Appleton & Co.) NY 1925, DJ	300 - 500
	w/o DJ	200 - 350
MS2560	**The Yellow Y** (Robert Schulkers Pub) Cinti 1926, DJ	175-250
	w/o DJ	50 - 75

Service, Robert W.

| MS3110 | **Ballads of a Bohemian** NY 1921, DJ | 50 - 75 |

Seton, Ernest Thompson

MS3130	**Monarch the Big Bear** NY 1904	50 - 75
MS3140	**The Trail of the Sandhill Stag** NY 1910	50 - 75
MS3150	**The Wild Animal Play** Phil 1900	100 - 150

Settle, Mary Lee

| MS3210 | **Know Nothing** NY 1960, DJ | 75 - 100 |

Sexton, Anne

| MS3310 | **To Bedlam and Part Way Back** (1st book) Bos 1960, DJ | 125 - 175 |

Shaara, Michael

| MS3410 | **The Broken Place** (1st book) NY 1968, DJ | 75 - 100 |
| MS3420 | **The Killer Angels** NY 1975, DJ | 25 - 50 |

Sillitoe, Alan

MS3510	**The Loneliness of the Long Distance Runner** Lon 1958, DJ	125 - 250
MS3520	**Saturday Night and Sunday Morning** Lon 1958, DJ	100 - 150
MS3530	**Without Beer or Bread** (1st book) Dulwich Village 1957, wrappers	300 - 500

Simak, Clifford D.

| MS3710 | **City** NY 1952, DJ | 300 - 500 |
| MS3720 | **Way Station** NY 1963, DJ | 200 - 300 |

Simpson, Mona

| MS3910 | **Anywhere But Here** NY 1987, DJ | 40 - 60 |

Sinclair, Upton

MS4010	**Dragon's Teeth** NY 1942, DJ	50 - 75
MS4021	**The Jungle** NY 1906, DJ, 1st issue w/"Doubleday" imprint on tp	200 - 300
MS4030	**Saved by the Enemy** (1st book) NY 1898	150 - 200

Smith, E. E.

| MS4210 | **The Skylark of Space** (1st book) Prov 1946, DJ | 200 - 300 |
| MS4211 | Prov 1947, DJ | 100 - 150 |

Smith, Ernest Braman (see Ernest Bramah)

Smith, Thorne

| MS4310 | **Topper** NY 1926, DJ | 600 - 800 |
| | w/o DJ | 75 - 125 |

Solzhenitsyn, Alekandr (1970 Nobel Laureate)

MS4410	**August 1914** NY 1987, 200 cys, slipcase	200 - 300
MS4420	**The Gulag Archipelago** 1918-1956 NY 1974, DJ	30 - 50
MS4430	**One Day in the Life of Ivan Denisovich** Lon 1963, DJ	100 - 150
MS4431	NY 1963, DJ (1st American ed)	50 - 75

Spark, Muriel

MS4710	**The Bachelors** Lon 1960, DJ	75 - 125
MS4720	**Child of Light** Essex 1951, DJ	125 - 250
MS4730	**The Comforters** Lon 1957, DJ	100 - 150
MS4740	**The Fan Farlo** Kent 1952, wrappers	100 - 150
MS4750	**Memento Mori** Lon 1959, DJ	75 - 125
MS4760	**The Prime of Miss Jean Brodie** Lon 1961, DJ	125 - 250
MS4770	**Robinson** Lon 1958, DJ	75 - 125
MS4780	**The Seraph and the Zambesi** Phil 1960, DJ	75 - 125
MS4790	**Tribute to Wordsworth** (1st book) Lon 1950, DJ	100 - 150

Spicer, Jack

MS4910	**After Lorca** (1st book) SF 1957, 26 cys, wrappers	300 - 500
MS4911	474 cys, wrappers	75 - 125
MS4920	**Lament for the Makers** Oakland 1962, 100 cys	200 - 300

Spillane, Mickey

MS5010	**The Big Kill** NY 1951, DJ	75 - 125
MS5020	**Day of the Guns** NY 1964, DJ	30 - 50
MS5030	**The Delta Factor** NY 1967, DJ	30 - 50
MS5040	**The Girl Hunters** NY 1962, DJ	30 - 50
MS5050	**I, the Jury** (1st book) NY 1947, DJ	200 - 300
MS5060	**My Gun is Quick** NY 1950, DJ	75 - 125
MS5070	**The Snake** NY 1964, DJ	30 - 50
MS5080	**Vengeance is Mine!** NY 1950, DJ	100 - 150

Stafford, William

MS5210	**Down in My Heart** (1st book) Elgin 1947, DJ	800 - 1200
MS5220	**Eleven Untitled Poems** Mt. Horeb 1968, 250 cys, wrappers, DJ	125 - 250
MS5230	**The Quiet of the Land** NY 1979, 26 cys, wrappers	200 - 300
MS5240	**Traveling Through the Dark** NY 1962, DJ	75 - 125
MS5250	**Weather** Mt. Horeb 1969, 207 cys, wrappers, DJ	125 - 200
MS5260	**West of Your City** Los Gatos 1960, cl	400 - 600
	wrappers	200 - 300

Stallone, Sylvester

| MS5410 | **Paradise Alley** (1st book) NY 1977, DJ | 30 - 50 |

Stein, Gertrude

MS5510	**Absolutely Bob Brown or Bobbed Brown** Pawlet 1955, 52 cys, envelope	400 - 600
MS5520	**An Acquaintance with Description** Lon 1929, 225 cys, glassine DJ	700 - 1000
MS5530	**Before the Flowers of Friendship Faded Friendship Faded** Paris 1931, 120 cys, DJ	800 - 1200

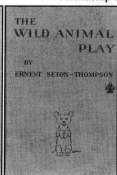

| MS2460 | MS3130 | MS3140 | MS3150 | MS3710 | MS3910 |

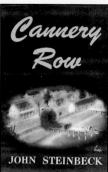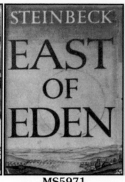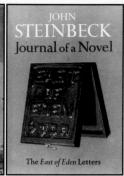

MS4310 (w/o DJ)	MS5901	MS5941

MS5971	MS6081	MS6180

MS5540 **Blood on the Dining Room Floor** NY 1948,
626 cys, slipcase — 250 - 350

MS5550 **A Book Concluding with As a Wife Has a
Cow: A Love Story** Paris 1926, 102 cys, DJ 2000 - 3500

MS5560 **Dix Portraits** Paris 1930, 400 cys, glassine DJ 300 - 400

MS5561 65 cys, DJ — 900 - 1200

MS5562 25 cys, glassine DJ — 2000 - 3000

MS5563 10 cys, glassine DJ — 7000 - 10000

MS5570 **Four Saints in Three Acts** NY 1934, DJ — 100 - 150

MS5580 **Have They Attacked Mary, He Giggled**
West Chester 1917, 200 cys, wrappers — 700 - 1000

MS5590 **How To Write** Paris 1931, 1000 cys, tissue DJ — 20 - 30

MS5600 **Matisse, Picasso, and Gertrude Stein with Two
Shorter Stories** Paris 1933, 500 cys, glassine
DJ, box — 400 - 600

MS5610 **Morceaux Choisis de la Fabrication des
Americains** Paris 1929, 400 cys, glassine DJ — 300 - 500

MS5611 85 cys, glassine DJ — 800 - 1200

MS5620 **Operas and Plays** Paris 1932, 500 cys, slipcase 700 - 1000

MS5630 **Portraits and Prayers** NY 1934, DJ — 400 - 600

MS5640 **Tender Buttons, Objects, Food, Rooms**
NY 1914, DJ — 300 - 500

MS5650 **Things As They Are: A Novel in Three Parts**
Pawlet 1950, 516 cys — 250 - 350

MS5651 Pawlet 1950, 26 cys — 700 - 1000

MS5660 **Three Lives** (1st book) NY 1909, 1000 cys — 1000 - 1500

MS5662 Lon 1915, 300 cys — 400 - 600

MS5663 Lon 1920, DJ (1st trade ed) — 250 - 350

MS5670 **Useful Knowledge** NY 1928, DJ — 250 - 350

MS5671 Lon 1928, DJ — 150 - 250

MS5680 **A Village Are You Ready Yet Not Yet**
Paris 1928, 102 copies, glassine DJ — 1000 - 1500

MS5681 10 cys, vellum — 2000 - 3000

MS5690 **The World Is Round** NY 1939, 350 cys, box 1000 - 1500

MS5691 NY 1939, DJ (1st trade ed) — 150 - 250

MS5692 Lon 1939, DJ — 150 - 250

Steinbeck, John (1962 Nobel Laureate)

MS5850 **America and Americans** NY 1966, DJ — 100 - 150

MS5870 **Bombs Away** NY 1942, DJ — 200 - 300

MS5880 **Burning Bright** NY 1950, DJ — 150 - 200

MS5881 Lon 1951 — 50 - 75

MS5901 **Cannery Row** NY 1945, DJ, 1st state, light
buff cloth — 300 - 500

MS5902 2nd state, yellow cloth — 100 - 150

MS5903 NY 1945 (advance review cy), blue wraps — 400 - 600

MS5904 Lon 1945, DJ — 150 - 200

MS5930 **The Collected Poems** NY 1976, 250 cys, DJ 100 - 150

MS5941 **Cup of Gold** (1st book) NY 1929, DJ, 1st state
w/top edge stained blue & "August, 1929" on
cr page — 5000 - 7000

MS5942 2nd state w/unstained top edge — 2000 - 3000

MS5943 NY 1936, DJ, top edge stained blue, maroon cloth 200 - 300

MS5944 NY 1936, blue cloth w/o publisher's name
on DJ spine — 200 - 300

MS5946 Lon 1937, DJ, blue cloth w/Heinemann
"windmill" on back cover — 2000 - 3000

MS5970 **East of Eden** NY 1952, 1500 cys, glassine
DJ, box — 700 - 1000

MS5971 NY 1952, DJ (1st trade ed) w/"Sept. 1952" on cr page 200 - 300

MS5972 Lon 1952, DJ — 200 - 300

MS5990 **El Galiban** Salinas 1919, high school yearbook
w/Steinbeck's contributions as editor — 2000 - 3000

MS6000 **The First Watch** NY 1947, 60 cys, envelope 2000 - 2500

MS6010 **Flight** Covelo 1984, 250 cys, slipcase — 300 - 500

MS6021 **The Forgotten Village** NY 1941, 1st issue
w/"May, 1941" on cr page, DJ — 50 - 75

MS6022 NY 1941 (Book League ed) — 20 - 30

MS6031 **The Grapes of Wrath** NY 1939, 1st state
w/yellow top edge, "April 1939" on cr
page & 1st ed notice on DJ flap — 1000 - 1500

signed — 3000 - 5000

MS6032 NY 1939 salesman's sample — 2000 - 3000

MS6033 Lon 1939, DJ (1st English ed) — 150 - 200

MS6035 NY 1940, 2 vol, box — 150 - 200

MS6036 NY 1939, later printings & later state DJs — 20 - 50

MS6050 **How Edith McGillicuddy Met RLS** Clev 1943,
152 cys — 2000 - 3000

MS6060 **In Dubious Battle** NY 1936, DJ, 99 cys, tissue
DJ, box — 3000 - 5000

MS6061 NY 1936, DJ (1st trade ed) yellow cl, "Pub.
Oct 1936" on cr page — 700 - 1000

MS6062 NY 1936, 2nd trade ed w/"Second Printing"
on DJ spine — 200 - 300

MS6063 Lon 1936, pub May, 1936, blue cl, DJ — 200 - 400

MS6064 Toronto 1936, DJ — 200 - 300

MS6065 NY 1937, DJ (Blue Ribbon reprint) — 150 - 200

MS6067 NY 1939, DJ (Modern Library ed) — 20 - 30

MS6080 **Journal of a Novel** NY 1969, 1000 cys — 150 - 250

MS6081 NY 1969, DJ (1st trade ed) — 50 - 75

MS6090 **A Letter From John Steinbeck** NY 1964,
orange wraps — 300 - 500

MS6100 **A Letter of Inspiration** West Covina 1980, 100 cys 50 - 75

MS6110 **Letters to Elizabeth** SF 1978, 500 cys, DJ — 200 - 300

MS6120 **The Log From the Sea of Cortez** NY 1951,
DJ "Pub. Sept. 1951" on cr page — 300 - 500

MS6121 Lon 1958, DJ — 200 - 300

MS6130 **The Long Valley** NY 1938, DJ, "Pub. Sept.
1938" on cr page, top edge stained red — 300 - 500

MS6131 Lon 1939, DJ — 75 - 100

MS6140 **Molly Morgan** Chi 1961, wrappers — 25 - 50

MS6150 **The Moon is Down** NY 1942, DJ, blue cl — 150 - 200

MS6151 NY 1942 (advance review ed) — 250 - 350

MS6152 NY 1942, 700 cys, wrappers — 200 - 400

MS6153 NY 1942 (play ed) wrappers — 200 - 400

MS6160 **Nothing So Monstrous** NY 1936, pub. Dec.
1936, 370 cys, tissue DJ — 700 - 1000

MS6171 **Of Mice and Men** NY 1937, DJ, 1st issue w/beige
cloth, top edge stained blue, pub "Feb, 1937" on
cr page, "and only moved because the heavy
hands were Pendula" on line 20, p 9 — 1500 - 2500

MS6172 NY 1937, DJ, 2nd issue w/o above words on line
20, p 9 & "bullet" removed from page # on p 88 300 - 500

MS6173 NY 1937 (advance review ed) 300 cys
w/review slip — 2000 - 3000

MS6174 NY 1937 salesman's sample (dummy)
w/shortened text, DJ? — 700 - 1000

MS6175 Lon 1937, DJ, "Pub. Sept. 1937" on cr page — 400 - 600

MS6176 NY 1937, DJ (BOMC ed) — 20 - 30

MS6177 NY 1938, DJ (Modern Library ed) — 30 - 40

MS6178 NY 1939, DJ (Sun Dial Press) — 20 - 30

MS6179 Paris 1947, DJ — 75 - 100

MS6180 NY 1947, DJ (World Pub. Co.) — 20 - 30

MS6181 NY 1958 (Bantam Paperback 1st printing) — 30 - 40

MS6182 NY 1970 (Limited Editions Club) 1500 cys,
glassine DJ, box — 150 - 200

MS6183 NY 1937 (play ed) beige cl, DJ — 300 - 500

MS6190 **Once There Was a War** NY 1958, DJ, pub
"Sept.1958" on cr page, top edge stained red — 200 - 300

MS6191	Lon 1959, DJ	50 - 75
MS6201	**The Pastures of Heaven** NY 1932, 1st state, "Pub. Oct. 1932" on cr page, DJ printed in blue, top edge stained black	1500 - 2500
MS6202	NY 1932, DJ, 2nd state pub by Robert Ballou	800 - 1200
MS6203	NY 1932, DJ, 3rd state w/tipped in title page	700 - 1000
MS6204	NY 1935, DJ, 4th state w/tan cl, top edge stained green	800 - 1200
MS6205	Clev 1946, DJ (Tower Books ed)	20 - 40
MS6206	NY 1963, DJ	20 - 30
MS6221	**The Pearl** NY 1947, DJ, "Pub. Nov. 1947" on cr page, brown cl w/top edge stained green, 1st state DJ w/Steinbeck looking left	200 - 300
MS6222	2nd state DJ w/Steinbeck looking right	150 - 200
MS6223	Lon 1948, DJ	30 - 40
MS6224	Toronto 1947, DJ	100 - 150
MS6240	**Pipe Dream** NY 1956, DJ, play from novel "Sweet Thursday"	20 - 40
MS6250	**The Red Pony** NY 1937, 699 cys, cellophane DJ, box	700 - 1000
MS6251	Toronto 1937, DJ	300 - 500
MS6252	NY 1945 (1st illustrated ed) beige cl, slipcase	50 - 75
MS6253	NY 1945 (BOMC ed) slipcase	15 - 25
MS6260	**A Russian Journal** NY 1948, DJ, pub "April 1948" on cr page w/top edge stained blue	100 - 150
MS6270	**Saint Katy the Virgin** NY 1936, 199 cys, glassine DJ	2000 - 3000
MS6280	**Sea of Cortez** NY 1941, DJ	300 - 400
MS6290	**The Short Reign of Pippin IV** NY 1957, DJ	100 - 150
MS6310	**Sweet Thursday** NY 1954, DJ	150 - 200
MS6311	Lon 1954, DJ	50 - 75
MS6320	**Their Blood Is Strong** SF 1938, wrappers	400 - 600
MS6321	SF 1938, 2nd printing	75 - 100
MS6331	**To a God Unknown** NY 1933, DJ, 1st issue w/Robert Ballou imprint DJ	1000 - 1500
MS6332	2nd issue w/Covici-Friede imprint	300 - 500
MS6340	**Tortilla Flat** NY 1935, DJ	800 - 1200
MS6341	NY 1935, wrappers (advance review cy)	1500 - 2000
MS6342	Lon 1935, DJ	1000 - 1500
MS6360	**Vanderbilt Clinic** NY 1947, wrappers	200 - 300
MS6370	**The Wayward Bus** NY 1947, DJ	100 - 150
MS6371	Lon 1947, DJ	50 - 75
MS6390	**The Winter of Our Discontent** NY 1961, "Pub. in 1961" on cr page, DJ	75 - 100
MS6391	NY 1961, 500 cys, acetate DJ	200 - 300
MS6392	Lon 1961, DJ	50 - 75

Stoker, Bram

MS6501	**Dracula** Lon 1897, 1st state w/o ads	8000 - 12000
MS6502	2nd state w/ads	3000 - 5000
MS6503	NY 1899 (1st American ed)	300 - 500
MS6505	NY 1965 (Limited Ed. Club reprint) box	150 - 200
MS6510	**The Lady of the Shroud** Lon 1909	200 - 300
MS6520	**The Mystery of the Sea** Lon 1902	200 - 300

Stoll, Clifford

MS6610	**The Cuckoo's Egg** NY, October 1989, DJ	30 - 50

Stone, Irving

MS6710	**Pageant of Youth** (1st book) NY 1933, DJ	50 - 75

Stone, Robert

MS6810	**Children of Light** Lon 1986, DJ	50 - 75
MS6811	NY 1986, DJ (1st American ed)	30 - 50
MS6820	**Dog Soldiers** Bos 1974, DJ	75 - 125
MS6830	**A Flag For Sunrise** NY 1981, DJ	50 - 75
MS6840	**A Hall of Mirrors** (1st book) Bos 1967, DJ	300 - 500

Stoppard, Tom

MS7010	**Lord Malquist and Mr. Moon** (1st book) Lon 1966, DJ	125 - 250
MS7020	NY 1968, DJ (1st American ed)	50 - 75

Storey, David

MS7110	**Flight into Camden** Lon 1960, DJ	100 - 150
MS7120	**This Sporting Life** (1st book) Lon 1960, DJ	200 - 300

Stout, Rex

Main character is Nero Wolfe; Triangle Books reprints in DJs are worth about $15-25.

MS7210	**Alphabet Hicks** NY 1941, DJ	100 - 150
MS7220	**And Four To Go** NY 1958, DJ	25 - 50
MS7230	**Black Orchids** NY 1942, DJ	150 - 250
MS7231	Lon 1943, DJ (1st English ed)	100 - 150
MS7240	**Corsage: A Bouquet of Rex Stout and Nero Wolfe** Bloomington 1977, 26 cys, DJ	200 - 300
MS7250	**The Doorbell Rang** NY 1965, DJ	25 - 50
MS7260	**Fer-De-Lance** NY 1934, DJ	200 - 300
MS7270	**The Final Deduction** NY 1961, DJ	25 - 50
MS7280	**The Golden Spiders** NY 1953, DJ	50 - 75
MS7281	Lon 1954, DJ (1st English ed)	25 - 50
MS7290	**How Like a God** (1st book) NY 1929, DJ	300 - 500
MS7300	**Mountain Cat** NY 1939, DJ	150 - 250
MS7310	**The Red Box** NY 1937, DJ	150 - 250
MS7311	Lon 1937, DJ (1st English ed)	100 - 150
MS7320	**Some Buried Caesar** NY 1939, DJ	150 - 250
MS7330	**Three Men Out** NY 1954, DJ	25 - 50
MS7340	**Triple Jeopardy** NY 1951, DJ	50 - 75

Stratton-Porter, Gene (see Porter, Gene Stratton)

Straub, Peter

MS7510	**Ishmael** (1st book) Lon 1972, 100 cys, wrappers, DJ	200 - 300

Stuart, Ian (Alastair MacLean)

MS7610	**The Satan Bug** Lon 1962, DJ	50 - 75
MS7611	NY 1962, DJ	40 - 60

Stuart, Jesse

The most widely known and collectible Appalachian writer, his books are frequently signed with interesting anecdotes. Authored about 50 novels and children's books; most first editions are $50-125.

MS7900	**Beyond the Dark Hills** NY 1938, DJ	250 - 350
MS7902	NY 1972, 950 cys, box	75 - 125
MS7910	**Come Gentle Spring** NY 1969, DJ	50 - 75
MS7920	**Daughter of the Legend** NY 1965, DJ	40 - 60
MS7930	**Foretaste of Glory** NY 1946, DJ	150 - 250
MS7940	**Harvest of Youth** (1st book) Howe, OK 1930, DJ	2000 - 3000
MS7950	**Man with the Bull Tongue Plow** NY 1934, DJ	500 - 700
MS7960	**Mongrel Mettle** NY 1944, DJ	150 - 250
MS7970	**Mr. Gallion's School** NY 1967, DJ	50 - 75
MS7980	**My World** Lexington 1975	15 - 25
MS7990	**Taps For Private Tussie** NY 1943, DJ	100 - 150
MS8000	NY 1943, DJ (BOMC reprint)	15 - 25
MS8010	**The Thread That Runs So True** NY 1950, DJ	75 - 125
MS8020	**To Teach To Love** NY 1970, DJ	30 - 50
MS8030	**Tree of Heaven** NY 1940, DJ	150 - 250

Stuart, W. J.

MS8310	**Forbidden Planet** NY 1956, DJ	150 - 250

Sturgeon, Theodore

MS8410	**Without Sorcery** (1st book) Phil 1948, 88 large paper cys	600 - 800
MS8411	Phil 1948, DJ (1st trade ed)	150 - 250

Styron, William

MS8510	**The Confessions of Nat Turner** NY 1967, DJ	75 - 125

MS6260

MS6290

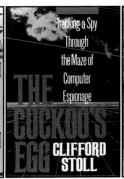

MS6610

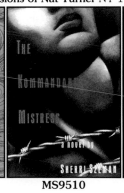

MS7920

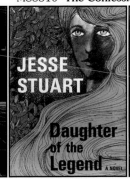

MS9510

MT1210

MT2110

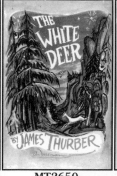
MT2650

MT2660

MT30??

MT3010

MT3021

MT3031 (w/o DJ)

MT3070

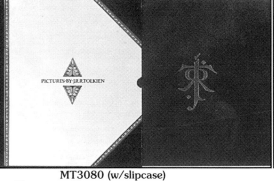
MT3080 (w/slipcase)

MT3102

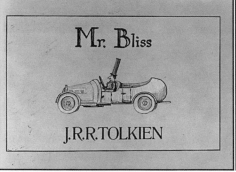
MT3120 MT3140 MT3141

MS8520	In the Clap Shack NY 1973, DJ	100 - 150
MS8530	Lie Down in Darkness (1st book) Ind 1951, DJ	200 - 300
MS8540	Shadrach LA 1979, 26 cys	300 - 500
MS8550	Sophies Choice NY 1976, 500 cys, box	150 - 250
MS8551	NY 1976, DJ (1st trade ed)	30 - 50
MS8560	This Quiet Dust NY 1982, 250 cys, slipcase	125 - 200

Swift, Graham

MS9010	Shuttlecock Lon 1981, DJ	200 - 300
MS9020	The Sweet Shop Owner (1st book) Lon 1980, DJ	200 - 300

Szeman, Sherri

MS9510	The Kommandant's Mistress (1st book) NY 1993, DJ	20 - 30

Tarkington, Booth

MT1011	Alice Adams NY 1921, DJ, 1st state w/"I can't see you why etc" line 14, p 419	150 - 250
MT1020	Beasley's Christmas Party NY 1909, DJ	100 - 150
MT1030	Cherry NY 1903, DJ	100 - 150
MT1041	The Gentleman From Indiana (1st book) NY 1899, 1st issue w/"eye" as last word, line 12, p 245	200 - 300
MT1051	The Magnificent Amberson's NY 1918, DJ, 1st state on white paper	200 - 300
MT1052	2nd state on grayish paper	125 - 200
MT1060	Monsieur Beaucaire NY 1900, DJ	125 - 200
MT1070	Penrod Garden City 1914, DJ	300 - 500

Tartt, Donna

MT1210	The Secret History NY 1992, DJ	40 - 60
	NY 1992, advance review cy, wrappers	50 - 75

Taylor, Peter

MT1310	A Summons to Memphis NY 1986, DJ	25 - 50

Taylor, Robert Lewis

MT1410	Adrift in a Boneyard (1st book) NY 1947, DJ	75 - 100
MT1420	The Travels of Jamie McPheeters NY 1958, DJ	25 - 50

Tennant, Emma

MT1610	The Time of the Crack (1st book) Lon 1973, DJ	100 - 150

Tevis, Walter

MT1810	The Color of Money Lon 1985, DJ	30 - 40
MT1820	The Hustler NY 1959, DJ	100 - 150

Theroux, Paul

MT2110	Waldo (1st book) Bos 1967, DJ	150 - 250

Thomas, D. M. (Donald Michael)

MT2210	Personal and Possessive (1st book) Lon 1964, DJ	300 - 500
MT2220	Two Voices Lon 1968, 50 cys, glassine DJ	300 - 500
MT2221	wrappers, glassine DJ	75 - 125
MT2222	NY 1968, wrappers (1st American ed)	50 - 75
MT2230	The White Hotel Lon 1981, DJ	100 - 150

Thomas, Dylan

MT2310	18 Poems Lon 1934, DJ, 250 cys	2000 - 3000
MT2320	Twenty-Five Poems Lon 1936, DJ	700 - 1000

Thurber, James

MT2610	Alarms and Diversions NY 1957, DJ	125 - 250
MT2620	Further Fables For Our Time NY 1956, DJ	125 - 250
MT2630	Is Sex Necessary? (1st book) NY 1929, DJ	300 - 500
MT2640	Thurber Country NY 1953, DJ	125 - 250
MT2650	The White Deer NY 1945, DJ	50 - 75
MT2660	The Wonderful O NY 1957, DJ	50 - 75

Tolkien, John R. R.

MT3000	The Adventures of Tom Bombadil Lon 1962, DJ	100 - 150
MT3001	NY 1962, DJ (1st American ed)	75 - 125
MT3002	Bos 1963, DJ	50 - 75
MT3010	Works from Tolkien's Library, signed in pencil by Tolkien, value of signature	150 - 250
MT3020	Farmer Giles of Ham Lon 1949, DJ	150 - 250
MT3021	Bos 1950, DJ	100 - 150
MT3022	NY 1950, DJ	125 - 250
MT3030	The Hobbitt Lon 1937, DJ	4000 - 6000
	w/o DJ	1200 - 1800
MT3031	Bos 1938, DJ (1st issue w/Hobbitt on tp)	1200 - 1500
	w/o DJ	300 - 500
MT3040	The Lord of the Rings Trilogy (The Fellowship of the Ring/The Two Towers/The Return of the King) Lon 1954-55, 3 vol pub separately w/DJ's	5000 - 7000
MT3041	NY 1954-56, 3 vol pub separately w/DJ's	700 - 1000
MT3042	Lon 1966, 3 vol, DJ's	200 - 300
MT3051	A Middle English Vocabulary (1st book) Oxford 1922, 1st state w/ads dated Oct 1921	800 - 1200
MT3052	2nd state w/ads undated	400 - 600
MT3070	Mr. Bliss Lon 1982, DJ	75 - 125
MT3072	Bos 1983, DJ	30 - 50
MT3080	Pictures by J.R.R. Tolkien Lon 1979, slipcase	100 - 150

MT3081	Bos 1979, slipcase	75 - 125
MT3100	**The Return of the King** Lon 1955, DJ	250 - 350
MT3102	Bos 1956, DJ	100 - 150
MT3120	**The Road Goes Ever On** Bos 1967, DJ	75 - 125
MT3130	**The Silmarillon** Lon 1977, DJ	75 - 125
MT3140	**Smith of Wootton Major** Lon 1967, DJ	75 - 125
MT3141	Bos 1967, DJ (1st American ed)	30 - 50
MT3160	**Tree and Leaf** Lon 1964, DJ	250 - 350
MT3162	Bos 1965, DJ	50 - 75

Toole, John Kennedy

MT3410	**A Confederacy of Dunces** (1st book) Baton Rouge 1980, DJ	250 - 350
MT3411	Lon 1981, DJ (1st English ed)	75 - 125

Toomer, Jean

MT3510	**Cane** (1st book) NY 1923, DJ	2000 - 3000
MT3520	**Essentials** Chi 1931, DJ	300 - 500
MT3530	**The Flavor of Man** Phil 1949, wrappers	100 - 150

Traver, Robert

MT4310	**Trouble-Shooter** NY 1943, DJ	100 - 150

Trevor, William

MT4610	**The Boarding House** Lon 1965, DJ	100 - 150
MT4620	**The Day We Got Drunk on Cake and Other Stories** Lon 1967, DJ	200 - 300
MT4630	**The Love Department** Lon 1966, DJ	100 - 150
MT4640	**The Old Boys** Lon 1964, DJ	100 - 150
MT4650	**A Standard of Behavior** (1st book) Lon 1958, DJ	300 - 500

Twain, Mark (see Samuel Clemens)

Tyler, Anne

MT6000	**The Accidental Tourist** NY 1985, DJ	50 - 75
MT6010	**Breathing Lessons** NY 1989, DJ	25 - 50
MT6011	NY 1988 (limited ed) box	75 - 125
MT6030	**The Clock Winder** NY 1972, DJ	700 - 1000
MT6040	**Dinner at the Homesick Restaurant** NY 1982, DJ	75 - 125
MT6041	Lon 1982, DJ (1st English ed)	50 - 75
MT6050	**Earthly Possessions** NY 1977, DJ	100 - 150
MT6060	**If Morning Ever Comes** (1st book) NY 1964, DJ	800 - 1200
MT6070	**Morgan's Passing** Lon 1977, DJ	50 - 75
MT6071	NY 1977, DJ (1st American ed)	75 - 125
MT6090	**Searching For Caleb** NY 1976, DJ	125 - 250
MT6100	**A Slipping-Down Life** NY 1970, DJ	200 - 300
MT6102	Lon 1983, DJ (1st English ed)	50 - 75
MT6120	**The Tin Can Tree** NY 1965, DJ	700 - 1000

Updike, John

MU5000	**Bech is Back** NY 1982, DJ	40 - 60
MU5010	**The Carpentered Hen** (1st book) NY 1958, DJ	300 - 500
MU5020	**Couples** NY 1968, DJ	30 - 50
MU5030	**The Music School** NY 1966, DJ	50 - 75
MU5040	**Of The Farm** NY 1965, DJ	75 - 125
MU5050	**Rabbit at Rest** NY 1990, DJ	25 - 50
MU5060	**Rabbit is Rich** NY 1981, DJ	25 - 50
MU5080	**Rabbit Redux** NY 1971, DJ	50 - 75
MU5100	**Rabbit Run** NY 1960, DJ	150 - 250
MU5120	**The Witches of Eastwick** NY 1984, DJ	50 - 75

Valin, Jonathan

MV0510	**Dead Letter** NY 1981, DJ	30 - 50
MV0520	**Final Notice** NY 1980, DJ	50 - 75
MV0530	**The Lime Pit** (1st book) NY 1980, DJ	100 - 150
MV0540	**Natural Causes** NY 1983, DJ	20 - 30

van Vogt, A. E.

MV0850	**Rogue Ship** Garden City 1965, DJ	40 - 60

Vance, Jack

MV1010	**Big Planet** NY 1957, DJ	200 - 300
MV1020	**Emphyrio** NY 1969, DJ	300 - 500
MV1030	**The Languages of Pao** NY 1958, DJ	200 - 300
MV1040	**To Live Forever** NY 1956, DJ	300 - 500
MV1050	**Vandals of the Void** Phil 1953, DJ	200 - 300

Vargas Llosa, Mario

MV1210	**The Time of the Hero** (1st book) NY 1966, DJ	50 - 75

Vercors (Gene Marcel Bruller)

MV1510	**Borderline** Lon 1954, DJ	50 - 75

Verne, Jules

MV1710	**Their Island Home** NY 1924, DJ	100 - 150

Vidal, Gore

MV2010	**City & the Pillar** NY 1948, DJ	75 - 125
MV2020	**Dark Green, Bright Red** NY 1950, DJ	75 - 125
MV2030	**The Judgment of Paris** NY 1952, DJ	75 - 125
MV2040	**Messiah** NY 1954, DJ	50 - 75
MV2050	**Myra Breckinridge** Bos 1968, DJ	25 - 50
MV2060	**Rocking the Boat** Bos 1962, DJ	25 - 50
MV2070	**Thirsty Evil** NY 1956, DJ	50 - 75
MV2080	**Visit to a Small Planet** Bos 1956, DJ	25 - 50
MV2090	**Williwaw** (1st book) NY 1946, DJ	200 - 300

Vinge, Joan D.

MV2410	**The Snow Queen** NY 1980, DJ (Hugo Award winner)	75 - 100

Vollmann, William T.

MV2800	**The Rainbow Stories** Lon 1989, DJ	75 - 125
MV2810	**You Bright and Risen Angels** Lon 1987, DJ	100 - 150
MV2820	**Whores for Gloria** NY 1991, DJ	25 - 35

Vonnegut, Jr., Kurt

MV3010	**Canary in a Cat House** Greenwich 1961	125 - 250
MV3020	**Cats Cradle** NY 1963, DJ	125 - 250
MV3030	**Player Piano** (1st book) NY 1952, DJ, w/Scribner's "A" on cr page	300 - 500

MT3162

MT3410

MU5040

MU5080

MV0530

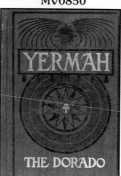

MV0850

MV1510   MV1710   MV2410   MV2820   MV3010   MW0140

MW1913	**MW1913 (title page)**		**MW1953**

MV3040 **The Sirens of Titan** NY 1959, pictorial
    wrappers-Pocketbook   50 - 75
MV3042 Bos 1961, DJ   300 - 500

Wain, John
MW0090 **Mixed Feelings** (1st book) Reading 1951,
    120 cys, wrappers   200 - 300

Wait, Frona Eunice
MW0140 **Yermah The Dorado** SF 1897, 500 cys   300 - 500

Walker, Alice
MW0210 **The Color Purple** NY 1982, DJ   50 - 75
MW0220 **Once** (1st book) NY 1968, DJ   200 - 300

Wallace, Edgar
MW0310 **The Mission That Failed** (1st book) Cape Town
    1898, wrappers   400 - 600
MW0320 **White Face** NY 1931, DJ   40 - 60

Wambaugh, Joseph
MW0410 **The Choirboys** NY 1975, DJ   20 - 30
MW0420 **The Glitter Dome** NY 1981, DJ   20 - 30
MW0430 **The New Centurions** (1st book) NY 1971, DJ 25 - 50

Warren, Robert Penn
MW0510 **All the King's Men** NY 1946, DJ   200 - 300
MW0512 NY 1989, 600 cys, box   800 - 1200
MW0520 **Blackberry Winter** Cummington 1946,
    280 cys, arches paper, DJ   700 - 1000
MW0530 **The Circus of the Attic** NY 1947, DJ   200 - 300
MW0540 **John Brown** (1st book) NY 1929, DJ   700 - 1000
MW0550 **Night Rider** Bos 1939, DJ   300 - 500
MW0560 **Or Else - Poem/Poems 1968-1974** NY 1974, DJ 200 - 300
MW0570 **Selected Poems: New and Old 1923-1966**
    NY 1966, 250 cys, DJ, box   300 - 500

Waterhouse, Keith
MW0710 **Billy Liar** Lon 1959, DJ   75 - 125
MW0720 **The Cafe Royal** (1st book) Lon 1955, DJ 125 - 250
MW0730 **There is a Happy Land** Lon 1957, DJ   100 - 150

Waugh, Evelyn
MW0810 **Black Mischief** Lon 1932, DJ   300 - 500
MW0811 Lon 1932, 250 cys   500 - 700
MW0820 **Decline and Fall** Lon 1929, DJ   700 - 1000
MW0830 **A Handful of Dust** Lon 1934, DJ   300 - 500
MW0840 **Helena** Lon 1950, DJ   125 - 250
MW0850 **Love Among the Ruins** Lon 1953, 350 cys,
    glassine DJ   300 - 500
MW0860 **The Loved One** Lon 1948, 250 cys   300 - 500
MW0870 **P.R.B. An Essay....** Lon 1926, errata slip 2000 - 3000
MW0880 **Remote People** Lon 1931, DJ   700 - 1000
MW0890 **Rossetti - His Life and Work** Lon 1928, DJ 2000 - 3000
MW0891 NY 1928, DJ   700 - 1000
MW0900 **Scoop** Lon 1938, DJ   400 - 600
MW0910 **Sword of Honor** Lon 1965, DJ   75 - 125
MW0920 **They Were Still Dancing** NY 1932, DJ 500 - 700
MW0930 **Vile Bodies** Lon 1930, DJ   700 - 1000
MW0940 **Wine in Peace and War** Lon 1947, DJ 125 - 250
MW0941 Lon 1947 100 cys   300 - 500
MW0950 **The World to Come** (1st book) 1916 8000 - 12000

Webb, Charles
MW1110 **The Graduate** (1st book) NY 1963, DJ   50 - 75

Weinbaum, Stanley G.
MW1210 **Dawn of Flame** (1st book) Jamaica, NY 1936,
    pub w/o DJ, w/intro by Keating   1200 - 1500
MW1220 w/intro by Palmer   2000 - 3000
MW1230 **The New Adam** Chi 1939, DJ   200 - 300

Welch, James
MW1310 **The Death of Jim Loney** NY 1979, DJ   50 - 75
MW1320 **Fools Crow** NY 1986, DJ   30 - 50
MW1330 **The Indian Lawyer** NY 1990, DJ   20 - 30
MW1340 **Riding the Earthboy 40** (1st book) NY 1971, DJ 100 - 150
MW1350 **Winter in the Blood** NY 1974, DJ   75 - 125

Weldon, Fay
MW1510 **The Fat Woman's Joke** (1st book) Lon 1967, DJ 75 - 125

Wellman, Manly Wade
MW1610 **The Invading Asteroid** (1st book) NY 1932, DJ 150 - 250
MW1620 **Who Fears the Devil?** Sauk City 1963 100 - 150

Wells, H. G. (Herbert George)
MW1710 **The Adventures of Tommy** Lon 1929, DJ 150 - 250
MW1720 **Certain Personal Matters** Covent Garden 1898,
    w/32 pp of ads dated "Spring 1897"   200 - 300
MW1730 **The Country of the Blind** Lon 1939, 30 cys 1200 - 1800
MW1731 280 cys   400 - 600
MW1740 **The Discovery of the Future** Lon 1902, red
    cl w/o "S" in Anticipations on cover 300 - 500
MW1741 red wrappers   200 - 300
MW1750 **The Door in the Wall** NY 1911, 600 cys,
    boards   1200 - 1800
MW1752 Lon 1915, 60 cys, boards   1000 - 1500
MW1761 **The Dream** Lon 1924, DJ, 1st issue w/plain
    top edge   150 - 250
MW1771 **The First Men in the Moon** Lon 1901, DJ,
    1st state in dark blue cl, gold stamped 1200 - 1800
MW1772 2nd state in light blue cl, black stamped 300 - 500
MW1780 **Floor Games** Lon 1911, DJ   150 - 250
MW1790 **The Food of the Gods** Lon 1904, DJ, w/18 pp
    of ads dated 20/7/04   250 - 350
MW1800 **In the Days of the Comet** Lon 1906, DJ,
    w/8 pp of ads dated 5/5/06   300 - 500
MW1811 **The Invisible Man** Lon 1897, 1st issue w/p 1
    numbered 2, 2 pp ads   500 - 700
MW1812 2nd issue w/page numbers corrected 250 - 350
MW1813 NY 1897 (1st American ed)   200 - 300
MW1820 **The Island of Doctor Moreau** Lon 1896,
    w/32 pp of ads   700 - 1000
MW1821 NY 1896, black cl   300 - 500
MW1830 **A Modern Utopia** Lon 1905, DJ   200 - 300
MW1840 **The Red Room** Chi 1896, 12 cys 1200 - 1800
MW1851 **The Sea Lady** Lon 1902, DJ, 1st state
    w/40 pp of ads dated July   250 - 350
MW1860 **The Secret Places of the Heart** Lon 1922, DJ 200 - 300
MW1870 **Select Conversations with an Uncle (Now Extinct)
    and Two Other Reminiscences** Lon 1895 300 - 500
MW1881 **The Stolen Bacillus** Lon 1895, 1st state
    w/32 pp of ads dated September 700 - 1000
MW1890 **Tales of Space and Time** NY 1899 300 - 500
MW1891 Lon 1900 (1st English ed)   200 - 300
MW1900 **Thirty Strange Stories** NY 1987   300 - 500
MW1911 **The Time Machine** (1st novel) Lon 1895,
    1st state w/16 pp of ads, gray cl, blue &
    purple stamping   2000 - 3000
MW1912 Lon 1895 blue wrappers   800 - 1200
MW1913 NY 1895 (1st American ed, 1st issue), name
    misspelled H.S. Wells on tp   1000 - 1500
MW1914 NY 1895 (2nd issue)   300 - 500
MW1920 **Tono Bungay** Lon 1909, DJ   200 - 300
MW1931 **Twelve Stories and a Dream** Lon 1903, DJ,
    1st state w/22 pp of ads dated 20/9/03 150 - 250
MW1940 **The War in the Air** Lon 1908, DJ 250 - 350
MW1951 **The War of the Worlds** Lon 1898, 1st state
    w/ads dated 1897   800 - 1200
MW1953 Armed Services Edition pocketbook, wrappers 20 - 30
MW1961 **The Wheels of Chance** Lon 1896, 1st state
    w/10 pp of ads, printer's imprint on p 314
MW1970 **When the Sleeper Wakes** Lon 1899 300 - 500
MW1971 NY 1899   100 - 150
MW1981 **The Wonderful Visit** Lon 1895, 1st state in
    red buckram w/covers blind-stamped 250 - 350
MW1982 2nd state stamped in gold   200 - 300
MW1990 **The World of William Clissold** Lon 1926,
    198 cys, 3 vol   300 - 500
MW2000 **The World Set Free** Lon 1914, DJ 200 - 300

Welty, Eudora
MW2110 **A Curtain of Green** (1st book) NY 1941, DJ 1200 - 1800

MW2120 **Delta Wedding** NY 1946, DJ   100 - 150
MW2130 **The Eye of the Story** NY 1978, 300 cys, slipcase   200 - 300
MW2140 **The Golden Apples** NY 1949, DJ   250 - 350
MW2150 **Ida M'Toy** Chi 1979, 350 cys   150 - 250
MW2160 **Losing Battles** NY 1970, 300 cys, acetate DJ, box   300 - 500
MW2161 NY 1970, DJ (1st trade ed)   40 - 60
MW2170 **Music From Spain** Greenville 1948, 775 cys, DJ   500 - 700
MW2180 **The Optimist's Daughter** NY 1972, 300 cys, box   200 - 300
MW2181 NY 1972, DJ (1st trade ed)   50 - 75
MW2190 **A Pageant of Birds** NY 1974, 26 cys   400 - 600
MW2191 300 cys   200 - 300
MW2200 **The Ponder Heart** NY 1954, DJ   125 - 250
MW2210 **Retreat** Winston-Salem 1981, 50 cys   200 - 300
MW2220 **The Robber Bridegroom** NY 1942, DJ   300 - 500
MW2230 **The Shoe Bird** NY 1964, DJ   150 - 250
MW2240 **Short Stories** NY 1949, 1500 cys, glassine DJ   125 - 250
MW2250 **A Sweet Devouring** NY 1979, wrappers, 26 cys   700 - 1000
MW2251 150 cys   300 - 500
MW2260 **The Wide Net** NY 1943, DJ   300 - 500

West, Nathanael
MW2410 **The Day of the Locust** NY 1939, DJ   2000 - 3000

Wharton, Edith
  Wrote about 50 books.
MW2511 **The Age of Innocence** NY 1920, DJ, 1st issue
    w/quotation from burial service on p 186   300 - 500
MW2520 **Crucial Instances** NY 1901, DJ   200 - 300
MW2531 **Ethan Frome** NY 1911, DJ, 1st issue w/perfect
    type in last line, p 135   3000 - 5000
MW2540 **The Greater Inclination** (1st book) NY 1899   300 - 500
MW2550 **The Touchstone** NY 1900   200 - 300

White, T. H.
MW2710 **The Elephant and the Kangaroo** NY 1947, DJ   75 - 125
MW2720 **Farewell Victoria** NY 1934, DJ   200 - 300
MW2730 **The Green Bay Tree** (1st book) Chi 1929,
    wrappers   300 - 500
MW2740 **The Once and Future King** Lon 1958, DJ   100 - 150

Wilde, Oscar
MW2810 **The Ballad of Reading Gaol** Lon 1898,
    30 cys, vellum   3000 - 5000
MW2811 Lon 1898, 99 cys, purple linen   2000 - 3000
MW2812 Lon 1898, 800 cys   800 - 1200
MW2813 NY 1928, 200 cys, DJ   200 - 300
MW2814 NY 1936, 1500 cys, box   200 - 300
MW2820 **Collected Works** Lon 1908, 14 vol, 80 cys,
    vellum   3000 - 5000
MW2821 Lon 1908, 1000 cys   700 - 1000
MW2830 **De Profundis** Lon 1905, 50 cys, vellum   3000 - 5000
MW2840 Lon 1905, 200 cys   1500 - 2000

Wilder, Laura Ingalls
MW3110 **Little House on the Prairie** NY 1933, DJ   75 - 125

Wilder, Thornton
MW3210 **The Bridge of San Luis Rey** Lon 1927, DJ   250 - 350
MW3211 NY 1927, DJ (1st American ed), 1st state w/tp
    printed in black   500 - 700
MW3212 NY 1927, DJ, 2nd state w/tp in green & black   300 - 500
MW3221 **The Cabala** (1st book) NY 1926, DJ, 1st issue
    w/"conversation" on line 13, p 196   200 - 300
MW3222 Lon 1926, DJ (1st English ed)   75 - 125
MW3230 **The Ides of March** NY 1948, 750 cys, DJ   150 - 250
MW3231 NY 1948, DJ (1st trade ed)   25 - 50
MW3240 **The Skin of Our Teeth** NY 1942, DJ   150 - 250

Williams, Tennessee
MW3411 **American Blues** NY 1948, wrappers, 1st issue
    w/author's name misspelled on cover   250 - 350
MW3420 **Baby Doll** NY 1956, DJ   75 - 125
MW3430 **Battle of Angels** (1st book) Murray 1945, wrappers   300 - 500
MW3440 **Cat on a Hot Tin Roof** Norfolk 1955, DJ   100 - 150
MW3450 **The Glass Menagerie** NY 1945, DJ   200 - 300
MW3460 **In the Winter of Cities: Poems** NY 1956, DJ   50 - 75
MW3470 **The Milk Train Doesn't Stop Here Anymore**
    Norfolk 1964, DJ   50 - 75
MW3480 **The Night of the Iguana** NY 1963, DJ   50 - 75
MW3490 **Period of Adjustment** NY 1960, DJ   50 - 75
MW3500 **The Rose Tatoo** NY 1951, DJ   100 - 150
MW3510 **A Streetcar Named Desire** Norfolk 1947, DJ   300 - 500
MW3520 **Suddenly Last Summer** NY 1958, DJ   75 - 125
MW3530 **Sweet Bird of Youth** NY 1959, DJ   75 - 125

Williams, William Carlos
MW3710 **Al Que Quiere A Book of Poems** Bos 1917,
    1000 cys, glassine DJ   300 - 500
MW3720 **The Build Up** NY 1952, DJ   75 - 125
MW3730 **The Clouds** Aurora 1948, 60 cys, signed, box   400 - 600
MW3731 250 cys, unsigned, box   200 - 300
MW3740 **The Cod Head** SF 1932, 125 cys, wrappers   700 - 1000
MW3750 **The Collected Earlier Poems** NY 1951, DJ   50 - 75
MW3760 **The Collected Later Poems** Norfolk 1950,
    100 cys, box   700 - 1000
MW3761 Norfolk 1950, DJ (1st trade ed)   50 - 75
MW3770 **Collected Poems 1921-1931** NY 1934, DJ   300 - 500
MW3780 **The Complete Collected Poems 1906-1938**
    Norfolk 1938, 50 cys, box   800 - 1200
MW3781 Norfolk 1938, DJ (1st trade ed)   200 - 300
MW3790 **The Desert Music and Other Poems** NY 1954,
    100 cys, glassine DJ, box   400 - 600
MW3791 NY 1954, DJ (1st trade ed)   75 - 125
MW3800 **The Farmer's Daughter** NY 1961, DJ   50 - 75
MW3810 **The Great American Novel** Paris 1923,
    300 cys, box   700 - 1000
MW3820 **In the American Grain** NY 1925, DJ   300 - 500
MW3830 **In the Money** Norfolk 1940, DJ   150 - 250
MW3840 **The Knife of the Times** Ithaca 1932,
    500 cys, DJ   700 - 1000
MW3850 **Kora in Hell: Improvisations** Bos 1920, DJ   300 - 500
MW3860 **Life Along the Passaic River** Norfolk 1938, DJ   200 - 300
MW3870 **Many Loves and Other Plays** NY 1961, DJ   50 - 75
MW3880 **A Novelette and Other Prose** Toulon 1932,
    wrappers   400 - 600
MW3890 **Paterson (Books 1-5)** NY 1946-58, separately
    published vols in DJs, each vol   125 - 250
MW3900 **The Pink Church** Columbus 1949, 375 cys,
    wrappers   150 - 250
MW3901 25 cys, wrappers   400 - 600
MW3910 **Poems** (1st book) Rutherford 1909, wrappers   12000 - 18000
MW3920 **The Selected Letters** NY 1957, 75 cys, box   700 - 1000
MW3930 **Selected Poems** Snake River Press 1981, 25 cys   200 - 300
MW3940 **Sour Grapes** Bos 1921, DJ   700 - 1000
MW3950 **Spring and All** Paris 1923, 300 cys, wrappers,
    glassine DJ   800 - 1200
MW3960 **The Tempers** Lon 1913, cl, glassine DJ   1500 - 2000
MW3970 **White Mule** Norfolk 1937, DJ   300 - 500

Williamson, Henry
MW4110 **The Flax of Dreams** (1st book) Lon 1921, 750 cys   300 - 500
MW4120 **The Gale of the World** Lon 1969, DJ   75 - 125

Wilson, Colin
MW4310 **The Philosopher's Stone** NY 1969, DJ   50 - 100

Wister, Owen
MW4500 **The Dragon of Wantley** Phil 1892   75 - 125
MW4510 **Lady Baltimore** NY 1906, 200 cys, vellum   200 - 300
MW4511 NY 1906, DJ (1st trade ed)   75 - 125
MW4520 **Lin McLean** NY 1898   125 - 250
MW4530 **The New Swiss Family Robinson** (1st book)
    Cambridge 1882   150 - 250
MW4540 **Red Men and White** NY 1896   150 - 250
MW4550 **The Virginian** NY 1902, DJ   300 - 500

Wodehouse, P. G. (Pelham G.) (also see Golf: F, H & P)
MW4710 **The Code of the Woosters** NY 1938, DJ   200 - 300
MW4720 **Love Among the Chickens** NY 1909, DJ   800 - 1200
MW4730 **The Pot Hunters** (1st book) Lon 1902, DJ   2000 - 3000
MW4740 **Uncle Fred in the Springtime** NY 1939, DJ   200 - 300
MW4750 **Uneasy Money** NY 1916, DJ   300 - 500

MW1971

MW3110 (w/o DJ)

MW3530

MW4500	MW4910	MW5130	MW5320	MW5330

MW5340   MW6411   MW6412

Wolf, Gary
MW4910 **Who Censored Roger Rabbit?** NY 1980, DJ   125 - 200

Wolfe, Gene
MW5010 **The Shadow of the Torturer** NY 1980, DJ   50 - 75

Wolfe, Thomas
MW5110 **From Death to Morning** NY 1935, DJ, Scribner's
    "A" on cr page, brown cl   200 - 300
MW5121 **Look Homeward, Angel** (1st book) NY 1929,
    DJ, 1st issue w/Scribner's seal on cr page in
    1st state DJ w/Wolfe's photo on back   2000 - 3000
MW5130 **Mannerhouse** NY 1948, DJ   75 - 125
MW5140 **Of Time and the River** NY 1935, DJ, "A" on
    cr page   200 - 300
MW5150 **The Story of a Novel** NY 1936, DJ, "A" on
    cr page   150 - 250

Wolfe, Tom
MW5310 **The Bonfire of the Vanities** NY 1987, DJ   75 - 125
MW5320 **The Electric Kool-Aid Acid Test** NY 1968, DJ   125 - 175
MW5330 **From Bauhaus to Our House** NY 1981, DJ   40 - 60
MW5340 **The Kandy-Kolored Tangerine-Flake Streamline**
    Baby NY 1965, DJ   50 - 75
MW5360 **Mauve Gloves and Madmen** NY 1976, DJ   25 - 50
MW5370 **The Pump House Gang** NY 1968, DJ   25 - 50
MW5380 **Radical Chic & Mau-Mauing the Flak Catchers**
    NY 1970, DJ   25 - 50
MW5390 **The Right Stuff** NY 1979, DJ   75 - 125

Woolf, Virginia
MW5610 **Beau Brummell** NY 1930, 550 cys, glassine
    DJ, slipcase   700 - 1000
MW5620 **The Captain's Death Bed** NY 1950, DJ
MW5621 Lon 1950 DJ   150 - 250
MW5630 **The Death of the Moth** Lon 1942, DJ   125 - 250
MW5631 NY 1942, DJ (1st American ed)   50 - 75
MW5640 **Jacob's Room** Lon 1922, 40 cys, DJ
MW5651 **Kew Gardens** Richmond 1919, 1st issue
    w/errata slip   250 - 350
MW5652 Lon 1927, 500 cys, DJ   700 - 1000
MW5660 **Night and Day** Lon 1919, DJ   200 - 300
MW5670 **A Room of One's Own** NY 1929, 492 cys   700 - 1000
MW5680 **Street Haunting** SF 1930, 500 cys, box   500 - 700
MW5690 **The Voyage Out** (1st book) Lon 1915, DJ   700 - 1000
MW5691 NY 1920, DJ (1st American ed)   300 - 500

Wouk, Herman
MW5910 **The Caine Mutiny** NY 1951, DJ   125 - 250
MW5920 **The City Boy** NY 1948, DJ   100 - 150
MW5930 **The Man in the Trench Coat** (1st book)
    NY 1941, wrappers   700 - 1000
MW5940 **This is My God** Bos 1987, 250 cys, slipcase   150 - 250

Wright, Harold Bell
    Reprints in DJ by A.L. Burt are worth $10-25.
MW6210 **Long Ago Told** NY 1919, DJ   200 - 300
MW6220 **Ma Cinderella** NY 1932, DJ   150 - 250
MW6230 **The Man Who Went Away** NY 1942, DJ   75 - 125
MW6240 **Mine with the Iron Door** NY 1923, DJ   75 - 125
MW6250 **Recreation of Brian Kent** Chi 1919, DJ   150 - 250
MW6260 **The Shepherd of the Hills** Chi 1907, DJ,
    w/pub "Sept., 1907" on cr page   300 - 500
MW6270 **That Printer of Udell's** (1st book) Chi 1903, DJ   200 - 300
MW6280 **Their Yesterdays** Chi 1912, DJ   150 - 250
MW6290 **The Winning of Barbara Worth** Chi 1911, DJ   200 - 300

Wright, Richard
MW6411 **Native Son** NY 1940, 1st state DJ w/synopsis
    on front   100 - 150
MW6412 2nd state DJ w/picture of black man   50 - 75
MW6420 **The Outsider** NY 1953, DJ   75 - 125
MW6430 **White Man Listen** NY 1957, DJ   50 - 75

Wylie, Elinor
MW6611 **Nets to Catch the Wind** (1st book) NY 1921, DJ,
    1st state paper not watermarked   200 - 300

Wylie, Philip
MW6710 **The Big Ones Get Away** NY 1940, DJ   100 - 150
MW6720 **Heavy Laden** (1st book) NY 1928, DJ   150 - 200

Wyndham, John
MW6910 **The Day of the Triffids** (1st novel) Lon 1951, DJ   150 - 250
MW6911 NY 1951, DJ   75 - 100
MW6920 **Jizzle** Lon 1954, DJ   100 - 150
MW6930 **The Kraken Wakes** Lon 1953, DJ   100 - 150
MW6940 **The Midwich Cuckoos** NY 1958, DJ   75 - 100
MW6950 **Re-Birth** NY 1955, DJ   150 - 250

Yeats, William Butler (1923 Nobel Laureate)
MY1010 **The Cat and the Moon and Certain Poems**
    Dublin 1924, 500 cys   250 - 350
MY1020 **Collected Works** Stratford-on-Avon 1908,
    8 vol, 1060 cys   1500 - 2500
MY1030 **The Cutting of an Agate** NY 1912, DJ   200 - 300
MY1032 Lon 1919, DJ (1st English ed)   150 - 250
MY1041 **Deirdre** Lon 1907, 1st state w/printer's imprint
    on p 48   300 - 500
MY1042 2nd state w/o imprint   200 - 300
MY1050 **Discoveries: A Volume of Essays** Dundrum
    1907, 200 cys   300 - 500
MY1060 **Essays** Lon 1924, DJ   200 - 300
MY1061 NY 1924, 250 cys   700 - 1000
MY1070 **Essays 1931 to 1936** Dublin 1937, 300 cys, DJ   300 - 500
MY1080 **The Golden Helmet** NY 1908, 50 cys   700 - 1000
MY1090 **The Green Helmet** Dundrum 1910, 400 cys,
    errata slip   200 - 300
MY1100 **Irish Fairy Tales** Lon 1892   300 - 500
MY1110 **The Kings Threshold** NY 1904, 100 cys, box   1000 - 1500
MY1120 **Later Poems** Lon 1922   250 - 350
MY1122 NY 1927, 250 cys, glassine DJ, box   300 - 500
MY1123 NY 1927 (1st American trade ed)   25 - 50
MY1130 **Mosada** (1st book) Dublin 1886, wrappers,
    lacks endpapers, 2 cys located   30000 - 50000
MY1140 **October Blast: Poems** Dublin 1927, 350 cys, DJ   300 - 500
MY1150 **Plays and Controversies** Lon 1923
MY1151 NY 1924, 250 cys   300 - 500
MY1160 **Poems** Lon 1895, 25 cys, vellum   2000 - 3000
MY1161 725 cys   700 - 1000
MY1170 **The Secret Rose** Lon 1897   300 - 500
MY1171 NY 1897 (1st American ed)   150 - 250
MY1180 **The Shadowy Waters** Lon 1900   200 - 300

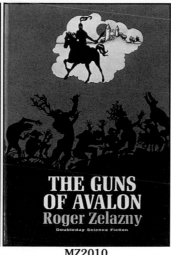

MZ2040	**MZ2010**

MY1190 **The Tables of the Law** Lon 1897, 110 cys   1000 - 1500
MY1192 Stratford 1914, 510 cys   300 - 500
MY1200 **Three Things** Lon 1929, 500 cys   200 - 300
MY1201 Lon 1929 wrappers (1st trade ed)   50 - 75
MY1210 **The Tower** Lon 1928, DJ   300 - 500
MY1211 NY 1928 DJ (1st American ed)   200 - 300
MY1220 **The Trembling of the Veil** Lon 1922,
    1000 cys, DJ   250 - 350
MY1230 **A Vision** Lon 1925, 600 cys, DJ   700 - 1000
MY1241 **The Wind Among the Reeds** Lon 1899,
    1st issue w/o errata slip   300 - 500
MY1242 2nd issue w/slip   100 - 150
MY1250 **The Winding Stair** NY 1929, 642 cys, DJ   300 - 500
MY1252 Lon 1933, DJ (1st English ed)   100 - 150
MY1253 NY 1933, DJ (1st American trade ed)   100 - 150

Zelazny, Roger
MZ2000 **Damnation Alley** NY 1969, DJ   50 - 75
MZ2010 **The Guns of Avalon** Garden City 1972, DJ   150 - 250
MZ2030 **Lord of Light** NY 1967, DJ   150 - 250
MZ2040 **Nine Princes in Amber** NY 1970, DJ   300 - 500

MOVIES

The motion picture is almost entirely a 20th century phenomenon. It probably came about as a result of Edward Muybridge's experiments with animal and human locomotion in the 1870s-1880s. Then George Eastman invented roll film in the 1880s. Thomas Edison, impressed with Muybridge's experiments, developed the Kinetoscope which used Eastman's film. A viewer peeped into the Kinetoscope to see the show. But the French created the first movie projector and commercial movies. In 1895, Auguste and Louis Lumière introduced *Sortie Des Ouvriers de L'Usine Lumière* to a skeptical but curious public. Edison soon offered performances on his Vitascope projector in New York. Another Frenchman, Georges Méliès, became the first to produce fantasy films. *Le Voyage Dans La Lune* (1902), was based on the Jules Verne novel *From the Earth to the Moon* (1873).

The earliest printed materials relating to commercial movies were handbills and posters. Theatre programs, photoplay novels, film annuals and technical books about film-making like *The Handbook of Kinematography* by Colin Bennett (1911) started in the early 1900s.

Movie History & Technique
Barnouw, Erik
MV4020 **The Magician and the Cinema** NY 1981, DJ   15 - 25
Bennett, Colin N.
MV4060 **The Handbook of Kinematography** Lon 1911   75 - 125
Cameron, James R.
MV4100 **Motion Picture Encyclopedia** 1948   20 - 25
Carr, Catherine
MV4140 **The Art of Photoplay Writing** 1914   20 - 25
Emerson, John & Anita Loos
MV4180 **Breaking Into the Movies** 1921   15 - 20

Fox, Charles Donald
MV4220 **Famous Film Folk** 1925, photos   25 - 35
Freeburg, Victor O.
MV4260 **Pictorial Beauty On the Screen** 1923   25 - 35
Fulton, A. R.
MV4300 **Motion Pictures** 1960, DJ   15 - 20
Hulfish, David S.
MV4340 **Cyclopedia of Motion Picture Work** 1914, 2 vol   75 - 125
Jacobs, Lewis
MV4380 **The Rise of the American Film** 1939   15 - 20
Lorentz, Pare & Morris Ernst
MV4420 **Censored** 1930   20 - 30
Lutz, E. G.
MV4460 **Animated Cartoons** 1923   35 - 40
Martin, Olga J.
MV4500 **Hollywoods Movie Commandments** 1937   20 - 25
Noble, Peter
MV4540 **The Negro In Films** 1969, DJ   20 - 25
Powell, A. Van Buren
MV4600 **The Photoplay Synopsis** 1919   15 - 20
Ramsaye, Terry
MV4660 **A Million and One Nights** 1926, 2 vol   150 - 200
Rathbun, John
MV4700 **Motion Picture Making and Exhibiting** 1914   35 - 50
Richardson, F. H.
MV4740 **Handbook of Projection** 1930, 5th ed, 2 vol   35 - 50
MV4745 **Motion Picture Handbook** 1912, 2nd ed   25 - 35
Sargent, Epes
MV4820 **Technique of the Photoplay** 1913, 2nd ed   25 - 30
Seldes, Gilbert
MV4860 **An Hour With the Movies and the Talkies** 1929   15 - 20
Smith, Albert E.
MV4900 **Two Reels and a Crank** 1952, DJ   15 - 25
Talbot, F. A.
MV4940 **Moving Pictures - How They Are Made and**
    Worked 1912   50 - 75
Tuska, Jon
MV4980 **The Filming of the West** 1976, DJ   20 - 30
Watts, Stephen (editor)
MV5060 **Behind the Screen** 1938   15 - 20
Weegee
MV5100 **Naked Hollywood** 1953, photo book, w/DJ   75 - 125
    w/o DJ   50 - 75

Movie Personalities (alphabetical by subject)
Astaire, Fred
MV5220 **Steps In Time** 1959   15 - 20
Barrymore, John
MV5260 **Confessions of an Actor** 1926, illus   20 - 25
Chaney, Lon
MV5300 **Outside the Law** Jacobson Hodgkinson, NY
    1926, wrappers   50 - 75
Chaplin, Charlie
MV5340 **Chaplin** Gerith Von Ulm 1940, DJ   20 - 30
MV5345 **The Great God Pan** Robert Payne 1952, DJ   15 - 20
MV5350 **The Little Fellow** Peter Coats & Thelma Niklaus 1951   12 - 15
MV5355 **My Trip Abroad** Chaplin 1922   25 - 30
Coogan, Jackie
MV5400 **Adventures of Tom Sawyer** 1931   20 - 25

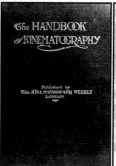

MV4020	**MV4060**	**MV5355**

| MV5535 | MV6530 | MV6540 | MV6590 | MV6600 | MV6620 |

| MV6640 | MV6645 | MV6690 |

Disney, Walt (see Disneyana)

Elsenstein, Sergei
| MV5480 | Film Form 1949 | | 22 - 30 |

Fairbanks, Douglas
MV5520	Doug and Mary Allene Talmey 1927	20 - 30
MV5525	Douglas Fairbanks Ralph Hancock & Letitia Fairbanks 1953	10 - 15
MV5530	Laugh and Live 1917	10 - 15
MV5535	Making Life Worth While 1918	10 - 15
MV5536	bound in suede	15 - 25
MV5540	Youth Points the Way 1924	10 - 15

Flaherty, Robert
| MV5580 | World of Robert Flaherty Richard Griffith 1953 | 15 - 20 |

Fox, William
| MV5620 | William Fox Upton Sinclair 1933, DJ | 30 - 50 |

Gish, Lillian
| MV5660 | Life and Lillian Gish Albert Bigelow Paine 1932, DJ | 30 - 40 |

Goldwyn
| MV5700 | The Great Goldwyn 1937 Alva Johnston | 20 - 25 |

Grace, Dick
| MV5740 | Squadron of Death 1929, DJ | 15 - 25 |

Griffith, D. W.
| MV5780 | When the Movies Were Young Mrs. D.W. Griffith 1925, DJ | 30 - 40 |

Hart, William S.
| MV5820 | My Life East & West Hart 1929 | 25 - 35 |

Laemmle, Carl
| MV5860 | Life & Adventures of Carl Laemmle John Drinkwater 1931, signed by author to Laemmle | 25 - 30 |

Marx, Groucho
| MV5900 | Beds 1930, photos, DJ | 150 - 200 |
| MV5905 | Many Happy Returns 1942, DJ | 15 - 20 |

Marx, Harpo
| MV5950 | Harpo Speaks 1961, DJ | 45 - 60 |

Mix, Tom
| MV5990 | Tony and His Pals H.M. & F.M. Christeson 1934 | 25 - 35 |

Monroe, Marilyn
MV6030	Marilyn Norman Mailer 1973, limited ed	200 - 300
MV6031	NY 1973, DJ (1st trade ed)	50 - 75
MV6032	NY 1973, DJ (Grosset & Dunlap reprint)	20 - 30
MV6040	My Story 1974	20 - 25

Reid, Wallace
| MV6100 | His Life Story Bertha Westbrook Reid 1923 | 15 - 25 |

Rin Tin Tin
MV6140	Little Folks Story of Rin Tin Tin 1927	15 - 25
MV6145	Story of Rin Tin Tin 1927, Whitman Pub, children's book w/color photos	15 - 20
MV6150	Strongheart, Story of a Wonder Dog 1926	15 - 20

Sennett, Mack
| MV6190 | Father Goose Gene Fowler 1934, DJ | 25 - 30 |
| MV6195 | King of Comedy Sennett 1954, DJ | 20 - 25 |

Talmadge Sisters
| MV6240 | Talmadge Sisters Margaret L. Talmadge 1924 | 20 - 25 |

Valentino, Rudolph
MV6280	Day Dreams Valentino 1923	30 - 50
MV6285	Secret Life of Rudolph Valentino	35 - 50
MV6290	Valentino As I Knew Him S. George Ullman 1927, DJ	15 - 25

Van Dyke, W. S.
| MV6330 | Van Dyke & the Mythical City of Hollywood Robert Cannon 1948, DJ | 20 - 25 |

Vidor, King
| MV6370 | A Tree is a Tree Vidor 1953, signed | 50 - 75 |

Zukor, Adolphe
| MV6440 | The House That Shadows Built Will Irwin 1928 | 15 - 20 |

Photoplays

Photoplays are novels illustrated with movie scenes. Published mainly from 1910 to 1940 by Grossett & Dunlap, A.L. Burt and others, they're usually clothbound with very colorful pictorial dust jackets. Grosset & Dunlap photoplays have eight plates and the A.L. Burt version has four plates. Soft cover photoplays (pictorial wrappers) were published by The Jacobson-Hodkinson Co. These are relatively scarce. Many of Lon Chaney's photoplays are soft cover with prices ranging from $40-75. There is no record of how many different photoplays were published; the number could exceed 1,000. Most are worth $10-15 with dust jacket and only several dollars without. Many collectors will not buy jacketless photoplays. The most valuable depict the horror or science fiction/fantasy genre, picture major stars such as Lon Chaney, Douglas Fairbanks, Jean Harlow, Rudolph Valentino or describe a major release such as *Tarzan and the Golden Lion* (1927). The listings are alphabetized according to title. Prices are for books with dust jackets in very good to fine condition.

MV6510	Adventures of Robinson Crusoe 1922 Harry Myers	20 - 35
MV6520	America 1924 D.W. Griffith film	20 - 30
MV6530	Barnum M.R. Werner	12 - 18
MV6540	The Beast of the City Jean Harlow	20 - 35
MV6550	Beau Geste 1926 Ronald Colman	15 - 20
MV6560	Beau Ideal 1931 Ralph Forbes	15 - 20
MV6570	Beau Sabreur 1928 Gary Cooper	15 - 20
MV6580	Birth of a Nation 1915 D.W. Griffith film	20 - 35
MV6590	The Black Pirate 1926 Douglas Fairbanks (color stills)	30 - 50
MV6600	Cobra Martin Brown, Rudolph Valentino	25 - 35
MV6610	The Covered Wagon 1923 Lois Wilson	15 - 20
MV6620	The Dawn Patrol Richard Barthelmess	40 - 75
MV6630	Dinner at Eight 1933 Jean Harlow	35 - 50
MV6640	Don Q's Love Story 1925 Douglas Fairbanks	25 - 30
MV6645	Douglas Fairbanks in Robin Hood (Douglas Fairbanks Pictures) 1922 wrappers	50 - 75
MV6650	Dr. Jekyll and Mr. Hyde 1932 John Barrymore	35 - 75
MV6660	Dr. Jekyll and Mr. Hyde 1941 Spencer Tracy, DJ only, no photos	20 - 30
MV6670	Dracula 1931 Bela Lugosi	100 - 300

MV6680	**Elephant Dance** 1937 Sabu	20 - 30
MV6690	**Fighting Back** H. C. Witwer	10 - 15
MV6710	**The Fleets In** Clara Bow	30 - 50
MV6720	**Flight** 1929 Jack Holt	30 - 40
MV6730	**Frankenstein** 1932 Boris Karloff	100 - 250
MV6740	**The Freshman** 1925 Harold Lloyd	25 - 35
MV6750	**The Gaucho** 1927 Douglas Fairbanks	25 - 35
MV6760	**The General** 1927 Buster Keaton	25 - 35
MV6770	**Girl of the Limberlost** Gene Stratton Porter silent film	20 - 30
MM5521	**Gone With the Wind** see Margaret Mitchell in Modern First Editions	
MV6780	**Grass** Meriam C. Cooper documentary	25 - 40
MV6790	**Greed** 1924 Evich Von Stroheim film	30 - 40
MV6800	**Hunchback of Notre Dame** 1923 Lon Chaney	45 - 75
MV6820	**The Iron Horse** 1924 John Ford film	20 - 30
MV6830	**The Jazz Singer** 1927 Al Jolson	25 - 45
MV6840	**Jungle Menace** Frank Buck	20 - 30
MV6850	**King Kong** 1933 no interior stills, end sheets only illustrated, rare, w/DJ	1000+
	w/o DJ	25 - 30
MV6860	**The King of Kings** 1927 Cecil B. DeMille film	20 - 35
MV6870	**The Lost World** 1925 Wallace Berry	35 - 75
MV6880	**Lilac Time** 1928 Gary Cooper, Clara Bow	35 - 75
MV6890	**Little Robinson Crusoe** 1924 Jackie Cooper	25 - 40
MV6910	**London After Midnight** Lon Chaney	100 - 200
MV6920	**The Lone Wolf Returns** Louis Vance	10 - 15
MV6930	**The Lost Patrol** 1934 John Ford film, DJ only	10 - 20
MV6940	**Love** (Anna Kavenina) Greta Garbo	35 - 50
MV6950	**Madam Sans-Gêne** Gloria Swanson	12 - 18
MV6960	**The Mark of Zorro** Douglas Fairbanks	30 - 45
MV6970	**The Marriage Playground** Edith Wharton	12 - 18
MV6980	**The Miracle Man** Frank Packard	10 - 15
MV6990	**Noahs Ark** 1928	20 - 35

MV7000	**Old Ironsides** Harry Carr	15 - 25
MV7010	**Orphans of the Storm** 1922 D.W. Griffith film	25 - 45
MV7020	**Outside the Law** Lon Chaney	
MV7030	**The Painted Lady** Larry Evans	10 - 15
MV7040	**The Patent Leather Kid** 1927 Richard Barthelmess	25 - 45
MV7050	**Peter Pan** 1925 Betty Bronson	25 - 40
MV7060	**Phantom of the Opera** 1925 Lon Chaney	100 - 200
MV7070	**Queen Christina** Faith MacKenzie, Greta Garbo	20 - 30
MV7080	**Romola** Lillian Gish	12 - 18
MV7100	**The Scarlet Letter** 1926	20 - 30
MV7110	**The Sea Beast** 1928 John Barrymore	25 - 40
MV7120	**She** 1917	90 - 150
MV7130	**Speedy** Harold Lloyd	15 - 25
MV7135	**A Story of Our Gang** Racine (Whitman) 1929 bds.	25 - 35
MV7140	**Strangers May Kiss** Norma Shearer	12 - 18
MV7150	**A Tale of Two Cities** Ronald Coleman	12 - 18
MV7160	**Tarzan and the Golden Lion** 1927	100 - 175

MV6760

MV6840

MV6880

MV6920

MV6950

MV6970

MV6980

MV7000

MV7020

MV7030

MV7070

MV7080

MV7130

MV7135

MV7140

MV7150

MV7170

MV7210

MV7230

MV7240

MV8780

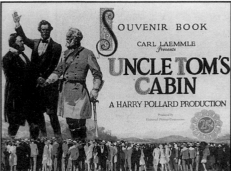

MV9080	**MV9640**	**MV9640**

	MV9700	**MV9780**

MV7170	**The Ten Commandments** 1922 Cecil B. DeMille film, Jeanie MacPherson	12 - 18
MV7180	**The Thief of Bagdad** Douglas Fairbanks	50 - 75
MV7190	**Three Bad Men** 1926	20 - 30
MV7200	**Tolable David** 1921 Richard Barthelmess	15 - 25
MV7210	**The Trail of '98** Robert Service	15 - 25
MV7230	**The Vagabond Lover** (Rudy Vallee)	12 - 18
MV7240	**'Way Down East** 1920 D.W. Griffith film, Joseph Grismer	12 - 18
MV7250	**When a Feller Needs a Friend** Jackie Cooper	12 - 18
MV7260	**The White Sister** 1923	20 - 30
MV7270	**The Wind** 1928	20 - 30
MV7280	**Wings** 1927	30 - 45

Reference Books and Annuals

MV8020	**Bluebook of the Screen** Ruth Wing (editor)	30 - 50
MV8040	**Film Daily Year Books** 1924-1929	30 - 50
MV8042	1930-1950	20 - 30
MV8044	1951-1964	20 - 25
MV8046	1965-1970	15 - 25
MV8080	**Motion Picture Almanac** Martin Quigley (editor) 1929	50 - 75
MV8100	**Motion Picture Studio Directory** 1918	75 - 125
MV8120	**Six United Showmen** United Artists campaign book 1938-39, large folio-size w/movie ads	50 - 70
MV8140	**Stars of the Movies** 1927	30 - 50
MV8160	**Stars of the Photoplay** 1924	30 - 50
MV8180	**Stars of the Photoplay** 1930	30 - 50
MV8200	**Theatrical Guide and Moving Picture Directory** Julius Cahn & Gus Hill 1921	40 - 60

Theatre Programs

Most theatre programs are soft-cover books, about 9"x12" in size, with photos and information about how the film was made. Some later programs from the 1950s-60s are hard cover. They were usually purchased in the theatre lobby for as little as 25¢. The silent movie programs are worth at least $25. Listings are alphabetical by title.

MV8500	**All Quiet on the Western Front** 1930 Lew Ayres	45 - 75
MV8520	**America** 1924 D.W. Griffith film	45 - 75
MV8530	**Beau Geste** 1926 Ronald Colman	20 - 30
MV8540	**Ben Hur** 1926 Ramon Navarro	25 - 40
MV8560	**The Best Years of Our Lives** 1946 Fredric March, Myrna Loy	30 - 50
MV8580	**The Better 'Ole** 1926	25 - 40
MV8590	**The Big Parade** 1925 King Vidor directed	25 - 40
MV8600	**The Birth of a Nation** 1915 D.W. Griffith film	50 - 85
MV8620	**The Black Pirate** 1926 Douglas Fairbanks	45 - 75
MV8640	**The Bridge On the River Kwai** 1957 William Holden	15 - 25
MV8660	**Can Can** Frank Sinatra	20 - 30
MV8680	**Civilization** 1916 Thomas Ince film	50 - 75
MV8700	**The Cockeyed World** 1929 Victor MacLaglen	35 - 50
MV8720	**The Covered Wagon** 1923 Lois Wilson	30 - 50
MV8740	**Cyrano de Bergerac** 1951 Jose Ferrer	15 - 25
MV8760	**Dinner at 8** 1933 Jean Harlow, John Barrymore	30 - 50
MV8770	**Don Juan** 1926 John Barrymore	45 - 60
MV8780	**East of Eden** 1955 James Dean	50 - 75
MV8800	**For Whom the Bell Tolls** 1943 Gary Cooper	30 - 50
MV8820	**The Four Horsemen of the Apocalypse** 1921 Rudolph Valentino	50 - 75
MV8840	**Gigi** 1958 Leslie Caron	15 - 25
MM5521	**Gone With the Wind** see Margaret Mitchell under Modern First Editions	
MV8860	**The Good Earth** 1937 Louise Rainer, Paul Muni	20 - 35

MV8880	**Grand Hotel** 1932 Greta Garbo, John Barrymore	45 - 75
MV8900	**The Great Dictator** 1940 Charlie Chaplin	50 - 75
MV8920	**The Great Ziegfeld** 1936 William Powell, Myrna Loy	30 - 50
MV8940	**The Greatest Show On Earth** 1952 Cecil B. DeMille film	20 - 30
MV8960	**Guys and Dolls** 1955 Marlon Brando	15 - 25
MV8980	**Hamlet** 1950 Lawrence Olivier	15 - 25
MV9000	**Hans Christian Anderson** 1952 Danny Kaye	15 - 25
MV9020	**Hearts of the World** 1918 D.W. Griffith film	50 - 75
MV9040	**Hells Angels** 1930 Jean Harlow, Ben Lyon, small hardcover	35 - 50
MV9060	**Henry V** 1946 Lawrence Olivier	15 - 25
MV9080	**Hunchback of Notre Dame** 1923 Lon Chaney	65 - 100
MV9100	**In Old Chicago** 1938 Tyrone Power, Alice Faye	30 - 50
MV9120	**The Iron Horse** 1924 John Ford directed	30 - 50
MV9140	**Ivan the Terrible** 1947 Sergei Elsenstein film	25 - 45
MV9160	**Joan of Arc** 1950 Ingrid Bergman	20 - 30
MV9180	**Julius Caesar** 1953 Marlon Brando	15 - 25
MV9200	**The King of Kings** 1927 Cecil B. DeMille film	20 - 35
MV9220	**Knights of the Round Table** 1954 Robert Taylor	15 - 25
MV9240	**La Dolce Vita** 1966 Frederico Fellini film	20 - 30
MV9260	**Lilac Time** 1928 Colleen Moore, Gary Cooper	45 - 60
MV9280	**Limelight** 1953 Charlie Chaplin	30 - 50
MV9300	**Moulin Rouge** 1953 Jose Ferrer	20 - 30
MV9320	**Noah's Ark** 1929 Delores Costello	30 - 50
MV9340	**Old Ironsides** 1926 George Bancroft	30 - 45
MV9360	**Quo Vadis** Robert Taylor	15 - 25
MV9380	**The Red Shoes** 1951 Moira Shearer	10 - 20
MV9400	**Riptide** 1934 Norma Shearer	30 - 50
MV9420	**The Robe** 1953 Richard Burton	20 - 30
MV9440	**Romeo and Juliet** 1936 Leslie Howard, Norma Shearer	20 - 35
MV9460	**Romola** 1924 Lillian Gish	20 - 30
MV9480	**Salome** 1918 Theda Bara	50 - 75
MV9485	**Salome** 1953 Rita Hayworth	20 - 30
MV9500	**Samson & Delilah** 1949 Cecil B. DeMille film	20 - 30
MV9520	**The Sand Pebbles** 1966 Steve McQueen	15 - 20
MV9540	**Scaramouche** 1923 Ramon Navarro	30 - 50
MV9560	**The Sea Beast** 1926 John Barrymore, Delores Costello	35 - 60
MV9580	**Stella Dallas** 1925 Samuel Goldwyn film	20 - 30
MV9600	**Tales of Hoffman** 1952 Moira Shearer	10 - 20
MV9620	**The Ten Commandments** 1923 Cecil B. DeMille film	25 - 40
MV9640	**The Thief of Bagdad** 1924 Douglas Fairbanks	45 - 75
MV9700	**Uncle Tom's Cabin** 1927 Carl Laemmle	30 - 50
MV9720	**The Vanishing American** 1925 Richard Dix	20 - 30
MV9740	**Way Down East** 1920 Lillian Gish, D.W. Griffith film	45 - 65
MV9760	**What Price Glory** 1926 Victor MacLaglen	45 - 60
MV9780	**Wings** 1927 "Buddy" Rogers, Clara Bow	45 - 75
MV9800	**The Winning of Barbara Worth** 1926 Ronald Colman, Vilma Banky	30 - 45

PHOTOGRAPHY

Photography books first became popular in the 19th century. Most from this period are either technical manuals like *The Ferrotype and How to Make It* by Edward Estabrooke NY 1872 ($200-300) or view books with images of people and places. Many of these view books contain original mounted photographs and are among the most valuable books of the 19th century. Alexander Gardner's *Photographic Sketch Book of the War* (NY 1866, $20,000-30,000) has 100 original albumen prints of the Civil War. Books with color photographs were actual hand-colored images since photomechanical color imaging was not invented until the late 19th century. The earliest photographic view book is *The Pencil of Nature* by Henry Fox Talbot (1846) with 24 calotype prints.

A major change occurred around 1890 when pictorialism was introduced. This was part of the photo-secessionist movement founded by Alfred Stieglitz. He wanted photographers to be like artists and not just recorders of reality; pictorialism is an art form similar to impressionist painting in that it attempts to create a mood or atmosphere. The movement's main literary vehicle was *Camera Work*, a quarterly journal founded by Alfred Stieglitz. It ran from 1903 to 1917, a total of 50 issues, and introduced great 20th century photographers like Stieglitz, Paul Strand, Gertrude Käsebier, Edward Steichen, and Alvin Langhorn Coburn. The images in *Camera Work* were photogravures, which were the products of a photographic printing process developed in the late 1800s with a resolution as fine as original mounted prints. A complete run of *Camera Work* could be worth $50,000-$75,000, with some individual issues ranging in the thousands. Issue #36 contains 16 photogravures by Stieglitz and may bring $10,000. "The Steerage," his most famous image, appeared in double issue 7-8 and may be worth $10,000 by itself. Symbolic of the 20th century union of photography and art was Stieglitz using his wife Georgia O'Keefe, a surrealist painter, as a model for many years.

A type of photography which ran counter to pictorialism was surrealism. Developed in the 1920s, it rejected photography as natural beauty and created odd and unusual photos, some with symbolic meaning. Man Ray (1890-1976) was in the forefront of this movement. He produced "Rayographs" (direct photographs of objects placed on light sensitive film to reveal shapes and patterns) and "solarization" (a reversal of an image, creating a negative instead of a positive image).

Life, a pictorial and documentary magazine which debuted in 1936, was to photojournalists what *Camera Work* was to pictorialists. Photojournalism was greatly aided by the development of hand-held cameras, fast shutter speeds, and very-light-sensitive film. Instant moments of emotion and action could now be captured. *Life* became a perfect vehicle for this art form and was the proving ground for important 20th century photographers like Margaret Bourke White, Alfred Eisenstadt, Louis Feininger, Robert Capa, and Philippe Halsman. For these and other pioneering photojournalists (Weegee, Jacob Riis, and Eugene Atget) favorite subjects were people and places in New York, Paris and other large cities. They photographed everything from glamorous movie stars to criminals and palaces to slums. Arthur Fellig, alias Weegee, is perhaps the most popular documentary photographer. He recorded the seamy and often violent aspects of New York during the 1940s-1950s.

Photojournalism was also used to catch newsworthy events. David Douglas Duncan photographed the Vietnam War in *War Without Heroes* (NY 1970).

Nature photography rose to prominence in the 19th century and continues to be very popular. The two American photographers best known for this art form are Ansel Adams and Edward Weston. Adams became a lifetime member of the Sierra Club in the early 1900s and devoted much of his life to studies in Yosemite and the Sierra Nevada mountain range. Weston spent most of his time in the 1920s-1940s photographing California, in particular Point Lobos off the coast. He created unusual photographs of shells, tree roots, vegetables and other common objects.

Books about the history of photography began appearing in the late 1800s. Since then, hundreds have been published about the major photographic eras. These books have themselves become collectible and in some cases very valuable.

Early camera manuals and catalogs for Kodaks, Leicas and other cameras, as well as technical manuals on photography are also valuable. Ansel Adams himself wrote a series of manuals in the 1940s-1950s.

Unlike Modern First Editions, in which the dust jacket and cover are the most critical aspects of a book's condition, a photography books' emphasis is on the images inside. Books which have soiled, torn, or creased photographs are going to be worth a lot less. The dust jacket adds value to most books; books by Adams, Weston, and Weegee are usually worth much more with jackets. This is especially true for books printed in the 1940s and earlier. For many early photography books, the dust jackets are very rare and add considerably to the value.

The following list is alphabetized by the photographers' or authors' last names. Handbooks and books on photography's history are in the second section. Prices are for books in fine condition with all original parts as applicable: dust jackets, slipcases, boxes, etc.

Books By or About Photographers

Abbott, Berenice

PG0030	**The Attractive Universe** Clev 1969, DJ	50 - 70
PG0038	**Berenice Abbott** NY 1970, DJ	50 - 75
PG0046	**Berenice Abbott Photographs** Wash 1990	50 - 75
PG0054	**Berenice Abbott's New York** NY 1978, 60 cys, 12 signed prints	2000 - 3000
PG0062	**Changing New York** NY 1929, DJ	200 - 300
PG0070	**Greenwich Village Today & Yesterday** NY 1948, DJ	125 - 250
PG0078	**A Portrait of Maine** NY 1968, DJ	50 - 75
PG0086	**Ten Photographs** Roslyn Heights 1976, 50 cys, 12 prints signed	2000 - 3000

Adams, Ansel

PG0120	**Ansel Adams** Bos 1980, DJ	125 - 250
PG0128	**Ansel Adams: An Autobiography** Bos 1985, DJ	50 - 75
PG0136	**Ansel Adams: Images 1923-1974** Bos 1974, DJ, slipcase	150 - 250
PG0137	Bos 1974, 1000 cys, slipcase, signed print	2000 - 3000
PG0139	NY 1981, DJ	100 - 150
PG0148	**Ansel Adams: The American Wilderness** Bos 1990, DJ	100 - 150
PG0156	**Arthur Putnam, Sculpture** SF 1932, 500 cys	1000 - 1500
PG0164	**Born Free and Equal** NY 1944, DJ	200 - 300
PG0172	**Death Valley** Redwood City 1954, DJ	300 - 500
PG0180	**The Eloquent Light** SF 1963, DJ	250 - 350
PG0182	NY 1980, DJ	75 - 125
PG0190	**Examples: The Making of 40 Photographs** Bos 1983, DJ	125 - 250
PG0198	**Fiat Lux** NY 1967, DJ	150 - 250
PG0206	**Images 1923-1974** Bos 1974, DJ/Slipcase	150 - 250
PG0214	**An Introduction to Hawaii** SF 1964, DJ	150 - 250
PG0222	**The Islands of Hawaii** SF 1958, DJ	250 - 350
PG0224	SF 1974, DJ	100 - 150
PG0232	**The Land of Little Rain** Bos 1950, DJ	200 - 300
PG0240	**Lights and Shadows of Yosemite** SF 1926	200 - 300
PG0248	**Making a Photograph** Lon 1939, DJ	150 - 250
PG0250	Lon 1948, DJ	100 - 150
PG0258	**My Camera in the National Parks** Bos 1950, DJ	250 - 350
PG0266	**My Camera in Yosemite Valley** Bos 1949, DJ	250 - 350
PG0274	**The Pageant of History in Northern California** SF 1954	150 - 250
PG0282	**Parmelian Prints of the High Sierras** SF 1927	20000 - 30000
PG0290	**Photographs of the South West** Bos 1976, DJ	150 - 250
PG0298	**Polaroid Land Photography** NY 1963, DJ	30 - 50
PG0306	**Portfolio One** SF 1948, 75 cys, 12 signed prints	20000 - 30000
PG0314	**Portfolio Two: The National Parks** SF 1950, 150 cys, 15 signed prints	20000 - 30000

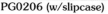
PG0206 (w/slipcase)

PG0610	**PG1155**	**PG2375**

PG0322	**Portfolio Three: Yosemite Valley** SF 1960, 258 cys, 16 signed prints	25000 - 35000
PG0330	**Portfolio Four: What Majestic Word** SF 1963, 110 cys, 15 signed prints	25000 - 35000
PG0338	**Portfolio V** NY 1971, 110 cys, 10 signed prints	20000 - 30000
PG0346	**Portfolio VI** NY 1974 110 cys, 10 signed prints	30000 - 40000
PG0354	**Portfolio VII** NY 1976, 115 cys, 12 signed prints	25000 - 35000
PG0362	**The Portfolios of Ansel Adams** NY 1977, DJ	150 - 250
PG0370	**Sierra Nevada: The John Muir Trail** Berkeley 1938, 500 cys	1000 - 1500
PG0378	**Singular Images** Bos 1974	50 - 75
PG0386	**Taos Pueblo** SF 1930	15000 - 20000
PG0394	**This is the American Earth** SF 1960, DJ	200 - 300
PG0402	**What Majestic Word; In Memory of Russell Varian** SF 1963, 200 cys	800 - 1200
PG0410	**Yosemite and the Range of Light** Bos 1979, DJ	100 - 150
PG0418	**Yosemite and the Sierra Nevada** Bos 1948, DJ	125 - 250
PG0426	**Yosemite Valley** SF 1959, DJ	150 - 250

Adams, W. I. Lincoln (also see Histories & Handbooks)

PG0460	**Photographing in Old England, With Some Snapshots in Scotland and Wales** NY 1910	100 - 150
PG0465	**Sunlight and Shadow** NY 1897	75 - 125

Anderson, A. J.

PG0490	**The ABC of Artistic Photography** NY 1910	1200 - 1800
PG0492	NY 1913	200 - 300

Annan, Thomas

PG0520	**Glasgow City Improvement Trust, Old Closes and Streets, A Series of Photogravures 1868-1899** Glasgow 1900, folio, 50 gravures	3000 - 5000

Atget, Eugene

PG0550	**Atget Photographie de Paris** NY 1930, 96 gravures	500 - 700
PG0555	**Atget's Gardens** NY 1979, DJ	50 - 75
PG0560	**Eugene Atget** Millerton 1980	20 - 30
PG0565	**Eugene Atget: A Selection of Photographs From the Mus'ee Carnavalet** NY 1985, DJ	50 - 75
PG0570	**A Vision of Paris** NY 1963, DJ	200 - 300
PG0572	NY 1980, DJ	50 - 75
PG0580	**The Work of Atget** Bos 1981, DJ	50 - 75
PG0585	**The World of Atget** NY 1964, DJ	75 - 125
PG0587	NY 1979, DJ	50 - 75

Avedon, Richard

PG0610	**Avedon Photographs 1947-1977** NY 1978, acetate DJ	50 - 75
PG0618	**Famous Photographer's Course** Westport 1964, 4 vol	75 - 125
PG0626	**In the American West, 1979-1984** NY 1985, DJ	75 - 125
PG0634	**Nothing Personal** NY 1964, DJ	125 - 200
PG0642	**Observations** NY 1959, slipcase	200 - 300
PG0650	**Photographs 1947-1977** NY 1978, glassine DJ	150 - 250
PG0651	Toronto 1978, plastic DJ	150 - 250
PG0660	**Portraits** NY 1976, DJ	50 - 75
PG0668	**Self Portrait in a Convex Mirror** SF 1984, 150 cys, canister, 27 sheets, 8 prints, sound disc	
PG0676	**What Becomes a Legend Most?** NY 1979, DJ	50 - 75

Bailey, David

PG0710	**Black and White Memories** Lon 1983, DJ	30 - 50

Bayer, Herbert

PG0740	**Herbert Bayer: Das Kunsterische Werk 1918-1938** Berlin 1982, wrappers	40 - 60
PG0746	**Herbert Bayer: Painter, Designer, Architect** NY 1967, DJ	50 - 75
PG0752	**Herbert Bayer: Photographic Work** LA 1977, 2500 cys, wrappers	30 - 50
PG0758	**Modern Art in Advertising** Chi 1945	20 - 30

Beaton, Cecil

PG0780	**British Photographers** Lon 1934	50 - 75
PG0785	**Cecil Beaton's New York** Phil 1938, DJ	75 - 125
PG0790	**The Glass of Fashion** Garden City 1954, DJ	50 - 75
PG0795	**Japanese** Lon 1959, DJ	40 - 60
PG0800	**The Magic Image** NY 1975, DJ	40 - 60
PG0805	**Portrait of New York** Lon 1948, DJ	50 - 75
PG0810	**The Wandering Years** Bos 1961, DJ	30 - 50

Bellocq, E. J.

PG0830	**Storyville Portraits** NY 1970, DJ	50 - 75

Berger, Charles

PG0850	**Image Tibet** SF 1973, DJ	50 - 75

Bidermanas, Izis

PG0870	**Paris Des Rêves** Lausanne 1950, 75 gravures, DJ	300 - 500
PG0880	**The World of Marc Chagall** NY 1968	100 - 150

Bischof, Warner

PG0900	**Japan** NY 1954, DJ	100 - 150
PG0910	**Our Leave in Switzerland** Zurich 1946-47, 200 gravures, DJ	100 - 150
PG0915	**Warner Bischof** NY 1966, 500 cys, wrappers	50 - 75
PG0920	**The World of Warner Bischof** NY 1959, DJ	100 - 150

Black, Alexander

PG0940	**Miss America: Pen & Camera Sketches of the American Girl** NY 1899	100 - 150
PG0945	**Miss Jerry** NY 1895	75 - 125
PG0950	**Photography Indoors and Out** Bos 1897	50 - 75
PG0955	**Time and Chance: Adventures with People and Print** NY 1937, DJ	50 - 75

Blossfeldt, Karl

PG0975	**Art Forms in Nature** Lon 1929, DJ, 120 gravures	300 - 500
PG0977	NY 1967, DJ	50 - 75
PG0985	**Urformen Der Kunst** Berlin 1929, DJ	300 - 500
PG0987	Berlin 1936, DJ	200 - 300

Bonaparte, Roland

PG1010	**Les Habitants de Suriname** Paris 1884, 61 gravures	2000 - 3000

Bonfils, Maison

PG1030	**Souvenir de Jerusalem** Leipzig 1895, 30 gravures	200 - 300

Bonney, M.

PG1050	**Europe's Children 1939-1943** NY 1943, DJ	100 - 150

Boubat, Edouard

PG1070	**Pauses** Paris 1983, DJ	50 - 75

Boughton, Alice

PG1090	**Photographing the Famous** NY 1928	100 - 150

Bourke-White, Margaret

PG1110	**"Dear Fatherland Rest Quietly"** NY 1946, DJ	75 - 125
PG1115	**Eyes on Russia** NY 1931, DJ	300 - 500
PG1120	**Halfway to Freedom** NY 1949, DJ	75 - 125
PG1125	**Interview with India** Lon 1950, DJ	75 - 125
PG1130	**Newsprint** Montreal 1939	75 - 125
PG1135	**Say, Is This the U.S.A.** NY 1941, DJ	75 - 125
PG1140	**They Called It the Purple Heart Valley** NY 1944, DJ	50 - 75
PG1145	**You Have Seen Their Faces** NY 1937, cl, DJ	150 - 250
PG1146	NY 1937, wrappers, DJ	75 - 125

Brady, Mathew

PG1155	**Mathew Brady** (James Horan) NY 1955, DJ	40 - 60
PG1160	**Mathew Brady's Great Americans** NY 1975, 2500 cys, 10 prints	300 - 500
PG1170	**Mr. Lincoln's Camera Man Mathew B. Brady** NY 1946, DJ	50 - 75
PG1175	**Mr. Lincoln's Contemporaries** NY 1951, DJ	50 - 75

Brandt, Bill

PG1200	**Camera in London** Lon 1948	200 - 300
PG1205	**The English at Home** Lon 1936	300 - 500
PG1210	**Literary Britain** Lon 1951, DJ	150 - 250
PG1215	**Perspective of Nudes** NY 1961, DJ	125 - 250
PG1220	**Shadow of Light** NY 1966, DJ	100 - 150

Brassai (Gyula Halsz)

PG1240	**Camera in Paris** Lon 1949	100 - 150
PG1245	**Conversations Avec Picasso** Paris 1964, wrappers	100 - 150

PG1250 **Fiesta in Seville** NY 1956, DJ 75 - 125
PG1255 **Histoire de Marie** Paris 1949, 2500 cys,
    wrappers, box 150 - 250
PG1260 **Les Sculptures de Picasso** Paris 1948, glassine DJ 75 - 125
PG1261 Lon 1949, DJ (English ed) 75 - 125
PG1265 **Paris de Nuit** Paris 1933 300 - 500
PG1270 **Picasso and Company** Garden City 1966, DJ 50 - 75
PG1275 **The Secret Paris of the 30's** NY 1976, DJ 30 - 50

Braun, Adolphe
PG1300 **Enseignement de L'Historie de L'Art** Paris
    1890-1900, 49 gravures, portfolio 200 - 300

Bravo, Manuel Alvarez
PG1320 **Dreams, Visions, Metaphors: The Photographs
    of Manuel Alvarez Bravo** Jerusalem 1983 20 - 30
PG1330 **Manuel Alvarez Bravo: Fotographias** Mexico
    1945, wrappers 300 - 500

Brodovitch, Alexey
PG1350 **Ballet** NY 1945, DJ 50 - 75

Bruce, Wallace
PG1370 **Panorama of the Hudson** NY 1903 50 - 75

Bruehl, Anton
PG1390 **Magic Dials, The Story of Radio and Television**
    NY 1939, DJ 50 - 75
PG1395 **Photographs of Mexico** NY 1933, 1000 cys 200 - 300

Bruguiere, Francis
PG1420 **Beyond This Point** Lon 1929, DJ 150 - 250
PG1425 **Bruguiere** NY 1977, DJ 30 - 50
PG1430 **The Evanescent City** SF 1925 75 - 125
PG1435 **A Project for a Theatrical Presentation of the
    Divine Comedy of Dante Alighieri** NY 1924 200 - 300
PG1440 **San Francisco** SF 1918, DJ 150 - 250

Bullock, Wynn
PG1460 **The Widening Stream** 1965, 2000 cys 100 - 150
PG1470 **Wynn Bullock** SF 1971, glassine DJ 200 - 300

Burdekin, Harold
PG1490 **London Night** Lon 1934, 150 cys, 50 gravures 200 - 300

Burri, Rene
PG1510 **The Gaucho** NY 1968, DJ 30 - 50

Buscovich, Mario
PG1530 **Manhattan Magic** NY 1937, wrappers 50 - 75
PG1535 **Paris** Paris 1928 100 - 150
PG1540 **Photographs by Mario Buscovich** NY 1930 50 - 75

Caffin, Charles H.
PG1570 **Photography as a Fine Art** NY 1901 100 - 150

Cali, Francois
PG1600 **Sortilèges de Paris** Paris 1952, DJ 100 - 150

Callahan, Harry
PG1630 **Harry Callahan** NY 1967, DJ 25 - 50
PG1640 **Harry Callahan** Albu 1988 20 - 30
PG1650 **Harry Callahan Photographs** NY 1981, wrappers 30 - 50
PG1660 **Landscapes 1941-1971** NY 1972, 25 cys,
    10 prints 3000 - 5000
PG1670 **The Multiple Image** Chi 1961, wrappers 75 - 125
PG1680 **Photographs: Harry Callahan** Santa Barbara
    1964, 1500 cys, slipcase 500 - 700
PG1690 **Photographs in Color** Tucson 1980, wrappers 30 - 50

Cameron, Julia Margret
PG1720 **Alfred, Lord Tennyson and His Friends**
    Lon 1893, 400 cys, 25 gravures 2000 - 3000
PG1725 **A Victorian Album** NY 1975, 100 cys, slipcase 200 - 300
PG1726 NY 1975, DJ (trade ed) 50 - 75
PG1735 **Victorian Photographs of Famous Men and
    Fair Women** Lon 1926, 450 cys 500 - 700
PG1736 NY 1926, 250 cys 500 - 700
PG1738 Bos 1973, DJ 50 - 75

Capa, Robert
PG1770 **The Battle of Waterloo Road** NY 1941, DJ 100 - 150
PG1780 **Death in the Making** NY 1938 150 - 250
PG1790 **Images of War** NY 1964, DJ 75 - 125
PG1795 **Invasion!** NY 1944, DJ 75 - 125
PG1805 **Report on Israel** NY 1950 50 - 75
PG1810 **Robert Capa** NY 1966, 61 gravures, wrappers 50 - 75
PG1815 **A Russian Journal** (John Steinbeck) NY 1948, DJ 100 - 150
PG1820 **Slightly Out of Focus** NY 1947, DJ 100 - 150

Caponigro, Paul
PG1850 **Megaliths** Bos 1986, DJ 75 - 125

PG1860 **Sunflower** NY 1974, wrappers 30 - 50
PG1870 **The Wise Silence** Bos 1983, DJ 100 - 150

Carroll, Lewis
PG1900 **Diaries of Lewis Carroll** NY 1954, 2 vol 30 - 50
PG1910 **Lewis Carroll, Photographer**
    Lon 1949, DJ 75 - 125
PG1920 **The Lewis Carroll Picture Book** Lon 1909 100 - 150

Cartier-Bresson, Henri
PG1950 **Beautiful Jaipur** Jaipur 1948 200 - 300
PG1960 **Cartier-Bresson's France** NY 1970, DJ 50 - 75
PG1970 **The Decisive Moment** Paris 1952, DJ, booklet
    insert 500 - 700
PG1971 NY 1952, DJ, booklet insert 400 - 600
PG1973 NY 1955, DJ, booklet insert 300 - 500
PG1980 **The Europeans** NY 1955, 114 gravures, folio 300 - 500
PG1990 **The Galveston That Was** NY 1966 100 - 150
PG2000 **Les Europeens** Paris 1955, 114 gravures, folio 300 - 500
PG2010 **Man and Machine** NY 1971, DJ 75 - 125
PG2020 **The People of Moscow** NY 1955, DJ 200 - 300
PG2030 **Photographs** NY 1963, DJ 30 - 50
PG2040 **Photographs by Cartier-Bresson** NY 1963, DJ 75 - 125
PG2041 Lon 1964, DJ 75 - 125
PG2050 **The World of Henri Cartier-Bresson**
    NY 1968, DJ 100 - 150

Cave, Henry W.
PG2080 **The Ruined Cities of Ceylon** Lon 1897,
    47 gravures 300 - 500

Clark, Larry
PG2110 **Teenage Lust** NY 1987, wrappers 75 - 125
PG2120 **Tulsa** NY 1971, wrappers 200 - 300
PG2122 NY 1985 75 - 125

Clergue, Lucien
PG2150 **Naissances D'Aphrodite** NY 1966, DJ 125 - 250
PG2160 **Née de la Vague** Montreal 1960, wrappers 125 - 250
PG2170 **Nude Work Shop** NY 1982, DJ 50 - 75

Coburn, Alvin Langdon
PG2200 **Alvin Langdon Coburn Photographer**
    Lon 1966, DJ 75 - 125
PG2201 NY 1966, DJ 75 - 125
PG2205 **The Book of Harlech** Harlech 1920 300 - 500
PG2210 **Chesterton** Lon 1914, 10 gravures, DJ 800 - 1200
PG2215 **The Door in the Wall** NY 1911, DJ, 600 cys,
    10 gravures 2000 - 3000
PG2225 **The Intelligence of Flowers** NY 1907, DJ 75 - 125
PG2235 **London** NY 1909, 20 gravures 3000 - 5000
PG2240 **Men of Mark** Lon 1913, 33 gravures 3000 - 5000
PG2245 **Moor Park** Lon 1914, 20 gravures, DJ 800 - 1200
PG2250 **More Men of Mark** Lon 1922, 33 gravures 800 - 1200
PG2260 **New York** Lon 1910, 20 gravures 3000 - 5000
PG2265 **The Novels and Tales of Henry James**
    NY 1907-09, 22 vol, 22 gravures 2000 - 3000
PG2270 **A Portfolio of Sixteen Photographs by Alvin
    Langdon Coburn** NY 1962, 16 gravures, 2000 cys 125 - 250

Cole, Ernest
PG2300 **House of Bondage** NY 1967, DJ 40 - 60

Cunningham, Imogen
PG2330 **Imogen Cunningham: A Portrait** Bos 1979, DJ 50 - 75
PG2340 **Imogen! Imogen Cunningham Photographs
    1910-1973** Seattle 1974 125 - 250
PG2350 **Photographs** Seattle 1970, DJ 125 - 200

Curtis, Edward S.
PG2375 **Edward S. Curtis** (Barbara A. Davis) SF 1985, DJ 40 - 60
PG2380 **The Flute of the Gods** NY 1909, DJ, 24 gravures 300 - 500
PG2390 **In the Land of the Head-Hunters: Indian Life
    and Indian Lore** Yonkers-on-Hudson 1915 300 - 500
PG2400 **The North American Indian** Cambridge 1907-30,
    20 vol text, 20 portfolios, 500 sets 125000 - 175000
PG2410 **Visions of a Vanishing Race** NY 1976, DJ 50 - 75

Daguerre, L. J. M.
PG2440 **L. J. M. Daguerre** Clev 1956, DJ 75 - 125

Davies, G. Christopher
PG2470 **On Dutch Waterways** Lon 1890, 12 gravures 500 - 700
PG2475 **The Rivers and Broads of Norfolk and Suffolk**
    Lon 1889, 48 gravures, wrappers 3000 - 5000

Davis, Robert
PG2510 **Man Makes His Own Mask** NY 1932,
    160 cys, box 125 - 200

Day, F. Holland
PG2540 Slave to Beauty Bos 1981, 60 cys   200 - 300
PG2541 Bos 1981, DJ (trade ed)   50 - 75
De Carava, Roy
PG2570 The Sweet Flypaper of Life NY 1955   75 - 125
De Lamater, R. S.
PG2600 Sunlight Pictures Hartford 1892   75 - 125
Delcroix, Eugene
PG2630 Patios, Stairways and Iron Lace Balconies of
        Old New Orleans New Orleans 1938, DJ   50 - 75
Disframer
PG2660 Disframer Danbury 1976, DJ   100 - 150
Dixon, Joseph
PG2690 The Vanishing Race Garden City 1913,
        80 gravures   200 - 300
Dobyns, Winifred
PG2720 California Gardens NY 1931   50 - 75
Doisneau, Robert
PG2750 1 2 3 4 5 Phil 1955, DJ   50 - 75
PG2760 Bistrots Paris 1960, wrappers   30 - 50
PG2770 My Paris NY 1972, DJ   50 - 75
PG2780 Paris NY 1956   200 - 300
Dorr, Nell
PG2810 The Bare Feet Bos 1962, DJ   75 - 125
PG2820 In a Blue Moon NY 1939, slipcase   125 - 250
PG2830 Life Dance Allendale, NJ 1975, 250 cys, DJ   100 - 150
PG2840 Mother and Child NY 1954, DJ   100 - 150
Drtikol, Frantisek
PG2870 Frantisek Drtikol Prague 1988   50 - 75
Dunbar, Paul Lawrence (see Modern First Editions)
Duncan, David Douglas
PG2900 Goodbye Picasso NY 1974, DJ   150 - 250
PG2910 Picassos Picassos NY 1961, DJ   150 - 250
PG2920 The Silent Studio NY 1976, DJ   40 - 60
PG2930 This is War! NY 1951, DJ   100 - 150
PG2940 War Without Heroes NY 1970, DJ   100 - 150
PG2950 Yankee Nomad: A Photographic Odyssey
        NY 1966, DJ   50 - 75
Edgerton, Harold
PG2980 Flash! Seeing the Unseen by Ultra High-Speed
        Photography Bos 1939, DJ   200 - 300
PG2982 Bos 1954, DJ   75 - 125
Eickemeyer, Carl
PG3010 Among the Pueblo Indians NY 1895   200 - 300
Eickemeyer, Rudolf Jr.
PG3040 Down South NY 1900   300 - 500
PG3045 The Old Farm NY 1901   150 - 250
PG3050 Winter NY 1903   150 - 250
Elder, Paul
PG3080 California the Beautiful SF 1911, DJ   50 - 75
PG3085 The Old Spanish Missions of California
        SF 1913, DJ   50 - 75
Elkus, Richard
PG3120 Alamos: A Philosophy in Living SF 1965
Elmendorf, Dwight
PG3150 A Camera Crusade Through the Holy Land
        NY 1912   50 - 75
PG3152 Lon 1913   50 - 75
Emerson, P. H.
PG3190 Birds, Beasts and Fishes of the Norfolk
        Broadland Lon 1895 (written by Emerson
        but photographer's identity unknown)   100 - 150
PG3195 The Compleat Angler Lon 1888, 250 cys,
        2 vol, 54 gravures   2000 - 3000
PG3196 Lon 1888 500 cys, 2 vol, 54 gravures   800 - 1200
PG3200 Marsh Leaves Lon 1895, 300 cys   1000 - 1500
PG3205 On English Lagoons Lon 1893, 100 cys,
        15 gravures   3000 - 5000
PG3206 Lon 1893 (1st trade ed)   300 - 500
PG3210 Pictures of East Anglian Life Lon 1888,
        275 cys, 32 gravures   3000 - 5000
PG3215 Wild Life on a Tidal Water Lon 1890,
        500 cys, 30 gravures   3000 - 5000
English, Douglas
PG3250 Photography For Naturalists Lon 1901   75 - 125

Ericson, A. W.
PG3280 Fine California Views Eureka 1975, 100 cys,
        1 orig print, DJ   150 - 250
Evans, Frederick
PG3310 Twenty Five Great Houses of France Lon, folio   200 - 300
PG3305 The Works of George Meredith
        NY 1909, 29 vol, gravures   800 - 1200
Evans, Walker
PG3340 American Photographs NY 1938, DJ   200 - 350
PG3342 NY 1962, DJ   100 - 150
MC5510 The Bridge (see **Hart Crane** in **Modern First Editions**)
PG3350 The Crime of Cuba Phil 1933, DJ   125 - 250
PG3355 First and Last NY 1978, DJ   150 - 250
PG3365 Let Us Now Praise Famous Men Bos 1941, DJ   100 - 150
PG3370 Many Are Called Bos 1966, DJ   50 - 75
PG3380 Walker Evans NY 1971, DJ   30 - 50
Farnsworth, Emma Justine
PG3410 In Arcadia NY 1892, 5 gravures   300 - 500
Fassbender, Adolf
PG3440 Pictorial Artistry NY 1937, 1000 cys   150 - 250
Feininger, Andreas
PG3470 The Face of New York NY 1954, DJ   50 - 75
PG3475 Feininger's Chicago NY 1980, 1000 cys, DJ   50 - 75
PG3480 Forms of Nature and Life NY 1966, DJ   50 - 75
PG3490 New York Chi 1945   50 - 75
PG3500 Stockholm Stockholm 1936   300 - 500
PG3510 The World Through My Eyes NY 1963   50 - 75
Fenton, Roger
PG3550 Roger Fenton of Crimble Hall Bos 1976, DJ   75 - 125
PG3560 Roger Fenton: Photographer of the Crimean
        War Lon 1954, DJ   50 - 75
Fiske, George
PG3590 In the Heart of the Sierras Yosemite Valley 1886 200 - 300
Flaherty, Robert
PG3620 Eskimos: A Portfolio of Six Photogravures
        NY 1920-21   800 - 1200
Frank, Robert
PG3655 The Americans NY 1968, wrappers   100 - 150
PG3657 NY 1969, DJ   100 - 150
PG3665 Indiens Pas Morts Paris 1956, DJ   50 - 75
PG3670 Indios Zurich 1956, DJ   100 - 150
PG3675 The Lines of My Hands NY 1989, glassine DJ   50 - 75
PG3680 Pull My Daisy (by Jack Kerouac) NY 1959, DJ   150 - 250
PG3690 Zero Reads a Book NY 1963   30 - 50
Freed, Leonard
PG3720 Black in White America NY 1967, wrappers   30 - 50
Freund, Gisele
PG3750 James Joyce in Paris: His Final Years NY 1965, DJ 50 - 75
Friedlander, Lee
PG3780 Flowers and Trees NY 1981, portfolio   150 - 250
Funke, Jaronir
PG3810 Prazske Kostely Prague 1946   75 - 125
Genthe, Arnold
PG3840 As I Remember NY 1936, DJ   100 - 150
PG3845 The Book of the Dance NY 1916, DJ   125 - 250
PG3855 The Gardens of Kijkuit Balt 1919   200 - 300
PG3860 Highlights and Shadows NY 1937   75 - 125
PG3865 Impressions of Old New Orleans NY 1926, DJ   75 - 125
PG3870 Isadora Duncan 24 Studies NY 1929, DJ   200 - 300
PG3875 Pictures of Old Chinatown NY 1908, DJ   125 - 250
PG3877 NY 1913, DJ   100 - 150
PG3885 Sanctuary, A Bird Masque NY 1914, DJ   75 - 125
PG3890 Walt Whitman in Camden Camden 1938,
        1100 cys, slipcase   100 - 150
Gibson, William Hamilton
PG3920 Eye Spy NY 1897   75 - 125
PG3925 Sharp Eyes NY 1891   75 - 125
Gleason, Herbert W.
PG3960 Our National Parks Bos 1901   100 - 150
PG3965 Steep Trails Bos 1918, DJ   50 - 75
PG3970 Through the Year With Thoreau Bos 1917, DJ   150 - 250
Guillot, Laure Albin
PG4000 Micrographie Decorative Paris 1931, 300 cys,
        20 prints   1000 - 1500
Haas, Ernst
PG4030 In America NY 1975, DJ   30 - 50

Hajek-Halke, H.
PG4060　Experimentelle Fotografie Bonn 1955　　150 - 250
Halsman, Philippe
PG4085　Dalí's Mustache NY 1954, DJ　　75 - 125
PG4090　The Frenchman NY 1949, wrappers　　30 - 50
PG4095　Halsman on the Creation of Photographic Ideas
　　　　NY 1963, DJ　　50 - 75
PG4100　Halsman Portraits NY 1983, DJ　　50 - 75
PG4105　Halsman Sight and Insight Garden City 1972, DJ　50 - 75
PG4110　The Jump Book NY 1959, DJ　　50 - 75
Hampton Camera Club (see Paul Lawrence Dunbar in
　Modern First Editions)
Hanscom, Adelaide
PG4140　The Rubaiyat of Omar Khayyam NY 1905,
　　　　28 gravures　　125 - 250
Harney, W. D.
PG4170　Art Work of Seattle & Alaska Racine 1907,
　　　　9 vol, 75 gravures　　800 - 1200
Hartmann, Sadakichi
PG4200　Composition in Portraiture NY 1909, DJ　　200 - 300
Haskins, William C.
PG4230　Canal Zone Pilot Panama 1908, wrappers,
　　　　2 rolled panoramas　　300 - 500
Haynes, F. Jay
PG4250　F. Jay Haynes Photographer (Robert Archibald,
　　　　Director) Helena 1981, DJ　　30 - 50
PG4255　Following the Equator with F. Jay Haynes
　　　　(Freeman Tilden) NY 1964, DJ　　50 - 75
PG4260　A Treatise on Portrait Painting Lon 1887　　100 - 150
PG4265　Following the Frontier with F. Jay Haynes
　　　　(Freeman Tilden) NY 1955, DJ　　40 - 60
Heath, David
PG4290　A Dialogue with Solitude NY 1965, DJ　　150 - 250
Henle, Fritz
PG4320　The American Virgin Islands: A Photographic
　　　　Essay NY 1971, portfolio　　100 - 150
PG4325　China NY 1943, DJ　　30 - 50
Hill, David Octavius
PG4350　An Early Victorian Album NY 1976, DJ　　50 - 75
Hill, Oliver
PG4380　The Garden of Adonis Lon 1923, 48 gravures　300 - 500
Hiller, Lejaren
PG4410　Surgery Through the Ages NY 1944　　125 - 250
Hine, Lewis
PG4440　America & Lewis Hine: Photographs 1904-1940
　　　　Millerton 1977, DJ　　50 - 75
PG4445　The Clothing Workers in Philadelphia Phil 1940, DJ 50 - 75
PG4450　Lewis Hine in Europe NY 1988, DJ　　50 - 75
PG4455　Men at Work NY 1932, DJ　　300 - 500
PG4460　Our Foreigners New Haven 1920, DJ　　150 - 250
PG4465　Portfolio 1 Rochester 1974, 50 cys, 10 prints 2000 - 3000
PG4470　Skyscraper NY 1933, DJ　　100 - 150
Hinton, A. Horsley
PG4500　Practical Pictorial Photography Lon 1900　　50 - 75
Hochova, Dagmar
PG4530　Dagmar Hochova Prague 1934, wrappers　　30 - 50
Hodges, John
PG4560　Photographic Lenses: How to Choose and
　　　　How to Use Lon 1895　　75 - 125
Holme, Charles
PG4590　Art is Photography Lon 1905　　300 - 500

Hoppe, E. O.
PG4620　The Book of Fair Women NY 1922, 500 cys,
　　　　32 gravures　　300 - 500
PG4625　Deutsche Arbeit Berlin 1930　　150 - 250
PG4630　The Fifth Continent Lon 1931, DJ　　75 - 125
PG4635　The Image of London NY 1930　　50 - 75
PG4640　London Types Taken From Life Lon 1926, DJ　50 - 75
PG4645　Picturesque Great Britain NY 1926, DJ, slipcase 100 - 150
PG4650　Romantic America NY 1927, slipcase　　100 - 150
Horn, Grace Chandler
PG4680　The Song of Hiawatha Chi 1911　　75 - 125
Horst, Horst P.
PG4710　Photographs of a Decade NY 1944, DJ　　150 - 250
PG4715　Salute to the Thirties NY 1971, DJ　　30 - 50
Hoyningen-Huene, Baron
PG4740　Baalbek & Palmyra NY 1946　　75 - 125
PG4745　Egypt NY 1943　　75 - 125
PG4750　Hellas NY 1943　　75 - 125
Huet, Michel
PG4780　Noir D'Ivoire Brazzaville 1950, 1550 cys　　50 - 75
PG4785　Viet Nam Paris 1951　　30 - 50
Huffman, Lawton
PG4810　Sun and Saddle Leather Bos 1915　　75 - 125
Hurrell, George
PG4840　50 Years of Photographing Hollywood The
　　　　Hurrell Style NY 1976, DJ　　40 - 60
Izis (Bidermanas)
PG4870　Israel NY 1958, DJ　　75 - 125
PG4875　Paris Des Reves Lausanne 1950, DJ　　100 - 150
Jackson, William Henry
PG4905　Descriptive Catalog of Photographs of
　　　　American Indians Wash 1877　　200 - 300
PG4910　Photographs of the Yellowstone National
　　　　Park and Views in Montana and Wyoming
　　　　Territories Wash 1873　　20000 - 30000
PG4915　Picture Maker of the Old West William H.
　　　　Jackson (Clarence Jackson) NY 1947, DJ　　75 - 125
PG4920　The Pioneer Photographer Yonkers-on-Hudson,
　　　　NY, DJ　　125 - 250
PG4925　Rocky Mountain Scenery NY 1885　　200 - 300
PG4930　Time Exposure NY 1940, DJ　　75 - 125
PG4935　Views of Western Scenery and Camp Life
　　　　Phil 1870s, 78 prints　　20000 - 30000
PG4940　Westward America NY 1942, DJ　　75 - 125
Jacobi, Lotti
PG4970　Lotti Jacobi Danbury 1978, DJ　　50 - 75
PG4980　Portfolio I Deering 1978, 25 cys,
　　　　10 signed prints　　2000 - 3000
Jennings, Payne
PG5010　Views on the Lancashire, Derbyshire and East
　　　　Coast Railway Lon 1900-1910, 60 prints, folio 2000 - 3000
Johnston, Francis B.
PG5040　The Early Architecture of North Carolina
　　　　Chapel Hill 1947, slipcase　　150 - 250
PG5045　Plantations of the Carolina Low Country
　　　　Charleston 1938, 1500 cys, DJ　　100 - 150
Kalisher, Simpson
PG5080　Railroad Men 1961　　30 - 50
Karsh, Yousuf
PG5110　Faces of Destiny Chi 1946　　75 - 125
PG5115　Faces of Our Time Toronto 1971, DJ　　40 - 60
PG5120　In Search of Greatness NY 1962, DJ　　25 - 50

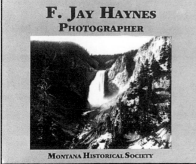

PG4250

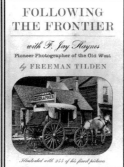

PG4265

185 PG4840

PG4915

PG6635

PG5125 **Karsh Portfolio** Toronto 1967, DJ   50 - 75
Kenna, Michael
PG5150 **The Hound of Baskervilles** SF 1985, 400 cys,
slipcase   300 - 500
Kertesz, Andre
PG5180 **Americana** NY 1979, wrappers   20 - 30
PG5185 **Andre Kertesz: Sixty Years of Photography...**
NY 1972, DJ   200 - 300
PG5190 **Day of Paris** NY 1945, DJ   300 - 500
PG5195 **Distortions** NY 1976, DJ   75 - 125
PG5200 **From My Window** Bos 1981, DJ   75 - 125
PG5205 **Hungarian Memories** Bos 1982, DJ   100 - 150
PG5210 **J'Aime Paris** NY 1974, DJ   75 - 125
PG5215 **Of New York** NY 1976, DJ   75 - 125
Klein, William
PG5250 **Moscow** Paris 1964, DJ   200 - 300
PG5251 NY 1964, DJ   200 - 300
PG5255 **New York** Lon 1956   300 - 500
PG5260 **Rome: The City and Its People** NY 1959, DJ   200 - 300
PG5265 **Tokyo** NY 1964, DJ   300 - 500
PG5270 **William Klein** Paris 1985, wrappers   75 - 125
Klute, Jeannette
PG5310 **Woodland Portraits** Bos 1954, box   125 - 250
Kolb, E. L.
PG5340 **Through the Grand Canyon From Wyoming
to Mexico** NY 1914, DJ   25 - 50
Koudelka, Josef
PG5370 **Gypsies** NY 1975, wrappers   30 - 50
PG5380 **Joseph Koudelka** Paris 1984, wrappers   30 - 50
Krauss, Dr. Freidrich
PG5410 **Streifzuge im Reiche der Frauenschonheit**
Leipzig 1903   200 - 300
Krull, Germaine
PG5430 **100 X Paris** Berlin 1929   200 - 300
PG5435 **Paris** Berlin 1928   75 - 125
Labrot, Syl
PG5470 **Pleasure Beach** NY 1976, DJ   150 - 250
Lambeth, Michel
PG5500 **The Confessions of a Tree Taster** Toronto
1987, 150 cys, 2 silver prints   200 - 300
Lang, Charles B.
PG5530 **Indians of Southern Mexico** Chi 1909,
560 cys, 141 gravures   800 - 1200
Lange, Dorothea
PG5560 **An American Exodus** NY 1939, DJ   100 - 150
PG5570 **Land of the Free** NY 1938, DJ   100 - 150
PG5580 **To a Cabin** NY 1973, DJ   50 - 75
Lartigue, Jacques Henri
PG5610 **Ami Guichard** Lusanne 1966   500 - 700
PG5620 **The Autochromes of J.H. Lartigue** NY 1981, DJ   50 - 75
PG5630 **Boyhood Photos of J.H. Lartigue**
Greenwich 1966   200 - 300
PG5631 Lausanne 1966   200 - 300
PG5640 **Diary of a Century** NY 1970, DJ   200 - 300
PG5642 Lon 1978, wrappers   30 - 50
PG5650 **The Jacques-Henri Lartigue Portfolio** NY 1977,
7500 cys, 10 prints, gravure   500 - 700
Laughlin, Clarence John
PG5680 **Ghosts Along the Mississippi** NY 1948, DJ   100 - 150
PG5682 NY 1961, DJ   50 - 75
Lee, Willis T.
PG5720 **The Face of the Earth as Seen From the Air**
NY 1922   100 - 150
Lembezat, Bertrand
PG5750 **Eve Noire** Paris 1952   50 - 75
Levy, Julien
PG5780 **Surrealism** NY 1936, DJ   75 - 125
List, Herbert
PG5820 **Herbert List, Photgraphien 1930-1970**
Munchen 1976, DJ   50 - 75
Lucas, Jan
PG5850 **Light and Shade** Lon 1947, DJ   30 - 50
Lummis, Charles
PG5880 **Mesa, Canon & Pueblo** NY 1925, DJ   50 - 75
Lyon, Danny
PG5910 **The Bike Riders** NY 1968, wrappers   100 - 150

PG5920 **The Destruction of Lower Manhattan**
NY 1969, DJ   100 - 150
Mapplethorpe, Robert
PG5950 **Certain People: A Book of Portraits**
Pasadena 1985, 5000 cys, DJ   200 - 300
PG5960 **Flowers** Bos 1990, DJ   50 - 75
PG5970 **Lady Lisa Lyon** NY 1983, DJ   50 - 75
PG5975 **The Power of Theatrical Madness** Lon 1986,
3000 cys   75 - 125
PG5980 **Robert Mapplethorpe 1970-1983** Lon 1985,
wrappers   30 - 50
PG5985 **A Season in Hell** NY 1986, 1000 cys,
8 gravures, slipcase   1200 - 1800
PG5990 **Some Women** Bos 1989, DJ   75 - 125
Matthies-Masuren, F.
PG6020 **Die Photographische Kunst** Halle 1904   300 - 500
Maxwell, Marius
PG6050 **Stalking Big Game With a Camera in
Equatorial Africa** Lon 1924, 568 cys   300 - 500
PG6051 Lon 1924, DJ (1st trade ed)   75 - 125
McAdie, Alexander
PG6080 **A Cloud Atlas** NY 1923, DJ   50 - 75
PG6085 **The Clouds & Fogs of San Francisco**
SF 1912, 50 cys   150 - 250
PG6090 **Fog** NY 1934, DJ   50 - 75
McCullin, Donald
PG6130 **Is Anyone Taking Any Notice?** Cambridge 1971   100 - 150
Meatyard, Ralph Eugene
PG6160 **The Family Album of Lucybelle Crater**
Millerton 1974, DJ   100 - 150
PG6165 **Father Louie** NY 1991, 100 cys, 1 orig print,
slipcase   200 - 300
Mennie, Donald
PG6200 **The Grandeur of the Gorges** Shanghai 1926,
1000 cys, 38 gravures, 12 silver prints   300 - 500
PG6205 **The Pageant of Peking** Shanghai 1920,
66 gravures   300 - 500
Meyer, Dr. Bruno
PG6230 **Weibliche Schonheit** Stuttgart 1905   200 - 300
Michals, Duane
PG6260 **Homage to Cavafy** Danbury 1978, 1000 cys   100 - 150
PG6265 **Take One and See Mt. Fujiyama and Other
Stories** Rochester 1976, wrappers   50 - 75
Misrach, Richard
PG6300 **Telegraph 3 A.M.** Berkeley 1974   100 - 150
Modotti, Tina
PG6330 **Tina Modotti A Fragile Life** NY 1975, DJ   75 - 125
Moholy-Nagy, Laszio
PG6360 **Experiment in Totality** NY 1950, DJ   75 - 125
PG6365 **Malerei, Photographie** Munich 1925   800 - 1200
PG6370 **Moholy Nagy** NY 1970, wrappers   30 - 50
PG6380 **Moholy-Nagy Experiment in Totality** NY 1950, DJ   75 - 125
PG6385 **Moholy-Nagy: Photographs and Photograms**
Munich 1978, DJ   50 - 75
PG6387 NY 1980, DJ   50 - 75
PG6395 **Montagen ins Blaue** Berlin 1980, wrappers   50 - 75
PG6400 **The New Vision** NY 1928, DJ   100 - 150
PG6405 **The Street Markets of London** Lon 1936   300 - 500
PG6410 **Vision in Motion** Chi 1947, DJ   75 - 125
Morgan, Barbara
PG6440 **Martha Graham** NY 1941, DJ   50 - 75
PG6445 **Prestini's Art in Wood** NY 1950, 1000 cys   75 - 125
Morris, Wright
PG6480 **The Cat's Meow** LA 1975, 125 cys, 1 orig print   200 - 300
PG6490 **God's Country and My People** NY 1968, DJ   50 - 75
PG6495 **The Home Place** NY 1948, DJ   100 - 150
PG6500 **The Inhabitants** NY 1946, DJ   100 - 150
PG6505 **Love Affair - A Venetian Journal** NY 1972, DJ   50 - 75
PG6510 **Wright Morris Photographs** Copenhagen 1981,
wrappers   25 - 50
Mortenson, William
PG6540 **The Model** SF 1937   25 - 50
PG6545 **Monsters and Madonnas** SF 1936, 20 gravures   150 - 250
PG6550 **Pictorial Lighting** SF 1947   25 - 50
Mucha, Alphonse
PG6580 **Alphonse Mucha Photographs** NY 1974, DJ   50 - 75

Muybridge, Eadweard
PG6610 Animal Locomotion Phil 1887, 11 vol,
      folio, 781 plates   30000 - 50000
PG6615 Animal Locomotion: The Muybridge Work
      at the University of Pennsylvania Phil 1888   300 - 500
PG6620 Animals in Motion Lon 1899   300 - 500
PG6622 Lon 1918   200 - 300
PG6624 Lon 1925   100 - 150
PG6635 Eadweard Muybridge (Kevin MacDonnell) Bos
      1972, DJ   30 - 50
PG6640 The Horse in Motion as Shown by
      Instantaneous Photography Bos 1882,
      5 heliotypes, 55 lithographs   1200 - 1800
PG6645 The Human Figure in Motion NY 1955, DJ 50 - 75
PG6650 Muybridge's Complete Human and Animal
      Locomotion NY 1979, 3 vol, DJs   100 - 150

Nadar, Felix
PG6680 Nadar NY 1976, DJ   75 - 125

Newman, Arnold
PG6710 Bravo Stravinsky Clev 1967, DJ   50 - 75
PG6720 One Mind's Eye Bos 1974, wrappers   30 - 50
PG6721 Bos 1974, DJ   50 - 75

Newton, Helmut
PG6750 Sleepless Nights NY 1978, DJ   50 - 75
PG6760 White Women NY 1976, DJ   50 - 75

Notman, William
PG6790 Portrait of a Period: A Collection of Notman
      Photographs 1856-1915 Montreal 1967   75 - 125

Nutting, Wallace
  All state or country "Beautiful" books are worth $50-75 with DJ and
$30-50 without.
PG6820 The Clock Book Framingham 1924, DJ   50 - 75
PG6825 Furniture Treasury Framingham 1928, DJ, 2 vol 150 - 250
PG6827 NY 1954, DJs, 2 vol   75 - 125
PG6835 New Hampshire Beautiful Framingham 1923, DJ 50 - 75
PG6840 Photographic Art Secrets NY 1928, DJ 100 - 150

Ockenga, Starr
PG6870 Mirror After Mirror Garden City 1976, DJ 50 - 75

O'Neal, Hank
PG6900 All the Kings Men NY 1989, 600 cys, box   800 - 1200

Ongania, Ferdinand
PG6930 Streets and Canals in Venice Venice 1896,
      100 plates, portfolio   800 - 1200

O'Sullivan, Timothy
PG6960 American Frontiers NY 1981, DJ   50 - 75
PG6970 Timothy O'Sullivan, America's Forgotten
      Photographer NY 1966, DJ   50 75

Outerbridge, Paul
PG7100 Paul Outerbridge, Jr.: Photographs NY 1980, DJ 50 - 75
PG7110 Photographing in Color NY 1940, DJ   300 - 500

Penn, Irving
PG7140 Flowers NY 1980, DJ   30 - 50
PG7150 Inventive Paris Clothes 1909-1939 NY 1977, DJ 50 - 75
PG7160 Moments Preserved NY 1960, DJ, slipcase 300 - 500
PG7170 Passage A Work Record NY 1991, DJ   30 - 50

Porter, Eliot
PG7200 All Under Heaven: The Chinese World
      NY 1983, 250 cys, 1 orig print, slipcase 500 - 700
PG7210 Baja California SF 1967, DJ   75 - 125
PG7230 Eliot Porter Bos 1987, DJ   50 - 75
PG7240 The Tree Where Man Was Born The African
      Experience NY 1972, DJ   50 - 75

Quennell, Peter
PG7270 Victorian Panorama Lon 1937, DJ   75 - 125

Ray, Man
PG7300 Electricite Paris 1931, 10 gravures   3000 - 5000
PG7305 La Photographie N'Est Pas l'Art Paris 1937,
      wrappers   300 - 500
PG7310 Les Souvenirs de Kiki Paris 1929 (10 halftones
      by Man Ray) 250 cys   100 - 150
PG7320 Man Ray: Photographs 1920-1934 Hartford
      1934, 104 gravures   800 - 1200
PG7321 Paris 1934, 104 gravures   800 - 1200
PG7330 Man Ray: Self Portrait Bos 1963, wrappers 50 - 75
PG7332 NY 1979   25 - 50

Renger-Patzsch, Albert
PG7360 Bestandige Welt Münster 1947   300 - 500

PG7370 Die Welt 1st Schon Münster 1948   300 - 500

Riboud, Marc
PG7400 Bangkok NY 1972, DJ   20 - 30
PG7410 The Three Banners of China NY 1966, DJ 50 - 75

Riefenstal, Leni
PG7430 The Last of the Nuba NY 1973, DJ   75 - 125

Riis, Jacob
PG7460 The Battle With the Slum NY 1902 100 - 150
PG7470 How the Other Half Lives NY 1901   75 - 125

Rinehart, Frank
PG7500 Rinehart's Indians Omaha 1899   300 - 500

Rodtschenko, Alexander
PG7530 Possibilities of Photography Koln 1982 50 - 75

Rogovin, Milton
PG7560 The Forgotten Ones Buffalo 1985   20 - 30

Roth, Sanford
PG7590 The French of Paris NY 1956, DJ   50 - 75

Rothstein, Arthur
PG7620 Look at Us... NY 1967, DJ   50 - 75
PG7630 Photo Journalism NY 1956, DJ   50 - 75

Rudinger, Hugo
PG7660 Architecture of the California Missions
      Berkeley 1958, DJ   75 - 125

Ryder, James F.
PG7690 Voigtlander and I in Pursuit of Shadow
      Catching Clev 1902   125 - 250

Salomon, Erich
PG7720 Beruhmte Zeitgenossen Stuttgart 1931, DJ 300 - 500
PG7730 Erich Salomon: Portrait of an Age NY 1967, DJ 125 - 200
PG7740 Portrait Einer Epoche Stuttgart 1963, DJ 125 - 200

Samaras
PG7770 Samaras Album NY 1971, 100 cys, 1 Polaroid
      print   500 - 700

Sander, August
PG7800 Men Without Masks Greenwich 1973, DJ 150 - 250

Saudek, Jan
PG7830 The World of Jan Saudek Millerton 1983, DJ 50 - 75

Schlemmer, Oskar
PG7860 Oskar Schlemmer und Die Abstracte Buhne
      Zurich 1961, wrappers   75 - 125

Scott, Arthur
PG7890 Nature Studies in Berkshire NY 1899 300 - 500

Seldes, Gilbert
PG7920 This is New York NY 1934   75 - 125

Sella, Vittoria
PG7950 The Exploration of the Caucasus Lon 1896,
      76 gravures, 4 maps   300 - 500
PG7955 Karadoram and Western Himalya NY 1912,
      2 vol, 32 gravures   300 - 500

Shadbolt, Cecil V.
PG7990 Walks in Palestine Lon 1988, 24 gravures 150 - 250

Shahn, Ben
PG8020 Ben Shahn Photographer, An Album From
      the Thirties NY 1973, DJ   50 - 75

Shawn, Ted
PG8050 The American Ballet NY 1926, DJ   75 - 125

Sheeler, Charles
PG8080 Charles Sheeler Artist in the American
      Tradition NY 1938, DJ   100 - 150
PG8085 The Great King of Assyria NY 1945   50 - 75
PG8090 Paintings, Drawings, Photographs NY 1939,
      wrappers   50 - 75

Sinsabaugh, Art
PG8120 Jargon 45 Highlands 1964, 1550 cys   300 - 500

Siskind, Aaron
PG8150 Aaron Siskind Photographs, John Logan
      Poems Rochester 1976
PG8155 Bucks County NY 1974, DJ   50 75
PG8160 Siskind: Photographs NY 1959, DJ   150 - 250
PG8170 The Siskind Variations Tor 1990, 190 cys 125 - 250

Slavin, Neal
PG8200 Portugal NY 1971   75 - 125

Smith, W. Eugene
PG8250 Let Truth be the Prejudice NY 1989, DJ 50 - 75

PG7270	PG8410 (photo page)	PG8560

PG8255 **Master of the Photographic Essay** Millerton
        1981, 1000 cys, signed gravure .... 300 - 500
PG8256 Millerton 1981, DJ (1st trade ed) .... 50 - 75
PG8265 **W. Eugene Smith** Millerton 1969, wrappers .. 30 - 50

Smythe, Frank
PG8300 **Alpine Ways** Lon 1942 .... 75 - 125
PG8305 **Rocky Mountains** Lon 1948 .... 50 - 75

Southworth and Hawes
PG8330 **The Spirit of Fact the Daguerreotypes of
        Southworth and Hawes 1843-1862** Bos 1976, DJ 50 - 75

Steichen, Edward
PG8360 **Camera Work #14** NY 1906 (quarterly w/7
        gravures by Steichen) .... 3000 - 5000
PG8365 **Carl Sandburg** NY 1941, DJ .... 50 - 75
PG8370 **The First Picture Book** NY 1930 .... 125 - 250
PG8372 NY 1992, 250 cys, box .... 300 - 500
PG8380 **Gardens in Color** Garden City 1944, DJ .. 30 - 50
PG8385 **A Life in Photography** Garden City 1963, DJ 100 - 150
PG8390 **The Picture Garden Book & Gardener's
        Assistant** NY 1942 .... 50 - 75
PG8395 **Steichen: The Master Prints 1895-1914**
        NY 1978, DJ .... 50 - 75
PG8400 **Steichen: The Photographer** NY 1929,
        925 cys, 48 gravures, slipcase .... 800 - 1200
PG8405 **The Vanity Fair Book** NY 1931 .... 100 - 150
PG8410 **Walden or Life in the Woods** Bos 1936,
        1500 cys, slipcase .... 300 - 500

Steiner, Ralph
PG8440 **A Point of View** Middletown 1978, DJ, slipcase 200 - 300

Stellmann, Louis
PG8470 **The Vanished Ruin Era** SF 1910 .... 125 - 250

Stephenson, William L.
PG8500 **The Battle of Little Big Horn** 1936, wrappers,
        5 mounted prints .... 300 - 500

Stibor, Miroslav
PG8530 **Miroslav Stibor** Prague 1990, DJ .... 30 - 50

Stieglitz, Alfred
PG8550 **Alfred Stieglitz** (Dorothy Norman) NY 1973, DJ 50 - 75
PG8560 **Alfred Stieglitz An American Seer** (Dorothy
        Norman) NY 1973, DJ .... 50 - 75
PG8570 **Alfred Stieglitz; Introduction to An American
        Seer** NY 1960, 2000 cys, DJ .... 50 - 75
PG8575 **Alfred Stieglitz, Photographer** Bos 1965 .. 50 - 75
PG8580 **Alfred Stieglitz Talking: 1925-1931**
        New Haven 1966 .... 50 - 75
PG8585 **America & Alfred Stieglitz** NY 1934, DJ .. 30 - 50
PG8590 **Camera Work** Millerton 1973, DJ .... 100 - 150
PG8595 **Camera Work #7-8** NY 1904 .... 12000 - 15000
PG8600 **Camera Work #36** NY 1911, 16 gravures 10000 - 12000
PG8605 **Exhibition of Photographs** Wash 1958, wrappers 30 - 50
PG8610 **Georgia O'Keefe, A Portrait** NY 1978, DJ,
        slipcase .... 100 - 150
PG8615 **Picturesque Bits of New York** NY 1897,
        12 gravures .... 3000 - 5000
PG8616 NY 1898, 12 gravures .... 3000 - 5000
PG8625 **Stieglitz Memorial Portfolio 1864-1946**
        NY 1947, 1500 cys, 18 silkscreens .... 800 - 1200
PG8630 **Waldo Frank; A Study** NY 1923, 500 cys,
        frontis print by Stieglitz .... 500 - 700

Stock, Dennis
PG8660 **Apache Boy** NY 1968, DJ .... 30 - 50
PG8665 **James Dean Revisited** NY 1978, DJ .... 20 - 30

PG8670 **Jazz Street** NY 1960, DJ .... 75 - 125

Stone, Sir Benjamin
PG8700 **Sir Benjamin Stone's Pictures** NY 1906, 2 vol 300 - 500

Strache, Wolf
PG8730 **Forms and Patterns in Nature** NY 1956, DJ 100 - 150

Strand, Paul
PG8760 **Ghana: An African Portrait** Millerton 1976, DJ 50 - 75
PG8765 **Living Egypt** Lon 1969, DJ .... 150 - 250
PG8770 **The Mexican Portfolio** NY 1940, 1000 cys,
        20 gravures .... 5000 - 7000
PG8771 NY 1967, 1000 cys, 20 gravures .... 1000 - 1500
PG8775 **Orgeval** Toronto 1990, 200 cys, 2 prints .. 125 - 200
PG8780 **Paul Strand, Sixty Years of Photography**
        Millerton 1976, DJ .... 100 - 150
PG8785 **A Retrospective Monograph: The Years
        1915-1946** and **The Years 1950-1968**
        Millerton 1971-72, 2 vol, DJs .... 200 - 300
PG8790 **Time in New England** NY 1950, DJ .... 150 - 250
PG8795 **Tir A'Mhurain: Outer Hebrides** Lon 1962, DJ 200 - 300
PG8797 NY 1968, DJ .... 150 - 250

Sudek, Josef
PG8830 **Praha** Prague 1948 .... 250 - 350

Szarkowski, John
PG8860 **The Face of Minnesota** St. Paul 1958, DJ 50 - 75
PG8865 **The Idea of Louis Sullivan** Minneapolis 1956 125 - 250
PG8870 **The Photographers Eye** NY 1966, DJ .... 20 - 30

Tabard, Maurice
PG8900 **Tabard** Paris 1987, DJ .... 50 - 75

Talbot, William Henry Fox
PG8930 **Fox Talbot and the Invention of Photography**
        Bos 1980, DJ .... 50 - 75
PG8935 **W.H.F. Talbot: A Weekend of Events at
        Lacock Abbey** Lacock, England 1978,
        25 cys, 9 facsimile calotype prints .... 800 - 1200

Thorek, Dr. Max
PG8970 **Camera Art as a Means of Self-Expression**
        Phil 1947, DJ .... 100 - 150
PG8975 **Creative Camera Art** Canton 1937 .... 125 - 250
PG8980 **The Creative Camera Art of Max Thorek**
        Chi 1984, 500 cys, wrappers .... 50 - 75

Tice, George
PG9010 **Hometowns** Bos 1988, DJ .... 50 - 75

Trager, Philip
PG9040 **Echoes of Silence** Danbury 1972, 1000 cys 50 - 75
PG9045 **Philip Trager: New York** Middletown 1980,
        100 cys, 1 orig print, DJ, slipcase .... 300 - 500

Traub, Charles
PG9070 **Beach** NY 1978, wrappers .... 20 - 30

Tress, Arthur
PG9100 **The Dream Collector** Richmond 1972, DJ 30 - 50
PG9105 **Shadow** NY 1975, wrappers .... 20 - 30

Ulmann, Doris
PG9130 **Handicrafts of the Southern Highlands**
        NY 1937, DJ .... 300 - 500
PG9132 NY 1946, DJ .... 125 - 250
PG9140 **A Portrait Gallery of American Editors**
        NY 1925, 375 cys, 43 gravures .... 500 - 700

Uzzle, Burk
PG9170 **Landscapes/Photographs** NY 1973, wrappers 30 - 50

Van Der Elsken, Ed
PG9200 **Life in Saint Germain Des Pres** Hamburg
        1957, DJ .... 100 - 150
PG9205 **Love on the Left Bank** Lon 1957, DJ .... 100 - 150
PG9210 **Sweet Life** NY 1966, DJ .... 125 - 250

Van Der Zee, James
PG9230 **James Van Der Zee** Dobbs Ferry 1973, DJ 100 - 150

Vishniac, Roman
PG9260 **Building Blocks of Life** NY 1971, DJ .... 20 - 30
PG9265 **A Day of Pleasure** NY 1969, DJ .... 30 - 50
PG9270 **Polish Jews** NY 1947, DJ .... 50 - 75

Wall, A. H.
PG9300 **Artistic Landscape Photography** Lon 1896 100 - 150

Wallihan, A. G.
PG9330 **Hoofs, Claws and Antlers of the Rocky
        Mountains by the Camera** Denver 1894 .. 125 - 250
PG9332 Denver 1902 .... 75 - 125

Warhol, Andy
PG9360 Andy Warhol's Exposures NY 1979, DJ   100 - 150
Weber, Bruce
PG9390 Bear Pond Bos 1990, DJ   75 - 125
PG9395 Bruce Weber NY 1989, DJ   100 - 150
Wedgwood, Tom
PG9430 Tom Wedgwood, the First Photographer Lon 1903 50 - 75
Weegee (Arthur Fellig)
PG9460 Naked City NY 1945, DJ   125 - 200
        w/out DJ   50 - 75
PG9465 Naked Hollywood NY 1953, DJ   75 - 125
        w/out DJ   50 - 75
PG9470 Weegee SF 1984, wrappers   20 - 30
PG9475 Weegee by Weegee NY 1961, DJ   30 - 50
PG9480 Weegee's Creative Camera NY 1959, DJ   50 - 75
PG9485 Weegee's People NY 1946, DJ   125 - 200
        w/out DJ   50 - 75
Welty, Eudora
PG9520 One Time, One Place: Mississippi in the Depression:
        A Snapshot Album NY 1971, 300 cys   125 - 250
PG9525 Photographs Jackson 1989, DJ   75 - 125
Weston, Brett
PG9560 A Personal Selection Carmel 1986, 300 cys,
        1 orig print, slipcase   800 - 1200
PG9565 Voyage of the Eye Millerton 1975, DJ   50 - 75
Weston, Edward
PG9590 50 Years Millerton 1973, 100 cys, original print 800 - 1200
PG9595 50th Anniversary Portfolio Carmel 1952,
        100 cys, 12 signed prints   15000 - 25000
PG9600 California and the West NY 1940, DJ   150 - 250
PG9601 Millerton 1978, 350 cys, 1 print, slipcase   600 - 800
PG9605 The Cats of Wildcat Hill NY 1947, DJ   250 - 350
PG9610 The Daybooks of Edward Weston Rochester
        1961, DJ, Vol I: Mexico   100 - 150
PG9611 Rochester 1966, DJ, Vol II: California   100 - 150
PG9615 Dedicated to Simplicity Toronto 1986, 150 cys 200 - 300
PG9620 Edward Weston NY 1932, 550 cys   1200 - 1800
PG9625 Edward Weston Wash 1966, wrappers   30 - 50
PG9630 Edward Weston: Nudes Millerton 1977, DJ   100 - 150
PG9635 Edward Weston Portfolio Roslyn Heights
        1971, 50 cys, 10 prints   3000 - 5000
PG9640 Edward Weston: Seventy Photographs
        Bos 1978, wrappers   30 - 50
PG9645 Edward Weston: The Flame of Recognition
        Millerton 1975   50 - 75
PG9650 Fifty Photographs NY 1947, DJ, 1500 cys
PG9655 Fit For a King NY 1939, DJ (cookbook w/4
        photos by Weston)   75 - 125
PG9660 Idols Behind Altars NY 1929, DJ   200 - 300
PG9665 My Camera on Point Lobos NY 1950   300 - 500
PG9667 NY 1968, DJ   100 - 150
PG9669 Bos 1950   300 - 500
PG9675 Seeing California with Edward Weston 1939   150 - 250
PG9680 Six Nudes of Neil, 1925 NY 1977, 25 cys,
        6 prints   2000 - 3000
PG9685 Weston's California Landscapes Bos 1984,
        slipcase   75 - 125
White, Minor
PG9710 Mirrors, Messages, Manifestations NY 1969, DJ 200 - 300
PG9715 Sequence 6 SF 1951, 25 cys, 14 signed prints 3000 - 5000
Williams, James Leon
PG9740 The Homes and Haunts of Shakespeare
        NY 1894, 30 gravures, folio   1200 - 1800
Wilson-Carmichael, Amy
PG9770 Lotus Buds Lon 1910, 50 gravures   100 - 150
Winningham, Geoff
PG9800 Going Texan Toronto 1972, DJ   30 - 50
Winogrand, Garry
PG9830 The Animals NY 1969, wrappers   20 - 30
PG9835 Women are Beautiful NY 1975, DJ   50 - 75
PG9836 NY 1975, wrappers   30 - 50
Woodbury, Walter E.
PG9860 Aristotypes and How To Make Them NY 1893 100 - 150
PG9865 The Encyclopaedic Dictionary of Photography
        NY 1899   100 - 150
PG9870 Photographic Amusements, Including a
        Description of a Number of Novel Effects
        Obtainable with a Camera NY 1898   75 - 125

Worthington, A. M.
PG9900 A Study of Splashes Lon 1908   200 - 300
Yavno, Max
PG9930 The Los Angeles Book Bos 1950, DJ   200 - 300
PG9935 The Photographs of Max Yavno LA 1981, DJ   50 - 75
PG9940 The San Francisco Book Bos 1948, DJ   200 - 300

Histories & Handbooks

Ackley, Clifford S.
PH1110 Private Realities: Recent American Photography
        Bos 1974, DJ   50 - 75
Adams, W. I. Lincoln (also By or About Photographers)
PH1210 In Natures Image: Chapters on Pictorial
        Photography NY 1898   50 - 75
Andrews, Ralph W.
PH1310 Photographers of the Frontier West: Their Lives
        and Their Works 1875 to 1915 NY 1965, DJ   50 - 75
PH1320 Picture Gallery Pioneers 1850 to 1875
        NY 1964, DJ   50 - 75
Barret, Andre
PH1410 Lumierè: Les Premierès Photographies en
        Couleurs Paris 1974   75 - 125
Beaton, Cecil
PH1510 British Photographers Lon 1944, DJ   100 - 150
PH1520 The Magic Image: The Genius of Photography
        From 1839 to the Present Day Bos 1975, DJ   50 - 75
Bensusan, A. D.
PH1610 Silver Images: History of Photography in Africa
        Cape Town 1966, DJ   75 - 125
Boni, Albert
PH1710 Photographic Literature NY 1962   200 - 300
PH1720 Photographic Literature 1960-1970 NY 1972 200 - 300
Bothamley, C. H.
PH1810 The Ilford Manual of Photography Lon 1890-95 50 - 75
Boughton, Alice
PH1910 Photographing the Famous NY 1928, DJ   300 - 500
Braive, Michel
PH2010 The Era of the Photograph: A Social History
        NY 1966, DJ   50 - 75
Brothers, Alfred
PH2110 Photography: Its History, Processes, Apparatus
        and Materials Lon 1892   300 - 500
Buckland, Gail
PH2200 First Photographs NY 1980, DJ   30 - 50
PH2210 Reality Recorded: Early Documentary
        Photography Bos 1974, DJ   50 - 75
Bull, Deborah
PH2310 Up the Nile: A Photographic Excursion, Egypt
        1839-1898 NY 1979   50 - 75
Capa, Cornell
PH2410 Behind the Great Wall of China, Photographs
        From 1870 to the Present NY 1972   50 - 75
Chamberlain, Samuel
PH2510 Fair is Our Land NY 1942, DJ   50 - 75
Coe, Brian
PH2610 The Birth of Photography: The Story of the
        Formative Years 1800-1900 NY 1977, DJ   50 - 75
PH2620 Colour Photography: The First Hundred Years
        1840-1940 Lon 1978, DJ   75 - 125
Coke, Van Deren
PH2710 The Painter and the Photograph Albu 1964   50 - 75
Colnaghi, P & D
PH2810 Photography: The First Eighty Years Lon 1976 30 - 50
Crawford, William
PH2910 The Keepers of Light, A History & Working Guide
        to Early Photographic Processes Dobbs Ferry 1979 30 - 50
Current, Karen
PH3010 Photography and the Old West NY 1978, DJ   75 - 125
Daniels, Patrick
PH3110 Early Photography NY 1978   30 - 50
Danziger, James
PH3210 Interviews With Master Photographers NY 1977 50 - 75
Darrah, William Culp
PH3310 Stereo Views: A History of Stereographs in
        America and Their Collection Gettysburg 1964, DJ 50 - 75

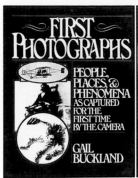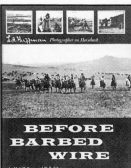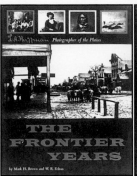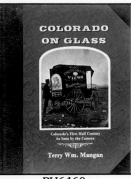

| PH2200 | PH5460 | PH5470 | PH6460 | PH6910 |

PH3410 **The World of Stereographs** Gettysburg 1977, DJ   25 - 50

Daval, Jean Luc
PH3510 **Photography, History of an Art** Geneva 1982, DJ 50 - 75

Doty, Robert
PH3610 **Photography in America** NY 1974, DJ   25 - 50
PH3620 **Photo-Session: Photography as a Fine Art**
         Rochester 1960, DJ   75 - 125
PH3622 NY 1978, DJ   40 - 60

Eastman, George
PH3710 **Chronicles of an African Trip** Rochester 1927   125 - 250
PH3720 **How to Make Good Pictures** Rochester 1913, wrappers
         (1st ed of a much reprinted popular handbook)   100 - 150

Eder, Josef Maria
PH3810 **Des Actions Chimiques de la Lumiere Colorée
         et de la Photographie en Couleurs Naturelles**
         Ghent 1881   300 - 500
PH3820 **Geschichte der Photographie** Halle, Prussia
         1932, 2 vol   200 - 300
PH3830 **The History of Photography** NY 1945, DJ   75 - 125

Edey, Maitland
PH3910 **Great Photographic Essays From Life** Bos 1978, DJ 30 - 50

Feininger, Andreas
PH4010 **Successful Color Photography** NY 1954, DJ   50 - 75
PH4020 **Total Picture Control - A Personal Approach
         to Photography** NY 1961, DJ   50 - 75

Friedman, Joseph
PH4110 **History of Color Photography** Bos 1944   75 - 125

Gassan, Arnold
PH4210 **A Chronology of Photography** Athens 1972   50 - 75

Gee, Helen
PH4310 **Photography of the Fifties** Tucson 1980   30 - 50

Gernsheim, Helmut
PH4410 **Beautiful London** Lon 1950, DJ   75 - 125
PH4412 Lon 1960, DJ   50 - 75
PH4420 **Churchill, His Life in Photographs** NY 1955, DJ   50 - 75
PH4425 **A Concise History of Photography** NY 1965, DJ   50 - 75
PH4430 **Creative Photography: Aesthetic Trends,
         1839-1960** Lon 1962   50 - 75
PH4435 **Focus on Architecture and Sculpture**
         Lon 1949, DJ   75 - 125
PH4440 **The History of Photography** NY 1955, DJ   250 - 350
PH4445 **The History of Photography From the
         Camera Obscura...** NY 1969, DJ   200 - 300
PH4450 **Masterpieces of Victorian Photography**
         Lon 1951, DJ   75 - 125
PH4455 **The Origins of Photography** NY 1982, DJ   75 - 125

Goodrich, L. Carrington
PH4510 **The Face of China: Photographs 1860-1912**
         Millerton 1978   20 - 30

Gräff, Werner
PH4610 **Es Kommt Der Neue Fotograf!** Berlin 1929   300 - 500

Green, Jonathan
PH4710 **Camera Work: A Critical Anthology** Millerton 1973 20 - 30
PH4720 **The Snapshot** Millerton 1974   30 - 50

Greenhill, Ralph
PH4810 **Early Photography in Canada** Toronto 1965   75 - 125

Harrison, Jerome
PH4910 **A History of Photography** NY 1887   200 - 300

Hicks, Wilson
PH5010 **Words and Pictures** NY 1952, DJ   50 - 75

PH5012 NY 1973, DJ   30 - 50

Hillier, Bevis
PH5110 **Victorian Studio Photographs** Bos 1976, DJ   30 - 50

Hodgson, Pat
PH5210 **Early War Photographs: 50 Years of War
         Photographs From the Nineteenth Century**
         Bos 1974, DJ   50 - 75

Holme, Charles
PH5310 **Art in Photography** Lon 1905   125 - 250
PH5320 **Colour Photography, and Other Recent
         Developments of the Art of the Camera**
         Lon 1908   125 - 250

Howarth-Loomes, B. E. C.
PH5410 **Victorian Photography** NY 1974   30 - 50

Huffman, L. A.
PH5460 **Before Barbed Wire** (Brown & Felton) NY 1956, DJ 50 - 75
PH5470 **The Frontier Years** (Brown & Felton) NY 1965, DJ 30 - 50

Jammes, Andre
PH5510 **The First Century of Photography Niepce
         to Atget** Chi 1977   30 - 50
PH5520 **French Primitive Photography** Millerton 1970   30 - 50

Jenkins, Reese V,
PH5610 **Image and Enterprise: Technology and the American
         Photographic Industry 1839-1925** Balt 1976   50 - 75

Jonquières, Henri
PH5710 **La Vieille Photographie Depuis Daguerre
         Jusqu'a 1870** Paris 1935   200 - 300

Juhl, Ernst
PH5810 **Camera Konst** Berlin 1903, glassine DJ   300 - 500

Kahmen, Volker
PH5910 **Photography as Art** Lon 1974   30 - 50

Karfeld, Kurt Peter
PH5960 **My Leica and I** Berlin 1937   75 - 125

Lacey, Peter
PH6010 **History of the Nude in Photography** NY 1964,
         wrappers   15 - 25

Lecuyer, Raymond
PH6110 **Histoire de la Photographie** Paris 1945,
         w/3-D glasses in pocket   700 - 1000

Liberman, Alexander
PH6160 **The Art and Technique of Color Photography**
         NY 1951, DJ   75 - 125

Livingston, Jane
PH6210 **The Art of Photography at National Geographic**
         Charlottesville 1988   30 - 50

Lorant, Stefan
PH6260 **Lincoln: His Life in Photographs** NY 1941, DJ   25 - 50

Lucie-Smith, Edward
PH6310 **The Invented Eye Masterpieces of Photography
         1839-1914** NY 1975   20 - 30

Lyons, Nathan
PH6410 **Vision and Expression** NY 1969, DJ   30 - 50

Mangan, Terry Wm.
PH6460 **Colorado on Glass** Silverton, CO 1975, DJ   50 - 75

Mendola, Raphael
PH6510 **The Chemistry of Photography** Lon 1889   75 - 125

Miller, Francis Trevelyan
PH6610 **The Photographic History of the Civil War**
         NY 1912, 10 vol   200 - 300

PH7210   PH7410   PH7710   PH7710 (photo page)   PH8110

About the Author

John Wade, a native of Ohio, has avidly pursued rare books for more than fifteen years. He began by frequenting used book stores and flea markets, where he made his earliest discovery: a first edition of Jack London's *Call of the Wild* for 25¢. He is now a dealer and collector. In 1984 he promoted one of the first books collectors' shows in the Mid-West. He has also assisted libraries and museums with indentifying their treasures. His other colleccting interests include autographs, manuscripts, photographs, and advertising ephemera.

Become a Collectibles Expert with Tomart Photo Price Guides

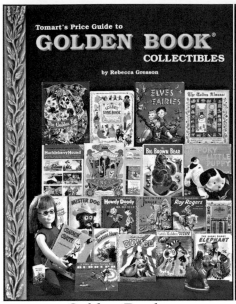

Golden Books

Over 3,000 color and black & white photos of Little Golden Books, Big Golden Books, Giant Golden Books and the rest of the Golden Books family with detailed descriptions and prices. Become an expert on more than 1 billion Golden Books in print, 8½" x 11", 240 pages, softbound. **$21.95 + P&H**

Star Wars

This pictorial value guide, produced under license from Lucasfilm, Ltd., includes thousands of photos, current value estimates, and a list of all licensees from 1977 through 1993. Compiled by collector Stephen J. Sansweet, and *AFD* editor T.N. Tumbusch, this authorized guide is the first to make use of Lucasfilm's records and toy archives. **$26.95 + P&H**

Available in February 1994

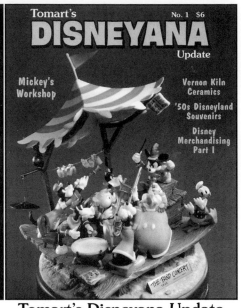

Tomart's Disneyana Update

Tomart's Disneyana Update will keep you informed on the vast amount of Disneyana merchandise and collectibles not previously listed in Tomart books, and items newly created by Disney licensees, theme parks, and other operations. Only Disney Merchandise and collectibles are covered in each update. This is not another Disney Magazine, but a vehicle to provide up-to-date information, availability, values, and other insights for Disneyana collectors.

$28.95 per year in U.S.

McDonald's Happy Meals

All premiums, boxes, bags, translites, and displays connected with McDonald's Happy Meal promotions are pictured with latest value estimates. Included are all regional and test items known to the author, Meredith Williams, publisher of the McDonald's Collector's newsletter. 8½" x 11", 160 pages. **$24.95 + P&H**

Kids Meal Collectibles

The companion book to Tomart's Price Guide to McDonald's Happy Meal Collectibles, this book describes Kids Meal premiums from 30 national and regional fast food restaurants. This valuable identification guide is crammed full of facts, photos, and little-known information. 200 pages, softbound. **$25.95 + P&H**

Magazines

Price guide to Time, Life, Look, TV Guide, Playboy, Sports Illustrated, Newsweek, Inside Sports, The Saturday Evening Post, and Sport Magazine issues published through 1993. Thousands of color and b&w photos and pricing for each issue with reasons for extra value. **$25.95 + P&H**

Available Fall 1994